Contents

Czech beer colour
section following p.152

Castles and chateaux
colour section following
p.280

◀◀ Telč ◀ Malá Strana, Prague

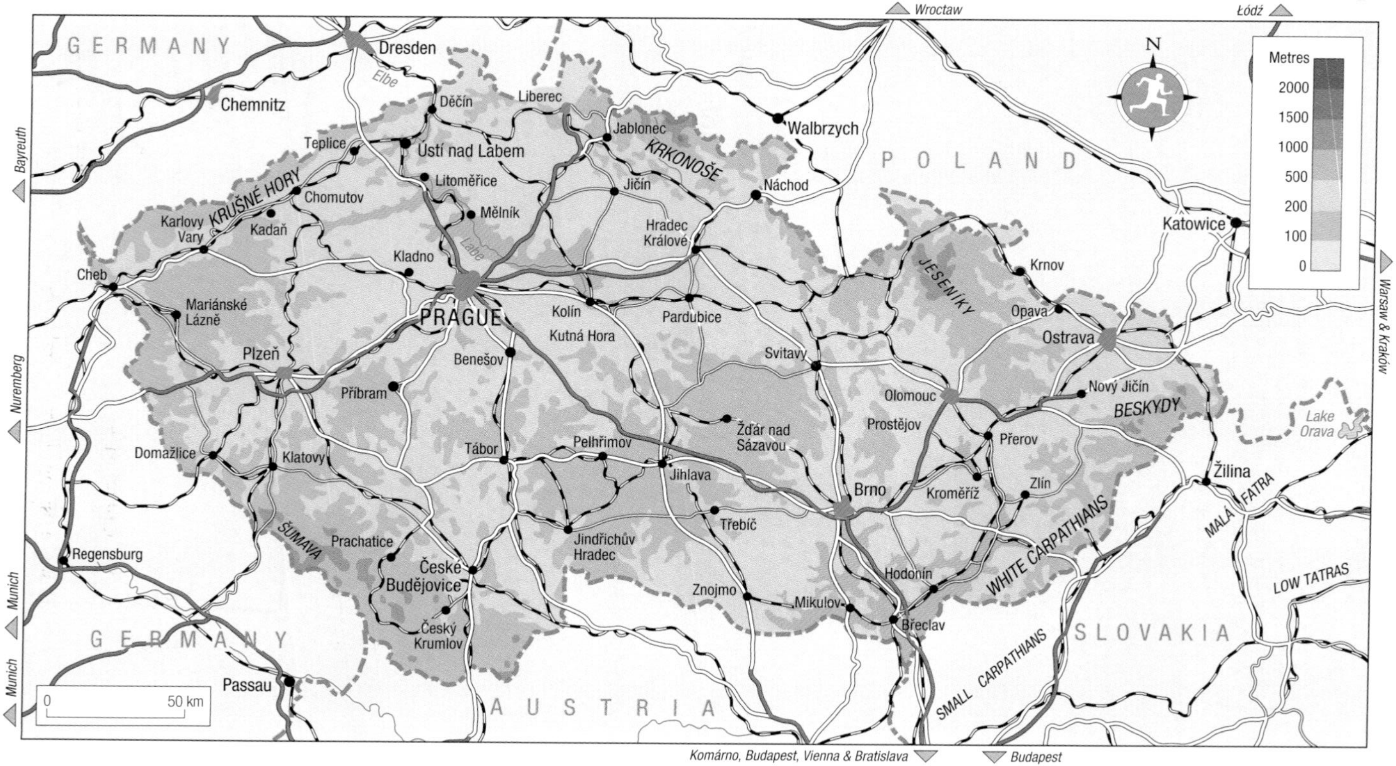

Metres
2000
1500
1000
500
200
100
0

Warsaw & Kraków

Lake Orava

LOW TATRAS

Łódź

Wrocław

Żilina

MALÁ FATRA

Katowice

SLOVAKIA

N

BESKYDY

Nový Jičín

Krnov

Ostrava

Opava

Přerov

Zlín

WHITE CARPATHIANS

POLAND

JESENÍKY

Olomouc

Prostějov

Brno

Hodonín

Břeclav

SMALL CARPATHIANS

Budapest

Wałbrzych

Náchod

Svitavy

Žďár nad Sázavou

Třebíč

Mikulov

Znojmo

Komárno, Budapest, Vienna & Bratislava

KRKONOŠE

Jablonec

Jičín

Hradec Králové

Pardubice

Liberec

Děčín

Ústí nad Labem

Mělník

Litoměřice

Labe

Kolín

Kutná Hora

Pelhřimov

Jihlava

Jindřichův Hradec

AUSTRIA

Dresden

Elbe

Kladno

PRAGUE

Benešov

Tábor

České Budějovice

Český Krumlov

Chemnitz

Teplice

Chomutov

Příbram

Prachatice

KRUŠNÉ HORY

Kadaň

ŠUMAVA

GERMANY

Karlovy Vary

Mariánské Lázně

Plzeň

Klatovy

Domažlice

Passau

GERMANY

Regensburg

50 km

0

Bayreuth

Nuremberg

Munich

Munich

4

Introduction to
The Czech Republic

The Czech Republic is famous for two things: the stunning beauty of its capital, Prague, and the outstanding quality of its beer. Few visitors, however, realize that the magnificence of the capital's buildings is also echoed in countless other towns and cities all across the country. For, in contrast to the political upheavals that have plagued the region, the Czech Republic has suffered very little physical damage over the centuries. Gothic castles and Baroque chateaux have been preserved in abundance, town after town in Bohemia and Moravia has retained its old medieval quarter, and even the wooden folk architecture of the rural regions has survived beyond all expectations.

In fact, it's easy to forget that the Czech Republic was once part of Communist Eastern Europe. Posters no longer exhort the country's citizens to fulfil the next five-year plan, and apart from the ubiquitous high-rise suburbs and the odd Soviet war memorial, you'd be hard pushed to envisage the bad old days. In 2004, there were genuine national celebrations at the country's accession to the **European Union**; putting aside their natural apathy towards politics, the Czechs rejoiced in the fact that they'd returned to the fold, and shed their old Eastern Bloc identity. That said, the political and economic upheavals in the country have been bewildering for those who lived through the Communist era, and along with the new-found freedom have come the usual suspects: multinational takeovers, the rise of the mafia and all the other sundry vices that plague the capitalist world. Few Czechs would want to turn the clock right back, but when the Communist Party can still garner over half a million votes, and the president is a confirmed Eurosceptic, it's clear that not everybody's happy with the changes in the new Republic.

Where to go

Before the fall of Communism, a staggering ninety percent of foreign tourists visiting the country never strayed from the environs of the Czech capital, **Prague**. While that no longer holds true, Prague is still the main focus of most people's trips to the Czech Republic, certainly English-speaking tourists. Of course, much of the attention heaped on Prague is perfectly justified. It is one of the most remarkable cities in Europe, having emerged virtually unscathed from two

Trains

The most relaxing way to travel round the Czech Republic is by train. The system, bequeathed by the Habsburgs in 1918, is one of the densest in Europe, and has changed little since those days, with less than ten percent of lines allowing train speeds of over 120kph. In addition, many are wonderfully scenic, such as the single-track one that winds its way through the Šumava. Heritage railways are well established now, too, with several old forest railways running steam-train excursions on summer weekends.

▲ Cervena Lhota

Fact file

- The Czech Republic is a landlocked country in the geographical centre of Europe, roughly equidistant from the Baltic and Adriatic seas, with a total area of 78,866 square kilometres.

- More than one-third of the country is made up of forest, mostly coniferous, while two-thirds of the land lies at an altitude below 500m. The highest point is Sněžka (1602m) in the Krkonoše on the Polish border, and the lowest point is Hřensko (115m) at the border with Germany on the River Labe (Elbe).

- The population is 10.2 million, of whom roughly 95 percent are Czech, with significant Roma, Slovak, Polish, Vietnamese and German minorities. The largest group of foreigners residing in the country is Ukrainian, with more than 125,000 nationals officially registered.

- The Czech nation is one of the least religious in Europe, with nearly 60 percent declaring themselves agnostic, 27 percent Roman Catholic and 2.5 percent Protestant.

- Total earnings from tourism make up 6 percent of GNP and the industry employs over 1 percent of the population.

- Since 2000, the country has been divided into thirteen administrative regions or kraje (not including Prague) the borders of which totally ignore all historical and cultural identities. Each kraj has its own elected regional assembly and a hejtman or president.

world wars. Baroque palaces and churches shout out from the cobbles, Gothic pinnacles spike the skyline, and Art Nouveau and functionalist edifices line the boulevards. However, it's also mobbed for much of the year, whereas elsewhere the country can be enjoyed in relative peace and quiet.

The rest of the Czech Republic divides neatly into two: Bohemia to the west and Moravia to the east. Prague is the perfect launching pad from which to explore the rolling hills and forests of Bohemia, at their most unspoilt in South Bohemia, whose capital is **České Budějovice**, a grid-plan medieval city and home to the original Budweiser beer. The real gem of the region is **Český Krumlov**, arguably the most stunning medieval town in the country, beautifully preserved in a narrow U-bend of the River

Vltava. The region also boasts other less well-known "**Rose Towns**", such as Jindřichův Hradec and Prachatice, which have preserved their Renaissance riches intact. To the west, **Plzeň** produces the most famous of all Czech beers, Pilsner Urquell, the original golden nectar from which all other lagers derive. Meanwhile, along the German border, a triangle of relaxing **spa towns** – Karlovy Vary, Mariánské Lázně and Františkovy Lázně – retain an air of their halcyon days in the last years of the Habsburg Empire. Pine-covered mountains form Bohemia's natural borders, and the weird **sandstone rock "cities"** of the České Švýcarsko and Český ráj and Krkonoše, in the north and east of the region, make for some of the most memorable landscapes.

Moravia, the eastern province of the Czech Republic, is every bit as beautiful as Bohemia, though the crowds thin out even more here. The largest city, **Brno**, has its own peculiar pleasures – not least its interwar functionalist architecture – and gives access to the popular Moravian karst region, or **Moravský kras**, plus a host of other nearby castles and chateaux. The southern borders of Moravia comprise the country's main **wine** region, while in the uplands that form the border with Bohemia are two of the most perfectly preserved medieval towns in the entire country, **Telč** and **Slavonice**. To the north, **Olomouc** is perhaps Moravia's most charming city, more immediately appealing than Brno, and just a short step away from the region's highest mountains, the **Jeseníky** in Moravian Silesia, and the **Beskydy**, renowned for their folk architecture.

Walking and hiking

The Czechs are keen walkers, and the country is crisscrossed with a dense, easily followed, network of way-marked, colour-coded paths ranging from a gentle stroll to a serious hike, leaving no excuse not to get into the countryside and take some exercise. All 1:50,000 hiking maps show the trails and each path has regular signposts, with distances and approximate walking times. To make sure you don't lose your way there's even a colour-coded marker or *značka* every 100m or so, maintained annually by teams of local volunteers.

When to go

I n general, the climate is continental, with short, fairly hot summers and chilly winters. **Spring** can be a good time to visit, as the days tend to warm quickly, with consistently pleasant, mild weather for most of May. This is also the blossom

Wooden churches

The Czech Republic boasts an impressive number of wooden churches. While timber-framed houses have, on the whole, been superseded by bricks and mortar, wooden churches have survived in many villages. One or two remain in Bohemia – there's even one in Prague – but the densest cluster is to be found in Moravia, in the Wallachian region of the Beskydy hills, where there's a varied collection of Roman Catholic wooden churches (see p.375).

season, when the fruit trees that line so many Czech roads are in full flower. **Autumn** is also recommended, with clear and settled weather often lasting for days on end in September and October. With much of the country heavily forested, this is also a great time to appreciate the changing colours of the foliage.

Winter can be a good time to come to Prague: the city looks beautiful under snow and there are fewer tourists to compete with. Other parts of the country have little to offer during winter (aside from skiing), and most sights stay firmly closed between November and March. **Summer**

▼ Folk festival, Strážnice

is, of course, still the season during which the largest number of tourists descend. Certainly, temperatures are at their highest, with the occasional heat wave pushing readings

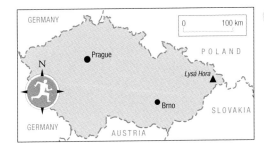

well above 30°C. While that can be advantageous if you fancy swimming in a lake or river, it's not fun in Prague, which is also at its most crowded in July and August.

Average temperatures (°C)

	Jan	Feb	Mar	Apr	May	Jun	Jul	Aug	Sep	Oct	Nov	Dec
Prague												
	-1	1	5	9	14	18	19	19	15	10	4	1
Brno												
	-3	0	4	9	14	17	19	18	14	9	4	-1
Lysá hora (Beskydy)												
	-6	-6	-3	2	7	10	11	11	8	4	-2	-5

Note that these are average daily temperatures. At midday in summer, Prague can be very hot. Equally, in mountainous regions like the Beskydy, it can get extremely cold and wet at any time of the year.

25

things not to miss

It's not possible to see everything that the Czech Republic has to offer in one trip – and we don't suggest you try. What follows is a subjective selection of the country's highlights, from ruined castles and striking Renaissance architecture to the best forested mountain ranges – all arranged in colour-coded categories to help you find the very best things to see, do and experience. All entries have a page reference to take you straight into the Guide, where you can find out more.

01 **Žďár nad Sazavou, Zelená Hora** Page **342** • Star-shaped Gothic-Baroque pilgrimage church by Giovanni Santini, dedicated to the martyr St John of Nepomuk.

02 **Rožnov pod Radhoštěm** Page **379** • Moravian town that's home to the largest and most impressive open-air folk museum in the Czech Republic.

04 **Český ráj** Page **267** • Natural playground within easy reach of Prague, with densely wooded hills, sandstone rock "cities" and a smattering of ruined castles.

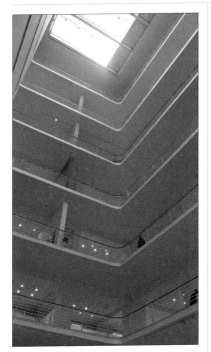

03 **Veletržní palác, Prague** Page **121** • The finest modern art museum in the Czech Republic, and a functionalist masterpiece in its own right.

05 **Třeboňsko** Page **171** • South Bohemian flatlands with the pretty walled town of Třeboň at its heart, surrounded by medieval carp ponds.

06 **Plzeň brewery** Page **207** • World-famous brewery where, in 1842, the world's first lager, Pilsner Urquell, was produced.

07 **Telč** Page **336** • Telč's vast, arcaded main square is one long parade of perfectly preserved sixteenth-century facades and gables, culminating in a handsome Renaissance chateau.

08 Prague's Jewish quarter Page **98** • Six synagogues, a town hall and a cemetery survive as a testament to over a thousand years of Jewish settlement and struggle.

09 Karlovy Vary Page **224** • Grandiose late nineteenth-century spa town lying in a steep valley, and home to the Czech Republic's premier film festival.

11 **Burčák** Page **41** • In autumn, make sure you try *burčák*, the young, misty, partially fermented Moravian wine whose arrival in the streets and bars marks the beginning of the annual wine harvest.

10 **Terezín** Page **244** • This Habsburg-era military fortress was transformed into a "model" Jewish ghetto by the Nazis, though in reality it was simply a transit camp en route to Auschwitz.

I ACTIVITIES I CONSUME I EVENTS I NATURE I SIGHTS I

12 **Litomyšl** Page **299** • This tiny Bohemian town, the birthplace of Bedřich Smetana, is home to a very handsome Renaissance chateau and the weird and wonderful Portmoneum, designed by self-taught artist Josef Váchal.

13 **Mariánské Lázně** Page **214** • Elegant fin-de-siècle Bohemian spa town set in verdant wooded hills – and once a firm favourite with European royalty.

14 **Pernštejn** Page **323** • Highly atmospheric hilltop Gothic castle with dizzying sheer walls and spectacular views across the wooded hills.

15 **České Švýcarsko (Bohemian Switzerland)** Page **253** • Switzerland it may not be, but this forested border region features outlandish sandstone outcrops and boat trips down the River Kamenice.

I ACTIVITIES I **CONSUME** I **EVENTS** I NATURE I SIGHTS I

16 **Roast pork, dumplings and cabbage** Page **38** • Known colloquially as *vepřo-knedlo-zelo*, this is the quintessential Czech comfort food and pub grub staple.

17 **Prague Castle** Page **68**
• Landmark castle that's home to the cathedral, royal palace, several museums and galleries – and the president.

18 **Český Krumlov** Page **182** • Medieval town of steep cobbled streets, picturesquely situated in a tight U-bend of the River Vltava.

19 **Obecní dům** Page **111** • Prague's Art Nouveau jewel from 1911, housing a café, several restaurants, an exhibition space and a concert hall.

20 **Moravský kras** Page **320** • Moravia's karst region, just outside Brno, replete with cave systems featuring superb stalactites and stalagmites and an underground river.

21 **Nové Město nad Metují** Page **286** • Pint-sized east Bohemian town with a picture perfect main square and a Baroque chateau with a rich and remarkable interior, reconstructed in 1908.

22 **Hiking in the Šumava** Page **190** • Bordering Germany and Austria, the rolling, wooded hills of the Šumava is an unspoilt terrain best explored on foot.

24 Strážnice folk festival

Page **344** • This Moravian folk jamboree is the country's biggest and most popular, with lots of impromptu music-making in addition to the official programme.

23 Budvar beer
Page **179** • Taste the original Budweiser beer in the one of the many pubs serving Budvar in České Budějovice.

25 Slavonice
Page **337** • Slavonice's tiny old town sports more pictorial sgraffito facades than any other town in the republic.

Basics

Basics

Getting there

Unless you're coming from a neighbouring European country, the quickest way to get to the Czech Republic is by plane. There are direct flights from just about every European capital to Prague, plus one or two to Brno. There are also one or two nonstop flights from North America to Prague, though you'll get a much wider choice – and often lower fares – if you fly via London or another more popular European gateway.

How much you pay to fly to the Czech Republic depends on the **season**, with the highest fares charged from Easter to October, and around Christmas and New Year. With budget airlines, of course, the earlier you book, the cheaper the prices.

Another option, if you're travelling from Britain or elsewhere in Europe, is to go by **train**, **bus** or **car** – this will take considerably longer than the plane and may not work out cheaper, but it's undoubtedly better for the environment. For more details, see below.

Flights from Britain and Ireland

You can book a direct flight to Prague from all over Britain, Ireland and Europe. The most competitive fares are with the budget airlines, though the national airlines British Airways (BA) and Czech Airlines (ČSA) have had to slash their prices accordingly.

If you book far enough in advance or can be flexible about your dates, you can get return **fares** to Prague for as little as £50–70 from a selection of British airports. From Ireland, return airfares start at around €100 return from Dublin. Of course, if you don't book early, prices can skyrocket. Since routes can change – and airlines can go under – with little notice, it's best to check the airport websites for the latest.

Flights from the US and Canada

Czech Airlines (ČSA) is the only airline to offer **nonstop flights** from North America to Prague. You'll get a much wider choice of flights and ticket prices, though, if you opt for a **indirect flight** with one or two changes

of plane, allowing you to depart from any number of North American cities and travel via one of the major European gateways.

Flying time from New York or Montréal direct to Prague is about eight hours. **Fares** depend very much on the flexibility of the ticket and on availability, with a New York–Prague return costing US$750–1000, and a Montréal–Prague return costing Can$900–1250.

Flights from Australia and New Zealand

Flight time from **Australia or New Zealand** to Prague is over twenty hours or more, depending on routes and transfer times. There's a wide variety of routes, with those touching down in Southeast Asia generally the quickest and cheapest. Given the length of the journey, you might want to include a night's stopover in your itinerary; indeed, some airlines include one in the price of the flight.

The cheapest direct scheduled flights to London are usually to be found on one of the Asian airlines. Average return **fares** (including taxes) from eastern gateways to London are Aus$1500–2000 in low season, around Aus$500 more in high season. You'll then need to add Aus$100–200 onto all these for the connecting flight to Prague. Return fares from Auckland to London range between NZ$2000 and NZ$3000 depending on the season, route and carrier.

By train

You can travel **by train** from **London** to Prague overnight in around twenty hours. Fares start at around £125 return but depend on the route you take and how far in advance you book your ticket.

Fly less – stay longer! Travel and climate change

Climate change is perhaps the single biggest issue facing our planet. It is caused by a build-up in the atmosphere of carbon dioxide and other greenhouse gases, which are emitted by many sources – including planes. Already, **flights** account for three to four percent of human-induced global warming: that figure may sound small, but it is rising year on year and threatens to counteract the progress made by reducing greenhouse emissions in other areas.

Rough Guides regard travel as a **global benefit**, and feel strongly that the advantages to developing economies are important, as are the opportunities for greater contact and awareness among peoples. But we also believe in travelling responsibly, which includes giving thought to how often we fly and what we can do to redress any harm that our trips may create.

We can travel less or simply reduce the amount we travel by air (taking fewer trips and staying longer, or taking the train if there is one); we can avoid night flights (which are more damaging); and we can make the trips we do take "climate neutral" via a carbon offset scheme. **Offset schemes** run by climatecare.org, carbonneutral .com and others allow you to "neutralize" the greenhouse gases that you are responsible for releasing. Their websites have simple calculators that let you work out the impact of any flight – as does our own. Once that's done, you can pay to fund projects that will reduce future emissions by an equivalent amount. Please take the time to visit our website and make your trip climate neutral, or get a copy of the *Rough Guide to Climate Change* for more detail on the subject.

Ⓦ**www.roughguides.com/climatechange**

To reach Prague by train you first have to take the **Eurostar** from St Pancras to **Brussels**. From Brussels, the most direct, and usually cheapest, route is **via Frankfurt**, from where there's an overnight service to Prague. Alternatively, from Brussels, you can take the **overnight service to Berlin** – it's longer and slightly more expensive, but the sleeper trains are superior and the timings might suit you better.

Although you can crash out on the seats, it makes sense to book a **couchette on your European train**; this costs an extra £15 one-way in a six-berth compartment, rising to £25 in a three-berth compartment. Couchettes are mixed-sex and allow little privacy; for a bit more comfort, you can book a bed in a single-sex two-berth **sleeper** for around £50.

Fares for continental rail travel are much more flexible than they used to be, so it's worth shopping around for the best deal, rather than taking the first offer you get. Tickets are usually valid for two months and allow as many stopovers as you want on the specified route. If you're travelling with one or more companions, you may be eligible for a further discount.

The cheapest way to book tickets is usually **online**, but you have to use several websites. For more details visit Ⓦwww.seat61.com. Alternatively, you can phone one of the agents listed on p.32.

By bus

One of the cheapest ways to get to the Czech Republic is **by bus**. There are direct services from London's Victoria Station more or less daily throughout the year. Coaches tend to depart in the evening, arriving eighteen hours later in Prague's main bus terminal, Florenc, in the early afternoon. The journey is bearable (just about), with short breaks every three to four hours, but only really worth it if you've left it too late to find a budget flight. Prices between companies vary only slightly (see p.32); a return ticket starts at around £70, less if you're under 26 or over 60.

By car

With two or more passengers, **driving** to the Czech Republic can work out relatively inexpensive. However, it is not the most relaxing option, unless you enjoy pounding along the motorway systems of Europe for the best part of a day and a night.

Eurotunnel operates a 24-hour train service carrying vehicles and their passengers from Folkestone to Calais. At peak times, services run every ten minutes, with the journey lasting 35 minutes. Off-peak fares in the high season start at £150 return (passengers included). The alternative is to catch one of the **ferries** between Dover and Calais, Boulogne or Dunkirk, or between Ramsgate and Ostend. Prices vary enormously but if you book in advance, summer fares can be as little as £70 return per carload. Journey times are usually around ninety minutes. If you're travelling from north of London, however, it might be worth taking one of the longer ferry journeys from Rosyth, Newcastle, Hull or Harwich.

Once you've made it onto the continent, you've got some **1000km of driving** ahead of you. Theoretically, you could make it in around twelve hours solid, but realistically it will take you longer. The most direct route from Calais or Ostend is via Brussels, Liège (Luik), Cologne (Köln), Frankfurt, Würzburg and Nuremberg (Nürnberg), entering the country at the **Waidhaus–Rozvadov** border crossing. Motorways in Belgium and Germany are free, but to travel on any motorways within the Czech Republic you'll need to buy the relevant tax disc, available from all border crossings and most post offices and petrol stations. If you're travelling by car you'll need proof of ownership or a letter from the owner giving you permission to drive the vehicle. You also need a red warning triangle in case you break down, a first-aid kit (all these are compulsory in the Czech Republic), and a "Green Card" for third-party insurance cover at the very least.

Airlines, agents and operators

Online booking

Ⓦ www.expedia.co.uk (UK), Ⓦ www.expedia.com (US), Ⓦ www.expedia.ca (Canada)
Ⓦ www.lastminute.com (UK)
Ⓦ www.opodo.co.uk (UK)
Ⓦ www.orbitz.com (US)

Ⓦ www.travelocity.co.uk (UK), Ⓦ www.travelocity.com (US), Ⓦ www.travelocity.ca (Canada), Ⓦ www.travelocity.co.nz (New Zealand)
Ⓦ www.travelonline.co.za (South Africa)
Ⓦ www.zuji.com.au (Australia)

Airlines

Aer Lingus UK ☎0870/876 5000, Republic of Ireland ☎0818/365 000, US & Canada ☎1-800/IRISH-AIR, New Zealand ☎1649/308 3355, South Africa ☎1-272/2168-32838; Ⓦ www.aerlingus.com.
Air Canada US & Canada ☎1-888/247-2262, UK ☎0871/220 1111, Republic of Ireland ☎01/679 3958, Australia ☎1300/655 767, New Zealand ☎0508/747 767; Ⓦ www.aircanada.com.
Air New Zealand New Zealand ☎0800/737 000, Australia ☎0800/132 476, UK ☎0800/028 4149, Republic of Ireland ☎1800/551 447, US ☎1-800/262-1234, Canada ☎1-800/663-5494; Ⓦ www.airnz.co.nz.
Air Transat Canada ☎1-866/847-1112, Ⓦ www.airtransat.com.
American Airlines ☎1-800/433-7300, UK ☎020/7365 0777, Republic of Ireland ☎01/602 0550, Australia ☎1800/673 486, New Zealand ☎0800/445 442; Ⓦ www.aa.com.
bmi UK ☎0870/607 0555 or 0870/607 0222, Republic of Ireland ☎01/283 0700, US ☎1-800/788-0555, Australia ☎02/8644 1881, New Zealand ☎09/623 4293, South Africa ☎11/289 8111; Ⓦ www.flybmi.com.
bmibaby UK ☎0871/224 0224, Republic of Ireland ☎1890/340 122; Ⓦ www.bmibaby.com.
British Airways UK ☎0844/493 0787, Republic of Ireland ☎1890/626 747, US & Canada ☎1-800/AIR-WAYS, Australia ☎1300/767 177, New Zealand ☎09/966 9777, South Africa ☎11/441 8600; Ⓦ www.ba.com.
Cathay Pacific Australia ☎13 17 47, New Zealand ☎09/379 0861, US ☎1-800/233-2742, Canada ☎1-800/268-6868, UK ☎020/8834 8888, South Africa ☎11/700 8900; Ⓦ www.cathaypacific.com.
Continental Airlines US & Canada ☎1-800/523-3273, UK ☎0845/607 6760, Republic of Ireland ☎1890/925 252, Australia ☎1300/737 640, New Zealand ☎09/308 3350; Ⓦ www.continental.com.
CSA (Czech Airlines) UK ☎0870/444 3747, Republic of Ireland ☎0818/200 014, US ☎1-800/223-2365, Canada ☎1-866/293-8702, Australia ☎1800/063 257; Ⓦ www.czechairlines.co.uk.
Delta US & Canada ☎1-800/221-1212, UK ☎0845/600 0950, Republic of Ireland ☎1850/882 031 or 01/407 3165, Australia ☎1300/302 849, New Zealand ☎09/977 2232; Ⓦ www.delta.com.

The Best to the East.

550 flights, 48 destinations, 24 countries, 1 airline
Fly Austrian to Prague and Ostrava. For more
information & booking visit **www.austrian.com**

Austrian

We fly for your smile.

easyJet UK ⓣ0905/821 0905, ⓦwww.easyjet.com.
Gulf Air Australia ⓣ1300/366 337, US ⓣ1-888/359-4853, UK ⓣ0870/777 1717, Republic of Ireland ⓣ0818/272 828, South Africa ⓣ11/268 8909; ⓦwww.gulfairco.com.
Jet2 UK ⓣ0871/226 1737, Republic of Ireland ⓣ0818/200 017; ⓦwww.jet2.com.
KLM (Royal Dutch Airlines) US & Canada ⓣ1-800/225-2525 (Northwest), UK ⓣ0870/507 4074, Republic of Ireland ⓣ1850/747 400, Australia ⓣ1300/392 192, New Zealand ⓣ09/921 6040, South Africa ⓣ0860/247 747; ⓦwww.klm.com.
Lufthansa US ⓣ1-800/399-5838, Canada ⓣ1-800/563-5954, UK ⓣ0871/945 9747, Republic of Ireland ⓣ01/844 5544, Australia ⓣ1300/655 727, New Zealand ⓣ0800/945 220, South Africa ⓣ0861/842 538; ⓦwww.lufthansa.com.
Malaysia Airlines Australia ⓣ13 26 27, New Zealand ⓣ0800/777 747, US ⓣ1-800/552-9264, UK ⓣ0871/423 9090, Republic of Ireland ⓣ01/676 1561, South Africa ⓣ11/880 9614; ⓦwww.malaysiaairlines.com.
Northwest/KLM US ⓣ1-800/225-2525, UK ⓣ0870/507 4074, Australia ⓣ1300/767 310; ⓦwww.nwa.com.
Qantas Airways Australia ⓣ13 13 13, New Zealand ⓣ0800/808 767 or 09/357 8900, US & Canada ⓣ1-800/227-4500, UK ⓣ0845/774 7767, Republic of Ireland ⓣ01/407 3278, South Africa ⓣ11/441 8550; ⓦwww.qantas.com.
Royal Brunei Australia ⓣ1300/721 271, New Zealand ⓣ09/977 2209, UK ⓣ020/7584 6660; ⓦwww.bruneiair.com.
Ryanair UK ⓣ0871/246 0000, Republic of Ireland ⓣ0818/303 030; ⓦwww.ryanair.com.
Singapore Airlines Australia ⓣ13 10 11, New Zealand ⓣ0800/808 909, US ⓣ1-800/742-3333, Canada ⓣ1-800/663-3046, UK ⓣ0844/800 2380, Republic of Ireland ⓣ01/671 0722, South Africa ⓣ11/880 8560 or 11/880 8566; ⓦwww.singaporeair.com.
SkyEurope UK ⓣ0905/722 2747, ⓦwww.skyeurope.com.
Thai Airways Australia ⓣ1300/651 960, New Zealand ⓣ09/377 3886, US ⓣ1-212/949-8424, UK ⓣ0870/606 0911, South Africa ⓣ11/268 2580; ⓦwww.thaiair.com.
United Airlines US ⓣ1-800/864-8331, UK ⓣ0845/844 4777, Australia ⓣ13 17 77; ⓦwww.united.com.
Virgin Atlantic US ⓣ1-800/821-5438, UK ⓣ0870/574 7747, Australia ⓣ1300/727 340, South Africa ⓣ11/340 3400; ⓦwww.virgin-atlantic.com.

Agents and operators

Blue Danube Tours US ⓣ1-800/268 4155 or 416/362 5000, ⓦwww.bluedanubeholidays.com. Extensive range of city breaks and package tours, plus tailor-made options.
ČEDOK ⓦwww.cedok.com. Former state-owned tourist board offering flights, accommodation and package deals.
Czech Active Tours US ⓣ269/327-0619, Australia ⓣ08/941 79 469; ⓦwww.czechactivetours.com. Group bike tours for small groups in the Czech Republic and neighbouring countries.
Czech & Slovak Heritage Tours US ⓣ1-888/427-8687, ⓦwww.czechheritage.com. Specialists in small-group bus tours of the Czech and Slovak republics.
ebookers UK ⓣ0871/223 5000, Republic of Ireland ⓣ01/431 1311; ⓦwww.ebookers.com or www.ebookers.ie. Low fares on scheduled flights and package deals.
etours Czech Republic ⓣ572 557 191, ⓦwww.etours.cz. Walking, cycling, birding and agricultural tours (for mixed and women-only groups) in the Czech Republic and central Europe.
Interhome UK ⓣ020/8891 1294, ⓦwww.interhome.co.uk. Around four hundred self-catering houses, cottages and apartments throughout the Czech Republic.
Martin Randall Travel UK ⓣ020/8742 3355, ⓦwww.martinrandall.com. Small-group cultural tours, led by experts on art, archeology or music. Tours include walking in Bohemia, a Moravian trip and, of course, Prague.
North South Travel UK ⓣ01245/608 291, ⓦwww.northsouthtravel.co.uk. Friendly, competitive travel agency, offering discounted fares worldwide. Profits are used to support projects in the developing world, especially the promotion of sustainable tourism.
Romantic Czech Tours US ⓣ206/527-7000, ⓦwww.romanticczechtours.com. Customized walking, biking and sightseeing tour operator specializing in the Czech Republic.
STA Travel US ⓣ1-800/781-4040, UK ⓣ0871/230 0040, Australia ⓣ13 47 82, New Zealand ⓣ0800/474 400, South Africa ⓣ0861/781 781; ⓦwww.statravel.com. Worldwide specialists in independent travel; also student IDs, travel insurance, car rental, rail passes and more. Good discounts for students and under-26s.
Trailfinders UK ⓣ0845/058 5858, Republic of Ireland ⓣ01/677 7888, ⓦwww.trailfinders.com. One of the best-informed and most efficient agents for independent travellers.

Rail contacts

Deutsche Bahn ☎0871/880 8066 (Mon–Fri 9am–
5pm), ⊛www.bahn.co.uk. Competitive discounted
fares for any journey from London across Europe, with
very reasonable prices for journeys passing through
Germany.

European Rail UK ☎020/7619 1083, ⊛www
.europeanrail.com. Rail specialist offering competitive
prices on international rail tickets from anywhere in
the UK.

Eurostar UK ☎0870/518 6186, outside UK
☎0044/12336 17575; ⊛www.eurostar.com. Latest
fares and youth discounts (plus online booking) on
the Eurostar, plus competitive add-on fares from the
rest of the UK.

Man in Seat 61 ⊛www.seat61.com. The world's
finest train website, full of incredibly useful tips and
links for rail travel anywhere in the world.

National Rail ☎0845/748 4950 (24hr), ⊛www
.nationalrail.co.uk. First stop for details of all train
travel within the UK – fares, passes, train times and
delays due to engineering works.

Rail Europe UK ☎0844/848 4064, US
☎1-888/382-7245, Canada ☎1-800/361-7245,
Australia ☎03/9642 8644, South Africa ☎11/628
2319; ⊛www.raileurope.com. SNCF-owned
information and ticket agent for all European passes
and journeys from London.

Trainseurope ☎0871/700 7722 (Mon–Fri
9am–5pm), ⊛www.trainseurope.co.uk. Agent
specializing in discounted international rail travel.

Bus contacts

Eurolines UK ☎0871/781 8181, ⊛www
.nationalexpress.com/eurolines. Tickets can also be
purchased from any National Express or Bus Éireann
agent.

Student Agency ☎020/7828 1001, ⊛www
.studentagency.cz. Despite the name, anyone can
travel with this Czech-based company, which runs a
regular bus service from London to Prague.

Ferry contacts

To find out the **cheapest fares** across the
Channel, check ⊛www.ferrysmart.co.uk.

DFDS Seaways UK ☎0871/522 9955, ⊛www
.dfdsseaways.co.uk. Newcastle to Amsterdam.

Eurotunnel UK ☎0870/535 3535, ⊛www
.eurotunnel.com. Folkestone to Calais through the
Channel Tunnel.

Norfolkline UK ☎0870/870 1020 (for Dover–
Dunkerque reservations) or 0844/499 0007 (for
Irish Sea reservations); ⊛www.norfolkline.com.

P&O Ferries UK ☎0871/664 5645, ⊛www
.poferries.com. Dover to Calais and Hull to Rotterdam
and Zeebrugge.

Sea France UK ☎0871/663 2546, ⊛www
.seafrance.com. Dover to Calais.

SpeedFerries UK ☎0871/222 7456, ⊛www
.speedferries.com. Dover to Boulogne.

Stena Line UK ☎0870/570 7070, Northern Ireland
☎0870/520 4204, Republic of Ireland ☎01/204
7733; ⊛www.stenaline.co.uk. Harwich to the Hook
of Holland.

Superfast Ferries UK ☎0870 420 1267, ⊛www
.superfast.ferries.org. Rosyth (near Edinburgh) to
Zeebrugge.

Transeuropa Ferries UK ☎01843/595522,
Belgium ☎059/340260, ⊛www.transeuropaferries
.co.uk. Ramsgate to Ostend.

Getting around

The Czechs run a very reliable, inexpensive, integrated public transport system. The train system, bequeathed by the Habsburgs in 1918, is one of the densest in Europe, and has changed little since those days. Wonderfully scenic, it can be extremely slow, so if you're in a hurry, it might be worth considering taking the bus. Bus and train timetables can be found in the "Travel details" section at the end of each chapter, and in more detail at ⊛jizdnirady.idnes.cz.

By train

The country's **train** system is run, for the most part, by Czech Railways or ČD (*České dráhy*; ☏840 112 113, ⊛www.cd.cz). Trains marked "Os" (*osobní* or *zastavkový*) are local trains that stop at just about every station, while those marked "R" (*rychlík or spěšný*) are faster, stopping only at major towns. Fast trains are further divided, in descending order of speed, into "SC" (SuperCity) – for which you must pay a supplement – "EC" (EuroCity), "IC" (InterCity) and "Ex" (express).

Fares are calculated according to distance (and speed of train), with a one-way (*jednoduchá*) ticket on a fast train from Prague to Brno, a journey of 255km, costing around 300Kč (£10/$15); return fares (*zpatečni*) are slightly less than double and two or more people travelling together get a discount (*sleva pro skupiny*). Note that up to two **children** aged 5 and under travel for free,

any extra kids and those aged from 6 to 15 travel half-price; those aged 15 to 25 can buy a summer-only Junior Pass (valid from June 21–Sept 20) for just 100Kč, entitling them to discounted fares. Once you've worked out when your train leaves (for which, see the box below), the best thing to do when buying a **ticket** (*jízdenka* or *lístek*) is to write down all the relevant information (date/time/destination) on a piece of paper and hand it to the ticket clerk.

For all international services (and any other trains marked with an "R" on the timetable), you can buy a **seat reservation** (*místenka*), but it's only really worth it if you're travelling at the weekend or want to be sure of a seat. Several stations now offer **bike rental** (April–Oct) for between 100 and 200Kč a day. At some locations, you can also return the bike to a different station; check the Czech railways website for further details.

Railway timetables

Large **train stations** (*nádraží*) have information desks and a simple airport-style arrivals and departures board, which includes information on delays under the heading *zpoždění*. However, smaller stations only have poster-style displays of arrivals (*příjezd*) and departures (*odjezd*), the former on white, the latter on yellow, with fast trains printed in red. All but the smallest stations have a comprehensive display of timings and route information. These **timetables** may seem daunting at first, but with a little practice they should become decipherable. First find the route you need to take on the diagrammatic map and make a note of the number printed beside it; then follow the timetable rollers through until you come to the appropriate number. Some of the more common Czech notes at the side of the timetable are *jezdí jen v …* (only running on …), or *nejezdí v* or *nechodí v …* (not running on …), followed by a date or a symbol: a cross or an "N" for a Sunday, a big "S" for a Saturday, two crossed hammers for a weekday, "A" for a Friday and so on. Small stations may simply have a board with a list of departures under the title *směr* (direction) followed by a town. Note that a **platform**, or *nástupiště*, is usually divided into two *kolej* on either side.

By bus

Buses (*autobusy*) go almost everywhere, and from town to town they're sometimes, though not always, faster than the train. Bear in mind, though, timetables tend to be designed around the needs of commuters, and tend to fizzle out at the weekend.

In many towns and villages, the **bus station** (*autobusové nádraží*) is adjacent to the train station, though you may be able to pick up the bus from the centre of town. The bigger terminals, like Prague's Florenc, are run with train-like efficiency, with airport-style departure boards and numerous platforms. Often you can book your ticket in advance, and it's essential to do so if you're travelling at the weekend or early in the morning on one of the main routes. For most minor routes, simply buy your ticket from the driver. Large items of luggage (*zavazadlo*) go in the boot, and you'll have to pay the driver for the privilege. Minor bus stops are marked with a rusty metal sign saying *zastávka*. If you want to get off, ask *já chci vystoupit?*; "the next stop" is *příští zastávka*.

Bus **timetables** (ⓦwww.vlak-bus.cz) are more difficult to figure out than train ones, as there are no maps at any of the stations. In the detailed timetables, each service is listed separately, so you may have to scour several timetables before you discover when the next bus is. A better bet is to look at the departures and arrivals board. Make sure you check on which day the service runs, since many run only on Mondays, Fridays or at the weekend (see the section "By train", above, for the key phrases).

Bus timetable symbols

X or crossed hammers – only on weekdays
S – Saturday only
N – Sunday only
b – Monday to Saturday
a – Saturday, Sunday and holidays only
P – Monday only
V – Friday only
c – schooldays only
g – daily except Saturday
d – Monday to Thursday
y – Tuesday to Friday

By car

The motorway system in the Czech Republic is very limited, and traffic outside the big cities is still pretty light. The only place where you might encounter difficulties is in the bigger cities and towns, where the lane system is confusing, tramlines hazardous and parking a nightmare. You have to be 18 or over to drive in the Czech Republic, and if you want to travel on long-distance motorways, you'll need a **motorway tax disc** or *dálniční známka*, which currently costs around 220Kč for one week, 330Kč for one month, and is available from all border crossings and most post offices and petrol stations.

If you're bringing your own car, you'll need proof of ownership, or a letter from the owner giving you permission to drive the car. A British or other EU **driving licence** is fine; all other drivers are advised to purchase an International Driving Licence. You also need a red warning triangle and high-visibility vest in case you break down, a first-aid kit, a set of spare light bulbs, spare glasses (for those who need them) and a "Green Card" (*zelená karta*) for third party insurance cover at the very least. An even better idea is to sign up with one of the national motoring organizations, which offer continental breakdown assistance and, in extreme circumstances, will get you and your vehicle brought back home if necessary.

Rules of the road

Rules and regulations on Czech roads are pretty stringent, with on-the-spot fines regularly handed out, up to a maximum of 2000Kč. The basic rules are driving on the right; compulsory wearing of seatbelts; headlights on at all times; children under 1.5m must travel in a child seat; hands-free mobiles only; and no alcohol at all in your blood when you're driving. Theoretically, Czechs are supposed to give way to pedestrians at zebra crossings, but few do. However, Czechs do give way to pedestrians crossing at traffic lights when turning right or left. You must also give way to trams, and, if there's no safety island at a tram stop, you must stop immediately and allow passengers to get on and off. As in other continental

Traffic signs

Průjezd zakázán	closed to all vehicles
Dálkov provoz	by-pass
Objížďka	diversion
Nemocnice	hospital
Choďte vlevo	pedestrians must walk on the left
Zákaz zastavení	no stopping
Rozsviť světla	switch your lights on
Bez poplatku	free of charge
Úsek častych nechod	area where accidents often occur
Nebezpečí smyku	slippery road
Při sněhu a náledí cesta uzavřena	road closed due to snow or ice
Pozor dětí	watch out for children

countries, a yellow diamond sign means you have right of way, a black line through it means you don't; it's important to clock this sign before you reach the junction since the road markings at junctions rarely make priorities very clear. A blank sign in a red circle means "no entry" except to those vehicles stated underneath (in Czech).

Vehicle crime is not unknown, so don't leave anything visible or valuable in the car. Restrictions on **parking** are commonplace in Czech towns – for a start, you should always park with your car facing the same direction as the traffic flow. Pay-and-display meters are the easiest system to decipher; more complicated are the voucher schemes, which require you to buy a voucher from a newsagent, tourist office or bookshop. Illegally parked cars will either be clamped or towed away – if this happens, phone ☏158.

Petrol (*benzín*) comes as *natural* (unleaded 95 octane), *super plus* (unleaded 98 octane), *special* (leaded 91 octane) and *nafta* (diesel); LPG or *plyn* is also available from some petrol stations. Petrol currently costs over 30Kč a litre (£1/$2). If you have car **trouble**, dial ☏1230 at the nearest phone and wait for assistance. For peace of mind it might be worth taking out an insurance policy that will pay for any on-the-spot repairs and, if necessary, ship you and your passengers home free of charge.

Speed limits are 130kph on motorways (if you travel any faster you will be fined), 90kph on other roads and 50kph in all cities, towns and villages – you need to remember these, as there are few signs to remind you. In addition, there's a special speed limit of 30kph for level crossings (you'll soon realize why if you try ignoring it). Many level crossings have no barriers, simply a sign saying "*pozor*" and a series of lights: a single flashing light means that the line is live; two red flashing lights mean there's a train coming.

Car and motorbike rental

All of the big international **car rental** companies have offices in Prague and Brno, and it's easy to book a car online before you travel. If you book in advance and shop around, prices can go as low as £15–20/$25–35 a day for a small car, £120/$180 a week. In order to rent a car, you'll need to be at least 21, have a clean licence, and have been driving for at least a year; all hire cars come with a valid motorway sticker. Motorbike rental is available from Motorbike Ventures (see the box on rental agencies below).

Cycling, hiking and boating

Cycling is a popular leisure activity in the Czech Republic, and the rolling countryside, though hard work on the legs, is rewarding. Facilities for bike rental (*půjčovna*) are improving, especially in the more touristy areas, and the increasing number of bike shops makes repairs possible and spare parts slightly easier to obtain. To take your bike (*kolo*) on the train, you must buy a separate ticket before taking it down to the freight

Czech rental agencies

Alimex Czech Republic ☏724 316 131, ⊛www.alimex.sk.

Czechocar Czech Republic ☏800 321 321, ⊛www.czechocar.cz.

Motorbike Ventures Czech Republic ☏773 453 184, US ☏1-925/348-9433; ⊛www.motorbikeventures.com.

Addresses

The street name is always written before the number in **addresses**. The word for street (*ulice/ulica*) is either abbreviated to *ul.* or simply missed out altogether. Other terms often abbreviated are *náměstí/námestie* (square), *třída/trieda* (avenue) and *nábřeží/nábrežie* (embankment), which become *nám.*, *tř./tr.* and *nánř./nábr.* respectively. Bear in mind when using a Czech index that "Ch" is considered a separate letter and comes after H in the alphabet. Similarly, "Č", "Ď", "Ľ", "Ř", "Š" and "Ž" are all listed separately, immediately after their non-accented cousins. Many towns and villages in the Czech republics were once inhabited by German minorities. In these places we have given the German name in brackets after the Czech, for example Mariánské Lázně (Marienbad).

section of the station, where, after filling in the mountains of paperwork, your bike should be smoothly sent on to its destination.

Hiking is a very popular pastime with young and old alike, the most enthusiastic indulging in an activity curiously known as going *na trampu*; dressing up in quasi-military gear, camping in the wilds, playing guitar and singing songs round the campfire. A dense network of paths covers the countryside. All trails are colour-coded with clear markers every 200m or so and signs indicating roughly how long it'll take you to reach your destination. Many walks are fairly easy-going, but it can be wet and muddy underfoot even in summer, so sturdy boots are a good idea, particularly if you venture into the mountains proper. There are no hiking guides in English, but it's easy enough to get hold of 1:50,000 maps that cover the whole country and detail all the marked paths in the area (see p.40).

The opportunity for travelling by **boat** (*loď*) is pretty limited, but there are a few services worth mentioning. From Prague, boats sail all the way upriver to Orlík, with a change of vessel at each of the dams on the way (see box, p.162), and downriver to Mělník, where the Vltava flows into the Labe (Elbe). There's also a summer service on Lake Lipno in South Bohemia (see p.191).

City transport

City transport is generally excellent, with buses (*autobus*), trolleybuses (*trolejbus*) and sometimes also trams (*tramvaj*) running from dawn until around midnight in most major towns (and all night in Prague and Brno). Ticket prices vary from place to place (10–20Kč for an adult, reduced rates for those aged 6–14, under-6s travel free), but are universally cheap. In Prague and Brno, it's a good idea to buy a pass (see the relevant city accounts).

With a few exceptions, you must buy your ticket (*lístek* or *jízdenka*) before getting on board. Tickets, which are standard for all types of transport, are available from newsagents, tobacconists and the yellow machines at major stops, and are validated in the punching machines once you're on board. There are no conductors, only plain-clothes inspectors (*revizoři*), who make spot checks and will issue an on-the-spot fine of 500Kč.

Taxis are cheap and plentiful. Beware, however, that tourists are seen as easy prey by some taxi drivers, especially in Prague. The best advice is to have your hotel or pension call you one, rather than pick one up on the street or at the taxi ranks.

Accommodation

Accommodation is likely to be by far the largest chunk of your daily expenditure, unless you're camping. Overall, standards in pensions, hotels and hostels have improved enormously. Only in Prague, and, to a lesser extent, in Brno, is it difficult to find reasonably priced accommodation. If you're going to Prague anytime from Easter to September or over Christmas and New Year, it's as well to arrange accommodation before you arrive.

Hotels, pensions and private rooms

On the whole, the country has come a long way from the bad old days when foreign visitors were shepherded into high-rise monstrosities and charged three times as much as locals for services that were uniformly bad. That said, old Communist hotel dinosaurs live on and "service with a snarl" is still occasionally encountered.

All **hotels** operate a star system, though it's self-regulatory and therefore none too reliable. Prices vary wildly and, unsurprisingly, tend to be much higher in areas that receive the most tourists. The vast majority of rooms now have en-suite bathrooms and TVs, with continental breakfast either included in the price or offered as an optional extra, and you'll find a restaurant and/or bar in almost every hotel.

Most guesthouses bill themselves as **pensions**. Again, prices and standards can vary widely, and a well-run pension can often be cheaper, friendlier and better equipped than many hotels. An alternative in some areas is to opt for **private rooms**. You can be sure that they will be clean and tidy, but in what proximity you'll be to your hosts is difficult to predict. You might be sharing

bathroom, cooking facilities and more with the family – Czech hospitality can be somewhat overwhelming, although meals other than breakfast are not generally included in the price. In some parts of the countryside you'll see plenty of signs saying either *ubytování* ("accommodation") or *pokoje* ("rooms") or *Zimmer Frei* ("rooms available" in German). In some towns and cities, you may be able to book rooms through the local tourist office (details are listed throughout the *Guide*).

Hostels and student rooms

Hostels in the Czech Republic vary enormously in size, quality and location. A smattering are affiliated to Hostelling International (ⓦ www.hihotels.com or ⓦ www .czechhostels.com), but there are plenty of good ones that aren't. If you want to book or plan ahead, visit one of the aforementioned websites or ⓦ www.hostels.com.

An alternative in the big university towns is **student accommodation** – known as *kolej* – which is let out cheap to travellers from June to August. Though often heavily booked up in advance by groups, they'll usually try their best to squeeze you in.

Accommodation price codes

All hotels and pensions in this book have been coded according to the following **price categories**, based on the rate for the least expensive double room during the summer season.

❶ 500Kč and under
❷ 501–1000Kč
❸ 1001–1500Kč
❹ 1501–2000Kč
❺ 2001–2500Kč
❻ 2501–3000Kč
❼ 3001–4000Kč
❽ 4001–5000Kč
❾ 5001Kč and over

Addresses can change from year to year, so to find out the most recent, go to the local tourist office.

Camping and other options

Campsites (*autokemping*) are plentiful all over the Czech Republic. Some are huge affairs, with shops, swimming pools, draught beer and so on; others, known often as *tábořiště*, are just a simple stretch of grass with ad hoc toilets and a little running water. Many sites feature chalets (*chaty* or *bungolovy*), which vary in size and facilities from rabbit hutches to mini-villas; prices start at around 400Kč for two people.

Very few campsites are open all year round, most opening in May and closing in September. Charges are pretty reasonable; two people plus car and tent cost from 250Kč. Campfires, though officially banned, are tolerated at many campsites, and the guitar-playing barbecues can go on until well into the night.

Mountain huts

In the mountains of the Krkonoše, there are a fair number of **mountain huts** (*bouda* or *chata*) scattered about the hillsides. Some are just like hotels and charge similar prices, but the more isolated ones are simple wooden shelters costing around 300Kč per person, with minimal facilities. A few are accessible by road, and most are only a few miles from civilization. Ideally, these should be booked in advance through the various accommodation agencies in the nearest settlements. The more isolated huts work on a first-come, first-served basis, but if you turn up before 6pm, you're unlikely to be turned away.

Eating and drinking

The good news is that you can eat and drink very cheaply in the Czech Republic: the food is filling and the beer flows freely. The bad news is that the kindest thing you can say about traditional Czech food is that it is hearty. That said, the choice of places to eat has improved enormously over the last decade. In Prague, at least, you could spend a whole week and never go near a dumpling, should you so wish. The Czechs themselves are very keen on pizza, and there are some very good pizzerias in the larger towns and cities. In Prague, and, to a lesser extent, Brno, you will even find some passably authentic ethnic restaurants ranging from Japanese and Lebanese to Balkan and French. For a comprehensive glossary of Czech food and drink terms, see the language section on p.419.

Where to eat

The division between cafés, bars, pubs and restaurants is pretty blurred. **Restaurants** (*restaurace* in Czech) are primarily there to serve you food, but some will also have a bar where you can simply have a drink. Away from the touristy towns, the **menu** (*jídelní lístek*), which should be displayed outside, is often in Czech only, and deciphering it without a grounding in the language can be quite a feat. Bear in mind that, on a traditional menu, the right-hand column lists the prices, while the far left column gives you the estimated weight of every dish in grams; if what you get weighs more or less, the price will alter accordingly (this applies in particular to fish).

Other places style themselves as *vinárna* or **wine-bars**, though they, too, often serve food. Equally, while many **cafés** (*kavárna* in Czech) realize most of their customers only want a drink and maybe a slice of cake,

Czech etiquette

It's common practice to **share a table** with other eaters or drinkers; *je tu volno?* ("Is this seat free?") is the standard question. **Waiter-service** is the norm, even in pubs, so sit tight and a beer should come your way. You may have to ask to see the **menu** (*jídelní lístek*) in pubs and some cafés to indicate that you wish to eat. When food arrives for your neighbours, it's common courtesy to wish them bon appetit (*dobrou chuť*). When you want to leave, simply say *zaplatím, prosím* (literally "I'll pay, please"), and your **tab** will be totted up. A modest form of **tipping** exists in all establishments, generally done by rounding up the bill to the nearest few crowns, though beware that the waiters haven't already done this for you. On leaving, bid your neighbours farewell (*na shledanou*).

many serve up cheap, hot snacks and even full meals. Czech **pubs** (*pivnice, hostinec* or *hospoda* in Czech) are on the whole the cheapest places to eat, and almost exclusively serve standard Czech food. Cheaper still is the local stand-up **bufet**, usually a self-service café serving basic, hot Czech meals.

Breakfast and snacks

Czechs generally have little time for **breakfast** (*snídaně*) as such. Many get up so early in the morning (often around 6am) that they simply start the day with a quick cup of coffee or tea. Most hotels will serve the "continental" basics of tea, coffee, rolls and cold cheese and meat. Bear in mind, though, that if you get up much past 10am you may as well join the country's working population for lunch.

Pastries (*pečivo*) are sold in bakeries (*pekařství*), but rarely in bars and cafés, so you'll probably have to eat them on the go. The ubiquitous croissant (*loupák*) and muffins are now widely available, but a traditional Czech pastry (*koláč*) is more like sweet bread; dry and fairly dense with only a little flavouring in the form of hazelnuts (*oříškový*), poppy-seed jam (*makový*), prune jam (*povidlový*) or a kind of sour-sweet curd cheese (*tvarohový*).

Czech morning rolls come in two basic varieties: *rohlík*, a plain finger roll, and *houska*, a rougher, tastier round bun. Czech **bread** (*chléb*) is some of the tastiest around when fresh. The standard loaf is a dense mixture of wheat and rye, which you can buy whole, in halves (*půl*) or quarters (*čtvrtina*). Fresh milk (*čerstvé mléko*) is available in most supermarkets either *plnotučné* (full fat) or

nízkotučné (semi-skimmed). Look out, too, for *kefír*, deliciously thick sourmilk, or *acidofilní mléko*, its slightly thinner counterpart.

The ubiquitous street **takeaway** is the hot dog or *párek*, a dubious-looking frankfurter (traditionally two – *párek* means a pair), dipped in mustard and served with a white roll (*v rohlíku*). A greasier option is *bramborák*, a thin potato pancake with flecks of bacon or salami. In larger towns, *felafal* or kebabs (known as *gyros*) form another popular takeaway choice, usually with pitta bread and salad. And, of course, there are now numerous multinational fast-food joints (most notably *McDonald's*) all over the country.

The stand-up **bufet** or *jídelna* is a dying breed, but you may still come across one or two. A cross between a British greasy spoon and an American diner, they're usually self-service (*samoobsluha*) and offer incredibly cheap basic food. While the *jídelna* declines, the **sandwich bar** (*sandvič*) bar goes from strength to strength, with more and more Czechs opting for a quick light lunch. Traditionally, the Czechs went for artistically presented open sandwiches known as *chlebíčky* – with combinations of gherkins, cheese, salami, ham and aspic – but the baguette, the Italian panini and the multinational wrap are now on the ascendancy.

Like the Austrians who once ruled over them, the Czechs have a grotesquely sweet tooth, and the **coffee-and-cake** hit is part of the daily ritual. The **cukrárna** is the place to go for cake-eating. There are two main types of cake: *dort*, like the German *Tort*, consist of layers of custard cream, chocolate and sponge, while *řez* are lighter square cakes, usually containing a bit of fruit. A *věneček*, filled with "cream", is the nearest you'll get to an éclair and a *kobliha* is a doughnut. One speciality to look out for is a *rakvička*, which literally means "little coffin", an extended piece of sugar like a meringue, with cream, moulded vaguely into the shape of a coffin. Whatever the season, Czechs have to have their daily fix of **ice cream** (*zmrzlina*), available from machines or scooped, either dispensed from little window kiosks in the sides of buildings, or dished out from within a *cukrárna*.

Czech cuisine

Czechs don't go big on starters, with the exception of **soup** (*polévka*), one of the country's culinary strong points. There are two types of **main course**: *hotová jídla* (ready-made meals), which should arrive swiftly, and *jídla na objednávku* or *minutky* (meals made to order), for which you'll have to wait. In either case, dishes are overwhelmingly based on **meat** (*maso*), usually pork, sometimes beef. The difficulty lies in decoding names such as *klašterní tajemství* ("mystery of the monastery") or even a common dish like *Moravský vrabec* (literally "Moravian sparrow", but actually just roast pork). **Fish** (*ryby*) is generally listed separately, or along with chicken (*drůbez*) and other fowl like duck (*kachna*). River trout (*pstruh*) and carp (*kapr*) – the traditional dish

at Christmas – are the cheapest and most widely available fish, and, although their freshness may be questionable, they are usually served, grilled or roasted, in delicious buttery sauces or breadcrumbs.

Side dishes (*přílohy*), most commonly served with fish and fowl, generally consist of either chips (*hranolky*) or potatoes (*brambory*), though with meat dishes you'll often be offered **dumplings** (*knedlíky*), one of the mainstays of Bohemian cooking. The term itself is misleading for English-speakers, since they look nothing like the English dumpling – more like a heavy white bread. *Houskové knedlíky* are made from flour and come in large slices (four or five to a dish), while *bramborové knedlíky* are smaller and made from potato and flour. Occasionally, you may be treated to *ovocné knedlíky* (fruit dumplings), the king of *knedlíky* and usually served with melted butter and soured cream as a sweet main course.

Fresh **salads** rarely rise above the ubiquitous *obloha*, with a bit of tomato, cucumber and lettuce, or cabbage (*zelí*), often swimming in a slightly sweet, watery dressing. *Šopský* salads, made with a feta-like cheese, are a pale imitation of Greek salads (often without olives), but are generally fresher and more substantial than most other salads on offer.

Vegetarians

Czech meat consumption remains one of the highest in the world. It's hardly suprising then that **vegetarianism** is still a minority sport. Needless to say, you're better off in Prague than anywhere else in the country. For a start, places which cater mostly for expats usually have one or two veggie options, and there are plenty of pizzerias.

Even in traditional Czech places, most menus have a section called *bezmasa* (literally "without meat") – don't take this too literally, though, for it simply means the main ingredient is not dead animal; dishes like *omeleta se šunkou* (ham omelette) can appear under these headings, so always check first. The staple of Czech vegetarianism is *smažený sýr*, a slab of melted cheese, deep-fried in breadcrumbs and served with tartare sauce (*tartarská omáčka*) – beware, though, as it's sometimes served *se šunkou* (with ham). Other types of cheese can also be deep fried, as can other vegetables: *smažené žampiony* (mushrooms) and *smaženy květák* (cauliflower). Emergency veggie standbys which most Czech pubs will knock up for you without too much fuss include *knedlíky s vejci* (dumplings and scrambled egg) or *omeleta s hráškem* (pea omelette).

Veggie phrases to remember are *"jsem vegeterián/vegeteriánka. Máte nejaké bezmasa?"* (I'm a vegetarian. Is there anything without meat?); for emphasis, you could add *"nejím maso nebo ryby"* (I don't eat meat or fish).

With the exception of *palačinky* (pancakes) filled with chocolate or fruit and cream, **desserts** (*moučníky*), where they exist at all, can be pretty unexciting.

Drinking

Traditional Czech **pubs** are smoky, male-dominated places, where most of the customers are drinking copious quantities of Czech beer by the half-litre. If you want a more mixed environment, you're better off heading for a wine cellar or café, where you'll get a wider selection of wine and spirits, but probably only bottled beer.

Coffee and tea

Coffee (*káva*) is drunk black and is usually available in espresso (*presso*) form: small, black and strong, though by no means as diminutive as in Italy. Occasionally, you may still come across the traditional Czech coffee, called somewhat hopefully *turecká* (Turkish) – it's really just hot water poured over ground coffee. Some places sell *ledová káva*, a weak, cold black coffee, while at the other end of the scale *Vídeňská káva* (Viennese coffee) is a favourite with the older generation, served with a dollop of whipped cream.

Tea (*čaj*) is drunk weak and without milk, although you'll usually be given a glass of boiling water and a tea bag so you can do your own thing – for milk, say "*s mlékem*". If you want really good tea, you should look out for a *čajovna,* one of the country's growing number of tea-houses: calm, no-smoking cafés that take their tea drinking very seriously.

Alcohol

Alcohol consumption among Czechs has always been high, and in the decade following the events of 1968 it doubled, as a whole generation found solace in drinking, mostly **beer** (*pivo*). The Czechs remain top of the world league table of beer consumption even now, though it's a problem that seldom spills out onto the streets; violence in pubs is uncommon and the only obnoxious drunks you're likely to see (in Prague at least) are members of British stag and hen parties. Czech beer ranks among the best in the world and the country remains the true home

of most of the lager drunk around the world today – see our colour insert for more on Czech beer.

The country's **wine** (*vino*) will never win over as many people as its beer, but since the import of French and German vines in the fourteenth century, it has produced a modest selection of medium-quality wines. The main wine region is South Moravia, though a little is produced around the town of Mělník. Most places list their wines by grape type and occasionally also by region – *Svatovařinecké* (Saint Laurent) is the most popular red and *Veltlínské zelené* (*Grüner Veltliner*) is a good, dry white, but the best stuff can only be had from the private wine cellars (*sklepy*), hundreds of which still exist out in the regions. A Czech speciality is *burčák*, a very young, fizzy, sweet, misty wine of varying (and often very strong) alcoholic content, which appears on the streets in the vine harvest season for three weeks in September.

All the usual **spirits** are on sale and known by their generic names, with rum and vodka dominating the market. The home production of brandies is a national pastime, and the most renowned of the lot is *slivovice*, a **plum brandy** originally from the border hills between Moravia and Slovakia. You'll probably also come across *borovička*, a popular Slovak firewater, made from pine trees; *myslivec* is a rough brandy with a firm following. There's also a fair selection of intoxicating herbal concoctions: *fernet* is a dark-brown bitter drink, known as *bavorák* (Bavarian beer) when it's mixed with tonic, while *becherovka* is a supposedly healthy herbal spirit made to a secret recipe from the Bohemian spa town of Karlovy Vary, with a very unusual, almost medicinal taste; it can also be mixed with tonic, when it's known as *beton*.

Although illegal in some parts of Europe, **absinthe** has enjoyed something of a renaissance in the Czech Republic. The preferred poison of Parisian painters and poets in the nineteenth century, absinthe is a nasty green spirit made from fermented wormwood. At 170 degrees proof, it's dangerous stuff and virtually undrinkable neat. To make it vaguely palatable, you need to set light to an absinthe-soaked spoonful of sugar, and then mix the caramelized mess with the absinthe.

The media

You'll find the full range of foreign newspapers at kiosks in city centres, large train stations and more touristy resorts. In Prague and Brno, you can usually get the European edition of the British broadsheet the *Guardian*, printed in Frankfurt, by mid-morning the same day. Similarly, the *International Herald Tribune* is printed in Europe and available the same day, and contains a useful distilled English version of the *Frankfurter Allgemeine Zeitung*. Elsewhere in the Czech Republic, foreign papers, where available, tend to be a day or two old.

The *Prague Post* (ⓦwww.praguepost.com) is an **English-language weekly** aimed at the expat community, but good for visitors, too; it's a quality paper with strong business coverage and a useful pull-out listings section. You'll find the best coverage of contemporary Czech politics in English in *The New Presence/Nová přítomnost*, a bilingual current affairs **magazine**, directly inspired by the Masaryk-funded *Přítomnost*, which was one of the leading periodicals of the First Republic.

It's a sign of the times that the most of **Czech press** is German-owned, and the most popular newspaper is a sensationalist tabloid. It's a similar story with **TV** – the majority of Czechs watch the foreign (mostly American) programming supplied by the country's two commercial channels.

Czech newspapers and magazines

The only Czech-owned mass circulation daily is the left-wing *Právo*, formerly the official mouthpiece of the Communist Party (when it was known as *Rudé právo* or "Red Justice"). Its chief competitor is *Mladá fronta dnes*, former mouthpiece of the Communist youth movement, now a very popular centre-right daily. *Lidové noviny* (the best-known *samizdat* or underground publication under the Communists and the equivalent of *The Times* under the First Republic) is now a much less respected right-wing daily, while the orange-coloured *Hospodářské noviny* is the Czech equivalent of the *Financial Times* or *Wall Street Journal*. The country's most popular newspaper is *Blesk*, a sensationalist tabloid with lurid colour pictures, naked women and reactionary politics. If all you want, however, is yesterday's (or, more often than not, the day before yesterday's) international sports results, pick up a copy of the daily *Sport*.

Czech TV and radio

The state-run **radio** broadcaster *Český rozhlas* has four stations: *ČR1 Radiožurnál* (94.6FM), which is mainly current affairs; *ČR2* (91.3FM), which features more magazine-style programming; and *ČR3 Vltava* (105FM), a culture and arts station that plays a fair amount of classical music. The president broadcasts his Sunday evening chat on *ČR1*; an English-language news summary goes out Monday to Friday at 5.30pm. The three top commercial channels are *Evropa 2* (88.2FM), *Radio Bonton* (99.7FM) and *Radio Kiss* (98FM), which dish out bland Euro-pop. More interesting is *Radio 1* (91.9FM), which plays a wide range of indie rock.

The most popular Czech **TV** channel is *Nova*, a commercial station that gets more than forty percent of the audience share, thanks to its mix of American sitcoms dubbed into Czech, talent and reality shows, striptease weather forecasts and comprehensive coverage of Czech football. It's followed closely behind by the similar *Prima*, the country's other commercial channel. Despite broadcasting better-quality programmes, the state-run *Česká televize* (Czech TV) has been eclipsed as far as ratings go; it currently has four **channels**, *ČT1* and *ČT2* (the latter is your best bet for foreign films with subtitles), plus rolling news on *ČT24* and the sports channel, *4 Sport*.

Festivals

There are remarkably few large-scale national festivals. Aside from the usual religious celebrations, most annual shindigs are arts-, music- and sports-based events, confined to a particular town or city. In addition, there are also folkloric events in the nether regions, the Strážnice folk festival in Moravia being by far the most famous.

Jan 6 nationwide – Epiphany (*Den tří králů*). The letters K + M + B (the initials of the three wise men) followed by the date of the new year are chalked on doorways across the capital to celebrate the "Day of the Three Kings" when the Magi came to worship Christ.

Zabijačka, Masopust & Easter moveable festivals nationwide – the "Slaughter of the Pig", known as *zabijačka*, takes place in rural parts towards the end of winter, when all other provisions are exhausted. Every bit of the animal is prepared for the feast that accompanies the event. As with Carnival (Mardi Gras), *Masopust* means literally "goodbye to meat", and prompts parties, concerts and masked parades in anticipation for the arrival of Lent. Easter heralds the age-old sexist ritual of whipping girls' calves with braided birch twigs tied together with ribbons (*pomlázky*). To prevent such a fate, the girls are supposed to offer the boys a coloured Easter egg and pour a bucket of cold water over them.

late April Olomouc – the country's most hortilogical town puts on a spectacular flower festival in the Výstaviště. ⊛ www.flora-ol.cz

April 30 nationwide – Burning of the Witches (*pálení čarodějnic*). Halloween comes early to the Czech Republic when bonfires are lit across the country, and old brooms thrown out and burned, as everyone celebrates the end of the long winter.

May 12–June 2 Prague – *Pražské jaro* (Prague Spring Festival). The country's biggest annual arts event and most prestigious international music festival begins on the anniversary of Smetana's death, with a procession from his grave in Vyšehrad to the Obecní dům where the composer's *Má vlast* (My Country) is performed in the presence of the president, and finishes with a rendition of Beethoven's *Ninth Symphony*. Tickets sell out fast – try writing a month in advance to the Prague Spring Festival box office at Hellichova 18, Malá Strana; ☎ 257 310 414, ⊛ www.festival.cz

mid-May Ostrava – despite its name, the city's *Janáčkův máj* is not a celebration of Janáček's music but a classical music festival. ⊛ www.janackuvmaj.cz

late May Chrudim – week-long (mostly Czech) puppet festival. ⊛ www.pim.cz

late May Prague – *Khamoro* is an international Roma festival of music, dance and film, with seminars and workshops. ☎ 222 518 554, ⊛ www.khamoro.cz

late May/early June Prague – week-long international puppet festival organized by Prague's chief puppetry institute. ⊛ www.puppetart.com

late May Vlčnov – the elaborate *Jízda králů* (Ride of the Kings) procession is a great opportunity to see Moravian folk costumes in all their glory. ⊛ jizdakralu.vlcnov.cz

early June Prague – *Tanec Praha* (Dance Prague). An international, three-week-long festival of modern dance that's an established highlight in the cultural calendar. ☎ 224 817 886, ⊛ www.tanecpha.cz

mid-June Český Krumlov – the town fills up for *Slavnost pětilisté růže* (Five-petalled Rose Festival), a three-day binge of medieval and Renaissance music, dancing, jousting and processions. ⊛ www.ckrumlov.info

mid-June Litomyšl – an impressive smattering of international stars come for the open-air Smetana Opera Festival, where there's a Czech (rather than Smetana) slant. ⊛ www.nulk.cz

mid-June Pelhřimov – two-day festival in which mad folk from around the globe try and break various obscure world records and do ludicrous things. ⊛ www.dobryden.cz

mid-June Strážnice – probably the oldest, largest and most traditional folk festival in central Europe, this is primarily a showpiece for Czech folk culture, with just a few international guests. ⊛ www.nulk.cz

late June Prague – concerts begin in mid-May, but the Respect music festival comes into its own at the end of the month, with a world music weekend held on the Štvanice island. ☎ 296 330 988, ⊛ www.respectmusic.cz

early July Karlovy Vary – the country's premier international film festival is one of Europe's top cinematic gatherings. ⊛ www.kviff.com

early July Hradec Králové – Rock for People. Well-established open-air pop/rock festival featuring

bands from all over Europe and America. ⓦwww
.rockforpeople.cz

mid-July Ostrava – **Colours of Ostrava** is the
country's biggest world music festival, held over a
summer weekend in the middle of the city. ⓦwww
.colours.cz

July to early Aug Telč – *Prázdniny Telči*, a
fortnight-long festival featuring folk music from
traditional to contemporary, Czech and global.
ⓦwww.prazdninyvtelci.cz

mid-Aug Mariánské Lázně – long-established
International Chopin Festival featuring music by
Chopin and other romantics. ⓦwww.chopinfestival.cz

mid-Aug Domažlice – Bohemia's biggest traditional
folk festival, with music, dancing and lots of amazing
costumes. ⓦwww.chodskeslavnosti.cz

late Aug Strakonice – international bagpipe festival
(MDF), featuring an amazing array of Czech and
foreign bagpipers. ⓦwww.dudackyfestival.cz

late Aug Valtice – Baroque music festival staged in
and around the town's beautiful chateau. ⓦwww
.festivalvaltice.cz

early Sept Žatec – *Dočesná* is a two-day festival
celebrating the town's most precious commodity,
hops.

mid-Sept Prague – *Pražský podzim* (Prague
Autumn Festival). Not quite as prestigious as the
spring festival, but with plenty of top-drawer classical
music performances held at the Rudolfinum. ⓦwww
.pragueautumn.cz

Sept–Oct Brno – *Moravský podzim* (Moravian
Autumn). The city's chief classical music festival, with
a different theme each year. ⓦwww.mhf-brno.cz

early Oct Plzeň – the *Pilsner Fest* is the town's
beery celebration of its status as the home of all lager.
ⓦwww.pilsnerfest.cz

mid-Oct Prague – *Pražský podzim* (Prague
Autumn Festival) is not quite as prestigious as the
spring festival, but there's still plenty of top-drawer
performances of classical music held at the
Rudolfinum. ⓦwww.pragueautumn.cz

early Dec Prague – annual music festival
celebrating the least known of the big four Czech
composers, Bohuslav Martinů. ⓦwww.martinu.cz

Dec 5 nationwide – on the eve of St Nicholas Day
(Dec 6), numerous trios, dressed up as St Nicholas
(*svatý Mikuláš*), an angel and a devil, tour the streets,
the angel handing out sweets and fruit to children
who've been good, the devil dishing out coal and
potatoes to those who've been naughty. The Czech
St Nicholas has white hair and a beard, and dresses not
in red but in a white priest's outfit, with a bishop's mitre.

Dec 24 nationwide – Christmas Eve (*Štědrý večer*)
is traditionally a day of fasting, broken only when the
evening star appears, signalling the beginning of the
Christmas feast of carp, potato salad, schnitzel and
sweetbreads. Only after the meal are the children
allowed to open their presents, which miraculously
appear beneath the tree, thanks not to Santa Claus,
but to Baby Jesus (*Ježíšek*).

Travel essentials

Costs

In general terms, the Czech Republic is an **inexpensive** place to visit, with the exception of accommodation, which is comparable with many EU countries. That said, price differences across the republic are quite marked: hotel costs in central Prague are exorbitant, while in some parts of the countryside, accommodation can be very reasonably priced. All other basic costs, like food, drink and transport, remain very cheap indeed. To put things in perspective, it's worth bearing in mind that the average monthly salary for Czechs is around 20,000Kč (£650/$1000).

Most sights and some cinemas, theatres and events offer **concessions** for senior citizens, the unemployed, full-time students and children under 16, with under-5s being admitted free almost everywhere – proof of eligibility will be required in most cases. Once obtained, **youth/student ID cards** soon pay for themselves in savings. Full-time students are eligible for the International Student Identity Card or ISIC (Ⓦ www.isiccard.com), which costs around £10/$15. If you're not a student, but you are under 26, you can get an International Youth Card, or IYTC, which costs the same as the ISIC and carries the same benefits.

Crime and personal safety

Almost all problems encountered by tourists in the Czech Republic are to do with petty crime. Because you're legally obliged to carry ID with you at all times, ideally your passport, or at the least a driving licence, it's a good idea to keep photocopies of these documents. Reporting thefts to the police is straightforward enough, though it takes some time to wade through the bureaucracy. The national **police** force (*Policie*), who wear navy blue, grey and white, are under the control of Ministry of Interior. However, if you do need the police – and above all if you're reporting a serious crime – you should always go to the municipal police, run by the local authorities and known as *Městská policie*; their uniforms differ from region to region, though black is a popular choice. In addition, there are various **private police** forces, who also dress in black – hence their nickname *Černí šerifové* (Black Sheriffs) – employed mostly by hotels and banks. They are allowed to carry guns, but have no powers of arrest, and you are not legally obliged to show them your ID.

Electricity

The Czech Republic uses the standard continental **220 volts AC**. Most European appliances should work as long as you have an adaptor for continental-style two-pin round plugs. North Americans will need this plus a transformer.

Emergency numbers

Emergencies ☏ 112
Ambulance ☏ 155
Police ☏ 158
Fire ☏ 150

Entry requirements

To enter the Czech Republic, citizens of the EU, US, Canada, Australia and New Zealand need only a full **passport**, valid for at least six months beyond your return date. UK citizens can stay up to 180 days; all other EU and US citizens, Australians and New Zealanders can stay up to ninety days. Citizens of most other countries require a **visa**, obtainable from a Czech embassy or consulate in the country of application (see Ⓦ www.mzv.cz for a list). All visitors must register with the police within three days of arrival (if you're staying in a campsite, hostel, pension or hotel, this will be done for you). If you do need a visa, note that they are no longer issued at border stations, but must be obtained in advance from a Czech embassy or consulate. If you wish to extend your visa or your stay, you

Embassies and consulates

Australia Klimentská 10, Prague ⊤251 018 350.
Belarus Sádky 626, Prague ⊤233 540 899.
Britain Thunovská 14, Prague ⊤257 402 111, ⓦwww.britain.cz.
Canada Muchova 6, Prague ⊤272 101 890, ⓦwww.canada.cz.
Ireland Tržiště 13, Prague ⊤257 530 061.
New Zealand Dykova 19, Prague ⊤222 514 672.
Poland Valdštejnská 8, Prague ⊤257 099 500, ⓦwww.ambpol.cz.
Russia Pod kaštany 1, Prague ⊤233 374 100.
Slovakia Pod hradbami 1, Prague ⊤233 113 051, ⓦwww.slovakemb.cz.
South Africa Ruská 65, Prague ⊤267 311 114.
Ukraine Charlese de Gaulla 29, Prague ⊤233 342 000.
US Tržiště 15, Prague ⊤257 530 663, ⓦwww.usembassy.cz.

need to go to the Foreigners' Police head-quarters in Prague.

Football

Despite failing to qualify for the 1998 and 2002 World Cups, the Czech national **football** team have generally enjoyed great success over the last couple of decades, and remain in the world top ten. As with most former Eastern Bloc countries, the best homegrown players have, almost without exception, chosen to seek fame and fortune abroad since the 1990s. As a result, domestic teams usually struggle in European competitions. The most consistent team in the *Českomoravského liga* (ⓦwww.fotbal.cz) is Sparta Praha, who have won the league ten times since 1994. The season runs from August to November and March to May, and matches are usually held on Saturdays. Tickets for domestic games are rarely more than 200Kč and four-figure crowds remain the norm.

Health

EU healthcare privileges apply in the Czech Republic, so on production of a European Health Insurance Card or **EHIC** (ⓦwww.ehic.org.uk), you are entitled to free emergency **hospital** treatment. Nevertheless, all visitors would do well to take out insurance to cover themselves against medical emergencies. Many medicines are available over the counter at a **pharmacy** (*lékárna*). Most are open Monday to Friday from 7.30am to 6pm, but some are open 24 hours (all pharmacies

should have directions to the nearest 24hr pharmacy posted in the window).

One of the most common problems visitors encounter – especially those who are staying anywhere near woodland below 1200m – are **ticks**, tiny parasites no bigger than a pin head, which bury themselves into your skin. Current medical advice is to pull them out carefully with small tweezers. There is a very slight risk of picking up some nasty diseases from ticks, such as encephalitis. Symptoms for the latter are initially flu-like, and if they persist, you should see a doctor immediately.

Ice hockey

Ice hockey (*lední hokej*) runs soccer a close second as the nation's most popular sport. Though, as with soccer, the fall of Communism prompted an exodus by the country's best players who left to seek fame and fortune in North America's National Hockey League (NHL), most notably Jaromír Jágr, the Czech team still ranks among the world's top five (ⓦwww.iihf.com). Domestic games take place on Saturdays and can take anything up to three hours; fast and physical, they make for cold but compelling viewing. The season starts at the end of September and culminates in the annual World Championships the following summer, when the fortunes of the national side are subject to close scrutiny, especially if pitched against the old enemy Russia, not to mention their former bed-mate and new rival, Slovakia.

Insurance

EU health care privileges apply, but you should get **travel insurance** to cover against theft, loss and illness or injury. For non-EU citizens, it's worth checking whether you are already covered by your home insurance or health plan before you buy a new policy. If you need to take out insurance, you might want to consider the policies offered by Rough Guides (see box below).

Internet

The Czechs are keen **internet** users and most cafés, restaurants, hotels, shops and museums have websites. With any luck your accommodation will have internet access and quite a few have wi-fi. Otherwise, you can get online at numerous cafés and bars in towns and cities: 30–50Kč an hour is the norm.

Laundry

Self-service **laundrettes** don't really exist, except in Prague, though you can get clothes beautifully service-washed or dry-cleaned for a reasonable price at a *čistírna* (dry cleaners) as long as you've got a few days to spare.

Mail

Outbound **post** is reasonably reliable, with letters or cards taking around five working days to Britain and Ireland, and one week to ten days to North America or Australasia. You can buy **stamps** (*známky*) from newsagents, tobacconists and some kiosks, as well as at post offices. Check ⓦwww.cpost .cz for the latest postal charges.

Maps

Most tourist offices sell good **maps** and all bookshops usually have a comprehensive

selection. Geodézie (ⓦwww.geodezie.cz) produce an excellent range of road maps; the 1:200,000 version is probably the best general car touring atlas, while the incredibly detailed 1:100,000 version is good for cyclists. SHOCart (ⓦwww.shocart.cz), along with several other competitors, do a series of 1:50,000 walking maps, which cover the whole of the Czech Republic, marking all the colour-coded paths which crisscross the countryside. Local **town plans** (*plán města*), showing bus, tram and trolleybus routes, should be available from most bookshops and some hotels.

Money

The **currency** in the Czech Republic is the **Czech crown,** or *koruna česká* (abbreviated to Kč or CZK), which is divided into one hundred relatively worthless hellers or *halíře* (abbreviated to h). At the time of going to press there were around 30Kč to the pound sterling, 25Kč to the euro and around 20Kč to the US dollar. For the most up-to-date exchange rates, consult the useful currency converter websites ⓦwww.oanda.com or ⓦwww.xe.com.

Notes come in 20Kč, 50Kč, 100Kč, 200Kč, 500Kč, 1000Kč, 2000Kč and (less frequently) 5000Kč denominations; **coins** as 1Kč, 2Kč, 5Kč, 10Kč, 20Kč and 50Kč, plus 50h. Notes of 2000Kč and 5000Kč are rarely used for transactions of less than 200Kč.

There are **ATMs** all over the Czech Republic, from which you can take out money using either a debit or credit card. **Banks** tend to give the best rates and charge the lowest commission when it comes to **changing money** and **traveller's cheques**; most are open Monday to Friday 9am to 5pm.

Rough Guides travel insurance

Rough Guides has teamed up with Columbus Direct to offer **travel insurance** that can be tailored to suit your needs. Products include a low-cost **backpacker** option for long stays; a **short break** option for city getaways; a typical **holiday package** option; and others. There are also annual **multi-trip** policies. Different sports and activities (trekking, skiing, etc) can be usually be covered if required.

See our website (ⓦwww.roughguides.com/website/shop) for eligibility and purchasing options. Alternatively, UK residents should call ☏0870/033 9988, Australians should call ☏1300/669 999 and New Zealanders should call ☏0800/559 911. All other nationalities should call ☏+44 870/890 2843.

Opening hours

Shops are generally open Monday to Friday from 9am to 5pm, though most supermarkets and tourist shops work longer hours. Smaller shops usually close for lunch for an hour sometime between noon and 2pm. Those shops that open on Saturday are generally shut by noon or 1pm, and very few open on Sunday. The majority of **pubs** and **restaurants** outside the big cities tend to close between 10pm and 11pm, with food often unavailable after 9pm.

Opening hours for **museums and galleries** are generally 10am to 6pm daily except Monday (when they are closed) all year round. Full opening hours are detailed in the text. Getting into **churches** can present more of a problem. Most are kept locked, with perhaps just the vestibule open, allowing you at least a glimpse of the interior, opening fully only for worship in the early morning (around 7 or 8am on weekdays, more like 10am on Sun) and/or the evening (around 6 or 7pm).

Phones

All **public telephones** have instructions in English, and if you press the appropriate button the language on the digital read-out will change to English. The **dialling tone** is a short pulse followed by a long one; the **ringing tone** is long and regular; **engaged** is short and rapid (not to be confused with the connecting tone, which is very short and rapid). The standard Czech response is *prosím*; the word for "extension" is *linka*. If you have any problems, ring ☏1181 to get through to international information. The

majority of public phones take only **phone cards** (*telefonní karty*). Best value are the **pre-paid phone cards** that give you much longer call time and can be used from any public or private phone. Simply call the toll-free access number and then punch in the PIN given on the card. If you're taking your **mobile/cell phone** (*mobilní*), check with your service provider whether it will work abroad and what the call charges will be. Mobiles bought for use in Europe, Australia and New Zealand should work fine, but a mobile bought for use in the US is unlikely to work unless it's tri-band.

Public holidays

National holidays (*Státní svátek*) were always a potential source of contention under the Communists, and they remain controversial even today. May Day, once a nationwide compulsory march under dull Communist slogans, remains a public holiday, though only the skinheads, anarchists and die-hard Stalinists take to the streets nowadays. Of the other *slavné májové dny* (Glorious May Days), as they used to be known, May 5, the beginning of the 1945 Prague Uprising, has been binned, and VE Day is now celebrated along with the Western Allies on May 8, and not on May 9, as it was under the Communists, and still is in Russia. September 28, the feast day of the country's patron saint, St Wenceslas, is now Czech State Day. Strangely, however, October 28, the day on which the First Republic was founded in 1918, is still celebrated, despite being a "Czechoslovak" holiday (and, under the Communists, Nationalization Day).

Useful telephone numbers

Phoning the Czech Republic from abroad
From Britain & Ireland ☏00 + 420 + number.
From the US & Canada ☏011 + 420 + number.
From Australia & New Zealand ☏0011 + 420 + number.

Phoning abroad from Czech Republic
To the UK ☏0044 + area code minus zero + number.
To Ireland ☏00353 + area code minus zero + number.
To the US & Canada ☏001 + area code + number.
To Australia ☏0061 + area code minus zero + number.
To New Zealand ☏0064 + area code minus zero + number.

Public holidays

January 1 New Year's Day (*Nový rok*)
Easter Monday (*Velikonoční pondělí*)
May 1 May Day (*Svátek práce*)
May 8 VE Day (*Den osvobození*)
July 5 Introduction of Christianity (*Den slovanských věrozvěstů Cyrila a Metoděje*)
July 6 Death of Jan Hus (*Den upálení mistra Jana Husa*)
September 28 Czech State Day (*Den české státnosti*)
October 28 Foundation of the Republic (*Den vzniku samostatného československého státu*)
November 17 Battle for Freedom and Democracy Day (*Den boje za svobodu a demokracii*)
December 24 Christmas Eve (*Štědrý den*)
December 25 Christmas Day (*Vánoce*)
December 26 Saint Stephen's Day (*Den sv Štěpana*)

Smoking

The Czechs are **keen smokers**, and you'll find very few no-smoking areas in cafés, pubs or restaurants, though there is no smoking on the public transport system. If you're a smoker and need a light, say *máte oheň?* Matches are *zápalky*.

Time

The Czech Republic is generally one hour ahead of **GMT** and six hours ahead of EST, with the clocks going forward in spring and back again some time in autumn – the exact date changes from year to year. Generally speaking, Czechs use the 24-hour clock.

Tipping

Tipping is normal practice in cafés, bars, restaurants and taxis, though it is usually done simply by rounding up the total. For example, if the waiter tots up the bill and asks you for 74Kč, you should hand him a 100Kč note and say "take 80Kč".

Toilets

Apart from the automatic ones in the big cities, **toilets** (*záchody*, *toalety* or *WC*) are few and far between. In some, you still have to buy toilet paper (by the sheet) from the attendant, whom you will also have to pay as you enter. Standards of hygiene can be low. Gentlemen should head for *muži* or *páni*; ladies should head for *ženy* or *dámy*. In dire straits you should make use of conveniences in restaurants and pubs, as most Czechs do.

Tourist information

You'll find most large towns and cities now have a **tourist office**, usually known as an *informační centrum*, specifically designed to assist visitors. Most will hand out (or sell for a small fee) basic maps and pamphlets on local sights. They may also be able to assist with finding accommodation, but don't rely on this. Hours vary and are detailed in the text. In those places where there is no information centre, your best bet is probably to try the reception at the nearest large hotel. In Prague, simply go to one of the branches of the **PIS** (*Pražská informační služba*), whose staff can book accommodation and theatre and concert tickets, and answer most questions.

Travellers with disabilities

Disabled access in the Czech Republic still has a long way to go, although attitudes are slowly changing and EU legislation has been put in place. Transport is a major problem. In Prague buses and all but the newest trams are inaccessible for wheelchairs, though some metro stations have facilities for the disabled, and the two railway stations (Hlavní nádraží and nádraží Holešovice) have self-operating lifts. Many towns and cities have cobbles and the general lack of ramps also make life hard on the streets. For a list of wheelchair-friendly hotels, restaurants, metro stations in **Prague**, order the **guidebook** *Accessible Prague/Přístupná Praha* from the Prague Wheelchair Association (*Pražská organizace vozíčkářů*), Benediktská 6, Staré Město (☎224 827 210, ⊛www.pov.cz). The association can organize a pick-up from Prague airport if you contact them well in advance, and can help with transporting wheelchairs.

Travelling with children

The attitude to **kids** is generally very positive. That said, you'll see few babies out in the open, unless snuggled up in their prams, and almost no children in pubs, cafés or even most restaurants. Children are generally expected to be unreasonably well behaved and respectful to their elders, and many of the older generation may frown at over-boisterous behaviour. Kids under six go free on public transport; 6- to 14-year-olds pay half-fare.

Websites

Czech language ⓦ www.bohemica.com. Czech language and culture – especially language. You can learn it online and there are lots of links to Czech sites. ⓦ www.locallingo.com. Download phrases and learn Czech online. The couple who run these two sites also run a blog, at blog.myczechrepublic.com.

General Czech information ⓦ www.czechsite.com, ⓦ www.myczechrepublic.com. Useful background information, up-to-date news and tourist links.

Maps ⓦ www.mapy.cz. This site will provide you with a thumbnail map to help you find any hotel, restaurant, pub, shop or street in the Czech Republic.

News ⓦ www.ctk-online.cz. Weekly news in English from the Czech News Agency (CTK).

Prague Post ⓦ www.praguepost.com. A very useful site, not just for the latest news, but also for Prague listings and tourist information.

Radio Prague ⓦ www.radio.cz/english. An informative site with updated news and weather as audio or text.

Welcome to the Czech Republic ⓦ www.czech.cz. Basic information in English, with details of the worldwide network of Czech Centres, run by the Czech Foreign Ministry.

Guide

Guide

Prague and around

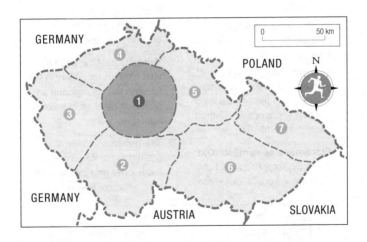

CHAPTER 1 # Highlights

✳ **Pražský hrad** Perched high above the city, and the seat of power for over a millennium, Prague Castle is home to the cathedral, the royal palace, several museums and art galleries, and the president. See p.68

✳ **Malá Strana terraced gardens** Ornamental Baroque gardens hidden away in the steep backstreets of Malá Strana. See p.85

✳ **Karlův most (Charles Bridge)** The city's wonderful medieval stone bridge, peppered with Baroque statuary, has been the main link between the two banks of the river for over five hundred years. See p.88

✳ **Staroměstské náměstí (Old Town Square)** Prague's busy showpiece square, dominated by the Art Nouveau Hus Monument and best known for its astronomical clock. See p.93

✳ **Josefov** Prague's former Jewish ghetto is still home to six synagogues and an atmospheric medieval cemetery. See p.98

✳ **Obecní dům** The most ornate and accessible of all Prague's Art Nouveau masterpieces, completed in 1911, now houses cafés, restaurants, exhibition spaces and a concert hall. See p.111

✳ **Veletržní palác** Prague's vast modern art gallery is the finest in the country and an architectural sight in its own right. See p.121

✳ **Tea-houses** A 1990s reaction against the smoky, boozy pub, tea-houses provide the perfect chill-out zone. See p.128

▲ Charles Bridge

Prague and around

W
ith some six hundred years of architecture virtually untouched by
natural disaster or war, few other cities in Europe look as good as
Prague. Straddling the winding River Vltava, with a steep wooded
hill to one side, the city retains much of its medieval layout, the street
facades remain smothered in a rich mantle of Baroque, and the historical core
has successfully escaped the vanities and excesses of postwar redevelopment.
During the decades of Soviet-imposed isolation, very few westerners visited
Prague. However, after the 1990s, all that changed, and the city is now one of
the most popular city break destinations in Europe.

Prague is surprisingly compact, its centre divided into two unequal halves by
the **River Vltava**. The steeply inclined left bank is dominated by the castle
district of **Hradčany**, which contains the most obvious sights – the castle, or
Hrad, itself, the city's cathedral, and the old royal palace and gardens – as well as
a host of museums and galleries. Between the castle hill and the river are the
picturesque Baroque palaces and houses of the **Malá Strana** (Little Quarter) –
around 150 acres of twisting cobbled streets and secret walled gardens – home
to the Czech parliament and most of the city's embassies, and dominated by the
green dome and tower of the church of sv Mikuláš.

The city's twisting matrix of streets is at its most confusing in the original
medieval hub of the city, **Staré Město** – (Old Town) – on the right bank of the
Vltava. The Karlův most (Charles Bridge), its main link with the opposite bank,
is easily the city's most popular historical monument, and the best place from
which to view Prague Castle. Staré Město's other great showpiece is its main
square, Staroměstské náměstí, with its famous astronomical clock. Within the
boundaries of Staré Město is the former Jewish quarter, or **Josefov**. The ghetto
walls and slums have long since gone and the whole area was remodelled at the
end of the nineteenth century, but six synagogues, a medieval cemetery and a
town hall survive as powerful reminders of a community that has existed here
for more than a millennium.

South and east of the old town is the large sprawling district of **Nové Město**,
whose main arteries make up the city's commercial and business centre. The
nexus is Wenceslas Square (Václavské náměstí), focus of the political upheavals
of the modern-day republic. Further afield lie various **suburbs**, most of which
were developed only in the last hundred years or so. The single exception is
Vyšehrad, one of the original fortress settlements of the newly arrived Slavs in
the last millennium, now the final resting place of leading Czech artists of the
modern age, including the composers Smetana and Dvořák.

If Prague's city centre is a revelation, the city's outer suburbs, where most of
the population live, are more typical of eastern Europe: seemingly half-built,

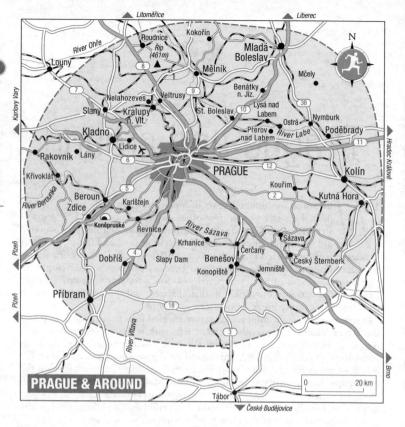

PRAGUE & AROUND

high-rise housing estates, known locally as *paneláky*, swimming in a sea of mud. However, once you're clear of the city limits, the traditional, provincial feel of **Bohemia** (Čechy) immediately makes itself felt. Many Praguers own a *chata* (country cottage) somewhere in these rural backwaters, and every weekend the roads are jammed with weekenders. Few places are more than an hour from the centre by public transport.

The most popular destinations for day-trippers are the castles of **Karlštejn** and **Konopiště**, both of which suffer from a daily swarm of coach parties. You'd do better to head north, away from the hills and the crowds, to the chateaux of **Nelahozeves**, in the village of Dvořák's birth, and nearby **Veltrusy**, or to the wine town of **Mělník**. The wooded hills around **Křivoklát** in the northeast or **Kokořín** in the southwest, both around 40km from Prague, are also good places to lose the crowds. Even further afield is the undisputed gem of the region, the medieval silver-mining town of **Kutná Hora**, 60km east of Prague, with a glorious Gothic cathedral.

Prague (Praha)

The Czechs have a legend for every occasion, and the founding of **PRAGUE** is no exception. Sometime in the seventh or eighth century AD, the Czech prince Krok (aka Pace) moved his people south from the plains of the River Labe (Elbe) to the rocky knoll that is now Vyšehrad (literally "high castle"). His youngest daughter, **Libuše**, who was to become the country's first and last female leader, was endowed with the gift of prophecy. Falling into a trance one day, she pronounced that they should build a city "whose glory will touch the stars", at the point in the forest where they would find an old man constructing the threshold of his house. He was duly discovered on the Hradčany hill overlooking the Vltava, and the city was named **Praha**, meaning "threshold". Subsequently, Libuše was compelled to take a husband and again fell into a trance, this time pronouncing that they should follow her horse to a ploughman, whose descendants would rule over them. Sure enough, a man called **Přemysl** (meaning "ploughman") was discovered and became the mythical founder of the Přemyslid dynasty, which ruled Bohemia until the fourteenth century.

So much for the legend. Historically, Hradčany and not Vyšehrad appears to have been the site of the first Slav settlement. The Vltava was relatively shallow at this point, and it probably seemed a safer bet than the plains of the Labe. Under the **Přemyslids** the city prospered, benefiting from its position on the central European trade routes. Merchants from all over Europe came to settle here, and in 1234 the first of Prague's historic towns, the **Staré Město**, was founded to accommodate them. In 1257, King Otakar II founded the **Malá Strana** on the slopes of the castle as a separate quarter for Prague's German merchants. When the Přemyslid dynasty died out in 1306, the crown was handed over by the Czech nobles to the Luxembourgs, and it was under **Charles IV** (1346–78) that Prague enjoyed its **first golden age**. In just thirty years, Charles transformed Prague into one of the most important cities in fourteenth-century Europe, establishing institutions and buildings that survive today – the Charles University, St Vitus Cathedral, the Charles Bridge, monasteries and churches – and founding an entire new town, **Nové Město**, to accommodate the influx of students and clergy.

Surprisingly enough, it was under a Habsburg, **Rudolf II** (1576–1612), that the city enjoyed its **second golden age**, inviting artists, scientists (and quacks) from all over Europe, and filling the castle galleries with the finest art. However, following the defeat of the Protestants at the 1620 **Battle of Bílá hora** (White Mountain) on the outskirts of the city, came the period the Czechs refer to as the **dark ages**, when the full force of the Counter-Reformation was brought to bear on the city's people. Paradoxically, though, the spurt of **Baroque rebuilding** during this period lent Prague its most striking architectural aspect, and the majority of the city's impressive palaces date from this period.

The next two centuries saw Prague's importance gradually whittled away within the Habsburg Empire. Two things dragged it out of the doldrums: the first was the **industrial revolution** of the mid-nineteenth century, which brought large numbers of Czechs in from the countryside to work in the factories; and the second was the contemporaneous **Czech national revival** or *národní obrození*, which gave Prague a number of symbolic monuments, such

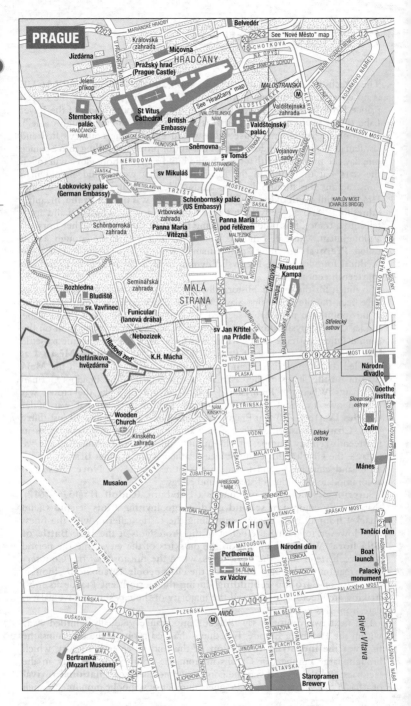

PRAGUE

Belvedér

MARIÁNSKÉ HRADBY

Královská
zahrada

Jízdárna

Jelení
příkop

Míčovna

CHOTKOVA

NA OPYŠI

STARÉ ZÁMECKÉ SCHODY

Pražský hrad
(Prague Castle)

HRADČANY

MALOSTRANSKÁ

Šternberský
palác

HRADČANSKÉ
NÁM.

St Vitus
Cathedral

See "Hradčany" map

British
Embassy

ZÁMECKÉ SCHODY

THUNOVSKÁ

VALDŠTEJNSKÁ

VALDŠTEJNSKÉ
NÁM.

Valdštejnská
zahrada

Valdštejnský
palác

MÁNESŮV MOST

NERUDOVA

JÁNSKÁ
SPORKOVA

Sněmovna

MALOSTRANSKÉ
NÁM.

sv Tomáš

Vojanovy
sady

sv Mikuláš

Lobkovický palác
(German Embassy)

BŘETISLAVOVA

TRŽIŠTĚ

MOSTECKÁ

KARLŮV MOST
(CHARLES BRIDGE)

VLAŠSKÁ

Schönbornská
zahrada

Vrtbovská
zahrada

Schönbornský palác
(US Embassy)

SASKÁ

Panna Maria
Vítězná

Panna Maria
pod řetězem

MALTÉZSKÉ
NÁM.

KARMELITSKÁ

HARANTOVA

Seminářská
zahrada

MALÁ
STRANA

HELLICHOVA

NOSTICOVA

Museum
Kampa

Čertovka

Kampa

Rozhledna
Bludiště

sv Vavřinec

VŠEHRDOVA

Střelecký
ostrov

Funicular
(lanová dráha)

Nebozízek

Hladová zeď'

K.H. Mácha

sv Jan Křtitel
na Prádle

ŘÍČNÍ

SEŘÍKOVÁ

ÚJEZD

VÍTĚZNÁ

MOST LEGII

Štefánikova
hvězdárna

PLASKÁ

MĚLNICKÁ

Národní
divadlo

Goethe
Institut

Slovanský
ostrov

Žofín

Wooden
Church

Kinského
zahrada

NÁM.
KINSKÝCH

PETŘÍNSKÁ

ZBOROVSKA

VODNÍ

JANÁČKOVO NÁBŘEŽÍ

Dětský
ostrov

Mánes

Musaion

HOLEČKOVA

DRTINOVA

KROFTOVA

ZUBATÉHO

ARBESOVO
NÁM.

PRESLOVA

EL. PEŠKOVÉ

MATOUŠOVA

KOŘENSKÉHO

JIRÁSKŮV MOST

STRAHOVSKÝ TUNEL

VIKTORA HUGA

V BOTANICE

SMÍCHOV

Tančící dům

MATOUŠOVA

Portheimka

ŠTEFÁNIKOVA

NÁM.
14. ŘÍJNA

LESNICKÁ

ZBOROVSKÁ

PECHÁČKOVA

Národní dům

Boat
launch

Palacký
monument

sv Václav

PLZEŇSKÁ

KARTOUZSKÁ

PLZEŇSKÁ

ANDĚL

LIDICKÁ

PALACKÉHO MOST

DUŠKOVA

MOZARTOVA

MRAZOVKA

MRAZOVKA

KŘÍŽOVÁ

RADLICKÁ

NA ZATLANCE

KMOCHOVA

ŠTĚRBOVA

BOZDĚCHOVA

NA BĚLIDLE

VRAZOVA

SVORNOSTI

JINDŘICHA

PLACHTY

STAROPRAMENNÁ

KLICPEROVA

VLTAVSKÁ

River Vltava

Bertramka
(Mozart Museum)

Staropramen
Brewery

PRAGUE AND AROUND

1

58

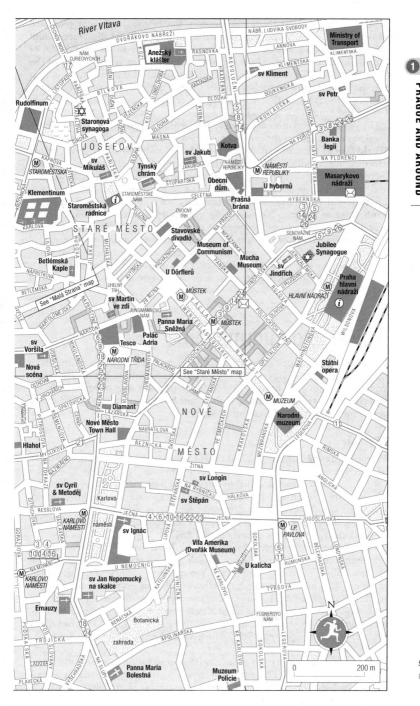

as its Národní divadlo (National Theatre), the Národní muzeum (National Museum), the Rudolfinum concert and exhibition hall and the Obecní dům (Municipal House). The national revival led eventually to the foundation of Czechoslovakia in 1918, which once again put Prague at the centre of the country's political events and marked the beginning of the city's third golden age, the **First Republic**. Architecturally, the first three decades of the twentieth century left Prague with a unique legacy of Art Nouveau, Cubist, Rondo-Cubist and Functionalist buildings.

The virtual annihilation of the city's Jews and the expulsion of the German-speaking community changed Prague forever, though the city itself survived **World War II** physically more or less unscathed and industrially intact, before disappearing completely behind the Iron Curtain. Internal centralization only increased the city's importance – it hosted the country's macabre show trials, and at one time boasted the largest statue of Stalin in the world. The city briefly re-emerged onto the world stage during the cultural blossoming of the **1968 Prague Spring**, but following the Soviet invasion in August of that year, Prague vanished from view once more. Just over twenty years later, the **1989 Velvet Revolution** finally toppled the Communist government without so much as a shot being fired. The city has been restored and transformed visually out of all recognition over the past two decades, and now has the difficult job of juggling its twin roles as a major tourist destination and the country's capital.

Arrival and information

Prague is one of Europe's smaller capital cities, with a population of one and a quarter million. The airport lies just over 10km northwest of the city centre, with only a bus link or taxi to get you into town. By contrast, both the **international train stations** and the main **bus terminal** are linked to the centre by the fast and efficient metro system.

By air

Prague's **Ruzyně** airport (☎220 113 314, ⓦwww.prg.aero), 10km northwest of the city centre, is connected to the city by minibus, bus and taxi. The Cedaz (ⓦwww.cedaz.cz) **shared minibus service** will take you (and several others) to your hotel for around 360Kč. The minibus also runs a scheduled service (daily 5.30am–9.30pm; every 30min), which stops first at Dejvická metro station, at the end of metro line A (20min) and ends up at náměstí Republiky (30min); the full journey currently costs 120Kč.

The cheapest way to get into town is on **local bus #119** (daily 5am to midnight; every 15–20min; 20min), which stops frequently and also ends its journey outside Dejvická metro station. You can buy your ticket from the public transport (DP) information desk in arrivals (daily 7am–10pm), or from nearby machines or newsagents. If you're going to use public transport while in Prague, you might as well buy a pass immediately (see p.62). If you arrive between midnight and 5am, you can catch the hourly night bus #510 to Divoká Šárka, the terminus for night tram #51, which will take you on to Národní in the centre of town.

Prague **taxi** drivers have a reputation for overcharging; one of the more reliable firms is AAA Taxi (☎14014, ⓦwww.aaataxi.cz), which has a rank outside arrivals. The journey to the centre should cost around 400–500Kč.

By train and bus

International trains arrive either at the old Art-Nouveau **Praha hlavní nádraží**, on the edge of Nové Město and Vinohrady, or at **Praha-Holešovice**, which lies in an industrial suburb north of the city centre. At both stations you'll find exchange outlets, 24-hour left-luggage offices (*úschovna zavazadel*) and accommodation agencies (plus a tourist office at Hlavní nádraží). Both stations are on metro lines, and Hlavní nádraží is just a five-minute walk from Václavské náměstí (Wenceslas Square).

Domestic trains usually wind up at Hlavní nádraží or the central **Masarykovo nádraží** on Hybernská, a couple of blocks east of náměstí Republiky. Slower trains and various provincial services arrive at a variety of obscure suburban stations: trains from the southwest pull into **Praha-Smíchov** (metro Smíchovské nádraží); trains from the east arrive at **Praha-Vysočany** (metro Českomoravská); trains from the west at **Praha-Dejvice** (metro Hradčanská); and trains from the south occasionally rumble into **Praha-Vršovice** (tram #6 or #24 to Václavské náměstí).

Virtually all long-distance international and domestic services terminate at Prague's main **bus terminal**, **Praha-Florenc** (metro Florenc), on the eastern edge of Nové Město. It's a confusing place, but it has a left-luggage office upstairs (daily 5am–11pm), and you can make a quick exit to the adjacent metro station.

Information

The tourist office is run by the **Prague Information Service** or **PIS** (Pražská informační služba), whose main branch is within the Staroměstská radnice on Staroměstské náměstí (April–Oct Mon–Fri 9am–7pm, Sat & Sun 9am–6pm; Nov–March Mon–Fri 9am–6pm, Sat & Sun 9am–5pm; ⓦwww.prague-info .cz). There are additional PIS offices at Rytířská 31, Staré Město (metro Můstek), in the main train station, Praha hlavní nádraží, plus an (April–Oct only) office in the Malá Strana bridge tower on the Charles Bridge.

You can pick up useful **listings** publications from the PIS, including *Culture in Prague/Česká kultura* (ⓦwww.ceskakultura.cz), a monthly English-language booklet listing major events, concerts and exhibitions, *Přehled*, a more comprehensive monthly listings magazine (in Czech only) and the weekly **English-language paper**, *Prague Post* (ⓦwww.praguepost.com), which carries selective listings.

City transport

The centre of Prague, where most of the city's sights are concentrated, is reasonably small and best explored on foot. At some point, however, in order to cross the city quickly or reach some of the more widely dispersed attractions, you'll need to use the city's cheap and efficient **public transport** system, known as

---

Prague Card

For those coming for a long weekend, it's worth considering buying the **Prague Card** (ⓦwww.praguecard.biz), which is valid for four days and gives free entry into over fifty sights within the city for 790Kč, plus another 330Kč for a travel pass. The one major omission is that the card doesn't include the sights of the Jewish Museum. All in all, the card will save you a lot of hassle, but not necessarily that much money. The card is available from all travel information and PIS offices (see above).

Prague addresses, house signs and numbers

In order to help locate **addresses** more easily, we have used the names of the city districts as they appear on street signs: Hradčany, Staré Město, etc. Prague's **postal districts**, which also appear on street signs, are too large to be of much help in orientation, since the city centre lies almost entirely within Prague 1.

In the older districts, many houses have retained their original medieval **house signs**, a system that is still used today, though predominantly by pubs, restaurants and wine bars, for example *U zeleného hroznu* (The Green Grape). In the 1770s, the Habsburgs, in their rationalizing fashion, introduced a numerical system, with each house in the city entered onto a register according to a strict chronology. Later, the conventional system of progressive **street numbering** was introduced; so don't be surprised if seventeenth-century pubs like *U medvídků* (The Little Bears) have, in addition to a house sign, two numbers, in this case 345 and 7. When written down the numbers are separated by a forward slash; on the building, the former Habsburg number appears on a red background, the latter modern number on blue.

dopravní podník or DP (Ⓦ www.dpp.cz), comprising the metro and a network of trams and buses. To get a clearer picture, invest in a city map that marks all the tram, bus and metro lines.

Tickets and passes

Tickets, passes and free maps are available from the DP **information offices** at both airport terminals (daily 7am–10pm), from Holešovice train station (Mon–Fri 7am–6pm) Můstek metro (Mon–Fri 7am–6pm), Muzeum metro (daily 7am–9pm); and Anděl metro (Mon–Fri 7am–6pm).

You don't need to provide photos or ID to buy a **travel pass** (*časová jízdenka*) for 24 hours (*na 24 hodin*; 100Kč), three days (*na 3 dny;* 330Kč) or five days (*na 5 dní;* 500Kč), though you must write your name and date of birth on the back of the ticket, and punch it to validate when you first use it. For a monthly pass (*měsíční*; 550Kč) you need ID and a passport-sized photo. In addition to the DP outlets, the 24-hour pass is also available from ticket machines.

Ticket machines, inside all metro stations and at some bus and tram stops, have a multitude of buttons, but for a single **ticket** (*lístek* or *jízdenka*) in the two central zones (*2 pásma*), there are just two basic choices. The 18Kč version (*limitovaná*) allows you to travel for up to 20 minutes on the trams or buses, or up to five stops within 30 minutes on the metro; you can change metro lines (but not buses or trams). The 26Kč version (*základní*) is valid for 75 minutes at **peak times** (Mon–Fri 5am–8pm) during which you may change trams, buses or metro lines as many times as you like. Half-price (*zvýhodněna*) tickets are available for children aged 6–14; under-6s travel free. Press the appropriate button – once for one ticket, twice for two and so on – and the enter (*výdej*) button, then insert your money. The machines do give change, but only accept coins. Tickets can also be bought, en masse, and rather more easily, from a tobacconist (*tabák*), street kiosk, newsagent, PIS office or any place that displays the yellow DP sticker. When you enter the metro, or board a tram or bus, you must validate your ticket by placing it in one of the electronic machines to hand.

Since there are no barriers, there's nothing to stop people from freeloading on the system. However, plain-clothes **inspectors** (*revizoři*) make spot checks and will issue an on-the-spot fine of 500Kč (950Kč if you don't cough up immediately) to anyone caught without a valid ticket or pass; controllers should show you their ID (a small metal disc), and give you a receipt (*paragon*).

The metro

Prague's futuristic, Soviet-built **metro** is fast, smooth and ultra-clean, running daily from 5am to midnight with trains every two minutes during peak hours, slowing down to every four to ten minutes by late in the evening. Its three lines (with a fourth planned) intersect at various points in the city centre and route plans are easy to follow. The stations are fairly discreetly marked above ground with the metro logo, in green (line A), yellow (line B) or red (line C). Once inside the metro, it's worth knowing that *výstup* means exit and *přestup* will lead you to one of the connecting lines at an interchange.

Trams and buses

The electric **tram** (*tramvaj*) system, in operation since 1891, negotiates Prague's hills and cobbles with remarkable dexterity. After the metro, trams are the fastest and most efficient way of getting around, running every five to eight minutes at peak times – check the timetables posted at every stop (*zastávka*), which list the departure times from that specific stop.

Tram #22, which runs from Vinohrady to Hradčany via the centre of town and Malá Strana, is a good way to get to grips with the lie of the land, and a cheap way of sightseeing, though you should beware of pickpockets. From Easter to mid-November, interwar **tram #91** runs from Výstaviště to the Tram Museum via Malá Strana and Prague Castle (Sat & Sun hourly noon–5pm) and back again; the ride takes forty minutes and costs 35Kč. **Night trams** (*noční tramvaje*; #51–58) run roughly every thirty to forty minutes from around midnight to 4.30am; the routes are different from the daytime ones, though at some point all night trams pass along Lazarská in Nové Město.

Unless you're staying in the more obscure suburbs, you'll rarely need to use Prague's **buses** (*autobusy*), which, for the most part, keep well out of the centre of town; they operate similar (though generally less frequent) hours to the trams, and route numbers are given in the text where appropriate. **Night buses** (*noční autobusy*) run hourly between midnight and 5am from náměstí Republiky.

Taxis, cars and bikes

Taxis come in all shapes and sizes, and, theoretically at least, are extremely cheap. However, many Prague taxi drivers will attempt to overcharge; the worst offenders, needless to say, hang out at the ranks closest to the tourist sights. Officially, the initial fare on the meter should be around 40Kč plus 28Kč per kilometre within Prague. It's best to have your hotel or pension call you one – you then qualify for a cheaper rate – rather than hail one or pick one up at the taxi ranks. The best firm, AAA Taxi ☎ 222 333 222 has metered taxis all over Prague.

You really don't need a **car** in Prague, since much of the city centre is pedestrianized and the public transport system is so cheap and efficient. The city authorities, quite rightly, make it very awkward for drivers to enter the city centre, and finding a **parking** space is also extremely difficult. Much of the centre is pay-and-display (Mon–Sat only); illegally parked cars will either be clamped or towed – if this happens, phone ☎ 158. A sensible option is to park near one of the metro stations out of the centre, several of which have park-and-ride schemes: try Hradčanská, Opatov or Skalka.

Prague has a handful of brave **cyclists** but the combination of cobbled streets, tram lines and sulphurous air is enough to put most people off. Bike rental facilities are not widespread, but if you're determined to cycle, head for City Bike, Králodvorská 5, Staré Město (☎ 776 180 284; metro Náměstí Republiky)

Boats on the Vltava

In the summer there's a regular **boat service** on the River Vltava run by the PPS (*Pražská paroplavební společnost*; ☏224 930 017, ⓦwww.paroplavba.cz) from just south of Jiráskův most on Rašínovo nábřeží (see map, p.106). There are also three or four boats a day to Troja (see p.124) in the northern suburbs (May to mid-Sept daily; April & mid-Sept to Oct Sat & Sun only; 200Kč return) and weekend services south to Slapy (May to mid-Sept Sat & Sun; 340Kč) and Mělník on two Sundays in July and August (490Kč return).

In addition, the PPS also offers **boat trips** around Prague (April to mid-Sept daily 1–2hr; 190–290Kč) on board a 1930s paddlesteamer. Several other boat companies run smaller boat trips around Charles Bridge. There are pedalos for hire from near the Charles Bridge and a wider range of boats from the northern tip of Slovanský ostrov.

or Praha Bike, Dlouhá 24, Staré Město (☏732 388 880, ⓦwww.prahabike.cz; metro Náměstí Republiky); both also organize group rides through Prague.

Accommodation

Compared to the price of almost everything else in Prague, **accommodation** is very expensive. If you can pay around 4000Kč (£130/$200) a night for a double room you'll find plenty of choice. At the other end of the scale, there are numerous hostels charging as little as 400Kč for a bed. However, there's a chronic shortage of decent, inexpensive to mid-range places. Searching the internet for special offers or for apartments will usually reap dividends.

Prague is pretty busy for much of the year, and doesn't have much of a **low season** (Nov–March excluding New Year) – February and November are probably the quietest months. If you're going to visit anytime from Easter to September, or over Christmas and New Year, you need to book well in advance either directly with the hotels or through one of the agencies listed on p.31. Prices are at their highest over the public holidays, but drop by as much as a third in the low season, and sometimes come down a bit in July and August when business custom is low.

If you arrive in Prague without having booked a room, you can turn to several **accommodation agencies**, most of which will book you into either a hotel or pension, and some of which can also help you find a hostel bed or a private room in an apartment. The largest agency is **AVE** (☏251 551 011, ⓦwww.avetravel.cz), who have desks at the airport, both international train stations, and several points throughout the city; they will book anything from hostels to hotels. **Pragotur** (☏221 714 130, ⓦwww.prague-info.cz), who have desks in various PIS tourist offices (see p.61), do the same, but specialize in private rooms.

Hotels and pensions

Prague boasts a huge variety of **hotels** and **pensions**, from big multinational chains to places with real character in the old town. With plenty of centrally located options, there's no need to stay out in the suburbs unless you're on a tight budget. The quietest central areas are on the left bank in Malá Strana and Hradčany; there's more choice, and more nightlife, in Staré Město and Nové Město.

Hradčany and Malá Strana

See the maps on p.68 and p.82.

Aria Tržiště 9 ⊕ 225 334 111, ⓦ www.ariahotel .net; metro Malostranská. Prague's first real stab at a boutique hotel, this superbly stylish, contemporary place has a stunning roof terrace and music-themed floors (and rooms) from jazz and rock to classical and opera. Doubles from 10,000Kč. ❾

Castle Steps Nerudova 7 ⊕ 257 216 337, ⓦ www.castlesteps.com; metro Malostranská. A variety of beautifully furnished rooms and apartments, some with unbelievable views, others with self-catering facilities. Free internet access at their office on Nerudova. ❺

Dientzenhofer Nosticova 2 ⊕ 257 316 830, ⓦ www.dientzenhofer.cz; metro Malostranská. Birthplace of its namesake, and a very popular pension due to the fact that it's one of the few reasonably priced places (anywhere in Prague) to have wheelchair access. ❼

Domus Henrici Loretánská 11, Hradčany ⊕ 220 511 369, ⓦ www.domus-henrici.cz; tram #22 or #23 from metro Malostranská to Pohořelec stop. Stylish, discreet hotel in a fab location, with just eight rooms/apartments, some with splendid views. Run in conjunction with *Domus Balthasar* on Mostecká, by the Charles Bridge. ❽

Dům U velké boty (The Big Shoe) Vlašská 30 ⊕ 257 532 088, ⓦ www.dumuvelkeboty .cz; metro Malostranská. The anonymity of this pension, in a lovely old building in the quiet backstreets, is one of its main draws. Run by a very friendly English-speaking couple, it has characterful, tastefully modernized rooms, some en suite, some not. Breakfast is extra, but worth it. ❼

U Karlova mostu Na Kampě 15 ⊕ 257 531 430, ⓦ www.archibald.cz; metro Malostranská. On a lovely tree-lined square, just off the Charles Bridge, the rooms in this former brewery have real character, despite the modern fittings. ❾

U krále Karla (King Charles) Úvoz 4, Hradčany ⊕ 257 532 869, ⓦ www.romantichotels.cz /ukralekarla; tram #22 or #23 from metro Malos-transká to Pohořelec stop. Possibly the most exquisite of all the small luxury hotels in Hradčany, with beautiful antique furnishings and stained-glass windows. It's a stiff walk from the nearest tram stop. ❾

U zlatého koníčka (Golden Horse House) Úvoz 8, Hradčany ⊕ 603 841 790, ⓦ www.goldenhorse.cz; tram #22 or #23 from metro Malostranská to Pohořelec stop. Small, plain, clean, en-suite rooms at real bargain prices in a perfect location on the way up to the Hrad. Breakfast in the brick-vaulted cellar is an extra 100Kč. ❹

U žluté boty (The Yellow Boot) Jánský vršek 11 ⊕ 257 532 269, ⓦ www.zlutabota .cz; metro Malostranská. Hidden away in a lovely old backstreet, this Baroque hotel has real character: the odd original ceiling, exposed beams, and in one room, a ceramic stove and authentic wood-panelling. ❼

Staré Město

See the map on p.90.

Avalon-Tara Havelská 15 ⊕ 224 228 083, ⓦ www.prague-hotel.ws; metro Můstek. Perfect location right over the market on Havelská, with seven very small, plainly furnished but clean rooms, some en suite. ❺

Černá liška (The Black Fox) Mikulášská 2 ⊕ 224 232 250, ⓦ www.cernaliska.cz; metro Staroměstská. Well-appointed rooms with lovely wooden floors. Some offer incredible views onto Old Town Square; quieter ones at the back. ❽

Expres Skořepka 5 ⊕ 224 211 801, ⓦ www.hotel -expres.com; metro Národní třída. Friendly little hotel with few pretensions: cheap and cheerful fittings, low prices and an excellent central location. ❹

Josef Rybná 20 ⊕ 221 700 901, ⓦ www .hoteljosef.com. This designer hotel exudes modern professionalism. The lobby is a symphony in off-white efficiency and the rooms continue the crisply maintained minimalist theme. ❾

Savic Hotel Jilská 7 ⊕ 221 700 901, ⓦ www.savichotelprague.com. Lovely original parquet flooring, repro mahogany furnish-ings and excellent service make this a very popular choice – book online for the best deals. ❼

U medvídků (The Little Bears) Na Perštýně 7 ⊕ 224 211 916, ⓦ www.umedvidku.cz; metro Národní třída. The plainly furnished rooms above this famous Prague pub are quiet considering the locale, and something of an Old Town bargain; booking ahead essential. ❼

U zlatého jelena (The Golden Stag) Štupartská 6 ⊕ 222 317 237, ⓦ www.hotel-u-zlateho-jelena.cz; metro Náměstí Republiky. Inexpensive little pension with spacious rooms very simply furnished with parquet flooring and repro ironwork. ❼

Unitas Bartolomějská 9 ⊕ 224 211 020, ⓦ www .unitas.cz; metro Národní třída. Set in a Franciscan nunnery, the *Unitas* offers simple twins as well as dorm beds in its *Art Prison* hostel (see p.66). No smoking or drinking. ❹

Nové Město

See the map on p.106.

Alcron Štepánska 40 ⊕ 222 820 000, ⓦ www .radisson.com; metro Muzeum/Můstek. Giant 1930s luxury hotel, just off Wenceslas Square, that has been superbly restored to its former Art Deco glory by the Radisson SAS chain. Doubles here are the most luxurious and tasteful you'll find in Nové Město. ❾

Bohemia Plaza Žitná 50 ☎224 941 000, ⓦwww .bohemiaplaza.com; metro Museum or I.P. Pavlova. Big, family-run patrician hotel with themed rooms, some stuffed with antiques, others with tasteful repro and more modern gear. ❼

Floor Na příkopě 13 ☎234 076 300, ⓦwww .floorhotel.cz; metro Náměstí Republiky. Situated right on one of Prague's premier pedestrianized shopping streets, on the edge of the Staré Město, this comfortable hotel goes for a predominantly modern look. ❼

Grand Hotel Evropa Václavské nám. 25 ☎224 215 387, ⓦwww.evropahotel.cz; metro Muzeum. Potentially the most beautiful hotel in Prague, built in the 1900s and sumptuously decorated in Art Nouveau style. Yet despite its prime location and its incredible decor, this place is run like an old Communist hotel – a blast from the past in every sense. The rooms are furnished in repro Louis XIV; non-en suites are cheaper. ❺

Salvator Truhlářská 10 ☎222 312 234, ⓦwww .salvator.cz; metro Náměstí Republiky. Very good location for the price, just a minute's walk from nám. Republiky, with small, clean rooms (the

cheaper ones without en-suite facilities), and a sports bar; advance booking advisable. ❻

Further afield

Unless otherwise stated, the hotels reviewed here are indicated off the map on p.106.

Alpin Velehradská 25, Žižkov ☎222 723 551, ⓦwww.alpin.cz; metro Jiřího z Poděbrad. Clean, bare, bargain rooms on the edge of Vinohrady and Žižkov. ❹

Crowne Plaza Koulova 15, Dejvice ☎224 393 111, ⓦwww.crowneplaza.cz; tram #8 from metro Dejvická to Podbaba terminus; see map, p.68. Prague's classic 1950s Stalinist wedding-cake hotel, with its dour socialist realist friezes and large helpings of marble, is now run by Austrians. ❽

Mánes Mánesova 46, Vinohrady ☎603 104 121, ⓦprague-pension-manes.ic.cz; tram #11 stop Vinohradská tržnice or metro Náměstí Míru. Clean and modern inside, very cheap, and close to a tram stop and a lovely park. ❹

Triška Vinohradská 105 ☎222 727 313, ⓦwww .hotel-triska.cz; metro Jiřího z Poděbrad. Large turn-of-the-twentieth-century hotel with comfortable rooms; they've made an effort with the interior decor, the service is good and it's close to the metro. ❻

Hostels

There are a fair few **hostels** in Prague catering for the large number of backpackers who hit the city all year round – these are supplemented by a host of more transient, high-season-only hostels. Visit ⓦwww.hostelworld.com to see the whole range and read reviews. Only a few stand out from the crowd and they're recommended below. Many offer double rooms at prices that undercut the hotels, but they are often very basic in comparison.

A handful of hostels give discounts to HI (Hostelling International; ⓦwww .hihostels.com) members and can be booked via the HI's online booking service, including the **Traveller's Hostels**, a chain that is particularly popular with US students. Its main booking office is at Dlouhá 33, Staré Město (☎224 826 662, ⓦwww.travellers.cz), where there is also a hostel (see below).

Art Prison Bartolomějská 9 ☎224 230 603, ⓦart-prison.prague-hostels.cz; metro Národní třída; see map, p.90. Set in a Franciscan nunnery and part of *Pension Unitas* (see p.65) – this hostel offers both simple twins and bargain dorm beds in converted secret police prison cells (Havel was kept in P6). No smoking or drinking. Twins from 1580Kč (❹); six-bed dorms from 400Kč.

Clown and Bard Bořivojova 102, Žižkov ☎222 716 453, ⓦwww.crownandbard.com; tram #5, #9 or #26 from metro Hlavní nádraží to Husinecká stop; see map, p.106. Žižkov hostel that's so laid-back it's horizontal, and not a place to go if you don't like

partying. Nevertheless, it's clean, undeniably cheap, stages events and has laundry facilities. Doubles from 1000Kč (❸); dorm beds from 300Kč.

Czech Inn Francouzská 76, Vinohrady ☎267 267 600, ⓦwww.czech-inn.com; tram #4, #22 or #23; see map, p.106. Upbeat, designer hostel that feels and looks like a hotel, with friendly and helpful staff and a choice of dorms and private rooms. Doubles from 1600Kč (❹); dorm beds from 390Kč.

Golden Sickle Vodičkova 10, Nové Město ☎222 230 773, ⓦwww.goldensickle.com; metro Národní třída; see map, p.106. Clean, modern, friendly hostel courtesy of IKEA, with a great central courtyard. Breakfast included. Doubles from 1400Kč (●); dorm beds from 450Kč.

Klub Habitat Na Zderaze 10, Nové Město ☎224 921 706, ⓦwww.hotelline.cz; metro Karlovo náměstí; see map, p.106. Perfectly serviceable hostel in a great location south of Národní. Book ahead. Dorm beds from 450Kč.

Miss Sophie's Hostel Melounová 3, Nové Město ☎296 303 530, ⓦwww.miss -sophies.com; metro I.P. Pavlova; see map, p.106. The most central of Prague's smart new designer hostels, offering everything from cheap dorm beds to fully equipped apartments. Doubles from 1790Kč (●); dorm beds from 400Kč.

Ritchie's Karlova 9 & 13, Staré Město ☎222 221 229, ⓦwww.ritchieshostel.cz; metro Staroměstská; see map, p.90. In the midst of the human river that is Karlova, this old town hostel has no in-house laundry or cooking facilities, but it's clean, with accommodation ranging from en-suite doubles to twelve-bed dorms. Doubles from 1650Kč (●); dorm beds 330Kč.

Sir Toby's Hostel Dělnická 24, Holešovice ☎283 870 635, ⓦwww.sirtobys.com; tram #1, #5, #25 or #26 from metro Vltavská; see map, p.120. Out in Holešovice, but just a tram-ride away from the centre, *Sir Toby's* is among the most welcoming and efficiently run hostels in Prague. Doubles from 1200Kč (●); dorm beds from 340Kč.

Traveller's Hostel Dlouhá 33, Staré Město ☎224 826 662, ⓦwww.travellers.cz; metro Náměstí Republiky; see map, p.90. Centrally located party hostel above the *Roxy* nightclub, but not the cleanest of places. The main booking office for a network of hostels, they will find you a bed in one of their other central branches if there's not enough room here. Doubles from 1300Kč (●); dorm beds from 400Kč.

Týn Týnská 19, Staré Město ☎224 808 333, ⓦtyn.prague-hostels.cz; metro Náměstí Republiky; see map, p.90. Small, basic rooms in Prague's most centrally located hostel, just metres from Old Town Square. Doubles from 1200Kč (●); six-bed dorms 400Kč.

Campsites

Prague abounds in **campsites**, most of which are relatively easy to get to on public transport. Facilities tend to be rudimentary and poorly maintained, but the prices reflect this, starting at around 350Kč for a tent and two people.

Džbán SK Aritma, Nad lávkou 5, Vokovice ☎235 358 554, ⓦwww.camp.cz/dzban; tram #20 or #26 from metro Dejvická to Nad Džbánem stop, 15min from tram stop and 4km west of the centre, near the Šárka valley. Large field with tent pitches, bungalows, shop, restaurant, tennis courts, lake swimming and gym. Open all year.

Herzog Trojská 161, Troja ☎283 850 472, ⓦwww .campherzog.cz; bus #112 from metro Nádraží Holešovice. Good location, one of several along the road to Troja chateau, situated in a large, shady back garden. Open all year.

Kotva U ledáren 55, Braník ☎244 466 085, ⓦwww.kotvacamp.cz. The oldest, and nicest, site, with a riverside location 20min by tram south of the city. Hostel and caravan accommodation is available too. Take tram #3, #16, #17 or #21 to Nádraží Braník stop. Open all year.

Sokol Troja Trojská 171a, Troja ☎233 542 908, ⓦwww.camp-sokol-troja.cz; bus #112 from metro Nádrazí Holešovice. Larger than Herzog and slightly further away from the Troja chateau and zoo, but well organized, with kitchen, laundry and restaurant on site. Open all year.

Hradčany

HRADČANY is wholly dominated by the city's omnipresent landmark, **Prague Castle**, or Pražský hrad, the vast hilltop complex that looks out over the city centre from the west bank of the River Vltava. Site of a Slav settlement in the seventh or eighth century AD, there's been a castle here since at least the late ninth century, and since then whoever has had control of the Hrad has exercized authority over the Czech Lands. It continues to serve as the seat of the president, and, being home to several museums and galleries, is open to the public.

The rest of the castle district, or Hradčany, has always been a mere appendage, its inhabitants serving and working for their masters in the Hrad. Even now,

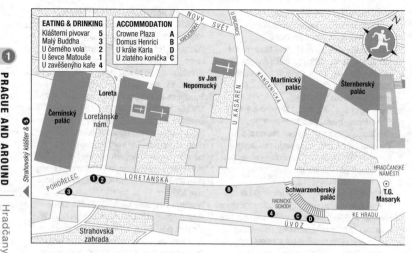

EATING & DRINKING		ACCOMMODATION	
Klášterní pivovar	5	Crowne Plaza	A
Malý Buddha	3	Domus Henrici	B
U černého vola	2	U krále Karla	D
U ševce Matouše	1	U zlatého koníčka	C
U zavěšenýho kafe	4		

despite the odd restaurant or *pivnice* (pub) in among the palaces (and even in the Hrad itself), there's very little real life here beyond the civil servants and the odd tourist group en route to the Hrad. All of this makes it a very peaceful and attractive area in which to take a stroll.

Stretched out along a high spur above the River Vltava, Hradčany shows a suitable disdain for the public transport system. There's a choice of **approaches** from Malá Strana, all of which involve at least some walking. From Malostranská metro station, most people take the steep short cut up the Staré zámecké schody, which brings you into the castle from its rear end. A better approach is up the stately Zámecké schody, where you can stop and admire the view, before entering the castle via the main gates. From April to October, you might also consider coming up through Malá Strana's wonderful terraced gardens, which are connected to the castle gardens (see p.76). The alternative to all this climbing is to take tram #22 or #23 from Malostranská metro, which tackles the hairpin bends of Chotkova with ease, and deposits you either outside the Královská zahrada (Royal Gardens) to the north of the Hrad, or, if you prefer, outside the gates of the Strahovský klášter (monastery), at the far western edge of Hradčany.

Pražský hrad (Prague Castle)

Viewed from the Charles Bridge, **Pražský hrad** (known to the Czechs simply as the Hrad), stands aloof from the rest of the city, protected, not by bastions and castellated towers, but by a rather austere palatial facade – an "immense unbroken sheer blank wall", as Hilaire Belloc described it – above which rises the great Gothic mass of St Vitus Cathedral. It's the picture-postcard image of Prague, and is spectacularly lit up at night, though for the Czechs the castle has been an object of disdain as much as admiration, its alternating fortunes mirroring the shifts in the nation's history. The golden age of Charles IV and Rudolf II and the dark ages of the later Habsburgs, interwar democracy and Stalinist terror – all have emanated from the Hrad. When the first posters appeared in December 1989 demanding "HAVEL NA HRAD" ("Havel to the Castle"), they weren't asking for his reincarceration. Havel's occupancy of the Hrad was the sign that the reins of government had finally been wrested from the Communist regime.

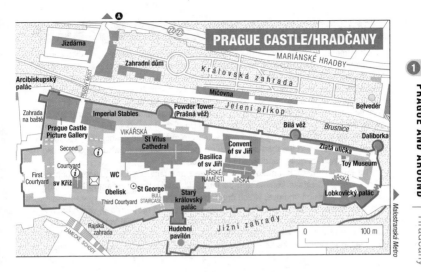

The site has been successively built on since the Přemyslid princes erected the first castle here in the ninth century, but two **architects** in particular bear responsibility for the present outward appearance of the Hrad. The first is **Nicolo Pacassi**, court architect to Empress Maria Theresa, whose austere restorations went hand in hand with the deliberate run-down of the Hrad until it was little more than an administrative barracks. For the Czechs, his grey-green eighteenth-century cover-up, which hides a variety of much older buildings, is unforgivable. Less apparent, though no less controversial, is the hand of **Josip Plečnik**, the Slovene architect who was commissioned by T.G. Masaryk, president of the newly founded Czechoslovak Republic, to restore and modernize the castle in his highly distinctive style in the 1920s.

The first and second courtyards

The **first courtyard**, which opens on to Hradčanské náměstí, is guarded by Ignaz Platzer's blood-curdling *Battling Titans* – two gargantuan figures, one on each of the gate piers, wielding club and dagger and about to inflict fatal blows on their respective victims. Below them stand a couple of impassive presidential sentries, sporting uniforms that deliberately recall those of the First Republic. The hourly **Changing of the Guard** is a fairly subdued affair, but every day at noon there's a much more elaborate parade, accompanied by a brass ensemble which appears at the first-floor windows to play a gentle, slightly comical, modern fanfare.

To reach the **second courtyard**, you must pass through the early Baroque Matyášova brána (Matthias Gate), originally a freestanding triumphal arch in the middle of the long since defunct moat, now set into one of Pacassi's blank walls. Grand stairways on either side lead to the presidential apartments in the south wing, and to the **Španělský sál** (Spanish Hall) and the **Rudolfova galerie** (Rudolf Gallery) in the north wing – two of the most stunning rooms in the entire complex. Sadly, both are generally out of bounds, though concerts are occasionally held in the Španělský sál.

Surrounded by monotonous Pacassi plasterwork, the courtyard itself is really just a through-route to the cathedral. The most visible intrusion is Anselmo Lurago's **chapel of sv Kříž**, which cowers in one corner. Its richly painted interior, dating

Visiting the castle

You're free to wander round the precincts of the **castle** (daily: April–Oct 5am–midnight; Nov–March 6am–11pm; ☏224 373 368, ⓦwww.hrad.cz). For the sights within the castle (excluding the cathedral) there are two main types of multi-entry **ticket** available: the *velký okruh* or long tour (350Kč), which gives you entry to most sights, including the Old Royal Palace, the Basilica and Convent of sv Jiří, the Prague Castle Picture Gallery and the Zlatá ulička; and the *malý okruh* or short tour (250Kč), which only covers the Old Royal Palace, the Basilica of sv Jiří and the Zlatá ulička. Tickets are valid for two days and available from several places, including the main information centre in the third courtyard, opposite the cathedral, where you can also hire an English-language audioguide (200Kč for 2hr).

The Muzeum hraček, Lobkovický palác and any temporary exhibitions such as those held in Císařská konírna and Jízdárna, all have different **opening hours** and separate admission charges, which are detailed in the text.

Within the castle precincts there are several **cafés** and **restaurants**, which are not quite as extortionate as you might expect from their location. If you simply want a quick cup of coffee, head for the *Café Poet*, which has tables outside in the shade and is hidden away in the peaceful and little-visited Zahrada na baště.

mostly from the mid-nineteenth century, used to house the cathedral treasury, a macabre selection of medieval reliquaries. In the north wing of the courtyard are the former **Císařská konírna** (Imperial Stables), which still boast their original, magnificent Renaissance vaulting dating from the reign of Rudolf II, and are now used to house temporary exhibitions (Tues–Sun 10am–6pm).

Obrazárna Pražského hradu (Prague Castle Picture Gallery)

The remnants of the imperial collection, begun by the Habsburg Emperor Rudolf II, are housed in the **Obrazárna Pražského hradu** (daily: April–Oct 10am–6pm; Nov–March 9am–4pm; 150Kč; ⓦwww.obrazarna-hradu.cz), opposite the old imperial stables. The surviving collection is definitely patchy, but it does contain one or two masterpieces that are well worth seeing, and visiting the gallery is a great way to escape the castle crowds. The illusionist triple portrait of Rudolf (when viewed from the left), and his Habsburg predecessors (when viewed from the right), by Paulus Roy, is typical of the sort of tricksy work that appealed to the emperor. One of the collection's finest paintings is **Rubens'** richly coloured *Assembly of the Gods at Olympus*, featuring a typically voluptuous Venus and a slightly fazed Jupiter. Even more famous is the surrealist portrait of Rudolf by Giuseppe Arcimboldo, portraying him as a collage of fruit, with his eyes as cherries, cheeks as apples and hair as grapes. Elsewhere, there's an early, very beautiful *Young Woman at her Toilet* by **Titian**, and a superbly observed *Portrait of a Musician* by one of his pupils, Bordone. **Veronese's** best offering is his portrait of his friend Jakob König, a German art dealer in Venice, who worked for, among others, Rudolf II. Look out, too, for **Tintoretto's** *Flagellation of Christ*, a late work in which the artist makes very effective and dramatic use of light.

St Vitus Cathedral

St Vitus Cathedral (March–Oct Mon–Sat 9am–6pm, Sun noon–6pm; Nov–Feb closes 4pm; ⓦwww.katedralapraha.cz; free) is squeezed so tightly into the third courtyard that it's difficult to get an overall impression of this chaotic Gothic edifice. Its asymmetrical appearance is the product of a long and chequered history, for although the foundation stone was laid in 1344, the cathedral was not completed until 1929 – exactly 1000 years after the death of Bohemia's most famous patron saint, Wenceslas.

The inspiration for the medieval cathedral came from Emperor Charles IV, who, while still only heir to the throne, had not only wangled an independent archbishopric for Prague, but had also managed to gather together the relics of Saint Vitus. Inspired by the cathedral at Narbonne, Charles commissioned the Frenchman **Matthias of Arras** to start work on a similar structure. Matthias died eight years into the job in 1352, with the cathedral barely started, so Charles summoned **Peter Parler**, a precocious 23-year-old from a family of great German masons, to continue the work, but he got no further than the construction of the choir and the south transept before his death in 1399.

Little significant work was carried out during the next four centuries, and the half-built cathedral became a symbol of the Czechs' frustrated aspirations of nationhood. Not until the Czech national revival of the nineteenth century did building begin again in earnest, with the foundation, in 1859, of the **Union for the Completion of the Cathedral**. A succession of architects oversaw the completion of the entire west end, and the building was transformed into a treasure-house of Czech art. The cathedral was finally given an official opening ceremony in 1929, though in fact work continued right up to and beyond World War II.

It's hard now to differentiate between the two building periods. Close inspection, however, reveals that the **western facade**, including the twin spires, sports the rigorous if unimaginative work of the neo-Gothic restorers (their besuited portraits can be found below the rose window), while the **eastern section** – best viewed from the Belvedér – shows the building's authentic Gothic roots. The south door (see Zlatá brána, p.73) is also pure Parler. Oddly then, it's above the south door that the cathedral's tallest steeple reveals the most conspicuous stylistic join: Pacassi's Baroque topping resting absurdly on a Renaissance parapet of light stone, which is itself glued onto the blackened body of the original Gothic tower.

The nave

The cathedral is the country's largest, and once inside, it's difficult not to be impressed by the sheer height of the **nave**. This is the newest part of the building, and, consequently, is decorated mostly with twentieth-century furnishings. The most arresting of these is the cathedral's modern **stained-glass** windows, which on sunny days send shafts of rainbow light into the nave. The effect is stunning, though entirely out of keeping with Parler's original concept, which was to have almost exclusively clear-glass windows. The most unusual windows are those by František Kysela, which look as though they have been shattered into hundreds of tiny pieces, a technique used to greatest effect in the rose window over the west door with its kaleidoscopic *Creation of the World* (1921). In keeping with its secular nature, two of the works from the time of the First Republic were paid for by financial institutions: the *Cyril and Methodius* window, in the third chapel in the north wall, was commissioned from Art Nouveau artist Alfons Mucha by the Banka Slavie; while on the opposite side of the nave, the window on the theme *Those Who Sow in Tears Shall Reap in Joy* was sponsored by a Prague insurance company.

Of the cathedral's 22 side chapels, the grand **Chapel of sv Václav**, by the south door, is easily the main attraction. Although officially dedicated to St Vitus, spiritually the cathedral belongs as much to the Přemyslid prince, Václav (Wenceslas, of Good King fame; see box, p.72), the country's patron saint, who was killed by his pagan brother, Boleslav the Cruel. Ten years later, in 939,

Good King Wenceslas

As it turns out, there's very little substance to the story related in the nineteenth-century Christmas carol, *Good King Wenceslas looked out*, by J.M. Neale, itself a reworking of the medieval carol *Tempus adest floridum*. For a start, **Václav** was only a duke and never a king (though he did become a saint); he wasn't even that "good", except in comparison with the rest of his family; the St Agnes fountain, by which "yonder peasant dwelt", wasn't built until the thirteenth century; and he was killed a full three months before the Feast of Stephen (Boxing Day) – the traditional day for giving to the poor, hence the narrative of the carol.

Born in 907, Václav inherited his title at the tender age of 13. His Christian grandmother, Ludmilla, was appointed regent in preference to Drahomíra, his pagan mother, who had Ludmilla murdered in a fit of jealousy the following year. On coming of age in 925, Václav became duke in his own right and took a vow of celibacy, intent on promoting Christianity throughout the dukedom. Even so, the local Christians didn't take to him, and when he began making conciliatory overtures to the neighbouring Germans, they persuaded his pagan younger brother, Boleslav the Cruel, to do away with him. On September 20, 929, Václav was stabbed to death by Boleslav at the entrance to a church just outside Prague.

Boleslav repented, converted, and apparently transferred his brother's remains to this very spot. Charles, who was keen to promote the cult of Wenceslas in order to cement his own Luxembourgeois dynasty's rather tenuous claim to the Bohemian throne, had Peter Parler build the present chapel on top of the original grave; the lion's head **door-ring** set into the north door is said to be the one to which Václav clung before being killed. The chapel's rich, almost Byzantine decoration is like the inside of a jewel casket: the gilded walls are inlaid with semi-precious Bohemian stones, set around ethereal fourteenth-century frescoes of the Passion; meanwhile the tragedy of Wenceslas unfolds above the cornice in the later paintings of the Litoměřice school.

Though a dazzling testament to the golden age of Charles IV's reign, it's not just the chapel's artistic merit which draws visitors. A door in the south wall gives access to a staircase leading to the coronation chamber (closed to the public) which houses the **Bohemian crown jewels**, including the gold crown of Saint Wenceslas, studded with some of the largest sapphires in the world. Closed to the public since 1867, the door is secured by seven different locks, the keys kept by seven different people, starting with the president himself – like the seven seals of the holy scroll from Revelation. Replicas of the crown jewels can be seen in the Lobkovický palác (see p.74).

The chancel and crypt

The **Tomb of Saint Jan of Nepomuk**, plonked in the middle of the ambulatory in 1736, is a work of grotesque excess, designed by Johann Bernhard Fischer von Erlach's son, Johann Michael, and sculpted in solid silver with free-flying angels holding up the heavy drapery of the baldachin. Where Charles sought to promote Wenceslas as the nation's preferred saint, the Jesuits, with Habsburg backing, replaced him with another Czech martyr, Jan of Nepomuk, who had been arrested, tortured, and then thrown – bound and gagged – off the Charles Bridge in 1393 on the orders of Václav IV, allegedly for refusing to divulge the secrets of the queen's confession. A cluster of stars was said to have appeared over the spot where he drowned, hence the halo of stars on every subsequent portrayal of the saint.

The Jesuits, in their efforts to get him canonized, exhumed his corpse and produced what they claimed to be his tongue – alive and licking, so to speak (it was in fact his very dead brain). In 1729, he duly became a saint, and, on the lid of the tomb, back-to-back with the martyr himself, a cherub points to his severed tongue, sadly no longer the "real" thing. The more prosaic reason for Jan Nepomucký's death was simply that he was caught up in a dispute between the archbishop and the king over the appointment of the abbot of Kladruby, and backed the wrong side. Jan was tortured on the rack along with two other priests, who were then made to sign a document denying that they had been maltreated; Jan, however, died before he could sign, and his dead body was secretly dumped in the river. The Vatican finally admitted this in 1961, some 232 years after his canonization.

Also in the chancel, check out the sixteenth-century marble **Imperial Mausoleum**, in the centre of the choir and surrounded by a fine Renaissance grille on which numerous cherubs are irreverently larking about. Commissioned by Rudolf II, it contains the remains of his grandfather Ferdinand I, his Polish grandmother Queen Anne, and his father Maximilian II, the first Habsburgs to wear the Bohemian crown. Rudolf himself rests beneath them, in one of the two pewter coffins in the somewhat cramped **Royal Crypt** (Královská hrobka). Rudolf's coffin (at the back, in the centre) features yet more cherubs, brandishing quills, while the one to the right contains the remains of Maria Amelia, daughter of the Empress Maria Theresa. A good number of other Czech kings and queens are buried here, too, reinterred last century in incongruously modern 1930s sarcophagi, among them the Hussite King George of Poděbrady, Charles IV and, sharing a single sarcophagus, all four of his wives. The exit from the crypt brings you out in the centre of the nave.

In fine weather, you can get a great view over the castle and the city from the cathedral's **Hlavná věž** (Great Tower; daily: March–Oct noon–4.15pm; Nov–Feb noon–3.15pm; free), the entrance to which is in the south aisle – be warned, there are around three hundred steps before you reach the top. Be sure, too, to check out Parler's **Zlatá brána** (Golden Gate), over the doorway to the south transept, which is decorated with a remarkable fourteenth-century mosaic of the Last Judgement, recently restored to something like its original, rich colouring.

Starý královský palác (Old Royal Palace)

Across the courtyard from the Zlatá brána, the **Starý královský palác** (Old Royal Palace) was home to the princes and kings of Bohemia from the eleventh to the sixteenth centuries. It's a sandwich of royal apartments, built one on top of the other by successive generations, but left largely unfurnished and unused for the last three hundred years. The original Romanesque palace of Soběslav I now forms the cellars of the present building, above which Charles IV built his own Gothic chambers; these days you enter at the third and top floor, built at the end of the fifteenth century.

Immediately beyond the antechamber is the bare expanse of the massive **Vladislavský sál** (Vladislav Hall), the work of Benedikt Ried, the German mason appointed by Vladislav Jagiello as his court architect. It displays some remarkable, sweeping rib-vaulting which forms floral patterns on the ceiling, the petals reaching almost to the floor. It was here that the early Bohemian kings were elected, and since 1918 every president from Masaryk to Havel has been sworn into office in the hall. In medieval times, the hall was also used for banquets and jousting tournaments, which explains the ramp-like **Riders' Staircase** in the north wing (now the exit). At the far end of the hall, to the right, there's an outdoor **viewing platform**, from which you can enjoy a magnificent view of Prague (at its best in the late afternoon).

The second defenestration

After almost two centuries of uneasy coexistence between Catholics and Protestants, matters came to a head over the succession to the throne of the Habsburg archduke **Ferdinand**, a notoriously intolerant Catholic. On May 23, 1618, a posse of more than one hundred Protestant nobles, led by Count Thurn, marched to the chancellery for a showdown with Jaroslav Bořita z Martinic and Vilém Slavata, the two Catholic governors appointed by Ferdinand I. After a "stormy discussion", the two councillors (and their personal secretary, Filip Fabricius) were thrown out of the window. As a contemporary historian recounted: "No mercy was granted them and they were both thrown dressed in their cloaks with their rapiers and decoration head first out of the western window into a moat beneath the palace. They loudly screamed ach, ach, oweh! and attempted to hold on to the narrow window-ledge, but Thurn beat their knuckles with the hilt of his sword until they were both obliged to let go".

In the southwest corner of the hall, you can gain access to the **Bohemian Chancellery** (Česká kancelář), scene of Prague's **second defenestration** (see box above). There's some controversy about the exact window from which the victims were ejected, although it's agreed that they survived to tell the tale, landing in a medieval dung heap below, and – so the story goes – precipitating the Thirty Years' War.

The Story of Prague Castle

Anyone can view the forty-minute film on the history of the castle by the Riders' Staircase, but you need a long tour ticket (or pay an extra 140Kč) to gain entry to **The Story of Prague Castle** (Příběh Pražského hradu), housed in the palace's subterranean Gothic and Romanesque chambers. This state-of-the-art, if slightly overlong, exhibition displays one or two exceptional works of art, like the *Vyšehrad Codex*, an illuminated manuscript made for the coronation of Vratislav II, first king of Bohemia, in 1086. There are also several historically charged items, such as the chain mail and helmet that may have belonged to St Václav. Also on display are the grave robes of several Přemyslids and the very impressive grave jewels of the Habsburgs. Don't miss the Communist dinner service from the 1970s, which rivals the Habsburgs for gilded kitsch, nor the small room containing replicas of the Bohemian crown jewels.

The Basilica of sv Jiří

The only exit from the Old Royal Palace is via the Riders' Staircase, which deposits you in Jiřské náměstí. Don't be fooled by the russet red Baroque facade of the **Basilica of sv Jiří** (St George) which dominates the square; inside is Prague's most beautiful Romanesque building, meticulously scrubbed clean and restored to re-create something like the honey-coloured stone basilica that replaced the original tenth-century church in 1173. The double staircase to the chancel is a remarkably harmonious late-Baroque addition and now provides a perfect stage for chamber music concerts. The choir vault contains a rare early thirteenth-century painting of the New Jerusalem from Revelation – not to be confused with the very patchy sixteenth-century painting on the apse – while to the right of the chancel, only partially visible, are sixteenth-century frescoes of the **burial chapel of sv Ludmila**, grandmother of St Wenceslas, who was strangled by her own daughter-in-law in 921 (see box, p.72). There's a replica of the recumbent Ludmila, which you can inspect at close quarters, in the south aisle. Also worth a quick peek is the Romanesque crypt, situated beneath the choir, which contains a macabre sixteenth-century green wax statue of Vanity, whose shrouded, skeletal body is crawling with snakes and lizards.

Jiřský klášter: nineteenth-century Czech art

The basilica was once the church of Bohemia's first monastery, the **Jiřský klášter** (daily 10am–6pm; 150Kč; Ⓦ www.ngprague.cz), which survives next door. Founded in 973 by Mlada, sister of the Přemyslid prince Boleslav the Pious, it was turned into a barracks by Joseph II in 1782, and now houses the Národní galerie's unexceptional **nineteenth-century Czech art collection**. The collection kicks off on the first floor with Antonín Machek's eye-catching series of 32 naive scenes depicting Bohemian rulers from Krok to Ferdinand IV. There are numerous works by members of the influential **Mánes family**. Antonín Mánes succeeded in getting the Czech countryside to look like Italy, and thus gave birth to Romantic Czech landscape painting. Three of his offspring took up the brush: Quido specialized in idealized peasant genre pictures; Amálie obeyed her father's wishes and restricted herself to a little gentle landscape painting; Josef was the most successful of the trio, much in demand as a portrait artist, and one of the leading exponents of patriotically uplifting depictions of national events (he himself took part in the 1848 disturbances in Prague).

Whatever you do, make sure you check out the paintings of Yugoslavia by **Jaroslav Čermák**, a man who lived life to the full, was decorated for his bravery by the Montenegran prince Nicholas I, and died of a heart attack at the age of just 48. František Ženíšek's depiction of the Přemyslid prince Oldřich eyeing up his future peasant princess, Božena, is typical of the dramatic patriotic painting that proved very popular with the late nineteenth-century Czech audience. **Mikuláš Aleš**, whose sgraffito designs can be seen on many of the city's nineteenth-century buildings, is under-represented, though you can admire his decorative depiction of the historical meeting between George of Poděbrady and Matthias Corvinus. Close by are the four saints that appear on the city's Wenceslas Monument by **Josef Václav Myslbek**, the father of Czech sculpture. Beyond hang several misty, moody streetscapes by Jakub Schikaneder.

Zlatá ulička and the castle towers

Around the corner from the convent is **Zlatá ulička** (Golden Lane), a seemingly blind alley of miniature sixteenth-century cottages in dolly-mixture colours, built for the 24 members of Rudolf II's castle guard. The lane takes its name from the goldsmiths who followed (and modified the buildings) a century later. By the nineteenth century, it had become a kind of palace slum, attracting artists and craftsmen, its two most famous inhabitants being Jaroslav Seifert, the Nobel prize-winning Czech poet, and Franz Kafka, who came here in the evenings in the winter of 1916 to write short stories. Finally, in 1951, the Communists kicked out the remaining residents and turned most of the houses into souvenir shops for tourists.

At no. 24, you can climb a flight of stairs to the **Obranná chodba** (defence corridor), which is lined with wooden shields, suits of armour and period costumes. The **Bílá věž** (White Tower), at the western end of the corridor, was the city's main prison from Rudolf's reign onwards. In the opposite direction, the corridor leads to **Daliborka**, the castle tower dedicated to its first prisoner, the young Czech noble Dalibor, accused of supporting a peasants' revolt at the beginning of the fifteenth century, who was finally executed in 1498. According to Prague legend, he learnt to play the violin while imprisoned here, and his playing could be heard all over the castle – a tale that provided material for Smetana's opera *Dalibor*.

To get inside the castle's other tower, the **Prašná věž** (Powder Tower) or Mihulka, which once served as the workshop of gunsmith and bell-founder Tomáš Jaroš, you'll have to backtrack to Vikářská, the street which runs along the north side of the cathedral. The Powder Tower's name comes from the lamprey (*mihule*), an eel-like fish supposedly bred here for royal consumption, though it's actually more noteworthy as the place where Rudolf's team of alchemists was put to work trying to discover the philosopher's stone. Despite its colourful history, the exhibition currently on display within the tower is dull, with just a pair of furry slippers and hat belonging to Ferdinand I to get excited about.

Lobkovický palác

The **Lobkovický palác** (daily 10.30am–6pm; 275Kč; ⓦ www.lobkowiczevents .cz), on the opposite side of Jiřská, was appropriated from the aristocratic family in 1939 and again in 1948 and has only recently been handed back. It now displays an impressive selection of the Lobkowicz family's prize possessions (with audioguide accompaniment by US-born William Lobkowicz himself), including an armoury and a vast art collection. Among them are a portrait of the four-year old Infanta Margarita Teresa (possibly by Velázquez), niece and first wife of Emperor Leopold I. The family has a long history of musical patronage (most notably Beethoven, who dedicated two of his symphonies to the seventh prince), and the original working manuscripts by Mozart and Beethoven on show are pretty impressive. Other highlights include Pieter Brueghel the Elder's sublime *Haymaking* from the artist's famous cycle of seasons, and two views of London by Canaletto. There's a decent **café** in the courtyard and classical music **concerts** daily at 1pm in the Baroque concert hall (tickets from the desk near the café).

The castle gardens

For recuperation and a superlative view over the rest of Prague, head for the **Jižní zahrady** (South Gardens), accessible via Plečnik's copper-canopied Bull Staircase on the south side of the third courtyard. Alternatively, make a short detour beyond the castle walls from the second courtyard, by crossing the **Prašný most** (Powder Bridge), erected in the sixteenth century to connect the newly established royal gardens with the Hrad. Beyond the bridge, opposite the Jízdárna (Riding School) – now an art gallery – is the entrance to the Royal Gardens or **Královská zahrada** (April–Oct daily 10am–6pm; free), founded by Emperor Ferdinand I on the site of a former vineyard. Today, this is one of the best-kept gardens in the capital, with fully functioning fountains and immaculately cropped lawns. Consequently, it's a very popular spot, though more a place for admiring the azaleas and almond trees than lounging around on the grass. It was here that tulips brought from Turkey were first acclimatized to Europe before being exported to the Netherlands, and every spring there's an impressive, disciplined crop.

Built into the gardens' south terrace is Rudolf's distinctive Renaissance ball-game court, known as the **Míčovna** (occasionally open to the public for concerts and exhibitions) and tattooed with sgraffito. At the far end of the gardens is Prague's most celebrated Renaissance legacy, the **Belvedér**, a delicately arcaded summerhouse topped by an inverted copper ship's hull, built by Ferdinand I for his wife, Anne. Unlike the gardens, the Belvedér is open most of the year and is now used for exhibitions of contemporary artists. At the centre of the palace's miniature formal garden is the **Zpívající fontána** (Singing Fountain), built shortly after the palace and so named from the musical sound of the drops of water falling in the metal bowls below. From the garden terrace you can enjoy an unrivalled view of the cathedral.

Chotkovy sady and the Bílkova vila

Adjacent to the Belvedér is the **Chotkovy sady**, Prague's first public park, founded in 1833. You can enjoy a superb view of the bridges and islands of the Vltava from its south wall, or check out the elaborate, grotto-like memorial to the nineteenth-century Romantic poet **Julius Zeyer**, from whose blackened rocks emerge life-sized, marble characters from his works.

Across the road from the park and hidden behind its overgrown garden, the **Bílkova vila** (Sat & Sun 10am–5pm; 50Kč; ⓦ www.ghmp.cz), at Mieckiewiczova 1, honours one of the most unusual Czech sculptors, František Bílek (1872–1941). Born in Chýnov (see p.169), in a part of South Bohemia steeped in Hussite tradition, Bílek lived a monkish life, spending years in spiritual contemplation, reading the works of Hus and other Czech reformers. The villa was built in 1911 to Bílek's own design, intended as both a "cathedral of art" and the family home. Inside, Bílek's extravagant religious sculptures line the walls of his "workshop and temple". In addition to his sculptural and relief work in wood and stone, often wildly expressive and spiritually tortured, there are also ceramics, graphics and a few mementoes of Bílek's life. His living quarters have also been restored and have much of the original wooden furniture, designed and carved by Bílek himself, still in place. Check out the dressing table for his wife, shaped like some giant church lectern, and the wardrobe decorated with a border of hearts, a penis, a nose, an ear and an eye plus the sun, stars and moon.

From Hradčanské náměstí to Strahovský klášter

The monumental scale and appearance of the rest of Hradčany, outside the castle, is a result of the **great fire of 1541**, which swept up from Malá Strana and wiped out most of the old dwelling places belonging to the serfs, tradesmen, clergy and masons who had settled here in the Middle Ages. With the Turks at the gates of Vienna, the Habsburg nobility were more inclined to pursue their major building projects in Prague instead, and, following the Battle of Bílá hora in 1620, the palaces of the exiled (or executed) Protestant nobility were up for grabs too. The newly ensconced Catholic aristocrats were keen to spend some of their expropriated wealth, and over the next two centuries they turned Hradčany into a grand architectural showpiece. As the Turkish threat subsided, the political focus of the empire gradually shifted back to Vienna and the building spree stopped. For the last two hundred years, Hradčany has been frozen in time, and, two world wars on, its buildings have survived better than those of any other central European capital.

Hradčanské náměstí

Hradčanské náměstí fans out from the castle gates, surrounded by the oversized palaces of the old Catholic nobility. For the most part, it's a tranquil space that's foresaken by the tour groups marching through, intent on the Hrad. The one spot everyone heads for is the ramparts in the southeastern corner, by the top of the Zámecké schody, which allow a fabulous view over the red rooftops of Malá Strana, past the famous green dome and tower of the church of sv Mikuláš and beyond, to the spires of Staré Město.

Schwarzenberský palác – the Czech Baroque art collection

The most outrageous, over-the-top, sgraffitoed pile on the square is the **Schwarzenberský palác**, at no. 2. It now houses the Národní galerie's **Czech Baroque art collection** (Tues–Sun 10am–6pm; 150Kč; ⓦ www.ngprague.cz)

– a vast hoard of only limited interest to the non-specialist. Chronologically, the collection begins on the second floor, where you get a brief glimpse of the overtly sensual and erotic **taste** of Rudolf II, who enjoyed works such as Hans von Aachen's sexually charged *Suicide of Lucretia* and Josef Heintz's riotous orgy in his *Last Judgement*. The paltry remains of Rudolf's *Kunstkammer* are pretty disappointing, but the adjacent room contains some superb woodcuts by the likes of Dürer, Holbein and Altdorfer, including some wonderfully imaginative depictions of Satan and the Whore of Babylon. The rest of the gallery, which is spread over three floors, is given over to the likes of Karel Škréta and Petr Brandl, whose paintings and sculptures spearheaded the Counter-Reformation and fill chapels and churches across the Czech Lands. Perhaps the most compelling reason to wade through the gallery is to admire the vigorous, gesticulating sculptures of Matthias Bernhard Braun and Ferdinand Maximilian Brokof.

Šternberský palác – European art from the Classical to the Baroque

A passage down the side of the Arcibiskupský palác leads to the early eighteenth-century **Šternberský palác** (Tues–Sun 10am–6pm; 150Kč; ⓦ www.ngprague .cz), which houses the Národní galerie's **European art collection**, mostly ranging from the fourteenth to the eighteenth century, but excluding works by Czech artists of the period (you'll find them in the Anežský klášter and the Schwarzenberský palác). The collection is relatively modest in comparison with those of other major European capitals, but a handful of masterpieces makes a visit worthwhile.

The collection begins on the **first floor** with Tuscan religious art, most notably a series of exquisite miniature triptychs by Bernardo Daddi, plus several striking triangular-framed portraits of holy figures by Pietro Lorenzetti, including a very fine *St Anthony the Abbot*, with long curly hair and beard. Before you move on, take a detour to the side room 11, which contains Orthodox icons from Venice, the Balkans and Russia. Moving swiftly into the gallery's large Flemish collection, it's worth checking out Dieric Bouts' *Lamentation*, a complex composition crowded with figures in medieval garb. Other works worth picking out are Caroto's effeminate *St John the Evangelist on Patmos*, in room 10, lazily dreaming of the apocalypse, and the two richly coloured Bronzino portraits in room 12. One of the most eye-catching works is Jan Gossaert's *St Luke Drawing the Virgin*, in room 13, an exercise in architectural geometry and perspective that used to hang in the cathedral.

The **second floor** is huge and best taken at a canter. Outstanding works here include Tintoretto's *St Jerome* (room 17), a searching portrait of old age; a wonderfully rugged portrait of a Spanish guerilla leader from the Peninsular War by Goya (room 22); and a mesmerizing *Praying Christ* by El Greco (room 23). Be sure, too, to have a look at the Činský kabinet (room 35), a small oval chamber smothered in gaudy Baroque Chinoiserie, and one of the palace's few surviving slices of original décor. Elsewhere, there are a series of canvases by the Brueghel family (room 26), Rembrandt's *Scholar in his Study* (room 29) and Rubens' colossal *Murder of St Thomas* (room 30), with its pink-buttocked cherubs hovering over the bloody scene. Nearby, in the vast (and uneven) Dutch section, there's a wonderful portrait of an arrogant "young gun" named Jasper by Frans Hals (room 31).

The **ground-floor** galleries contain one of the most prized paintings in the whole collection: the *Feast of the Rosary* by Albrecht Dürer, in room 1, depicting, among others, the Virgin Mary, the Pope, the Holy Roman

Emperor, and even a self-portrait of Dürer himself (top right). This was one of Rudolf II's most prized aquisitions (he was an avid Dürer fan), and was transported on foot across the Alps to Prague (he didn't trust wheeled transport with such a precious object). Also in this room are several superb canvases by Lucas Cranach the Elder. The only other ground-floor room worth bothering with is room 3, harbouring Hans Raphons's multi-panelled *Passion Altar* – look out for *Christ in Purgatory* featuring some wicked devils, especially the green she-devil with cudgel.

Martinický palác – Museum of Mechanical Musical Instruments
Compared to the other palaces on the square, the **Martinický palác** (daily 10am–6pm; 100Kč; ⓦ www.martinickypalace.cz), at no. 8 in the far north-western corner, is one of the more modest piles, built in 1620 by one of the councillors who survived the second defenestration (see p.74). Its rich sgraffito decoration, which continues in the inner courtyard, was only discovered during restoration work in the 1970s. On the facade, you can easily make out Potiphar's wife making a grab at a naked and unwilling Joseph. Guided tours of the interior are available, which, along with a series of fine Renaissance ceilings, holds the **Museum of Mechanical Musical Instruments** or Muzeum hudebních strojů. It's an impressive collection ranging from café orchestrions and fairground barrel organs to early wax phonographs and portable gramophones. Best of all, though, is the fact that almost every exhibit is in working order, as the curators will lovingly demonstrate.

From Nový Svět to Loretánské náměstí
At the other end of Hradčanské náměstí, Kanovnická heads off towards the northwest corner of Hradčany. Nestling in this shallow dip, **Nový Svět** (meaning "New World", though not Dvořák's) provides a glimpse of life on a totally different scale from Hradčanské náměstí. Similar in many ways to the Zlatá ulička in the Hrad, this cluster of brightly coloured cottages, which curls around the corner into Černínská, is all that's left of Hradčany's medieval slums, painted up and sanitized in the eighteenth and nineteenth centuries. Despite having the same scope for mass tourist appeal as Zlatá ulička, it remains remarkably undisturbed, save for a few swish wine bars and **Gambra**, a surrealist art gallery at Černínská 5 (March–Oct Wed–Sun noon–6pm; Nov–Feb Sat & Sun noon–5.30pm; free), which sells works by, among others, the Czech animator **Jan Švankmajer** and his late wife Eva.

Up the hill from Nový Svět, Loretánské náměstí is dominated by the phenomenal 135-metre-long facade of the **Cernínský palác** (Černín Palace), decorated with thirty Palladian half-pillars and supported by a swathe of diamond-pointed rustication. For all its grandeur, it's a miserable, brutal building, whose construction nearly bankrupted future generations of Černíns, who were forced to sell the palace in 1851 to the Austrian state. Since the First Republic, the palace has housed the **Ministry of Foreign Affairs**, and during the war it was, for a while, the Nazi *Reichsprotektor's* residence. On March 10, 1948, it was the scene of Prague's third – and most widely mourned – defenestration. Only days after the Communist coup, **Jan Masaryk**, only son of the founder of Czechoslovakia and the last non-Communist in the cabinet, plunged 14m to his death from a top-floor bathroom window. Whether it was suicide (he had been suffering from depression, partly induced by the country's political path) or murder will probably never be satisfactorily resolved, but for most people Masaryk's death cast a dark shadow over the newly established regime.

The facade of the **Loreta** (Tues–Sun 9am–12.15pm & 1–4.30pm; 110Kč; Ⓦwww.loreta.cz), immediately opposite the Černínský palác, was built by the Dientzenhofers, a Bavarian family of architects, in the early part of the eighteenth century, and is the perfect antidote to the Černíns' humourless monster. It's all hot flourishes and twirls, topped by a tower which lights up like a Chinese lantern at night, and by day clanks out the hymn *We Greet Thee a Thousand Times* on its 27 Dutch bells.

The facade and the cloisters are, in fact, just the outer casing for the focus of the complex, the **Santa Casa**, founded in 1626 and smothered in a mantle of stucco depicting the building's miraculous transportation from the Holy Land. Legend has it that the Santa Casa (Mary's home in Nazareth), under threat from the heathen Turks, was transported by a host of angels to a small laurel grove (*lauretum* in Latin, hence Loreta) in northern Italy. News of the miracle spread across the Catholic lands, prompting a spate of copycat shrines. During the Counter-Reformation, the cult was actively encouraged in an attempt to broaden the popular appeal of Catholicism. The Prague Loreta is one of fifty to be built in the Czech Lands, each of the shrines following an identical design, with pride of place given to a limewood statue of the Black Madonna and Child encased in silver.

Behind the Santa Casa, the Dientzenhofers built the much larger **Church of Narození Páně** (Church of the Nativity), which is like a mini-version of sv Mikuláš, down in Malá Strana. The Santa Casa's serious financial backing is evident in the **treasury** on the first floor of the west wing, much ransacked over the years but still stuffed full of gold. The light fittings are a Communist period piece, but most folk come here to gawp at the master exhibit, an outrageous Viennese silver monstrance designed by Fischer von Erlach in 1699, and studded with diamonds taken from the wedding dress of Countess Kolovrat, who had made the Loreta sole heir to her fortune.

Strahovský klášter (Strahov Monastery)

Continuing westwards from Loretánské náměstí you come to Pohořelec, an arcaded street-cum-square, which leads to the **Strahovský klášter** (Ⓦwww.strahovmonastery.cz), founded in 1140 by the Premonstratensian order. Having managed to evade Joseph II's 1783 dissolution of the monasteries, it continued to function until shortly after the Communists took power, when it was closed down and most of its inmates thrown into prison, though the monks have since returned.

It's the monastery's two ornate **libraries** (daily 9am–noon & 1–5pm; 80Kč), though, that are the real reason for visiting Strahov. The first library you come to is the later and larger of the two, the **Filosofický sál** (Philosophical Hall), built in some haste in the 1780s in order to accommodate the books and bookcases from Louka, a Premonstratensian monastery in Moravia that failed to escape Joseph's decree. The walnut bookcases are so tall they touch the library's lofty ceiling, which is busily decorated with frescoes by the Viennese painter Franz Maulbertsch on the theme of the search for truth. The other main room is the low-ceilinged **Teologický sál** (Theological Hall), studded with ancient globes, its wedding-cake stucco framing frescoes on a similar theme, executed by a monk seventy years earlier. Outside the hall, the library's oldest book, the ninth-century gem-studded *Strahov Gospel*, is displayed – look out, too, for the cabinet of books documenting Czech trees, each of which has the bark of the tree on its spine.

If you leave the monastery through the narrow doorway in the eastern wall, you can reach the hill of Petřín (see p.87). Alternatively, tram #22 or #23 runs from outside Strahov's main entrance back down to the centre of town.

Malá Strana

MALÁ STRANA, Prague's picturesque Little Quarter, sits below the castle and is, in many ways, the city's most entrancing area. Its peaceful, often hilly, cobbled backstreets have changed very little since Mozart walked them during his frequent visits to Prague between 1787 and 1791. Despite the quarter's minuscule size – it takes up a mere 600 square metres of land squeezed in between the river and Hradčany – it's easy enough to lose the crowds, many of whom never stray from the well-trodden route that links the Charles Bridge with the castle. Its streets conceal a whole host of quiet terraced gardens, as well as the wooded hill of Petřín, which together provide the perfect inner-city escape. The **Church of sv Mikuláš**, by far the finest Baroque church in Prague, and the **Kampa Museum**, with its unrivalled collection of works by František Kupka, are the two major sights.

Malostranské náměstí

The main focus of Malá Strana has always been the sloping, cobbled **Malostranské náměstí**, which is dominated and divided into two by the church of sv Mikuláš. Trams and cars hurtle across it, regularly dodged by a procession of people – some heading up the hill to the Hrad, others pausing for coffee and cakes at the numerous bars and restaurants hidden in the square's arcades and Gothic vaults.

Towering above the square, and the whole of Malá Strana, is the church of **sv Mikuláš** or St Nicholas (daily: March–Oct 9am–5pm; Nov–Feb 9am–4pm; 70Kč; ⓦwww.psalterium.cz), easily the most magnificent Baroque building in the city, and one of the last great structures to be built on the left bank, begun in 1702. For Christoph Dientzenhofer, a German immigrant from a dynasty of Bavarian architects, this was his most prestigious commission and is, without doubt, his finest work. For the Jesuits, who were already ensconced in the adjoining college, it was their most ambitious project yet in Bohemia, and the

Mozart in Prague

Mozart made the first of several visits to Prague with his wife Constanze in 1787, staying with his friend and patron Count Thun in what is now the British Embassy (Thunovská 14). A year earlier, his opera *The Marriage of Figaro*, which had failed to please the opera snobs in Vienna, had been given a rapturous reception at Prague's Nostitz Theater (now the Stavovské divadlo; see p.97); and on his arrival in 1787, Mozart was already flavour of the month, as he wrote in his diary: "Here they talk about nothing but Figaro. Nothing is played, sung or whistled but Figaro. Nothing, nothing but Figaro. Certainly a great honour for me!" Encouraged by this, he chose to premiere his next opera, *Don Giovanni*, later that year, in Prague rather than Vienna. He arrived with an incomplete score in hand, and wrote the overture at the Dušeks' Bertramka villa in Smíchov (now the Mozart Museum; see p.126), dedicating it to the "good people of Prague". Apart from a brief sojourn while on a concert tour, Mozart's fourth and final visit to Prague took place in 1791, the year of his death. The climax of the stay was the premiere of Mozart's final opera, *La Clemenza di Tito*, commissioned for the coronation of Leopold II as King of Bohemia (and completed while on the coach from Vienna to Prague). The opera didn't go down quite as well as previous ones – the Empress is alleged to have shouted "German hogwash" from her box. Nevertheless, four thousand people turned out for the funereal memorial service, held in Malá Strana's church of sv Mikuláš to the strains of Mozart's *Requiem Mass*.

ACCOMMODATION

Aria	D
Castle Steps	C
Dientzenhofer	G
Dům U velké boty	A
Nosticova	F
U Karlova mostu	E
U žluté boty	B

RESTAURANTS

Barbar	17
David	7
Hergetová cihelna	13
Kampa Park	14
Nebozízek	16
Rybářský klub	18
U Maltézských rytířů	10
U modré kachničky	15

CAFÉS & TEA-HOUSES

Bohemia Bagel	11
Cukrkávalimonáda	12
Malý Buddha	1
Savoy	19
U zavěšenýho kafe	3
U zeleného čaje	4

PUBS & BARS

Baráčnická rychta	5
Jo's Bar	8
Klášterní pivovar	2
U kocoura	6
U malého Glena	9

Strahovský klášter

Prážský hrad (Prague Castle)

British Embassy

Palace gardens

Valdštejnský palác

Jízdárna

MALOSTRANSKÁ

Franz Kafka Museum

Lichtenštejnský palác

Lékárna Dittrich

sv Tomáš

Sněmovna

Valdštejnská zahrada

sv Josef

Vojanovy sady

sv Mikuláš

Panna Maria pod řetězem

Bridge Tower

Buquoyský palác

Čertovka

Lobkovický palác (German Embassy)

Schönbornský palác (US Embassy)

Vrtbovská zahrada

Panna Maria Vítězná

České muzeum hudby

Atelier Josefa Sudka

sv Jan Křtitel Na Prádle

Kampa

Střelecký ostrov

Rudolfinum

Klementinum

KARLOVO NÁBŘ

MALÁ STRANA

River Vltava

N

Strahovský klášter

Petřín

Rozhledna

Bludiště

sv Vavřinec

Růžový sad

Štefánikova hvězdárna

K H Mácha

Nebozízek

Funicular Railway

Hladová zeď

Wooden Church

Smíchov

0   100 m

ultimate symbol of their stranglehold on the country. When Christoph died in 1722, it was left to his son Kilian Ignaz Dientzenhofer, along with Kilian's son-in-law, Anselmo Lurago, to finish the project, which they did with a masterful flourish, adding the giant green dome and tower – now among the most characteristic landmarks on Prague's left bank. Sadly for the Jesuits, they were able to enjoy the finished product for just twenty years, before they were banished from the Habsburg Empire in 1773.

Nothing about the relatively plain west facade prepares you for the High Baroque **interior**, dominated by the nave's vast fresco, by Johann Lukas Kracker, which portrays some of the more fanciful miraculous feats of St Nicholas. Apart from his role as Santa Claus, he is depicted here rescuing sailors in distress, saving women from prostitution by throwing them bags of gold, and reprieving from death three unjustly condemned men. Even given the overwhelming proportions of the nave, the dome at the far end of the church, built by the younger Dientzenhofer, remains impressive, thanks, more than anything, to its sheer height. Leering over you as you gaze up at the dome are four terrifyingly oversized and stern Church Fathers, one of whom brandishes a gilded thunderbolt, while another garottes a devil with his crozier, leaving no doubt as to the gravity of the Jesuit message.

Occasional exhibitions are staged in the church's gallery, which gives you a great chance to look down on the nave and get closer to the frescoes. It's also possible to climb the *věž* or **belfry** (April–Oct daily 10am–6pm), for fine views over Malá Strana and the Charles Bridge. Before you leave, check out the exceptional Rococo pulpit wrought in pink scagliola, busy with cherubs, a pieta and topped by an archangel on the point of beheading some unfortunate. And don't miss the church's superb organ, its white case and gilded musical cherubs nicely offsetting the grey pipes.

Nerudova, Tržiště and Vlašská

The most important of the various streets leading up to the Hrad from Malostranské náměstí is **Nerudova**, named after the Czech journalist and writer Jan Neruda (1834–91), who was born at *U dvou slunců* (The Two Suns), at no. 47, an inn at the top of the street. His tales of Malá Strana immortalized bohemian life on Prague's left bank, though he's perhaps best known in the West via the Chilean Nobel prize-winner, Pablo Neruda, who took his pen-name from the lesser-known Czech. Historically, this was the city's main quarter for craftsmen, artisans and artists, though the shops and restaurants that line Nerudova now are mostly predictably and shamelessly touristy. Architecturally, the Baroque houses that line the steep climb up to the Hrad are fairly restrained, many retaining their medieval barn doors, and most adorned with their own peculiar house signs (see p.62).

Running (very) roughly parallel to Nerudova – and linked to it by several picturesque side streets and steps – is **Tržiště**, which sets off from the south side of Malostranské náměstí. Halfway up on the left is the **Schönbornský palác**, now the US Embassy. The entrance, and the renowned gardens, are nowadays watched over by closed-circuit TV and twitchy Czech policemen – a far cry from the dilapidated palace in which Kafka rented an apartment in March 1917, and where he suffered his first bout of tuberculosis.

As Tržiště swings to the right, bear left up **Vlašská**, home to yet another **Lobkovický palác**, now the German Embassy. In the summer of 1989, several thousand East Germans climbed over the garden wall and entered the embassy compound to demand West German citizenship, which had been every

German's right since partition. The neighbouring streets were soon jam-packed with abandoned Trabants, as the beautiful palace gardens became a muddy home to the refugees. Finally, the Czechoslovak government gave in and organized special trains to take the East Germans over the federal border, cheered on their way by thousands of Praguers, and thus prompted the exodus that eventually brought down the Berlin Wall.

Valdštejnský palác and around

To the north of Malostranské náměstí, up Tomášská, lies the **Valdštejnský palác**, which takes up the whole of the eastern side of **Valdštejnské náměstí** and Valdštejnská. As early as 1621, Albrecht von Waldstein started to build a palace that would reflect his status as commander of the Imperial Catholic armies of the Thirty Years' War. By buying, confiscating, and then destroying 26 houses, three gardens and a brick factory, he succeeded in ripping apart a densely populated area of Malá Strana to make way for one of the first, largest and, quite frankly, most undistinguished Baroque palaces in the city – at least from the outside. The Czech upper house, or **Senát**, is now housed in the palace, and can be visited on a guided tour at weekends (Sat & Sun: April–Sept 10am–5pm; Oct–March 10am–4pm; free; ⓦwww.senat.cz). The former stables contain the **Pedagogické muzeum** (Tues–Sun 10am–12.30pm & 1–5pm; 40Kč; ⓦwww .pmjak.cz), a small exhibition on Czech education and, in particular, the influential teachings of Jan Amos Komenský (1592–1670) – often anglicized to John Comenius – who was forced to leave his homeland after the victory of Waldstein's Catholic armies, eventually settling in Protestant England.

The palace's formal gardens, the **Valdštejnská zahrada** (April–Oct daily 10am–6pm) – accessible from the palace's main entrance, from the piazza outside Malostranská metro and also from a doorway in the palace walls along Letenská – are a good place to take a breather from the city streets. The focus of the gardens is the gigantic Italianate *sala terrena*, a monumental loggia decorated with frescoes of the Trojan Wars, which stands at the end of an avenue

▲ Valdštejnská zahrada

of sculptures by Adriaen de Vries. The originals, which were intended to form a fountain, were taken off as booty by the Swedes in 1648 and now adorn the royal gardens in Drottningholm. In addition, there are a number of peacocks, a carp pond, a massive semicircular grotto with mysterious doors, and an old menagerie that's now home to a mini-parliament of eagle owls.

One of the chief joys of Malá Strana is its steeply terraced **palace gardens** (palácové zahrady; daily: April 9am–6pm; May & Sept 10am–7pm; June & July 10am–9pm; Aug 10am–8pm; Oct 10am–6pm; 80Kč; ⓦ www.palacovezahrady .cz), hidden away behind the Baroque palaces on Valdštejnská, on the slopes below the castle. There are five small, interlinking gardens in total, dotted with little pavilions, terraces of vines, and commanding superb views over Prague. If you're approaching from below, you have the choice of two entrances, one on Valdštejnské náměstí and one on Valdštejnská. You can also exit or enter via the Jižní zahrady (see p.76) beneath the Hrad itself.

The Prague tourist industry is obsessed with Kafka, and, not content with the small museum on the site of his birthplace (see p.102), there is now a much larger **Franz Kafka Museum** (daily 10am–6pm; 120Kč; ⓦ www .kafkamuseum.cz) hidden away down Cihelná, in the courtyard of the *Hergetová cihelna* restaurant, with its delightful fountain of two gentlemen urinating. The first section includes photos of the ghetto into which Kafka was born, an invoice from his father's shop, with the logo of a jackdaw (*kavka* in Czech), copies of his job applications, requests for sick leave and one of his reports on accident prevention in the workplace. Upstairs, audiovisuals and theatrical trickery is employed in order to explore the torment, alienation and claustrophobia Kafka felt throughout his life and expressed through his writings. For more on Kafka's life and works, see p.102.

Southern Malá Strana

Karmelitská is the busy cobbled street that runs south from Malostranské náměstí along the base of Petřín towards the suburb of Smíchov, becoming Újezd at roughly its halfway point. Between here and the River Vltava are some of Malá Strana's most picturesque and secluded streets. The island of **Kampa**, in particular, makes up one of the most peaceful stretches of riverfront in Prague and the modern art collection on display in the **Museum Kampa** is definitely worth a visit.

Before you set off to explore this part of town, however, you should pop through the doorway at no. 25, on the corner of Karmelitská and Tržiště, to see one of the most elusive of Malá Strana's many Baroque gardens, the **Vrtbovská zahrada** (April–Oct daily 10am–6pm), founded on the site of the former vineyards of the **Vrtbovský palác**. Laid out on Tuscan-style terraces, dotted with ornamental urns and statues of the gods by Matthias Bernhard Braun, the gardens twist their way up the lower slopes of Petřín to an observation terrace, from where there's a spectacular rooftop perspective on the city.

Maltézské náměstí and around

From the trams and traffic of Karmelitská, it's a relief to cut across to the calm restraint of **Maltézské náměstí**, one of a number of delightful little squares between here and the river. It takes its name from the Order of the Knights of St John of Jerusalem (better known by their later title, the Maltese Knights), who in 1160 founded the nearby church of **Panna Maria pod řetězem** (Saint Mary below-the-chain), so called because it was the knights' job to guard the Judith Bridge. The original Romanesque church was pulled down by the

Knights themselves in the fourteenth century, but only the chancel and towers were successfully rebuilt by the time of the Hussite Wars. The two bulky Gothic towers are still standing and the apse is now thoroughly Baroque, but the nave remains unfinished and open to the elements.

The Knights have reclaimed (and restored) the church and the adjacent Grand Priory, which backs onto **Velkopřevorské náměstí**, another pretty little square to the south, which echoes to the sound of music from the nearby Prague conservatoire. Following the violent death of John Lennon in 1980, Prague's youth established an ad hoc shrine smothered in graffiti tributes to the ex-Beatle along the Grand Priory's garden wall. On the opposite side of the square from the priory, behind a row of chestnut trees, is the Rococo **Buquoyský palác**, built for a French family and appropriately enough now the French Embassy.

Kampa

Heading for **Kampa**, the largest of the Vltava's islands, with its cafés, old mills and serene riverside park, is the perfect way to escape the crowds on the Charles Bridge, from which it can be accessed easily via a staircase. The island is separated from the left bank by Prague's "Little Venice", a thin strip of water called **Čertovka** (Devil's Stream), which used to power several mill-wheels until the last one ceased to function in 1936. The northern half of the island is centred on an oval main square, **Na Kampě**, studded with slender acacia trees and cut through by the Charles Bridge; the southern half is a public park, with riverside views across to Staré Město.

Housed in an old riverside water mill by the side of the park, the **Museum Kampa** (daily 10am–6pm; 120Kč; ⓦ www.museumkampa.cz) is dedicated to the private art collection of Jan and Meda Mládek. As well as temporary exhibitions, this stylish modern gallery also exhibits the best of the Mládeks' collection, including a whole series of works by the Czech artist František Kupka, seen by many as the father of abstract art. These range from early Expressionist watercolours to transitional pastels like *Fauvist Chair* from 1910, and more abstract works, such as the seminal oil paintings, *Cathedral* and *Study for Fugue in Two Colours* from around 1912. The gallery also displays a good selection of Cubist and later interwar works by the sculptor Otto Gutfreund and a few collages by postwar surrealist Jiří Kolář.

Panna Maria Vítězná

Halfway down busy Karmelitská is the rather plain church of **Panna Maria Vítězná** (Mon–Sat 9.40am–5.30pm, Sun 1–6pm; free; ⓦ www.pragjesu.com), begun in early Baroque style by German Lutherans in 1611, and later handed over to the Carmelites. The main reason for coming here is to see the **Pražské Jezulátko** or *Bambino di Praga*, a high-kitsch wax effigy of the infant Jesus as a precocious 3-year-old, enthroned in a glass case illuminated with strip lights, donated by one of the Lobkowicz family's Spanish brides in 1628. Attributed with miraculous powers, the *pražské Jezulátko* became an object of international pilgrimage equal in stature to the Santa Casa in Loreta, similarly inspiring a whole series of replicas. It continues to attract visitors (as the multilingual prayer cards attest) and boasts a vast personal wardrobe of expensive swaddling clothes – approaching a hundred separate outfits at the last count – regularly changed by the Carmelite nuns. If you're keen to see some of the infant's outfits, there's a small museum, up the spiral staircase in the south aisle. Here, you get to see his lacy camisoles, as well as a selection of velvet and satin overgarments sent from all over the world. There are also chalices, monstrances and a Rococo crown studded with diamonds and pearls to admire.

Ceské muzeum hudby (Czech Music Museum)

The city's **České muzeum hudby** (daily except Tues 10am–6pm; 100Kč; ⓦ www.nm.cz) is housed in a former Dominican nunnery on the opposite side of Karmelitská. Temporary exhibitions are held on the ground floor of the magnificently tall main hall (formerly the nunnery church), while the permanent collection begins upstairs. The first exhibition kicks off with a crazy cut-and-splice medley of musical film footage from the last century alongside a display of electric guitars and an early Tesla synthesizer. Next up is August Förster's pioneering quarter-tone grand piano from 1924 – you can even listen to Alois Hába's microtonal *Fantazie no. 10* composed for, and performed on, its three keyboards. After this rather promising start, the museum settles down into a conventional display of old central European instruments from a precious Baumgartner clavichord and an Amati violin to Neapolitan mandolins and a vast contrabass over 2m high.

Ateliér Josefa Sudka

A little further south, Karmelitská becomes Újezd. Hidden behind the buildings on the east side of the street, at no. 30, is a faithful reconstruction of the **Ateliér Josefa Sudka** (Tues–Sun noon–6pm; free; ⓦ www.sudek-atelier.cz), a cute little wooden garden studio, where Josef Sudek (1896–1976), the great Czech photographer, lived with his sister from 1927. Sudek moved out to Úvoz 24 (also now a photo gallery) in 1958, but he used the place as his darkroom to the end of his life. The twisted tree in the front garden will be familiar to those acquainted with the numerous photographic cycles he based around the studio. The building has a few of Sudek's personal effects and is now used for temporary photography exhibitions.

Petřín

The scaled-down version of the Eiffel Tower is the most obvious landmark on the wooded hill of **Petřín**, the largest green space in the city centre. The tower is just one of the exhibits built for the 1891 Prague Exhibition, whose modest legacy includes the **funicular railway** or *lanová dráha* (every 10–15min; daily 9am–11.20pm), which climbs up from a station just off Újezd. As the carriages pass each other at the halfway station of Nebozízek, you can get out and soak in the view from the restaurant of the same name. At the top of the hill, it's possible to trace the southernmost perimeter wall of the old city – popularly known as the **Hladová zed'** (Hunger Wall) – as it creeps eastwards back down to Újezd, and northwestwards to the Strahovský klášter. Instigated in the 1460s by Charles IV, it was much lauded at the time (and later by the Communists) as a great public work which provided employment for the burgeoning ranks of the city's destitute (hence its name); in fact, much of the wall's construction was paid for by the expropriation of Jewish property.

Follow the wall southeast and you come to the **Štefánikova hvězdárna** (times vary; ⓦ www.observatory.cz), run by star-gazing enthusiasts. The small astronomical exhibition inside is hardly worth bothering with, but if it's a clear night, a quick peek through the observatory's two powerful telescopes is a treat. Follow the wall northwest and you'll come to Palliardi's twin-towered church of **sv Vavřinec** (St Lawrence), from which derives the German name for Petřín – Laurenziberg.

Opposite the church is a series of buildings from the 1891 Exhibition, starting with the diminutive **Rozhledna** (April daily 10am–5pm; May–Sept daily 10am–10pm; Oct daily 10am–6pm; Nov–March Sat & Sun 10am–5pm; 60Kč), an octagonal interpretation – though a mere fifth of the size – of the Eiffel Tower which shocked Paris in 1889, and a tribute to the city's strong cultural and political links with Paris at the time; the view from the public gallery is terrific in fine weather. The nearby **Bludiště** (times as above; 50Kč), a mini neo-Gothic castle – complete with mock drawbridge – features a **mirror maze** and an action-packed, life-sized diorama of the Prague students' and Jews' victory over the Swedes on the Charles Bridge in 1648.

Staré Město

STARÉ MĚSTO, literally the Old Town, is Prague's most central, vital ingredient. Most of the capital's busiest markets, shops, restaurants and pubs are in this area, and during the day a gaggle of shoppers and tourists fills its complex and utterly confusing web of narrow streets. The district is bounded on one side by the river, on the other by the arc of Národní, Na příkopě and Revoluční, and at its heart is **Staroměstské náměstí**, Prague's showpiece main square, easily the most magnificent in central Europe.

The fire of 1541, which ripped through the quarters on the other side of the river, never reached Staré Město, though the 1689 conflagration made up for it. Nevertheless, the victorious Catholic nobles built fewer large palaces here than on the left bank, leaving the medieval street plan intact with the exception of the Klementinum (the Jesuits' powerhouse) and the Jewish quarter, Josefov, which was largely reconstructed in the late nineteenth century (see p.98). Like so much of Prague, however, Staré Město is still, on the surface, overwhelmingly Baroque, built literally on top of its Gothic predecessor to guard against the floods which plagued the town.

In their explorations of Staré Město, most people unknowingly retrace the **králová cesta**, the traditional route of the coronation procession from the medieval gateway, the Prašná brána (see p.111), to the Hrad. Established by the Přemyslids, the route was followed, with a few minor variations, by every king until the Emperor Ferdinand IV in 1836, the last of the Habsburgs to bother having himself crowned in Prague. It's also the most direct route from the Charles Bridge to Staroměstské náměstí, and therefore a natural choice. However, many of the real treasures of Staré Město lie away from the *králová cesta*, so if you want to escape the crowds, it's worth heading off into the quarter's silent, twisted matrix of streets, then simply following your nose. For details of specific sights to the south of Karlova, see p.97.

Karlův most (Charles Bridge)

The **Karlův most**, or Charles Bridge – which for over four hundred years was the only link between the two halves of Prague – is by far the city's most familiar monument. It's an impressive piece of medieval engineering, aligned slightly askew between two mighty Gothic gateways, but its fame is due almost entirely to the magnificent, mostly Baroque statues, additions to the original structure, that punctuate its length. Individually, only a few of the works are outstanding, but taken collectively, set against the backdrop of the Hrad, the effect is breathtaking.

The bridge was begun in 1357 to replace an earlier structure that was swept away in 1342 by one of the Vltava's frequent floods. Charles IV commissioned his young German court architect, Peter Parler, to carry out the work, which was finally completed in the early fifteenth century. For the first four hundred years it was known simply as the Prague or Stone Bridge – only in 1870 was it officially named after its patron. Since 1950, the bridge has been closed to vehicles, and is now one of the most popular places to hang out, day and night: the crush of sightseers never abates during the day, when the niches created by the bridge-piers are occupied by souvenir hawkers and buskers, but at night things calm down a bit, and the views are, if anything, even more spectacular.

A bronze **crucifix** has stood on the bridge since its construction, but its gold-leaf Hebrew inscription, "Holy, Holy, Holy Lord", from the Book of Isaiah, was added in 1696, paid for by a Prague Jew who was ordered to do so by the city court, having been found guilty of blasphemy before the cross. The first of the sculptures wasn't added until 1683, when a bronze statue of **sv Jan of Nepomuk** appeared as part of the Jesuits' persistent campaign to have him canonized (see p.72); this later inspired hundreds of copies, which adorn bridges throughout central Europe. On the base, there's a bronze relief depicting his martyrdom, the figure of John now extremely worn through years of being touched for good luck. The statue was such a propaganda success with the Catholic Church authorities that another 21 were added between 1706 and 1714. These included works by Prague's leading Baroque sculptors, including Matthias Bernhard Braun and Ferdinand Maximilian Brokof; the remaining piers (and a few swept away in the 1890 flood) were filled in with unimaginative nineteenth-century sculptures.

The bridge towers, at each end of the bridge, can be climbed for a bird's eye view of the masses pouring across. The **Malostranské mostecké věže** (mid-March to Oct daily 10am–6pm; 70Kč) are two unequal towers, connected by a castellated arch, which form the entrance to the bridge. The smaller, stumpy tower was once part of the original Judith Bridge (named after the wife of Vladislav I, who built the twelfth-century original); the taller is crowned by one of the pinnacled wedge-spires more commonly associated with Prague's right bank. The **Staroměstská mostecká věž** (daily: March 10am–6pm; April & Oct 10am–7pm; May–Sept 10am–10pm; Nov–Feb 10am–5pm; 70Kč) is arguably the finest bridge tower of the lot, its eastern facade still encrusted in Gothic cake-like decorations from Peter Parler's workshop. The severed heads of twelve of the Protestant leaders were displayed here for ten years, following their executions on Staroměstské náměstí in 1621 (see p.93). In 1648, it was the site of the last battle of the Thirty Years' War, fought between the besieging Swedes and an ad hoc army of Prague's students and Jews, which trashed the western facade of the bridge tower.

Křížovnické náměstí to Malé náměstí

Pass under the Staré Město bridge tower and you're in **Křížovnické náměstí**, an awkward space hemmed in by its constituent buildings and, with traffic hurtling across the square, a dangerous spot for unwary pedestrians. The two striking churches facing onto the square are worth exploring. The half-brick church of **sv František z Assisi** was built in the 1680s to a design by Jean-Baptiste Mathey for the Czech Order of Knights of the Cross with a Red Star, the original gatekeepers of the old Judith Bridge. The design of the church's interior, dominated by its huge dome, decorated with a fresco of The Last Judgement by Václav Vavřinec Reiner, and rich marble furnishings, served as a blueprint for numerous subsequent Baroque churches in Prague. The **Muzeum Karlova mostu** (daily 10am–8pm; 150Kč; ⓦwww.muzeumkarlovamostu.cz), next door, houses an exhibition on the history of the Charles Bridge. Those with an interest in stonemasonry and engineering will enjoy the exhibition; everyone else will probably get more out of the archive film footage.

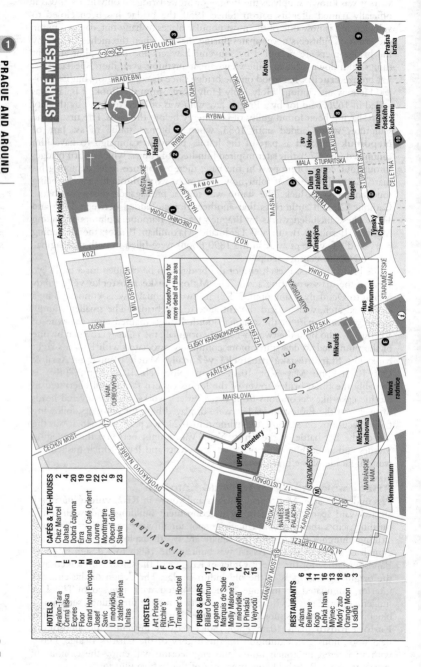

STARÉ MĚSTO

HOTELS

Avalon-Tara	I
Černá liška	E
Expres	J
Floor	H
Grand Hotel Evropa	M
Josef	B
Savic	G
U medvídků	K
U zlatého jelena	D
Unitas	L

HOSTELS

Art Prison	L
Ritchie's	F
Týn	C
Traveller's Hostel	A

PUBS & BARS

Billard Centrum	17
Legends	7
Marquis de Sade	8
Molly Malone's	1
U medvídků	K
U Pinkasů	21
U Vejvodů	15

CAFÉS & TEA-HOUSES

Chez Marcel	2
Dahab	4
Dobrá čajovna	20
Érra	19
Grand Café Orient	10
Louvre	22
Montmartre	12
Obecní dům	9
Slavia	23

RESTAURANTS

Ariana	6
Bellevue	14
Kogo	11
Lehká hlava	16
Mlýnec	13
Modrý zub	18
Orange Moon	5
U sádlů	3

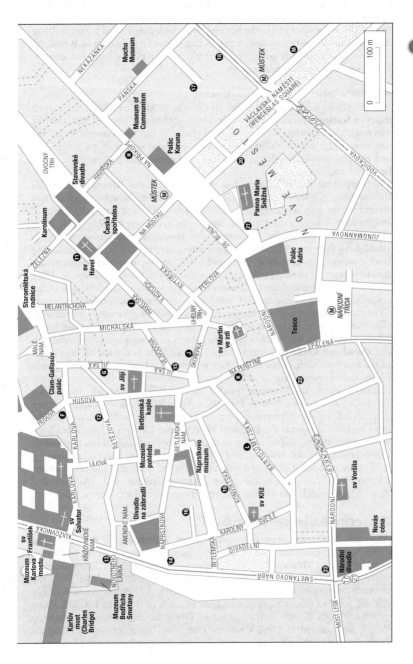

Over the road is the church of **sv Salvátor**, its facade prickling with saintly statues that are lit up enticingly at night. Founded in 1593, but not completed until 1714, sv Salvátor marks the beginning of the Jesuits' rise to power and, like many of their churches, its design copies that of the Gesù church in Rome. It's worth a quick look, if only for the frothy stucco plasterwork and delicate ironwork in its triple-naved interior.

Karlova and the Klementinum

Running from Křižovnické náměstí all the way to Malé náměstí is the narrow street of **Karlova**, packed with people wending their way towards Staroměstské náměstí, their attention divided between checking out the souvenir shops and not losing their way. With Europop blaring out from several shops, jesters' hats and puppets in overabundance, the whole atmosphere can be oppressive in the height of summer.

As they stroll down Karlova, few people notice the **Klementinum**, the former Jesuit College on the north side of the street, which covers an area second in size only to the Hrad. In 1556, Ferdinand I summoned the Jesuits to Prague to help bolster the Catholic cause in Bohemia, eventually putting them in control of the entire university and provincial education system. In establishing their great Catholic seat of learning they bought up the surrounding land, demolishing more than thirty old town houses, and, over the next two hundred years, gradually building themselves a palatial headquarters. In 1773, soon after the Klementinum was completed, the Jesuits were turfed out of the country and the building handed over to the university authorities.

For the moment, the Klementinum houses the National Library's collection of over five million volumes, but much of the original building has been left intact. The **entrance**, on Karlova, lets you into a series of rather plain courtyards, with the **Zrcadlová kaple** (Mirrored Chapel) immediately to the left on the far side of the first courtyard; its interior of fake marble, gilded stucco and mirror panels boasts fine acoustics but is only open for concerts. Nearby is the visitors' entrance, where thirty-minute guided tours (daily: Jan–March 10am–4pm; April–Oct 10am–8pm; Nov & Dec 10am–6pm; 220Kč; ⓦwww.klementinum .net) set off for the Klementinum's two most easily accessible attractions. The most spectacular sight is the **Barokní sál** (Baroque Library), a long room lined with leather tomes, whose ceiling is decorated by one continuous illusionistic fresco praising secular wisdom, and whose wrought-iron gallery balustrade is held up by wooden barley-sugar columns. Upstairs, at roughly the centre of the Klementinum complex, is the Jesuits' **Astronomická věž** (Astronomical Tower), from which you can enjoy a superb view over the centre of Prague.

Staroměstské náměstí

All streets in the old town eventually lead to **Staroměstské náměstí** (Old Town Square), easily the most spectacular square in Prague, and the traditional heart of the city. Most of the brightly coloured houses look solidly eighteenth-century, but their Baroque facades hide considerably older buildings. From the eleventh century onwards, this was the city's main marketplace, known simply as Velké náměstí (Great Square), to which all roads in Bohemia led, and where merchants from all over Europe gathered. When the five towns that made up Prague were united in 1784, it was the Old Town Square's town hall that was made the seat of the new city council, and for the next two hundred years the square was the scene of the country's most violent demonstrations and battles. Nowadays, it's busy all year round with tourists: gathering to watch the town hall's astronomical clock chime, admiring the Hus Monument and simply soaking up the atmosphere.

The square's most recent arrival is the colossal **Jan Hus Monument**, a turbulent sea of blackened bodies – the oppressed to the right, the defiant to the left – out of which rises the majestic moral authority of Hus himself (for more on whom, see p.194), gazing to the horizon. For the sculptor Ladislav Šaloun, a maverick auto-didact, the monument was his life's work. Commissioned in 1900 when the Art Nouveau style of the Viennese Secession was at its peak, it was strangely old-fashioned by the time it was completed in 1915. It would be difficult to claim that it blends in with its Baroque surroundings, yet this has never mattered to the Czechs, for whom its significance goes far beyond aesthetics. The Austrians refused to hold an official unveiling; in protest, on July 6, 1915, the 500th anniversary of the death of Hus, Praguers smothered the monument in flowers. Since then it has been a powerful symbol of Czech nationalism: in March 1939, it was draped in swastikas by the invading Nazis, and in August 1968, it was shrouded in funereal black by Praguers, protesting at the Soviet invasion. The inscription along the base is a quote from the will of Comenius, one of Hus's later followers, and includes Hus's most famous dictum, *Pravda vítězí* (Truth Prevails), which has been the motto of just about every Czech revolution since then.

Staroměstská radnice

It wasn't until the reign of King John of Luxembourg (1310–46) that Staré Město was allowed to build its own town hall, the **Staroměstská radnice**. Short of funds, the citizens decided against an entirely new structure, buying a corner house on the square instead and simply adding an extra floor; later on, they added the east wing, with its graceful Gothic oriel and obligatory wedge-tower. Gradually, over the centuries, the neighbouring merchants' houses to the west were incorporated into the building, so that now it stretches all the way across to the richly sgraffitoed **Dům U minuty**, which juts out into the square.

On May 8, 1945, on the final day of the Prague Uprising, the Nazis still held on to Staroměstské náměstí, and in a last desperate act set fire to the town hall – one of the few buildings to be irrevocably damaged in the old town in World War II. The tower was rebuilt immediately, but only a crumbling fragment remains of the neo-Gothic **east wing**, which once stretched almost as far as the church of sv Mikuláš. Set into the paving nearby, 27 **white crosses** commemorate the Protestant leaders who were condemned to death on the orders of the Emperor Ferdinand II, following the Battle of Bílá hora. They were publicly executed in the square on June 21, 1621: 24 enjoyed the nobleman's privilege and had their heads lopped off; the three remaining commoners were hung, drawn and quartered.

Today, the town hall's most popular feature is its *orloj* or **Astronomical clock** – on the hour (daily 8am–8pm), a crowd of tourists gathers in front of the tower to watch a mechanical dumbshow by the clock's assorted figures. The apostles shuffle past the top two windows, bowing to the audience, while perched on pinnacles below are the four threats to the city as perceived by the medieval mind: Death carrying his hourglass and tolling his bell, the Jew with his moneybags (since 1945 minus his stereotypical beard), Vanity admiring his reflection, and a turbaned Turk shaking his head. Beneath the moving figures, four characters representing Philosophy, Religion, Astronomy and History stand motionless throughout the performance. Finally, a cockerel pops out and flaps its wings to signal that the show's over; the clock then chimes the hour.

The powder-pink facade on the south side of the town hall now forms the **entrance** to the whole complex. The town hall is a popular place to get married, but casual visitors can also join a **guided tour** to see the inside (Mon 11am–5pm, Tues–Sun 9am–6pm). Despite being steeped in history, there's not much of interest here, apart from a few decorated ceilings, a couple of Renaissance portals, the atmospheric Romano-Gothic cellars, and a Gothic **chapel**, designed by Peter Parler. Visitors also get to see the clock's **apostles** close up – and if you're there just before the clock strikes the hour, you can watch them going out on parade; the figures all had to be re-carved by a local puppeteer after the war. Temporary art exhibitions are held on the ground floor (50Kč); you can climb the **tower** (60Kč) for a panoramic sweep across Prague's spires; and on the fourth floor, there's a vast **model** of contemporary Prague (free).

Church of sv Mikuláš and palác Kinských

The destruction of the east wing of the town hall in 1945 rudely exposed Kilian Ignaz Dientzenhofer's church of **sv Mikuláš** (Mon noon–4pm, Tues–Sat 10am–4pm, Sun noon–3pm), built for the Benedictines in 1735. The south front is decidedly luscious – Braun's blackened statuary pop up at every cornice – promising an interior to surpass even its sister church of sv Mikuláš in Malá Strana, which Dientzenhofer built with his father immediately afterwards (see p.81). Inside, however, it's a much smaller space, theatrically organized into a series of interlocking curves. It's also rather plainly furnished, partly because it was closed down by Joseph II and turned into a storehouse, and partly because it's now owned by the very "low", modern, Czechoslovak Hussite Church. Instead, your eyes are drawn sharply upwards to the impressive stuccowork, the wrought-iron galleries and the trompe l'oeil frescoes on the dome.

The largest secular building on the square is the Rococo **palác Kinských** (Tues–Sun 10am–6pm; Ⓦwww.ngprague.cz), designed by Kilian Ignaz Dientzenhofer and built by his son-in-law Anselmo Lurago. In the nineteenth century it became a German *Gymnasium*, which was attended by, among others, Franz Kafka (whose father ran a haberdashery shop on the ground floor). The palace is perhaps most notorious, however, as the venue for the fateful speech by the Communist prime minister, Klement Gottwald, who walked out on to the grey stone balcony one snowy February morning in 1948, flanked by his Party henchmen, to address the thousands of enthusiastic supporters who packed the square below. It was the beginning of *Vítězná února* (Victorious February), the bloodless coup that brought the Communists to power and sealed the fate of the country for the next 41 years.

The Národní galerie currently uses the top two floors for a vast permanent collection of **Czech landscapes** (Tues–Sun 10am–6pm; 100Kč; Ⓦwww .ngprague.cz) – hardly a popular choice and a slightly perverse one given the gallery's prime location. The works range from nineteenth-century views of old Prague, by the Mánes family and the Impressionists Slavíček, Hudeček and Jakob Schikaneder, to temporary contemporary exhibits.

Týnský chrám and Ungelt

Staré Město's most impressive Gothic structure, the mighty **Týnský chrám** (Mon–Fri 10am–1pm & 3–5pm; free; Ⓦtynska.farnost.cz), whose two irregular towers, bristling with baubles, spires and pinnacles, rise like giant antennae above the arcaded houses which otherwise obscure its facade, is a far more imposing building than sv Mikuláš. Like the nearby Hus monument, the Týn church, begun in the fourteenth century, is a source of Czech national pride. In an act of defiance, George of Poděbrady, the last Czech and the only Hussite

King of Bohemia, adorned the high stone gable with a statue of himself and a giant gilded *kalich* (chalice), the mascot of all Hussite sects. The church remained a hotbed of Hussitism until the Protestants' crushing defeat at the Battle of Bílá hora, after which the chalice was melted down to provide the newly ensconced statue of the Virgin Mary with a golden halo, sceptre and crown.

Despite being one of the main landmarks of Staré Město, it's well-nigh impossible to appreciate the church from anything but a considerable distance, since it's boxed in by the houses around it, some of which are actually built right against the walls. The church's lofty, narrow nave is bright white, punctuated at ground level by black and gold Baroque altarpieces. The pillar on the right of the chancel steps contains the red marble **tomb of Tycho Brahe**, the famous Danish astronomer, who arrived in Prague wearing a silver and gold false nose, having lost his own in a duel in Rostock. Court astronomer to Rudolf II for just two years, Brahe laid much of the groundwork for Johannes Kepler's later discoveries – Kepler getting his chance of employment when Brahe died of a burst bladder in 1601 after joining Petr Vok in one of his notorious binges.

Behind the Týn church lies the **Týn** courtyard, also known by its German name, **Ungelt** (meaning "No Money", a pseudonym used to deter marauding invaders), which, as the trading base of German merchants, was one of the first settlements on the Vltava. A hospice, church and hostel were built for the use of the merchants, and by the fourteenth century the area had become an extremely successful international marketplace; soon afterwards the traders moved up to the Hrad, and the court was transformed into a palace. The whole complex has since been restored, and the courtyard is home to various shops, restaurants, and a luxury hotel.

Dům U zlatého prstenů

Back on Týnská, you'll come to the handsome Gothic town house of **Dům U zlatého prstenů** (House of the Golden Ring; Tues–Sun 10am–6pm; Ⓦ www .citygalleryprague.cz), now used by the City of Prague Gallery to show off some of its twentieth-century Czech art. If you're not heading out to the modern art museum in the Veletržní palác (see p.121), then this is a good taster. The permanent collection is spread over three floors, arranged thematically, while the cellar provides space for installations by up-and-coming contemporary artists; there's also a nice café across the courtyard.

On the first floor, symbolism looms large, with *Destitute Land*, Max Švabinský's none-too-subtle view of life under the Habsburg yoke, and a smattering of works by two of Bohemia's best-loved eccentrics, Josef Váchal and František Bílek. There's a decent selection of dour 1920s paintings, too, typified by *Slagheaps in the Evening II* by Jan Zrzavý, plus the usual Czech Surrealist suspects, Josef Šíma, Toyen and Jiří Štyrský. More refreshing is the sight of Eduard Stavinoha's cartoon-like *Striking Demonstrators 24.2.1948*, an ideological painting from 1948 that appears almost like Pop Art. Antonín Slavíček's easy-on-the-eye Impressionist views of Prague are displayed on the second floor, along with works by Cubist Emil Filla. Also on this floor, you'll find Zbyšek Sion's absinthe nightmare and the strange perforated metal sheets of Alena Kučerova.

From Celetná to Anežský klášter

Celetná, whose name comes from the bakers who used to bake a particular type of small loaf (*calty*) here in the Middle Ages, leads east from Staroměstské náměstí direct to the Prašná brána, one of the original gateways of the old town. It's one of the oldest streets in Prague, lying along the former trade route from the old town market square, as well as on the *králová cesta*.

Two-thirds of the way along Celetná, at the junction with Ovocný trh, is the **Dům U černé Matky boží** (House at the Black Madonna), built as a department store in 1911–12 by Josef Gočár and one of the best examples of Czech Cubist architecture in Prague (see p.116). Appropriately enough, the building now houses a small but excellent **Muzeum českého kubismu** (Museum of Czech Cubism; Tues–Sun 10am–6pm; 100Kč; ⓦ www.ngprague .cz). There's a little bit of everything, from sofas and sideboards by Gočár himself to paintings by Emil Filla and Josef Čapek, plus some wonderful sculptures by Otto Gutfreund.

Celetná ends at the fourteenth-century Prašná brána (see p.111), beyond which is náměstí Republiky, at which point, strictly speaking, you've left Staré Město behind. Back in the old town, head north from Celetná into the backstreets which conceal the Franciscan church of **sv Jakub** or St James (Mon–Sat 9.30am–noon & 2–4pm, Sun 2–4pm), with its distinctive bubbling, stucco portal on Malá štupartská. The church's massive Gothic proportions – it has the longest nave in Prague after the cathedral – make it a favourite venue for organ recitals, Mozart masses and other concerts. After the great fire of 1689, Prague's Baroque artists remodelled the entire interior, adding huge pilasters, a series of colourful frescoes and more than twenty side altars.

Anežský klášter – medieval Czech art

Further north through the backstreets, the **Anežský klášter** (Convent of St Agnes), Prague's oldest surviving Gothic building, stands within a stone's throw of the river as it loops around to the east. It was founded in 1233 as a Franciscan convent for the Order of the Poor Clares, and takes its name from Anežka (Agnes), youngest daughter of Přemysl Otakar I, who left her life of regal privilege to become the convent's first abbess. Anežka herself was beatified in 1874 to try to combat the spread of Hussitism among the Czechs, and was officially canonized on November 12, 1989, just four days before the Velvet Revolution. The convent now houses the Národní galerie's **medieval Czech art collection** (Tues–Sun 10am–6pm; 150Kč; ⓦ www.ngprague.cz), in particular the Gothic art, which first flourished here under the patronage of Charles IV.

The exhibition is arranged chronologically, starting with a remarkable silver-gilt casket from 1360 used to house the skull of sv Ludmila. The nine panels from the altarpiece of the Cistercian monastery at Vyšší Brod in South Bohemia, from around 1350, are among the finest in central Europe: the *Annunciation* panel is particularly rich iconographically. The real gems of the collection, however, are the six panels by **Master Theodoric**, who painted over one hundred such paintings for Charles IV's castle chapel at Karlštejn (see p.153). These larger-than-life half-length portraits of saints, church fathers and so on, are full of intense expression and rich colours, their depictions spilling onto the embossed frames. The three late fourteenth-century panels by the **Master of Třeboň** show an even greater variety of balance and depth, and the increasing influence of Flemish paintings of the period. Since the quality of the works in the gallery's largest room is pretty uneven, it's worth moving fairly swiftly on to the smaller rooms beyond, where you'll find woodcuts by Cranach the Elder, Dürer and the lesser-known Hans Burgkmair – the seven-headed beast in Dürer's *Apocalypse* cycle is particularly memorable. Finally, don't miss the superb sixteenth-century wood sculptures, including an incredibly detailed scene, *Christ the Saviour and the Last Judgement*, in which Death's entrails are in the process of being devoured by a frog.

Southern Staré Město

The southern half of Staré Město is bounded by the **králová cesta** (the corona-tion route) to the north, and the curve of **Národní** and **Na příkopě**, which follow the course of the old fortifications, to the south. There are no showpiece squares like Staroměstské náměstí here, but the complex web of narrow lanes and hidden passageways, many of which have changed little since medieval times, makes this an intriguing quarter to explore, and one where it's easy to lose the worst of the crowds.

Around the Stavovské divadlo

South of Celetná lies **Ovocný trh**, site of the old fruit market, its cobbles fanning out towards the back of the lime-green and white **Stavovské divadlo** (Estates Theatre). Built in the early 1780s for the entertainment of Prague's large and powerful German community, the theatre is one of the finest Neoclassical buildings in Prague, reflecting the enormous self-confidence of its patrons. The Stavovské divadlo has a place in Czech history too, for it was here that the Czech national anthem, *Kde domov můj* (Where is My Home), was first performed, as part of the comic opera *Fidlovačka*, by J.K. Tyl. It is also of great appeal to Mozart fans, since it was here, rather than in the hostile climate of Vienna, that the composer chose to premiere both *Don Giovanni* and *La Clemenza di Tito*. This is, in fact, one of the few opera houses in Europe which remains intact from Mozart's time, though it underwent major refurbishment during the nineteenth century – it was here that Miloš Forman filmed the concert scenes for his Oscar-laden *Amadeus*.

West of the Stavovské divadlo, the junction of Melantrichova and Rytířská is always teeming with people pouring out of Staroměstské náměstí and heading for Wenceslas Square. Clearly visible from Melantrichova is Prague's last surviving **open-air market** – it runs the full length of the arcaded Havelská, and sells everything from celery to CDs, with plenty of souvenirs and wooden toys in between.

Betlémské náměstí

Betlémské náměstí is named after the **Betlémská kaple** (Tues–Sun: April–Oct 10am–6.30pm; Nov–March 10am–5.30pm; 50Kč), whose high wooden gables face on to the square. The chapel was founded in 1391 by religious reformists, who, denied the right to build a church, proceeded instead to build the largest chapel in Bohemia, with a total capacity of three thousand. Sermons were delivered not in the customary Latin, but in Czech, the language of the masses. From 1402 to 1413, **Jan Hus** preached here (see box, p.194), regularly pulling in more than enough commoners to fill the chapel. Hus was eventually excommunicated for his outspokenness, found guilty of heresy and burnt at the stake at the Council of Constance in 1415. The chapel continued to attract reformists from all over Europe for another two centuries until it was handed over to the Jesuits. The chapel was demolished following the expulsion of the Jesuits in 1773, and only three outer walls now remain from the medieval building, with patches of their original biblical decoration. The rest is a scrupulous reconstruction by Jaroslav Fragner, using the original plans and a fair amount of imaginative guesswork.

At the western end of the square stands the **Náprstkovo muzeum** (Tues–Sun 10am–6pm; 80Kč; ⓦ www.nm.cz), whose founder, Czech nationalist Vojta Náprstek, was inspired by the great Victorian museums of London while in exile following the 1848 revolution. Despite the fact that the museum could clearly do with an injection of cash, it still manages to put on some excellent temporary ethnographic exhibitions, and does a useful job of promoting tolerance of different cultures. The permanent collection of Náprstek's American, Australasian and Oceanic collections occupies the top two floors.

Muzeum Bedřicha Smetany

A few blocks west, in a gaily decorated neo-Renaissance building on the river-front, is the **Muzeum Bedřicha Smetany** (daily except Tues 10am–noon & 12.30–5pm; 50Kč; ⓦwww.nm.cz). Bedřich Smetana (1824–84) was without doubt the most nationalistic of all the great Czech composers, taking an active part in the 1848 revolution and the later national revival movement. He enjoyed his greatest success as a composer with *The Bartered Bride*, which marked the birth of Czech opera. However, he was forced to give up conducting in 1874 with the onset of deafness, and eventually died of syphilis in a mental asylum. Sadly, the museum fails to capture much of the spirit of the man, though you get to see his spectacles and the garnet jewellery of his first wife.

Josefov

It is crowded with horses; traversed by narrow streets not remarkable for cleanliness, and has altogether an uninviting aspect. Your sanitary reformer would here find a strong case of overcrowding.

Walter White, *A July Holiday in Saxony, Bohemia and Silesia* (1857)

Less than half a century after Walter White's comments, all that was left of the former ghetto of **JOSEFOV** were six synagogues, the town hall and the medieval cemetery. At the end of the nineteenth century, it was decided that Prague should be turned into a beautiful bourgeois city, modelled on Paris. The key to this transformation was the "sanitization" of the ghetto, a process, begun in 1893, which reduced the notoriously malodorous backstreets and alleyways of Josefov to rubble and replaced them with block after block of luxurious five-storey mansions. The Jews, the poor, the Gypsies and the prostitutes were cleared out so that the area could become a desirable residential quarter, rich in Art Nouveau buildings festooned with decorative murals, doorways and sculpturing.

In any other European city occupied by the Nazis in World War II, what little was left of the old ghetto would have been demolished. But although Prague's Jews were transported to the new ghetto in Terezín and eventually Auschwitz, the Prague ghetto was preserved by Hitler himself in order to provide a site for his planned "Exotic Museum of an Extinct Race". By this grotesque twist of fate, Jewish artefacts from all over central Europe were gathered here, and now make up one of the richest collections of Judaica in Europe.

Visiting Josefov

All the major sights of Josefov – the five synagogues and the cemetery – (ⓦwww .jewishmuseum.cz) are covered by an all-in-one 480Kč **ticket**, valid for one day only and available from any of the quarter's numerous ticket offices. If you don't want to visit the Staronová synagoga, the ticket costs just 300Kč. **Opening hours** vary but are basically daily except Saturday, April to October from 9am to 6pm, and from November to March between 9am and 4.30pm.

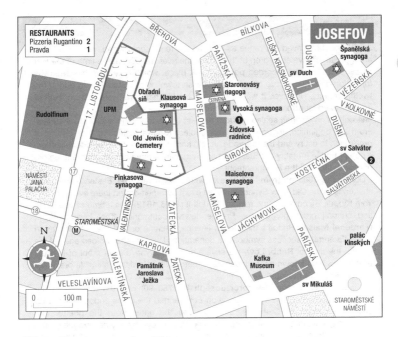

The former ghetto

Geographically, Josefov lies to the northwest of Staroměstské náměstí, between the church of sv Mikuláš and the River Vltava. The warren-like street plan of Josefov disappeared during the sanitization, and through the heart of the old ghetto runs the ultimate bourgeois avenue, **Pařížská**, a riot of turn-of-the-twentieth-century sculpturing, spikes and turrets, home to swanky boutiques and cafés. If Josefov can still be said to have a main street, though, it is really the parallel street of **Maiselova**, named after the community's sixteenth-century leader. The sheer volume of tourists that visit Josefov has brought with it the inevitable rash of stalls flogging dubious "Jewish" souvenirs, and the area is now something of a tourist trap. Yet to skip this part of the old town is to miss out on an entire slice of the city's cultural history.

Staronová synagoga and Židovská radnice

Walking down Maiselova, it's impossible to miss the steep sawtooth brick gables of the **Staronová synagoga** or Altneuschul (Old-New Synagogue), so called because when it was built it was indeed very new, though as time went on, it became anything but. Begun in the second half of the thirteenth century, it is, in fact, the oldest functioning synagogue in Europe, one of the earliest Gothic buildings in Prague and still the religious centre for Prague's Orthodox Jews. Since Jews were prevented by law from becoming architects, the synagogue was probably constructed by the Franciscan builders working on the convent of sv Anežka. Its five-ribbed vaulting is unique in Bohemia; the extra, purely decorative rib was added to avoid any hint of a cross.

When entering the synagogue (Ⓦ www.synagogue.cz), men are asked to cover their heads – paper *kippahs* are usually available, though a handkerchief will do. To get to the **main hall**, you must pass through one of the two low

99

Prague's Jews

Jews probably arrived in Prague as early as the tenth century and, initially at least, are thought to have settled on both sides of the river. In 1096, at the time of the first crusade, the earliest recorded **pogrom** took place, which may have hastened the formation of a much more closely knit "Jewish town" within Staré Město during the twelfth century. However, it wasn't until much later that Jews were actually herded into a **walled ghetto** (and several centuries before the word "ghetto" was actually first coined, in Venice), sealed off from the rest of the town and subject to a curfew. From the beginning, though, they were subject to laws restricting their choice of profession to usury and the rag trade; in addition, some form of visible identification, a cap or badge (notably the Star of David), remained a more or less constant feature of Jewish life until the Enlightenment.

During the **1389 pogrom**, 3000 Jews were massacred over Easter, some while sheltering in the Old-New Synagogue – an event commemorated there every year on Yom Kippur. By contrast, the reign of Rudolf II (1576–1612) was a time of economic and cultural prosperity for the Prague Jewish community. The Jewish mayor, **Mordecai Maisel**, Rudolf's minister of finance, became one of the richest men in Bohemia and the success symbol of a generation. This was the "golden age" of the ghetto: the time of **Rabbi Löw**, the severe and conservative chief rabbi of Prague, who is now best known as the legendary creator of the Jewish "golem" (a precursor of Frankenstein's monster).

It was the enlightened **Emperor Joseph II** (1780–90) who did most to lift the restrictions on Jews. His 1781 Toleration Edict ended the dress codes, opened up education to all non-Catholics, and removed the gates from the ghetto. The community paid him homage in the following century by officially naming the ghetto Josefov, or Josefstadt. It was not until the **1848 revolution**, however, that Jews were granted equal status as citizens and permitted to settle outside the ghetto. Gradually, the more prosperous Jewish families began to move to other districts of Prague, leaving behind only the poorest Jews and strictly Orthodox families, who were rapidly joined by the underprivileged ranks of Prague society: Gypsies, beggars, prostitutes and alcoholics. By 1890, only twenty percent of Josefov's population was Jewish, yet it was still the most densely populated area in Prague.

After the **Nazi occupation** of Prague on March 15, 1939, the city's Jews were subject to an increasingly harsh set of regulations, which saw them again barred from most professions, placed under curfew, and compelled once more to wear the yellow Star of David. In November 1941, the first transport of Prague Jews set off for the new ghetto in Terezín, 60km northwest of Prague. Of the estimated 55,000 Jews in Prague at the time of the Nazi invasion, over 36,000 died in the camps. Many survivors emigrated to Israel and the USA. Of the 8000 who registered as Jewish in the Prague census of 1947, a significant number joined the Communist Party, only to find themselves victims of Stalinist anti-Semitic wrath during the 1950s.

It's difficult to calculate exactly how many Jews now live in Prague – around a thousand were officially registered as such prior to 1989 – though their numbers have undoubtedly been bolstered by a new generation of Czech Jews who have rediscovered their roots, and by the new influx of Jewish Americans and Israelis.

vestibules from which women are allowed to watch the proceedings. Above the entrance is an elaborate tympanum covered in the twisting branches of a vine tree, its twelve bunches of grapes representing the tribes of Israel. The simple, plain interior is mostly taken up with the elaborate wrought-iron cage enclosing the *bimah* in the centre. In 1354, Charles IV granted Jews a red flag inscribed with a Star of David – the first such community known to have adopted the symbol. The red standard currently on display was originally a gift to the community from Emperor Ferdinand II for helping fend off the Swedes in 1648.

Just south of the synagogue is the **Židovská radnice** (Jewish Town Hall), one of the few such buildings to survive the Holocaust. Founded and funded by Maisel in the sixteenth century, it was later rebuilt as the creamy-pink Baroque house you see now, housing an overpriced kosher restaurant. The belfry, permission for which was granted by Ferdinand III, has a clock on each of its four sides, plus a Hebrew one stuck on the north gable that, like the Hebrew script, goes "backwards".

Pinkasova synagoga

Jutting out at an angle on the south side of the Old Jewish Cemetery (see below), with its entrance on Široká, the **Pinkasova synagoga** was built in the 1530s for the powerful Pinkas family, and has undergone countless restorations over the centuries. In 1958, the synagogue was transformed into a chilling memorial to the 77,297 Czech Jews killed during the Holocaust. Of all the sights of the Jewish quarter, the **Holocaust memorial** is perhaps the most moving, with every bit of wall space taken up with the carved stone list of victims, stating simply their names, dates of birth and dates of transportation to the camps. It is the longest epitaph in the world, yet it represents only the merest fraction of those who died in the Nazi ghettos and concentration camps. All that remains of the synagogue's original decor is the ornate *bimah* surrounded by a beautiful wrought-iron grille, supported by barley-sugar columns. Upstairs in a room beside the women's gallery, there's now a harrowing exhibition of drawings by children from the Jewish ghetto in Terezín (see p.244), most of whom later perished in the camps.

Starý židovský hřbitov (Old Jewish Cemetery)

At the heart of Josefov is the **Starý židovský hřbitov** (Old Jewish Cemetery), which was established in the fifteenth century, and closed in 1787, by which time there were an estimated 100,000 buried here, one on top of the other, as many as twelve layers deep. The volume of visitors has meant that the graves have been roped off to protect them, and a one-way system introduced: you

▲ Old Jewish Cemetery

enter from the Pinkasova synagoga, on Široká, and leave by the Klausová synagoga (see below). Get there before the crowds – a difficult task at most times of the year – and you'll find a poignant reminder of the ghetto, its inhabitants subjected to inhuman overcrowding even in death. The rest of Prague recedes beyond the sombre ash trees and cramped perimeter walls, the haphazard headstones and Hebrew inscriptions casting a powerful spell.

Obřadní síň and the other synagogues

Immediately on your left as you leave the cemetery is the **Obřadní síň**, a lugubrious neo-Renaissance house built in 1906 as a ceremonial hall by the Jewish Burial Society. Appropriately enough, it's now devoted to an exhibition on Jewish traditions of burial and death, good to peruse before you head off into the cemetery.

Close to the entrance to the cemetery is the **Klausová synagoga**, a late-seventeenth-century building, founded in the 1690s by Mordecai Maisel on the site of several medieval prayer halls (*klausen*), in what was then a notorious red-light district of Josefov. The ornate Baroque interior contains a rich display of religious objects from embroidered *kippah* to *Kiddush* cups, and explains the very basics of Jewish religious practice.

On Kafka's trail

Franz Kafka was born on July 3, 1883, above the *Batalion* Schnapps bar on the corner of Maiselova and Kaprova (the original building has long since been torn down, but a gaunt-looking modern bust now commemorates the site). He spent most of his life in and around Josefov. His father was an upwardly mobile small businessman from a Czech-Jewish family of kosher butchers (Kafka himself was a vegetarian), his mother from a wealthy German-Jewish family of merchants. The family owned a haberdashery shop, located at various premises on or near Staroměstské náměstí. In 1889, they moved out of Josefov and lived for the next seven years in the beautiful Renaissance Dům U minuty, next door to the Staroměstská radnice, during which time Kafka attended the *Volksschule* on Masná (now a Czech primary school), followed by a spell at an exceptionally strict German *Gymnasium*, located on the third floor of the palác Kinských.

At 18, he began a law degree at the German half of the Karolinum, which was where he met his lifelong friend and posthumous biographer and editor, Max Brod. Kafka spent most of his working life as an accident insurance clerk, until he was forced to retire through ill health in 1922. Illness plagued him throughout his life and he spent many months as a patient at the innumerable spas in *Mitteleuropa*. He was engaged three times, twice to the same woman, but never married, finally leaving home at the age of 31 for bachelor digs on the corner of Dlouhá and Masná, where he wrote the bulk of his most famous work, *The Trial*. He died of tuberculosis at the age of 40 in a sanatorium just outside Vienna, on June 3, 1924, and is buried in the Nový židovský hřbitov in Žižkov (see p.119).

Nowadays, thanks to his popularity with Western tourists, Kafka has become an extremely marketable commodity, with his image plastered across T-shirts, mugs and postcards all over the city centre. A ludicrous statue of Kafka riding on the shoulders of the golem has recently been erected outside the Spanish Synagogue and now provides photo opportunities for tourists. The best place to head for, though, is the small **Kafka museum** (Expozice Franze Kafky; Tues–Fri 10am–6pm, Sat 10am–5pm; 50Kč), on the site of Kafka's birthplace next door to the church of sv Mikuláš, which retells Kafka's life simply but effectively with pictures and quotes (in Czech, German and English). There's also a larger, more sophisticated Kafka museum over in Malá Strana (see p.85).

Founded and paid for entirely by Mordecai Maisel, the neo-Gothic **Maiselova synagoga**, set back from the neighbouring houses on Maiselova, was, in its day, one of the most ornate synagogues in Josefov. Nowadays, its bare whitewashed turn-of-the-twentieth-century interior houses an exhibition on the history of the Czech Jewish community up until the 1781 Toleration Edict, its glass cabinets filled with gold and silverwork, *hanukkah* candlesticks, *torah* scrolls and other religious artefacts.

East of Pařížská, up Široká, stands the **Španělská synagoga** (Spanish Synagogue), built in 1868. By far the most ornate synagogue in Josefov, every available surface of its stunning, gilded Moorish interior is smothered with a profusion of floral motifs and geometric patterns, in vibrant reds, greens and blues, which are repeated in the synagogue's huge stained-glass windows. The interior houses an interesting exhibition on the history of Prague's Jews from the time of the 1848 emancipation. Lovely, slender, painted cast-iron columns hold up the women's gallery, where the displays include a fascinating set of photos depicting the old ghetto at the time of its demolition. There's a section on Prague's German-Jewish writers, including Kafka, and information on the planned Nazi museum and the Holocaust.

Around náměstí Jana Palacha

As Kaprova and Široká emerge from Josefov, they meet at **náměstí Jana Palacha**, named after the student from the Faculty of Philosophy on the east side of the square who killed himself in protest against the 1968 invasion. The north side of the square is taken up by the **Rudolfinum** or Dům umělců (House of Artists), designed by Josef Zítek and Josef Schulz. One of the proud civic buildings of the nineteenth-century national revival, it was originally built to house an art gallery, museum and concert hall for the Czech-speaking community. In 1918, however, it became the seat of the new Czechoslovak parliament, only returning to its original purpose in 1946. It's now one of the capital's main exhibition and concert venues, home to the **Czech Philharmonic**, with a wonderfully grand café on the first floor.

UPM – the Decorative Arts Museum

A short way down 17 listopadu from the square is the **UPM**, or Uměleckoprůmyslové muzeum (Tues 10am–7pm, Wed–Sun 10am–6pm; 120Kč, free Tues 5–7pm; Ⓦ www.upm.cz), installed in another of Schulz's worthy nineteenth-century creations, richly decorated in mosaics, stained glass and sculptures. Literally translated, this is a "Museum of Decorative Arts", though the translation hardly does justice to what is one of the most fascinating museums in the capital. The museum's consistently excellent temporary exhibitions are staged on the ground floor, with the permanent collections on the floor above. Audioguides are available (30Kč) though they're by no means essential, as there's lots of information and labelling in English.

The displays start with the **Votive Hall** (Votivní sál), which is ornately decorated with trompe l'oeil wall hangings, lunette paintings and a bewhiskered bust of Emperor Franz-Josef I. Next door is the **Story of a Fibre**, which displays textile exhibits, ranging from a sixteenth-century Brussels tapestry of Samson bringing down the temple to some 1930s curtains by the Surrealist artist Toyen. The room is dominated by a double-decker costume display: above, there are richly embroidered religious vestments from the fifteenth to eighteenth centuries; below, fashionable attire from the eighteenth century to contemporary catwalk concoctions.

More rooms are planned to open on this side of the Votive Hall, but at the time of going to press, you have to backtrack to reach the **Arts of Fire**, home to the museum's impressive glass, ceramic and pottery displays, ranging from eighteenth-century Meissen figures to Art Nouveau vases by Bohemian glass-makers such as Lötz. To catch the best examples of Cubist works, head for the room's Gočár-designed Cubist bookcase, and look out, too, for Jan Zrzavy's three-piece glass mosaic from the 1930s.

The **Print and Images** room is devoted mainly to Czech photography, and includes numerous prints from the art form's interwar heyday, including several of František Drtikol's remarkable 1920s geometric nudes, Jaromír Funke's superb still-lifes and Josef Sudek's contemplative studio shots. Finally, in the **Treasury**, there's a kind of modern–day cabinet of curiosities: everything from ivory objets d'art and seventeenth-century Italian *pietro dure* or hardstone mosaics, to miniature silver furniture and a goblet made from rhino horn.

Nové Město

NOVÉ MĚSTO is the city's main commercial and business district, housing its long-established big hotels, cinemas, nightclubs, fast-food outlets and depart-ment stores. Architecturally, it comes over as big, bourgeois and predominantly late nineteenth century, yet Nové Město was actually founded way back in 1348 by Emperor Charles IV as an entirely new town – three times as big as Staré Město – intended to link the southern fortress of Vyšehrad with Staré Město to the north. Large market squares, wide streets, and a level of town planning far ahead of its time were employed to transform Prague into the new capital city of the Holy Roman Empire. In fact, it quickly became one of the city's poorer quarters, renowned as a hotbed of Hussitism and radicalism throughout the centuries. In the second half of the nineteenth century, the authorities set about a campaign of slum clearance similar to that inflicted on the Jewish quarter; only the churches and a few important historical buildings were left standing, though Charles' street layout survived pretty much intact. The leading architects of the day began to line the wide boulevards with ostentatious examples of their work, which were eagerly snapped up by the new class of status-conscious businessmen – a process that continued well into the twentieth century, making Nové Město the most architecturally varied part of Prague.

The obvious starting point, and probably the only place in Prague most visitors can put a name to, is Wenceslas Square, known to the Czechs as **Václavské náměstí**, hub of the modern city and somewhere you'll find yourself passing through again and again. The two principal, partially pedestrianized, streets which lead off it are **Národní třída** and **Na příkopě**, which together form the *zlatý kříž* (golden cross), Prague's commercial axis. The *zlatý kříž*, and the surrounding streets, also contain some of Prague's finest late nineteenth-century, Art Nouveau and twentieth-century architecture. The rest of Nové Město, which spreads out northeast and southwest of the square, is less explored and, for the most part, heavily residential.

Václavské náměstí (Wenceslas Square)

The natural pivot around which modern Prague revolves, and the focus of the Velvet Revolution of November 1989, **Václavské náměstí** (Wenceslas Square) is more of a wide, gently sloping boulevard than a square as such. It's scarcely a conventional – or even convenient – space in which to hold mass demonstrations, yet the square's **history of protest** goes back to the 1848 revolution, whose violent denouement began here on June 12 with a peaceful open-air Mass organized by Prague students. On the crest of the nationalist disturbances, the square – which had been known as Koňský trh (Horse Market) since medieval times – was given its present name. Naturally enough, it was one of the rallying points for the jubilant milling crowds on October 28, 1918, when Czechoslovakia's independence was declared. At the lowest point of the Nazi occupation, on July 3, 1942, some two weeks after the capture of Reinhard Heydrich's assassins (see p.113), over 200,000 Czechs gathered to swear allegiance to the Third Reich. Just six years later, in February 1948, a similar-sized crowd showed their support for the Communist coup. Then in August 1968, it was the scene of some of the most violent confrontations between the Soviet invaders and local Czechs. On January 16, 1969, at the top of the square, Jan Palach set fire to himself in protest at the continuing occupation of the country by Warsaw Pact troops. And, of course, it was here that night after night, in late November 1989, more than 250,000 people crammed into the square, until the Communist old guard finally threw in the towel.

Up the square

The busiest part of Wenceslas Square and a popular place to meet up before hitting town is around **Můstek**, the city's most central metro station, at the northern end of the square. The area is dominated by the **Palác Koruna**, a hulking wedge of sculptured concrete and gold, built for an insurance company in 1914 by Antonín Pfeiffer, one of Jan Kotěra's many pupils. The building is a rare mixture of heavy constructivism and gilded Secession-style ornamentation, but the *pièce de résistance* is the palace's pearly crown that lights up at night.

Opposite Palác Koruna is a recent neo-functionalist glass building, accompanied by two much older functionalist shops from the late 1920s, designed by Ludvík Kysela and billed at the time as Prague's first glass curtain-wall buildings. Along with the former *Hotel Juliš* (see below), they represent the perfect expression of the optimistic mood of progress and modernism that permeated the interwar republic. The second of the Kysela buildings was built as a **Baťa** store, flagship of a chain of functionalist shoeshops built for the Czech shoe magnate, Tomáš Baťa, one of the greatest patrons of avant-garde Czech art, whose company's assets were nationalized by the Communists in 1948 and partially restored to the family after 1989.

Twenty-five years earlier, Czech architecture was in the throes of its own version of Art Nouveau, one of whose earliest practitioners was Jan Kotěra. The **Peterkův dům**, a slender essay in the new style, was his first work, written at the age of 28. Kotěra, a pupil of the great architect of the Viennese Secession, Otto Wagner, eventually moved on to a much more brutal constructivism. Another supreme example of Czech functionalism, a few doors further up at no. 22, is the **Hotel Juliš**, designed by Pavel Janák, who had already made his name as one of the leading lights of the short-lived Czech Cubist (and later Rondo-Cubist) movement (see p.116).

Further up on the same side of the square is the former **Melantrich** publishing house, whose first-floor balcony was handed over to the opposition speakers of the Občanské fórum (Civic Forum) on the second night of the demonstrations in November 1989. Now a branch of Marks & Spencer, Melantrich faces two of the most ornate buildings on the entire square, the Art Nouveau **Grand Hotel Evropa** and its slim neighbour, the *Hotel Meran*, both built in 1903–05. They represent everything the Czech modern movement stood against, chiefly, ornament for ornament's sake, not that this has in any way dented their renown.

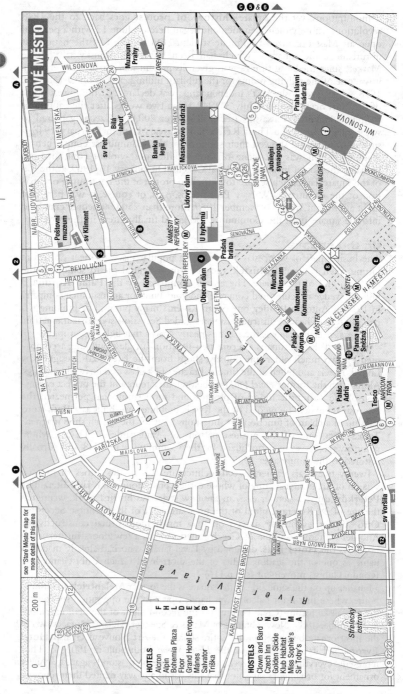

NOVÉ MĚSTO

WILSONOVA

Muzeum Prahy Ⓜ

FLORENC Ⓜ

TĚŠNOV

KLIMENTSKÁ

SVOBODY

PETRSKÁ

Bílá labuť

sv Petr

NA POŘÍČÍ

Banka legií

NA FLORENCI

Masarykovo nádraží

Praha hlavní nádraží

WILSONOVA

ZLATNICKÁ

HAVLÍČKOVA

⑤ ⑨ ㉖

NÁBŘ. LUDVÍKA

Poštovní muzeum

SOUKENICKÁ

KLIMENTSKÁ

BIBLICKÉ

NA POŘÍČÍ

HYBERNSKÁ

③ ㉔

⑤ ㉔

SENOVÁŽNÉ NÁM.

JERUZALÉMSKÁ

Jubilejní synagoga

HLAVNÍ NÁDRAŽÍ Ⓜ

sv Kliment ℹ

Lidový dům

⑭㉖

③

sv Kliment

③

NÁMĚSTÍ REPUBLIKY Ⓜ

U hybernů

SENOVÁŽNÁ

⑭ Ⓑ

⑨ ㉔

HRADEBNÍ

⑤ ⑭

REVOLUČNÍ

③

Kotva

②

DLOUHÁ

NÁMĚSTÍ REPUBLIKY Ⓜ

④ Obecní dům

Prašná brána

NEKÁZANKA

PANSKÁ

Ⓔ

ROZHODIN

POLITICKÝCH VĚZŇŮ

BENEDIKTSKÁ

HAŠTALSKÉ NÁM.

NA FRANTIŠKU

U MILOSRDNÝCH

CELETNÁ

OVOCNÝ TRH

Mucha Museum

Muzeum Komunismu

⑦

⑧

PANSKÁ

JINDŘIŠSKÁ

JINDŘIŠSKÁ

KOZÍ

OBECNÍHO DVORA

ANENSKÁ

TÝNSKÁ

STAROMĚSTSKÉ NÁM.

Palác Koruna

MŮSTEK Ⓜ

MŮSTEK

Ⓓ

⑨

Panna Maria Sněžná

VÁCLAVSKÉ NÁM.

DUŠNÍ

ELIŠKY KRÁSNOHORSKÉ

TÝNSKÁ

MELANTRICHOVA

MALÉ NÁM.

⑩

JUNGMANNOVO NÁM.

JOSEFOV

PAŘÍŽSKÁ

MAISLOVA

MARIÁNSKÉ NÁM.

MICHALSKÁ

JILSKÁ

Palác Adria

JUNGMANNOVA

NÁRODNÍ TŘÍDA Ⓜ

Tesco

⑥ ⑨

KAPROVA

KARLOVA

HUSOVA

NA PERŠTÝNĚ

NÁRODNÍ

⑪

17 LISTOPADU

17

MARIÁNSKÉ NÁM.

BETLÉMSKÉ NÁM.

BARTOLOMĚJSKÁ

KONVIKTSKÁ

MÁNESŮV MOST

DVOŘÁKOVO NÁBŘEŽÍ

KAROLINY SVĚTLÉ

DIVADELNÍ

sv Voršila

KŘIŽOVNICKÁ

LÁVKA

NÁPRSTKOVA

SMETANOVO NÁBŘ.

⑫

KARLŮV MOST (CHARLES BRIDGE)

River Vltava

⑫

MOST LEGIÍ

Střelecký ostrov

⑱

⑱

⑥ ㉒㉓

see "Staré Město" map for more detail of this area

⑰

⑱

⑫

⑱ ㉒ ㉓

200 m

0

HOTELS

Alcron   F
Alpin   H
Bohemia Plaza   L
Floor   D
Grand Hotel Evropa   E
Mánes   K
Salvator   B
Tříška   J

HOSTELS

Clown and Bard   C
Czech Inn   N
Golden Sickle   G
Klub Habitat   I
Miss Sophie's   M
Sir Toby's   A

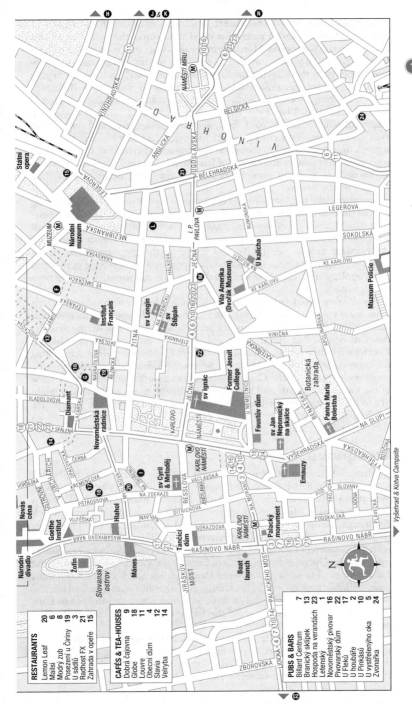

RESTAURANTS
Lemon Leaf	20
Maitsi	6
Modrý zub	8
Posezení u čiriny	19
U sádlů	3
Radhost FX	21
Zahrada v opeře	15

CAFÉS & TEA-HOUSES
Dobrá čajovna	9
Globe	18
Louvre	11
Obecní dům	4
Slavia	12
Velryba	14

PUBS & BARS
Billard Centrum	7
Branický sklípek	13
Hospoda na verandách	23
Letenský	1
Novoměstský pivovar	16
Pivovarský dům	22
U Fleků	17
U houbaře	2
U Pinkasů	10
U vystřeleného oka	5
Zvonařka	24

Vyšehrad & Kotva Campsite

107

The Wenceslas Monument and the Národní muzeum

A statue of St Wenceslas (sv Václav) has stood at the top of the square since 1680, but the present **Wenceslas Monument**, by the father of Czech sculpture, Josef Václav Myslbek, was only unveiled in 1912. It's worthy and heroic but pretty unexciting, with the Czech patron saint sitting resolutely astride his mighty steed, surrounded by smaller-scale representations of four other Bohemian saints – his grandmother Ludmilla, Procopius, Adalbert and Agnes – added in the 1920s. In 1918, 1948, 1968, and again in 1989, the monument was used as a national political noticeboard, festooned with posters, flags and slogans and, even now, it remains the city's favourite soapbox venue. A few metres below the statue, a simple memorial to the *obětem komunismu* (the victims of Communism) is adorned with flowers and photos of **Jan Palach** and Jan Zajíc, both of whom set themselves alight in protest against the continuing occupation of their country by the Soviets.

Dominating the top, southern end of Wenceslas Square sits the broad, brooding hulk of the **Národní muzeum** (daily: May–Sept 10am–6pm; Oct–April 9am–5pm, closed first Tues of month; 120Kč; ⓦwww.nm.cz), built by Josef Schulz and modelled on the great European museums of Paris and Vienna. Along with the Národní divadlo (see p.110), this is one of the great landmarks of the nineteenth-century Czech national revival, sporting a monumental gilt-framed glass cupola, worthy clumps of sculptural decoration and narrative frescoes from Czech history.

The museum is old-fashioned and underfunded, but it's worth taking at least a quick look at the ornate marble entrance hall and the splendid monumental staircase leading to the **Pantheon** of Czech notables at the top. Arranged under the glass-domed hall are 48 busts and statues of distinguished bewhiskered Czech men (plus a couple of token women and Czechophile Slovaks), including the universally adored T.G. Masaryk, the country's founding president, whose statue was removed by the Communists from every other public place. The rest of the museum is dowdy and badly labelled, though those with children might like to head upstairs for the fossils and stuffed animals. The museum's temporary exhibitions, displayed on the ground floor, can be very good indeed, so it's always worth checking to see what's on.

Wilsonova

At the southern end of Wenceslas Square is some of the worst blight that Communist planners inflicted on Prague – above all, the six-lane highway of **Wilsonova** that effectively cuts off the Národní muzeum from Wenceslas Square. Alongside the Národní muzeum stands the former **Prague Stock Exchange**, completed in the 1930s, rendered redundant by the 1948 coup, turned into the "socialist" **Federal Assembly** in 1971 and closed down again with the breakup of Czechoslovakia in 1993. Next door is the grandiose **Státní opera** (State Opera; ⓦwww.opera.cz), built by the Viennese duo Helmer and Fellner. Opened in 1888 as the Neues Deutsches Theater, it was one of the last great building projects of Prague's once all-powerful German minority. The velvet and gold interior is still as fresh as it was when the Bohemian-born composer Gustav Mahler brought the traffic to a standstill, conducting the premiere of his *Seventh Symphony*.

The last building on this deafening freeway is **Praha hlavní nádraží**, Prague's main railway station. One of the final glories of the dying empire, it was designed by Josef Fanta and officially opened in 1909 as the Franz-Josefs Bahnhof. Arriving in the subterranean modern section, it's easy to miss the station's surviving Art Nouveau parts. The original entrance on Wilsonova still exudes imperial confidence, with its wrought-iron canopy and naked figurines clinging to the sides of the towers. You can sit and admire the main foyer from the *Fantová kavárna* (daily 6am–11pm); it's also worth heading north from the foyer to take a peek at the ceramic pillars in the former station restaurant (now a secondhand clothes shop).

Národní and Na příkopě

Národní and **Na příkopě** trace the course of the old moat, which was finally filled in 1760. Their boomerang curve marks the border between Staré Město and Nové Město (strictly speaking, the dividing line runs down the middle of both the streets). Ranged around here is a variety of stylish edifices, including some of the city's most flamboyant Art Nouveau buildings.

Jungmannovo náměstí and around

Heading west from Můstek, before you hit Národní třída proper, you must pass through **Jungmannovo náměstí**, which takes its name from Josef Jungmann (1772–1847), a prolific writer, translator and leading light of the Czech national revival, whose pensive, seated statue was erected here in 1878. This small, ill-proportioned square boasts one of Prague's most endearing architectural curiosities, Emil Králíček and Matěj Blecha's unique **Cubist streetlamp** (and seat) from 1912, which is currently crumbling away beyond the Jungmann statue in the far eastern corner of the square.

On the south side stands the square's most imposing building, the chunky, vigorously sculptured **Palác Adria**. It was designed for the Italian insurance company Reunione Adriatica di Sicurità in the early 1920s by Pavel Janák and Josef Zasche, with sculptural extras by Otto Gutfreund and a central *Seafaring* group by Jan Štursa. Janák was a pioneering figure in the short-lived, prewar Czech Cubist movement; after the war, he and Josef Gočár attempted to create a national style of architecture appropriate for the newly founded republic. The style was dubbed Rondo-Cubism – semicircular motifs are a recurrent theme – though the Palác Adria owes as much to the Italian Renaissance as it does to the new national style. The building's *pasáž* still retains its wonderful original portal featuring sculptures by Bohumil Kafka, depicting the twelve signs of the zodiac.

Through the unpromising courtyard back near the Jungmann statue, you can gain access to the church of **Panna Maria Sněžná** (St Mary-of-the-Snows). Once one of the great landmarks of Wenceslas Square, towering over the backs of the old two-storey houses that lined the square, it's now barely visible from

---

The Masakr – November 1989

On the night of Friday, November 17, 1989, a 50,000-strong, officially sanctioned student demo, organized by the students' union, SSM (League of Young Socialists), worked its way down Národní with the intention of reaching Wenceslas Square. Halfway down the street they were confronted by the *bílé přílby* (white helmets) and *črvené barety* (red berets) of the hated riot police. For what must have seemed like hours, there was a stalemate as the students sat down and refused to disperse, some of them handing out flowers to the police. Suddenly, without any warning, the police attacked, and what became known as the **masakr** (massacre) began. No one was actually killed, though it wasn't for want of trying by the police. Under the arches of Národní 16, there's a small symbolic bronze relief of eight hands reaching out for help, a permanent shrine in memory of the hundreds who were hospitalized in the violence.

any of the surrounding streets. Charles IV, who founded the church, envisaged a vast coronation church on a scale comparable with St Vitus Cathedral, on which work had just begun. Unfortunately, the money ran out shortly after completion of the chancel; the result is curious – a church that is short in length, but equal to the cathedral in height. The thirty-metre-high vaulting – which collapsed on the Franciscans who inherited the half-completed building in the seventeenth century – is awesome, as is the gold and black Baroque altar that touches the ceiling. To get an idea of the intended scale of the finished structure, take a stroll through the **Františkánská zahrada**, to the south of the church, which links up with one of the arcades off Wenceslas Square.

Národní třída

Three-quarters of the way down **Národní** on the north side is an eye-catching duo of Art Nouveau buildings designed by Osvald Polívka in 1907–8. The first, at no. 7, was built for the **pojišťovna Praha** (Prague Savings Bank), hence the beautiful mosaic lettering above the windows advertising *život* (life insurance) and *kapital* (loans), as well as help with your *důchod* (pension) and *věno* (dowry). Next door, the more ostentatious **Topičův dům**, built for a publishing house, provides the perfect accompaniment, with a similarly ornate wrought-iron and glass canopy.

At the end of Národní, overlooking the Vltava, is the gold-crested **Národní divadlo** (National Theatre), proud symbol of the Czech nation. Refused money by the Habsburg state, Czechs of all classes dug deep into their pockets to raise funds for the venture themselves. The foundation stones were laid in 1868, and in June 1881 the theatre opened with a premiere of Smetana's opera *Libuše*. In August of the same year, fire ripped through the building, destroying everything except the outer walls. Within two years the whole thing was rebuilt – even the emperor contributed this time – opening once more to the strains of *Libuše*. The grand portal on the north side of the theatre is embellished with suitably triumphant allegorical figures, and inside, every space is taken up with paintings and sculptures by leading artists of the Czech national revival.

Standing behind and in dramatic contrast to the National Theatre is its state-of-the-art extension, the modern glass box of the **Nová scéna** (New Stage), designed by Karel Prager, the leading architect of the Communist era, and completed in 1983. It's one of those buildings most Praguers love to hate – it has been memorably described as looking like "frozen piss" – though compared to much of Prague's Communist-era architecture, it's not bad.

Na příkopě

Heading northeast from Můstek metro station, at the bottom end of Wenceslas Square, you can join the crush of bodies ambling down **Na příkopě** (literally "on the moat"). The street has been an architectural showcase for more than a century and was once lined on both sides with grandiose Habsburg-era buildings; the Art Nouveau **U Dörflerů**, at no. 7, from 1905, with its gilded floral curlicues, is one of the few survivors along this stretch.

There are another couple of interesting buildings at nos. 18 and 20, designed by Polívka over a twenty-year period for the **Zemská banka** and connected by a kind of Bridge of Sighs suspended over Nekázanka. The style veers between 1890s neo-Renaissance and later Art Nouveau elements, such as Jan Preisler's gilded mosaics and Ladislav Šaloun's attic sculptures. It's worth nipping upstairs to the main banking hall of what is now the **Živnostenka banka**, at no. 20, to appreciate the financial might of Czech capital in the last decades of the Austro-Hungarian Empire. Yet more financial institutions, this time from the dour 1930s, line the far end of Na příkopě, as it opens up into náměstí Republiky, including the state's palatial **Národní banka** (National Bank).

Mucha Museum

Dedicated to probably the most famous of all Czech artists in the West, the **Mucha Museum** (daily 10am–6pm; 120Kč; Ⓦ www.mucha.cz), housed in the Kaunicky palác on Panská, southwest of Senovážné náměstí, is very popular indeed. **Alfons Mucha** (1860–1939) made his name in fin-de-siècle Paris, where he shot to fame after designing the Art Nouveau poster *Gismonda* for the actress Sarah Bernhardt. "Le Style Mucha" became all the rage, but the artist himself came to despise this "commercial" period of his work, and in 1910 moved back to his homeland and threw himself into the national cause, designing patriotic stamps, banknotes and posters for the new republic.

The whole of Mucha's career is covered in the permanent exhibition, and there's a good selection of informal photos taken by the artist himself of his models – and even one of Paul Gauguin (with whom he shared a studio) playing the harmonium with his trousers down. The only work not represented here is his massive *Slav Epic*, but the excellent video (in English) covers the decade of his life he devoted to this cycle of nationalist paintings. In the end, Mucha paid for his Czech nationalism with his life; dragged in for questioning by the Gestapo after the 1939 Nazi invasion, he died shortly after being released.

Muzeum komunismu (Museum of Communism)

It took an American expat to open Prague's first museum dedicated to the country's troubled Communist past. Situated above a branch of *McDonald's*, and in the same building as a casino, the **Muzeum komunismu** (daily 9am–9pm; 180Kč; Ⓦ www.muzeumkomunismu.cz) can be found (with some difficulty) on the first floor of the Palác Savarin, Na příkopě 10. The exhibition gives a brief (and rather muddled) rundown of Czech twentieth-century history, accompanied by a superb collection of Communist statues, uniforms and propaganda posters. The politics are a bit simplistic – the popular postwar support for the Party is underplayed – but it's worth tracking down for the memorabilia alone. There's a mock-up of a Communist classroom, a chilling StB (secret police) room and plenty of film footage of protests throughout the period. Wrangles with the landlord may mean the place will move premises in the future so check the website.

Náměstí Republiky

The oldest structure on **náměstí Republiky** is the **Prašná brána** (Powder Tower; mid-March to Oct daily 10am–6pm; 70Kč), one of the eight medieval gate-towers that once guarded Staré Město. The present tower was begun by Vladislav Jagiello in 1475, shortly after he had moved into the royal court, which was situated next door at the time. A small historical exhibition inside traces the tower's architectural metamorphosis up to its present remodelling by the nineteenth-century restorer Josef Mocker. Most people, though, ignore the displays and climb straight up for the modest view from the top.

Attached to the tower, and built on the ruins of the old royal court, the **Obecní dům** (Municipal House) is by far the city's most exciting Art Nouveau building, one of the few places that still manages to conjure up the atmosphere of Prague's fin-de-siècle café society. Conceived as a cultural centre for the Czech community, it's probably the finest architectural achievement of the Czech national revival. Designed by Osvald Polívka and Antonín Balšánek, it is extravagantly decorated inside and out with the help of almost every artist connected with the Czech Secession. From the lifts to the cloakrooms, just about all the furnishings remain as they were when the building was completed in 1911.

The simplest way of soaking up the interior – peppered with mosaics and pendulous brass chandeliers – is to have a drink in the cavernous **café**, or a meal in the *Francouská restaurace* or the *Plzeňská restaurace* in the basement. For a closer inspection of the building's spectacular interior (which includes paintings by Alfons Mucha, Jan Preisler and Max Švabinský, among others), you can sign up for one of the regular **guided tours** (160Kč; daily 10am–7pm; ⓦwww .obecnidum.cz). Several rooms on the second floor are given over to temporary art exhibitions, while the building's **Smetanova síň**, Prague's largest concert hall, stages concerts, including the opening salvo of the Pražské jaro (Prague Spring Festival) – traditionally a rendition of Smetana's *Má vlast* (My Country) – which is attended by the president.

Karlovo náměstí and around

The streets south of Národní and Wenceslas Square still run along the medieval lines of Charles IV's town plan, though they're now lined with grand nineteenth- and twentieth-century buildings. Of the many roads which head down towards Karlovo náměstí, **Vodičkova** is probably the most impressive, curving southwest for half a kilometre from Wenceslas Square into Prague's biggest square, **Karlovo náměstí**, created by Charles IV as Nové Město's cattle market (Dobytčí trh). Unfortunately, the square's once impressive proportions are no longer so easy to appreciate, obscured by a tree-planted public garden and cut in two by the busy thoroughfare of Ječná. The Gothic **Novoměstská radnice** (May–Sept Tues–Sun 10am–6pm; 40Kč) or New Town Hall, at the northern end of the square, sports three steep, triangular gables embellished with intricate blind-tracery. It was built, like the one on Staroměstské náměstí, during the reign of King John of Luxembourg, though it has survived rather better, and is now one of the finest Gothic buildings in the city. It was here that Prague's **first defenestration** took place on July 30, 1419, when the radical Hussite preacher Jan Želivský and his penniless religious followers stormed the building, mobbed the councillors and burghers, and threw twelve or thirteen of them out of the town hall windows onto the pikes of the Hussite mob below. Václav IV, on hearing the news, suffered a stroke and died just two weeks later. So began the long and bloody Hussite Wars. Nowadays, you can visit the site of the defenestration, and climb to the top of the tower (added shortly afterwards) for a view over central Prague.

Following the defeat of Protestantism two centuries later, the Jesuits demolished half the east side of the square to build their college and the accompanying church of **sv Ignác** (St Ignatius), begun in 1665. The statue of St Ignatius, which sits above the tympanum surrounded by a sunburst, caused controversy at the time, as until then only the Holy Trinity had been depicted in such a way. The church, modelled, like so many Jesuit churches, on the Gesù in Rome, is quite remarkable inside, a salmon-pink and white confection, with lots of frothy stuccowork and an exuberant powder-pink pulpit dripping with gold drapery, cherubs and saints.

Cathedral of sv Cyril and Metoděj (Heydrich Martyrs' Monument)

West off Karlovo náměstí, down Resslova, the noisy extension of Ječná, is the Orthodox cathedral of **sv Cyril and Metoděj** (Tues–Sun: April–Oct 10am–5pm; Nov–March 10am–4pm; 60Kč), originally constructed for the Roman Catholics by Bayer and Dientzenhofer in the eighteenth century, but since the

The assassination of Reinhard Heydrich

The assassination of Reinhard Heydrich in 1942 was the only attempt the Allies ever made on the life of a leading Nazi. It's an incident which the Allies have always billed as a great success in the otherwise rather dismal seven-year history of the Czech resistance. But, as with all acts of brave resistance during the war, there was a price to be paid. Given that the reprisals meted out on the Czech population were entirely predictable, it remains a controversial, if not suicidal, decision to have made.

The target, **Reinhard Tristan Eugen Heydrich**, was a talented and upwardly mobile anti-Semite (despite rumours that he was partly Jewish himself), a great organizer and a skilful concert violinist. He was a late recruit to the Nazi Party, signing up in 1931 after his dismissal from the German Navy for dishonourable conduct towards a woman. However, he swiftly rose through the ranks of the SS to become second in command to Himmler and, in the autumn of 1941, *Reichsprotektor* of the puppet state of *Böhmen und Mähren* – effectively, the most powerful man in the Czech Lands. Although his rule began with brutality, it soon settled into the tried-and-tested policy that Heydrich liked to call *Peitsche und Zucker* (literally, "whip and sugar").

On the morning of May 27, 1942, as Heydrich was being driven by his personal bodyguard, *Oberscharführer* Klein, in his open-top Mercedes from his house north of Prague to his office in Hradčany, three Czechoslovak agents (parachuted in from England) were taking up positions in the northern suburb of Libeň. The first agent, Valčík, gave the signal as the car pulled into Kirchmayer Boulevard (now V Holešovičkách). Another agent, a Slovak called Gabčík, pulled out a gun and tried to shoot. The gun jammed, at which Heydrich, rather than driving out of the situation, ordered Klein to stop the car and attempted to shoot back. At this point, the third agent, Kubiš, threw a bomb at the car. The blast injured Kubiš and Heydrich, who immediately leapt out and began firing at Kubiš. Kubiš, with blood pouring down his face, jumped on his bicycle and fled downhill. Gabčík meanwhile pulled out a second gun and exchanged shots with Heydrich, until the latter collapsed from his wounds. Gabčík fled into a butcher's, shot Klein – who was in hot pursuit – in the legs and escaped down the backstreets.

Meanwhile back at the Mercedes, a baker's van was flagged down by a passer-by, but the driver refused to get involved. Eventually, a small truck carrying floor polish was commandeered and Heydrich was taken to the Bulovka hospital. Heydrich died eight days later from the fragments of horsehair and wire from the car seat which had infected his spleen, and was given full Nazi honours at his Prague funeral; the cortège passed down Wenceslas Square, in front of a crowd of thousands. As the home resistance had forewarned, revenge was quick to follow. The day after Heydrich's funeral service in Berlin, the village of **Lidice** (see p.155) was burnt to the ground and its male inhabitants murdered; two weeks later, the men and women of the village of **Ležáky** (see p.299) suffered a similar fate.

The plan to assassinate Heydrich had been formulated in the early months of 1942 by the Czechoslovak government-in-exile in London, without consultation with the Czech Communist leadership in Moscow, and despite fierce opposition from the resistance within Czechoslovakia. Since it was clear that the reprisals would be horrific, the only logical explanation for the plan is that this was precisely the aim of the government-in-exile's operation – to forge a solid wedge of resentment between the Germans and Czechs. In this respect, if in no other, the operation was ultimately successful.

1930s the main base of the Orthodox church in the Czech Republic. Amid all the traffic, it's extremely difficult to imagine the scene here on June 18, 1942, when seven of the Czechoslovak secret agents involved in the most dramatic assassination of World War II (see box above) were besieged in the church by over seven hundred SS. Acting on a tip-off by one of the Czech resistance who turned himself in, the Nazis surrounded the building just after 4am and fought a pitched battle for over six hours, trying explosives, flooding and any other method they could think of to drive the men out of their stronghold in the crypt. Eventually, all seven agents committed suicide rather than give themselves up. There's a plaque at street level on the south wall commemorating those who died, and an exhibition on the whole affair in the crypt itself, which has been left pretty much as it was; the entrance is underneath the church steps on Na Zderaze.

The islands and the embankments

Magnificent turn-of-the-twentieth-century mansions line the Vltava's right bank, almost without interruption, for some two kilometres from the Charles Bridge south to the rocky outcrop of Vyšehrad. It's a long walk, even just along the length of **Masarykovo** and **Rašínovo nábřeží**, though there's no need to do the whole lot in one go; you can hop on a tram (#17 or #21) at various points, drop down from the embankments to the waterfront itself, or escape to one of the two islands connected to them, Střelecký ostrov and Slovanský ostrov, better known as Žofín.

The islands

Access to either of the two islands in the central section of the Vltava is from close to the Národní divadlo. The first, **Střelecký ostrov**, or Shooters' Island, is where the army held their shooting practice, on and off, from the fifteenth until the nineteenth century. Closer to the left bank and accessible via the most Legií (Legion's Bridge), it became a favourite spot for a Sunday promenade and is still popular, especially in summer.

The second island, **Slovanský ostrov**, more commonly known as **Žofín** (after the island's concert hall, itself named after Sophie, the domineering mother of the Emperor Franz-Josef I), came about as a result of the natural silting of the river in the eighteenth century. By the late nineteenth century it had become one of the city's foremost pleasure gardens, where, as the composer Berlioz remarked, "bad musicians shamelessly make abominable music in the open air and immodest young males and females indulge in brazen dancing, while idlers and wasters … lounge about smoking foul tobacco and drinking beer". On a decent day, things seem pretty much unchanged from those heady times. Concerts, balls and other social gatherings take place here in the cultural centre, and there's a decent beer garden round the back; rowing boats can be rented in the summer.

Along the embankment

Most of the buildings along the waterfront are private apartments and therefore inaccessible. One exception to this, and architecturally atypical of this part of Prague, is the striking white functionalist mass of the **Mánes** art gallery (Tues–Sun 10am–6pm; 25Kč), halfway down Masarykovo nábřeží. Designed in open-plan style by Otakar Novotný in 1930, it spans the narrow channel between Slovanský ostrov and the waterfront, close to the onion-domed Šítek water tower. The gallery is named after Josef Mánes, a traditional nineteenth-century landscape painter and Czech nationalist, and stages contemporary art exhibitions. Clearly visible from Mánes is the **Tančící dům** (Dancing House), also known as "Fred and Ginger" after the shape of the building's two towers, which look vaguely like a couple ballroom dancing. It was designed in the 1990s by the Canadian-born Frank O. Gehry and the Yugoslav-born Vlado Milunič, and stands next door to the block of flats where Havel lived before becoming president (when he wasn't in prison).

Further along the embankment, at **Palackého náměstí**, the buildings retreat for a moment to reveal an Art Nouveau sculpture to rival Šaloun's monument in Staroměstské náměstí (see p.93): the **Monument to František Palacký**, the great nineteenth-century Czech historian, politician and nationalist, by Stanislav Sucharda. Like the Hus Monument, which was unveiled three years later, this mammoth project – fifteen years in the making – had missed its moment by the time it was completed in 1912, and found universal disfavour. The critics have mellowed over the years, and nowadays it's appreciated for what it is – an energetic and inspirational piece of work. Ethereal bronze bodies, representing the world of the imagination, shoot out at all angles, contrasting sharply with the plain stone mass of the plinth and, below, the giant, grimly determined, seated figure of Palacký himself, representing the real world.

Vyšehradská and Ke Karlovu

Behind Palackého náměstí, off **Vyšehradská**, the intertwined concrete spires of the **Emauzy** monastery are an unusual modern addition to the Prague skyline. The monastery was one of the few important historical buildings to be damaged in the last war, in this case by a stray Anglo-American bomb that was meant to land on Dresden. The cloisters can be visited (June–Sept Mon–Sat 9am–4pm; Oct–May Mon–Fri 9am–4pm; 30Kč; Ⓦwww.emauzy.cz) and contain some extremely valuable Gothic frescoes. Heading south from here, Vyšehradská descends to a junction, where you'll find the entrance to the **Botanická zahrada** (daily 9am–6pm), the university's botanic gardens laid out in 1897 on a series of terraces up the other side of the hill. Though far from spectacular, the garden is one of the few patches of green in this part of town, and the 1930s greenhouses (*skleníky*; 25Kč) have been restored to their former glory.

On the far side of the gardens, Apolinářská runs along the south wall and past a grimly Gothic red-brick maternity hospital with steep, stepped gables, before joining up with **Ke Karlovu**. Head north up here and right into Na bojišti, where you'll find **U kalicha** (Ⓦwww.ukalicha.cz), the pub immortalized in the opening passages of the consistently popular comic novel *The Good Soldier Švejk*, by Jaroslav Hašek. In the story, on the eve of the Great War, Švejk (Schweik to the Germans) walks into *U kalicha*, where a plain-clothes officer of the Austrian constabulary is sitting drinking and, after a brief conversation, finds himself arrested in connection with the assassination of Archduke Ferdinand. Whatever the pub may have been like in Hašek's day (and even then, it wasn't his local), about the only authentic thing you'll find inside today – albeit at a price – is the beer.

Further north along Ke Karlovu, set back behind wrought-iron gates, is a more rewarding place of pilgrimage, the russet-coloured **Vila Amerika** (Tues–Sun: April–Sept 10am–1.30pm & 2–5.30pm; Oct–March 9.30am–1.30pm & 2–5pm; 50Kč; Ⓦwww.nm.cz), now a museum devoted to the Czech composer **Antonín Dvořák** (1841–1904), who lived for a time on nearby Žitná. Even if you've no interest in Dvořák, the house is a delight, built as a Baroque summer palace around 1720 and one of Kilian Ignaz Dientzenhofer's most successful secular works. Easily the most famous of all Czech composers, Dvořák, for many years, had to play second fiddle to Smetana in the orchestra at the Národní divadlo, where Smetana was the conductor. In his 40s, Dvořák received an honorary degree from Cambridge before leaving for the "New World", and his gown is one of the few items of memorabilia to have found its way into the museum's collection. However, the tasteful period rooms echoing with the composer's music and the tiny garden dotted with Baroque sculptures compensate for what the display cabinets may lack.

Vyšehrad

At the southern tip of Nové Město, around 3km south of the city centre, the rocky red-brick fortress of **VYŠEHRAD** (Ⓦ www.praha-vysehrad.cz) – literally "High Castle" – has more myths attached to it than any other place in Bohemia. According to Czech legend, this is the place where the Slav tribes first settled in Prague, where the "wise and tireless chieftain" Krok built a castle, and whence his youngest daughter Libuše went on to found Praha itself (see p.57). Alas, the archeological evidence doesn't bear this claim out, but it's clear that Vratislav II (1061–92), the first Bohemian ruler to bear the title "king", built a palace here to get away from his younger brother who was lording it in the Hrad. Within half a century the royals had moved back to Hradčany and into a new palace, and from then on Vyšehrad began to lose its political significance.

Keen to associate himself with the early Přemyslids, Emperor Charles IV had a system of walls built to link Vyšehrad to the newly founded Nové Město, and decreed that the *králová cesta* (coronation route) begin from here. These fortifications were destroyed by the Hussites in 1420, but over the next two hundred years the hill was settled again, until the Habsburgs turfed everyone out in the mid-seventeenth century and rebuilt the place as a fortified barracks, only to convert it into a public park in 1866. By the time the Czech national revival movement became interested in Vyšehrad, only the red-brick fortifications were left as a reminder of its former strategic importance; they rediscovered its history and its legends, and gradually transformed it into a symbol of Czech nationhood. Today, Vyšehrad is a perfect place from which to escape the human congestion of the city and watch the sun set behind the Hrad.

Czech Cubism in Vyšehrad

Even if you harbour only a passing interest in modern architecture, it's worth seeking out the cluster of **Cubist villas** below the fortress in Vyšehrad. Whereas Czech Art Nouveau was heavily influenced by the Viennese Secession, it was Paris rather than the imperial capital that provided the stimulus for the short-lived but extremely productive Czech Cubist movement. In 1911, the Skupina výtvarných umělců or SVU (Group of Fine Artists) was founded in Prague and quickly became the movement's organizing force. **Pavel Janák** was the SVU's chief theorist, **Josef Gočár** its most illustrious exponent, but **Josef Chochol** was the most successful practitioner of the style in Prague.

Cubism is associated mostly with painting, and the unique contribution of its Czech offshoot was to apply the theory to furniture (some of which is now on permanent display at the Muzeum českého kubismu, see p.96) and **architecture**. In Vyšehrad alone, Chochol completed three buildings, close to one another below the fortress, using prismatic shapes and angular lines to produce the sharp geometric contrasts of light and dark shadows characteristic of Cubist painting.

The most impressive example of Czech Cubist architecture, brilliantly exploiting its angular location, is Chochol's apartment block **nájemný obytný dům** at Neklanova 30; begun in 1913 for František Hodek, and now housing a restaurant on the ground floor. Further along Neklanova, at no. 2, there's Antonín Belada's Cubist street facade, and around the corner is the largest project of the lot – Chochol's **Kovařovicova vila**, which backs onto Libušina. From the front, on Rašínovo nábřeží, it's possible to appreciate the clever, slightly askew layout of the garden, designed right down to its zigzag garden railings. Further along the embankment is Chochol's largest commission, the **rodinný trojdům**, a large building complex with a heavy mansard roof, a central "Baroque" gable with a pedimental frieze, and room enough for three families.

The fortress

There are several **approaches to the fortress**: if you've come by tram #3, #7, #16, #17 or #21, which trundle along the waterfront to Výtoň stop, you can either wind your way up Vratislavova and enter through the Cihelná brána, or take the steep stairway from Rašínovo nábřeží that leads up through the trees to a small side entrance in the west wall. Alternatively, from Vyšehrad metro station, walk west past the ugly Kongresové centrum Praha, and enter through the twin gateways, between which lies the *Špička* **information centre** (daily: April–Oct 9.30am–6pm; Nov–March 9.30am–5pm).

However you come, head for the blackened sandstone church of **sv Petr and Pavel**, rebuilt in the 1880s by Josef Mocker in neo-Gothic style (with further, even more ruthless additions in the 1900s) on the site of an eleventh-century basilica. The twin openwork spires are now the fortress's most familiar landmark, and you should be able to view the church's polychrome interior, though hours can be erratic (May–Sept Mon, Wed, Thurs & Sat 9am–noon & 1–5pm, Fri 9am–noon, Sun 11am–noon & 1–5pm; 30Kč).

Vyšehradský hřbitov (Vyšehrad Cemetery)

One of the first initiatives of the national revival movement was to establish the **Vyšehradský hřbitov** (daily: March, April & Oct 8am–6pm; May–Sept 8am–7pm; Nov–Feb 8am–5pm; free; Ⓦ www.slavin.cz), which spreads out to the north and east of the church. It's a measure of the part that artists and intellectuals played in the foundation of the nation, and the regard in which they are still held, that the most prestigious graveyard in the city is given over to them: no soldiers, no politicians, not even the Communists managed to muscle their way in here (except on artistic merit).

To the uninitiated only a handful of figures are well known, but for the Czechs the place is alive with great names (there is a useful plan of the most notable graves at the entrance nearest the church). Ladislav Šaloun's grave for **Dvořák**, situated under the arches, is one of the more showy, with a mosaic inscription, studded with gold stones, glistening behind wrought-iron railings. **Smetana**, who died twenty years earlier, is buried in comparatively modest surroundings near the Slavín monument. The Prague Spring Festival begins on the anniversary of his death (May 12) with a procession from his grave to the Obecní dům.

The grave of the Romantic poet **Karel Hynek Mácha** was the assembly point for the 50,000-strong demonstration on November 17, 1989, which triggered the Velvet Revolution. This was organized to commemorate the 50th anniversary of the Nazi closure of all Czech higher education institutions in 1939.

The focus of the cemetery, though, is the **Slavín monument**, a bulky stele covered in commemorative plaques and topped by a sarcophagus and a statue representing Genius. It's the communal resting place of over fifty Czech artists, including the painter Alfons Mucha, the sculptors Josef Václav Myslbek and Ladislav Šaloun, the architect Josef Gočár and the opera singer Ema Destinnová (see p.174).

The suburbs

By the end of his reign in 1378, Charles IV had laid out his city on such a grand scale that it wasn't until the industrial revolution hit Bohemia in the mid-nineteenth century that the first **suburbs** began to sprout up around its boundaries. A few were rigidly planned, with public parks and grid street plans;

most grew with less grace, trailing their tenements across the hills and swallowing up existing villages on the way. Most still retain a distinctive individual identity, and are free from the crowds in the centre, all of which makes them worth checking out on even a short visit to the city.

Vinohrady

Southeast of Nové Město is the predominantly late nineteenth-century suburb of **VINOHRADY**, Prague's most resolutely bourgeois suburb up until World War II. In one of its two main squares, **náměstí Jiřího z Poděbrad** (metro Jiřího z Poděbrad), stands Prague's most celebrated modern church, **Nejsvětější Srdce Páně** (Most Sacred Heart of Our Lord), built in 1928 by Josip Plečník, the Slovene architect responsible for much of the remodelling of the Hrad. It's a marvellously eclectic and individualistic work, employing a sophisticated potpourri of architectural styles: a Neoclassical pediment and a great slab of a tower with a giant transparent face in imitation of a Gothic rose window. Plečník also had a sharp eye for detail; note the little gold crosses set into the brickwork both inside and out, and the celestial orbs of light suspended above the heads of the congregation.

Žižkov

Though they share much the same architectural heritage, **ŽIŽKOV**, unlike Vinohrady, is a traditionally working-class area, and was a Communist Party stronghold even before the war, earning it the nickname Red Žižkov. Its peeling turn-of-the-twentieth-century tenements are home to a large proportion of Prague's Romany community. The main reason for venturing into Žižkov is to visit the ancient landmark of Žižkov hill and the city's main Olšany cemeteries, at the eastern end of Vyšehradská.

Žižkov TV tower

At over 100m in height, the Televizní vysílač or **Žižkov TV tower** (daily 10am–11pm; 150Kč; Ⓦ www.tower.cz) is the tallest building in Prague – and the most unpopular. Close up, it's an intimidating futuristic piece of architecture, made all the more disturbing by the addition of several statues of giant babies crawling up the sides, courtesy of artist David Černý. Begun in the 1970s in a desperate bid to jam West German television transmission, the tower only become fully operational in the 1990s. In the course of its construction, however, the Communists saw fit to demolish part of a nearby Jewish cemetery that had served the community between 1787 and 1891; a small section survives to the northwest of the tower. From the fifth-floor café or the viewing platform on the eighth floor, you can enjoy a spectacular view across Prague. To get to the tower, take the metro to Jiřího z Poděbrad and walk northeast a couple of blocks.

The cemeteries

The first one you come to as you approach from the west, the largest of the **Olšanské hřbitovy** (Olšany cemeteries; metro Flora) – each of which is bigger than the entire Jewish quarter – was created for the victims of the great plague epidemic of 1680. The perimeter walls are lined with glass cabinets, stacked like shoeboxes, containing funereal urns and mementoes, while the graves themselves are a mixed bag of artistic achievement, reflecting funereal fashions of the day as much as the character of the deceased. The cemetery's two most famous incumbents are an ill-fitting couple: Klement Gottwald, the country's first Communist president, whose ashes were removed from the mausoleum on Žižkov hill after

1989 and reinterred here; and the martyr Jan Palach, the philosophy student who set himself alight in protest at the continuing Soviet occupation in January 1969.

Immediately east of Olšany is the **Nový židovský hřbitov** or New Jewish Cemetery (April–Sept Mon–Thurs & Sun 9am–4.30pm, Fri 9am–2.30pm; Oct–March closes 1hr earlier), founded in the 1890s when the one by the Žižkov TV tower was full. It's a melancholy spot, particularly in the east of the cemetery, where large, empty allotments wait in vain to be filled by the generation who perished in the Holocaust. In fact, the community is now so small that it's unlikely the graveyard will ever be full. Most people come here to visit **Franz Kafka**'s grave, 400m east along the south wall and signposted from the entrance (for more on Kafka, see p.102). He is buried, along with his mother and father (both of whom outlived him), beneath a plain headstone; the plaque below commemorates his three sisters who died in the camps.

Žižkov hill

Žižkov hill (also known as Vítkov) is the thin green wedge of land that separates Žižkov from Karlín, a grid-plan industrial district to the north. From its westernmost point, which juts out almost to the edge of Nové Město, is probably the definitive panoramic view over the city centre. It was here, on July 14, 1420, that the Hussites enjoyed their first and finest victory at the **Battle of Vítkov**, under the inspired leadership of the one-eyed general, Jan Žižka (hence the name of the district). Ludicrously outnumbered by more than ten to one, Žižka and his fanatically motivated troops thoroughly trounced Emperor Sigismund and his papal forces.

Despite its overblown totalitarian aesthetics, the giant concrete **Žižkov monument** (Ⓦ www.pamatnik-vitkov.cz) that graces the crest of the hill was actually built between the wars as a memorial to the Czechoslovak Legion who fought against the Habsburgs – the gargantuan equestrian statue of the mace-wielding Žižka, which fronts the monument, is reputedly the world's largest. The building was later used by the Nazis as an arsenal, and eventually became a Communist hacks' mausoleum. In 1990, the remaining bodies were cremated and quietly reinterred in the Olšany cemeteries. Inside, a museum and café are due to be completed in 2009.

To get to the monument, take the metro to Florenc, walk under the railway lines and then up the steep lane U památníku. On the right as you climb the hill is the **Armádní muzeum** (Tues–Sun 10am–6pm; free; Ⓦ www.militarymuseum.cz), guarded by a handful of unmanned tanks, howitzers and armoured vehicles. The Czechs have a long history of manufacturing top-class weaponry for world powers (Semtex is probably their best-known export), so it's no coincidence that one of the two Czech words to have made it into the English language is pistol (from *pišťale*, a Hussite weapon) – the other is *robot*, incidentally. The museum contains a balanced account of both world wars, as well as telling the story of the Czechoslovak Legion, the Heydrich assassination (see box, p.113) – you can see the Reichsprotektor's soft-top Mercedes – and the 1945 Prague Uprising.

Holešovice and Bubenec

The late nineteenth-century districts of **HOLEŠOVICE** and **BUBENEČ**, tucked into a huge U-bend in the Vltava, have little in the way of magnificent architecture but make up for it with two huge splodges of green: to the south, **Letná**, where Prague's largest gatherings occur; and to the north, the **Stromovka park**, bordering the Výstaviště funfair and international trade fair grounds. Holešovice is also home to the **Veletržní palác**, Prague's impressive modern art museum.

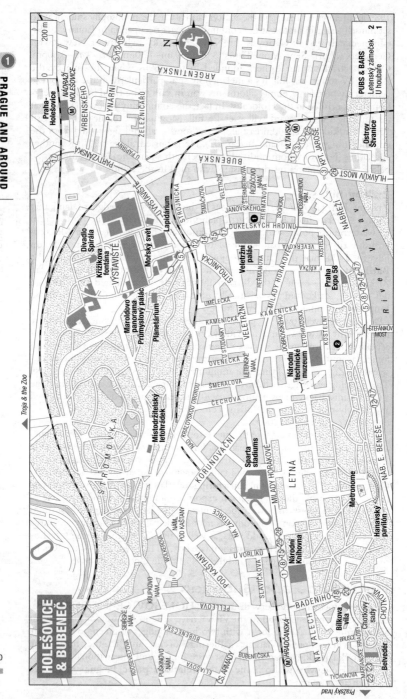

▲ Troja & the Zoo

HOLEŠOVICE & BUBENEČ

Praha-Holešovice Ⓜ

NÁDRAŽÍ
HOLEŠOVICE

VRBENSKÉHO

PLYNÁRNÍ

ŽELEZNIČÁŘŮ

U PAPÍREN

PARTYZÁNSKÁ

ARGENTINSKÁ

Divadlo
Spirála

Křížíkova
fontána
VÝSTAVIŠTĚ

Mořský svět

Lapidárium

Národovo panorana
Průmyslový palác

Planetárium

Mistodržitelský
letohrádek

S T R O M O V K A

NA KRÁLOVSKOU OBOROU

KORUNOVAČNÍ

Sparta
stadiums

MILADY HORÁKOVÉ

NAD KRÁLOVSKOU OBOROU

Národní
Knihovna

NAM.
POD KAŠTANY

U VORLÍKU

POD KAŠTANY

SLAVÍČKOVA

WOLKEROVA

KRUPKOVO
NÁM.

SIBIŘSKÉ
NÁM.

PELLÉOVA

BUBENEČSKÁ

HROBOVETOVA

PUŠKINOVO
NÁM.

ELIÁŠOVA

ČS. ARMÁDY

BUBENEČSKÁ

HRADČANSKÁ Ⓜ

NA VALECH

BADENIHO

Bílkova
vila

K BRUSCE

MÁRIANSKÉ HRADBY

TYCHONOVA

CHOTKOVA

Chotkovy
sady

Belvedér

▼ Pražský hrad

STROJNICKÁ

SMÁČKOVA

VELETRŽNÍ

STERNBERKOVA

ŘEZÁČOVO
NÁM.

HEŘMANOVA

JANOVSKÉHO

SOCHORA

STRESSEMEROVO
NÁM.

DUKELSKÝCH HRDINŮ ❶

VÝSTAVIŠTĚ

Veletržní
palác

HEŘMANOVA

VERKOVA

KŘÍŽKA

VEVERKOVA

KOSTELNÍ

Praha
Expo 58

UMĚLECKÁ

VELETRŽNÍ

KAMENICKÁ

U STUDÁNKY

KAMENICKÁ

DOBROVSKÉHO

LETOHRADSKÁ

KOSTELNÍ

Národní
technické
muzeum

❷

OVENECKÁ

LETENSKÉ
NÁM.

ŠMERALOVA

ČECHOVA

LETNÁ

NÁB. E. BENEŠE

12-17

Praha-
Holešovice Ⓜ

VLTAVSKÁ Ⓜ

KPT. JAROŠE

HLÁVKŮV MOST

N Á B Ř E Ž Í

R i v e r   V l t a v a

ŠTEFÁNIKŮV
MOST

Metronome

Hanavský
pavilón

Ostrov
Štvanice

0 ——— 200 m

N

Letná: the Stalin monument

Prague's most famous monument is one that no longer exists. The **Stalin monument**, the largest in the world, stood on **Letná**, the high plateau hovering above the city across the river to the north of Staré Město. A thirty-metre-high granite sculpture portraying a procession of people being led to Communism by the Pied Piper figure of Stalin, it was popularly dubbed *tlačenice* (the crush) because of its resemblance to a Communist-era bread queue. Designed by Jiří Štursa and Otakar Švec, it took 600 workers 500 days to erect the 14,200-ton monster. Švec, the sculptor, committed suicide shortly before it was unveiled, as his wife had done three years previously, leaving all his money to a school for blind children, since they at least would not have to see his creation. It was eventually revealed to the cheering masses on May 1, 1955 – the first and last popular celebration to take place at the monument. Within a year, Khrushchev had denounced his predecessor and, after pressure from Moscow, the monument was blown to smithereens by a series of explosions spread over a fortnight in 1962. All that remains above ground is the statue's vast concrete platform and steps, on the southern edge of the Letná plain, now graced with David Černý's symbolic giant red **metronome** (which is lit up at night); it's also a favourite spot for skateboarders and another good viewpoint.

Národní technické muzeum (National Technical Museum)

Belying its dull title, the **Národní technické muzeum** (Ⓦ www.ntm.cz) on Kostelní is surprisingly interesting. The showpiece hangar-like main hall contains an impressive gallery of motorbikes, Czech and foreign, and a wonderful collection of old planes, trains and automobiles from Czechoslovakia's industrial heyday between the wars, when the country's Škoda cars and Tatra soft-top stretch limos were really something to brag about. The oldest car in the collection is Laurin & Klement's 1898 *Präsident*, more of a motorized carriage than a car; the museum also boasts the world's oldest Bugatti. Other displays trace the development of early photography, and feature a collection of some of Kepler's and Tycho Brahe's astrological instruments. At the time of writing, the whole place was undergoing a restoration that should be completed by 2010.

Veletržní palác (Trade Fair Palace)

Situated at the corner of Dukelských hrdinů and Veletržní, some distance from the nearest metro station, the **Veletržní palác** (Tues–Sun 10am–6pm; 250Kč including English audioguide; Ⓦ www.ngprague.cz), or Trade Fair Palace, gets nothing like the number of visitors it should. For not only does the building house the Národní galerie's excellent nineteenth- and twentieth-century Czech and international art collection, it is also an architectural sight in itself. A seven-storey building constructed in 1928 by Oldřich Tyl and Josef Fuchs, it is Prague's ultimate functionalist masterpiece, not so much from the outside, but inside, where its gleaming white vastness is suitably awesome. The gallery itself, stretching over six floors, is virtually impossible to view in its entirety.

To reach the Veletržní palác by **public transport**, catch tram #5 or #14 from náměstí Republiky, tram #12 from Malostranská metro, tram #17 from Staroměstská metro, or tram #12 or #17 from Nádraží Holešovice to Veletržní. *U houbaře* (The Mushroom), opposite the museum at Dukelských hrdinů 30, is a good **pub**, and there's *Ouky Douky*, a groovy **café-bar** and secondhand bookshop, one block east at Janovského 14.

Foreign art

As good a place as any to start is the bluntly named **Foreign art** exhibition on the first floor. There are one or two gems here, beginning with **Gustav Klimt**'s mischievous *Virgins*, a mass of naked bodies and tangled limbs painted over in psychedelic colours, plus one of the square landscapes he used to enjoy painting during his summer holidays in the Salzkammergut.

Egon Schiele's mother came from the South Bohemian town of Český Krumlov, the subject of a tiny, gloomy, autumnal canvas, *Dead Town*. The gallery also owns one of Schiele's most popular female portraits, wrongly entitled *The Artist's Wife*, an unusually graceful and gentle watercolour of a seated woman in green top and black leggings. In contrast, *Pregnant Woman and Death* is a morbidly bleak painting, in which Schiele depicts himself as both the monk of death and the life-giving mother.

Perhaps the most influential foreign artist on show is **Edvard Munch**, whose two canvases hardly do justice to the considerable effect he had on a generation of Czech artists after his celebrated 1905 Prague exhibition. Look out, too, for **Oskar Kokoschka**'s typically vigorous landscapes, dating from his brief stay in Prague in the 1930s.

Czech art 1900–30

Chronologically, it's best to head up to the third floor, where the **Czech art 1900–30** collection confronts you with **Otakar Švec**'s life-sized *Motorcyclist*, a great three-dimensional depiction of the optimistic speed of the modern age. These are followed by a whole series of works by **František Kupka**, who was Czech by birth, but lived and worked in Paris from 1895. In international terms, Kupka is by far the most important Czech painter of the twentieth century, having secured his place in the history of art by being (possibly) the first artist in the western world to exhibit abstract paintings. His seminal *Fugue in Two Colours (Amorpha)*, one of two abstract paintings Kupka exhibited at the Salon d'Automne in 1912, is displayed here, along with some earlier, pre-abstract paintings.

The Edvard Munch retrospective exhibited in Prague in 1905 prompted the formation in 1907 of the first Czech modern art movement, Osma (The Eight), one of whose leading members was **Emil Filla**, whose *Ace of Hearts* and *Reader of Dostoyevsky* – in which the subject appears to have fallen asleep, though, in fact, he's mind-blown – are both firmly within the Expressionist genre. However, it wasn't long before several of the Osma group were beginning to experiment with Cubism. Filla eventually adopted the style wholesale, helping found the Cubist SVU in 1911. **Bohumil Kubišta**, a member of Osma, refused to follow suit, instead pursuing his own unique blend of Cubo-Expressionism, typified by the wonderful self-portrait, *The Smoker*, and by the distinctly Fauvist *Players*.

To round out the Czech Cubist picture, there's furniture and ceramics (and even a Cubist chandelier) by Gočár, Janák and Chochol, as well as sculptures by **Otto Gutfreund**, a member of SVU, whose works range from the Cubo-Expressionist *Anxiety* (1911–12) to the more purely Cubist *Bust* (1913–14). After World War I, Gutfreund switched to depicting everyday folk in technicolour, in a style that prefigures Socialist Realism. His life was cut short in 1927, when he drowned while swimming in the Vltava. **Josef Čapek**, brother of the playwright, Karel, is another Czech clearly influenced by Cubism, as seen in works such as *Accordion Player*, but like Kubišta, Čapek found Filla's doctrinaire approach difficult to take, and he left SVU in 1912.

Nineteenth- and twentieth-century French art

Also on the third floor, the **French art** collection features anyone of note who hovered around Paris in the fifty years from 1880 onwards. There are few masterpieces here, but it's all high-quality stuff, most of it either bought for the gallery in 1923, or bequeathed by art dealer Vincenc Kramář in 1960.

The collection kicks off with several works by **Auguste Rodin**, particularly appropriate given the ecstatic reception that greeted the Prague exhibition of his work in 1902. Rodin's sculptures are surrounded by works from the advance guard of Impressionism: Courbet, Delacroix, Corot, Sisley and early Monet and Pissarro. Among the other works here, there's a characteristically sunny, Provençal *Green Wheat* by **Vincent van Gogh**, and a *Moulin Rouge* by Toulouse-Lautrec, with Oscar Wilde looking on. Beyond, the loose brushwork, cool turquoise and emerald colours of **Auguste Renoir**'s *Lovers* are typical of the period of so-called High Impressionism. *Bonjour Monsieur Gauguin* is a tongue-in-cheek tribute to Courbet's painting of a similar name, with **Paul Gauguin** donning a suitably bohemian beret and overcoat. Also on display is the only known self-portrait by **Henri Rousseau**, at once confident and comical, the artist depicting himself, palette in hand, against a boat decked with bunting and the recently erected Eiffel Tower.

There's also a surprisingly good collection of works by **Pablo Picasso**, including several paintings and sculptures from his transitional period (1907–08), and lots of examples from the heights of his Cubist period in the 1910s; his *Landscape with Bridge* from 1909 uses precisely the kind of prisms and geometric blocks of shading that influenced the Czech Cubist architects. In addition, you'll find a couple of late paintings by Paul Cézanne, a classic *pointilliste* canvas by Georges Seurat and Cubist works by Braque. *Joaquine*, painted by **Henri Matisse** in 1910–11 clearly shows both Fauvist and Oriental influences. Look out too for Marc Chagall's *The Circus*, a typically mad work from 1927, and a rare painting by Le Corbusier himself, which clearly shows the influence of Fernand Léger, one of whose works hangs close by.

Czech art 1930–2000

On the second floor, the section covering **Czech art from 1930 to 2000** gives a pretty good introduction to the country's artistic peaks and troughs. There's too much stuff here – paintings, sculptures and installations – to take in at one go; below are one or two highlights.

First off, there's a wild kinetic-light sculpture by **Zdeněk Pešánek**, a world pioneer in the use of neon in art, who created a stir at the 1937 Paris Expo with a neon fountain. Devětsil, founded back in 1920, was the driving force of the Czech avant-garde between the wars, and is represented here by **Toyen** (Marie Čermínová) and her lifelong companion **Jindřich Štyrský**, and by abstract photographic works. One Czech artist who enthusiastically embraced Surrealism was **Josef Šíma**, who settled permanently in Paris in the 1920s; several of his trademark floating torsoes and cosmic eggs can be seen here.

Fans of Communist kitsch should make their way to the small **Socialist Realism** section, with works such as the wildly optimistic *We Produce More, We Live Better*, and Eduard Stavinoha's cartoon-like *Listening to the Speech of Klement Gottwald, Feb 21, 1948*. Note, too, the model of Otakar Švec's now demolished Stalin statue, which once dominated central Prague. In the 1960s, **performance art** was big in Czechoslovakia, and it, too, has its own section. Inevitably, it's difficult to recapture the original impact of some of the "happenings", but photographs, such as those of Zorka Ságlová's *Laying out Nappies near Sudoměř*, give you a fair idea of what you may have missed.

The gallery owns several works by **Jiří Kolář** – pronounced "collage" – who, coincidentally, specializes in collages of random words and reproductions of other people's paintings. The rest of the contemporary Czech art collection is interesting enough, if taken at a canter. Ivan Kafka's phallic *Potent Impotency* installation should raise a smile, and there's the occasional overtly political work such as *Great Dialogue* by Karel Nepraš, in which two red figures lambast each other at close quarters with loudspeakers.

Výstaviště and Stromovka

Five-minutes' walk north up Dukelských hrdinů takes you to the front gates of the **Výstaviště** (Tues–Fri 2–10pm, Sat & Sun 10am–10pm; free; ⓦwww .incheba.cz), a motley assortment of buildings, originally created for the 1891 Prague Exhibition, that have served as the city's main trade fair arena and funfair ever since. From 1948 until the late 1970s the Communist Party held its rubber-stamp congresses in the flamboyant stained-glass and wrought-iron **Průmyslový palác** at the centre of the complex.

The grounds are at their busiest on summer weekends, when hordes of Prague families descend on the place to down hot dogs and drink beer. Apart from the annual fairs and lavish special exhibitions, there are a few permanent attractions, such as the city's **Planetárium** (daily 11am–8pm; 10Kč; ⓦwww.planetarium .cz), which has static displays and videos (60Kč), but no telescopes (for which you need to go to the Štefánikova hvězdarna – see p.87); the **Maroldovo panorama** (April–Oct Tues–Fri 2–5pm, Sat & Sun 10am–5pm; 20Kč), a giant diorama of the 1434 Battle of Lipany (see p.389); and the **Lunapark**, a run-down funfair and playground for kids. In the long summer evenings, there's also an open-air **cinema** (*letní kino*), and regular performances by the **Křižíkova fontána** (ⓦwww.krizikovafontana.cz), dancing fountains devised for the 1891 Exhibition by the Czech inventor František Křižík, which perform a music and light show to packed audiences; for the current schedule, ask at the tourist office, or check the listings magazines or the website ⓦwww.krizikovafontana.cz. Lastly, to the right as you enter the fairgrounds, there's the excellent and much overlooked **Lapidárium** (Tues–Fri noon–6pm, Sat & Sun 10am–6pm; 40Kč; ⓦwww.nm.cz), official depository for the city's monumental sculptures that have been under threat from demolition or the weather in the last century or so.

To the west is the *královská obora* or royal enclosure, more commonly known as **Stromovka**. Originally a game park for the noble occupants of the Hrad, it's now Prague's largest and leafiest public park. From here, you can wander northwards to Troja and the city's zoo (see opposite), following a path that leads under the railway, over the canal, and on to the Císařský ostrov (Emperor's Island) – and from there to the right bank of the Vltava. The hourly bus #112 will take you back to metro Nádraží Holešovice.

Troja

Though still well within the municipal boundaries, the suburb of **TROJA**, across the river to the north of Holešovice and Bubeneč, has a distinctly provincial air. Its most celebrated sight is Prague's only genuine chateau, the late seventeenth-century **Trojský zámek** (April–Sept Tues–Sun 10am–6pm; Nov–March Sat & Sun 10am–5pm; 100Kč; bus #112 from metro Nádraží Holešovice), perfectly situated against a hilly backdrop of vines. Despite renovation and a rusty red repaint, its plain early Baroque facade is no match for the action-packed, blackened figures of giants and titans who battle it out on the chateau's monumental balustrades. The star exhibits of the **interior** are the gushing frescoes depicting the victories of the Habsburg Emperor Leopold I (who reigned from 1657 to 1705) over the Turks, which cover the grand hall. You also get to wander through the chateau's pristine, trend-setting, French-style formal **gardens**, the first of their kind in Bohemia.

On the other side of U trojského zámku, which runs along the west wall of the chateau, is the city's capacious **zoo** (daily: March 9am–5pm; April, May, Sept & Oct 9am–6pm; June–Aug 9am–7pm; Nov–Feb 9am–4pm; 100Kč; Ⓦwww .zoopraha.cz). Founded in 1931 on the site of one of Troja's numerous hillside vineyards, the zoo has had a lot of money poured into it and now has some very imaginative animal enclosures. All the usual animals are on show – including elephants, hippos, giraffes, zebras, big cats and bears – and kids, at least, will enjoy themselves. In the summer you can take a chairlift (*lanová dráha*) from the duck pond over the enclosures to the top of the hill, where the prize exhibits – a rare breed of miniature horse known as Przewalski – hang out. Other highlights include the red pandas, the giant tortoises, the Komodo dragons and the bats that fly past your face in the Twilight Zone.

Another reason for coming out to Troja is to visit the city's **Botanická zahrada** (daily: April 9am–6pm; May–Sept 9am–7pm; Oct 9am–5pm; Nov–March 9am–4pm; 120Kč; Ⓦwww.botanicka.cz), hidden in the woods to the north of the zámek. The botanic gardens feature a vineyard, a Japanese garden, several glasshouses and great views over Prague. A little higher up the hill there's also a spectacular, curvaceous greenhouse, **Fata Morgana** (Tues–Sun only), with butterflies flitting about amid the desert and tropical plants. The Fata Morgana – which, incidentally, means "mirage" in Czech – is hugely popular, and there are vast queues at the weekend.

Dejvice to Smíchov

Spread across the hills to the northwest of the city centre are the leafy garden suburbs of **Dejvice** and **Střešovice**, peppered with fashionable villas built between the wars for the upwardly mobile Prague bourgeoisie and commanding magnificent views across the north of the city.

In Střešovice, you'll find Prague's local transport museum, **Muzeum MHD** (April to mid-Nov Sat & Sun 9am–5pm; 35Kč; Ⓦwww.dpp.cz), at Patočkova 4 – to get there take tram #1, #8, #15, #18, #25 or the historic tram #91 to Vozovna Střešovice. Housed in a 1909 tram shed, the majority of its exhibits are red-and-cream municipal trams from the last century, though there are one or two buses and trolleybuses too, and an exhibition covering everything from horse-drawn trams to the Soviet-built metro.

Müllerova vila

The most famous of Prague's interwar villas is the Loosova vila or **Müllerova vila** (Tues, Thurs, Sat & Sun: April–Oct 9am, 11am, 1pm, 3pm & 5pm; Nov–March 10am, noon, 2pm & 4pm; 300Kč; plus 100Kč for an English guide; ☎224 312 012, Ⓦwww.mullerovavila.cz) at Nad hradním vodojemem 14. Designed by the Brno-born architect, **Adolf Loos** – regarded by many as one of the founders of modern architecture – and completed in 1930, it's a typically uncompromising box, wiped smooth with concrete rendering. Loos' most famous architectural concept, the *Raumplan*, or open-plan design, is apparent in the living room, which is overlooked by the dining room on the mezzanine level, and, even higher up, by the boudoir, itself a *Raumplan* in miniature. The house is also decorated throughout in the rich materials and minimal furnishings that were Loos' hallmark: green and white Cipolino marble columns, with an inset aquarium in the living room and mahogany panelling for the dining room ceiling. To visit the house, you must phone in advance as each guided tour is limited to seven people; to get there, take tram #1, #2 or #18 to Ořechovka.

Hvězda

A couple of kilometres southwest of Dejvice, trams #1, #2 and #18 terminate close to the hunting park of **Hvězda** (Tues–Sun: April & Oct 10am–5pm; May–Sept 10am–6pm; 30Kč; ⓦwww.pamatniknarodnihopisemnictvi.cz), one of Prague's most beautiful and peaceful parks. Wide, green avenues of trees radiate from a bizarre star-shaped building (*hvězda* means "star" in Czech) designed by the Archduke Ferdinand of Tyrol for his wife in 1555. It houses a small exhibition on the **Battle of Bílá hora** (White Mountain), the first battle of the Thirty Years' War, which took place in 1620 a short distance southwest of Hvězda. However, it's the building itself – decorated with delicate stuccowork and frescoes – that's the greatest attraction; it makes a perfect setting for the chamber music concerts occasionally staged here.

Musaion (Folk Museum)

The Kinský family's Neoclassical summer palace, built in 1827, sits on the southern edge of Petřín hill, and now houses the **Musaion** (Tues–Sun: May–Sept 10am–6pm; Oct–April 9am–5pm; 80Kč; ⓦwww.nm.cz), the city's ethnographic museum. The permanent collection is spread out over ten or so galleries on the *piano nobile*, with some of the most intriguing exhibits in room 7, which displays fearsome masks and rattles from the pre-Lent Masopust festival, a Čaramura costume bestrewn with eggs and snails, and, of course, garlanded *pomlázky*, with which the boys beat the girls at Easter. The Christmas section (room 9) is another highlight, with its spectacular *Betlém* (Bethlehem) scene set amid a rocky papier-maché townscape. The best approach to the museum is through the park from náměstí Kinských, Újezd or Petřín itself (see p.87), rather than up the busy road of Holečkova.

Bertramka (Mozart Museum)

In the hills above the late nineteenth-century suburb of **Smíchov** is Prague's Mozart Museum, known as the **Bertramka** (daily: April–Oct 9am–6pm; Nov–March 9.30am–4pm; 110Kč; ⓦwww.bertramka.com), where, so the story goes, the composer put the finishing touches to his *Don Giovanni* overture the night before the premiere at the Stavovské divadlo (see p.97). As long ago as 1838, the villa was turned into a shrine to Mozart, though thanks to a fire on New Year's Day 1871 very little survives of the house he knew – not that this has deterred generations of Mozart-lovers from flocking here. These days, what the museum lacks in memorabilia, it makes up for with its Rococo ambience, lovely garden and regular Mozart recitals. To get to Bertramka, take the metro to Anděl, walk a couple of blocks west or go one stop on a tram up Plzeňská, then turn left up Mozartova.

Zbraslav

One of Prague's more intriguing museums is situated in the little-visited village of **ZBRASLAV**, 10km south of the city centre, though within the municipal boundaries. Přemyslid King Otakar II built a hunting lodge here, which was later turned into a Cistercian monastery. Nowadays, **Zámek Zbraslav** (Tues–Sun 10am–6pm; 80Kč; ⓦwww.ngprague.cz) shelters the Národní galerie's remarkably extensive Asian art collection. Downstairs you can see Japanese art from seventeenth-century travelling altarpieces and cracked glaze porcelain to late nineteenth-century lacquerwork and exquisite landscapes on silk. Upstairs, there's a vast array of Chinese exhibits from Neolithic axes and ancient funerary art to Ming vases, dishes and even roof tiles. Highlights include an incredibly naturalistic eleventh-century wooden statue of one of the Buddha's aged disciples, a large standing gilded and lacquered Burmese Buddha, and an erotic Yab-Yum, a central icon of Tantric Buddhism.

Appropriately enough, the museum has a tea-house (*čajovna*) in the cloisters, and plenty of grass outside on which to picnic. To reach the gallery, take bus #129, #241, #243, #255 or #360 from metro Smíchovské nádraží or the local train from Smíchovské nádraží to Praha-Zbraslav.

Eating and drinking

While traditional **Czech food** still predominates in the city's pubs, the choice of places to eat is vast compared with the rest of the country – you can spend a whole week eating out and never go near a dumpling. Like most Czechs, Praguers are very keen on pizza, and there's now a range of restaurants serving up everything from sushi to Afghan, some at stratospheric prices.

Not surprisingly, the places in the main tourist areas along Mostecká and Karlova, on either side of the Charles Bridge, and on Staroměstské náměstí and Wenceslas Square, tend to be overpriced, relying on their location, rather than the quality of their food, to bring in custom. Venture instead into the backstreets and you're more likely to find better service, better value and perhaps even better food.

Snacks and fast food

Paneria (ⓦ www.paneria.cz) provides **sandwiches**, toasted panini and pastries for Prague's hungry office workers; there are branches at Kaprova 3 and Maiselova 4 (both metro Staroměstská) and all over town. Expat favourites include the self-service breakfast, **bagel** and soup outfit, *Bohemia Bagel*, Lázeňská 19 (ⓦ www.bohemiabagel.cz; metro Malostranská) and Masná 2 (metro Staroměstská), both of which have an internet café attached. More varied and upmarket sandwiches, wraps and pastries can be had from *Bakeshop Praha*, Kozí 1 (metro Náměstí Republiky), which has a few eat-in bar stools.

Obviously the usual multinational burger chains have their outlets splattered all over Prague. For something more uniquely Czech, head for *Havelská Koruna*, Havelská 21 (metro Můstek), an authentic no-frills, self-service *jídelna* serving **Czech comfort food** classics such as *sekaná*, goulash and *zelí*, all for under 50Kč (you pay at the exit). For authentic, cheap Indian **veggie** canteen food, look no further than *Beas*, Týnská 19 (ⓦ www.beas-dhaba.cz; metro Malostranská/ Náměstí Republiky). Local veggies head for the multinational health food café *Country Life*, Melantrichova 15 and Jungmannova 1 (closed Sat; metro Můstek). *Dahab Yalla*, Dlouhá 33 (metro Náměstí Republiky), and *Anis*, Jungmannova 21 (closed Sun; metro Národní třída), serve felafel and **Middle Eastern** snacks.

Cafés

At the beginning of the twentieth century, Prague boasted a **café society** to rival that of Vienna or Paris. A handful of these classic Habsburg-era haunts have survived, or been resurrected, and should definitely be sampled. The cafés listed

Prague's tea-houses

Prague's **tea-houses** are a post-Communist phenomenon, though they have their historical roots in the First Republic. Partly a reaction to the smoke-filled, alcohol-driven atmosphere of the ubiquitous Czech pub, and partly a reaction against the multinational, fast-food culture that has now arrived in Prague, tea-houses tend to be non-smoking, slightly hippified places to enjoy a quiet cuppa and chill out. The tea-drinking is taken very seriously and there's usually a staggering array of leaves on offer, some commanding pretty high prices.

Dahab Dlouhá 33, Staré Město ⓦwww.dahab.cz; metro Náměstí Republiky. The mother of all Prague tea-houses, a vast Bedouin tent of a place serving tasty Middle Eastern snacks, couscous and hookahs to a background of funky world music. Daily noon–1am.

Dobrá čajovna Václavské nám. 14, Nové Město ⓦwww.tea.cz; metro Můstek/Muzeum. Mellow, rarefied tea-house, with an astonishing variety of teas (and a few Middle Eastern snacks) served by waiters who slip by silently in their sandals. Mon–Fri noon–9.30pm, Sat & Sun 3–9.30pm.

Malý Buddha Úvoz 46, Malá Strana; tram #12, #20, #22 or #23 one stop from metro Malostranská. Typical Prague tea-house decor, with a Buddhist altar in one corner and (mainly) vegetarian Vietnamese snacks on the menu. A very useful haven just down from the Hrad. Tues–Sun 1–10.30pm.

U zeleného čaje (The Green Tea) Nerudova 19, Malá Strana; tram #12, #22 or #23 one stop from from metro Malostranská. A great little stop-off for a pot of tea or a veggie snack en route to or from the Hrad; the only problem is getting a place at one of the four tables. Daily 11am–10pm.

below are a mixed bunch. The majority serve just coffee and cakes, and more often than not, alcohol; others also serve up cheap and filling (though rarely gourmet) meals.

Malá Strana

Cukrkávalimonáda Lázeňská 7; metro Malostranská. Very professional and well-run café, serving good brasserie-style dishes as well as coffee and croissants, with tables overlooking the church of Panna Maria pod řetězěm. Daily 8.30am–8pm.

🏃 **Savoy** Vítězná 5 ⓦwww.ambi.cz; tram #6, #9, #12, #20, #22 or #23. Classic L-shaped Habsburg-era café from 1893 with a superb, high neo-Renaissance ceiling; you can just have a drink and snack, but the seafood-dominated menu is also very good. Mon–Fri 8am–10.30pm, Sat & Sun 9am–10.30pm.

U zavěšenýho kafe Úvoz 6; metro Malostranská. A pleasant, if smoky, crossover café/pub, serving cheap beer and traditional Czech food in a handy spot on the way up or down from the Hrad. A "hanging coffee" is one that has been paid for by the haves for the have-nots who drop in. Daily 11am–midnight.

Staré Město

Chez Marcel Haštalská 12 ⓦwww.chezmoi.cz; metro Náměstí Republiky. Effortlessly chic French

café-bistro. A good place to grab a coffee or a tarte tatin, read a French mag or eat some moderately priced brasserie staples. Mon–Sat 8am–1am, Sun 9am–1am.

Érra Konviktská 11; metro Národní třída. Vaulted cellar café in the backstreets off Betlémské náměstí that's popular with a fashionable mixed straight/gay crowd. Tasty salads and snacks on offer too. Daily 10am–midnight.

🏃 **Grand Café Orient** Ovocný trh 19; metro Náměstí Republiky. Superb reconstruction of a famous Cubist café from 1911 on the first floor of the Cubist museum. Cakes, pancakes and coffee. Daily 9am–9pm.

Montmartre Řetězová 7; metro Staroměstská. Surprisingly small, barrel-vaulted café that was once a famous First Republic dance and cabaret venue, frequented by fin-de-siècle types. Daily 8am–11pm.

Nové Město

Globe Pštrossova 6 ⓦwww.globebookstore.cz; metro Národní třída/Karlovo náměstí. Large, buzzing café, at the back of the English-language bookstore of the same name, that's a serious expat hangout, but enjoyable nevertheless. Live music Fri & Sat eve. Daily 10am–midnight.

🏃 **Louvre** Národní 20 🌐 www.kavarny.cz
/louvre; metro Národní třída. Turn-of-the-twentieth-century café, closed down under the Communists, but now a very popular refuelling spot for Prague's shoppers. Dodgy colour scheme, but high ceiling, mirrors, daily papers, lots of cakes, a billiard hall and window seats overlooking Národní. Daily 8am–11pm.

🏃 **Obecní dům** náměstí Republiky 5 🌐 www .obecni-dum.cz. The vast *kavárna*, with its famous fountain, is in the more restrained south

hall of this huge Art Nouveau complex, and has recently been glitteringly restored – an aesthetic treat. Daily 7.30am–11pm.

Slavia Národní 1; metro Národní třída. Famous 1920s riverside café that has a special place in the city's cultural and political history. Despite losing much of its character, it still pulls in a mixed crowd from shoppers and tourists to older folk and the pre- and post-theatre mob. Daily 9am–11pm.

Velryba (The Whale) Opatovická 24; metro Národní třída. One of the most determinedly cool, student cafés in Prague. Smoky, loud and serving cheap Czech food (plus several veggie options) and a wide range of malt whiskies. Daily 11am–2am.

Restaurants and wine bars

Prague's restaurant scene has greatly improved in the last few years. Prices have also shot up, yet even in the city's top restaurants, you can't guarantee faultless food or **service**, so keep an open mind, and check the bill. In addition to the odd unscrupulous waiter, beware of the mark-up on wine and watch out for extras: you will often find a **cover charge** for bread, music and for everything you touch, including the almonds you thought were courtesy of the house.

Hradčany

U ševce Matouše (The Cobbler Matouš)
Loretánské nám. 4 ☎ 220 514 536; tram #22 or #23 from metro Malostranská to Pohořelec stop. A large steak and chips, for around 300Kč, is the speciality of this former cobbler's, which is one of the few half-decent places to eat in the castle district. Bottled beer only. Daily 11am–4pm & 6–11pm.

Malá Strana

Barbar Všehrdova 17 ☎ 257 312 246.
Unpretentious cellar restaurant with big cheap salads, savoury (mostly veggie) pancake dishes and sweet crêpes (*palačinky*) on offer. Daily noon–midnight.

🏃 **David** Tržiště 21 ☎ 257 533 109, 🌐 www .restaurant-david.cz. Formal, small, family-run restaurant that specializes in doing classic Bohemian cuisine full justice; main dishes go for around 400–600Kč. Daily 11.30am–11pm.

Hergetová cihelna Cihelná 2b ☎ 257 535 534, 🌐 www.kampagroup.com. Slick, smart restaurant, run by the *Kampa Park* family, specializing in pasta dishes and tasty pizzas cooked in a wood-fired oven for around 250Kč. The riverside summer terrace overlooks Charles Bridge. Daily 11.30am–1am.

Kampa Park Na Kampě 8b ☎ 257 532 685, 🌐 www.kampagroup.com. Pink house exquisitely located right by the Vltava on Kampa Island with a superb fish and seafood menu, with main dishes

around 600–900Kč, top-class service and tables outside in summer. Daily 11.30am–1am.

Nebozízek (Little Auger) Petřínské sady 411
☎ 257 515 329, 🌐 www.nebozizek.cz. Situated at the halfway stop on the Petřín funicular. The view is superb, there's an oudoor terrace and a traditional Czech menu heavy with game dishes for 300–400Kč. Daily 11am–11pm.

Rybářský klub U sovových mlýnů 1 ☎ 257 534 200; tram #12, #20, #22 or #23 from metro Malostranská to Hellichova. Freshwater fish – carp, catfish, eel, pike and others – simply prepared for under 250Kč, at this unpretentious riverside restaurant, situated in the park on Kampa Island. Daily noon–11pm.

U Maltézských rytířů (The Maltese Knights)
Prokopská 10 ☎ 257 533 666, 🌐 www .umaltezskychrytiru.cz; tram #12, #20, #22 or #23 from Malostranská metro. One of the best Gothic cellars in Prague in which to sample faultless local cuisine (particularly venison) and excellent apple strudel. Most main dishes are 300–400Kč. Daily 1–11pm.

U modré kachničky Nebovidská 6 ☎ 257 320 308, 🌐 www.umodrekachnicky.cz. Intimate little restaurant, decorated with murals and antiques. Mouthwatering dishes, including many Czech favourites – such as roast duck with pears – given the gourmet treatment. Main dishes for under 500Kč. Branch at Michalská 16 ☎ 224 213 418; metro Národní třída. Daily 11.30am–11.30pm.

Staré Město and Josefov

Ariana Rámová 6, Staré Město ☏ 222 323 438, ⓦ www.sweb.cz/kabulrest; metro Náměstí Republiky. Welcoming Afghan restaurant serving up authentic spicy kebabs and veggie dishes (150–250Kč) a stone's throw from the Old Town Square. Daily 11am–11pm.

Bellevue Smetanovo nábřeží 18, Staré Město ☏ 222 221 443, ⓦ www .bellevuerestaurant.cz; metro Národní třída. The outstanding views of Charles Bridge and the Hrad, formal setting, and imaginatively prepared international cuisine mean that main courses are 500–800Kč and you need to book ahead. Daily noon–3pm & 5.30–11pm.

Kogo Havelská 27, Staré Město ☏ 224 214 543, ⓦ www.kogo.cz; metro Můstek. Divided into two intimate spaces by a passageway, and with a small courtyard out back, this place offers decent pasta, pizza and salads for around 250Kč, served by courteous and efficient waiters. There are other branches at Na příkopě 22 (metro Můstek) and Karlovo nám. 10 (metro Karlovo náměstí). Mon–Fri 8am–11pm, Sat & Sun 9am–11pm.

Lehká hlava (Clear Head) Boršov 2, Staré Město ☏ 222 220 665, ⓦ www.lehkahlava .cz; metro Staroměstská. Exotic, cave-like veggie restaurant, just off Karoliny Světlé, offering tapas, soups, salads, pasta and quesadillas for 75–150Kč – book ahead for the evening. Daily 11.30am–11.30pm.

Mlýnec Novotného lávka 9, Staré Město ☏ 221 082 208, ⓦ www.mlynec.cz; metro Staroměstská. International cuisine (which has occasionally garnered Michelin stars) and a fabulous terrace overlooking the Charles Bridge and the Hrad. Mains 500–700Kč. Daily noon–3pm & 5.30–11pm.

Orange Moon Rámová 5, Staré Město ☏ 222 325 119 ⓦ www.orangemoon.cz. Popular Burmese restaurant that cooks up spicy curries for under 200Kč, washed down with Czech beer. Daily 11.30am–11.30pm.

Pizzeria Rugantino Dušní 4, Josefov ☏ 222 318 172; metro Staroměstská. This pizzeria, just off Dlouhá, is the genuine article: an oak-fired oven, gargantuan thin bases, numerous toppings, and Bernard on tap. Mon–Sat 11am–11pm, Sun 5–11pm.

Pravda Pařížská 17, Josefov ☏ 222 326 203, ⓦ www.pravdarestaurant.cz; metro Staroměstská. Trendy restaurant on Prague's chicest street.

Service is attentive and the excellent menu ranges from Cajun to Vietnamese, with home-made pasta dishes around 360Kč and main dishes starting at around 600Kč. Daily noon–1am.

Nové Město

Lemon Leaf Na Zderaze 14 ☏ 224 919 056, ⓦ www.lemon.cz; metro Karlovo náměstí. Attractive, popular Thai restaurant, with hot and spicy meat and fish curries: lunch for 130Kč; dinner for 150–200Kč. Mon–Thurs 11am–11pm, Fri 11am–12.30am, Sat 12.30pm–12.30am, Sun 12.30–11pm.

Modrý zub (Blue Tooth) Jindřišská 5 ☏ 222 212 622, ⓦ modryzub.com; metro Můstek. Inexpensive Thai rice and noodle dishes (130–150Kč) in a place, just off Wenceslas Square, that has a modern wine-bar feel to it. Daily 11am–11pm.

Posezení u Čiriny Navrátilova 6 ☏ 222 231 709; metro Karlovo náměstí. Little family-run place, with only a handful of tables inside, leather benches in pleasant wooden alcoves, and a summer terrace. Classic Slovak home cooking for around 200Kč. Mon–Sat 11am–11pm.

U sádlů (The Lard) Klimentská 2 ☏ 224 813 874, ⓦ www.usadlu.cz; metro Náměstí Republiky. Deliberately over-the-top themed medieval banqueting hall serving inexpensive, hearty food (150–250Kč) and lashings of frothing Budvar. There's another branch at Balbínova 22, Vinohrady; metro Muzeum/náměstí Míru. Daily 11am–11.30pm.

Zahrada v opeře (Opera Garden) Legerova 75 ☏ 224 239 685, ⓦ www.zahradavopere .cz; metro Muzeum. Striking modern interior and beautifully presented food from around the world at democratic prices (main dishes 200–400Kč). The entrance is around the back of the building. Daily 11.30am–1am.

Further afield

Mailsi Lipanská 1, Žižkov ☏ 222 717 783; metro Jiřího z Poděbrad. Prague's only Pakistani restaurant is a friendly, unpretentious place that's great for a comfort curry for around 300Kč, as hot as you can handle. Daily noon–3pm & 6pm–midnight.

Radost FX Café Bělehradská 120 Vinohrady; ⓦ www.radostfx.cz; metro I.P. Pavlova. One of the best veggie menus in town (dishes under 200Kč) and funky music draw a large expat posse, particularly for the Sunday brunch. Daily 11am–midnight.

Pubs and bars

The Prague **pub** scene is diverse, with a mix of expat American-style bars, "Irish" pubs and smarter establishments offering alternatives to the traditional Czech *pivnice*: smoky, male-dominated places, primarily designed for drinking copious quantities of Czech beer. Food, where served, is almost always of the traditional Czech variety – cheap and filling, but ultimately it could shorten your life by a couple of years.

Hradčany

Klášterní pivovar (Monastery brewery) Strahovské nádvoří; tram #22 or #23 from metro Malostranská to Pohořelec stop. Smart new micro-brewery in the Strahovský klášter (Strahov monastery), offering their own excellent dark and light St Norbert beers and Czech pub grub to thirsty tourists. Daily 10am–11pm.

U černého vola (The Black Ox) Loretánské nám. 1; tram #22 or #23 from metro Malostranská to Pohořelec stop. Great traditional Prague pub doing a brisk business providing the popular light beer Velkopopovický kozel in huge quantities to thirsty local workers, plus a few basic pub snacks. Daily 10am–10pm.

Malá Strana

Baráčnická rychta Tržiště 23 (down a narrow passageway leading south off Nerudova); ⓦ www .baracnickarychta.cz; metro Malostranská. A real survivor – a small smoky backstreet *pivnice* squeezed in between the embassies, and still frequented mostly by Czechs. Mon–Sat 11am–11pm, Sun 11am–9pm.

Jo's Bar Malostranské nám. 7; metro Malostranská. A narrow bar that was the original American expat/backpacker hangout. It no longer has quite the same vitality, but it's still a good place to hook up with other travellers. Downstairs is *Jo's Garáž*. Daily 11am–2am.

U kocoura (The Cat) Nerudova 2; metro Malostranská. One of the few famous old pubs left on Nerudova, serving Budvar, plus the obvious Czech stomach-fillers. Daily 11am–11pm.

U malého Glena Karmelitská 23 ⓦ www .malyglen.cz; metro Malostranská. Smart-looking pub/jazz bar that attracts a fair mixture of Czechs and expats thanks to its better-than-average food and live music in the basement. Daily 10am–2am.

Staré Město

Legends Týn (Ungelt) ⓦ www.legends.cz; metro Náměstí Republiky. Heaving, loud, full-blown expat bar in the Týn courtyard, which shows the big TV sports events and has disco theme nights. Daily 11am–1am.

Marquis de Sade Templová 8; metro Náměstí Republiky. Great space: huge high ceiling, big comfy sofas, and a leery, mostly expat crowd. Awful beer and limited snacks, but a good place to start the evening or end it. Daily 4pm–3am.

Molly Malone's U Obecního dvora 4 ⓦ www .mollymalones.cz; metro Staroměstská. The best of Prague's Irish pubs with Irish staff, an open fire, draught Kilkenny and Guinness, and decent Irish-themed food. Mon–Thurs & Sun 11am–1am, Fri & Sat 11am–2am.

U medvídků (The Little Bears) Na Perštýně 7 ⓦ www.umedvidku.cz; metro Národní třída. A Prague beer hall going back to the thirteenth century and still much as it ever was (turn right when you enter, to avoid the new bar to the left). The Budvar comes thick and fast, and the food is pub standard. Mon–Sat 11.30am–11pm, Sun 11.30am–10pm.

U Vejvodů Jilská 4 ⓦ www.restauraceuvejvodu.cz; metro Národní třída. This atmospheric beer hall is now one of Pilsner Urquell's very successful chain of pubs, serving poshed-up pub food. Mon–Sat 10am–4am, Sun 11am–3am.

Nové Město

Billard Centrum V cípu 1 ⓦ www.billardcentrum .cz; metro Můstek. Den of table football, table tennis, bowling, snooker and pool with Černá hora beer to quench your thirst. Daily 11am–2am.

Branický sklípek Vodičkova 26; metro Můstek. Convenient downtown pub decked out like a pine furniture showroom, serving typical Czech food, and jugs of Prague's Braník beer. The rough and ready *Branická formanka* next door opens and closes earlier. Mon–Fri 9am–11pm, Sat & Sun 11am–11pm.

Novoměstský pivovar Vodičkova 20 ⓦ www .npivovar.cz; metro Národní třída. Micro-brewery which serves its own well-tapped misty 11° home brew, plus Czech food, in a series of bright, sprawling modern beer halls. Mon–Fri 10am–11.30pm, Sat 11.30am–11.30pm, Sun noon–10pm.

Pivovarský dům Corner of Lipová/Ječná; metro Karlovo náměstí. Busy micro-brewery dominated by its big shiny copper vats, serving excellent light, mixed and dark unfiltered beer (plus banana, coffee and wheat varieties), and all the standard Czech pub dishes (including *pivný sýr*). Daily 11am–11.30pm.

U Fleků Křemencova 11 ⓦ www.ufleku.cz; metro Karlovo náměstí. Famous medieval *pivnice* where the unique dark 13° beer, Flek, has been exclusively brewed and consumed since 1499. Seats over 500 German tourists at a go, serves short measures (0.4l), slaps an extra charge on for the music and still you have to queue. This is a tourist trap and the only

reason to visit is to sample the beer, which you're best off doing during the day. Daily 9am–11pm.
U Pinkasů Jungmannovo nám. 16; ⓦwww .upinkasu.cz; metro Můstek. Famous as the pub where Pilsner Urquell was first served in Prague in 1843, this place is a blast from the past, with old-style service-with-a-snarl, Pilsner and standard Czech food. Daily 9am–2am.

Further afield

Hospoda na verandách Nádražní 90, Smíchov; metro Anděl. The official Staropramen brewery tap, and *the* place to taste Prague's most popular beer. Daily 11am–11pm.
Letenský zámeček Letenské sady, Holešovice ⓦwww.letenskyzamecek.cz; tram #1 or #25 from metro Vltavská to Letenské náměstí. The beer garden, with its great views down the Vltava, is popular with the locals; the *Ullman* restaurant inside is much more upmarket, and serves upgraded Czech cuisine. Daily 11am–11.30pm.

U houbaře (The Mushroom) Dukelských hrdinů 30, Holešovice; tram #5 from metro Náměstí Republiky to Veletržní. Comfortable pub serving Pilsner Urquell and pub food, perfectly placed directly opposite the Veletržní palác (Museum of Modern Art). Daily 11am–midnight
U vystřeleného oka (The Shot-Out Eye) U božích bojovníků 3, Žižkov; metro Florenc. Big, loud, smoky, heavy-drinking pub just south of Žižkov Hill, off Husitská, with (unusually) good music playing and lashings of Měšťan beer, plus absinthe chasers. Mon–Sat 3.30pm–1am.
Zvonařka (The Bell) Šafaříkova 1, Vinohrady; ⓦwww.zvonarka.cz; tram #6 or #11 from metro I. P. Pavlova to Nuselské schody. The slick, futuristic interior belies the very traditional Czech food and beer on offer, while the terrace has great views over the Nuselské schody and Botič valley. Mon–Sat 11am–2am, Sun 11am–midnight.

Entertainment and the arts

For many Praguers, **entertainment** is confined to an evening's drinking in one of the city's beer-swilling *pivnice*. If you're looking for a bit more action, check the **listings** sections in *Prague Post* (ⓦwww.praguepost.com), or the Czech listings monthly *Culture in Prague/Česká kultura* (ⓦwww.ceskakultura .cz), and keep your eyes peeled for flyers and posters. You can obtain **tickets** from the box office (*pokladna*) of the venue concerned, but you might find it easier to go to one of the city's numerous **ticket agencies** – it will cost more, but might save a lot of hassle. Ticketpro has branches all over the city, with outlets in the Staroměstská radnice (Old Town Hall), Staroměstské náměstí, Staré Město (Mon–Fri 9am–6pm, Sat & Sun 9am–5pm; ⓦwww .ticketpro.cz) and in the Lucerna *pasáž*, Štěpánská 61, Nové Město (daily 9am–1pm & 1.30–5.30pm).

Clubs and live venues

While most Praguers go to bed pretty early, a dedicated minority, including many of the city's expats and tourists, stay up until the wee hours. To service this crowd, Prague has a good selection of late-night pubs and bars (see above) and a handful of half-decent **clubs**. Local techno DJs rule the roost, with the odd international name dropping in for a residency; there are also a few good one-off raves throughout the year (scour the fly posters). Many clubs double as **live music venues**, hosting everything from Czech reggae to thrash; in addition, a surprising array of world music bands find their way to Prague.

Rock, pop and dance music

Major Western **bands** often include Prague in their European tours and, to be sure of a full house, many offer low-price tickets. Czech bands play almost every night in the city's clubs and discos – a selection of the better venues is listed below, though you should always check local listings before setting out.

Abaton Na Košince 8, Libeň ☎602 324 434, ⓦwww.prostorabaton.cz; metro Palmovka. Cavernous factory venue in the suburbs that hosts some of the city's best raves and gigs.

Futurum Zborovská 7, Smíchov ☎257 328 571, ⓦwww.musicbar.cz; metro Anděl. Smíchov's turn-of-the-twentieth-century Národní dům is the unlikely home of this impressive, high-tech club which hosts Czech bands and DJs playing anything from retro nights to house. Daily 8pm–3am.

Mecca U Průhonu 3, Holešovice ☎283 870 522, ⓦwww.mecca.cz; tram #5, #12 or #15 from metro Nádraží Holešovice to U Průhonu. Despite being out in Prague 7, this converted factory is one of the best, and most popular, clubs in the city. Café/restaurant daily 11am–11pm; club Fri & Sat until 6am.

N11 Národní třída 11, Nové Město ☎222 075 705, ⓦwww.n11.cz; metro Národní třída. Funky, medium-sized, central club with several bars, an OK restaurant, a decent sound system and DJs who play a whole range of dance tunes from hip-hop to Latin, plus the occasional live act. Tues–Thurs & Sun 8pm–4am, Fri & Sat 7pm–5am.

Palác Akropolis Kubelíkova 27, Žižkov ☎296 330 911, ⓦwww.palacakropolis.cz; tram #5, #9 or #26 to Lipanská. Two live venue spaces and a whole complex of bars in scruffy Žižkov, this place is the nerve centre of the city's alternative and world music scene and puts on the most eclectic programme of gigs in Prague. Live venue doors open 7pm.

Radost FX Bělehradská 120, Vinohrady ☎224 254 776, ⓦwww.radostfx.cz; metro I.P. Pavlova. Still the slickest (and longest-running) all-round dance club venue in Prague; good veggie café upstairs (see p.130). Daily until 4am.

Roxy Dlouhá 33, Staré Město ☎224 826 296, ⓦwww.roxy.cz; metro Náměstí Republiky. The centrally located *Roxy* is a great little venue: a laid-back rambling old theatre with an interesting programme of events from arty films and exhibitions to exceptional live acts and house DJ nights. Daily from 7pm.

Jazz

Prague has a surprisingly long indigenous jazz tradition, and is home to a handful of good **jazz clubs**. With little money to attract acts from abroad, the artists are almost exclusively Czech and tend to do virtually the entire round of venues each month. The one exception to all this is *AghaRTA*, which attracts a few big names each year. More often than not, it's a good idea to book a table at the clubs listed below – this is particularly true of *AghaRTA* and *Reduta*.

AghaRTA Jazz Centrum Železná 16, Staré Město ☎222 211 275, ⓦwww.agharta.cz; metro Můstek. Probably the best jazz club in Prague, with a good mix of Czechs and foreigners and a consistently good programme of gigs. Daily 7pm–1am.

Blues sklep Liliová 9, Staré Město ☎774 624 677, ⓦwww.bluessklep.cz; metro Staroměstská. Old town cellar club that puts on jazz, flamenco, ragtime and blues. Daily 7pm–2.30am.

Reduta Národní 20, Nové Město ☎224 912 246, ⓦwww.redutajazzclub.cz; metro Národní třída. Prague's best-known jazz club – Bill Clinton played his sax here in front of Havel – obviously attracts a very touristy crowd, but also some decent acts. Gigs daily from 9.30pm; box office open from 3pm.

U malého Glena Karmelitská 23, Malá Strana ☎257 531 717, ⓦwww.malyglen.cz; tram #12 or #22 one stop from metro Malostranská. Tiny downstairs stage worth checking out for its eclectic mix of Latin jazz, be-bop and blues. Live music 9.30pm–1am.

Ungelt Jazz & Blues Club Týn 2, Staré Město ☎224 895 748, ⓦwww.jazzblues.cz; metro Náměstí Republiky. A good cellar venue that pulls in lots of tourists due to its central location, and puts on a decent selection of music, with the emphasis on blues. Daily 7pm–2am.

Gay and lesbian Prague

Prague has a small but well-established **gay and lesbian** scene, with its spiritual heart in leafy Vinohrady and neighbouring Žižkov. Check listings at ⓦgayguide .net/europe/czech/Prague, and once in the city, get hold of the bimonthly gay magazine *Amigo*, which has a shop at Příčná 7, Nové Město (Tues–Sat 11am–7pm; ☎222 233 250, ⓦwww.amigo.cz). You'll also find useful flyers at the places listed below. At many clubs, you'll be given a drinks ticket, which you must keep hold of or be liable to a hefty minimum charge.

Arco Voroněžská 24, Vinohrady ☏ 271 740 734, ⊛ www.arco-guesthouse.cz; tram #4, #22 or #23 from metro Náměstí Míru to Krymská. Gay internet café and guesthouse. Mon–Fri 8am–1am, Sat & Sun 9am–1am.

Babylonia Martinská 6, Staré Město ☏ 224 232 304, ⊛ www.amigo.cz/babylonia; metro Národní třída. Prague's most central gay sauna, with steam baths, pools and massage. Daily 2pm–3am.

Friends Bartolomějská 11, Staré Město ☏ 221 211 920, ⊛ www.friends-prague.cz; metro Národní

třída. Friendly, laid-back mixed gay/lesbian cellar bar in the centre of the old town. Daily 6pm–3am.

The Saints Polská 32, Vinohrady ☏ 222 250 326, ⊛ www.praguesaints.cz; metro Náměstí Míru. Small gay bar run by British expats that attracts an older crowd. A good place to go to find out about the scene. Daily 7pm–4am.

Termix Třebízského 4a, Vinohrady ☏ 222 710 462, ⊛ www.club-termix.cz; metro Jiřího z Poděbrad. Stylish mixed gay/lesbian club, with lots of dancing, as well as chill-out and dark rooms. Daily 10pm–5am.

The arts

Alongside the city's numerous cafés, pubs and clubs, there's a rich **cultural life** in Prague. Music is everywhere, especially in the summer, when the streets, churches, palaces, opera houses, concert halls and even the gardens are filled with the strains of classical music. Prague boasts three opera houses, three excellent orchestras and a couple of festivals that attract top-class international artists. Even if you don't understand Czech, there are theatre performances worth catching – there's a strong tradition of mime, "black light theatre" (visual trickery created by "invisible" actors dressed all in black), and puppetry, and many cinemas show films in their original language, with some even showing Czech films with English subtitles.

By far the biggest annual event is the Pražské jaro (Prague Spring), the country's most prestigious **international music festival**, which traditionally begins on May 12, the anniversary of Smetana's death. The main venues are listed on below, but keep an eye out for concerts in the city's churches and palaces, gardens and courtyards; note that evening performances tend to start fairly early, either at 5 or 7pm.

Main opera houses and concert halls

Národní divadlo (National Theatre) Národní 2, Nové Město ☏ 224 901 448, ⊛ www.narodni -divadlo.cz; metro Národní třída. Prague's grandest nineteenth-century theatre is the living embodiment of the Czech national revival movement, and continues to put on a wide variety of mostly, though by no means exclusively, Czech plays, plus the odd opera and ballet. Worth visiting for the decor alone. Box office daily 10am–6pm.

Obecní dům – Smetanova síň náměstí Republiky 5, Nové Město ☏ 222 002 336, ⊛ www .obecni-dum.cz; metro Náměstí Republiky. This fantastically ornate Art Nouveau concert hall is where the Prague Spring festival usually kicks off, and is also home to the excellent Prague Symphony Orchestra (⊛ www.fok.cz). Box office Mon–Fri 10am–6pm.

Rudolfinum Alšovo nábřeží 12, Staré Město ☏ 224 893 352, ⊛ www.rudolfinum.cz; metro Staroměstská. A truly stunning neo-Renaissance concert hall from the late nineteenth century that's

home base for the Czech Philharmonic (⊛ www .ceskafilharmonie.cz). The Dvořákova síň is the large hall; the Sukova síň is the chamber concert hall. Box office Mon–Fri 10am–6pm, plus 1hr before performance.

Státní opera Praha (Prague State Opera) Wilsonova 4, Nové Město ☏ 224 227 266, ⊛ www .opera.cz; metro Muzeum. A sumptuous nineteenth-century opera house, built by the city's German community, which once attracted star conductors such as Mahler and Zemlinsky. Now it's the number two venue for opera, with a repertoire that tends to focus on Italian pieces. Box office Mon–Fri 10am–5.30pm, Sat & Sun 10am–noon & 1–5.30pm, plus 1hr before performance.

Stavovské divadlo (Estates Theatre) Ovocný trh 1, Staré Město ☏ 224 215 001, ⊛ www.narodni -divadlo.cz; metro Můstek. Prague's oldest opera house, which witnessed the premiere of Mozart's *Don Giovanni*, hosts a mixture of opera, ballet and straight theatre (with simultaneous headphone translation available). Box office daily 10am–6pm, plus 30min before performance.

Theatres

Černé divadlo Jiřího Srnce Reduta, Národní 20, Nové Město ☎ 222 933 487, ⓦ www.redutajazzclub .cz; metro Národní třída. One of the founders of Laterna magika, Jiří Srnec puts on "black light" shows that are a cut above the competition at various venues around Prague. Box office daily 11am–9pm.

Divadlo Archa Na poříčí 26, Nové Město ☎ 221 716 333, ⓦ www.archatheatre.cz; metro Florenc. By far the most exciting, innovative venue in Prague, with two very versatile spaces, plus an art gallery and a café. The programming includes music, dance and theatre, with an emphasis on the avant-garde. English subtitles or translation often available. Box office Mon–Fri 10am–6pm, plus 2hr before performance.

Divadlo Image Pařížská 4, Staré Město ☎ 222 329 191, ⓦ www.imagetheatre.cz; metro Staroměstská. One of the more innovative and entertaining of Prague's ubiquitous "black light theatre" venues. Box office daily 9am–8pm.

Divadlo minor Vodičkova 6, Nové Město ☎ 222 231 351, ⓦ www.minor.cz; metro Karlovov náměstí. The former state puppet theatre puts on children's shows most days, plus adult shows on occasional evenings – sometimes with English subtitles. Box office Mon–Fri 9am–1.30pm & 2.30–8pm, Sat & Sun 11am–8pm.

Divadlo Spejbla a Hurvínka Dejvická 38, Dejvice ☎ 224 316 784, ⓦ www.spejbl-hurvinek.cz; metro Dejvická/Hradčanská. Features the indomitable puppet duo, Spejbl and Hurvínek, created by Josef Skupa earlier this century and still going strong as one of the few puppets-only theatres in the country. Box office Tues, Thurs & Fri 10am–2pm & 3–6pm, Wed 10am–2pm & 3–7pm, Sat & Sun 1–5pm.

Laterna magika (Magic Lantern) Nová scéna, Národní 4, Nové Město ☎ 224 931 482, ⓦ www .laterna.cz; metro Národní třída. The National Theatre's Nová scéna, one of Prague's most modern and versatile stages, is the main base for Laterna magika, founders of multimedia and "black light" theatre way back in 1958. Their slick productions continue effortlessly to pull in crowds of tourists. Box office Mon–Sat 10am–8pm.

Národní divadlo marionet Žatecká 1, Staré Město ☎ 222 324 565, ⓦ www.riseloutek.cz; metro Staroměstská. This company's rather dull marionette version of Mozart's *Don Giovanni* (ⓦ www.mozart.cz) has proved extremely popular, but it also puts on more interesting kids' shows at the weekends. Box office Wed 3.30–6pm plus 1hr before performance.

Ponec Husitská 24a, Žižkov ☎ 224 817 886, ⓦ www.divadloponec.cz; metro Hlavní nádraží or Florenc. Former cinema, now an innovative dance venue and centre for the annual Tanec Praha dance festival in June/July. Box office Mon–Fri 5–8pm plus 1hr before performance.

Švandovo divadlo Štefánikova 57, Staré Město ☎ 234 651 111, ⓦ www.svandovodivadlo.cz; metro Anděl. Pioneering, exciting and experimental, *Švandovo* is a great addition to the Prague theatre scene. Productions are in Czech (many with English subtitles), there's a great bar and often gigs too. Box office Mon–Fri 11am–7pm, Sat & Sun 5–7pm.

Cinemas

Aero Biskupcova 31, Žižkov ☎ 271 771 349, ⓦ www.kinoaero.cz; tram #9, #10, #16 or #19, stop Biskupcova. Crumbling art-house cinema that shows rolling mini-festivals, retrospectives and independent movies.

Evald Národní 28, Nové Město ☎ 221 105 225, ⓦ www.cinemart.cz; metro Národní třída. Prague's most centrally located art-house cinema shows a discerning selection of new releases and classics.

Lucerna Vodičkova 36, Nové Město ☎ 224 216 972, ⓦ www.lucerna.cz; metro Můstek. Without doubt the most ornate commercial cinema in Prague, decked out in Moorish style by Havel's grandfather, in the *pasáž* that the family once owned.

MAT Studio Karlovo nám. 19, Nové Město ☎ 224 915 765, ⓦ www.mat.cz; metro Karlovo náměstí. Tiny café and cinema popular with the film crowd, with an eclectic programme of shorts, documentaries and Czech films with English subtitles. Entrance is on Odborů.

Ponrepo – Bio Konvikt Bartolomějská 11, Staré Město ☎ 224 237 233; metro Národní třída. Black-and-white classics, dug out from the National Film Archives. Membership cards (150kč) can only be bought Mon–Fri 3–6pm, and you need to bring a photo.

Shopping, sports and activities

Czechs produce quality CDs, books and, of course, smoked meats and alcohol at reasonable prices; you can also find the odd bargain in goods like glass, ceramics and wooden toys. The backstreets of Malá Strana and Staré Město are good for interesting little **shops**, or follow Praguers to Nové Město and the covered shopping malls in and around Wenceslas Square. The two **sports** that draw in the biggest crowds are soccer and ice hockey; getting a ticket is easy (and cheap) enough on the day – only really big matches sell out.

Shopping

The superb **English-language bookstore**, Anagram, Týn 4, Nové Město (Mon–Sat 10am–8pm, Sun 10am–7pm; ⓦwww.anagram.cz; metro Náměstí Republiky), has lots of books on Czech politics and culture, plus a small secondhand section. The Globe, Pštrossova 6 (daily 10am–midnight; ⓦwww .globebookstore.cz; metro Národní třída/Karlovo náměstí), is an expat bookstore par excellence – both a social centre and superbly well-stocked store, with an adjacent café and friendly staff. You can get most foreign **newspapers and magazines** at the kiosks at the bottom of Wenceslas Square, outside metro Můstek.

Prague has two main **department stores** in Nové Město; Kotva, náměstí Republiky 8; and Tesco, Národní 26. If it's food, flowers or wooden toys that take your fancy, visit Havelská, Staré Město (Mon–Fri 8am–6pm, Sat & Sun 9am–6pm; metro Můstek), the only open-air fruit and veg **market** in central Prague.

For rock, folk, jazz and classical **music**, head to Bontonland, Palác Koruna, Václavské náměstí 1 (Mon–Fri 9am–7pm, Sat 9am–1pm; ⓦwww.bontonland .cz; metro Můstek), Prague's biggest music store, in the *pasáž* at the bottom of Wenceslas Square.

Sports and activities

Prague's (and the Czech Republic's) most successful **football** (soccer) club is Sparta Praha (ⓦwww.sparta.cz), who play in claret and white (in honour of Arsenal's original strip) at the 18,500 all-seater Letná stadium (5min walk from metro Hradčanská, or take tram #1, #8, #15, #25 or #26); international matches are also regularly played there. The city's second most successful team, Slavia Praha (ⓦwww.slavia.cz), have won the title just twice since the last war (1996 and 2008) and play at Eden stadium on Vladivostocká in Vršovice (tram #22 or #23 from metro Náměstí Míru or tram #6, #7 or #19, stop Kubánské náměstí). Sparta Praha (ⓦwww.hcsparta.cz) is Prague's top **ice hockey** team; their *zimní stadión* (winter stadium) is at Za elektrárnou (metro Nádraží Holešovice), next door to the Výstaviště exhibition grounds in Holešovice. Prague's only other first-division team are Slavia Praha (ⓦwww .hc-slavia.cz), who won the league for the first time ever in 2003 and play at the *zimní stadión* at Eden (see above for travel details).

For a refreshing **swim**, head for Divoká Šárka, Vokovice (June–Aug daily 9am–7pm; tram #20 or #26 from metro Dejvická to the Divoká Šárka terminus). Idyllically located in a craggy valley to the northwest of Prague, with two small outdoor pools filled with cold, fresh and clean spring water, it provides plenty of shade, and food and drink are available. The most famous of Prague's outdoor pools is Plavecký stadion Podolí, Podolská 74 (daily 6am–9.45pm; ☎241 433 952, ⓦwww.pspodoli.cz; Podolí, tram #3, #16, #17 or #21, stop Kublov), set against a sheltered craggy backdrop, with a children's wading pool and water slide, grass and draught beer.

Moving on from Prague

If you're catching a **train out of Prague**, don't leave buying your ticket until the last minute, as the queues can be long and slow, and make sure you check from which station your train is departing. You can buy domestic tickets (*vnitrostátní jízdenky*) at the "basic check-in" (*základní odbavení*) windows, whereas international train tickets (*mezinárodní jízdenky*) *must be bought at the* "complex check-in" (*komplexní odbavení*) *windows* at either Praha hlavní nádraží or Praha-Holešovice. For **buses out of Prague**, you may need to head out to one of the more obscure bus terminals, all of which are easy enough to reach by metro. To find out which one you want, ask at any of the PIS offices in town (see p.61) or check the comprehensive (and extremely complicated) timetables at Praha-Florenc: *stání* is the bus stand; *odjezd* is the departure time.

Listings

Dentist Emergency dentist at Palackého 5, Nové Město (metro Můstek).

Embassies and consulates Australia, Klimentská 10, Nové Město ☎296 578 350; metro Náměstí Republiky. Britain, Thunovská 14, Malá Strana ☎257 402 111, @www.britain.cz; metro Malostranská. Canada, Muchova 6 ☎272 101 890, @www.canada .cz; metro Hradčanská. Ireland, Tržiště 13, Malá Strana ☎257 530 061; metro Malostranská. New Zealand, Dykova 19 ☎222 514 672; metro Jiřího z Poděbrad. Poland, Valdštejnská 8, Malá Strana ☎257 530 388, @www.ambpol.cz; metro Malostranská. Slovakia, Pod hradbami 1, Dejvice ☎233 113 051, @www.slovakemb.cz; metro Dejvická. South Africa, Ruská 65, Vršovice ☎267 311 114; metro Flora. US, Tržiště 15, Malá Strana ☎257 530 663, @www .usembassy.cz; metro Malostranská.

Hospitals The main hospital is Nemocnice Na Homolce, Roentgenova 2, Motol (bus #167 from metro Anděl), which runs a 24hr emergency service and has English-speaking doctors. If it's an emergency, dial ☎155 for an ambulance and you'll be taken to the nearest hospital.

Left luggage Prague's main bus and train stations have lockers and/or a 24hr left-luggage office (*úschovna zavazadel*), with instructions in English.

Lost property The main train stations have lost property offices – look for the sign *ztráty a nálezy* – and there's a central municipal office at Karoliny Světlé 5, Staré Město (Mon–Fri only). If you've lost your passport, get in touch with your embassy (see opposite).

Pharmacies 24hr chemist at Palackého 5, Nové Město (metro Můstek).

Police If you wish to extend your visa or your stay, you need to go to the Cizinecká policie (Foreigners' Police), Olšanská 2, Žižkov. In an emergency dial ☎158.

Post office 24hr office/poste restante at Jindřišská 14, Nové Město.

Central Bohemia

Few capital cities can boast such extensive unspoilt tracts of wooded country-side so near at hand as Prague. Once you leave the half-built high-rise estates of the outer suburbs behind, the softly rolling hills and somnolent villages of central **Bohemia** (Čechy) take over.

To the north, several chateaux grace the banks of the Vltava, including that of the wine-producing town of **Mělník**, on the Labe (Elbe) plain. Beyond Mělník lie the wooded gorges of the **Kokořínsko** region, too far for a day-trip unless you've your own transport, but perfect for a weekend in the country. One of the most obvious day-trip destinations is to the east of Prague: **Kutná Hora**, a medieval silver-mining town with one of the most beautiful Gothic cathedrals in the country and a macabre gallery of bones in the suburb of **Sedlec**.

Further south, there are several minor sights along the winding, picturesque **Sázava valley**. Probably the most impressive chateau near Prague is **Konopiště**, the ill-fated Archduke Franz Ferdinand's Boehmian seat, set in exceptionally beautiful and expansive grounds. Southwest of Prague, a similar mix of woods and rolling hills surrounds the popular castle of **Karlštejn**, a gem of Gothic architecture, dramatically situated above the River Berounka. There are numerous possibilities for walking in the region around Karlštejn and, further upstream, in the forests of **Křivoklátsko**. Immediately west of Prague, there are two places of pilgrimage: **Lány** is the resting place of the founder of the modern Czechoslovak state and summer residence of the president; and **Lidice**, razed to the ground by the SS, recalls the horror of Nazi occupation.

Transport throughout Bohemia is fairly straightforward, thanks to a comprehensive network of suburban railway lines and regional bus services, though connections can be less than smooth and journeys slow. However, if you're planning to see a few places outside Prague, or one of the destinations more difficult to reach, it might be worth hiring a car (see p.35).

North along the Vltava

One of the quickest and most rewarding trips out of the capital is to follow the Vltava as it twists northwards across the plain towards the River Labe at Mělník. This is the beginning of the so-called **zahrada Čech** (Garden of Bohemia), a flat and fertile region whose cherry blossoms are always the first to herald the Bohemian spring and whose roads in summer are lined with stalls overflowing with fruit and vegetables. But the real reason to venture into this relatively flat landscape is to visit the **chateaux** that lie along the banks of the river, all easily reached by train from Prague's Masarykovo nádraží.

Nelahozeves and around

NELAHOZEVES is entirely dominated by its monumentally large **zámek** (Tues–Sun 9am–noon & 1–5pm; 45–350Kč; @ www.zamek-nelahozeves.cz), constructed in the 1550s by Italian builders for one of the lackeys of the Habsburg Ferdinand I, and totally smothered in sgraffito. Unfortunately, the original owner backed the wrong side in the Thirty Years' War, and in 1623 the chateau was snapped up by the incredibly wealthy Polyxena Lobkowicz. The best of the family heirlooms now reside in Prague (see p.76), but there's enough of interest here to warrant signing up for one of the two available **guided tours**. The highlights of the hour-long *trasa I* (85Kč) are the chateau's two masterpieces, Rubens' *Hygeia and the Serpent* and Veronese's *David with the Head of Goliath*; the thirty-minute *trasa II* (45Kč), meanwhile, gets you into the Rytířský sál (Knights' Hall), the best-preserved Renaissance chamber in the chateau. You have to pay around 200Kč extra to have an English-speaking guide.

Fans of **Antonín Dvořák** (1841–1904), who was born and bred here, under the shadow of the chateau, should seek out his family home, or **rodný dům** (1st & 3rd weeks of the month Wed–Sun 9.30am–noon & 1–5pm; 2nd & 4th weeks of the month Wed–Fri 9.30am–noon & 1–5pm; 30Kč), at the house (no. 12) next door to the post office. Originally apprenticed to a butcher, on the recommendation of his schoolmaster Dvořák was instead sent to the Prague Organ School and went on to become director of the Prague conservatoire and by far the country's most famous composer. If there's someone around at the house, you can have a quick look at the great man's rocking chair and various other personal effects.

Practicalities

To reach the chateau by train, get out at Nelahozeves zámek, the first station after Kralupy nad Vltavou (40–50min). There are a couple of pubs in town, but the nicest place to **eat** is the *Zámecká restaurace* in the courtyard of Nelahozeves zámek, where you can quaff Lobkowicz wine or beer with your meal. Look out, too, for the Sunday evening **Dvořák concerts** performed in the zámek (Ⓦ www.bdiscovery.org), from April to September.

Veltrusy

On the other side of the Vltava lies the village of **VELTRUSY**, which has its own **zámek** (April–Oct Tues–Sun 8.30am–5pm; Ⓦ www.zamek-veltrusy.cz) set in beautiful grounds to the north. The classic Baroque symmetry of the chateau is more hospitable than the one at Nelahozeves, its green shutters and four hennaed wings pivoting round a bulbous, domed building that recalls earlier country houses in France or Italy. It was built in the early eighteenth century as a plaything for the upwardly mobile Chotek family, its 290 acres of surrounding woodland perfect for a little light hunting. It was also the unlikely venue for the world's first trade fair, which took place in 1754 under the title "The Veltrusy Large Trade Fair of Products of the Czech Kingdom", and drew a distinguished audience including Empress Maria Theresa. The chateau puts on a changing roster of temporary exhibitions, and you can also take a tour round the greenhouses and gardens of the **zámecký park**, which is liberally dotted with fallow deer, follies, peacocks and woodpeckers.

To get to Veltrusy by **train**, get off at the station after Nelahozeves zámek, called simply Nelahozeves. From here it's a 1.5km walk to the zámek across the busy road bridge, or a slightly longer walk across the smaller bridge further south. There are also regular **buses** to Veltrusy from Prague's Florenc bus station.

Mělník

Occupying a spectacular, commanding site at the confluence of the Vltava and Labe rivers, **MĚLNÍK** (Ⓦ www.melnik.info), 33km north of Prague, lies at the heart of Bohemia's tiny wine-growing region. The town's history goes back to

---

Řip

Czech legend holds that the founding father of the nation, called Praotec Čech ("Forefather Czech"), led a group of his Slavic followers to the top of **Řip** (461m), some 20km north of Nelahozeves, sometime around the sixth century AD, and proclaimed all the land around as Čechy. The name has certainly stuck – Čechy translates as "the Czech Lands" or Bohemia – and the legend itself renders the hill a fairly important point of pilgrimage. Řip is an upside-down bowl of a hill that forms an intriguing lump in this otherwise monotonous landscape, and is quite a popular summertime hike. At the top, the twelfth-century Romanesque rotunda of **sv Jiří a Vojtěch** (April & Oct Wed–Sun 9am–4pm; May–Sept Tues–Sun 9am–6pm; 20Kč) commemorates the legend. The ascent is not difficult, and judging from the splendid views of flat fields spreading across the horizon, it's not hard to recognize the peaceful agrarian roots of the Czech nation. Getting to Řip is easiest from Ctiněves train station (change at Vraňany), 2km east of the hill, although there are more (and faster) trains to Roudnice, 5km north along the red-marked path.

the ninth century, when it was handed over to the Přemyslids as part of Ludmila's dowry on her marriage to Prince Bořivoj (see p.386). Ludmila was born here and it became the residence of the dowager queens of Bohemia until the Habsburgs took over the Czech Lands. Ludmila is also credited with introducing vines to the area, but viticulture only became the town's economic mainstay after Charles IV, aching for a little of the French wine of his youth, introduced grapes from Burgundy (over which he also ruled).

The old town

Mělník's greatest monument is its Renaissance **zámek** (daily 10am–5pm; 80Kč; @www.lobkowicz-melnik.cz), perched high above the flat plains. The present building, its courtyard covered in familiar sgraffito patterns, is now back in the hands of its last aristocratic owners, the Lobkowicz family, who have restored the chateau's magnificently proportioned rooms, which also provide great views out over the plain. Visits are by guided tour only, and allow you to see a handful of rooms filled with period furniture, old maps and family memorabilia. You can also visit the **wine cellars** (25Kč) and sample the plonk (70–350Kč).

Below the chateau, vines cling to the south-facing terraces, as the land plunges into the river below. From beneath the great tower of Mělník's onion-domed church of **sv Petr and Pavel**, next door to the chateau, there's an even better view of the rivers' confluence (to the left) and the subsidiary canal (straight ahead), once so congested with vessels that traffic lights had to be introduced to avoid accidents. The church itself contains a compellingly macabre **ossuary** or *kostnice* (Tues–Fri 9.30am–12.30pm & 1.15–4pm, Sat & Sun from 10am; 30Kč), filled with more than 10,000 bones of medieval plague victims, fashioned into weird and wonderful skeletal shapes by students in the early part of the nineteenth century.

The rest of the old town is pleasant enough for a casual stroll. One half of the main square, **náměstí Míru**, is lined with Baroque arcades typical of the region, and there's an old medieval gateway nearby, the **Pražská brána**, which has been converted into an art gallery. If you've time to kill, head for the unusual collection of old Czech prams in the **Regionalní muzeum** (Tues–Sun 9am–noon & 1–5pm; 30Kč; @www.muzeum-melnik.cz), at no. 54 on the main square.

Practicalities

The main line from Prague veers northwest beyond Nelahozeves, so it's easiest to take a fast **train** from Prague's Hlavní nádraží to Všetaty, and change, which gets you to Mělník in around an hour. A regular **bus** also leaves Prague's Nádraží Holešovice and Florenc (50min). To reach the older part of town from the **bus station**, simply head up Krombholcova in the direction of the big church tower; the **train station** is a little further from the old town, a couple of blocks northeast of the bus station, down Jiřího z Poděbrad. At present PPS boats (@www.paroplavba.cz) only make the trip from Prague to Mělník twice over the course of the summer, but it's worth enquiring about more frequent passenger services.

The **tourist office** (May–Sept daily 9am–5pm; Oct–April Mon–Fri 9am–5pm; ☎315 627 503), on náměstí Míru, can help with such information and with **accommodation**. In the shadow of the chateau to the south you'll find the relatively plush *Hotel Jaro*, 17 listopadu 174 (☎315 626 852, @www .hoteljaro.cz; ❸). The nearest **campsite** (closed Christmas & New Year) is around 750m north of the old town, on Klášterní (a continuation of Fügnerova).

For **food and drink**, the *Zámecká restaurace* (closed Mon) is as good (and cheap) a place as any to sample the local wine (and enjoy the view): the Ludmila rosé is the most sought after Mělník wine, though the vineyards produce red and white, too. Equally good views can be had from the *Stará škola* restaurant, behind the church; otherwise, you could try *Na hradbách*, on náměstí Míru, which serves up big portions of rabbit and game, with local wines, in a cosy brick and wood-panelled interior and a little courtyard.

Kokořínsko

Northeast of Mělník, you leave the low plains of the Labe for a plateau region known as **Kokořínsko**, a hidden pocket of wooded hills which takes its name from the Gothic castle rising through the treetops at its centre. The sandstone plateau has weathered over the millennia to form sunken valleys and bizarre rocky outcrops, providing great scope for some gentle hiking. With picturesque valleys, such as the Kokořínský důl, dotted with well-preserved, half-timbered villages and riddled with marked paths, the area is popular with Czechs and Germans alike.

At the centre of the region is the village of **KOKOŘÍN** (⊛www.kokorin .cz), whose dramatic setting and spectacular fourteenth-century **hrad** (April & Oct Sat & Sun 9am–4pm; May & Sept Tues–Sun 9am–4pm; June–Aug Tues–Sun 9am–5pm; 70Kč; ⊛www.hrad-kokorin.cz) greatly inspired the Czech nineteenth-century Romantics. The castle is a perfect hideaway, ideal for the robbers who used it as a base after it fell into disrepair in the sixteenth century. Not until the end of the nineteenth century did it get a new lease of life, from a jumped-up local landowner, Václav Špaček, who bought himself a title and refurbished the place as a family memorial. There's precious little inside and no incentive to endure the guided tour (*okruh I*), as you can explore the ramparts and enjoy the view from the tallest tower on your own (*okruh II – věž*; 20Kč).

If you've got your own car, Kokořínsko makes a pleasant day-trip from Prague. On public **transport**, take a bus or train to Mělník and change there, or catch the local train from Mělník to Mšeno, from where it's a three-kilometre walk west to Kokořín on the green-marked path. Finding **accommodation** shouldn't be a problem, with plenty of private rooms available in Kokořín and Kanina 2km further east. There are also several lovely pensions: try *Milča* (☎603 461 723, ⓔmilca@kokorin.cz; ➌), in the southern part of Kokořínský důl, its rooms decked out with antique wooden furniture, or *Penzion v údolí* (☎605 775 612, ⓔpenzion.v.udoli@seznam.cz; ➌), a farmhouse near Vojtěchov, 5km north of the hrad, with three modern, wood-panelled attic rooms. There's also a simple **campsite** (March–Oct; ⊛www.taboriste-kokorin.websnadno.cz) in the woods near the hrad, about 1km north up the main valley.

East of Prague: the Polabí

The scenery **east of Prague** is as flat as it is around Mělník, a rich blanket of fields spreading over the Labe (Elbe) plain – known as the **Polabí** – as far as the eye can see. The Labe has a lovely track/cycle path running along it, linking several minor sights, such as the open-air folk museum at **Přerov nad Labem**, and a few modest towns, the most impressive of which is **Kolín**. Although not on the River Labe, **Mladá Boleslav** attracts a fair few visitors thanks to its Škoda car museum.

Mladá Boleslav

MLADÁ BOLESLAV (Jungblunzau), 50km or so northeast of Prague, is where Václav Laurin and Václav Klement set up a bicycle factory in the mid-nineteenth century. They went on to produce the country's first car in 1905, and in the 1920s merged with the Škoda industrial empire, which has its main manufacturing base in Plzeň (see p.205). The word škoda actually means "shame" or "pity" in Czech – and might have been avoided had it not been the name of the founding father of the Czech car industry, Emil Škoda. In actual fact, Škoda was, for many decades, a great source of national pride – that is, until it was bought for a song by Volkswagen in the 1990s. Today, around half the population of the town works at the car factory.

The main reason for coming here is to visit the **Škoda Auto Muzeum** (daily 9am–5pm; 50Kč; Ⓦwww.skoda-auto.cz), which exhibits more than 25 old Škodas and Laurin & Klements in its showroom. The exhibition starts off, as the factory itself did, with an L & K bicycle and a couple of motorbikes. There are also several vintage vehicles and a 1917 fire engine, but the vast majority of the cars date from the 1920s and 1930s – big, mostly black, gangster-style motors. The museum is in the modern Škoda building at třída Václava Klementa 294, 1km northeast of the town centre near the edge of the massive car plant, and very badly signposted. Diagonally opposite the museum, and handy for orientation, is a park with a palatial neo-Baroque Gymnasium at the far end. Close by, there's a wonderfully provincial Art Nouveau theatre from 1912, brightly painted in white, gold and blue.

The **staré město** lies to the east of the River Jizera, in a tight bend of one of its tributaries, the Klenice. It has only a little of interest: its sgraffitoed **stará radnice** has a *vyhlídková věž* or lookout tower (May–Sept Tues–Fri 1–5pm, Sat & Sun 10–11.30am & 12.30–5pm; 10Kč), and the Gothic **hrad**, tucked into the southernmost part of town, used as a barracks by the Habsburgs, and now home to the recently revamped local museum, **Muzeum Mladoboleslavska** (May–Oct Tues–Sun 9am–noon & 1–5pm; Nov–April closes 4pm; 30Kč; Ⓦwww.muzeum-mb.cz), which has a particularly fine collection of twentieth-century marionettes.

Practicalities

Trains from Prague take just over an hour to reach Mladá Boleslav hlavní nádraží, 1km or so southwest of the stare město; on arrival, you can change to a local train which will take you to Mladá Boleslav město train station, just round the corner from the Škoda Auto Muzeum. **Accommodation** is pricey; the *Zlatý kohout* (Ⓣ326 721 937, Ⓦwww.zlatykohout.cz; Ⓢ) opposite the radnice, is an ancient building with plenty of character. If you're just looking for somewhere to **eat**, head for the *Rybářská* fish restaurant, next to *Hotel U hradu*, beside the castle entrance.

Along the Labe

Back in the Polabí proper, one of the most popular destinations is the **open-air museum** or **skansen** (May–Oct Tues–Sun 9am–5pm; Dec Fri–Sun 10am–4pm; 50Kč; Ⓦwww.polabskemuzeum.cz) of folk architecture at the village of **PŘEROV NAD LABEM**. Founded in 1895, the name (*skanzen* in Czech) comes from the first such museum founded in a Stockholm suburb in 1891. The Communists were keen on *skanzens*, as collectivization and urbanization continued to wipe out traditional rural communities, along with their distinctive folk culture and wooden architecture. The various half-timbered and stone buildings in the *skanzen* were brought here plank by plank from nearby villages, some from Přerov itself. Particularly evocative is the reconstructed eighteenth-century village school, with a portrait of the Austrian emperor taking pride of place amid the Catholic icons, and a delicate paper theatre that was used in drama lessons. Close by, on the other side of the village's small sgraffitoed zámek, is a **Muzeum moto & velo** (April–Oct Tues–Sun 9am–noon & 1–5pm), with over fifty bicycles including an 1885 boneshaker from Coventry and the first bike ever made by Laurin & Klement.

On the other side of the River Labe, 6km or so upstream, is the village of **OSTRÁ**, where Dr Stuart's Botanicus (Ⓦ www.botanicus.cz), one of the Czech Republic's most successful cosmetics businesses, has established a **historické centrum**, a kind of late-medieval settlement complete with timber-framed houses and extensive organic herb and vegetable gardens. You can wander round the complex at any time (Tues–Sun: May, June & Sept 10am–4pm; July & Aug 10am–5pm; 90Kč), convert your crowns into medieval *Groše*, and then have a bit to eat and drink or try your hand at rope-making or blacksmithery. It's best, though, to time your visit to coincide with one of the centre's many special events (195Kč – half price if you turn up in medieval costume). Costumed festivities range from Roman Saturnalia to a tea festival, accompanied by jesters, fencers and performers.

Another 10km upstream is the town of **NYMBURK**, where the writer **Bohumil Hrabal** (1914–97) spent his childhood. His stepfather worked in the local brewery, which now dutifully names its beers after his stories. There's a small exhibition on Hrabal at the **Polabské muzeum** on Tyršova (Tues–Sun 9am–4pm; 15Kč), with lots of family photos, his writing desk and a twenty-minute video (in Czech). You can also visit the Hrabals' *chata* in Kersko, on the opposite bank of the Labe from Ostrá – pick up a map from the **tourist office** (daily 9am–6pm; Ⓦ www.mesto-nymburk.cz) in the diminutive, Renaissance fomer radnice on the main square. Nymburk itself farily undistinguished, but it still retains its double moat around the staré město and an impressive swathe of restored medieval **fortifications** at the eastern edge of town.

Practicalities

The easiest way to travel along the Labe is by **bicycle**, which you can rent from the **train station** at Lysá nad Labem, which is about 6km north Přerov. Ostrá has its own train stop, just 1km from the village, and there's a popular lakeside **campsite**, *U vody* (mid-April to mid-Sept), near the river. Nymburk's train station is four blocks north of the old town.

The best place to **stay** is the *Hotel Ostrov* (☎325 514 602, Ⓦ www.hotelostrov .cz; ❺), which has lots of amenities (including billiards, skittles and sauna), a short walk from the centre of town in the wooded park on the south side bank of the Labe. Further afield, one of area's finest hotels, the seveneteenth-century *Chateau Mčely* (☎325 600 000, Ⓦ www.chateaumcely.com; ❾), lies 12km or so north of Nymburk; beautifully decorated double rooms start at a pricey 5500Kč, but the place really lives up to its billing as a luxurious forest retreat. **Eating** options are widest in Nymburk, where you've got the popular *Pizzeria Castello* on the main square, náměstí Přemyslovců, and the more formal *L'Escargot*, in the old post office on Tyršova (closed Sun eve; Ⓦ www.ustareposty .cz), which offers beautifully presented and imaginative dishes.

Poděbrady

Continuing along the Labe another 7km brings you to **PODĚBRADY**, birth-place of Jiří of Poděbrady, the only Hussite (and last Czech) king of Bohemia (see p.389). The town's riverside **zámek** (May–Oct Tues–Sun 9am–5pm; 10Kč;

www.polabskemuzeum.cz), where Jiří was born, houses a small exhibition on the man himself, the town's theatre and cinema, and the **pension** Na zámku (☎325 611 266, ⓦwww.nazamku.info; ❹), with tastefully converted en-suite rooms. Since the 1920s, Poděbrady has been better known as a spa town, with a large park running north–south from the train station more or less to the zámek. Close to the impressive floral clock is the Lázeňská italská kavárna, a daytime **café** that's a 1970s period piece.

Kolín

In addition to its railway sidings and industrial plants, **KOLÍN** (ⓦwww.kolin.cz) – 15km southeast of Poděbrady up the Labe – has actually managed to preserve its central medieval core. One of numerous towns in Bohemia founded by German colonists in the thirteenth century, its streets are laid out in chessboard fashion. The central, cobbled **Karlovo náměstí** is a picture-perfect main square, with an imposing Renaissance **radnice** covered in sgraffito and decorated with four rose-coloured panels from the nineteenth century, and four unusual Baroque gables on the west side.

Kolín's most ancient monument is tucked away in the southeast corner of the old town. On raised ground at the end of Karlova, on a rather cramped site, stands the Gothic church of **sv Bartoloměj** (April–June & Oct Sat 10am–4pm, Sun 1–4pm; July–Sept Mon–Sat 10am–4pm, Sun 1–4pm; 30Kč; ⓦwww.bartolomej-kolin.cz), begun in 1261. The church's fairly gloomy nave is suffused with an unusually intense blue light from the modern stained-glass windows, which disturbs the otherwise resolutely medieval ambience. But it's the choir, rebuilt and extended in the fourteenth century by Peter Parler, which provides the highlight, taking up almost half the church with its seven chapels, intricate tracery and spectacular ribbed vaulting. On the weekend, you can climb the church's belfry or **zvonice** (40Kč) for a view over the staré město.

Like many towns in Bohemia and Moravia, Kolín once had a significant **Jewish community**, which was all but wiped out in the Holocaust. The ghetto was situated in the southwest corner of the old town, in what is now Na Hradbach and Karoliny Světlé, and after descending into dereliction over the course of six decades, is now largely cleaned up. There's a plaque commemorating the 2200 Jews deported in June 1942 at Na Hradbach 157; inside is the **tourist office** (May–Oct Mon 9am–noon & 1–5pm, Tues–Fri 9am–5pm, Sat 10am–3pm; Nov–April Mon–Fri 9am–5pm; ☎321 712 021, ⓦwww.mukolin.cz), from where you can take guided tours of the renovated seventeenth-century **synagogue** (Tues–Fri 9.15am & 1.30pm, Sat & Sun 9am & 12.30pm; 40Kč), hidden in the rear courtyard. Though much that was damaged or has disappeared in the intervening years, the bright, stuccoed interior still contains portions of Hebrew writings lovingly restored on the walls, amid flourishing floral designs. This mini-complex once contained a Jewish school and residence for the rabbis, though these have long since been turned into offices. The synagogue is no longer active, but because of the building's fine acoustics, concerts are held here on occasion; ask at the tourist office. A few streets away on Sluneční, outside the former city walls, is an overgrown **Jewish cemetery** – a faint image of the famous one in Prague.

Practicalities

Kolín is an important railway junction and its **train station** is ten-minutes' walk east of the old town. **Hotels** include the comfortable, modern Hotel Theresia, Na Petříně (☎321 711 117, ⓦwww.hoteltheresia.cz; ❺), on a busy road west of the old town, and two excellent, smaller places in the old town: Pension pod věží, Parléřova 40 (☎246 030 246, ⓦpod-vezi.hotel.cz; ❸), or

U rabína, near the synagogue on Karoliny Světlé (℡&℻ 321 724 463; ❸). In addition to the hotel **restaurants**, there's *Café Monet*, a really nice place in the northeast corner of the square, or *Oliver*, a pizza place opposite. Kolín is closely associated with **František Kmoch** (1848–1912), king of Bohemian oompah music, and the each June town hosts an international brass band festival, **Kmochův Kolín** (ⓦwww.kmochuvkolin.cz), with a wide range of music from Kmoch to Dvořák and a huge parade of bands from all over the country.

Kutná Hora and around

For 250 years or so, **KUTNÁ HORA** (Kuttenberg) was one of the most important towns in Bohemia, second only to Prague, thanks to the silver deposits in the area. German miners were invited to work the seams, and around 1300 Václav II founded the royal mint here, importing Italian craftsmen to run it. At the end of the fourteenth century its population was equal to London's, its shantytown suburbs straggling across what are now green fields and its ambitious building projects rivalling those of the capital itself. However, when the price of silver collapsed during the sixteenth century and the mines began to dry up, Kutná Hora's wealth and importance came to an abrupt end – when the Swedes marched on the town during the Thirty Years' War, they had to be bought off with beer rather than silver.

Today, Kutná Hora is a provincial town with a population of just over 20,000, but its monuments, the superb Gothic cathedral, and the remarkable monastery

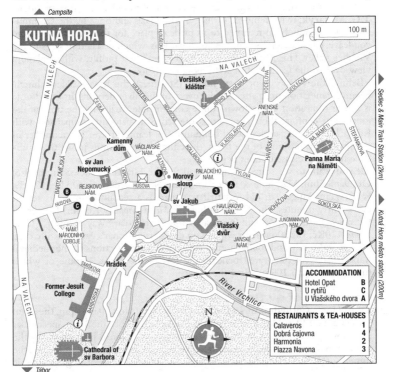

and ossuary in the suburb of **Sedlec**, make it one of the most enjoyable of all possible day-trips from Prague. In addition to the new influx of tourists, Kutná Hora has also benefited from a large injection of cash from the American tobacco giant Phillip Morris, whose factory is the town's chief employer.

The Town

The small, unassuming houses that line the town's medieval lanes and main square, **Palackého náměstí**, give little idea of its former glories. A narrow alleyway on the south side of the square, however, leads to the leafy Havlíčkovo náměstí, on which lies the **Vlašský dvůr** (Italian Court), originally conceived as a palace by Václav II, and for three centuries the town's bottomless purse. It was here that Florentine minters produced the Prager Groschen (*pražské groše*), a silver coin widely used throughout central Europe until the nineteenth century. The building itself has been mucked about with over the years, most recently – and most brutally – by nineteenth-century restorers, who left only the fourteenth-century oriel window (capped by an unlikely looking wooden onion dome) and the miner's fountain unmolested. The original minters' workshops have been bricked in, but the outlines of their little doors and windows are still visible in the courtyard. On the thirty-minute **guided tour** (daily: March & Oct 10am–5pm; April–Sept 9am–6pm; Nov–Feb 10am–4pm; 80Kč) – available in English – you get to see some silver Groschen, learn about the minters' hard life and admire the medieval royal chapel, which shelters a superb full-relief fifteenth-century altarpiece depicting the Death of Mary, and which was spectacularly redecorated in 1904 with Art Nouveau murals.

Outside the court is a statue of the country's founder and first president, **T.G. Masaryk**; twice removed – once by the Nazis and once by the Communists – it has now been returned to its pride of place for the third time. Before you leave, take a quick look at the court gardens, which descend in steps to the Vrchlice valley. This is undoubtedly Kutná Hora's best profile, with a splendid view over to the Cathedral of sv Barbora (see below).

Behind the Vlašský dvůr is **sv Jakub** (St James), the town's oldest church, begun a generation or so after the discovery of the silver deposits. Its grand scale is a clear indication of the town's quite considerable wealth by the time of the fourteenth century, though in terms of artistry it pales in comparison with Kutná Hora's other ecclesiastical buildings. The leaning tower is a reminder of the precarious position of the town, the church's foundations prone to subsidence from the disused mines below.

If you want to see some of these, head for the **Hrádek** (Tues–Sun: April & Oct 9am–5pm; May, June & Sept 9am–6pm; Nov 10am–6pm; ☏327 512 159, Ⓦwww.cms-kh.cz), an old fort that was used as a second mint. Tours set off every thirty minutes. The "Town of Silver" (*Město stříbra*; 60Kč; 1hr) focuses on the silver museum; more fun (book ahead) is the popular "Way of Silver" (*Cesta stříbra*; 110Kč; 1hr 30min), for which you don period miner's garb of white coat, helmet and torch, and follow a guide through narrow sections of the medieval mines that were discovered beneath the fort in the 1960s – some of which tunnel more than 100m below the surface.

Cathedral of sv Barbora

Kutná Hora's **Cathedral of sv Barbora** (May–Sept Mon 10am–4pm, Tues–Sun 9am–5.30pm; Oct–March 10am–4pm; 50Kč) is arguably the most spectacular and moving ecclesiastical building in central Europe. Not to be outdone by the great monastery at Sedlec (see opposite) or the St Vitus Cathedral in Prague, the miners of Kutná Hora began financing the construction of a great Gothic cathedral of their own, dedicated to St Barbara, the patron saint of miners and gunners. The foundations were probably laid by Parler in the 1380s, but work was interrupted by the Hussite wars, and the church remained unfinished until the late nineteenth century, despite being worked on in the intervening centuries by numerous architects, including Master Hanuš, Matouš Rejsek and Benedikt Ried.

The approach road to the cathedral, **Barborská**, is lined with a parade of gesticulating Baroque saints and cherubs that rival the sculptures on the Charles Bridge; and on the right-hand side is the palatial seventeenth-century former **Jesuit College**. The cathedral itself bristles with pinnacles, finials and flying buttresses that support its most striking feature, a **roof** of three tent-like towers added in the sixteenth century, culminating in unequal, needle-sharp spires.

Inside, cold light streams through the numerous plain glass windows, illuminating the lofty **nave** and Ried's playful ribbed vaulting, which forms branches and petals stamped with coats of arms belonging to Václav II and the local miners' guilds. The wide spread of the five-aisled nave is remarkably uncluttered: the multi-tiered tester of the Gothic pulpit – half-wood, half-stone – creeps tastefully up a central pillar, matching black and gold Renaissance confessionals lie discreetly in the north aisle, while nearby the filigree work on the original Gothic choirstalls echoes the cathedral's exterior. Look up, and you'll see virtually an entire chamber orchestra of gilded putti disporting themselves over the Baroque organ case.

The **ambulatory** boasts an array of early twentieth-century stained glass, but it's the medieval frescoes preserved in the southernmost chapels that really stand out. In the Smíšek chapel, there's a wonderful orchestra of angels in the vaulting and a depiction of the Queen of Sheba on one of the walls. Two chapels further along is the minters' chapel, its walls decorated with fifteenth-century frescoes showing the Florentines at work.

The rest of the staré město

On Rejskovo náměstí, the squat, polygonal **Kašna** (fountain), built by Rejsek in 1495, strikes a very odd pose: peppered with finials and replete with blind arcading, it was actually designed as the decorative casing for a reservoir and now houses a roofless shop selling sculptures (Ⓦ www.nemeth.cz). At the bottom of the sloping Šultyskovo náměstí is a particularly fine **Morový sloup** (Plague Column), giving thanks for the end of the plague of 1713; while just around the corner from the top of the square is one of the few Gothic buildings to survive the 1770 fire, the **Kamenný dům**, built around 1480, with an oriel window and a steep gable, covered in an ornate sculptural icing. This now contains an unexceptional local museum (Tues–Sun: April & Oct 9am–5pm; May, June & Sept 9am–6pm; July & Aug 10am–6pm; Nov 10am–4pm; 40Kč). A couple of blocks down Poděbradova stands Kilian Ignaz Dientzenhofer's unfinished Ursuline convent or **Voršilský klášter** (April & Oct Sat & Sun 9am–4pm; May–Sept Tues–Sun 9am–5.30pm; free). Only three sides of the convent's ambitious pentagonal plan were actually finished, its neo-Baroque church being added in the late nineteenth century while sv Barbora was being restored.

Sedlec

Buses #1 and #4 run from the inner ringroad, 3km northeast to **SEDLEC** (Ⓦ www.sedlec.info), once a separate village but now a suburb of Kutná Hora. Adjoining Sedlec's defunct eighteenth-century Cistercian monastery (now the largest tobacco factory in Europe, owned by Phillip Morris) is the fourteenth-century church of **Nanebevzetí Panny Marie** (Mon–Sat 9am–noon & 1–5pm; 30Kč) redesigned in the eighteenth century by Giovanni Santini, who specialized in melding Gothic with Baroque. Here, given a plain French Gothic church gutted by the Hussites, Santini set to work on the vaulting, adding his characteristic sweeping stucco rib patterns, relieved only by the occasional Baroque splash of colour above the chancel steps.

Cross the main road, following the signs, and you'll come to the monks' graveyard, where an ancient Gothic chapel – again redesigned by Santini, leans heavily over the entrance to the macabre subterranean **kostnice** (daily: April–Sept 8am–6pm; March & Oct 9am–noon & 1–5pm; Nov–Feb 9am–noon & 1–4pm; 50Kč; Ⓦ www.kostnice.cz), the mother of all ossuaries, full to overflowing with human bones. When holy earth from Golgotha was scattered over the graveyard in the twelfth century, all of Bohemia's nobility wanted to be buried here. Victims of the plague and the Hussite wars brought the bones count to over 40,000 complete sets. In 1870, worried about the ever-growing piles, the authorities commissioned František Rint to do something creative with them. He rose to the challenge and moulded out of bones four giant bells, one in each corner of the crypt, designed wall-to-ceiling skeletal decorations, including the Schwarzenberg coat of arms, and, as the centrepiece, put together a chandelier made out of every bone in the human body. Rint's signature (in bones) is at the bottom of the steps.

Practicalities

The simplest way to get to Kutná Hora is to take a **bus** from Prague's Florenc bus station (1hr 15min). Fast **trains** from Prague's hlavní nádraží take around an hour (some involve a change at Kolín – not to be confused with Kolín zastávka). The main **train station** (Kutná Hora hlavní nádraží) is a long way out of town, near Sedlec, but there's usually a shuttle service ready to leave for Kutná Hora město train station, nearer the centre of town.

The town has a highly efficient system of orientation signs and, at almost every street corner, a pictorial list of the chief places of interest (beware, though, that the train station signposted is not the main one). The **tourist office** is on Palackého náměstí (April–Oct Mon–Fri 9am–6.30pm, Sat & Sun 9am–5pm; Nov–March Mon–Fri 9am–5pm; Ⓣ 327 512 378, Ⓦ www.kutnahora.cz), with another small office by the cathedral. The best **accommodation** is ⚑ Hotel Opat (Ⓣ 327 536 900, Ⓦ www.hotelopat.cz; ④), a really nicely furnished place on Husova, right in the old town; other possibilities include the comfortable U vlašského dvora, just off Havlíčkovo náměstí (Ⓣ 327 514 618, Ⓦ www .vlasskydvur.cz; ④), with a decent restaurant and a sauna, and a simple, inexpensive pension, U rytířů, on Rejskovo náměstí (Ⓣ&Ⓕ 327 512 256; ②). The nearest **campsite** is the unlikely-sounding Santa Barbara, northwest of the town centre in a large suburban garden on Česká (April–Oct).

You're spoilt for choice for **eating and drinking**: try Piazza Navona, an excellent Italian-run pizzeria with tables on Palackého náměstí; Harmonia on Husova, which serves up traditional Czech food and has an outdoor terrace, or Calaveros, a Czech-Mex themed restaurant in a lovely Renaissance house on Šultysova. There's also a branch of the reliable tea-house chain, Dobrá čajovna, on Jungmannovo náměstí.

The Sázava valley

A short train ride **southeast** of Prague is enough to transport you from the urban sprawl of the capital into one of the prettiest regions of central Bohemia. The best way to visit the **Sázava valley** or **Posázaví** (Ⓦ www.posazavi.com)

is on the wonderfully entitled *Posázavský Pacifik*, the scenic railway line that winds its way slowly south down the Vltava from Prague, and then east along the steep and craggy valley. The region's chief sight is **Konopiště**, the Archduke Franz Ferdinand's Bohemian getaway, which lies just south of the Sázava.

Vojenské technické muzeum (Military Technical Museum)

Those of a military bent will enjoy the **Vojenské technické muzeum** (June & Sept Sat & Sun 9am–5pm; July & Aug Wed–Sun 9am–5pm; free; ⓦ www.vhu .cz), which occupies a field between the villages of Lešany and Krhanice, 43km by the slow-stopping *Posázavský Pacifik* from Prague. Pride of place in the museum goes to the "Pink Tank", a Soviet IS2 tank that once served as a war memorial in Prague, but was painted pink in 1991 by the artist David Černý in protest against the post-1968 Soviet occupation. The rest of the museum's lovingly preserved military vehicles are housed in giant hangars: highlights include a Nazi mobile soup tureen, a mock-up of the Iron Curtain and more than 350 tanks and rockets – there's even a Scud missile launcher. To reach the museum, cross the river from Krhanice train station and take the path immediately to the right – a ten-minute walk.

Sázava

Rising majestically above the slow-moving Sázava river, another 30km or so upstream, is the **Sázavský klášter** and **zámek** (April & Oct Sat & Sun 9am–noon & 1–4pm; May–Aug Tues–Sun 9am–noon & 1–6pm; Sept Tues–Sun 9am–noon & 1–5pm; 70Kč, 140Kč for a 1hr guided tour in English; ⓦ www .klaster-sazava.cz). The monastery was founded by the eleventh-century Prince Oldřich, on the instigation of a passing hermit called **Prokop** (St Procopius), whom he met by chance in the forest. Prokop became the first abbot of what was initially a Slavonic monastery, and, for a while, Sázava became an important centre for the dissemination of Slavonic texts. Later, a large Gothic church was planned, and this now bares its red sandstone nave to the world, incomplete but intact. The chancel was converted into a Baroque church, later bought by the Tiegel family, who started to build themselves a modest chateau. Of this architectural miscellany, only the surviving Gothic frescoes – of a sophistication unmatched in Bohemian art at the time – are truly memorable. The village itself thrived on the glass trade, and the rest of the monastery's guided tour concentrates on the local glassware.

The quickest way to reach Sázava by **train** is to change at Čerčany; the train station (Sázava-Černé Budy) is a fifteen-minute walk across the river from the monastery. For simple **accommodation** try the *Hostinec za vodou* (☎777 802 827, ⓦ www.sazavahostineczavodou.cz; ❶), right by the road bridge, which serves huge **meals** on its summer terrace.

Český Šternberk

Several bends later in the Sázava river, the village of **ČESKÝ ŠTERNBERK** is overlooked by the great castellated mass of its **hrad** (April & Oct Sat & Sun 9am–5pm; May & Sept Tues–Sun 9am–5pm; June–Aug Tues–Sun 9am–6pm; 85Kč, 150Kč for a 50min guided tour in English; ⓦ www.hradceskysternberk .cz), strung out along a knife's edge above the river. It's a breathtaking sight, rising out of thick woods, though not much remains of the original Gothic castle, headquarters of the powerful Šternberk family, who have refurbished it beautifully. The highlight of the guided tour is the Italian stuccowork that survives from the seventeenth century. Even if you don't take the tour, it's worth popping your head into the main courtyard, where there's usually a display of birds of prey, one of Count Šternberk's chief interests. Fifteen-minutes' walk through the woods behind the castle, there's a lookout tower (*rozhledna*) with great views over the hrad and valley.

If you're coming by **train**, get out at Český Šternberk zastávka, one stop beyond Český Šternberk's main station. The fur-strewn *Hradní restaurace* provides cheap, hot Czech **food**; if you need to **stay**, head for the smart and vast *Parkhotel* (☎317 855 168, ⓦwww.parkhoteldt.cz; ❸), near the station, with spectacular views over to the castle.

Konopiště

About 50km southeast of Prague, **Konopiště** (April & Oct Tues–Fri 9am–noon & 1–3pm, Sat & Sun 9am–noon & 1–4pm; May–Aug Tues–Sun 9am–noon & 1–5pm; Sept Tues–Fri 9am–noon & 1–4pm, Sat & Sun 9am–5pm; Nov Sat & Sun 9am–noon & 1–3pm; ⓦwww.zamek-konopiste.cz) is best known as the last residence of the **Archduke Franz Ferdinand**, heir to the Habsburg throne from 1896 until his assassination in Sarajevo in 1914. The archduke and his wife, Sophie Chotek, were shunned by the Habsburg court, due to the fact that Sophie was a mere countess, and not an archduchess, and so preferred this former Gothic castle and its wooded grounds to his official residence in Vienna. In addition to remodelling the chateau into its current appearance, the archduke shared his generation's voracious appetite for hunting, eliminating all living creatures foolish enough to venture into the grounds. However, he surpassed all his contemporaries by recording, stuffing and displaying a significant number of the 171,537 birds and animals he shot between the years 1880 and 1906, the details of which are recorded in his *Schuss Liste* displayed inside.

There's a choice of **guided tours**. The *I okruh* (125Kč) explores several salons, which contain some splendid Renaissance cabinets and lots of Meissen porcelain, while the *II okruh* (125Kč) takes you through the chapel, past the stuffed bears and deer teeth, to the assorted lethal weapons of one of the finest armouries in Europe. Both the above tours take roughly fifty minutes, and, include the hunting trophies. The *III okruh* (200Kč) takes an hour, is restricted to just eight people, and concentrates on the personal apartments of the archduke and his wife. Occasionally there are tours in English – for which you must pay extra – so ask at the box office before you sign up or phone ahead and book one (☎301 721 366).

Even if you don't fancy a guided tour, there are plenty of other things to do in Konopiště. In the main courtyard of the chateau, you can pop into the purpose-built **Střelnice** (Shooting Range; 30Kč), where the archduke honed his skills as a marksman against moving mechanical targets, all of which have been lovingly restored. Tucked underneath the south terrace is the **Muzeum sv Jiří** (30Kč), which is stuffed floor to ceiling with more than 800 artefacts – from paintings to statuettes and trinkets – relating to St George, the fictional father of medieval chivalry, with whom the archduke was obsessed. Much the best reason to come to Konopiště, though, is to explore its 555-acre **zámecký park**, which boasts a marked red path around the largest lake, sundry statuary, an unrivalled rose garden with a café and several greenhouses (35Kč) and a deer park. There are also regular one-hour **falconry** demonstrations in the chateau's grounds (April & Oct Sat & Sun 10am–noon & 2–4pm; May–Sept Tues–Sun same times) in English and Czech.

Practicalities

The train from Prague to **Benešov u Prahy** – the nearest train station – takes around an hour. The castle is then a pleasant two-kilometre walk west of the station along the red- or yellow-marked path (buses are relatively infrequent, though there are taxis). In fine weather, you could come equipped with a picnic; otherwise, there are several basic **food** stalls by the main car park, and decent Czech meals available in the nineteenth-century *Stará Myslivna*, on the path to the castle, and in the bistro in the main courtyard.

Since train connections are good from Prague, there's no compulsion **to stay** the night. If you do, try the luxurious rooms and apartments in *Pension Konopiště* (☏317 702 658, ⓦwww.pension-konopiste.cz; ⑥), by the chateau car park. There's a **campsite** (May–Sept), with a swimming pool, 1km southeast of the castle, near the ugly *Motel Konopiště*. Further afield, those with their own transport, seeking a bit of luxury, should head for the *Hotel Pecínov* (☏603 177 842, ⓦwww.hotelpecinov.cz; ⑨), a converted **fortress** with sumptuously decorated rooms, a pool and a riding school, 5km southeast of Benešov, off route 112. Another 3km down the road, you can stay in *Zámek Jemniště* (☏603 819 651, ⓦwww.jemniste.cz; ⑦), an even more winsome Baroque **chateau** with beautifully appointed apartments and extensive grounds; book ahead, though, as the place is a very popular wedding venue. At the other end of the scale, the nearby *Kršňův dvůr* (☏603 215 380, ⓦwww.krisnuvdvur.cz) is an organic farm run by the Czech **Hare Krishna** movement; visitors are welcome and there's a veggie feast on Sundays at 2pm. You don't have to be a devotee to stay, though you are asked to help out with the farm. The nearest train station, Městečko u Benešova, is just 100m away.

Příbram

Lying some 60km southwest of Prague, **PŘÍBRAM** (Pibrans) was once a royal silver-mining town, but it's more notorious among Czechs for its uranium mines, where thousands of political prisoners worked and died in appalling conditions in the 1950s. All mining operations ceased in 1991, and there's now an extensive and smartly laid-out mining museum or **Hornické muzeum** (April–Oct Tues–Sun 9am–5pm; Nov–March Tues–Fri 9am–4pm; 40Kč; ⓦwww.muzeum-pribram.cz), in the southwestern suburb of Březové Hory (Birkenberg) accessible via bus #1 or #14 from the train station. Architecturally, the most impressive building is the splendidly ornate pithead of the **Ševčínský šachta** (Ševčín Shaft), built in 1879, and now used for temporary exhibitions. Other buildings contain displays on mineralogy, palaeontology, the history of mining and on the forced labour of the Communist period. There's also a late nineteenth-century miner's cottage with an exhibition on toy- and puppet-making, and at least 180m of mining railway stuffed full of uranium mining equipment. If you walk for ten minutes back along the main road to the second section of the museum, you can also take a short train trip down one of the old mineshafts, the **Prokop Adit**, in the company of a retired miner, after which you're encouraged to pay a visit to the nearby miners' **pub** *Na vrších* (April–Oct). The forced labour camp from the 1950s, **Vojna u Příbrami** (times as above; 60Kč), 5km south of Příbram, has been turned into a museum, memorial and art gallery; take bus #7 or #10 to Žežice, then follow the blue-marked path.

Dukla Praha

Since 1997, Příbram has also been the home town of the successor to the old army football team, **Dukla Praha** – immortalized in the pop song *All I Want for Christmas is a Dukla Prague Away-Kit* by British punk band Half Man Half Biscuit (@www .phespirit.info/music/dukla_prague.htm) – after they were forced to leave the capital due to financial difficulties, and merge with the town's local team to become Marila Příbram (@www.fkmarila.cz). The team plays in Příbram's Na Litavce stadium, a couple of kilometres south of the town centre.

More popular than the mining museum, though, is the beautiful Marian shrine of **Svatá hora** (@svata-hora.cz), whose pepperpot domes crown a wooded hill to the east of the town. According to legend, the first shrine was built here in the thirteenth century, but was transformed out of all recognition by the Jesuits, who in 1658 employed Carlo Lurago to produce the striking set-piece of Italianate Baroque you see now. The best way to reach the shrine is via the Svatohorské schody or covered stairway built by Kilian Ignaz Dientzenhofer in 1728, off Dlouhá, east of the main square. From the stairs, you enter the arcaded ambulatory, which surrounds the main church, whose restored frescoes, dating from the late nineteenth century, recount the shrine's history. Thick stuccowork surrounds the hell, fire and damnation ceiling paintings, with cherubs fighting and hugging, skulls surrounded by swags made from bones, and egg timers on more skulls. At the centre of the complex is the pilgrim church or basilica, its balustrade dotted with saintly statuary; inside, pride of place goes to a kitsch Gothic statue of the Madonna and Child, whose clothes are regularly changed.

The photographer, **František Drtikol** (1883–1961) was born in Příbram and there's now a permanent display of his works in the **Zámeček-Ernestium** (Tues–Fri 9am–5pm; 30Kč; @www.galerie-drtikol.com), the Archbishop of Prague's former residence, just north of the main square, behind the town council building. Thanks to Prague's UPM, the exhibition has some great Drtikol prints, ranging from his early Art Nouveau works to later Art Deco nudes and avant-garde pieces. Drtikol was deeply drawn to eastern philosophy and in 1935 he sold his studio and abandoned photography to devote himself entirely to painting and theosophy.

Practicalities

Příbram itself is around 50km southwest of Prague along motorway route 4. The easiest way to get there on **public transport** is by bus (1hr) from Prague's Na Knížecí bus station, next to metro Anděl; the train from Prague's Smíchovské nádraží takes longer and often involves a change at Zdice, on the main line to Plzeň. The town centre is a short walk east of the train and bus stations; the mining museum is 1.5km to the southwest. Příbram is not a great place to stay, though the *Modrý hrozen* (☎318 628 007, @www.modryhrozen .cz; ❺), on the main square, is a pleasant and comfortable enough **hotel**, boasting a restaurant with an original seventeenth-century ceiling. The best **pub** around is the *Březohorka*, on the other side of the square from the mining museum; back in the town centre, there's *U Havlínů* pub, to the east of the main square on Václavské náměstí.

Czech beer

**The Czechs drink more beer than anyone else in the
world, downing approximately a pint a day for every
man, woman and child in the country – in fact, more
beer than water is drunk here. The drink's history is
deeply embedded in the national culture: after all,
this is the country that invented the first Pilsner, or
golden lager, as well as being home to the world's
most prized hops from Žatec (Saaz). Others beers just
don't get a look in, with imported beer accounting for
just one percent of the domestic market.**

History of beer

The Czechs' greatest claim to beer fame is that they invented the world's original Pilsner beer. The real story is a bit more complicated than that. By the late 1830s, the German-speaking inhabitants of **Plzeň** (Pilsen) were unhappy with the top-fermented, dark, cloudy local beer. In disgust, they founded the *Bürgerliche Brauhaus* and employed a Bavarian brewer, Josef Groll, who, on October 5, 1842, produced the world's first lager, a bottom-fermented beer stored in cool caves. The pale Moravian malt, the famous Žatec (Saaz) hops and the local soft water produced a clear, golden beer that caused a sensation. Cheap, mass-produced glass appeared on the market and showed off the new beer's colour and clarity beautifully. The newly built railway network meant that the drink could be transported all over central Europe, and soon the new Pilsner-style beers became all the rage across the continent.

Brewing methods remained traditional until the fall of Communism, after which the larger breweries almost all opted for modernization: pasteurization, de-oxidization, rapid maturation and carbon dioxide injections – all of which resulted in longer shelf-life, less taste and more fizz. The republic's smaller breweries were either swallowed up or went to the wall. By the mid-1990s, there were just sixty Czech breweries left, with the biggest – all but Budvar (see p.179) – owned by multinationals. However, in the last decade a new breed of micro-breweries has sprung up all over the country, eschewing modern technology and producing some of the tastiest, most individual brews you'll ever encounter.

Brewing pans, Budweiser brewery, Ceske Budejovice ▲

U Fleků brewery bar, Prague ▼

The pivnice experience

The best Czech *pivnice*, or pubs, are straightforward affairs: wooden tables, benches, beermats and an endless supply of beer. The clientele are mostly male, there's rarely any music and, apart from the odd game of cards or dominoes, drinking (though not necessarily getting drunk) is the chief pursuit. All you have to do is sit down and place a beermat in front of you, and soon enough a waiter will walk round with a large tray of frothing mugs and slap one down on your table. He'll then give you a little paper tab on which he'll keep a tally of your consumption. You should then raise your glass to your companions, say *na zdraví* (cheers) and start drinking. As you near the end of the glass, before you've even begun to worry about catching the waiter's eye, you'll be served another. At which point it becomes clear why Czechs don't go in for pub crawls. With table service the norm, you need a serious strength of will (and a clear head) to get up and leave. Most pubs serve traditional, inexpensive Czech food, which should help soak up some of the alcohol.

▲ The Good Soldier Švejk bar sign

▼ Pilsner Urquell advertising

Czech beer terms

čepované pivo – draught beer
černé – dark-coloured beer
kvasnicové pivo – yeast beer
lahvové pivo – bottled beer
malé pivo – small beer, served as 0.3l
nefiltrované – unfiltered (cloudy) beer
nepasterované – unpasteurized beer
pivo – beer, served as 0.5l
polotmavé – a "half-dark" beer
pšeničné pivo – wheat beer
řezané – "cut" beer, a mixture of light and dark beers
světlé – light-coloured beer
tmavé – dark-coloured beer
točené pivo – draught beer

▼ Pub in Prague

Beer label ▲

Beer hall ▼

Micro-breweries

▶▶ **Brno – Pegas** (see p.319). Hotel and cavernous micro-brewery, serving both dark and light beers, as well as wheat beer and a heady golden 16° *speciál*.

▶▶ **Harrachov – Novosad** (see p.280). The town's glassworks has a brewery-restaurant serving superb unfiltered, unpasteurized beers, including a rare 8° brew to quench the thirst of the local glass-workers.

▶▶ **Klatovy – Modrý abbé** (see p.210). Not strictly speaking a micro-brewery, but it serves beers from the nearby brewery at Kouť na Šumavě, as well as Platan beers.

▶▶ **Loket – Svatý Florián** (see p.230). Family-run brewery hotel, restaurant and pub in a beautiful town, producing just one delicious brew, a cloudy, amber 13° lager.

▶▶ **Olomouc – Moritz** (see p.362). Simple, unpretentious, non-smoking brewpub, with two cloudy *světlé* beers, one wheat beer and a cloudy 13° amber brew.

▶▶ **Olomouc – Svatováclavský pivovar** (see p.362). Olomouc's other brewpub, just off the main square, offers an almost black 13° *černe pivo* and an equally strong wheat beer.

▶▶ **Prague – U Fleků** (see p.131). This may be the ultimate tourist trap, but for the pub's legendary dark chocolatey 13° lager it's worth it.

▶▶ **Prague – Pivovarský dům** (see p.131). Prague's most popular micro-brewery pub has been going since the late 1990s – the regular light, dark and wheat beers are the ones to plump for.

▶▶ **Štramberk – Městský pivovar** (see p.375). Lovely little brewery pub with atmospheric Gothic cellars and a great tap room, on the main square of this pretty hilltop village.

▶▶ **Zvíkov – Zlatá labuť** (see p.162). Conveniently located close to Zvíkov castle, this hotel-brewery serves an excellent cloudy 11° yeast beer, a super-dark 13° *speciál* and occasional top-fermented ales.

Along the Berounka river

The green belt area to the **west of Prague** is easily the most varied of the regions around the city, and consequently one of the most popular escapes for citizens of the Czech capital. The **River Berounka** carves itself an enticingly craggy valley up to Charles IV's magnificent country castle at **Karlštejn**, the busiest destination of all, while further upstream is the more isolated stronghold of **Křivoklát**.

Karlštejn and around

KARLŠTEJN (Karlstein) is a small ribbon of a village, strung out along one of the tributaries of the Berounka. No doubt it was once pretty and unassuming; it now boasts an exclusive golf course and is jam-packed with tacky souvenir stands and tourists visiting its **hrad** (Tues–Sun: March 9am–noon & 1–3pm; April & Oct 9am–noon & 1–4pm; May, June & Sept 9am–5pm; July & Aug 9am–6pm; ☎311 681 617, ⓦwww.hradkarlstejn.cz), which occupies a spectacular, defiantly unassailable position above the village. Designed in the fourteenth century by Matthias of Arras for Emperor Charles IV as a giant safe-box for the imperial crown jewels and his large personal collection of precious relics, it quickly became Charles' favourite retreat from the vast city he himself had masterminded. Women were strictly forbidden to enter the castle, and the story of his third wife Anna's successful break-in (in drag) became one of the most popular Czech comedies of the nineteenth century.

Ruthlessly restored in the late nineteenth century, the castle now looks far better from a distance, with its giant wedge towers rising above a series of castellated walls. Most of the rooms on the hour-long Tour 1 (*trasa I*) contain only the barest of furnishings, the empty spaces taken up by uninspiring displays on the castle's history (120Kč, 220Kč for a guided tour in English). Far more interesting is Tour 2 (*trasa II*), which takes longer (June–Oct only; 1hr 20min; 300Kč), must be booked in advance, and is restricted to fifteen visitors at a time. This allows you to enter the Emperor's chambers in the **Mariánská věž**, where Charles shut himself off from the rest of the world, with any urgent business passed to him through a hole in the wall of the tiny ornate chapel of **sv Kateřina**. The castle's finest treasure is the **Chapel of sv Kříž**, connected by a wooden bridge that leads onto the highest point of the castle, the **Velká věž**. In the Emperor's day, only a select few could enter this gilded treasure-house, whose six-metre-thick walls contain 2200 semi-precious stones and 128 beautiful fourteenth-century panels painted by the masterful Master Theodoric. The imperial crown jewels, once secured here behind nineteen separate locks, were removed to Hungary after an abortive attack by the Hussites, while the Bohemian jewels are stashed away in Prague's cathedral.

Practicalities

Trains for Karlštejn leave Prague's Smíchovské nádraží roughly every hour, and take about 35 minutes to cover the 28km. The village is ten-minutes' walk across the river from the station, and it's a further fifteen- to twenty-minute climb up to the castle entrance. If you're looking for somewhere to grab a beer and a fairly bog-standard bite to **eat**, try hunting-lodge-style *U Janů*, which has an outdoor terrace, or the *Koruna*, both on the main street. Alternatively, bring a picnic and eat by the banks of the river.

There are many **accommodation** options in Karlštejn, but only a masochist would choose to stay here. If you are stuck for some reason, your best bet is the

Hotel Mlyn (☎311 744 411, ⓦwww.hotelmlynkarlstejn.cz; ⓔ), a well-run converted mill and fishing lodge on the same side of the river as the train station, ten-minutes' walk downstream. Karlštejn's **campsite** (all year) is on the opposite bank, upstream from the village, and allows fires, but there's a nicer site at **Řevnice** (April–Sept), two stops on the train before Karlštejn, with a small pool, restaurant and draught beer.

Around Karlštejn and the Český kras

There are some great possibilities for **hiking** in the countryside around Karlštejn; just make sure you buy yourself a decent map that shows the marked paths. You could also go for a swim at the popular flooded quarry, **Malá Amerika**, a couple of kilometres north of the castle.

From **SRBSKO** (one stop beyond Karlštejn), a red-marked path winds its way through the woods to **sv Jan pod Skalou** (St John Under the Rock), a strikingly situated monastery, as the name suggests, underneath a steep bluff in a landscape full of dramatic craggy flourishes. Designed by Christoph Dientzenhofer, the monastery was used as a training camp for the Communist secret police, but is now an ecological research centre. This is also the place where the country's remaining aristocrats were imprisoned following the 1948 coup. You can catch a bus back to Prague easily enough from Vráž, 1km or so north.

Another option from Srbsko is to take the yellow-marked path west into the **Český kras** (Bohemian Karst). The geology of this region has fascinated scientists since the early nineteenth century, but the one set of caves open to the public, the **Koněpruské jeskyně** (daily: April–June & Sept 8am–4pm; July & Aug 8am–5pm; Oct 8am–3pm; 100Kč; ⓦwww.caves.cz), 3km west of Srbsko, lay undiscovered until 1950. Much more fascinating than the dripstone decorations, however, was the simultaneous discovery of an illegal fifteenth-century mint.

Křivoklátsko

Further up the Berounka is the beautiful, mixed woodland of **Křivoklátsko**. Just out of reach of day-trippers, it's an altogether sleepier place than the area around Karlštejn. There are several castles in the region, and you could happily spend days exploring the countryside on a network of well-marked footpaths.

The agonized twists (*křivky*) of the Berounka river give the region its name and cast up its highest crags, which cluster round the lofty hrad of **Křivoklát** (March, April & Oct Tues–Sun 9am–noon & 1–3pm; May & Sept Tues–Sun 9am–noon & 1–4pm; June–Aug Tues–Sun 9am–noon & 1–5pm; Nov & Dec Sat, Sun 9am–noon & 1–3pm; ⓦwww.krivoklat.cz). First mentioned in the twelfth century, Křivoklát (Pürglitz) enjoyed the royal patronage of the Přemyslids, whose hunting parties were legendary. Charles IV also spent the early part of his childhood here before being sent off to Burgundy. From the outside, it's an impressive stronghold, dominated by the round tower in which English alchemist Edward Kelley was incarcerated for two and a half years for failing to reveal the secret of the philosopher's stone to Rudolf II. Kelley was, by all accounts, a slippery character, a swindler and a seducer, with a hooked nose and no ears (they were cut off by the Lancastrians as a punishment for forgery). In an attempt to escape, he jumped out of the window, only to break his leg so badly it had to be amputated.

The castle was saved from rack and ruin (and heavily renovated) by the Fürstenbergs at the end of the nineteenth century, and there's now a choice of two guided tours. The 70-minute *I okruh* (100Kč, 150Kč in English) takes in most of the castle's good points, including the dungeon and pit, and the Královský sál (Royal Hall) and the chapel. The last two, dating back to the thirteenth century, have kept their original late-Gothic vaulting, studded with corbels carved with colourful figureheads, and retain an austere beauty quite at odds with the castle's reputation as a venue for bacchanalian goings-on. An appealing alternative for those with kids (or an aversion to guided tours) is *2 okruh* (70Kč, 100Kč for a tour in English), a 35-minute scramble around the fortifications. During the high season, there are regular weekend events and concerts – visit the website to find out more.

Practicalities

Virtually all journeys by **train** from Prague to Křivoklát require a change at Beroun. If you've time to kill, pop into the family-run *Pivovarský Berounský medvěd*, Tyršova 135, next to Beroun railway station, a three-tun, in-house brewery pub and restaurant in a former sugar factory. **Buses** from the Praha-Dejvice terminal run frequently only at weekends (90min). The **information centre** (June & Sept Sat & Sun 10am–6pm; July & Aug Tues–Sun 10am–6pm), right in the centre of the village, can advise on walks and can also book **accommodation**; *Sýkora* (☏ 313 558 114, ⓦ hotel-sykora.krivoklatsko.com; ❸) is a simple family-run place close by. There are also plenty of **campsites** in the vicinity, such as *Višňová II* (June–Aug) by the river.

Lidice

The small mining village of **LIDICE**, 18km northwest of Prague, hit the world headlines on June 10, 1942, at the moment when it ceased to exist. On the flimsiest pretext, it was chosen as the scapegoat for the assassination of the Nazi leader Reinhard Heydrich (see p.113). All 173 men from the village were rounded up and shot by the SS, the 198 women were sent off to Ravensbrück concentration camp, and the 89 children either went to the camps or, if they were considered Aryan enough, were packed off to "good" German homes, while the village itself was burnt to the ground.

Knowing all this as you approach Lidice makes the modern village seem almost perversely unexceptional. At the end of the straight, tree-lined main street, 10 června 1942 (June 10, 1942), there's a dour concrete memorial with a small but horrific **museum** (daily: March & Oct 9am–5pm; April–Sept 9am–6pm; Nov–Feb 9am–4pm; 80Kč) where you can watch a short film about Lidice, including footage shot by the SS themselves as the village was burning. The spot where the old village used to lie is just south of the memorial, now merely smooth green pasture punctuated with a few simple symbolic reminders and a chilling bronze memorial to the 82 local children who never returned. After the massacre, the "Lidice shall live" campaign was launched and villages all over the world began to change their name to Lidice. The first was Stern Park Gardens, Illinois, soon followed by villages in Mexico and other Latin American countries. From Coventry to Montevideo, towns twinned themselves with Lidice, so that rather than "wiping a Czech village off the face of the earth", as Hitler had hoped, the Nazis inadvertently created a symbol of anti-fascist resistance.

There's no place nor reason to stay, and most people come here as a day-trip from Prague on one of the regular buses from Praha Dejvická, getting off at the turn-off to the village on the main road.

Lány

On summer weekends, Škoda-loads of Czech families, pensioners and assorted pilgrims make their way to **LÁNY**, a plain, grey village on a hill by the edge of the Křivoklát forest, 12km beyond Kladno. They congregate in the town's pristine cemetery to pay their respects to one of the country's most important historical figures, **Tomáš Garrigue Masaryk**, the founding father and president of Czechoslovakia from 1918 to 1935.

The Masaryk plot is separated from the rest of the cemetery (*hřbitov*) by a little wooden fence and flanked by two bushy trees. Tomáš is buried alongside his American wife, Charlotte Garrigue Masaryková, who died some fifteen years earlier, and their son Jan, who became foreign minister in the post-1945 government, only to die in mysterious circumstances shortly after the Communist coup (see p.79). The Masaryks were joined by their daughter, Alice, who founded the Czechoslovak Red Cross and died in exile in 1966.

After laying their wreaths, the crowds generally wander over to the presidential summer **zámek** (Ⓦwww.hrad.cz), with its blue-liveried guards, on the other side of the village. The chateau still serves as the president's out-of-town retreat, and its rooms are strictly out of bounds, but the large English **park**, orangerie and deer park, which were landscaped by Josip Plečnik, are open to the public (April–Oct Wed & Thurs 2–6pm, Sat & Sun 10am–6pm; free). To get to Lány, either change buses at Kladno, or take the slow train to Chomutov from Prague's Masarykovo nádraží, alighting at Stochov – the nearest station to Lány, 3km away to the southwest – which boasts a presidential waiting room.

Travel details

Trains

Benešov u Prahy to: Městečko u Benešova (hourly; 20min); Postupice (hourly; 15min).
Beroun to: Křivoklát (10–13 daily; 30–45min).
Čerčany to: Český Šternberk (7–8 daily; 1 hr); Sázava (7–8 daily; 30min).
Mělník to: Litoměřice město (every 1–2hr; 35min); Mladá Boleslav (5 daily; 1hr 30min); Mšeno (6 daily; 40min); Ústí nad Labem (every 1–2hr; 1hr).
Prague Hlavní nádraží to: Benešov (hourly; 40min–1hr 5min); Beroun (hourly; 40min); Čerčany (hourly; 55min); Kolín (1–2 hourly; 45min); Kutná Hora (4 daily; 55min–1hr); Mladá Boleslav (every 2hr; 1hr 15min–1hr 50min); Poděbrady (hourly; 50min–1hr).
Prague Holešovice to: Kolín (5 daily; 40min).
Prague Masarykovo nádraží to: Kladno (hourly; 40–55min); Kolín (hourly; 1hr 10min); Nelahozeves (every 1–2hr; 40min–60min); Roudnice nad Labem (every 2hr; 45min); Stochov (hourly; 1hr–1hr 15min); Stratov (hourly; 40min).

Prague Smíchov to: Beroun (5–9 daily; 50min–1hr); Karlštejn (1–2 hourly; 30min); Příbram (2–4 daily; 1hr 15min); Řevnice (1–2 hourly; 25min).

Buses

Prague (Černý Most) to: Přerov nad Labem and Poděbrady (up to 3 daily; 30min/50min).
Prague (Dejvická) to: Kladno (1–2 hourly; 45–50min); Lidice (1–2 hourly; 25–35min).
Prague (Florenc) to: Konopiště (up to every 45min; 1hr); Kutná Hora (Mon–Fri 1 daily; 1hr 15min); Mělník (up to 10 daily; 50min); Mladá Boleslav (frequently; 1hr 15min).
Prague (Na Knížecí) to: Příbram (hourly; 45min–1hr).
Prague (Opatov) to: Průhonice (every 30min–1hr; 15min).
Prague (Želivského) to: Kutná Hora (up to 5 daily; 1hr 15min); Sázava (5–12 daily; 1hr 10min).

2

South Bohemia

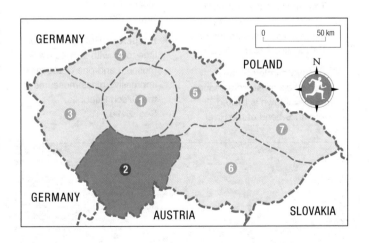

CHAPTER 2 # Highlights

✳ **Tábor** Stroll through a labyrinth of medieval streets designed to confuse potential aggressors in this former Hussite headquarters. See p.164

✳ **Zámek, Jindřichův Hradec** This chateau's forbidding exterior conceals one of the finest Italianate Renaissance interiors in the country. See p.173

✳ **Třeboň** Perfectly preserved walled town and spa set amid the medieval carp ponds of Třeboňsko. See p.175

✳ **Český Krumlov** South Bohemia's most picturesque medieval town is tucked into an S-bend of the River Vltava and overlooked by a Renaissance castle. See p.182

✳ **Hiking through the Šumava** The most unspoilt mountain range in the Czech Republic is the perfect place to do some summer hiking. See p.190

✳ **Sgraffito in Prachatice** This tiny walled town, on the edge of the Šumava mountains, boasts the finest sgraffito facades in Bohemia. See p.192

✳ **Kašperské Hory** Pretty little town with a motorcycle museum and one of the most impressive glass museums in the Czech Republic. See p.198

▲ The Šumava

South Bohemia

S outh Bohemia (Jižní Čechy), more than any other region, conforms to the popular myth of Bohemia as a bucolic backwater of rolling hills and endless forests. A century of conspicuous industrialization and destruction from two world wars have pretty much passed it by. The only city to speak of is the regional capital, **České Budějovice**, which makes up for its urban sprawl with a good-looking old town and a beer of no less standing. The rest of the countryside is dotted with a series of exceptionally beautiful medieval walled towns, known collectively as the **Rose Towns** after the emblems of the two most powerful families: the red rose of the Rožmberks and the black rose of the lords of Hradec. Both dynasties died out at the beginning of the seventeenth century, and many of their prize possessions, which have been in almost terminal decline ever since, ended up in the hands of the Bavarian-based Schwarzenberg family.

Český Krumlov is by far the most popular of the Rose Towns; others, like **Pelhřimov** and **Třeboň**, are equally well preserved, if not quite as picturesquely located. The latter lies in an uncharacteristically flat part of the country, known as **Třeboňsko**, a unique ecosystem of medieval fish ponds that still supply much of the country's Christmas carp. Bohemia's chief river, the **Vltava**, runs through South Bohemia and provides the setting for the region's most popular **castles**, some, like **Zvíkov**, almost monastic in their simplicity, and others, such as **Orlík**, **Hluboká** and **Rožmberk**, marvels of aristocratic decadence.

To the south, the **Šumava**, which forms the natural border with Austria and Germany, is one of the most unspoiled mountain ranges in the country. The German-speaking foresters and traders who settled on the northern slopes have left their mark on the architecture of the Bohemian towns and villages in that area. Following the postwar expulsions, however, the local population is now greatly reduced, their number augmented by a seasonal influx of walkers, fishermen, canoeists and inland beachniks, drawn by the natural beauty of the region, which is probably the least affected by acid rain in the Czech Republic.

Regional **transport** in South Bohemia isn't as bad as might be expected, given the overwhelmingly hilly, rural nature of the terrain. Travelling by train allows you to experience more of the countryside, and even parts of the Šumava are served by a scenic single-track railway that winds its way from České Budějovice to Český Krumlov, along the shores of Lake Lipno and then north to Prachatice. While they can be less frequent than trains, buses go virtually everywhere and are almost invariably faster.

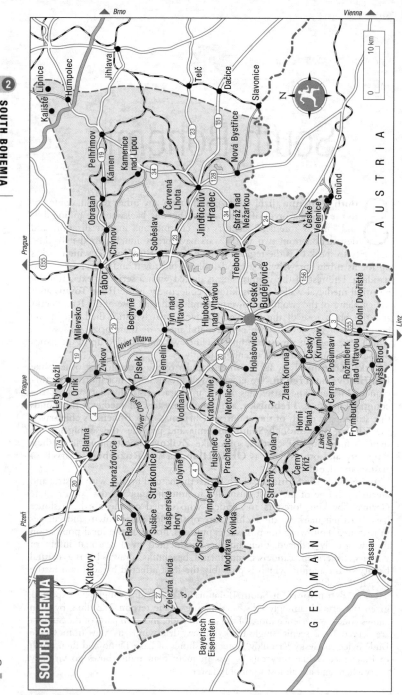

SOUTH BOHEMIA

Brno

Vienna

Prague

Prague

Plzeň

Linz

AUSTRIA

GERMANY

Kaliště
Lipnice
Humpolec
Jihlava
Telč
Dačice
Slavonice
Pelhřimov
Kamenice
nad Lipou
Kámen
Obrataň
Červená
Lhota
Jindřichův
Hradec
Nová Bystřice
Gmünd
Chýnov
Soběslav
Stráž nad
Nežárkou
České
Velenice
Tábor
Třeboň
Bechyně
Týn nad
Vltavou
České
Budějovice
Milevsko
River Vltava
Hluboká
nad Vltavou
Zvíkov
Písek
Temelín
Holašovice
Zlatá
Koruna
Český
Krumlov
Rožmberk
nad Vltavou
Dolní Dvořiště
Lety
Kožlí
Orlík
Vodňany
Kratochvíle
Netolice
Černá v Pošumaví
Vyšší
Brod
Blatná
River Otava
Husinec
Horní
Planá
Frymburk
Horažďovice
Strakonice
Volyně
Prachatice
Volary
Lake
Lipno
Rabí
Sušice
Kašperské
Hory
Vimperk
Strážný
Černý
Kříž
Klatovy
Srní
Modrava
Kvilda
Železná
Ruda
Bayerisch
Eisenstein
Passau

0   10 km

N

19
34
23
151
128
24
156
3
E55
29
20
4
174
22
27

160

Up the Vltava

South of Prague and the Slapy dam, the **River Vltava** has been transformed into a series of long, winding lakes, which remain a favourite destination for Czechs in the summer. The campsites, many of them fairly ad hoc affairs, are full to capacity, campfires burning every night. There are also two **castles** worth visiting: **Orlík** and **Zvíkov**, both of which overlook the Vltava. They're difficult to reach without your own transport; a possible base is the nearby pretty town of **Písek**, which is easily accessible by bus or train.

Orlík nad Vltavou

With its vanilla-coloured rendering and mock castellations, you're unlikely to be disappointed by your first impressions of **Orlík** (which means "little eagle"), a creamy nineteenth-century castle that juts out into this wide stretch of the Vltava. No doubt the view was a great deal more spectacular before the valley was dammed in the 1960s; nowadays the water laps rather tamely at the foot of the castle, and concrete has been injected into its foundations to prevent it from being swept away.

As some of the region's greatest self-propagandists, the Schwarzenbergs turned this old Gothic **hrad** (Tues–Sun: April & Oct 9am–4pm; May & Sept 9am–5pm; June–Aug 9am–6pm; 150Kč; ⓦwww.schwarzenberg.cz) into a pseudo-Gothic money-waster in the second half of the nineteenth century. There's nothing among the faience, weaponry and military memorabilia on the hour-long guided tour to hint at its seven-hundred-year history, and even the gardens were only laid out in the last century, but if you're interested in the Schwarzenbergs, this is one of the best places to find out about them.

For moderately priced traditional **food**, head for the restaurant U Toryka (closed Mon & Nov–March), just below the castle; for cheaper options, try the café in the orangery, or head off into the castle grounds for a picnic. There are also a handful of cheap restaurants in the village of Orlík, 1km or so south of the castle. Of the many **campsites** in the area, the nearest is 3km downriver (but 7km by road) at Velký Vír (May–Sept; ⓣ382 275 192, ⓦwww.velkyvir .cz), which has bungalows for rent and two restaurants. En route, there's a nice **pension**, U Nováků (ⓣ774 721 721; ❸), with a friendly pub downstairs serving cheap food and Gambrinus and Purkmistr beers.

Roma memorial at Lety

It took fifty years, but in 1995 a memorial at **Lety** was finally erected, 7km west of Orlík, to the Czech Roma who died here during World War II. Between 1942 and 1943, some 1300 Roma passed through the transit camp in Lety, amid what is now a rather insensitively placed pig farm (which is still a source of great contention and unhappiness for Roma), en route to Auschwitz. Thousands more were imprisoned in Hodonín, Moravia. About a quarter of those interned at Lety died in the camp – in the end around ninety percent of the prewar Czech Roma population was killed. Touching the raw nerve of Czech–Roma relations, it is inevitable that the memorial has provoked controversy, not least because of the accusation that the camp was staffed not by Germans, nor even Sudeten Germans, but by Czechs. The small-scale memorial is made up of a series of slabs of rock, already overgrown, with an information panel in Czech, Romany and English. To get there, take the road from Lety to Kožlí u Orlíka, and follow the inconspicuous sign *památník* into the woods, a fifteen-minute walk.

②

> ### Boats on the Vltava
>
> There are **boat services** from Orlík to Zvíkov (April–June & Sept to mid-Oct Sat & Sun 3 daily; July & Aug Tues–Sun 5 daily; 50min; 80Kč one way), which also head north to the Orlík dam (100Kč), via the Velký Vír, Radava, Podskalí and Trhovky campsites. For a boat tour of the area, there are irregular round-trip excursions from the pier below Orlík castle (45min; 100Kč). For more information on the timetable, call ☏382 275 333 or check ⓦwww.lodnidopravaorlikslapy.cz.

Zvíkov

Fourteen kilometres upstream, hidden amid the woods of an isolated rocky promontory at the confluence of the Vltava and the Otava, is the bare medieval husk of **Zvíkov** (April & Oct Sat & Sun 9.30am–noon & 12.30–3.30pm; May & Sept Tues–Sun 9.30am–noon & 1–4pm; June–Aug Tues–Sun 9am–5pm; tours in English; ⓦwww.pamatky-jc.cz), its simplicity a welcome relief after Orlík. You can wander at will among the light honey-coloured stone buildings, left to rack and ruin by the Rožmberks as long ago as the fifteenth century, then further destroyed by imperial troops during the Thirty Years' War. A small dusty track passes under three gatehouses before leading to the central courtyard, which boasts a simple, early Gothic, two-storey arcade, reconstructed in the nineteenth century from the few bays that still stood. Even the meagre offerings in the museum are more than compensated for by the absence of tour groups, the cool stone floors and the wonderful views over the water. The chapel's faded fifteenth-century frescoes feature a particularly memorable scene "where nimbed souls in underpants float uncomfortably through a forest", as one critic aptly described it.

Buses from Písek (weekdays only) generally only go as far as the village of **ZVÍKOVSKÉ PODHRADÍ**, 1km south of Zvíkov, from where the castle is signposted. Here you'll find spotless **accommodation** at the *Pivovarský dvůr* (☏382 285 660, ⓦwww.pivovar-zvikov.cz; ❸), a micro-brewery with a restaurant and pub that serves up several superb Zlatá labuť *kvasnicové* (yeast) beers.

Písek

Twenty kilometres south of Zvíkov, the pretty little town of **PÍSEK** takes its name from the gold-producing sand (*písek*) of the Otava. Gold fever has waxed and waned in the town over the centuries and at present commercial exploration, mostly around the village of Mokrsko, has been suspended. The likelihood of any company getting the go-ahead to mine looks very slim indeed. Meanwhile, an annual gold-panning championship is still held every August on the river around Kestřany.

Arrival, information and accommodation

The main **bus** and **train stations** are both 1km or so south of town, at the end of Nádražní (buses #1, #3, #11 from Budovcova, a five-minute walk from Velké náměstí). Pisek has a useful **information centre** (Sept–June Mon–Fri 9am–5pm; July & Aug daily 9am–6pm; ☏382 213 592, ⓦwww.icpisek.cz) at Hejduková 97, just off the main square, which offers **internet**, organizes accommodation and has a computerized information screen outside.

Hotel City (☏380 424 500, ⓦwww.hotel-city.cz; ❹) is a smart Gothic **hotel**, with a vaulted restaurant, in the old town at Alšovo náměstí 35. Conveniently central, *Bílá růže* (ⓦwww.hotelbilaruze.cz, ☏382 214 931; ❸), in the

Communist-era edifice on Fráni Šrámka 169, several steps above the church of Povýšení sv Kříže, has a decent, spacious restaurant. The **pension** *U Kloudů* (☏ 382 210 802; ❷) on Nerudova 66, with a café-bar and bustling restaurant downstairs, is cheaper – follow Heyduková through Havlíčkovo náměstí. The two closest **campsites** to Písek are a way out of town and a couple of kilometres from the nearest train stations: *Soutok* (May–Oct) is to the south, nearest Putim station, while *Vrcovice* (all year) is north of town, nearest Vrcovice station.

The Town

Písek experienced its last gold rush in the thirteenth century, but its prosperity was later demolished by the Thirty Years' War. The chief reminder of those days is the town's wonderful, 111-metre-long, **medieval stone bridge** (Kamenný most), which predates even the Charles Bridge in Prague and which likewise accrued a fine selection of beatific Baroque statuary during the Counter-Reformation. Located in the westernmost edge of the staré město, it is now closed to traffic.

From the bridge, it's a short hop to the main square, **Velké náměstí**, overlooked by the magnificent golden yellow Baroque **radnice**. Behind the town hall, at the far end of the courtyard, you'll find the entrance to the **Prácheňské muzeum** (Tues–Sun: March–Sept 9am–6pm; Oct–Dec 9am–5pm; 30Kč), which occupies the only surviving wing of the medieval riverside castle, built by Přemysl King Otakar II in the thirteenth century and destroyed by fire in 1532. The highlight of this vast museum is the Gothic Knights' Hall, which has retained its original black floor tiles, and contains a model of how the castle once looked. The rest of the museum is also worth a quick canter for its unusually frank account of the area's history, including a section on the Gypsy concentration camp of Lety (see p.161), and the events of 1968 and 1989.

A few doors down the main square from the radnice is the pretty little former monastery church of **Povýšení sv Kříže**, with its gabled sgraffitoed facade. It has a superbly kitsch Baroque main altar, sporting a golden sunburst in the shape of a love heart and a backdrop of blue, ruched curtains dotted with gold stars. Several other buildings around the town boast more recent sgraffito decoration, mostly the work of the late nineteenth-century artist (and local student) Mikuláš Aleš. A short walk up Fráni Šrámka brings you to the

---

Temelín

The cooling towers of **Temelín**, which rise up beside the main road from Písek to České Budějovice, are a chastening sight. Built to a Soviet design technically similar to the one used at Chernobyl, Temelín was designed to be the largest nuclear power station in the world – reason enough to give the place a wide berth. A long campaign of protest by local and international (mostly Austrian) groups persuaded the first post-Communist government to postpone the opening of the power station, which is situated on a tectonic fault line. However, in 1992, the US energy giant Westinghouse was commissioned to complete at least two of the four reactor units. Eight years later the establishment was officially opened. Temelín now provides twenty percent of the nation's electricity, as does the republic's only other (much older) nuclear reactor in the south Moravian town of Dukovany. You can visit the information centre (daily: Sept–June 9am–4pm; July & Aug 9am–5.30pm; free; ☏ 381 102 639, ⊛ www.cez.cz) which shows a 3-D movie on the building of the reactors. The staff eagerly distribute propaganda brochures and posters showing the cooling towers at sunset.

Putimská brána, the only remaining bastion, adjoined by a number of quiet backstreets heading east. These lead to a small market that takes place under the aegis of the 74-metre-high, onion-domed *hláska* (watchtower) of the Dominican church.

Eating and drinking

For a filling Bohemian **meal**, settle in at *U Reiňerů*, alongside the peaceful Palackého sady, or try *Na Ostrově*, on a leafy island in the river just downstream of the bridge, complete with kids' playground and mini-golf. Typical Czech food is also served at the pleasant *U Kamenného mostu*, which has views onto the river and the old bridge from its summer garden. The simple *Tandoor* (closed Sat), next door to the information centre, serves Indian food; a good place for a beer is the nearby *Bar Monika*.

Tábor and around

Founded in 1420 by religious exiles from Prague, 88km to the north, **TÁBOR** – named after the mountain where the transfiguration of Christ took place – was the spiritual and strategic centre of the social and religious revolution that swept through Bohemia in the first half of the fifteenth century. It gave its name to the radical wing of the reformist Hussite movement, the **Táborites**, whose philosophy – that all people should be equal on earth as in heaven – found few friends among the church hierarchy and feudal-minded nobility of the time, Hussite or Catholic. Under constant threat of physical attack, they developed into a formidable fighting force, declaring war on the established Church and remaining undefeated until 1452, when the town was taken by a force led by the moderate Hussite King Jiří of Poděbrady.

Anti-authoritarianism persists here, and despite the efforts of the Jesuits and others over the centuries, Tábor still claims the smallest percentage of

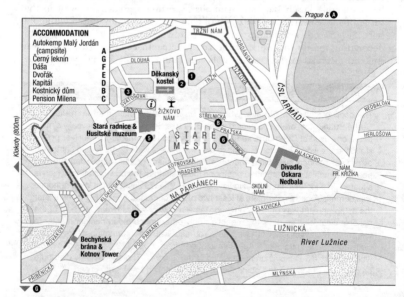

Catholics in the country. Considering its pugnacious history, though, and despite being a major bus and rail junction, Tábor is a relatively quiet little town nowadays, especially in the beautifully preserved **old quarter**, which is virtually devoid of traffic and has kept its labyrinthine street plan. In the staré město's back alleys, many houses have retained their rich sgraffito decoration and pretty Renaissance gables, while the country's premier **museum** devoted to the Hussite movement occupies a spot on the attractive main square.

There are also several appealing **day-trips** possible around Tábor, some of which are just a short train journey from the town.

Arrival and information

Fast trains from Prague take under two hours to reach Tábor. The **train and bus station** is a twenty-minute walk or short bus ride (buses #11 and #13) east of the staré město, in the new town or **nové město**. You can leave luggage in the train station, where there's also a small **information centre** (June–Sept Mon–Fri 9.30–11.45am & 12.30–5pm, Sat 9–11.45am & 12.30–5pm; ☏972 552 980) that can help with accommodation.

To reach the staré město, walk west from the train or bus station through Husovo náměstí, noting the unusual **statue of Jan Hus** by local sculptor František Bílek (you can see more of his work at the nearby village of Chýnov; see p.169). Two blocks past the statue on Erbenova is *Netc@fé*, a good spot to access the **internet**. Continue down třída 9 května until you reach the busy náměstí Fr. Křižíka, which straddles the new and old towns. The efficient **tourist office**, on the west side of square at Žižkovo náměstí 2 (May–Sept Mon–Fri 8.30am–7pm, Sat & Sun 10am–4pm; Oct–April Mon–Fri 9am–4pm; ☏381 486 230, ⓌWwww.tabor.cz), can arrange private rooms and has maps on the excellent **cycling trails** in the Táborsko region. From the square head up Palackého into the old town.

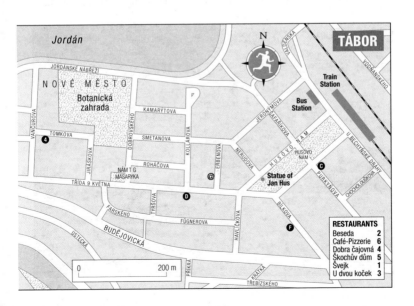

Accommodation

Tábor has a range of **hotels** and **pensions** to choose from. All the **campsites** are well out of the centre. The best is *Autokemp Malý Jordán*, with basic chalets (June–Sept; ☎ 381 235 103, ⓦ atc-mj.unas.cz; buses #20 & #21), north of town in the woods between Lake Jordán – formed by the oldest dam in Europe (built in 1492) and once a favourite spot for baptizing children – and its smaller sister lake.

Černý leknín Příběnická 695 ☎ 381 256 405. Probably the best place to stay in town, in the grandiose neo-Gothic villa beyond the Bechyňská brána. Comfortable en suites at moderate prices, with a sauna and swimming pool on site. ❹

Dáša Bílková 735 ☎ 381 256 253, ⓦ www .travelguide.cz/pensiondasa. Pleasant pension close to the station off Husovo náměstí, with a sauna. ❷

Dvořák Hradební 3037 ☎ 381 251 290, ⓦ www .orea.cz. In an old brewery south of the main square, this sleek hotel has comfortable rooms with satellite TV and internet. Swimming pool and sauna on site. ❻

Kapitál Třída 9 května 617 ☎ 381 256 096, ⓦ www .hotel-kapital.cz. Big hotel near the bus and train station, with basic rooms and a decent restaurant. ❸

Kostnický dům Střelnická 220 ☎ 603 516 188, ⓦ www.tabor.cz/kostnickydum. Inviting central pension in a small Renaissance house (just nine beds) off the main square. ❷

Pension Milena Husovo nám. 529 ☎ 381 254 755, ⓦ www.pensionmilena.cz. Cheap, simple rooms, some en suite, near the train station. ❷

The Town

The layout of the **staré město**, with its vast maze of narrow medieval streets designed to confuse the enemy, has changed little since its foundation back in the fifteenth century. No fewer than twelve streets lead onto the central square, **Žižkovo náměstí**, with its brightly coloured houses and stunning variety of gables and gargoyles, all of which had to be rebuilt after fires in the fifteenth and sixteenth centuries. The square is dominated by the **Děkanský kostel**, with its unusual triple gable; for a bird's-eye view of Tábor's web of streets, climb the 199 steps of the church's extremely tall **belltower** (May–Aug daily 10am–5pm; Sept & Oct Sat & Sun same hours if weather allows); try to time your climb

▲ Tábor

The Táborites

It was on Tábor's main square in 1420 that the **Táborites** threw theological caution to the wind and set up a religious commune under the principle *není nic mé a nic tvé, než všecko v obec rovně mají* ("nothing is mine, nothing is yours, everything is common to all"). Large urns were set up in the square and anyone – male or female – wishing to live in the commune had first to place all their possessions in them, after which they were given work on a daily rota. Men and women were granted equal rights, there was a complete ban on alcohol, and from the stone table which still stands outside the stará radnice, communion was given to the people "in both kinds" – as opposed to the established practice of reserving the wine (the blood of Christ) for the priesthood. The Hussites had this last symbolic act emblazoned on their flag – a red chalice on a black background – which, like the rousing religious war songs they sang before going into battle, struck fear into the crusaders from thirty nations who came against them.

not to coincide with the hourly tolling, as you have to pass very near the bell to reach the top.

Matching the church's triple gable on the west side of the square are the three steeply stepped neo-Gothic gables of the **stará radnice**, which houses the impressive **Husitské muzeum** (April–Oct daily 8.30am–5pm; Nov–March Tues–Fri same hours; ⑩ www.husmuzeum.cz; 60Kč). Inside, in among the nasty-looking pikes, there's a model of medieval Tábor, and several versions of Myslbek's late nineteenth-century statue of **Jan Žižka**, the Táborites' brilliant, blind military leader (traditionally depicted with one eye still functioning), which stands on the square in front of the church. You can also peek inside the Gothic hall, with its diamond rib-vaulting and irreverent medieval corbels. The museum runs hourly tours of a small section of the huge network of **underground passages** (*podzemí*; same hours); originally used to store beer barrels, they also served as a refuge from fire and siege, and as the town prison.

As for the rest of the town, its hotchpotch of backstreets, enlivened by the occasional sgraffito flourish, are perfect for a spot of aimless wandering – there's a great view of the surrounding countryside from the town's southern walls along Na parkánech. Head down Klokotská to the **Bechyňská brána**, the town's only remaining gateway; the adjoining Kotnov tower, now housing the **Muzeum života a práce středověké společnosti** (Museum of Life and Work in Medieval Society; May–Sept daily 8.30am–5pm; Oct–April by appointment on ☏ 381 254 286; 40Kč), has display cases full of farm tools and dioramas of house-building, and shows a video in English on medieval life in Bohemia. You can climb the tower (20Kč) for a sweeping panorama of the town.

One of the most endearing and least pompous of Bohemia's Counter-Reformation monasteries, the pilgrimage church and monastery of **Klokoty** lies a steep down-and-up scramble 1km west of the old town (turn right off Klokotská up Sady). An ensemble of nine onion domes rises above the peeling walls, forming the corner towers of a set of cloisters with a lovely rose garden as its centrepiece. The church, surprisingly, has a flat and unadorned ceiling, but the putti-strewn pulpit and main altar don't disappoint. For tours, available in English, call at least two days in advance on ☏ 381 232 584.

Eating, drinking and entertainment

You can enjoy traditional **Czech food** and Budvar and Bernard beers at *Beseda* (closed Sun), the popular, old-fashioned restaurant at no. 5 at the top of

Žižkovo náměstí, whose patio spills out onto the square itself. *U dvou koček*, Svatošova 310, west of the Děkanský kostel, is a bit of a tourist trap but offers dark Purkmistr beer and light Pilsner to go with good solid cooking; there's also the *Dobrá čajovná* (tea-house) at Tomkova 2. It's worth trying the reasonably priced Czech food in the small restaurant in the Škochův dům, while a good place to meet the locals is the *Švejk*, a lively **pub-cum-restaurant** hidden behind the building that houses *Beseda*, and adorned with the Good Soldier's portraits. For a wide selection of thin-crust pizzas, try the little *Café-Pizzerie*, with a small terrace on Kostinická.

Tábor has its very own **theatre**, Divadlo Oskara Nedbala, on Palackého, though the plays are all in Czech, and a rock **club**, *Orion*, on náměstí Fr. Křižíka, featuring the occasional live band. Biggest of the annual **festivals** is the Táborská setkání (Tábor Meetings) held around the middle of September – be prepared for a lot of medieval fooling around.

Around Tábor

Roughly thirty minutes west of Tábor, **Bechyně**, a tranquil little town blessed with a dramatic setting, makes a good day-trip. East of Tábor, there are several more possibilities: **Chýnov**, where the turn-of-the-twentieth-century sculptor František Bílek built his own house, now a museum to his exceptional talents, and, for those with an interest in the country's motorcycling history, **Kámen**. Even **Pelhřimov** is possible as a day-trip by train or bus, though you're more likely to pass through en route to Moravia. Devotees of Jaroslav Hašek can journey even further east beyond Humpolec to **Lipnice**, to pay their respects to the last resting place of the author of *The Good Soldier Švejk*.

Bechyně

Roughly every hour, a dinky electric train covers the 24-kilometre journey from Tábor to the soporific spa and pottery-producing town of **BECHYNĚ**. The line from Tábor to Bechyně was the empire's first electrified line when it was opened in 1903, and on alternate Saturdays from mid-June to mid-September, you can travel there and back on the original train (departs Tábor around 10am, returns around 2pm). As you enter the town, both rail and road cross a spectacular viaduct over the Lužnice gorge, known locally as the "Rainbow". The old town teeters on the edge of the gorge, ten-minutes' walk southwest of the station down Libušina.

At the far side of the uninspiring main square, which has long since lost its function as a marketplace, is the **Alšova jihočeská galerie** (May–Sept daily 9am–noon & 12.30–5pm; 50Kč), housed in the old town castle brewery, which has an impressive collection of locally produced ceramics and hosts regular international exhibitions. Opposite is the medieval granary, now home to the **Muzeum Vladimíra Preclíka** (June–Sept Tues–Sun 10am–5pm; 50Kč), containing over a hundred of Preclík's works, including paintings, drawings and sculptures. Just beyond lies the Rožmberks' Renaissance **zámek** (June–Sept Tues–Sun 10am–5pm; Oct–May call ☏381 213 143, ⓦwww.zamek-bechyne.cz; tour in English 120Kč), whose interiors are adorned with Renaissance frescoes and Baroque stuccowork. The tour takes you through the apartments of Petr Vok, the last of the Rožmberks, and a spectacular room with sixteenth-century vaulting supported by a single, tree-like column. The Franciscan **monastery** nearby is now a school, but the church, boasting a fine crystal vaulting, is open on Sundays for mass, and the gardens host summer concerts and afford excellent views of the gorge. Also worth exploring is the

Hasičské muzeum (Firefighting Museum; May, June & Sept Thurs–Sun 9am–noon & 1–5pm; July & Aug Tues–Sun same hours; 30Kč) on the main square, interesting less for its old fire engines than for its memorabilia from fire stations round the world. There's also a well-kept **Jewish cemetery** just beyond the old town walls on Michalská; ask at the museum. Lastly, for a **view** over the square, you can climb the belfry of the church of sv Matěj (summer daily 10am–5pm; 20Kč).

Practicalities

The last **train** back to Tábor leaves at around 8pm; the last **bus** an hour or so later (weekdays only). The helpful **tourist office** (☎381 213 822, ⓦwww .avantitravel.cz) on the main square leads tours of the town and can arrange private **accommodation**. Otherwise, head for the pension *U Pichlů* (☎603 927 893, ⓦwww.penzionupichlu.cz; ❷), a lovely little Baroque cottage at no. 141 on the main square, with a restaurant and ceramics shop downstairs; alternatively, there's the rather pricey *Hotel Panská* (☎381 212 550, ⓦwww .hotel-bechyne.cz; ❹) at the upper end of the square, where you can also book tickets for the castle. Another good choice is the *Hotel Jupiter* (☎381 212 631, ⓦwww.laznefelicitas.cz; ❸) a late nineteenth-century villa on Libůšina, which has a decent restaurant and offers spa treatments. *Protivínka*, with its terrace seating and Czech dishes, is the best of the **restaurants** lining the main square.

Chýnov

The little village of **CHÝNOV**, three stations east of Tábor, is the birthplace of the sculptor **František Bílek** (1872–1941), whose former home (though not his birthplace), the **Bílkův dům** at Údolní 133 (mid-May to mid-Oct Tues–Sun 10am–noon & 1–5pm; ☎381 297 624; 50Kč) is an absolute must if you're in the area. Far from being a simple house-museum, this is a remarkable piece of architecture, designed by Bílek himself in 1897. Built in red brick, with a large overhanging wooden roof and balcony, it stands out, above all, thanks to Bílek's biblical plaster relief on the south facade, and the miniature wooden chapel on the north side of the house. A large part of the interior is taken up with Bílek's studio, which is suffused with natural light and filled with studies for his large-scale works, but there is no attempt to re-create the home as it would have been in his day; instead, the building simply serves as a gallery for his works. Trained in Paris, Bílek was clearly influenced by Art Nouveau, though the tortured gestures and expressions of his subjects are derived more from the religious fervour which imbues all his work, which he himself described as "a sacrifice for the recovery of the brethren".

The Bílkův dům is on the south side of the river, beyond the main part of town, signposted off Bilkova (also route 19), a good 1.5km from Chýnov train station. On the way you'll pass a small **information centre** (Mon 9–11.30am & noon–4pm, Tues & Thurs noon–5.30pm, Wed noon–4pm, Fri 9–11.30am & noon–2.30pm; ☎381 297 647) at no. 7 on the main square.

Kámen

There's a sporadic branch-line service between Tábor and Pelhřimov, but you'll have to take the bus along route 19 to reach the one-street village of **KÁMEN** (meaning "Rock"), whose castle was once a fortified staging post between these two strongly pro-Hussite walled towns. In 1974, after centuries of neglect, the castle was reopened to display – somewhat incongruously – a collection of **vintage motorcycles** (April & Oct Sat & Sun 9am–noon & 1–4pm; May–Sept Tues–Sun 9am–noon & 1–5pm; 50Kč). Some wonderful old

Czech bikes are on display, from the very first Laurin & Klement Model TB from 1899 – not much more than a bicycle with a petrol tank tacked on – to stylish examples from the heyday of Czech biking between the wars. Other machines include ČZs and Jawas, which may have cut some ice back in the 1940s when they were designed, but now only exacerbate the country's environmental problems. You have to join the short guided tour (in Czech) of the castle before reaching the machines.

Pelhřimov

If you're heading east into Moravia and need a place to stay, make for the tiny, sleepy medieval town of **PELHŘIMOV**, just 16km further east along route 19. Barely 200m across, the walled town still retains two sixteenth-century tower gates, on one of which, the **Rynárecká brána**, two rams tirelessly butt each other on the hour. In one corner of the pretty, cobbled main square stands the beautiful Renaissance **Šrejnarovsky dům**, and the Venetian-red sixteenth-century **zámek Říčanskych**, both now part of the local **museum** (May–Oct Tues–Sun 9am–noon & 1–5pm; Nov–April Tues–Fri 9am–noon & 1–4pm; 30Kč). The nearby church of sv Bartoloměje has a splendid, 61-metre-high **belfry** (May–Sept Mon–Fri 9am–noon & 12.30–5pm, Sat & Sun from 10am), which you can climb for a bird's-eye panorama of the náměstí and surrounding streets. On the main square itself, opposite the museum, it's surprisingly easy to miss a minor work of Cubist architecture by Pavel Janák, who in 1913 adapted the Baroque **Fárův dům** at no. 13 into a slightly bizarre combination of pale pink Baroque and Cubism. You can get a good feel for the angled interior by stopping for a drink at the *Vinárna U brány* upstairs. If you're on the Cubist trail, head through the chateau's archway and a short distance north up Na Hradišti and Strachovská to Janák's **Drechselův dům** at no. 331, right by the town brewery. The maroon and mustard colour scheme looks snazzy, especially on the stripey columns of the garden canopy, but it's not on the quietest of roads.

On the second weekend of June the rather unlikely **Festival of Records and Curious Performances** takes place, during which Czech eccentrics attempt to enter the *Guinness Book of World Records* by whatever means necessary: recent records include a church built with 50,000 matches, 157 people on one tractor, and a man with 82 socks on one foot, while "Železný Zekon" ("Iron Zekon") allowed seven cars to roll over him while lying on a bed of 970 nails. A museum cataloguing these great feats, the **Muzeum rekordů a kuriozit** (June–Sept daily 9am–5pm; Oct–May call to arrange a visit; ☎565 321 226, ⓦwww .dobryden.cz; 40Kč), is in the Dolní (Jihlavská) brána, east of the main square. Inside, you can see the world's longest paper chain, the longest shawl (just over 158km long) and a bicycle made entirely of wood, among other delights.

Practicalities

The **train** station is, unfortunately, a good 2km south of the town centre, and the **bus** station is about halfway along the road into town. The **tourist information centre** (May–Sept Mon–Thurs 8.30am–12.30pm & 1–5pm, Fri 8.30am–12.30pm & 1–7pm, Sat & Sun 9am–12.30pm & 1–5pm; Oct–April Mon–Thurs 8.30am–12.30pm & 1–5pm, Sat 8.30am–12.30pm; ☎565 326 924, ⓦwww.pelhrimovsko.cz), no. 10 on the main square, has maps and can help with accommodation.

Pelhřimov still brews its own **beer**, which you can sup to your heart's content at *U Vlasáků*, next to the brewery, beyond the chateau; they also do passable Czech **food**, though the atmosphere is decidedly grungy. In addition to housing

Jaroslav Hašek

Stories about **Jaroslav Hašek** – many propagated by the author himself – have always been a mixture of fact and fiction, but at one time or another he was an anarchist, dog-breeder, lab assistant, bigamist, cabaret artist and people's commissar in the Red Army. He alternately shocked and delighted both close friends and the public at large with his drunken antics and occasional acts of political extremism. When, towards the end of his life, he made his home in the *Česká koruna* pub in Lipnice, he wrote happily, "Now I live bang in the middle of a *pivnice*. Nothing better could have happened to me." Few friends attended his funeral, and none of his family, with the exception of his 11-year-old son, who had met his father only two or three times. In a final act of contempt, the local priest would only allow his body to be buried alongside the cemetery wall, among the unbaptized and suicide victims. Before long, however, the protagonist in Hašek's *The Good Soldier Švejk* had become the most famous (fictional) Czech of all time, culminating in Hašek's "canonization" by the Communist regime – his works even being published by the military publishing house.

a simple and cheap restaurant, the Secessionist-era *Hotel Slávie* (☎565 321 540, ⓦwww.hotelslavie.pel.cz; ❷), at no. 29 on the main square, is also one of the nicest **places to stay**. *Penzion Lucerna* (☎565 333 333, ⓦwww.penzionlucerna .cz; ❷), behind the chateau, has an arcaded patio and offers decent, clean, if somewhat bland, rooms. There's also a restaurant serving Czech food.

Lipnice nad Sázavou

Around 20km northeast of Pelhřimov, just beyond Humpolec and the Prague–Brno motorway, in the midst of some glorious Bohemian countryside, is the village of **LIPNICE NAD SÁZAVOU**. Here, Bohemia's ultimate bohemian, the writer **Jaroslav Hašek**, died on January 3, 1923, his most famous work still unfinished. The village has changed little over the intervening years; the pub he lived and drank in is still going strong, and the **hrad** (April, Sept & Oct Sat & Sun 10am–4pm; May & June Tues–Sun 10am–4pm; July & Aug Tues–Sun 9am–6pm; ⓦwww.hrad-lipnice.cz; 40Kč), ruined even in Hašek's day, is still partly rubble. A flattering bust of the author has been erected on the way up to the castle, and his gravestone is a little less ignominious these days (see box above). Beside the castle, in the house where he died, the **Memorial to Jaroslav Hašek** (June–Sept Tues–Sun 9am–noon & 1–4pm; guided tours in Czech only) is respectfully vague about Hašek's less-than-rosy side, not least the alcoholism that eventually killed him. The pub is now run by his grandson, as is the *Penzion U České koruny*, where the writer also had an apartment (☎569 486 126, ⓦwww.hasektour.cz; rooms ❷, Hašek's apartment ❸). There are no easy transport links from Tábor or Pelhřimov, but roughly six buses a day (Mon–Fri) make the fourteen-kilometre trip from Havlíčkův Brod on the mainline from Prague to Brno.

Třeboňsko

The **Třeboňsko** region, with the picturesque town of **Třeboň** at its heart, is unlike the rest of South Bohemia – characterized not by rolling hills but by peat bogs, flatlands and fish ponds. This monotonous marshland, broken only by the occasional Gothic fortress, was moulded into an intricate system of canal-linked **ponds** (totalling over 6000) as early as the fifteenth century, ushering in profitable times for the nobles who owned the land. The fish industry still dominates the region, and around September the ponds are drained to allow the fish to be "harvested". Larger ponds, like the Rožmberk, are drained only every two years, and for several days people from the surrounding district gather to feast, sing and participate in a great local event that's worth seeking out if you're in the vicinity. **Wildlife** also thrives on the soggy plains – as do mosquitoes in the summer.

Jindřichův Hradec

JINDŘICHŮV HRADEC (Neuhaus) is the largest of the towns set among Třeboňsko's fish ponds. Hemmed in by walls and water, it's typical of the region – blessed with a glorious medieval past and a particularly appealing **zámek** – and, structurally at least, untouched by modern conflicts.

Arrival and accommodation

To get to the staré město from the **bus and train stations** to the north, it's a fifteen-minute walk along Nádražní, then left down Klášterská. This brings you to the edge of the old town, where the walls have long since been replaced by

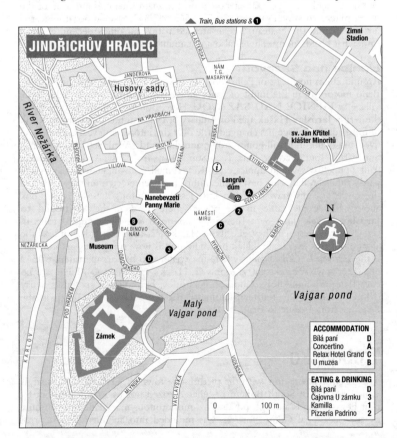

a park, the Husovy sady. You could also catch bus #1 or #4, which drop you on the main square. There's a **tourist office** on Panská (Mon–Fri 8am–5pm, Sat 8am–noon; ☎384 363 546, Ⓦwww.jh.cz), just off the main square, which has internet access. They should also have information about the state-owned **narrow-gauge railway** (*úzkorozchodná železnice*) run by JHMD (Ⓦwww .jhmd.cz), that winds its way north to Obrataň and south to Nová Bystřice, with occasional steam trains on both the branch lines. In the Langrův dům on the square is the **internet café** *EsNet*.

On the main square, the best of the **hotels** are the *Concertino* (☎384 362 320, Ⓦwww.concertino.cz; ❹) and the *Relax Hotel Grand* (☎384 361 252, Ⓦwww .relaxhotel.cz; ❸), which has a sauna. Better value, though, is the characterful *Bílá paní* (☎384 363 329, Ⓦwww.hotelbilapani.cz; ❸), in a lovely old house right by the chateau at Dobrovského 5, with a stylish restaurant on the ground floor. Another option is *U muzea* (☎384 361 698, Ⓦwww.umuzea.jhweb.cz; ❷), a pension in an apricot-coloured building opposite the museum; its restaurant has a summer terrace.

The Town

Although the staré město was robbed of much of its rich medieval dressing by a fire in 1801, the main square, **náměstí Míru**, still displays an attractive array of wealthy merchants' houses, sporting brightly coloured early nineteenth-century facades, and an exceptionally fine Baroque Trinity column. Only one house, the **Langrův dům** from 1579, hints at the Renaissance riches that were once the norm here. The diamond vaulting in the arcaded ground floor and the sgraffito biblical scenes that cover the façade bear closer inspection, especially the depiction of Jonah being swallowed by what looks like a giant crocodile, on the side of the oriel window.

Rybniční leads down from the main square to a bridge that bisects the Vajgar fishpond, creating a small harbour. From here, the town's thirteenth-century **zámek** (Tues–Sun: April & Oct 10am–3.15pm; May & Sept 10am–4.15pm; June–Aug 9am–4.15pm; Ⓦwww.zamek-jindrichuvhradec.eu) – chief residence of the lords of Hradec, and later the Černíns – is picturesquely mirrored in the water, its forbidding exterior giving no hint of the exuberant interior renovations by Italian architects in the sixteenth century, which make a visit here a must.

To get to the main entrance, head down Dobrovského. You have a choice of three fifty-minute **guided tours**, occasionally in English (220Kč for all three; 390Kč for all three in English), which set off from the second courtyard. *Trasa A* (Tues–Sun: April & Oct 10am–noon & 1–4pm; May & Sept 10am–noon & 1–5pm; June–Aug 9am–noon & 1–5pm; 100Kč, 180Kč in English), the *Adamovo stavení*, leads you through the Neoclassical and Baroque "Green Rooms", and past Petr Brandel's painting of St Joseph curing the lepers; *trasa B* (May & Sept Sat & Sun 10am–4.15pm; June–Aug Tues–Sun 9am–4.15pm; 90Kč, 160Kč in English), the *Gotický hrad*, explores the Gothic interiors, and features the starkly beautiful thirteenth-century chapel, fourteenth-century frescoes and the black kitchen; *trasa C* (June–Aug Tues–Sun 9am–4.15pm; 90Kč, 160Kč in English), the *Procházka staletími*, takes you round the slender, triple-tiered, Renaissance loggia (which you can view without a guide) and the Černíns' bizarre collection of dog portraits, as well as gaining you entrance to the chateau's pride and joy, the striking bubble-gum-pink garden rotunda, known as the Rondel, with its incredible gilded stuccowork. The chateau's **Černá věž** (Black Tower), accessible from the second courtyard, is accessible without a guided tour (May Sat & Sun 9am–3pm; June–Sept Tues–Sun 9am–3pm, depending on the weather; 25Kč), and you can peek through the windows into the Rondel anytime.

With most tour groups visiting only the chateau, hardly anyone explores the cobbled alleyways northwest of the main square at the top of Komenského. You can climb the tall **tower** (April–June & Sept–Dec Sat & Sun 10am–noon & 1–4pm; July & Aug daily 10am–noon & 1–4pm) of the Gothic church of Nanebevzetí Panny Marie, which is situated exactly on the fifteenth meridian east of Greenwich, and pay a visit to the former Jesuit seminary on Balbínovo náměstí, founded by Adam II of Hradec and Catherine de Montfort in 1604, and now home to the local **museum** (April–Dec Tues–Sun 8.30am–noon & 12.30–5pm; June–Sept daily same hours; 40Kč). Its chief exhibit is a 3-D Bethlehem Nativity scene – the world's largest – created over the course of sixty years by Tomáš Krýza (1838–1918), with fully mechanized figures. Other highlights include a seventeenth-century pharmacy and the reconstructed parlour of opera singer Ema Destinnová, who lived nearby in Stráž nad Nežárkou (see below).

Eating and drinking

The **restaurant** in the *Bílá paní* is a reasonable place for typical Czech dishes, and there's a pleasant tea-house, *Čajovna U zámku* (closed Mon), near *Bílá paní*. The wood-oven pizzas baked expertly by *Pizzeria Padrino*, náměstí Míru 158, are easily the best in town. The *Kamilla*, on Pražská, ten-minutes' walk north of the main square along Panská and Klášterská, is a lively **pub** with Regent on tap.

Červená Lhota

In the middle of nowhere, off the main road between Jindřichův Hradec and Soběslav, the red sugar-lump zámek of **Červená Lhota** (Feb & March Sat & Sun 10am–4pm; April Tues–Thurs 10am–5pm, Fri–Sun 10am–7pm; May Tues–Thurs

Ema Destinnová

Halfway between Jindřichův Hradec and Třeboň lies the town of Stráž nad Nežárkou (Platz an der Naser), whose chateau was once the estate of Czech diva **Ema Destinnová** (1878–1930) – her initials "ED" are emblazoned on the gates – one of the world's premier sopranos of the early twentieth century. Born Ema Kittlová, she took her stage name as a tribute to her first singing teacher. She won huge critical acclaim in Berlin at the age of just 19 as Santuzza in *Cavalleria rusticana*. As Donna Anna in Mozart's *Don Giovanni* at Covent Garden, she sang so well that they had her back for every performance for the next ten years. She sang opposite Enrico Caruso in the London premiere of *Madame Butterfly*, was chosen by Richard Strauss for the Berlin premiere of *Salome*, and enjoyed eight seasons as the *prima donna* at New York's Metropolitan Opera. However, she also had strong ties to the Czech independence movement, and in 1916, during the height of World War I, she decided to return to Stráž for a visit, where she was arrested for smuggling revolutionary plans over the border. She was sentenced to confinement at her estate – though given that the penalty for espionage was, in fact, death without trial, Destinnová got off relatively lightly.

When the war ended, Destinnová threw herself into promoting Czech opera and went on a European tour with an exclusively Czech repertoire. Her great days as a diva were over, however, and she spent her last twelve years writing plays, novels and poetry and living off the fish she caught from the Nežárka river. After her death in Stráž from a stroke at the age of 52, Destinnová was given a lavish burial at Prague's Vyšehrad cemetery, and in 1996 the Czech treasury placed her image on its new 2000Kč note. Her **zámek** (May, June & Sept Sat & Sun 10am–4pm; July & Aug Tues–Sun 9am–5pm; Ⓦ www.zamekstraz.cz) offers a choice of guided tours – if you're interested in the diva's life, choose *trasa 2* (60Kč) or the longer *trasa 4* (110Kč).

10am–6pm, Fri–Sun 10am–7pm; June–Aug daily 9am–9pm; Sept Tues–Sun 10am–7pm; Oct Tues–Sun 10.30am–7pm; Dec Sat & Sun 10am–6pm; 60Kč; tour in English 120Kč; ⓦ www.cervenalhota.com) is reflected perfectly in the still waters that surround it. This breathtaking sight – a Gothic water fort converted into a Renaissance retreat for the rich in 1551 – appears on almost every regional tourist handout, but its isolated location makes it a nightmare to reach on public transport. Given this, and the unremarkable nature of the chateau's interior, it's really only for dedicated fans of **Karl Ditters von Dittersdorf**, Mozart's composing chum who died here in 1799. That said, the lakeside grounds around the chateau are perfect for a picnic, and in high season there are boats for hire, and a horse and carriage available in which to take a turn. You can also **stay** at *U zámku Červená Lhota* (ⓣ 384 384 305; ❷), in some of the chateau's outbuildings.

Třeboň

Right in the midst of some of the region's largest fishponds, the charming spa town of **TŘEBOŇ** (Wittingau) is as medieval and minute as they come. The entire **staré město** is made up of just four streets, a fourteenth-century monastery and a chateau.

Arrival, information and accommodation

Třeboň's main **train station** is 2km north of the old town, off the road to Tábor; Třeboň lázně station is only ten-minutes' walk east of the old town. A couple of express trains stop at the latter station en route to Vienna, via Gmünd. However, there are no direct trains to or from České Budějovice or Jindřichův Hradec; to connect with them, you're best heading for the **bus station** – which has a left-luggage facility – a ten-minute walk northwest of the old town along Jiráskova.

The local **tourist office** (May–Sept Mon–Fri 9am–6pm, Sat & Sun 10am–noon & 1–6pm; Oct–April Mon–Fri 9am–5pm, Sat 9am–noon; ⓣ 384 721 169, ⓦ www.itrebon.cz), on the main square in the old town, can book **private rooms** and has **internet access**. There are also two **hotels** on the main square: the *Bílý koníček* (ⓣ 384 721 213, ⓦ www.hotelbilykonicek.cz; ❸) is prettier outside than in, but offers quite cheap en-suite rooms; the *Zlatá hvězda* (ⓣ 384 757 111, ⓦ www.zhvezda.cz; ❹), closer to the zámek on the opposite side, has much more comfortable rooms with TV for roughly twice the price. Another option is *U míšků* (ⓣ 384 721 698, ⓦ www.misek.cz; ❹), a pension and café-gallery, with a tiny indoor pool, in a prettily gabled building just north of the main square at Husova 11. For **camping** (and swimming), head for the *Autocamp Třeboň*, which also has bungalows (ⓦ www.autocamp-trebon.cz; May–Sept); it's situated south of the Svět pond, near the mausoleum.

The Town

The houses lining the long, thin main square, **Masarykovo náměstí**, make an attractive parade, but the *Bílý koníček* (*White Horse*) – now a hotel – built in 1544, steals the show with a stepped gable of miniature turrets. For a bird's-eye view of the square, climb the town hall's white **tower** from 1566 (summer daily 11am–4.30pm) opposite the *Bílý koníček*. As for the rest of the **staré město**, three gateways (including the impressive double south gate, next to the local brewery) and the entire ring of walls have survived from the sixteenth century, though many houses suffered badly during the last great fire in 1781. Just south of the main square, the **Regent Brewery**, founded in the fourteenth-century, is still operating. Tours of the cellar allow you to sample its lagers and pale ales (ⓣ 384 721 319, ⓦ www.pivovar-regent.cz).

Out of all proportion to the rest of the town is the huge Renaissance **zámek** (April–Oct Tues–Sun 9am–noon & 1–4pm; June–Aug closes 5.15pm; out of season call ☎384 721 193), built by Petr Vok, a colourful character, notoriously fond of sex, drugs and alchemy, friend of the mad Emperor Rudolf II, legendary thrower of parties, and the last heir of the Rožmberk family. The chateau, daubed in blinding white sgraffito and taking up almost a fifth of the town, is a pretty clumsy affair, but the interior is definitely worth visiting. There's a choice of three 45-minute guided tours: best go for *trasa A* (60Kč), which concentrates on Petr Vok and the chateau's Renaissance legacy. The Baroque and nineteenth-century period furniture imported by the later owners, the Schwarzenbergs, forms the bedrock of *trasa B* (80Kč), while *trasa C* (50Kč) focuses on the stables, dungeons and the unusual dogs' kitchen. For a guided tour in English, you'll need to ring ahead and pay 80–100Kč extra. Next to the chateau and equal in size to the old town is a very pleasant "English park", where the town's spa patients can take a stroll (daily dawn–dusk). Here you'll find the entrance to the castle's exhibition **Třeboňsko – krajina a lidé** (Třeboňsko – Man and the Landscape; April & Oct Tues–Sun 9am–5pm; May–Sept daily 9am–5pm; 50Kč), featuring well-designed displays and video presentations on the region's history and natural landscape.

South of the town is the Svět pond, beside which stands the local **fishery**, which handles the region's huge fish harvest and, most importantly, its *kapr* (carp) culling. **Carp**, not turkey, is the centrepiece of the Christmas meal in the Czech Lands, traditionally sold live and wriggling from town squares across the country, then transferred to the family bathtub until the big day. In summer you can take a 45-minute **cruise** of the pond (☎777 834 716; 100Kč).

The Schwarzenberg mausoleum

Head south out of Třeboň towards Borovany along the gravel path that skirts lakeshore, and you'll pick up signs to the **Schwarzenberg mausoleum** (Schwarzenberská hrobka; April, May, Sept & Oct Tues–Sun 9am–4pm; June–Aug Tues–Sun 9am–5pm; 50Kč), twenty-minutes' walk from the town centre. Hidden among the silver birch trees south of the Svět pond, it's a rather subdued, out-of-the-way site for a family so fond of ostentatious displays of wealth. The building itself is equally strange: a seemingly brand-new neo-Gothic building, with a bare chapel above and a dark crypt below (guided tours only).

Třeboň was the first Bohemian town to be bought up by the Bavarian-based Schwarzenberg family in 1660 who, having sided with the Habsburgs in the Counter-Reformation, became the unofficial heirs of ousted or defunct Czech aristocrats like the Vítkovci and Rožmberks. By 1875, the family owned more estates in Bohemia than anyone else and decided to "honour" Třeboň by establishing the family mausoleum in the town. After 1945, the family's possessions were expropriated and, along with all their fellow German-speakers, they were thrown out of the country.

Eating and drinking

For a taste of the local beer, there's no better place to go than the Regent brewery's own **pub**, a simple *pivnice* just inside the brewery archway. The very popular local fish **restaurant** *Šupina & Šupinka* lies opposite, in the twin buildings; if it's full, try the *Malá bašta*, on Masarykovo náměstí, which offers similar dishes. If you're camping and cooking your own food, head for the *rybárna* (fishmonger), which has fresh produce, right by the carp pools, to the south of town.

Česke Budějovice and around

The flat, urban sprawl of **ČESKÉ BUDĚJOVICE** (Budweis) comes as a surprise after the small-town nature of the rest of South Bohemia. But first impressions are deceptive, for at its heart it's a laid-back city, no more cosmopolitan than anywhere else in the region, with a perfectly preserved staré město that attracts a good number of Bavarian and Austrian tourists. Any renown it has is due to its local brew Budvar, also confusingly known (except in the US) under its original German name, **Budweiser** (see box, p.179).

Founded by King Otakar II in 1265 as a German merchants' colony, České Budějovice grew wealthy from its medieval silver mines and its position on the old salt route from Linz to Prague. Much of it was wiped out in the seventeenth century by war and fire, but, perhaps because it remained a loyal Catholic stronghold in a hotbed of Hussitism, the Habsburgs lavishly reconstructed most of it in the eighteenth century, and miraculously, in the face of two centuries of rapid industrial growth, the city's **staré město** remains carefully preserved.

Arrival and information

A ten-minute walk from the **train and bus stations** – the train station has a branch of the tourist office (Mon–Fri 9am–4pm, Sat 9am–noon & 12.30–3pm) and **left-luggage** facilities – down Lannova třída will bring you to Na sadech, the busy ring road that encloses the staré město in place of the greater part of the old town walls.

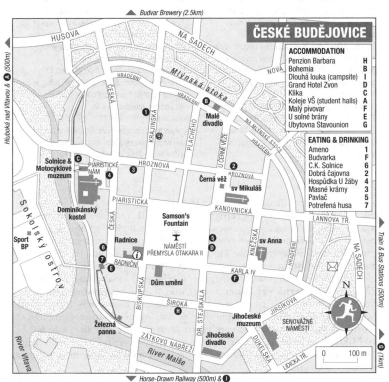

The **tourist office** in the town hall on the main square (May–Sept Mon–Fri 8.30am–6pm, Sat 8.30am–5pm, Sun 10am–noon & 12.30–4pm; Oct–April Mon–Fri 9am–4pm, Sat 9am–noon & 1–3pm; ☎386 801 413, ⓦwww .c-budejovice.cz) can help book accommodation. Sign onto the **internet** at *Na půdě*, at Krajinská 28 (ⓦwww.napude.cz).

A number of scenic **cycling trails** wend their way through and beyond České Budějovice; during the warmer months the paths along the river and on Sokolský ostrov are particularly popular. You can pick up an excellent cycling map from the tourist office and rent bikes at Sport BP (☎387 318 439, ⓦwww .sportbp.cz), on Sokolský ostrov.

Accommodation

České Budějovice's popularity with Austrians and Germans means that **hotels and pensions** tend to charge over the odds. From July to September rooms are available in **student halls** (*Koleje VŠ*), west of the Vltava at Studentská 15 (☎387 774 201; ❷); take bus #1 or #3 from Na Sadech. An even cheaper option is the *Ubytovna Stavounion* (book through the tourist office; ❶), a bunkhouse at Novohradská 3, southeast of the centre (bus #11 from the train station), offering clean, simple rooms with shared facilities and a lunchtime café. You can **camp** or rent a **bungalow** at the *Dlouhá louka* (☎387 203 601, ⓦwww.dlouhalouka .cz; all year), southwest of the centre on Litvínovská silnice (bus #16; stops running around 7pm) from Lidická třída near the Jihočeské muzeum.

Penzion Barbara Široká 15 ☎736 426 742, ⓦwww.penzionbarbara.cz. Just seven spacious, sunny rooms in this small, modern pension its own restaurant (Mon–Fri). ❸
Bohemia Hradební 20 ☎386 354 500, ⓦwww .hotelbohemiacb.cz. A comfortably modernized hotel on the northern edge of the old town, with its own little courtyard and vaulted cellar restaurant. ❹
Grand Hotel Zvon náměstí Přemysla Otakara II 28 ☎387 601 601, ⓦwww.hotel-zvon.cz. Luxurious hotel occupying one of the former burgher palaces right on the spectacular main square. ❻

Klika Hroznová 25 ☎387 318 171, ⓦwww .hotelklika.cz. Modern, tastefully furnished rooms in a hotel-restaurant, nicely situated by an arm of the Malše, on the western edge of the old town. The restaurant has a summer terrace and a winter garden, both overlooking the river. ❹
Malý pivovar Karla IV 8–10 ☎386 360 471, ⓦwww.malypivovar. Slick, Budvar-run hotel, in an arcaded burgher house just off the main square, with tasteful, modern en-suite rooms. ❺
U solné brány Radniční 11 ☎386 354 121, ⓦwww.hotelusolnebrany.cz. Tucked into the old town walls, this small hotel has pleasant, relaxed service and tasteful, plain rooms with satellite TV. ❹

The Town

České Budějovice's medieval grid plan leads inevitably to the town's showpiece, the magnificent **náměstí Přemysla Otakara II**, one of Europe's largest squares. The buildings are supremely elegant, testifying to the last three centuries of German burgher power, but it's the square's arcades, its magnificent Baroque radnice, whose clock tinkles out tunes, and the octagonal **Samson's Fountain** – once the only tap in town – that make the greatest impression. It was German merchants, too, who paid in silver and salt for the 72-metre-high **černá věž** (Black Tower), one of the few survivors of the 1641 fire, which leans gently to one side of the square. Its roof gallery (April–June, Sept & Oct Tues–Sun 10am–6pm; July & Aug Mon–Sat 10am–6pm; 25Kč) provides a superb view of the staré město. Next to the tower, the cathedral of **sv Mikuláš**, a church of Gothic proportions heavily overlaid with eighteenth-century plasterwork and furnishings, features a spectacular white marble pulpit trimmed with gold.

The streets immediately off the square – Krajinská, Česká and Kněžská – are worth a wander, and in fine weather you can join the townsfolk promenading by the banks of the Malše, where parts of the original town walls have survived. Here too you'll find some of České Budějovice's oldest buildings, such as the fifteenth-century prison tower, named after its most infamous torture instrument, **Železná panna** (literally "Iron Maiden"). All that is left of the bishop's palace is his serene **garden**, occasionally accessible in summer through a small gateway in the walls a little further on. At the second bridge as you head north, a right turn down Hroznová will lead you round into Piaristické náměstí, where the rough-looking, thoroughly medieval **solnice** (salt store) stands; it was later used as the town's arsenal and now houses the impressive **Motocyklové muzeum** (Motorcycle Museum; Tues–Sun 10am–6pm; 50Kč), with several vintage makes lining its narrow two floors.

Typically with regional museums, you'll need an interest in stuffed birds, mushrooms, armoury, coins and the like when visiting the grandiose **Jihočeské muzeum** (Tues–Sun 9am–12.30pm & 1–5.30pm; ⓦ www.muzeumcb.cz; 80Kč), southeast of the old town on Dukelská; it does occasionally put on interesting temporary shows.

The Budvar brewery

The **Budvar brewery**, 2.5km up the road to Prague, on Karolíny Světlé, has a modern *pivnice* (daily 10am–10pm) inside the nasty titanium-blue headquarters;

Budvar vs Budweiser

As far as taste goes, Czech **Budvar** bears little resemblance to the bland American Budweiser, or Bud as it's universally known – it wins hands-down. However, the fact that several of the world's beers stake a claim to the same name has caused more than a century of problems.

In fact, the name Budweiser simply refers to something from Budweis, the German name for what is now České Budějovice. The Czechs would like to argue that a Budweiser beer must come from Budweis, just as a Würzburger wine must come from Würzburg. The Americans would beg to differ. The story traditionally begins in the US in 1876, when German immigrant Carl Conrad got his brewer friend Adolphus Busch to produce a beer called Budweiser, as beers with German names sold well in the States. It wasn't until 1895 that the Czech-speakers of Budweis founded České akciový pivovar (now Budějovický Budvar), and started selling their own Budweiser beer. After several years of conflict, the Czechs and the American brewers, now known as **Anheuser-Busch**, came to an agreement in 1911, essentially allowing the Czechs to sell Budweiser in Europe, but not in America.

In the 1990s, the two breweries locked horns once more, with the scales tipped even more heavily in Anheuser-Busch's favour. Not only were the American brewers now the largest brewing company in the world, the Czechs, post-Communism, were desperate for cash to try and modernize their operation. A takeover seemed the most obvious solution. However, the Czech government, backed up by Britain's Campaign for Real Ale (CAMRA), campaigned strongly against the deal, and the brewery has remained in state hands ever since. In 2005, the other brewery in České Budějovice, which produces Samson beer, decided to join the fray. Founded by the town's German-speaking citizens in 1795 as the **Budweiser Bürgerbräu**, this brewery was selling Budweiser Bier as long ago as 1802, and has cannily recommenced production much to the annoyance of its rivals. The latest twist in the tale occurred in 2007, when Anheuser-Busch signed a deal with Budvar agreeing to distribute and market Budvar in the US under the name "Czechvar". Nevertheless, litigious skirmishes between the various breweries look to continue well into the future.

despite appearances, the beer and food are both inexpensive. To visit, you need to book one of the hour-long tours – ask for the *anglický text* (daily 9am–4pm; ☎387 705 341, ⓦwww.budweiser.cz; 100Kč). To get there, take bus #2 from the old town or a slow-stopping train to Tábor, and get off at the first stop (České Budějovice severní zastávka).

Eating, drinking and entertainment

Typical Czech **meals** are easy to come by. On the east side of the main square, *Pavlač* has a wide-ranging menu, with a few vegetarian dishes and special: ties like veal in cranberry sauce with almonds. Always busy, *Potrefená husa*, at Česká 66, behind the town hall, dishes up hearty meals on its big roof terrace overlooking the river, while *Hospůdka U žáby* (closed Sun), opposite the Motorcycle Museum, serves cheap pub food. For something different, try the hefty burritos and tasty pizza at *Ameno*, Krajinská 31.

Drinking is obviously important in České Budějovice. After a lengthy restoration, the nationally renowned ⚜ *Masné krámy*, formerly a sixteenth-century covered meat market, is open once more and is an atmospheric place to have a drink. The *Budvarka* pub in the hotel *Malý pivovar* is the best spot to quaff Budvar, since it's run by the brewery itself. For chilling out, there's no better place than the *Dobrá čajovna*, on Hroznová 16, right behind the Černá věž, a typically relaxing branch of the tea-shop chain.

The city's largest **theatre**, the Jihočeské divadlo (ⓦwww.jihoceskedivadlo.cz), stages plays, but non-Czech speakers will do better to listen to the local **chamber orchestra** at the Koncertní síň Otakara Jeremiáše (☎386 353 561), next to the church of sv Anna on Kněžská. More raucous **nightlife** is thin on the ground, though *C.K. Solnice*, on Česká, has occasional live jazz and rock, enlivening its rather rough interior.

The Českobudějovická pánev

To the northwest of České Budějovice lies the flat basin of soggy land known as the **Českobudějovická pánev**. Most people head for **Hluboká**, whose chateau receives over a quarter of a million tourists each year. Its neo-Gothic pastiche is not to everyone's taste – in which case you'd be better off seeking out the more elusive gems of **Holašovice's** folk-Baroque architecture or **Kratochvíle's** simple Renaissance beauty.

Hluboká nad Vltavou

HLUBOKÁ NAD VLTAVOU (Frauenberg), 8km northwest of České Budějovice, is a modest little village which sits below possibly the republic's most famous **zámek** (April, Sept & Oct Tues–Sun 9am–5.30pm; May & June Tues–Sun 9am–6pm; July & Aug daily 9am–6pm; last tour 90min before closing; compulsory guided tours 220Kč). Originally founded as a Přemyslid stronghold as early as the thirteenth century, the royal family sold the property to the Lords of Hradec in 1562, only to confiscate it in 1622 after the Hradec clan backed the Protestant side in the Thirty Years' War. Eventually, it was given to the arriviste Schwarzenberg family, who, during the course of the nineteenth century made Hluboká their chief seat, and spent some of their considerable fortune turning it into its present crenellated, mock-Gothic incarnation. In 1945, when all the German estates were nationalized, the Schwarzenbergs decamped with most of the loot, but they've since returned and filled the interior with the odds and ends they left behind at their numerous other castles.

If Hluboká's reproduction interiors fail to move you, seek sanctuary in the former riding school. This now houses the **Alšova jihočeské galerie** (daily: May–Sept 9–11.30am & 12.30–6pm; Oct–April 9–11.30am & 12.30–4pm; Ⓦwww.ajg.cz; 50Kč), a permanent collection of Gothic religious art, Dutch and Flemish sixteenth- to eighteenth-century masters and a large hall filled with a superb collection of twentieth-century Czech art, including Art Nouveau works by Bílek and Jan Preisler, a smattering of Cubist canvases by Čapek, Kubišta and Filla, a good selection of Surrealist paintings by the likes of Toyen and Štyrský, and 1960s Pop Art. The chateau and gallery aside, the very beautiful English-style grounds are reason enough to make the trip, though keep an eye out for wild boars that are reputed to roam here.

Practicalities

Regular **buses** run from České Budějovice, dropping passengers in the main square. In addition, two out-of-the-way **train** stations (nominally) serve the village: Hluboká nad Vltavou, 3km to the southwest on the Plzeň line; and Hluboká nad Vltavou-Zámostí, 2km to the east on the main line to Prague. There's also a **cycling path** (#12) from České Budějovice to Hluboká along the Vltava; ask the tourist office for a map.

The village has plenty of **places to stay**, but prices are no lower than in České Budějovice; ask at the **tourist office** (☎387 966 164, Ⓦwww.visitshluboka.cz), opposite the church on Zborovská, about private rooms. Alternatively, hotel *Apartment Hluboká* (☎387 967 777, Ⓦwww.kamille.cz; ❹), at Masarykova 972, has ten modern apartments (each with kitchen and two bedrooms), while in the nearby *Hotel Bakalář* (☎387 983 530, Ⓔhotelbakalar@seznam; ❸) at no. 69 you can rent bicycles. There's also the lakeside *Křivonoska* **campsite** (late May to Sept; Ⓦwww.krivonska.cz), 3km to the northwest up route 105.

Holašovice

If you have the time (and preferably your own car or bike), it's worth making a quick detour to the UNESCO-protected village of **HOLAŠOVICE**, 15km west of České Budějovice off the road to Lhenice, where you can see some of the finest examples of **Baroque folk architecture** unique to this part of Bohemia. The stone farmhouses (including the two pubs *U Vojty* and *Jihočeská hospoda*) date from the first six decades of the nineteenth century, and face onto the original green. Every house on the square follows the same basic design, though the decorative details on barn doors and gables are unique to each. Other nearby villages display similar architectural treats – like Záboří, 2km north, and Dobčice, another 2km west – but none can compete with the consummate effect of Holašovice. Ask about private **rooms** at the **tourist centre** (open in season only Tues–Sun 9am–5pm; ☎387 982 145, Ⓦwww .holasovice.eu), at the corner of the square.

Kratochvíle

Further west along route 145, and 2km beyond Netolice, lies **Kratochvíle** (Kurzweil), without doubt the most charming Renaissance chateau in Bohemia. It stands unaltered since its rapid six-year construction by Italian architects between 1583 and 1589, commissioned by the last generation of Rožmberks to while away the time – the literal meaning of *kratochvíle*. The attention to detail is still clearly visible in the exquisite stuccowork and painted vaults, but the rest of the place is now given over to the **Museum of Animated Film** (April & Oct Sat & Sun 9am–noon & 1–4pm; May & Sept Tues–Sun 9am–noon & 1–4.15pm; June–Aug Tues–Sun 9am–noon & 1–5.15pm), which is aimed primarily at a young, domestic audience, with original puppet "actors" and drawings from well-known Czech kids' cartoons. However, the thoughtfully laid out exhibition, demonstrating all the painstaking processes involved in animation, should interest anyone, particularly with Josef Lada's amusing drawings of the Good Soldier Švejk and two typically disturbing sculptures by Jan Švankmajer. Kratochvíle is served by several daily **buses** plying the České Budějovice–Prachatice route, though as usual service is cut short at weekends.

The foothills of the Šumava

An alternative to heading up the Českobudějovická pánev is to aim for the large bulge of forest, known as the **Blanský les**, to the southwest of České Budějovice. Its highest point is **Mount Kleť** (1083m), which stands slightly apart from the rest of the Šumava range and looks all the more impressive for it, towering above the Vltava basin to the north. From the summit on a clear day, you can see the undulating forested peaks of the Šumava laid out before you. As well as the obligatory TV tower, the hill is the site for the astronomical **Observatoř Kleť** (July & Aug Tues–Sun hourly guided tours 10.30am–3.30pm; Nov & March– June Sat & Sun only; ☏380 711 242, ⓦwww.klet.org; 40Kč). You can reach the top either by hopping into a single-seat chairlift (Wed–Sun hourly 10am–5pm) or opting for a stiff but enchanting four-kilometre hike through the woods. To reach the chairlift from České Budějovice or Český Krumlov, catch a train to the idyllic rural station at Holubov and walk the last 4km via Krasetín.

There's little **accommodation** in this neck of the woods, aside from a few private rooms and a basic **campsite** (May–Sept) in **ZLATÁ KORUNA** (Goldenkron), a tiny village on the Vltava, 6km along the line from Holubov. Here you can visit the strongly fortified **Cistercian monastery** (Tues–Sun: April, May, Sept & Oct 9am–noon & 1–4pm; June–Aug 8am–noon & 1–5pm; ☏380 743 126, ⓦwww.zlatakoruna.cz; tour in English 170Kč), founded in 1263 by Přemysl King Otakar II. As a wealthy bastion of Catholicism, it suffered badly at the hands of the Hussites, but parts of the original medieval structures survive. In one building there's a worthy museum on Czech literature, but the main focus is the vaulted chapterhouse dating from 1280 and the Gothic church, built in part by Peter Parler's masons and one of the first to employ ribbed vaulting without any accompanying capitals.

Český Krumlov

Squeezed into a tight S-bend of the Vltava, in the foothills of the Šumava, **ČESKÝ KRUMLOV** (Krumau) is one of the most exquisite towns in the Czech Republic. Rose-brown houses tumble down steep slopes to the blue-green river below, creating a magical effect whose beauty has barely changed in the last three hundred years. Under the Communists, few foreign visitors made it here, but nowadays the huge rise in tourism has made this the one place outside Prague where the warren of narrow streets can get uncomfortably crowded with day-trippers, including a steady parade of young backpackers. The whole town is a UNESCO-designated site, but with rich pickings now on offer, many of its residents are renovating their properties, causing great concern among conservationists, who foresee overdevelopment and insensitive restoration – not to mention the loss of character that occurs when virtually every building is turned over to pensions and restaurants. For all that, it's a place that never fails to impress.

▲ Český Krumlov

Arrival and information

The old town is divided into two by the twisting snake of the River Vltava: the circular **staré město** on the right bank and the **Latrán quarter** on the hillier left bank. The best way to explore Český Krumlov is by foot. The **train station** lies twenty-minutes' walk north of the old town up a precipitous set of steps, while the main **bus station** is closer to the heart of things, on the right bank. The **tourist office** on náměstí Svornosti (daily: April, May & Oct 9am–6pm; June & Sept 9am–7pm; July & Aug 9am–8pm; Nov–March 9am–5pm; ☎380 704 622, ⓦwww.ckrumlov.cz) has **internet** access and helps with accommodation, as does the **UNIOS** office (daily: June–Aug 9am–noon & 1–7pm; Sept–May 9am–noon & 1–6pm; ⓦwww.unios.cz), at the zámek's entrance, which also provides information about the castle and sells bus tickets to Prague. You can also go online at the **internet café** inside the zámek gates.

In summer, you can **rent kayaks**, **canoes** and **rafts** from the Vltava agency (ⓦwww.ckvltava.cz), Kájovská 62, and paddle downstream (a shuttle minibus brings you back). They also rent out **bikes** and **catamarans** on Lake Lipno (see p.191).

Accommodation

Accommodation is not in short supply, but the town gets crowded in high season. As well as the places listed below, there are numerous small pensions and **private rooms** in town – Parkán and Rooseveltova are literally heaving with them – and many lively **hostels**. The popular HI *Travellers Hostel* at Soukenická 43 (☎380 711 345, ⓦwww.travellers.cz; ❷) has bike rental, a barbecue and internet access; even better is *Hostel Ryba* (☎380 711 801; ❷) with a nice river terrace and pub. Several **campsites** dot the Vltava south of town; one of the best is *Kemp Český Krumlov* (☎777 640 946, ⓦwww .kempkrumlov.cz), on the south side of the river just past Nové Spolí, with bike and canoe rental and a restaurant.

▲ Grafitový důl (500m)　　　　　　　　▲ Train Station (1km)

RESTAURANTS, PUBS & TEA-HOUSES

Cikánská jizba	4
Dobrá čajovna	1
Eggenberg	2
Laibon	5
Maštal	6
Na louži	9
Papa's Living Restaurant	3
Rybářská bašta	7
U písaře Jana	8

0 ——— 100 m

ACCOMMODATION

Pension Barbakán	H
Kemp Český Krumlov (campsite)	J
Hotel Leonardo	D
Hotel Na louži	E
Hotel Růže	G
Hostel Ryba	I
Travellers Hostel	C
U města Vídně	A
Ve věži	B
Zlatý anděl	F

Budějovická brána

Jelení zahrada

PoleČnice

CHVALSÍNSKÁ SILNICE

Convent of Poor Clares

Zámecké divadlo

PLÁŠŤOVÝ MOST

Krumlovský zámek

LATRÁN

Zámecká zahrada

MOST NA PLÁŠTI

NA OSTROVĚ

Former arsenal

LATRÁN

NOVÉ MĚSTO

Brewery

DLOUHÁ

MĚSTO

Pohádkový dům

Muzeum marionet

STARÉ

SOUKENICKÁ

ŠIROKÁ

RADNIČNÍ

MASNÁ

NÁPLAVKA

River Vltava

Schiele Centrum

Radnice

NÁMĚSTÍ SVORNOSTI

PARKÁN

Regionální muzeum

RYBÁŘSKÁ

HORNÍ

KAPLICKÁ

KOSTELNÍ

Church of sv Vít

Městské sady

ROOSEVELTOVA

N

LINECKÁ

ČESKÝ KRUMLOV

HORSKÁ

160

Bus Station (250m)

J ▼

Pension Barbakán Kaplická 26 ☎ 380 717 017, ⓦ www.barbakan.cz. A wonderfully refurbished pension with tastefully decorated rooms and a terraced dining area that overlooks the stone viaduct and old town. ❸

Hotel Leonardo Soukenicka 33 ☎ 380 725 911, ⓦ www.hotel-leonardo.cz. Just off náměstí Svornosti, the elegant *Leonardo* has eleven spacious, smartly appointed rooms and friendly, attentive staff. ❻

Hotel Na louži Kájovská 66 ☎ 380 711 280, ⓦ www.nalouzi.cz. An excellent hotel, kitted out with antique furniture, and situated above a great pub near the Schiele Centrum. ❸

Hotel Růže Horní 154 ☎ 380 772 100, ⓦ www.hotelruze.cz. Originally built by the Rožmberks to house their guests, the *Růže* is right in the heart of

the staré město, with pool, sauna, casino and the odd original Renaissance feature. ❾

U města Vídně Latrán 77 ☎ 380 720 111, ⓦ www.hmv.cz. An upscale hotel offering refurbished rooms in a sixteenth-century bakery at the edge of the old town. Facilities include internet access and a small gym. ❼

Ve věži Pivovarská 28 ☎ 380 711 742. Several bargain rooms hidden inside one of the town's medieval bastions, right by the Eggenberg Brewery. ❸

Zlatý anděl náměstí Svornosti 10 ☎ 380 712 310, ⓦ www.hotelzlatyandel.cz. Tall, thin hotel in one of the Renaissance houses on the old town square, with no lift, but stylish decor – ask for a room overlooking the square. ❻

The Town

Český Krumlov's **history** is dominated by those great seigneurs of the region, the Rožmberks and the Schwarzenbergs. Thanks to special privileges won after the Battle of Leipzig in 1813, the Schwarzenbergs were permitted to keep a private army of twelve soldiers dressed in Napoleonic uniform (who also doubled as the castle's private orchestra), one of whom would sound the bugle at 9am every morning from the thirteenth-century round tower. In 1945, Krumau awoke abruptly from this semi-feudal coma when the Schwarzenbergs and the majority of the town's inhabitants, who were also German-speaking, were booted out; three years later, repopulated by Czech-speakers, the town went back into aspic as the Iron Curtain descended. Now the economy relies increasingly heavily on the ebb and flow of foreign tourists, a dependency that has thrown up the dubious delights of a waxworks and a torture museum, neither of which is worth visiting.

Krumlovský zámek

For centuries, the focal point of the town has been its chateau, **Krumlovský zámek** in the **Latrán quarter**, as good a place as any to begin. Once you've passed through the first gateway, you enter the sprawling first courtyard, which belongs to the older, lower castle. Cross the *medvědí příkop* (bear moat), where the latest batch of unfortunate bears is incarcerated, and head for the beautifully restored castle tower, the **Zámecká věž** (daily: April–May, Sept & Oct 9am–5pm; June–Aug 9am–6pm; 45Kč), for a superb view over the town. There are two hour-long **guided tours** (Tues–Sun: April, May, Sept & Oct 9am–5pm; June–Aug 9am–6pm), occasionally in English: go for *trasa 1* (100Kč, 230Kč for an English tour), which takes you through the surviving Renaissance rooms, the Rococo excesses of the blue and pink marble chapel, and the Maškarní sál, a ballroom exquisitely decorated with trompe l'oeil murals of *commedia dell'arte* scenes. *Trasa 2* (100Kč, 180Kč for an English tour) concentrates on portraits of the Schwarzenbergs and doles out rich helpings of nineteenth-century opulence.

The castle's unique gem, however, is its ornate eighteenth-century Rococo **Zámecké divadlo** (May–Oct Tues–Sun 45min tours 10am, 11am, 1pm, 2pm & 3pm; 200Kč, 350Kč for an English tour), on the other side of the covered Plášťový most, a many-tiered viaduct with a superb view over the town. This is one of the few Rococo theatres in the world to retain so much of its original scenery and wardrobe. An ingenious system of flies and flats meant that a typical comic opera of the kind the theatre specialized in could have more than forty scene changes without interrupting the action. It's worth booking at the ticket office at least one day in advance for a tour.

Another covered walkway takes you high above the town into the unexpectedly expansive and formal terraced **Zámecká zahrada** (daily: April & Oct 8am–5pm; May–Sept 8am–7pm), whose tranquillity is disturbed only by the operas and ballets performed in the gardens' modern, revolving, open-air theatre (*otáčivé hlediště*) during July and August; details from the tourist office.

The staré město and around

Latrán, lined with shabby, overhanging houses, leads to a wooden, ramp-like bridge that connects with the **staré město**. There's a compelling beauty in the old town, whose precarious existence is best viewed from the circling River Vltava. Turning right down Dlouhá, where the houses glow red at dusk, will bring you to the site of the town's former arsenal. From here, if the river's not swollen, you can walk across the gangplanks of the footbridge to Rybářská, which then follows the left bank to the southernmost bridge, taking you back into the old town.

Heading straight up the soft incline of Radniční brings you to the main square, **náměstí Svornosti** – look back for a great view of the castle.

Schiele in Krumau

In 1911, the Austrian painter **Egon Schiele** decided to leave Vienna and spend some time in Krumau, his mother's home town. During his brief sojourn here, Schiele painted a number of intense townscapes, like *Houses and Roofs near Krumau* and *Dead City*, in which he managed to make even the buildings look sexually anguished. At the time, he was not making much money from his art, and was forced to shuffle from rooming house to rooming house with his 17-year-old lover, Wally Neuzil, a model handed down to him by Gustav Klimt. Finally he succeeded in buying a studio, a crumbling Baroque cottage by the river in Plešivec, south of the old town. Schiele and his bohemian companions, Erwin Osen and Moa Mandu, caused more than a little controversy in this resolutely petit-bourgeois town – hiring young local girls for nude modelling and painting Wally naked in the orchard were among his more famous faux pas. Forced to leave before the year was out, he vowed never to return.

Under the Communists, the town made no attempt to advertise Schiele's brief but productive stay; now, however, Schiele is for Krumlov what Kafka is for Prague. Fans of the artist should head for the **Schiele Centrum** (daily 10am–6pm; Ⓦwww.schieleartcentrum.cz; 120Kč), a vast, rambling art complex housed in a fifteenth-century former brewery on Široká, where a smattering of the artist's lithographs, watercolours and pencil sketches – including one of Český Krumlov – are on permanent display. In addition, there's some furniture designed by the artist for his studio, a small exhibition on Schiele's life, and regular shows by contemporary artists.

Occupying one side of the cobbled square is the former **radnice**, which was created out of two and a half Gothic houses, and sports a strikingly long, white, Renaissance entablature of blind arcading. To the southeast, the high lancet windows of the church of **sv Vít** rise vertically above the ramshackle rooftops. Inside, the church retains its Gothic lierne vaulting, patches of medieval fresco and the remarkable tomb of Vilém of Rožmberk. One or two of the later furnishings are notable, too, particularly the Rococo organ case and the fabulously gilded pulpit.

If you continue east off the square, down Horní, you'll meet the beautiful sgraffitoed sixteenth-century Jesuit college, which now houses the *Hotel Růže*, among other things. Opposite the *Růže*, the local **museum** (Regionalní muzeum; March, April & Oct–Dec Tues–Fri 9am–4pm, Sat & Sun 1–4pm; May, June & Sept daily 10am–5pm; July & Aug daily 10am–6pm; Ⓦwww.muzeum .ckrumlov.cz; 50Kč) puts on small, temporary exhibitions relating to the history of the town. Also on display is a model of the town and the two-thousand-seat theatre at nearby Hořice, where elaborate Passion Plays have been staged on and off since 1816.

Kids and adults alike will appreciate a couple of museums located on either side of the Vltava; the **Muzeum marionet** (Marionette Museum; March–Oct daily 10am–7pm; Ⓦwww.marionettemuseum.com; 70Kč), in the former church of sv Jošt at Latrán 6, where old and new puppets from the National Marionette Theatre hang rather eerily from the wooden ceiling; and the **Pohádkový dům** (Fairytale House; Jan–March Sat & Sun 10am–6pm; April–Dec daily 10am–6pm; 80Kč), at Radniční 29, where Czech puppets, mainly from the eighteenth and nineteenth centuries, are displayed alongside an original mechanical theatre from 1815.

Eating and drinking

As far as **eating** goes, there's certainly plenty of choice – the same goes for pubs. For **teas** from around the world, slip into the *Dobrá čajovna* opposite the internet café inside the zámek gates. *Na louži*, at Kájovská 66, is the town's most historic **pub**, with fine food to boot, or else there's the Eggenberg Brewery tap, *Eggenberg*, which also puts on occasional live events and gigs (Ⓦ www.eggenberg.cz).

Cikánská jizba Dlouhá 31. Nifty, cheap little place with a country theme and lots of Czech, Slovak and gypsy specialities including goulash and *halušky*. Closed Sun.

Laibon Parkán 105. A surprisingly long, all-vegetarian menu with specialities from twelve countries and great riverside seating.

Maštal náměstí Svornosti 2. Smoky Gothic cellar restaurant on the main square serving typical Czech pub food and local beers.

Papa's Living Restaurant Latrán 13. This cosy, vaulted restaurant offers funky ribs, steaks, Italian and veggie dishes.

Rybářská bašta Kájovská 54. Excellent, reasonably priced fish restaurant in the Krčinův dům off Na louži.

U písaře Jana Horní 151. Elegant, tasteful restaurant with stucco decoration on the ceiling and a vast menu, including several fish dishes.

Nightlife and entertainment

Theatre performances take place in the **open-air revolving theatre** (*otáčivé hlediště*), in the castle gardens (June–Sept; Ⓦ www.jihoceskedivadlo.cz), and there's an **open-air cinema** 500m or so west of the main road junction, off route 39 to Volary.

Catering to the huge potential tourist audience, Český Krumlov hosts many, many cultural events throughout the summer. If you arrive in town at the weekend nearest the solstice, you'll witness the **Five-Petalled Rose Festival** (*Slavnosti pětilisté růže*), an excuse for the townsfolk to don medieval dress worn in the days of the Rožmberks, as well as let off fireworks, sing, dance and generally make merry. The town also hosts several **music festivals** (Ⓦ www.czechmusicfestival.com): a chamber music festival in June or early July, one dedicated to early music, held in mid-July, an international one which takes place over three weeks in August (Ⓦ www.festivalkrumlov.cz), plus a pop (*bigbít*) festival in mid-July and a jazz festival in late August (Ⓦ www.jazz-krumlov.cz).

The Šumava

The dense pine forests and peat bogs of the **Šumava** region (Ⓦ www.sumava-info.cz or Ⓦ www.sumava.net) stretch along the Austrian and German borders southwest of Český Krumlov, part of the much larger Böhmerwald which spreads across into Bavaria and forms one of the last remaining wildernesses in central Europe. The original inhabitants of this sparsely populated region were German-speaking foresters, who scraped a living from its meagre soil – their Austrian lilt and agricultural poverty separating them from their "civilized" Sudetenland brothers in western and northern Bohemia. Up until the declaration of the First Republic in 1918, the economic armlock of the all-powerful Schwarzenberg and Buquoy dynasties kept the region in a permanent semi-feudal state. Even in the nineteenth century, peasants had to have permission from their landlords to marry, and their customary greeting to the local squire was *Brotvater* (literally "Breadfather").

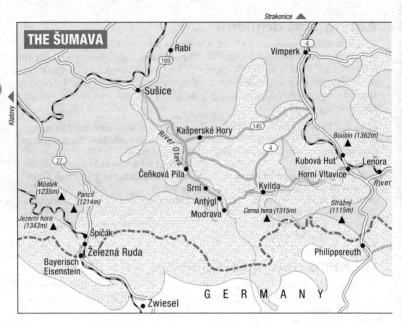

THE ŠUMAVA

Strakonice

Rabí

Vimperk

Sušice

Kašperské Hory

Boubín (1362m)

River Otava

Kubová Huť

Lenora

Čeňkova Pila

Horní Vltavice

River

Srní

Kvilda

Můstek (1235m)

Pančíř (1214m)

Antýgl

Jezerní hora (1343m)

Modrava

Černá hora (1315m)

Strážný (1115m)

Špičák

Železná Ruda

Philippsreuth

Bayerisch Eisenstein

G E R M A N Y

Zwiesel

Following the expulsion of the German-speakers in 1945, all links with the past were severed, and despite financial incentives for Czechs to move here the Šumava has remained underpopulated. Poor, provincial and out of the way compared to the rest of the former Sudetenland, it had the added misfortune of lying alongside one of the most sensitive stretches of the East–West border during the Cold War – in the 1970s, large areas of forest along the south shore of Lake Lipno were closed off by the military. Much of this land has now been relinquished, the border dismantled, and contact between the two areas re-established, all of which has revived the area considerably. Ironically, while the Iron Curtain was there, the area was protected from overdevelopment, and local campaigners are fighting to keep it that way. As a consequence, most of the roads to the south of Lake Lipno are still closed to vehicles except bicycles.

Aside from the region's one truly medieval town, **Prachatice**, the majority of visitors come here for the scenery, which is among the most unspoilt in the country, thanks to the lack of heavy industry and minimal acid rain damage. Most tourists crowd round the northern shore of the artificial **Lake Lipno**, creating their own peculiar brand of beach culture, while others head for the hills, which rise up more gently than those on the Austrian and German side. The deepest part of the forest, hugging the German and Austrian borders between Lake Lipno and Železná Ruda, is preserved as the **Šumava National Park** (Národní park Šumava), where tiny villages blend into the silent hills, meadows and peat bogs. The most scenic way of **getting around**, apart from walking, is the single-track České Budějovice–Volary train line. Local buses are much more convenient, though services peter out at weekends. Look out, too, for the special **summer bus** services, which run up to five times daily through the heart of the national park. Due to its gently hilly landscape, the park is also great **cycling** territory, and in summer,

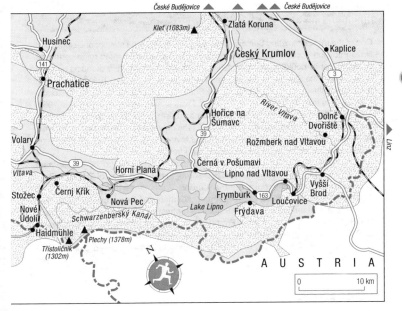

Czechs often float down the Vltava in **canoes**, which can be rented from towns along the river.

Rožmberk nad Vltavou

Buses from Český Krumlov follow the Vltava valley to the pretty village of **ROŽMBERK NAD VLTAVOU** (Rosenberg), which is tucked into a U-bend of the river, and overlooked by a spectacular, sgraffitoed **fortress** which teeters on a knife's edge high above it. As the name suggests, its *raison d'être* was as the headquarters of the powerful and single-minded Rožmberk family, regional supremos from the thirteenth century until their extinction in 1611. Only one round tower remains from the Rožmberk era, though the highlight of the interior, the castle's banquet hall with its sixteenth-century Italian frescoes, is also a Rožmberk legacy. The rest of the interior speaks little of that family, but volumes of its later French owners, the Buquoys, who stuffed the dull, mannerless rooms with heavy neo-Gothic furnishings and instruments of torture – the latter are displayed in the Katovna. There's a choice of 45-minute **guided tours** (April & Oct Sat & Sun 9am–4pm; May & Sept Tues–Sun 9am–4pm; June–Aug Tues–Sun 9am–5pm; Ⓦwww.hrad-rozmberk.eu): *trasa 1* (100Kč, 180Kč for an English tour) takes in the castle interior, while *trasa 3* (40Kč) climbs the tower, and *trasa 2* (130Kč, 210Kč, for an English tour) combines the two.

Finding **accommodation** down in the village is relatively easy, with many private rooms on offer. Otherwise, the *Hotel Růže* (Ⓣ380 749 715, Ⓦwww .hotelruze.rozmberk.cz; ❸) has well-appointed rooms and a restaurant, while the *Hotel Studenec* (Ⓣ380 749 818, Ⓦwww.hotel-studenec.com; ❸), 1km up a hill north of the village, off route 160 to Český Krumlov, rents out canoes and bikes and has a **restaurant** with a wonderful view over the valley.

Hiking in the Šumava

One of the most interesting Šumava hikes sets off from Ovesná station, one along from Nová Pec (and occasionally request only). Follow the yellow-marked route northwest through gigantic boulders and thick forest to Perník (1049m), before dropping down to Jelení, where the **Schwarzenberský kanál** emerges from a tunnel. Built at the turn of the eighteenth century, to transport the Šumava's valuable timber straight to the Danube (less than 40km due south), the canal was abandoned as a waterway in 1962. A little further on you reach **Medvědí kámen** (Bären Stein), marking the spot where the last bear in the Šumava was shot in 1856. The only threat to hikers now is the lynx, which was reintroduced hereabouts in 1985. Moving on, you should reach the village station at Černý Kříž in around six hours (14km) from Ovesná.

From Nové Údolí (only accessible by train, bike or foot), hard by the German border, you can take the red-marked trail south, 5km to the peak of **Třístoličník** or Dreisesselberg (1302m) right on the border. From here, it's another 5km to Trojmezí, the meeting-point of the German, Austrian and Czech borders, and 1km further to the summit of the Czech Šumava's highest peak, **Plechý** or Plöckenstein (1378m), on the Austrian border. From Plechý you could make the steep descent to Plešné jezero, a glacial lake that sits in the shadow of the sheer northeast face of the mountain, from which it's another 8km via the green-marked path to Nová Pec train station.

Vyšší Brod

Upriver from Rožmberk, just fifteen minutes south by bus, **VYŠŠÍ BROD** (Hohenfurth) is notable for its white **Cistercian monastery** on the western edge of town, founded in the thirteenth century in response to the Přemyslids' founding of nearby Zlatá Koruna (see p.182). Its proximity to the border and its extreme wealth gave rise to a set of immodest fortifications that withstood two sieges by the Hussites. Despite its pews, the essentially Gothic klášterní kostel was for the exclusive use of the monks, who sat in the fancy gilded stalls that take up almost half the church – only on religious holidays were the locals allowed in at the back. In the blue side chapel rests Petr Vok, the last of the Rožmberks, who died of drink and drugs but was nonetheless given pride of place as the monastery's rich patron. Suppressed during the Communist period, Vyšší Brod is once more inhabited by monks.

The only way to see the church's interior is by **guided tour** (50min; May–Sept Tues–Sat 9.30–11.30am & 12.30–5pm; Oct–April booking necessary ☎380 746 674, Ⓦwww.vyssibrod.cz; 120Kč), which also takes you through the beautiful Gothic chapterhouse and ends with the star attraction, a frescoed Rococo library decorated with 24-carat gold, accessible only via a secret door in one of the bookcases. The monastery's outer buildings house a mildly diverting **Poštovní muzeum** (April–Oct Tues–Sun 9am–noon & 1–5pm; 50Kč), charting the history of the republic's postal system since the late medieval period, with displays of period uniforms, old phones and typewriters, new stamps and old stage coaches.

Practicalities

There are **buses** from Rožmberk to Vyšší Brod, or you can catch a **train** from Rybník, 10km east on the Prague–Linz main line (get out at Vyšší Brod klášter, not Vyšší Brod, for the monastery). Local buses and trains continue 10km to Lipno nad Vltavou, at the eastern edge of Lake Lipno, where a host of other facilities is available (see opposite).

If you need a **place to stay**, try *Hotel Šumava* (℡380 746 574, 🌐www.hotel -sumava.cz; ❸), in a lovely old building on the main square at Náměstí 47, with a plain, pleasant restaurant. At the opposite corner of the square stands the *Hotel Panský dům* (℡380 746 669, 🌐www.hotelpanskydum.cz; ❸) with simple, clean en-suite rooms and a restaurant. There are also several private rooms and pensions, including *Pension Inge* (℡380 746 482, 🌐www.pensioninge.cz; ❷), right under the monastery, which has a decent restaurant and rents out boats and canoes; you can even stay in cheap, hostel-type accommodation in the monastery itself (℡380 746 457; ❶). The *Pod hrází* **campsite** (June to mid-Sept) is a basic riverside site with cold showers only, a short walk along route 163 towards Lipno nad Vltavou. If you do walk there, be sure to take the red route to the viewpoint at Čertova stěna (Devil's Walls), a giant scree of granite slabs that tumble into the river below.

Lake Lipno

Upstream from the giant paper mill at Loučovice on the Vltava, a dam marks the southeastern end of **Lake Lipno**. The barrage turns the turbines of a huge underground hydroelectric power station, and on the face of it, there's not much to get excited about. The northern shore is punctuated by small beach resorts, which have developed rapidly over the last thirty years, originally to give workers some well-needed fresh air, now with more of an eye to attract euros from across the border. The area is popular with Czechs, Germans and Austrians, so the **hotels** are often full in July and August, but you're rarely far from **private rooms** – look for the "Unterkunft/ubytování" signs dotted about – or a **campsite**, often with cheap bungalows for rent. **Buses** link most places, supplemented by trains from Černá v Pošumaví westwards.

Lipno nad Vltavou and Frymburk

About the only reason to come to **LIPNO NAD VLTAVOU** is to take the one- or two-hour **cruise** on the lake. From May to October around two boats leave daily from the small pier in town. The town has a couple of run-down hotels, though you're almost certainly better off trying any of the numerous pensions signposted off the road to Frymburk, or one of the campsites by the lake. Note that the train station at Lipno is situated below the dam, a couple of kilometres east of the town itself. A local **tourist office** (June–Aug Mon–Fri 9am–noon & 1–7pm; Sept–May closes 4pm; ℡380 736 053, 🌐www.lipnoservis .cz) is situated on the main road. Beyond Lipno, you can hardly miss the largest development on the lake, **Lipno Marina** (🌐www.landal.cz), with its swimming pool complex Aquaworld, yacht rental and the nearby **campsite** *Autocamp Modřín* (May–Sept; ℡380 736 272, 📧camp@lipno.info).

Some 9km along the shore from Lipno is **FRYMBURK** (Friedberg), the most attractive village on the lake, with its delicate white, octagonal spire and leafy, oval main square. **Accommodation** is plentiful; first choice on the square is the family-run *Hotel Maxant* (℡380 735 229, 🌐www.lipnonet.cz /maxant; ❹), which has a sauna and pool; *Hotel Vltava* (℡380 735 605, 🌐www.hotel-vtlava.com; ❺), opposite, is the flashiest accommodation in the village, with a sauna, tennis court, massage services and mountain bike rental. The well-run, lakeside *Camping Frymburk* (May–Sept) lies just 500m from the village back along route 163 to Lipno, with cycle and boat rental, and bungalows available. A car **ferry** from Frymburk to Frýdava just across on the south shore runs roughly every one to two hours.

Horní Planá

HORNÍ PLANÁ (Oberplan), 7km west of Černá, is the lake's chief resort, and has a useful **tourist office** (July & Aug daily 8am–6pm; Sept–May Mon–Fri 7.30–11.15am & noon–4pm; ⓦ www.horniplana.cz) in the Česká spořitelna building on the leafy main square, which can help you fix up accommodation, rents out **mountain bikes** and has **internet**.

A little cultural distraction can be experienced at the birthplace (*rodný domek*) of the German-speaking writer and painter **Adalbert Stifter**, who cut short his life in 1868 by slashing his throat to escape cancer of the liver. The house (April–June & Sept Tues–Sun 10am–noon & 1–6pm; July & Aug daily 10am–noon & 1–6pm; Oct to mid-Dec Tues–Sat 9am–noon & 1–4pm), on the road into town from the east (Palackého 22), is now a small memorial to his life and work; his statue stands behind the church, and there's another memorial to him overlooking the waters of the Plešné jezero, which sits below Plechý (Plockenstein) close to the meeting of the German, Austrian and Czech borders, the Trojmezí.

There's no shortage of **accommodation**. The smart *Pension Šejko* (ⓣ 380 738 330, ⓦ www.sejko.cz; ❸), a short way along the road to the lakeshore, with decent en-suite rooms, is a good choice. Or there's the large *Hotel Na pláží* (ⓣ 380 738 231, ⓦ www.hotel-plaz.cz; ❸), with its own restaurant and kids' playground, situated, as the name suggests, opposite the beach – ask for a room overlooking the lake. A more tranquil option, however, is to stay in the water-front village of **JENIŠOV**, a couple of kilometres south of Horní Planá, which consists of several hotels and pensions. The local **campsite** (May–Oct; also with bungalows) is more pleasant than the sites in Horní Planá.

Prachatice and around

The slopes of Libín (1096m) merge into the Otava and Vltava plain by the amiable little market town of **PRACHATICE** (Prachatitz), dubbed by the tourist authorities as the "Gateway to the Šumava". Most people do indeed come here en route to the Šumava, but it's a beautiful medieval town in its own right, as well as being a useful base for visiting **Husinec**, birthplace of Jan Hus (see p.194). Founded in 1325, Prachatice flourished in the following century, when it controlled the all-important salt trade route into Bohemia. A fire in 1507 is responsible for the uniformly sixteenth-century appearance of the town and its famous collection of sgraffito facades.

A short walk uphill from the bus and train stations brings you to Malé náměstí, the main square-cum-crossroads of the nondescript new part of town. Everything of interest is contained within the walls of the tiny circular **staré město**, reached through the bulky fifteenth-century **Písecká brána**, a gateway with a

---

Border crossings

Before 1989, the main road from Horní Planá northwest to Volary was punctuated at regular intervals by little red signs warning about the impending Iron Curtain; all villages on the right bank of the Vltava were closed to road vehicles, and trains were the only legal means of transport. The military have now given up their patch, and today there are numerous **border crossings** into Austria and Germany, with varying restrictions. The only 24-hour checkpoints open to all vehicles are Přední Výtoň/ Guglwald and Strážný/Philippsreuth, 50km to the west. In between there are six more crossing points, open only to cyclists and/or pedestrians, all with more limited opening hours – check with the local tourist office for the current restrictions.

faded mural showing Vilém of Rožmberk on horseback and, above it, in among the battlements, the red rose symbol of his family, who acquired the town briefly in 1501.

The gate's double arches open out on the small Kostelní náměstí, where old women sell spices and vegetables in the shade of the trees. The Gothic church of **sv Jakub**, with its steeply pitched, rather peculiar red-ribbed roof, is the oldest building and most obvious landmark in town. Inside, the short, tall nave is decorated with delicate lierne vaulting; the Baroque main altar, meanwhile, is much more in-your-face, with four gilded barley-sugar columns wreathed in vines dividing gold and silver relief scenes of the Nativity. Prachatice is best known, however, for the exquisitely decorative **Heydlův dům** to the left, which sports bizarre depictions of men clubbing each other to death. Next door is the Latin school or **Literátská škola**, also crowned with miniature Renaissance battlements, and which local heroes Hus and Žižka are said to have attended in their youth.

At this point the cobbles open out into the old town square, **Velké náměstí**, which has a thoroughly Germanic air. Its most striking aspect is the riot of **sgraffito** on the facades of many of the buildings; if you haven't already come across the style, Prachatice is as good a place as any to get to grips with it. The technique – extremely popular in the sixteenth century and revived in the nineteenth – involves scraping away painted plaster to form geometric, monochrome patterns or even whole pictorial friezes, producing a distinctive lace-work effect. The most lavish example of this style is the arcaded **Rumpálův dům**, at no. 41 on the east side of the square, which depicts a ferociously confused battle scene. At no. 45 is another arcaded building, the former **solnice** or salt house (also known as the Bozovského dům), through which the town accrued its enormous wealth in the Middle Ages and which features Vilém of Rožmberk once more on horseback. In between the two, at no. 43, the **Muzeum české loutky a cirkusu** (Museum of Czech puppets and circus; Tues–Sun 9am–5pm; 50Kč) has an amazing collection of marionettes, some by the likes of Mikuláš Aleš and Jiří Trnka, as well a travelling "House of Fun" from 1890 and a working puppet theatre.

On the west side of the square, the sixteenth-century **stará radnice** is decorated with copies of Hans Holbein's disturbing, apocalyptic parables, employing a much more sophisticated use of perspective; just a few doors down stands the **nová radnice**, whose sgraffito dates from the late nineteenth century. One of the fanciest houses on the square is the **Sittrův dům**, on the north side, now the local museum (March–June & Sept–Dec Tues–Fri 9am–4pm, Sat & Sun 10am–4pm; July & Aug Tues–Sun 9am–5pm; 25Kč), distinguished not by its sgraffito, but by its colourful painted facade and ornate Renaissance gable. Four doors down at no. 9 is the **Knížecí dům**, which hides its sgraffito round the side, on which you'll find, among other things, a stag hunt, several devils and an elephant, a mermaid with two tails and Joseph being put into the pit by his brothers. On Poštovní, just off the diagonally opposite corner of the square, you can find the **Muzeum krajky** (Lace Museum; April–Oct & Dec Tues–Fri 10am–5pm, Sat 9am–4pm, Sun 10am–3pm; ⓦmuzeumkrajky.euweb.cz), displaying lace from the republic and other European countries.

Practicalities

The **tourist office** (mid-June to mid-Sept Mon–Fri 9am–6pm, Sat & Sun 10am–noon & 1–5pm; mid-Sept to mid-June Mon–Fri 8am–4.30pm; ⓦwww .prachatice.cz) in the old town hall, can help find private rooms in the town. *Hotel Parkán* (☏388 311 868, ⓦwww.hotelparkan.cz; ❸), on Věžní, is probably the nicest **place to stay**, with en-suite facilities and TVs in all its rooms, and a solid Czech restaurant; to get there head up Křišťanova by sv Jakub and take the first left. Alternatively, head for the *Hotel Koruna* (☎388 310 177, ⓦwww .pthotel.cz; ➋), tucked away down an alleyway in the southwestern corner of the main square; the en-suite rooms are spartan, but the wood-beamed restaurant is cosy. Infrequent buses will drop you close to the riverside *Blanický mlýn* **campsite** (all year; ☎388 337 152, ⓦwww.blanicky-mlyn.cz), 12km south off route 141, with bungalows and rooms in the main building.

Prachatice's Indian **restaurant**, 🍴 *Tandoor*, Horní 165 (closed Sun & daily 3–5.30pm), on a backstreet to the west of the square, is a remarkable find; an Indian chef cooks up delicious tandoori dishes, masalas, kormas and thalis. For traditional Czech food, head for the simple, cheap **pub** *Národní dům*, to the left of the local museum. On Poštovní, downstairs near the lace museum, there's the friendly tea-house *Čajovná U hrušky*. To go online, head for the **internet café** upstairs at Club 111 on Křišťanova. The town's big summer bash, the **Slavnosti solné Zlaté stezky**, is a medieval knees-up held at a weekend towards the end of June to commemorate Prachatice's location at the crossroads of former trade routes.

Husinec

Six kilometres north of Prachatice is the unassuming village of **HUSINEC**, birthplace of **Jan Hus**, the man whose death in 1415 triggered the Hussite revolution. In the nineteenth century, when interest in Hus began to emerge after the dark years of the Counter-Reformation, the poet Jan Neruda visited Husinec and was horrified to find Hus' former home shabby and neglected. No expense has been spared since, with the family house at nos. 36 & 37 converted into a **museum** (Památník M.J. Husa; May–Sept Tues–Sun 9am–noon & 1–4pm; 25Kč) and many of Hus' old haunts in the surrounding region turned into points of pilgrimage over the nineteenth century. That said, few visitors come nowadays to the museum's small exhibition – it has only one original room, a tiny garret on the top floor. To

Jan Hus

The legendary preacher – and Czech national hero – **Jan Hus** (often anglicized to John Huss) was born in the Husinec around 1372. From a childhood of poverty, he enjoyed a steady rise through the Czech education system, taking his degree at Prague's Karolinum in the 1390s, and eventually being ordained as a deacon and priest around 1400. Although without doubt an admirer of the English religious reformer John Wycliffe, Hus was by no means as radical as many of his colleagues who preached at the Betlémská kaple. Nor did he actually advocate many of the more famous tenets of the heretical religious movement that took his name: Hussitism. In particular, he never advocated giving communion "in both kinds" (bread and wine) to the general congregation.

In the end, it wasn't the disputes over Wycliffe, whose books were burned on the orders of the archbishop in 1414, that proved Hus' downfall, but an argument over the sale of indulgences to fund the papal wars that prompted his unofficial trial at the Council of Constance in 1415. Having been guaranteed safe conduct by Emperor Sigismund himself, Hus naively went to Constance to defend his views, and was burnt at the stake as a heretic. The Czechs were outraged, and Hus became a national hero overnight, inspiring thousands to rebel against the authorities of the day. In 1965, the Vatican finally overturned the sentence, and the anniversary of his death (July 6) is now a national holiday.

give you an idea of Hus' place in the Czech nationalist canon, take a look at the stirring multicoloured sgraffito illustration on no. 42. Getting to Husinec is easiest on one of the regular **buses** from Prachatice; the train station lies 3km east of the village.

Lake Lipno to Vimperk

The scenic train ride from Lake Lipno to Vimperk takes you deep into the Šumava forest; it's worth breaking the journey at some point to delve further into the woods, particularly northwest of Volary, which lies 18km south of Prachatice. At **LENORA**, there's a glass factory (and shops), several old, wooden, Šumava cottages and a picturesque covered wooden bridge over the river. You can stay in *Zámeček Lenora* (☎388 438 861; ❷), a hotel situated in an old country house, with its own restaurant and a spacious courtyard. There are some great walks possible from the next station along, Záton, 1.5km northeast of which, in the hamlet of Kaplice, is the primitive *Boubínský prales* campsite (all year).

From Záton station, a green-marked path skirts the ancient **Boubínský prales** (Boubín Virgin Forest) that occupies the slopes of Boubín (1362m). It's forbidden to walk among the pines and firs of the forest, some of which are more than 400 years old, but the green markers take you 4km around the perimeter past a small deer park and on to the summit; from here you can get back to the rail line without retracing your steps by following the blue-marked path 4km to the station at the ski resort of **KUBOVÁ HUŤ**, where there are several hotels and pensions to choose from, including the vast *Ingo Hotel Arnika* (☎338 436 326, ⓦwww.hotel-arnika.cz; ❸), with sauna, pool and bike rental, and the modern mega ski-chalet, *Amber Hotel Kuba* (☎246 030 246; ❹), which also rents out bikes in the summer.

Vimperk and Volyně

From Horní Vltavice, a few local buses cover the 13km to the 24-hour Strážný–Philippsreuth German border crossing; trains continue for 13km to **VIMPERK** (Winterberg), where the first printing press in Bohemia was established in 1484 – a few decades after Gutenberg's invention. The business of the day goes on in the lower part of town, leaving the steep narrow streets of the **staré město** virtually deserted. The leafy main square, náměstí Svobody, is overlooked by the town's **hrad**, built in the thirteenth century by Otakar II, and last owned by the Schwarzenbergs. The castle, a stiff fifteen-minute hike up from the centre, has been knocked about a bit over the centuries, and now houses the local **museum** (May–Oct Tues–Sun 9am–noon & 1–4pm; 20Kč), with little of interest beyond a selective display of local glassware – and great views over the old town.

Despite its relative lack of local attractions, Vimperk is another possible base for exploring this part of the Šumava. There are a couple of **hotels** by the train station, but that leaves you a good 1.5km from the town centre down Nádražní. A better bet is to head for the *Amber Hotel Anna*, Kaplířova 168 (☎388 412 050; ❹), a lovely old building right in the centre that's been rather brutally modernized, but is a very comfortable place to stay all the same. A good option for families, the quiet *Penzion Róza* (☎604 783 358, ⓦwww .penzionroza.cz; ❷), at náměstí Svobody 10, has three comfortable apartments. The nearest **campsite** is *Vodník* (May–Oct; ☎388 415 656, ⓦwww .autokempvodnik.cz), at Hájná Hora, 1km or so up the hill to the west of town. For a cheap Platán **beer** and some traditional **food**, head for the

Hospoda na náměstí on náměstí Svobody. The **tourist office** (summer Mon–Fri 9am–5pm, Sat & Sun 9am–noon & 12.30–4pm; out of season Mon–Fri 9am–4pm) is at náměstí Svobody 8.

A train line from Vimperk to Strakonice runs along the winding River Volyňka. It's worth stopping briefly in **VOLYNĚ** to catch a glimpse of its extremely pretty **radnice**, which features typical Czech-style arcades, sgraffitoed walls, and – rather surprisingly – an onion-shaped cupola.

Strakonice

The remaining, mountainous part of the Šumava is only accessible from the east by an infrequent bus service. The railway meanwhile veers northwards to **STRAKONICE** (Strakonitz), which qualifies as a large industrial town in these parts. It grew up as a textile town in the nineteenth century, and its factories now produce an unusual trio of products: Turkish fez hats, ČZ motorcycles, and *dudy*, the Bohemian equivalent of bagpipes.

There's a museum on these very subjects in the town's large thirteenth-century **hrad** (Tues–Sun: May, June, Sept & Oct 8am–4pm; July & Aug 9am–5pm; Ⓦwww.muzeum.strakonice.cz; 30Kč), at the confluence of the Volyňka and the Otava, on the south bank of the latter. It's a fun place to explore: there are plenty of old motorbikes to admire, an international selection of *dudy* in everything from velvet to sheepskin, and a fez-making machine. You also get to climb the castle watchtower, Rumpál. If you're really into *dudy*, check out the **International Bagpipe Festival** (Ⓦwww.dudackyfestival.cz) held in the castle courtyard every other August, which attracts a regular contingent from Scotland and elsewhere.

The rest of the town, on the other side of the river, can't quite match the eclectic attractions of the castle, though **Velké náměstí** boasts two very attractive late nineteenth-century buildings – one a savings bank, the other the old radnice – facing each other across the square. Both are designed in florid neo-Renaissance style, and decorated with pretty floral and folk-inspired murals and friezes. East along Lidická, on the south side of the street, there's also a former butchers' stalls worth inspecting, a lovely little Baroque building with a brightly coloured naïve relief in the gable showing a butcher about to slaughter a bull.

Practicalities

From the **train** and **bus stations**, it's a five-minute walk to the castle down Alfonse Šťastného then right down Bezděkovská. The excellent **information centre** (Mon–Fri 8am–6pm) in the *mapové centrum*, in the main gateway of the castle, can book private rooms; the main **tourist office** (May–Sept Mon–Fri 8am–6pm, Sat 8am–1pm; Oct–April Mon–Fri 8am–4pm; ☎383 700 700, Ⓦwww.strakonice.net) is on Velké náměstí.

As for **hotels**, try the *Fontána* (☎383 321 440, Ⓦwww.hotelfontana .infohelp.cz; ❷), northeast of the main square on Lidická – it doesn't look much from the outside, but it's smart enough inside. Another possibility is the *Hotel Bílá růže* (☎383 321 946, Ⓦwww.hotelruzest.cz; ❷), at Palackého náměstí 80, two blocks down off the main square, which has a Chinese restaurant. There's a **campsite**, *Autokemp Podskalí* (June to mid-Sept; ☎383 322 024), by the banks of the Otava, fifteen-minutes' walk west along Pod Hradem, which runs south of the castle.

Strakonice brews its own **beer**, across the river from the castle, and you can sup the local Nektar (and Dudák) nearby at *U zborova*, a rough-and-ready pub at Bavorova 20, which heads off north from the western end of the main square; more civilized is the wood-panelled **restaurant** serving Budvar in the *Fontána*, or the twin, tastefully appointed restaurants *Kalich* and *U Madly* (both closed Sun), opposite the tourist office on Velké náměstí.

Rabí and Sušice

There are several ruined castles along the banks of the River Otava beyond Strakonice, but by far the most impressive – and the largest in Bohemia – are the vast and crumbling fortifications of the castle at **RABÍ**, 25km away by train (change at Horažd'ovice). A key fortress in the Hussite Wars, and allegedly the place where the Hussite general Jan Žižka lost his second eye, it was deliberately allowed to fall into rack and ruin in the eighteenth century for fear of its strategic value should it fall into the wrong hands. The village sold the **hrad** to the state for one crown in 1920, and recent renovation work, aimed at stabilizing some of the more dangerously disintegrating bits, has now allowed the public access to most of the site (April & Oct Sat & Sun 9am–noon & 1–3pm; May & Sept Tues–Sun 9am–noon & 1–4pm; June–Aug Tues–Sun 9am–noon & 1–5pm; Ⓦwww.rabi.cz). You can enter the courtyards (*nadvoří*; 20Kč) easily enough, but to visit the interior (*okruh palác*) or the ramparts and towers (*okruh věž*), you need to sign up for a guided tour (45min; 40Kč each or 75Kč for two, 90Kč/125Kč for tours in English).

A few stops on from Rabí is **SUŠICE** (Schüttenhofen), which means just one thing to the Czechs – matches. The local SOLO match factory (*sirkárna*) is one of the largest in Europe, and dominates the domestic market. Aside from that, there's little evidence of the town's wealthy medieval past, which, like Prachatice's, was based on the salt trade. The exception is the main square, náměstí Svobody, which boasts a handful of striking Renaissance houses; the most arresting are the **Rozacínovský dům** at no. 48, with a fantastic sgraffito-toed gable sporting several tiers of mini-pilasters, and the **Voprchovský dům** at no. 40, featuring a similarly eye-catching gable with a triple tier of blind arcading. The latter now houses the **muzeum Šumavy** (May–Oct Tues–Sat 9am–noon & 12.45–5pm, Sun 9am–noon; 30Kč), established as far back as 1880, with exhibits ranging from local glassware to fifteenth-century woodcarvings and, of course, the match-making industry, though it's the carefully restored interior that makes it worth a visit.

Practicalities

Sušice's **train station** is a regrettable 2.5km northeast of the town centre, with only infrequent bus connections; if you arrive by bus, make sure to get off at the town centre and not at the train and bus station, if you have the option. Sušice has a couple of decent inexpensive **hotels**: the excellent *Sport Hotel Pekárna* (Ⓣ376 526 869; ❷), with the added attraction of a bowling alley, is located at T.G. Masaryka 129, on the road in from the train station. Closer to the square is the *Hotel Svatobor* (Ⓣ376 526 490, Ⓦwww.hotel-svatobor.cz; ❶), at T.G. Masaryka 116, which is slightly better than it looks from the outside. In addition, there's a nice little upbeat pension, *Milli* (Ⓣ376 526 598, Ⓦwww.sweb .cz/pension.milli; ❷), down Kostelní. Both hotels have their own restaurants, and there's a pizzeria at the *Pekárna*. If you're looking to camp, you're best off heading up the Otava to one of the riverside **campsites** like *Annín* (May–Oct), 7.5km south of Sušice, and a favourite spot for canoeists. The **tourist office** (Mon–Fri 9am–noon & 12.30–4.30pm; Ⓦwww.sumava.net/icsusice) is in the radnice, on the square.

Kašperské Hory

One bus a day from Vimperk (more frequently from Sušice) heads for **KAŠPERSKÉ HORY** (Bergreichenstein), an old German mining village on the River Otava, positioned below the semi-ruined castle of Kašperk that was built by Charles IV to guard over the local gold mines. The town's smartest building is its pristine Renaissance **radnice** with its three perfect eighteenth-century gables, featuring – from left to right – a Czech lion, a clock and the town's mining emblem.

In addition, the town's **muzeum Šumavy** (May–Oct Tues–Sat 9am–noon & 12.45–5pm, Sun 9am–noon; 40Kč), on the main square, below the church, displays some wonderful local glassware on its top floor, ranging from fourteenth-century to turn-of-the-twentieth-century gear, with pieces by local firms such as Lötz, Schmid and Kralik, from the neighbouring town of Klášterský Mlýn (Klöstermühle). In the late nineteenth century, Lötz in particular won many prizes in Brussels and Paris for its Tiffany-style iridescent glass vases and weird vegetal shapes, many of which inexplicably escaped the auctioneer's hammer and ended up here.

Also on the main square is the **Moto muzeum** (June–Sept daily 9am–5.30pm), containing one of the finest collections of old motorbikes in the country, displayed rather surprisingly in the building's attic. More than forty bikes line the eaves, all in pristine condition, and ranging from interwar BMW boxers to domestic trials bikes; pride of place, though, goes to a beautiful red 1928 Indian.

Practicalities

At the western edge of the town there's the Šumava National Park's main **information centre** (June & Sept Mon–Fri 8am–3.30pm, Sat 9.30am–3.30pm; July & Aug daily 9.30am–3.30pm; Oct–May Mon–Fri 8am–3.30pm; ℡376 582 734, ⓦwww.npsumava.cz), a good place to go if you plan to explore the mountains.

Plush **accommodation** is available at the *Park Hotel Tosch* (℡376 582 592, ⓦwww.tosch-parkhotel.cz; ❺) on the northwest corner of the main square, catering mostly for German tourists. *Tosch's* rival is *Aparthotel Šumava 2000* (℡376 546 910, ⓦwww.sumava2000.cz; ❺), a Best Western chain hotel also on the square, which has an **internet café**. At the other end of the scale is the *Turistická ubytovňa* (℡724 265 683; ❶), behind the church; theoretically, it's open all year, but it's advisable to come early or to book in advance. There is also a host of pensions and private rooms on the outskirts of town. You can get a decent bite to **eat** and a Gambrinus and Radegast beer at the *Pod věží* restaurant (closed Sun), at the upper end of the square.

Srní and around

The most remote part of the Šumava National Park lies south and west of Kašperské Hory, and while there are few attractions in the way of museums or churches, it's the unblemished mountains that people come to see. The first stop of note south of Kašperské Hory is **ČEŇKOVA PILA**, a spot made up of little more than the *Pension Bystřina* (℡376 599 221; ❶; usually reserved for the whole season) and a bridge across the Vydra stream, where composer Bedřich Smetana is said to have been inspired to write the swirling flute introduction to his symphonic poem "Vltava" from *Má vlast*.

A few kilometres further on, the cute village of **SRNÍ** has a wooden-shingled church and a few hotels and pensions, such as the Communist-era twin hotels

Srní (☎376 599 222, ⓦwww.hotelysrni.cz; ❷) and *Šumava* (☎376 599 212; ❷), with indoor pool, sauna, weight room, bowling and restaurant. A few kilometres deeper into the forest, **ANTÝGL** is nothing more than a few wooden houses that make up the picturesquely situated *Campingplatz Antýgl*, a very popular **campsite** with basic lodging (May–Oct; ☎376 599 331; ❶). Nearby, *Hotel Antýgl* (☎376 599 444; ❶) is a cheap but clean place with a very good, if smoky, restaurant. Srní and Antýgl both make fine bases for **hikes** in the area. One popular walk from Antýgl is to take the red-marked path 6km along the boulder-strewn Vydra stream back down to Čeňkova Pila; you can make a longer day of it by returning via roundabout paths such as the blue-marked trail to Srní and eventually, via another red-marked path, to Modrava, or the yellow-marked trail that descends from Srní back down to the Vydra.

The quiet settlements of **MODRAVA**, 3km south of Antýgl, and **KVILDA**, another 4km further east, are both surrounded by peat bogs. The latter boasts the highest altitude in the whole republic (1049m) and the neo-Gothic church of sv Štěpán. These were restricted areas when the Iron Curtain was draped just a few kilometres beyond; because of this, the landscape is refreshingly underdeveloped, but there are just enough pensions and simple restaurants today to keep visitors happy. Buses from Sušice wind their way up here at fairly regular intervals.

Železná Ruda and Špičák

The northwestern tip of the Šumava centres on the town of **ŽELEZNÁ RUDA** (Eisenstein), 2km from the German border and best approached on the scenic railway line or bus from Klatovy (see p.210). In its triple role as a border town, ski resort and summer hiking base, the place has certainly lost much of its original charm. Souvenir shops, filled with "traditional" Czech art and garden gnomes, plus the odd strip club, attempt to coax every last euro out of the Germans who come here. In many ways, you're better off using quieter neighbouring resorts like Špičák as a base. Local sights are confined to the ludicrously oversized wooden onion dome over the nave of the village church, and the small **muzeum Šumavy** (Tues–Sat 9am–noon & 12.45–5pm, Sun 9am–noon; 20Kč), local repository for glassware and folk art, which is connected to the small **tourist office** (daily 8am–12.30pm & 1.30–6pm; ☎376 397 033, ⓦwww.sumava.net/itcruda).

Still, if you need to stock up on provisions or draw some cash, then Železná Ruda is a good place to come. The *Šumava* **restaurant**, opposite the Spar supermarket, is reasonably priced, and, as far as **accommodation** goes, you're spoilt for choice: try the *Bultas* (☎376 397 123; ❷), which has its own restaurant. An electronic board on the main road at the centre of town shows availability of many hotels and pensions, and provides a free phone from which you can call them. Finally, the town's **campsite**, *U mlýna* (June–Sept), lies 1km or so out of town up route 27. The nearest **train station** to the centre is Železná Ruda město, 500m north up the road to Špičák. **Germany** and the Czech Republic share the Železná Ruda/Bayerisch Eisenstein station on the border itself, 3km southwest of the town centre; hourly trains terminate 70km away at Plattling, with connections on to Regensburg.

From **ŠPIČÁK**, one stop back along the railway from Železná Ruda, a two-stage, year-round chairlift can take you to the top of **Pancíř** (1214m; 60Kč return). The first stage takes you as far as Hofmanky and the comfortable *Hotel Horizont* (☎376 365 111, ⓦwww.sumavanet.cz/horizont; ❸). Also convenient is the *Hotel Bohemia* (☎376 397 514, ⓦwww.hotelbohemia.be; ❸), near the main road in Špičák. Towards the German border, there are two idyllically situated glacial **lakes** – Černé jezero and Čertovo jezero – surrounded by forests, which you can reach via the yellow-marked path from Špičák station.

Travel details

Trains

Connections with Prague: České Budějovice (up to 14 daily; 2hr 15min–3hr); Písek (2 daily; 2hr 30min); Strakonice (2 daily; 2hr 55min); Sušice (1 daily; 3hr 40min); Tábor (10–14 daily; 1hr 35min–2hr 20min).

České Budějokvice to: Brno (4–5 daily; 4hr 20min); Černý Kříž (up to 6 daily; 2hr 20min–2hr 45min); Český Krumlov (8 daily; 45–55min); Horní Planá (6 daily; 1hr 55min–2hr 15min); Linz (2–3 daily; 2hr 10min–2hr 35min); Písek (3–5 daily; 50min–1hr 35min); Plzeň (12–13 daily; 2hr–3hr 25min); Strakonice (13–15 daily; 50min–1hr 30min); Tábor (14–19 daily; 50min–2hr 10min); Volary (up to 5 daily; 2hr 35min–3hr).

Český Krumlov to: Horní Planá (6 daily; 55min).

Plzeň to: Špičák (3–4 daily; 2hr 5min–2hr 15min); Železná Ruda (3–4 daily; 2hr 10min–2hr 20min).

Tábor to: Bechyně (7–9 daily; 50min); České Budějovice (14–19 daily; 50min–2hr 10min); Jihlava (1–2 daily; 2hr 40min–3hr); Milevsko/Písek (8–9 daily; 40min–1hr 30min); Pelhřimov (5–9 daily; 55min–1hr 25min).

Volary to: Prachatice (5–7 daily; 40–45min); Vimperk/Strakonice (5–6 daily; 1hr/2hr 30min).

Buses

Connections with Prague: České Budějovice (up to 8 daily; 2hr 30min–3hr 25min); **Český Krumlov** (2–6 daily; 2hr 40min–3hr 25min); Orlík/Písek (up to 15 daily; 1hr 30min/2hr); Pelhřimov (up to 15 daily; 1hr 35min–2hr 30min); Rabí/Sušice (up to 4 daily; 2hr 30min/2hr 45min); Strakonice/Prachatice (up to 15/7 daily; 2hr/2hr 30min); Tábor (up to 20 daily; 1hr 15min–1hr 55min); Volary (1 daily; 3hr 5min).

České Budějovice to: Český Krumlov (36 daily; 25–50min); Hluboká nad Vltavou (hourly; 15–40min); Holašovice (up to 7 daily; 30–35min); Jindřichův Hradec (up to 22 daily; 1hr 5min); Prachatice (up to 15 daily; 50min–1hr 15min); Tábor (5–17 daily; 1hr–1hr 35min); Třeboň (up to 14 daily; 30–40min).

Český Krumlov to: Horní Planá (2–8 daily; 55min–1hr); Lipno nad Vltavou (up to 4 daily; 1hr 5min–1hr 15min); Rožmberk/Vyšší Brod (6 daily; 40/55min); Zlatá Koruna (up to hourly; 15min).

Jindřichův Hradec to: České Budějovice (up to 20 daily; 1hr–1hr 15min); Pelhřimov (up to 4 daily; 50min–1hr 10min); Slavonice (up to 3 daily; 1hr 15min).

Pelhřimov to: Humpolec (up to 20 daily; 30min); Jihlava (up to 15 daily; 35min–1hr); Kámen (up to 15 daily; 20–35min).

Tábor to: Bechyně (up to 17 daily; 35–55min); Kámen (up to 8 daily; 25min–1hr).

Sušice to: Srní/Modrava (up to 4 daily; 55min/1hr 20min).

West Bohemia

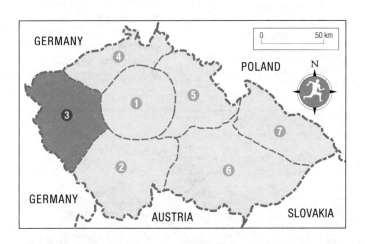

CHAPTER 3 # Highlights

✳ **Pilsner Urquell Brewery**
Take a guided tour of Plzeň's famous brewery, home of the original lager – complete with a tasting session. See p.207

✳ **Kladruby monastery** A Baroque–Gothic masterpiece by Czech-Italian architect Giovanni Santini. See p.209

✳ **Domážlice** This Bohemian town in the middle of the border region is renowned for its folk traditions and summer festival. See p.212

✳ **Mariánské Lázně** Elegant fin-de-siècle spa, once the favourite watering hole of European royalty, set in gentle wooded hills.
See p.215

✳ **Karlovy Vary** Grandiose late nineteenth-century spa, stretched out along the steeply wooded Teplá Valley, and host of the country's most prestigious film festival.
See p.224

✳ **Loket** Miniature walled town, squeezed into a U-bend of a river, with a gothic castle encircled by some of the region's most beguiling streets. See p.230

▲ Kladruby monastery

West Bohemia

For centuries, the rolling hills of **West Bohemia** (Západní Čechy) have been a buffer zone between the Slav world and the German-speaking lands. Encouraged by the Czech Přemyslid rulers, the border regions were heavily colonized by neighbouring Germans from the twelfth century onwards. The German settlers provided urgently needed skilled craftsmen and miners for the Bohemian economy, and for much of their history vast swathes of the region were almost exclusively German-speaking.

With the emergence of nationalism, and the subsequent rise of the pro-Nazi Sudeten German Party in the 1930s, the region became deeply divided along ethnic lines. The violent expulsions of the entire German-speaking population after World War II left vast areas of the countryside and several large towns virtually empty. Czechs and Slovaks were encouraged to resettle the area after the war; many Czechs used abandoned rural homes as country cottages, yet the countryside, particularly close to the border, remains eerily underpopulated even today.

The economic mainstay of the region for the last century has been the sprawling capital city of **Plzeň**, home of the Škoda engineering works and centre of the country's beer industry. It's not the most picturesque of places, but it does have a certain nineteenth-century grandeur, and has appeal for anyone who thirsts for Czech beer. Within easy reach of Plzeň is the monastery of **Kladruby**, monument to the outstanding architectural genius of Giovanni Santini, the master of "Baroque-Gothic". Further south, the historic border town of **Domažlice** is one of the best-preserved towns in the region, and a jumping-off point to neighbouring Šumava.

The main draw of West Bohemia, however, is its famous triangle of spas: **Mariánské Lázně**, **Františkovy Lázně** and **Karlovy Vary**. Conveniently scattered near the German border, these three Bohemian resorts were the Côte d'Azur of Habsburg Europe. Following the wholesale nationalization of the spa industry under Communism, every factory and trade union received an annual three weeks' holiday at a *lázně dům* (spa pension) in a bid to demonstrate what a success socialism was proving to be. Today, taking "the cure" remains very popular not only with Czechs – as a serious treatment for a multitude of ills – but also with Russia's nouveaux riches, and, of course, with the neighbouring Germans. All three spa towns are very attractive visually, but they do tend to be full of the plethoric and elderly, so if you need a break from cure-seekers, head for nearby **Cheb** or **Loket**, both beautifully preserved towns and largely crowd-free.

This being one of the most sparsely populated regions in the country, **public transport** is somewhat patchy. However, excellent rail and bus links exist between the major towns, so unless you're heading for the back of beyond, getting around without a car should present few problems.

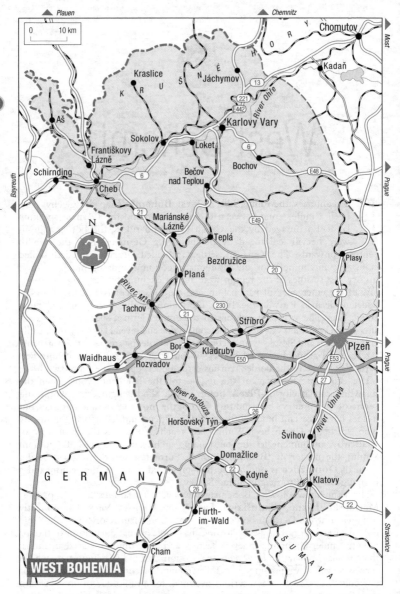

▲ Plauen
▲ Chemnitz

Chomutov

Kadaň

Kraslice · N É · Jáchymov · 13

K R U Š · River Ohře

Aš

Sokolov · Loket · Karlovy Vary

Františkovy
Lázně · Bochov · 6 · E48

Schirnding · Bečov
nad Teplou

Cheb

Mariánské
Lázně · E49

Teplá

Bezdružice · Plasy

Planá · 20

River Mže

Tachov · 230 · 27

Stříbro

Bor · Kladruby · E50 · Plzeň · E53

Waidhaus · 27

Rozvadov · River Radbuza · River Uhlava

Horšovský Týn · 26

Švihov

G E R M A N Y · Domažlice

Kdyně · Klatovy

22 · 26

Furth-
im-Wald

Cham · Š U M A V A

0   10 km

N

WEST BOHEMIA

Plzeň and around

PLZEŇ (Pilsen) was built on beer and bombs. Founded in 1295 and now with a population of around 165,000, it's by far the largest city in Bohemia after Prague, but as recently as 1850 it was a small town of just 14,000, most of whom were German-speakers. In 1859, an ironworks was founded and quickly snapped up by the Czech capitalist **Emil Škoda**, under whose control it drew an ever-increasing number of Czechs from the countryside. Within thirty years, the overall population of the town had trebled, while the number of Germans had decreased. Although initially simply an engineering plant, the Habsburgs transformed the ironworks into a huge armaments factory (second only to Krupps in Germany), which, inevitably, was a key acquisition for the Germans when they annexed Czechoslovakia, and soon attracted the attention of Allied bombers during World War II. In 1945, General Patton's **US Third Army** liberated much of West Bohemia, including Plzeň. Under the Communists, Plzeň diversified even further, producing trams, trains and buses, not to mention dodgy Soviet-designed nuclear reactors. Sadly, unlike Škoda's car-producing arm, based in Mladá Boleslav (see p.142), Škoda Plzeň is struggling, although Plzeň itself has attracted large-level foreign investment and is undergoing something of a minor renaissance.

Despite the city's overwhelmingly industrial character, Plzeň has its compensations: a large student population, eclectic late nineteenth-century architecture, and an unending supply of (probably) the best **beer** in the world – all of which make it a justifiably popular stop-off on the main railway line between Prague and the West.

Arrival and information

Fast trains from Prague take around ninety minutes to reach Plzeň, making it possible to visit on a long day-trip from the capital. The town's **train stations** are works of art in themselves: there are numerous minor ones within the city boundaries, but your most likely point of arrival is Plzeň hlavní nádraží, the ornate main station east of the city centre. It has a **left-luggage** office (*úschovna zavazadel*) and coin-operated luggage boxes. The irredeemably ugly **bus terminal**, for all national and international arrivals, is on the west side of town. From both the bus or main train stations, the city centre is just a short walk away – or a few stops on tram #2 from the bus station; trams #1 and #2 from the train station.

Plzeň's main **tourist office** at no. 41 on the main square, náměstí Republiky (April–Sept daily 9am–7pm; Oct–March Mon–Fri 10am–5pm, Sat & Sun 10am–3.30pm; ℡378 035 330, ⓦwww.info.plzen-city.cz), offers **internet** access. Outside hours try *Internet Café Neila* (ⓦwww.neila.cz) at Palackého náměsti 24.

Accommodation

Rooms don't come cheap in Plzeň's **hotels**, but the university offers cheap dorm accommodation in the summer holidays at its **student hostels**, about 1km north of the centre at Bolevecká 34 (℡377 259 384; ❶; tram #4 north along Karlovarská); if in doubt about availability ask at the CKM agency on Dominikánská (Mon–Fri 8am–6pm; ℡377 236 393). There are two **campsites** with bungalows – *Bílá hora* (April–Sept; ℡377 562 225), 28 října, and *Ostende* (May–Sept; ℡377 520 194, ⓦwww.ostende.webnode.cz) – both of which are just under 5km north of the centre on the far side of the Velký rybník, where Plzeňites go to swim on summer days. To get to *Bílá hora*, take bus #20 from náměstí Republiky, or #39 from Sady Pětatřicátníků and get off at the last stop; for *Ostende*, do the same but alight at Bílá Hora train station (the three or four daily slow trains from Plzeň to Žatec also stop here) and catch bus #30 for the remaining stops.

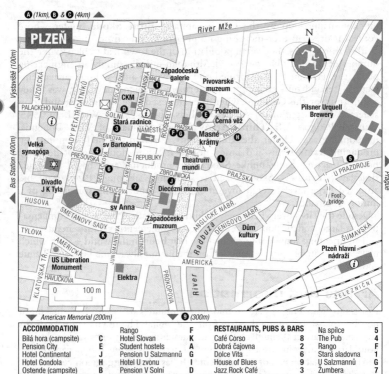

ACCOMMODATION		RESTAURANTS, PUBS & BARS	
Bílá hora (campsite)	**C**	Café Corso	**8**
Pension City	**E**	Dobrá čajovna	**2**
Hotel Continental	**J**	Dolce Vita	**6**
Hotel Gondola	**H**	House of Blues	**9**
Ostende (campsite)	**B**	Jazz Rock Café	**3**
Rango	**F**	Na spílce	**5**
Hotel Slovan	**K**	The Pub	**4**
Student hostels	**A**	Rango	**F**
Pension U Salzmannů	**G**	Stará sladovna	**1**
Hotel U zvonu	**I**	U Salzmannů	**G**
Pension V Solní	**D**	Žumbera	**7**

Pension City Sady 5 května 52 ☏ 377 326 069, ⓦ www.pensioncityplzen.cz. Small, very central pension on the northeastern edge of the old town, with plainly furnished rooms with TV. En suites are a little pricier. ③

Hotel Continental Zbrojnická 8 ☏ 377 235 292, ⓦ www.hotelcontinental.cz. Dating from 1895 and painstakingly restored, the *Continental* has rooms with phones and satellite TV, plus a café and restaurant. ⑤

Hotel Gondola Pallova 12 ☏ 377 327 253, ⓦ www.hotelgondola.cz. Small hotel on the tranquil edge of the old town, with well-appointed, en-suite singles and doubles with satellite TV. There's a laundry service and free internet access too. ④

🏃 **Rango** Pražská 10 T377 329 969, ⓦ www .rango.cz. Small, family-run hotel in a sixteenth-century house, with sunny, tastefully

designed rooms, free internet, and satellite TV. ⑤

Hotel Slovan Smetanovy sady 1 ☏ 377 227 256, ⓦ hotelslovan.pilsen.cz. Sombre, rather dreary Communist-style hotel fronting a peaceful park, with a wonderfully ornate stairwell. Some rooms are en suite; laundry service is available. ②–⑤

Pension U Salzmannů Pražská 8 ☏ 377 235 855, ⓦ www.usalzmannu.cz. Cosy double rooms are available at Plzeň's oldest pub. Free wi-fi. ④

Hotel U zvonu Pražská 8 27 ☏ 378 011 855, ⓦ www.hotel-uzvonu.cz. Owned by a former hockey player for the Czech national team, this modern hotel has a wide range of amenities and spotless, spacious rooms. ⑥

Pension V Solní Solní 8 ☏ 377 236 652, ⓦ www .volny.cz/pensolni. Small pension – with just three rooms – in a sixteenth-century house just off náměstí Republiky. The best value in town. ③

The City

Stepping out of Plzeň hlavní nádraží onto Americká, you're confronted by a range of ugly Communist-era buildings. Close by, the River Radbuza – one of four rivers running through Plzeň – doesn't bear close inspection, but the

Pilsner Urquell Brewery on its eastern bank certainly does. The lively **old town** has an interesting mix of museums and varied architecture.

The brewery

Most people come to Plzeň to sample its famous beer, the original Plzeňský Prazdroj or **Pilsner Urquell** (its more familiar Germanized export name). Beer has been brewed in the town since its foundation in 1295, but it wasn't until 1842 that the local *Bürgerliche Brauhaus* produced the first pale gold Pilsner-style beer, after a near-riot by the townsfolk over the declining quality of their beer. The new brew was a bottom-fermented variety, which quickly became popular across central Europe, spawning thousands of paler imitations under the generic name of Pilsner – hence the brewers' addition of the suffix Prazdroj or Urquell (meaning "original"), to show just who thought of it first. The superiority of Plzeň's beer is allegedly due to a combination of the soft local water and world-renowned Žatec hops.

For a **guided tour** of the **brewery** (1hr 45min; 150Kč; ☎ 377 062 888, Ⓦ www.prazdroj.cz; available in English), you can either book in advance or simply show up and join one of the scheduled groups (May–Sept 10.30am, 12.30pm, 2pm & 4pm; Oct–April 12.30pm, 2pm & 4pm). Tours include a beer-tasting session and a brief and gloriously tacky video show, as well as a look at the cellars. If the technological details of brewing don't appeal, you could just settle for the real thing at the vast *Na spílce* **pub** (Ⓦ www.naspilce.com), the Czech Republic's largest (Mon–Thurs & Sat 11am–10pm, Fri 11am–11pm, Sun 11am–9pm), beyond the brewery's triumphal arch. The arch itself, built in 1892 to commemorate the beer's fiftieth birthday, has been depicted on every authentic bottle of Pilsner Urquell ever since. Alternatively, you could try the historical angle at the Pivovarské muzeum (see p.208), or time your visit with Plzeň's annual **beer festival**, held early in October, as a preamble to the Munich Bierfest.

The old town

Laid out in grid fashion by Václav II in 1295, the old town is still dominated by the exalted heights of the Gothic cathedral of **sv Bartoloměje** (St Bartholomew; April–Sept Wed–Sat 10am–4pm; Oct–Dec Wed–Fri 10am–4pm; 30Kč), stranded awkwardly in the middle of the main square, **náměstí Republiky**. Inside, the late-Gothic vaulting of the Šternberská kaple, with its delicate pendant boss, is worth a look, but the cathedral's prize possession is its thirteenth-century wooden statue of the Plzeň Madonna in the Beautiful Style, on the high altar. The church used to boast two towers, but one was struck by lightning in 1525 and never rebuilt. The cathedral's remaining **spire** reaches a height of more than 100m, making it the tallest in the country; you can climb up to the viewing platform (*vyhlídková věž*; daily 10am–6pm) – which doubled as the town's lookout post – for a bird's-eye view of the local industrial complexes.

The rest of the main square presents a full range of architectural styles: some buildings, like the squat, grey *Hotel Central*, built in the 1960s; others, like the Italianate **stará radnice** (old town hall; daily 8am–6pm), dating from the sixteenth century but smothered in sgraffito in the early twentieth century. Plzeň became an unlikely imperial capital in 1599 when the Emperor Rudolf II based himself next door, at no. 41, for the best part of a year in an effort to avoid the ravages of the Prague plague. The vast majority of Plzeň's buildings, however, hail from the city's heyday at the turn of the twentieth century. In the old town, this resulted in some wonderful variations on historical themes and Art Nouveau motifs, particularly to the north and west of the main square. West of Sady Pětatřicátníků, and south of Husova, late-nineteenth-century residential apartments boast vestiges of ornate mosaics and sculpturing, now barely visible beneath the black layer of pollution that's eating away at their fanciful facades.

On Sady Pětatřicátníků itself stands the flamboyant late-nineteenth-century **Divadlo J.K. Tyla** (July & Aug daily 9am–4pm), named after Josef Kajétan Tyl, composer of the Czech national anthem, who died in Plzeň in 1856. Diagonally opposite the theatre is the city's imposing red-brick **Velká synagóga** (April–Oct daily except Sat 10am–6pm; Nov Mon–Fri 10am–4pm, Sun 10am–5.45pm; 55Kč), resplendent with its brightly coloured chevroned roof and twin onion domes topped by gilded Stars of David. The largest surviving synagogue in the country, and claiming to be Europe's second-largest, it was built in 1888, when it could just about have seated Plzeň's entire Jewish population of nearly 3500. The city's few remaining Jews use the winter synagogue at the back of the building, while the partially restored main hall now serves as a concert venue and exhibition space. The ornate interior, which boasts an organ at the east end, also contains a permanent exhibition on the history of the local Jewish community.

A ten-minute walk to the east is the copper-topped **Západočeské muzeum** (Tues–Sun 10am–6pm; Ⓦwww.zcm.cz; 20Kč), Plzeň's largest museum, if not its most interesting. It's a neo-Baroque extravaganza with an ornate interior, and was built in the nineteenth century to help educate the peasants who were flocking to the city. Temporary exhibitions are housed on the upper floor, but the real reason to visit is for the impressive town armoury (Plzeňská městská zbrojnice) – established by Charles IV. The little-visited **Diecézní muzeum** (April–Oct Tues–Sun 10am–6pm; 20Kč), nearby in the cloisters of the former Franciscan monastery on Františkánská, is more intriguing, worth a look for the Gothic chapel of sv Barbora (Saint Barbara). The beautiful rose-coloured frescoes here, dating from the 1460s, depict Barbara's martyrdom, which was gruesome even by biblical standards. Condemned to death by her father for converting to Christianity, she was racked, birched, carded with a metal comb, forced to lie on a bed of shards, slashed with red-hot blades, paraded naked, dragged up a mountain and finally beheaded – upon which her father was struck down by lightning.

If you want to get a glimpse of a dozen or so well-known Czech personalities gathered in one place, head for the **Theatrum mundi**, on Křižíkovy sady, east of the main square. In 2001 the local artists Vladivoj Kotyza and Miroslav Čech covered one of the building's walls with a vast mural (200 square metres), featuring an unusual meeting of famous Czechs, including Jan Žižka, King Wenceslas II and Emil Škoda. A block or so north, the excellent **Západočeská galerie** (Sun & Tues–Fri 10am–6pm, Sat noon–6pm; Ⓦwww.zpc-galerie.cz; 30Kč) puts on temporary exhibitions of modern Czech art in a Gothic building at Pražská 13. Its impressive permanent collection of Czech art (its Baroque paintings by Brandl and Škreta and sculptures by Braun are especially worthwhile) is housed in the distinctive elongated vaults of the town's Gothic butchers' stalls or **Masné krámy** (times as above), which stand opposite the city's sixteenth-century water tower or **Černá věž** (now a commercial art gallery).

At the east end of Veleslavínova, the popular **Pivovarské muzeum** (Brewery Museum; daily: April–Dec 10am–6pm; Jan–March 10am–5pm; 100Kč) is housed in what was originally a Gothic malthouse and later a pub. Ask the curator to get the old Würlitzer organ going while you check out numerous exhibits on the city's long tradition of brewing – including the smallest beer barrel in the world (a mere one-centimetre cubed) and case after case of kitsch

Baroque beer mugs. The next-door pub, *Na parkáně*, serves a rare *kvasnicové pivo* (yeast beer) from Pilsner Urquell.

Eating and drinking

Though there are plenty of hotel restaurants in town, several other places offer a more satisfying experience. For **drinks**, the *Na spílce* pub (see p.207), *Na parkáně* (see above) and *U Salzmannů* (see p.206), the town's famous wood-panelled pub at Pražská 8, remain dependable bets.

Café Corso Smetanovy sady 6. Laid-back, if a bit sterile, bar. Popular with locals who come to watch sports on the large-screen TV.

Dobrá čajovna Perlová 10. Sample a bewildering variety of teas from around the world at Plzeň's enduring branch of the ubiquitous tea-house chain.

Dolce Vita Prešovská 5. One of the best Italian joints in town, with a geranium-filled courtyard and occasional live music.

The Pub Prešovská 16, ⊛www.thepubworld .com. Pilsner Urquell's latest franchise concept is a party-animal place where you can tap your own unpasteurized beer and pay by volume.

Rango Pražská 10. An inviting cellar restaurant specializing in well-prepared Greek and Italian dishes – like penne in vodka sauce with ham and mushrooms or grilled zucchini with basil and thyme – which you can wash down with a bottle from Tuscany.

Stará sladovna Malá 3. Gut-busting Czech food and a wide choice of beers in suitably dark, medieval environs.

Žumbera Bezručova 14. Lively restaurant with wood-beam ceilings, Czech staples and well-executed South American grilled dishes. There's also a music club upstairs.

Entertainment

Plzeň's wonderful Beaux-Arts **Divadlo J.K. Tyla** is the city's main venue for opera and ballet. Most other concerts and cultural events take place at the Dům kultury on Americká, though the **Festival of Folk Songs** (known as Porta and held over the first weekend in July) is held in the Vystaviště, on Radčická, off Palackého náměstí, while the **International Folklore Festival** in mid-June takes place at various sites around town. Vystaviště is also home to the city's summer-only open-air **cinema** (*letní kino*). Elektra, an art-house cinema complex at Americká 24, also has a restaurant and occasional live music. Live concerts are held every Wednesday in the *Jazz Rock Café*, Sedláčkova 18, and in the *House of Blues*, Černická 10.

Kladruby

It's difficult not to be moved by the **Benedictine monastery** (April & Oct Sat & Sun 9am–4pm; May & Sept Tues–Sun 9am–4pm; June–Aug Tues–Sun 9am–5pm; tour in English 100Kč, tour with English text 70Kč; ⊛kladruby.euweb.cz) at **KLADRUBY** (Kladrau), 35km west of Plzeň – particularly if you manage to catch a Christmas concert or join the August music festival. Designed by Giovanni Santini, arguably the most original Baroque architect to work in the Czech Lands, the monastery was founded by Vladislav I in 1114 (he's buried here, too) and was once the largest and richest monastery in Bohemia. Gutted by the Hussites and again during the Thirty Years' War, the whole place was transformed when the Counter-Reformation had set in – the monastery according to blueprints by Kilian Ignaz Dientzenhofer, and the church under Santini's supervision. This huge church, now restored, is the main attraction, where the original Romanesque and Gothic elements blend imperceptibly with Santini's idiosyncratic additions. The original lantern tower has been converted into an extravagant Baroque cupola, which filters a faded pink light into the transepts, themselves covered in stars and zigzags mirrored on the cold stone paving below.

The easiest way to get from Plzeň to Kladruby on public transport is to go as far as **STŘÍBRO** (Mies) by train, and then change onto one of the fairly frequent local buses, which leave from the bus station in the town centre and cover the last 6km to Kladruby. Dramatically poised over the Mže (Mies) river, Stříbro itself was previously the vague frontier post between the German- and Czech-speaking districts, its tidy square sporting arguably the most beautiful Renaissance **radnice** in Bohemia, paid for by the town's long-extinct silver mines (*stříbro* means silver).

Klatovy and around

Tightly walled in and nervously perched on high ground, **KLATOVY** (Klattau) warns of the approaching border with Germany. Founded by Přemyslid King Otakar II in 1260, the town's great prosperity in the middle ages is still visible in the main square, but it can't compete with the Rose Towns further east. Still, there's enough here to pass a couple of hours; with Plzeň only an hour away by train it's another possible day-trip, or a potential base for exploring the northwest tip of the nearby Šumava region (see p.187).

Arrival, information and accommodation

Klatovy's main **train and bus stations** are more than 1km northwest of the old town (bus #1 or #2 to the main square); Klatovy-město station, just under 1km south of the old town, is only served by slow trains to and from Sušice. Accommodation, including private rooms, can be organized through the **tourist office** by the Černá věž on the main square (Mon–Fri 9am–5pm; ☏376 347 240, Ⓦwww.latovy.cz/icklatovy). There's an **internet café** at Václavská 19, two blocks northeast of the square.

Decent **pensions** in the old town include *U Hejtmana* on ulice kpt. Jaroše (☏376 317 918; ❷), just off the main square, and *Hotel Ennius*, in a Renaissance building at Randova 111 (☏376 320 567, Ⓦwww.sweb.cz/ennius; ❸), with a thriving restaurant. The same people run the *Hotel Centrál*, Masarykova 300 (☏376 314 571, Ⓦwww.centralkt.cz; ❸), between the old town and the stations. There's also an excellent **campsite**, *Sluneční mlýn* (May–Sept), with a swimming pool, bungalows and tent space. By an old water mill on the River Úhlava, it's signposted a couple of kilometres along the road to Domažlice.

The Town

Klatovy's best feature is undoubtedly the cluster of tall buildings jostling for position in the southwest corner of the cramped town square, **náměstí Míru**. The facade of the Renaissance radnice is decorated with 1920s sgraffito and features two liberation plaques: one to the Russians (who liberated the country), and one to the Americans (who liberated the town). Tucked in beside the town hall is the 76-metre-high, sixteenth-century **Černá věž** (Black Tower; April & Oct Sat & Sun 9am–noon & 1–4pm; May–Sept Tues–Sun 9am–noon & 1–5pm), the clearest evidence of the town's bygone prosperity. Its pinnacled parapet, once a lookout post, offers views of the forests at the Bavarian border and, closer at hand, across the rooftops to the smaller and later **Bílá věž** (see opposite).

Next to the Černá věž, Dientzenhofer's white **Jezuitský kostel** exudes incense and cooled air from its curvaceous interior. It's emblazoned with frescoes, including a spectacularly theatrical trompe l'oeil main altar and backdrop. More fascinating, though, are the church's musty **katakomby** (catacombs; times as for the Černá věž; 40Kč), where Jesuits and other wealthy locals are preserved in varying stages of decomposition beneath the radnice; the entrance is round the side of the church. Next door is **U bílého jednorožce** (At the White Unicorn), a seventeenth-century Baroque *lékárna* or apothecary (Tues–Sun 9am–noon & 1–5pm), which functioned until 1964 and has since become a UNESCO-registered monument. The bottles and pots are all labelled in Latin, with swirling wooden pillars flanking the shelves, and a unicorn's horn (strictly speaking, a tusk from an arctic narwhal), the pharmacists' mascot, jutting out into the centre. The back room, where the drugs were mixed, comes complete with ghoulish flasks of dried goat's blood and pickled children's intestines.

It's worth strolling over to the **Bílá věž** (White Tower), built during the Renaissance, but later Baroquified. Next door stands the Gothic church, **Arciděkanský chrám**, whose spires sport charming gilded crowns slipped on like rings on fingers. Inside, the church retains its medieval stellar vaulting, and features a fetching shell-shaped baldachin, held up by barley-sugar columns. Beyond the church and Bílá věž are the impressive remains of the town's medieval walls, which, if followed south, will bring you to the **Vlastivědné muzeum Dr. Hostaše**, on Hostašova, more interesting for its salmon-pink Austro-Hungarian architecture than for its humdrum exhibits (May–Sept & Dec Tues–Sun 9am–noon & 1–5pm; Jan–April, Oct & Nov Tues–Fri 9am–noon & 1–5pm; 30Kč).

Eating and drinking

You can enjoy Czech staples and admire Klatovy's main square from the tables outside the *Beseda* **restaurant**. Better value is the *Tep*, at the northwest corner of the square, which serves a wide range of dishes (even Argentine). The *Stará rychta*, on Denisova, west of the main square, is the town's liveliest **pub**, and serves Gambrinus; best for beer is the *Modrý abbé* (closed Sat), at the northern edge of the old town on Dobrovského. For a non-alcoholic drink, make for the cosy ✴ *U naší milé Paní* (ⓦ www.jasmin.cz), on Pavlíkova in a turret behind the Arciděkanský chrám – a mixture of tea-house and ceramics shop.

Švihov

Ruined castles are ten-a-penny in these border regions; the virtue of the one at **ŠVIHOV**, 11km north of Klatovy, is that it still looks like a proper castle – and it's easy to reach by train, from either Plzeň or Klatovy. It was begun in 1480 by the Rožmberks as a vast concentric structure, with traditional double fortifications creating an inner and outer castle surrounded by a moat. Suspicious of such an unusually well-fortified stronghold, the Habsburgs ordered the owners to tear down the eastern section, and what remains today is a kind of cross-section of a castle, partially surrounded by its original moat. The highlights of the fifty-minute guided tour (April & Oct Sat & Sun 9.30am–noon & 1–3pm; May & Sept Tues–Sun 9.30am–noon & 1–4pm; June–Aug Tues–Sun 9.30am–noon & 1–5pm; ⓦ www.cestujme.cz/svihov; 50Kč) are the late-Gothic chapel by Benedikt Ried and a very fine Renaissance strapwork ceiling. The castle also frequently hosts concerts of classical music and theatrical performances (ask at Klatovy's tourist office for details).

Domažlice and around

Just 15km from the German border, **DOMAŽLICE** (Taus) is an attractive little town in one of the few border areas that has always been predominantly Czech-speaking. For centuries the town was the local customs house, and the Chodové, as the folk round here are known, were given the task of guarding the border with Bavaria, but in 1707 the town lost much of its former importance when the border was fixed. Domažlice's biggest bash is the annual Chod folk festival, **Chodské slavnosti**, held in August.

Arrival, information and accommodation

The town's main **train station**, called simply Domažlice, is 1km east of town; the Domažlice město station, five-minutes' walk south of the old town down Jiráskova, is served only by slow trains to Bor and Tachov. The main **bus terminal** lies just north of the main square, on Poděbradova. You'll find the town's helpful **tourist office** (June–Sept Mon–Fri 7.30am–5pm, Sat & Sun 10am–2pm; Oct–May Mon–Fri 7.30am–4pm; ☎379 725 852, ⓦwww.idomazlice.cz) on the south side of the main square, near the nineteenth-century radnice.

There are plenty of simple family-run **pensions** in the old town. *Café-Pension Tiffany* (☎379 725 591, ⓦwww.tiffany.wz.cz; ❷) offers brightly coloured rooms beside the church at Kostelní 102, while *Hotel Sokolský dům* (☎379 720 084, ⓦwww.sokolskydum.cz; ❸) on the west side of the main square is tastefully furnished with a decent restaurant. Also good is the snug *Penzion Konšelský šenk*

The Chodové

"The spearhead of the Slavic march into central Europe", as writer Josef Škvorecký described them, the **Chodové** are one of the few Czech peoples to have kept their identity. Very little is certain about their origin, but their name comes from *choditi* (to walk about), and undoubtedly refers to their traditional occupation as guardians of the frontier. Since the earliest times, their proud independence was exploited by a succession of Bohemian kings, who employed them as border guards in return for granting them freedom from serfdom, plus various other feudal privileges.

However, after the Battle of Bílá hora, the Habsburgs were keen to curb the power of the Chodové, and the whole region was handed over lock, stock and barrel to one of the victorious generals, Wilhelm Lamminger von Albenreuth (also known as Lomikar). At first the Chodové tried to reaffirm their ancient privileges by legal means, but when this proved fruitless, with the encouragement of one **Jan Sladký** – better known as **Kozina** – they simply refused to acknowledge their new despot. Seventy of the rebels were thrown into the prison in Prague, while Kozina was singled out to be publicly hanged in Plzeň on November 28, 1695, as an example to the rest of the Chodové. From the gallows, Kozina prophesied the death of Lomikar "within a year and a day" – the general died as Kozina foresaw, from a stroke following a banquet held to celebrate Kozina's demise.

Although the empire prevailed, the Chodové never allowed the loss of their freedom to quash their ebullience or their peculiar local dialect, which still survives in the villages. Stubbornly resistant to Germanization, they carried the banner of Czech national defiance through the Dark Ages. Even now, of all the regions of Bohemia, Chodsko is closest to its cultural roots, known above all for its local dialect and rich local costumes, still worn on Sundays and religious holidays, and for its *dudy* (bagpipes), now played only in folk ensembles and at festivals. If you're interested in seeing a typical Chodové village, it's worth visiting **Klenčí pod Čerchovem**, 10km from Domažlice.

(☎379 720 200, ⓦwww.konselskysenk.cz; ❷), at Vodní 33, in the backstreets just south of the square, with pleasant en-suite rooms and an excellent pizzeria. The riverside *Babylon* **campsite** (mid-May to Sept), 6km south, is accessible by bus or train.

The Town

Like many small Bohemian towns, Domažlice starts and ends at its main square, **náměstí Míru**, a long, thin affair, positioned along an exact east–west axis. Flanked by uninterrupted arcades under every possible style of colourful gable, the pretty, elongated cobbled square seems like a perfect setting for a Bohemian-Bavarian skirmish. Halfway down one side, the thirteenth-century **church tower** or *věž* (April–Sept daily 9am–noon & 1–5pm; 30Kč), now leaning to one side quite noticeably, used to double as a lookout post; ascending its 196 steps provides a bird's-eye view of the whole area. The **Děkanský kostel** itself, whose entrance is round the corner in Kostelní, has a wonderful series of Baroque frescoes, colourful furnishings and a fine trompe l'oeil scenic backdrop for the gilded main altar.

Domažlice's other remaining thirteenth-century round tower lies to the southwest, down Chodská, and belongs to the **Chodský hrad**, seat of the Chodové self-government until it fell into the hands of Wilhelm Lamminger von Albreneuth. The castle's **Muzeum Chodska** (mid-April to mid-Oct Mon–Fri 9am–noon & 1–4pm; mid-Oct to mid-April daily 9am–noon & 1–5pm; 30Kč) worthily traces the town's colourful history.

More fascinating by half, though, is the **Muzeum Jindřicha Jindřicha**, east of the old town just beyond the medieval gateway (mid-April to mid-Oct Tues–Sun 9am–noon & 1–4pm; rest of the year Mon–Fri 9am–noon; 15Kč), and founded by local composer Jindřich Jindřich. The extensive collection includes Chod folk costumes, ceramics and other regional items, displayed in a mocked-up cottage interior, along with a room devoted to the prolific Chod writer Jan Vrba.

Eating and drinking

The straightforward *Ural* (closed Sun), on the north side of the main square, is a typical Czech **pub-restaurant** serving the local, dark beer, Purkmistr 11. Much more memorable, though, is the friendly, medieval-styled ☘ *U Meluzinn*, which serves creative takes on hearty Czech food one block south of the square at Vodní 19. Domažlice has its own **brewery** by the bus station, though no brewery tap; head for the *Štika*, a real drinkers' pub serving the local brew, on the road out to Plzeň.

Horšovský Tyn

A lazy afternoon could happily be spent at **HORŠOVSKÝ TYN** (Bischofteinitz), just 10km north of Domažlice. Its main square, **náměstí Republiky**, is a pictur-esque grassy, sloping affair centred on the church of sv Petr and Pavel, and lined with Gothic houses sporting brightly coloured Baroque facades. At the top end, surrounded by a goat-inhabited moat, is the quadrilateral sgraffitoed **zámek** (April & Oct Sat & Sun 9am–noon & 1–4pm; May & Sept Tues–Sun 9am–noon & 1–4pm; June–Aug closes 5pm; ☎379 423 111, ⓦwww.horsovsky-tyn.cz), one of the most popular in West Bohemia and transformed by the Lobkowicz family into a rich Renaissance pile. There's a rather complicated choice of **guided tours**: the hrad tour (*trasa 1*; 1hr; 50Kč) takes you through the renovated bishop's palace, including the reconstructed interior of the early Gothic bishop's chapel. The zámek tour (*trasa 2*; 1hr; 60Kč) covers living quarters from the sixteenth to twentieth centuries, plus a gallery lined with portraits of Czech rulers; the kuchyně tour (*trasa 3*; 40min; 30Kč) features a trawl round the kitchens, tacky china chandeliers equipped with their original Edison bulbs and other delights; the purkrabství tour (*trasa 4*; 50min; 30Kč) leads visitors around the reconstructed riding school; the erbovní sál tour (*trasa 5*; 30min; 20Kč) takes you through the rooms with sixteenth-century heraldry paintings; and the Mitsuko tour (*trasa 6*; 40min; 30Kč) presents the legacy of Mitsuko Aoyama, descendant of a Japanese samurai family, who married Count Coudenhove-Kalergi in 1892. Behind the chateau, the vast **Zámecký park** stretches northwards, complete with hidden chapels, a large lake and hosts of peacocks. It's a ten-minute walk to the centre from the train station: head east up Nádražní to the main crossroads, then north over the river, and the main square will appear on your right. If you want **to stay**, try one of two good hotels on the square: the simple *Hotel Šumava* (☏379 422 800, ⓦwww.hotel.htyn.cz; ❷), or the more sophisticated *Hotel Gurman* (☏379 410 020; ❹), right by the castle.

Mariánské Lázně and around

Until the end of the eighteenth century, what is now **MARIÁNSKÉ LÁZNĚ** was unadulterated woodland. It was not until the 1790s that the local abbot, Karel Reitenberger, and a German doctor, Josef Nehr, took the initiative and established a spa here. Within a hundred years, Marienbad (as it was known in its heyday) had joined the clique of world-famous European spas, boasting a clientele that ranged from writers to royalty. Inveterate spa-man Goethe was among the earliest of the VIPs to popularize the place, and a few generations later it became the favourite holiday spot of King Edward VII, a passion he shared with his pal, the Emperor Franz-Josef I. During World War I, even the incorrigibly infirm Franz Kafka spent a brief, happy spell here with Felice Bauer, writing "things are different now and good, we are engaged to be married right after the war", though in fact they never were.

Today, Mariánské Lázně is much less exclusive, though no less attractive. The riotous, late nineteenth-century architecture has been restored to its former

The spa tradition

Following the Habsburg tradition, **spa treatments** remain extremely popular in the Czech Republic, which boasts more than 35 spa resorts (*lázně*). One of the chief perks of the Communist system, they were a form of healthcare open to all and usually paid for by one's employers (ie the state). Children, the elderly and the generally ill and infirm are still prescribed spa treatments by their doctors – it is often very difficult to book a cure, with huge waiting lists. Nowadays, the spas also attract an increasing number of Germans, Austrians and wealthy Russians, for whom stays are still relatively inexpensive compared to Western prices. At a few resorts, such as Mariánské Lázně, you can book in for half- or full-day "treatments", but most are intended for longer stays (three weeks is the norm for those sent by their doctors). If you're paying "foreign rates" for your visit, you don't actually have to be ill to be treated. Some people find spa resorts rather like open hospitals, but many are beautifully situated deep in the countryside, with fresh air and constitutionals very much part of the cure.

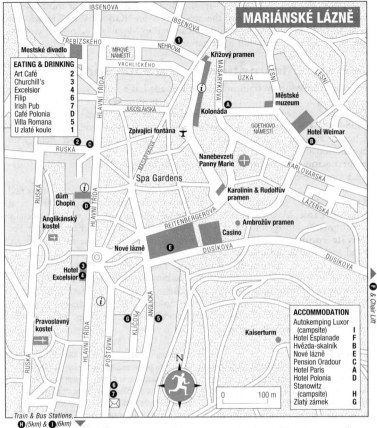

exuberance, and the whole place has been successfully brought back to life. Above all, though, it's the spa's beautiful setting, amidst thick forested hills, that remains its most beguiling asset. The air is cool and refreshing and the centre of the spa is more or less free of cars (parking is a fineable offence), all of which comes as something of a relief after the usual traffic-choked streets – it's even forbidden to smoke in the centre.

The basic treatment involves drinking the mineral waters from the spa's natural springs, for which many guests use their own ornate drinking vessels called *becher*. These curious miniature teapots each have a spout through which you sip the waters, thus preventing discolouration of the teeth. The waters come in an amazing variety: alkaline, chlorinated, carbogaseous and even radioactive, though they usually share one common characteristic: they are all pretty foul, or at least an acquired taste. In addition – and this is the more appealing bit – you can bathe in hot springs or sapropelic muds, breathe in pungent fumes or indulge in a new generation of complementary therapies, such as ultrasound and aerosol treatment, ultraviolet light baths, acupuncture and electrotherapy. Each spa resort tends to specialize in "curing" a particular ailment. For example, Františkovy Lázně is the best place for gynaecological problems, Luhačovice for respiratory diseases, and Karlovy Vary for digestive complaints. The most famous (and most oversubscribed) of the spa resorts are Karlovy Vary, Třeboň and Mariánské Lázně in Bohemia, and Luhačovice in Moravia. The official website, Ⓦ www.spas.cz, contains full information.

Arrival, information and accommodation

Passengers arriving by train or bus are unloaded at a suitably discreet distance from the spa, some 3km south of the centre; trolleybus #5 runs to the former Kaiserstrasse, now Hlavní třída. The **tourist office** (daily 10am–noon & 1–6pm; ☎354 622 474, Ⓦ www.marienbad.cz or www.marianskelazne.cz), in the dům Chopin at Hlavní 47, has maps and basic information, can help with accommodation and features its own **internet** café. For comprehensive **spa information**, stop by the **information centre** in the Kolonáda (daily 10am–12.30pm & 1–5pm).

Mariánské Lázně has a vast choice of **spa hotels** run by Hungarian-owned *Danubius Hotels* (☎354 655 550, Ⓦ www.marienbad.cz), whose office is at Lečebné Lázně, Masaryková 22. These are all fairly pricey (up to ⑨), especially in summer, and those undergoing spa treatments will always get first refusal. For **private rooms**, ask at the tourist office, or, if you have your own transport, head southeast to the suburbs of Úšovice.

There are two **campsites**: *Autokemping Luxor* (May–Sept; ☎354 623 504, Ⓦ www.luxor.karlovarsko.com), which is awkwardly located several kilometres to the west of the train station in Velká Hled'sebe, along the road to Cheb (bus #6 to Velká Hled'sebe, then walk 1km south down the Plzeň road); and *Stanowitz* (April–Oct; ☎354 624 673, Ⓦ www.stanowitz.com), in the village of Stanoviště, 5km south of Mariánské Lázně.

Hotels

Hotel Esplanade Karlovarská 438 ☎354 676 111, Ⓦ www.esplanade-marienbad.cz. The snazziest hotel in town, with comfortable, a/c rooms with all conceivable amenities. ⑨

Hvězda-skalnik Goethovo nám. 7 ☎354 631 111, Ⓔ hvezda@marienbad.cz. Yet another comfortable, opulent pile in the centre of town, offering various spa treatments. ⑥

🏃 **Nové lázně** Reitenbergerova 53 ☎354 644 111, Ⓔ novelazne@marienbad.cz. With its full-blown 1890s opulence, if you're here for the cure, this is the place to stay. The 180 well-appointed rooms are tastefully decorated and there's a wide range of spa treatments on offer. ⑧

Pension Oradour Hlavní třída 43 ☎354 624 304, Ⓦ www.penzionoradour.wz.cz. The best budget accommodation in the centre, with large rooms (no en-suite facilities) and its own car park. ③

Hotel Paris Goethovo nám. 15 ☎354 628 894, Ⓔ hotelparis@seznam.cz. This white-yellow, comfortable hotel stands directly above the Kolonáda, providing delightful views. ⑤

Hotel Polonia Hlavní třída 50 ☎354 622 861, Ⓦ www.hotelpolonia.cz. Simply modernized, but dripping with original fin-de-siècle features in the foyer and the café. Cheaper rooms with shared facilities are also available. ③

Zlatý zámek Klíčová 4 ☎354 623 924, Ⓔ manaskova@seznam.cz. Clean to the point of sterility, but exceptional value for its central locale. ②

The Spa

The most recently built of Bohemia's famous triangle of spas, Mariánské Lázně is the most consistently flamboyant. As far as the eye can see, sumptuously regal buildings rise up from the pine-clad surrounds, most dating from the second half of the nineteenth century. For all the sculptural theatricality and invention, there's an intriguing homogeneity in the fin-de-siècle opulence, with each building dressed up, almost without exception, in buttery Kaisergelb (imperial yellow) and white plasterwork.

Hlavní třída

Hlavní třída, the spa's main thoroughfare, is several kilometres long, and forms an almost uninterrupted parade of luxury, four-storey mansions (most of which are hotels), glass shops or granny-filled cafés. The vast majority are thoroughly in keeping with the fin-de-siècle ambience of the place. There are, however, one or two hideous modern hotels built over the last decade, though even these have failed to impinge on the most impressive final section of the street, where layer upon layer of shapely balconies overlook the spa gardens. Several of the shops here sell tins of *oplatky*, the ubiquitous sugar- or chocolate-filled wafers that make the waters you are about to taste infinitely more palatable. At no. 47 is the Bílá labuť' (The White Swan), a modest three-storey building where Frédéric Chopin stayed in 1836 on his way from Paris to Warsaw. Known as the **dům Chopin**, it serves as the spa's tourist office (see opposite), and has a tiny museum dedicated to the composer (mid-April to mid-Oct Tues, Thurs & Sun 2–5pm) on the second floor.

The spa's **synagogue**, which stood on Hlavní třída itself, was burnt down in 1938 on *Kristallnacht*, and no trace now remains. By contrast, the spa's small, red-brick **Anglikánský kostel** (Anglican church; Tues–Sun 9am–noon & 12.30–4pm) survives, hidden in the trees behind the *Hotel Bohemia*. Abandoned by its royal patrons and neglected under the Communists, the restored church is now used as an exhibition space. All that remains of the interior, however, is the pulpit, a rose window and a plaque to its most famous patron, King Edward VII. Better preserved is the nearby neo-Byzantine **Pravoslavský kostel** (Russian Orthodox church; daily: May–Oct 9am–noon; Nov–April 9.30–11.30am & 2–4pm; 20Kč) on Ruská, the road parallel to Hlavní třída. Dating from 1902, the rather plain interior is made remarkable by the spectacular iconostasis that won the Grand Prix de France at the 1900 Paris World Exhibition. Designed in the shape of a miniature Orthodox church, and made from enamel and porcelain, it is coated in more than 9kg of gold and cobalt, and is reputedly the largest piece of porcelain in the world. Mass is still held in the church every Sunday.

The Kolonáda and around

The focal point of the spa, overlooking the town, is the gently curving **Kolonáda**. Easily the most beautiful wrought-iron colonnade in Bohemia, it's rather like a whale-ribbed nineteenth-century railway station without the trains, and despite the lurid 1970s ceiling frescoes, the atmosphere is genteel and sober. In summer, there are daily concerts by Bohemian bands, occasional performances by the local symphony orchestra, and overpriced carriage rides (*drožky*) around the spa (200Kč for 10min). Adjoining the northern tip of the colonnade is the spa's first and foremost spring, the **Křížový pramen**, housed, along with two other springs, in its very own Neoclassical colonnade (daily 6am–6pm) and reputed to be good for one's kidneys. There are two more springs in the southern suburb of Úšovice.

Beyond the southern end of the Kolonáda stands the **zpívající fontána**, a computer-controlled dancing fountain, no great beauty, which does its thing to a popular piece of classical music roughly every two hours. Beyond and, more importantly, out of earshot of the fountain, is the elegant Neoclassical colonnade of the **Karolinin and Rudolfův pramen**, whose springs spurt forth water round the clock.

Behind and above the colonnades lies **Goethovo náměstí**, which boasts an aluminium, seated statue of Goethe; the original was carried off by the retreating Nazis, leaving just the granite plinth, to which the Czechs added a commemorative postwar plaque in Czech, Latin and French (but, significantly, not German). On his last visit in 1823, Goethe stayed at the house on the corner that now houses the **Městské muzeum** (Tues–Sun 9.30am–5.30pm). On the ground floor, displays trace the spa's history; upstairs, along with period furnishings from Goethe's time, there are historical sections that are frank about the spa's German roots (and about the American liberation), but silent on the postwar expulsions that more or less cleared the spa of its remaining inhabitants.

The square is overlooked by yet more giant, ochre spa buildings, including the former **Hotel Weimar**, at no. 9, in which King Edward VII preferred to stay (above the central portico there's a well-concealed German Gothic plaque commemorating his visit). Below, at the centre of the square, is the unusual octagonal church of **Nanebevzetí Panny Marie** (Assumption of the Virgin Mary), built in 1844–48 and decorated inside in rich neo-Byzantine style. Still further down the hill are two buildings definitely worth checking out. The first is the old **Casino** building, now the spa's main social centre, with a faded dance hall (discos held most nights) of fin-de-siècle marbled elegance; the other is the equally ornate **Nové lázně** (see p.216). Over a century old, it accepts "outpatients" for nude wallows in the colonnaded Roman baths, massages, mud baths and peat packs (Mon–Fri 2–8pm, Sat 9am–8pm; booking recommended at least two weeks in advance; all heftily priced in euros); you can also stay here. Ask for a carbon dioxide bath in *kabina 1*, which was fitted out for Edward VII and large enough to encompass his considerable bulk.

Eating, drinking and entertainment

Café Polonia, at Hlavní třída 50, is Mariánské Lázně's most opulent surviving **café**, its stucco decoration as rich as its cakes. *Art Café*, off Hlavní třída at Ruská 315, is a little less stuffy and has a wide assortment of filling pancakes and occasional live music. **Restaurants** include the moderately expensive *Villa Romana* on Anglická, a pretty stylish number, and romantic *U zlaté koule*, just east of Mírové náměstí at Nehrova 26, featuring live violin and piano in the evenings. *Churchill's* pub and restaurant, near the *Excelsior* on Hlavní třída, serves Czech food, pizzas and salads, which you can wash down with Guinness or local beers. A solid bet for straightforward Czech food is *Filip* at Poštovní 96, while next door is the lively *Irish Pub*.

There's usually a fair bit of highbrow **entertainment** on offer, including an international music festival in early summer, operetta in the theatre, weekly concerts by the Marienbad Symphony Orchestra, an annual week-long Chopin festival in mid-August (@www.chopinfestival.cz), plus a biannual Chopin music competition for young pianists. You could also try your hand in the splendid surroundings of the old **casino**.

Teplá

A relaxing day-trip from Mariánské Lázně is the monastery at **TEPLÁ** (Tepl), 15km to the east off route 24, whose abbots used to own the springs at Mariánské Lázně. The **Klášter premonstrátů** (May–Sept Mon–Sat 9am–5pm, Sun 11am–5pm; Feb–April & Oct–Dec Mon–Sat 9am–3.30pm, Sun 11am–3.30pm; @www.klastertepla.cz; 100Kč) – used as an army barracks until the 1960s, then renovated after 1989 – is 1km east of the village along the Toužim road. It's easy enough to spot, thanks to the plain stone towers of the original twelfth-century monastery church, though the rest of the monastery carries the universal stamp of the Baroque Counter-Reformation, courtesy of the Dientzenhofers. The real reason to come here is to see the neo-Baroque library (*nová knihovna*); built in the 1900s, it boasts almost edible stucco decoration, triple-decker bookshelves and swirling black iron balconies framed by white pilasters. You can **stay**, or simply tuck into excellent hearty **meals**, at *Hotel Klášter Teplá* (☎353 392 264, Ⓦwww.hotelklastertepla.cz; ③), a converted barn that also hosts organ concerts in summer.

If your next stop is Karlovy Vary, be sure to take the train, which winds its way painstakingly slowly but picturesquely for 50km, via Teplá, through the **Slavkovský les**, the thick forest that lies between the two spas.

Cheb

CHEB (Eger), 10km from the German border, is a typical Czech frontier town, with prostitutes lining the main roads and Vietnamese stallholders occupying the centre of town. For many Western visitors it's their first taste of the Czech Republic and, for most, it's a slightly bewildering introduction. Cheb is a beautiful historic town, but it is also primarily a German one, and

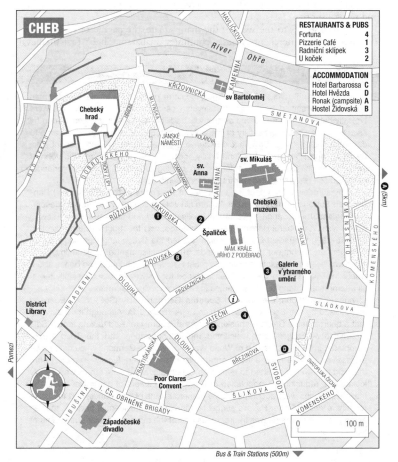

CHEB

RESTAURANTS & PUBS	
Fortuna	4
Pizzerie Café	1
Radniční sklípek	3
U koček	2

ACCOMMODATION	
Hotel Barbarossa	C
Hotel Hvězda	D
Ronak (campsite)	A
Hostel Židovská	B

River Ohře

HAVLÍČKOVA

KŘIŽOVNICKÁ

sv Bartoloměj

KAMENNÁ

MLÝNSKÁ

JERONÝMOVA

Chebský hrad

SMETANOVA

JÁNSKÉ NÁMĚSTÍ

KOLÁROVA

DOBROVSKÉHO

TRAKY ZBRY

sv. Mikuláš

sv. Anna

DOMINIKÁNSKÁ

KAMENNÁ

Chebské muzeum

ÚZKÁ

RŮŽOVA

JAKUBSKÁ

❶

❷

Špalíček

NÁM. KRÁLE JIŘÍHO Z PODĚBRAD

ŽIDOVSKÁ Ⓑ

Galerie v'ýtvarného umění ❸

SKOLNÍ

KOMENSKÉHO

HRADEBNÍ

DLOUHÁ

PROVAZNICKÁ

District Library

ⓘ

JATEČNÍ ❹

Ⓒ

SLÁDKOVA

DLOUHÁ

FRANTIŠKÁNSKÁ

BŘEZINOVA

Ⓓ

SVOBODY

SVATOPLUKA ČECHA

Pomezí ◄

N

Poor Clares Convent

I. ČS. OBRNĚNÉ BRIGÁDY

LIBUŠINA

ŠLIKOVA

KOMENSKÉHO

Západočeské divadlo

0   100 m

Ⓐ (5km) ►

Bus & Train Stations (500m) ▼

postwar expulsion of the German-speaking population left it with an identity crisis of mammoth proportions (see box below). Money was poured into the town, but Czechs were reluctant to move here (not so Roma, Hungarians and Slovaks, who were financially encouraged here to work). The root of the malaise lay in the authorities' ambivalence to Cheb, simultaneously encouraging its future and denying its past. Nevertheless, the town's historic centre – though overrun by German day-trippers for much of the summer – is worth an afternoon stop-off.

The Town

Cheb's showpiece main square, **náměstí Krále Jiřího z Poděbrad**, is named after one of the few Czech leaders the Egerländer ever willingly supported. Established in the twelfth century, but today lined with handsome, mostly seventeenth-century, houses with steeply pitched red roofs, this was the old Marktplatz, the commercial and political heart of Egerland for eight centuries. The batch of half-timbered buildings huddled together at the bottom of the square, known as **Špaliček** (*Stöckl* in German), forms a picturesque ensemble; originally medieval German-Jewish merchant houses, they now house a café and several shops.

In the backstreets to the west of the main square, the parade of seventeenth-century German merchants' houses continues unabated. Cheb's first medieval

Egerland

Most Germans still refer to Cheb as **Eger**, the name given to the town by the German colonists who settled here from the eleventh century onwards. The settlers were typically hard-working and proud of their folk traditions and peculiar dialect. Aided by its status as a Free Imperial City of the Holy Roman Empire, the town soon came to dominate trade between Bavaria and Bohemia. Shunted around between Babenbergs, Swabians and Přemyslids, Egerland finally accepted the suzerainty of King John of Luxembourg in 1322, in return for certain privileges, and in fact the Egerländer remained self-governing until well into the nineteenth century.

Hardly surprising, then, that the town was at the centre of the (anti-Semitic) **Pan-German Schönerer movement** of the late nineteenth century, which fought desperately against the advance of Czech nationalism, aided and abetted (as they saw it) by the weak and liberal Habsburg state. Here, too, was the most vociferous protest against the 1897 Badeni Decrees, which granted the Czech language equal status with German throughout the Czech Lands. The establishment of Czechoslovakia in 1918 was seen as a serious setback by most Egerländer, who made no bones about where their real sympathies lay; Eger remained the only town to successfully rebuff all attempts at putting up street names in Czech as well as German.

Thus, in the 1930s, the pro-Nazi **Sudeten German Party** (SdP) found Egerland receptive to its anti-Semitism as much as to its irredentism. Although it's estimated that a quarter of the German-speaking voters stubbornly refused to vote for the SdP, the majority of Egerländer welcomed their incorporation into the Third Reich, completed in 1938. At the end of World War II, only those Germans who could prove themselves to have been actively anti-fascist (Czechs were luckily exempted from this acid test) were permitted to remain on Czechoslovak soil; the others were bodily kicked out, reducing the population of Cheb to 27 percent of its prewar level. The mass expulsions were accompanied by numerous acts of vengeance, and the issue remains a delicate one. Havel's suggestion in his first presidential address that an apology to the Germans was in order was one of the most unpopular statements of his entire presidency.

Jewish ghetto is recalled in the street name, Židovská (Jewish Street), though the community was wiped out in a bloody pogrom in 1350; Jews were later expelled on another two occasions, in 1430 and 1502. Nothing remains of the 500-strong Jewish community that came under sustained attack during the 1930s as the Sudeten German Party rose to prominence in the region. Fascist thugs butchered a pig in the local synagogue shortly before its official opening, and *Kristallnacht* demolished what was left.

Chebské muzeum and art gallery

Behind Špalíček, on náměstí Krále Jiřího z Poděbrad 3, lurks the **Chebské muzeum**, which first opened to the public in 1874 (April–Sept Tues–Sun 9am–12.30pm & 1–5pm; Oct–March Wed–Sun same hours; ⓦwww .muzeumcheb.cz; 50Kč). The building in which it's housed was once the Stadthaus where **Albrecht von Waldstein** (better known as Wallenstein from the trilogy by Schiller, written during the author's stay here in 1791), generalissimo of the Thirty Years' War, was murdered in 1634 following a decree by Emperor Ferdinand II. The museum pays great attention to this event, and the heavy Gothic woodwork of his reconstructed bedroom provides an evocative setting for Waldstein's murder, graphically illustrated on the walls; however, Cheb's more recent history is studiously avoided. (For more on Waldstein, see p.221.)

The **Galerie výtvarného umění** (Gallery of Fine Arts; daily 9am–noon & 12.30–5pm; ☏354 422 450; 80Kč), in the Baroque nová radnice at no. 16 on the square, seems strangely out of context in a town with such rich traditions of its own, focusing as it does on Czech modern art. Kicking off with the 1890 generation, led by Jan Preisler and Antonín Procházka, there are several memorable paintings depicting Prague cityscapes, including the Belvedere, St Vitus Cathedral, and a red-and-cream city tram. More surprising is the large contingent of Cubist and Fauvist canvases, including a vivid blue *River Otava* by Václav Špála. In place of the usual Socialist Realism, a thought-provoking postwar collection rounds off the gallery.

Beyond the main square

Cheb's two largest buildings, dating from the town's early history, are out of keeping with the red-roofed uniformity of the seventeenth-century *Altstadt*. The church of **sv Mikuláš**, with its unusual roof, zigzagged like the spine of a stegosaurus, was restored by renowned local-born architect Balthasar Neumann in the eighteenth century. Only the bulky towers remain from the original thirteenth-century building, conceived as a monumental Romanesque basilica, and very few of the original furnishings survive. Most of what you see is neo-Gothic infill, but there are two fine Renaissance tombs inside the porch of the south door.

In the northwestern corner of the town walls, by the River Ohře (Eger), is the **Chebský hrad** (April–Oct daily 9am–6pm; ⓦwww.chebskyhrad.cz; 30Kč), or Kaiserburg as it used to be known; the sprawl of ruins built on and with volcanic rock is all that remains of the twelfth-century castle bequeathed by that obsessive crusader, the Holy Roman emperor Frederick Barbarossa, in 1179 on the foundations of a Slavic hill fort. Among the Baroque fortifications, the Gothic Černá věž (Black Tower) presents an impressive front and offers peeks at Cheb's rooftops through its tiny windows. In the northeastern corner, the lower storey of the ruined chapel with its beautifully carved Romanesque capitals will give you an idea of the castle of Barbarossa's time.

Practicalities

It's a none too pleasant ten-minute walk from the ugly postwar **train station**, north along Svobody, to the old town. The **tourist office**, at no. 31 on the main square (Mon–Fri 9am–5pm, Sat & Sun 9am–12.30pm & 1–5pm; ☎354 440 302, ⓦwww.mestocheb.cz), has information about the annual festivals, such as the autumn Jazz Jamm and the summer organ concerts, **internet access**, and can also help with private **accommodation**. *Hotel Hvězda* (☎354 422 549; ❸) is a decent option on the main square, but you'd be better off at *Hotel Barbarossa* (☎354 423 446, ⓦwww.hotel-barbarossa.cz; ❹), which has forty smart rooms on Jateční, just off the square. A cheaper alternative is the *Hostel Židovská* at Židovská 7 (☎354 423 401; reception 8am–noon & 4–8pm; ❷). The best of the **campsites** by the artificial lake Jesenice, 5km east of Cheb off the road to Karlovy Vary, is *Ronak* (☎354 436 899, ⓦwww.ronak.cz), with bungalows and basic lodging year round.

There are several **places to eat** on the main square – catering for German tourists, they're not bad for a drink; *Fortuna* is the best, with its straightforward Czech dishes and terrace seating. *Pizzeria café*, just off the square on Jakubská, has good pizza, but for something more traditional try *U koček* (closed Sat & Sun eve) for old Bohemian cuisine, at Kamenná 1, or *Radniční sklípek*, a cosy wine cellar on the main square. Kino Art (☎354 423 312), Kamenná 5, puts on interesting art-house **films**.

Františkovy Lázně

"The present Františkovy Lázně has nothing of historic interest", wrote Nagel's Guide in the 1960s, casually dismissing a town hailed by Goethe as "paradise on earth". Yet while **FRANTIŠKOVY LÁZNĚ** (Franzensbad), 5km north of Cheb and linked by train, may not boast any individual architectural gems, it is, in many ways, the archetypal spa town.

Originally known as Egerbrunnen, the spa was founded in 1793 and named Franzensbad after the then Habsburg Emperor Franz I. Laid out in the early nineteenth century, the Neoclassical architecture of the period finds its way into every building – even the cinema has Doric pillars – and virtually every conceivable building has been daubed in the soft yellowish colour of Kaisergelb. The centre of the spa is barely five streets across, and surrounded on all sides by a backdrop of luscious greenery. The virtual absence of vehicles and rowdy nightlife makes it the most peaceful of the spas, though as patients stagger about and white-coated attendants stride purposefully between buildings, it can resemble a large, open-plan hospital.

The Town

From the ochre-coloured train station, the road opens out onto the former *Kurpark* or **Městské sady**, whose principal path leads diagonally to a white, wooden bandstand at the head of pedestrianized **Národní**, the spa's modestly elegant main boulevard. Beethoven stayed at no. 7 in 1812, as the German plaque by the entrance recalls; while *U tří lilie*, the eponymous garden café further down, features in a poem by the Czech surrealist Vítězslav Nezval. You can sit and take in the scene from an alfresco table at one of the street's cafés.

At the bottom of Národní, a plain Neoclassical rotunda shelters the **Františkův pramen** (Franzensquelle; in season daily 9–11.30am & 12.30–4.30pm). While

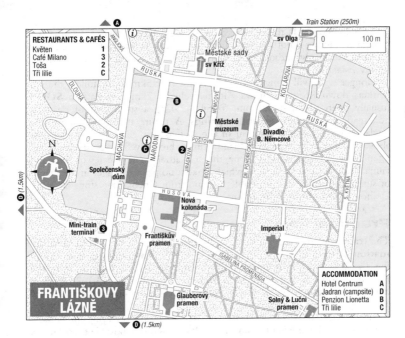

RESTAURANTS & CAFÉS

Květen	1
Café Milano	3
Toša	2
Tři lilie	C

ACCOMMODATION

Hotel Centrum	A
Jadran (campsite)	D
Penzion Lionetta	B
Tři lilie	C

FRANTIŠKOVY LÁZNĚ

the faithful queue to have their receptacles filled from the dazzling brass pipes, the real spa snobs retire to drink from their beakers by the fruit-encrusted sphinxes or under the nearby modern colonnade. Don't worry if you've come unprepared, as you can buy a plastic cupful, though, like most spa water, it's pretty unpalatable, on this occasion due to its high sulphur content. Don't be surprised to see a number of women touching the feet (and particularly another more specific part which is in danger of getting rubbed off) of a repulsive bronze cherub who sits holding a phallic fish, not far from the spring: in addition to treating diseases of the motor system and heart, Frantižkovy Lázně specializes in the treatment of gynaecological problems, and popular myth has it that giving the angel a good rub will ensure fertility. You've a greater choice of tipple at the **Glauberovy pramen** (daily 7–11.30am & 12.30–8pm; if closed, head for the tap outside), to the south: you can get your spa water salty or not; hot or cold.

The Neoclassical church of **sv Kříž**, dating from 1820, strikes an appropriately imperial pose at one end of Jiráskova, another riot of princely mansions with wrought-iron balconies. More intriguing is **sv Olga**, a richly decorated Russian Orthodox church on Kollárova. Set apart from the other spa buildings, and a favourite with visiting Germans, is Františkovy Lázně's finest spa villa, the **Imperial**, its corner balconies held up by caryatids. In the **Městské muzeum**, dr. Pohoreckého 8 (Tues–Sun 10am–5pm; 30Kč), you can see photographs of previous generations of Teutonic guests being subjected to gruesome nineteenth-century cures.

Walks and excursions

As with all the Bohemian spas, the formal parks quickly give way to untamed woodland, the difference being that in Františkovy Lázně the landscape is almost entirely flat, which is easier on the legs but shorter on views.

A two-kilometre **walk** through the silver birches will take you to Lake Amerika, though swimming is not advisable. In dry weather a **mini-train**, or *mikrovláček* (2–5pm; 20Kč) also heads there, supplemented in summer by another, the hourly *Frantovláček*.

A longer walk will bring you to Cheb, just over 5km south; follow the red markers down Klostermannova. Alternatively, it's 7km northeast to **SOOS** (usually open till 6pm or 7pm; ☎354 542 033), a small area of peatland pockmarked with **hot gaseous springs**. A nature trail raised above the bogland allows closer inspection of the springs that gurgle and bubble just above the surface, staining the land with a brown-yellow crust. A unique phenomenon in mainland Europe, the area attracts rare species of flora and fauna – not to mention insects, which make it no place to linger in the height of summer. Soos is also accessible by train from Cheb: three stops to Nový Drahov on the Luby u Chebu line.

Practicalities

The **train station** is a ten-minute walk north of the centre. The local **information office** (daily 10am–5pm; ☎354 208 990, ⓦwww.franzensbad.cz) is in the *Tři lilie* (see p.222). Additional offices exist at FL-Tour, Americká 2, by the bus stop (Mon–Fri 6am–6pm, Sat & Sun 8am–2pm; ☎354 543 162, ⓦwww .frantiskolazensko.cz) and at Spa Directory Information, Jiráskova 3 (Mon–Fri 10am–4pm).

With large numbers of Czech patients plus some tourists vying for **beds**, it can sometimes be difficult to find a room. It's occasionally possible to stay in spa hotels for one night, but spa guests always have priority. Probably the nicest place to stay is the elegant *Tři lilie*, Národní třída 3 (☎354 208 900, ⓔtrililie @franzensbad.cz; ⓞ), which was built when the spa was founded and has been sensitively modernized. Other options include the *Hotel Centrum* (☎354 543 156, ⓦwww.spahotelcentrum.cz; ❹), at Anglická 392, with a basic range of amenities, several spa treatments and a somewhat secluded location next to a park, and the small, cheaper *Penzion Lionetta* (☎607 560 793, ⓦwww.lionetta.cz; ❸), on a short alley off Národní třída, with massages on offer. The *Jadran* **campsite** (April–Oct; ☎354 542 412, ⓦweb.quick.cz/atc.jadran), with wooden **bungalows** and a half-timbered hotel with simple rooms (❷), is 1.5km southwest of the town by the lake at Jezerní 84; you can get there on the mini-train, and can hire boats once you're there.

Almost all spa hotels have reasonable **restaurants**; the *Tři lilie* is the best (and most expensive), and also has a pleasant café. *Květen*, on Národní, is locally renowned for its French cuisine, while *Café Milano*, next to the *mikrovláček* on Máchova, is a popular outdoor place. *Toša* on Jirasková ulice serves decent coffee and cakes.

Karlovy Vary and around

KARLOVY VARY is the undisputed king of the famous triangle of Bohemian spas, with by far the most illustrious guest list of European notables. What makes it special is its wonderful hilly setting, its Belle Epoque mansions piled on top of one another along the steeply wooded banks of the endlessly twisting River Teplá. It is best known throughout the world by its German name, **Karlsbad** (Carlsbad in its anglicized form), and it was German-speakers who made up the vast majority of the town's population until their forced expulsion in 1945.

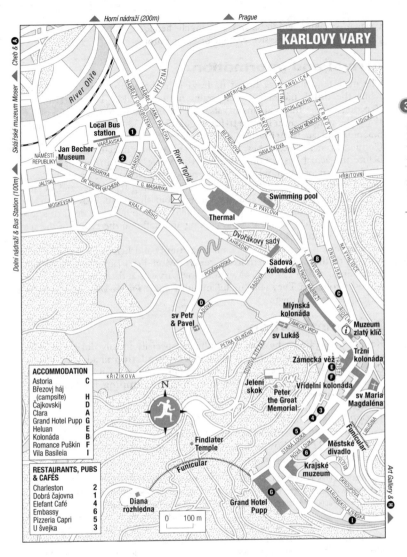

KARLOVY VARY

Horní nádraží (200m)

Prague

Cheb & A

Skláŕské muzeum Moser

Dolní nádraží & Bus Station (100m)

River Ohře

River Teplá

Local Bus station ❶

VITĚZNÁ

NÁBŘEŽÍ JANA PALACHA

NÁBŘEŽÍ OSVOBOZENÍ

VARŠAVSKÁ

Jan Becher Museum ❷

NÁMĚSTÍ REPUBLIKY

T. G. MASARYKA

BULHARSKÁ

JALTSKÁ

DR DAVIDA BECHERA

T. G. MASARYKA

MOSKEVSKÁ

KRÁLE JIŘÍHO

AMERICKÁ

ANGLICKÁ

KVĚTNA

JIRÁSKOVA

VRCHLICKÉHO

SVERMOVA

LIDICKÁ

BOŽENY NĚMCOVÉ

BEZRUČOVA

HAVLÍČKOVA

HŘBITOVNÍ

Swimming pool

I. P. PAVLOVA

Thermal

Dvořákovy sady

ZAHRADNÍ

PODĚBRADSKÁ

SÁDOVÁ

Sadová kolonáda

MLÝNSKÉ NÁBŘEŽÍ

I. P. PAVLOVA

NA VYHLÍDCE

ONDŘEJSKÁ

❸

sv Petr & Pavel ❾

Mlýnská kolonáda

ZÁMECKÝ VRCH

sv Lukáš

PETRA VELIKÉHO

SADOVÁ STEZKA

Muzeum zlatý klíč ⓘ

VÁŽNÍ

Tržní kolonáda

KŘIŽÍKOVA

Zámecká věž

TRŽIŠTĚ

Vřídelní kolonáda

ACCOMMODATION
Astoria	C
Březový háj (campsite)	H
Čajkovskij	D
Clara	A
Grand Hotel Pupp	G
Heluan	E
Kolonáda	B
Romance Puškin	F
Vila Basileia	I

RESTAURANTS, PUBS & CAFÉS
Charleston	2
Dobrá čajovna	1
Elefant Café	4
Embassy	6
Pizzeria Capri	5
U švejka	3

N

Jelení skok

Peter the Great Memorial

sv Maria Magdaléna

LIBUŠINA

Funicular

❸

❹

STARÁ LOUKA

NOVÁ LOUKA

Městské divadlo

Findlater Temple

Funicular

Krajské muzeum

❻

MARIÁNSKOLÁZEŇSKÁ

TYLOVA

ŠKROUPOVA

Art Gallery & ⒽH

Diana rozhledna

0   100 m

Grand Hotel Pupp ❼

❶

Despite this violent uprooting, the spa has survived and continues to attract an international clientele – largely Russian – which annually doubles the local population. This is further supplemented in the summer by thousands of able-bodied day visitors, the greatest number of whom are, naturally, German.

Tradition credits the Emperor Charles IV (or rather one of his hunting dogs) with discovery of the springs (hence Karlsbad); in fact, the village of Vary (which means "boiling" in Czech) had existed for centuries before Charles' trip, though he did found a German town here in around 1350 and set a precedent for subsequent Bohemian rulers by granting Karlsbad various privileges. By the nineteenth century its position at the meeting point of two great

German-speaking empires, and the much heralded efficacy of its waters, ensured the most impressive visitors' book in Europe.

Arrival and information

The main train station or **horní nádraží** is to the north of the River Ohře, while the **dolní nádraží** (where trains arrive from Mariánské Lázně arrive), off Západní, and the **bus station**, on Varšavská, are next to each other, south of the river. The dolní nádraží has a **left-luggage** office (6.30–11.10am & 11.40am–5.55pm) and an **information** centre (Mon–Fri 8am–noon & 12.30–4pm). Coming from Prague by bus, get off at Tržnice, the rather more central stop before the actual bus station. Wherever you arrive, you're in the unattractive, northern part of town, where the otherwise invisible local residents live and shop. The spa proper stretches south along the winding Teplá Valley and, in fact, the best way to approach Karlovy Vary is from the south. However, to do that you need your own transport, in which case you'll have a devil of a job finding somewhere safe to park, as parking and traffic in the centre of the spa are strictly controlled.

For general information, advice on **treatments** and help with accommodation, go to the main **information centre** (Mon–Fri 10am–6pm, Sat & Sun 10am–5pm; ☎353 224 097, ⓦwww.karlovyvary.cz), at Lázeňská 1, near the Mlýnská kolonáda. They sell a useful, monthly guide *Promenáda*, which you can pick up all around town.

Accommodation

Karlovy Vary can get busy in the summer, especially in July during the film festival (see p.230), so it's best to book **accommodation** in advance. Failing that, W Privat, an office on náměstí Republiky (Mon–Fri 8.30am–5pm, Sat 9am–1pm), can organize **private rooms**. If you're **camping**, head for the site with bungalows (②) near the *Hotel Gejzír* (April–Oct; ☎353 222 662, ⓦwww.hotelgejzir.cz) on Slovenská, south and upstream from the *Grand Hotel Pupp*; take bus #20 from the Divadelní náměstí. Three kilometres further south, in the village of **Březová**, lies the popular campsite *Březový háj* (April–Oct; ☎353 222 665, ⓦwww.brezovy-haj.cz), also with bungalows (buses from Tržnice every 1–2hr Mon–Fri).

Astoria Vřídelní 92 ☎353 335 111, ⓦwww.astoria-spa.cz. Central, quiet spa hotel with well-appointed rooms, bang opposite the Kolonáda. ④

Čajkovskij Sadová 44–46 ☎353 237 515, ⓦwww.cajkovskij.com. Once a cheap pension, now a luxury hotel, located in a quiet backstreet below the Orthodox church. ⑥–⑧

Clara Na kopečku 23 ☎353 449 983, ⓦwww.volny.cz/pensionclara. Very comfortable pension out of town beyond the railway station, at rock-bottom prices for this spa. ③

Grand Hotel Pupp Mírové nám. 2 ☎353 109 111, ⓦwww.pupp.cz. They don't come better (nor more expensive) than this outside Prague – 6800Kč a double and upwards – but though the decor is stunning, the service is not as good as it should be for the price. ⑨

Heluan Tržiště 41 ☎353 321 111, ⓦwww.heluan.cz. Peaceful hotel, with spacious, tastefully uncluttered en-suite rooms. ⑤

Kolonáda I.P. Pavlova 8 ☎353 345 555, ⓔreservation@kolonada.cz. Very plush and efficient place; rooms have all mod cons, and there's even a sauna, and an acceptable cellar restaurant. ⑨

Romance Puškin Tržiště 37 ☎353 222 646, ⓔinfo@hotelromance.cz. Decent doubles with breakfast, in the central section of the spa. ⑥

Vila Basileia Mariánskolázeňská 2 ☎353 224 132, ⓕ353 227 804. Secluded late nineteenth-century villa at the quiet, southern end of the spa, close to the *Pupp*, with just six large en-suite rooms. ④

The Spa

Unfortunately, many visitors' first impressions of Karlovy Vary are marred by the unavoidable sight of the **Thermal** sanatorium, an inexcusable concrete scab, built in the 1970s, for whose sake a large slice of the old town bit the dust. It serves as home base for the annual film festival, and there's a certain perverse appeal to the faded 1970s kitsch interior decor, but the most useful aspect of the Thermal is its open-air *bazén*, a spring-water **swimming pool** set high up above the river (Mon–Sat 8.30am–9.30pm, Sun 9am–9.30pm; 80Kč per hr). The poolside view over the town is wonderful, but don't be taken in by the clouds of steam – the water is only tepid.

On the other side of the River Teplá from the *Thermal*, the late nineteenth-century grandeur of Karlovy Vary begins to unfold along the riverbanks. The first of a series of colonnades designed by the Viennese duo Helmer and Fellner is the **Sadová kolonáda**, a delicate white-and-grey colonnade made of wrought iron. As the valley narrows, the river disappears under a wide terrace in front of Josef Zítek's graceful **Mlýnská kolonáda** (Mühlbrunnen Colonnade), whose forest of columns shelters four separate springs, each one more scalding than the last. At the next bend in the river stands the **Tržní kolonáda**, designed by Helmer and Fellner as a temporary structure, but one whose intricate whitewashed woodwork has lasted for over a century. Directly opposite is the **dům Zawojski** (now the Živnostenska banka), one of the best Art Nouveau houses in the spa, with its green wrought-iron and gilded detailing. Rising above the colonnade is the **Zámecká věž** (Schlossberg), the only link with the spa's founder, Charles IV, built on the site of his original hunting lodge.

Most powerful of the twelve springs is the **Vřídlo** or Sprudel, which belches out more than 2500 gallons of water every hour. The old wrought-iron **Vřídelní kolonáda** (daily 6am–7pm) was melted down for armaments by the Nazis, and only finally replaced in the 1970s by a rather uninspiring modern building. The smooth marble floor allows patients to shuffle up and down

▲ Karlovy Vary

Marx in Karlsbad

A certain **Mr Charles Marx** from London (as he signed himself in the visitors' book) visited the spa several times towards the end of his life, staying at the former *Hotel Germania*, at Zámecký vrch 41, above the Mühlbrunnen Colonnade. He was under police surveillance each time, but neither his daughter Eleanor's letters (she was with him on both trips) nor the police reports have much to say about the old revolutionary, except that he took the waters at 6am (as was the custom) and went on long walks. The Communists couldn't resist the excuse to set up a Karl Marx Museum, just down from the Mühlbrunnen Colonnade, at the house where Marx used to visit his doctor. Somewhat unbelievably, it was the only one of its kind in the entire Communist world, Lenin being the orthodox choice. Needless to say, it has long since been dismantled, and is now the even duller Muzeum zlatý klíč.

contentedly, while inside the glass rotunda the geyser pops and splutters, shooting hot water 12m upwards. Ensuing clouds of steam obscure what would otherwise be a perfect view of Kilian Ignaz Dientzenhofer's Baroque masterpiece, the church of **sv Maria Magdaléna**, pitched nearby on a precipitous site. The light, pink interior, full of playful oval shapes, contrasts strikingly with the relentlessly nineteenth-century air of the rest of the town.

If you've forgotten your cure cup, you can buy the faintly ridiculous *becher* vessels from one of the many souvenir shops. The purpose behind these is to avoid colouring your teeth with the water, though plenty of people cut costs and buy a plastic cup. Popular wisdom has it that "when the disorder becomes a disease, doctors prescribe the hot waters of Carlsbad" – in other words, it's strong stuff. In the eighteenth century, the poor were advised to drink up to five hundred cups of the salty waters to cure the disease of poverty. The German playwright Schiller (who came here on his honeymoon in 1791) drank eighteen cups and lived to tell the tale, but generally no more than five to seven cups a day are recommended.

Stará and Nová louka

South of the Sprudel is Karlovy Vary's most famous shopping street, the **Stará louka**, described rather mystifyingly by Le Corbusier as "a set of *Torten* (cakes) all the same style and the same elegance". Its shops, which once rivalled those in Vienna's Kärntnerstrasse, increasingly exude the snobbery of former days – there's even a branch of Versace at the far end of the street. Don't miss the Moser shop at Tržiště 7 (everyone who's anyone, from Stalin to the Shah, has had a Moser glass made for them), where you can buy some of the local glassware, made in the factory in the suburb of Dvory, just off the Cheb road.

At the end of Stará louka is the **Grand Hotel Pupp**, named after its founder, the eighteenth-century confectioner Johann Georg Pupp. Rebuilt in the late nineteenth-century by the ubiquitous Helmer and Fellner, *Pupp* was *the* place to be seen, a meeting place for Europe's elite. Despite the odd spot of careless modernization and rather snotty service, it boasts an interior that can't fail to impress, and the cakes are allegedly still made to Mr Pupp's own recipe. On the opposite bank, the former Kaiserbad – now known rather more prosaically as Lázně I – is another sumptuous edifice, designed like a theatre by Helmer and Fellner, with a luscious velvet and marble interior.

Back around the corner in Nová louka, the spa's richly decorated, creamy white **Městské divadlo** is another Helmer and Fellner construction, where Dvořák gave the premiere of his *New World Symphony* in 1893. What makes this place special, though, is that the frescoes and main curtain were executed by a group of painters that included a young **Gustav Klimt**, later to become one of the most famous figures in the Viennese Secession. If you ask at the box office, you should be able to get a glimpse of the auditorium.

A short distance beyond the casino is the spa's main **Galerie umění** (Tues–Sun 9.30am–noon & 1–5pm), on Goethova stezka, which contains a small but interesting cross-section of twentieth-century Czech canvases, and a disappointingly limited selection of glassware. The most interesting of Karloy Vary's museums is the **Sklářské muzeum Moser** (daily 9am–5pm; 80Kč; Ⓦwww.moser-glass.com), Kpt. Jaroše 19, out of the centre (bus #1, #9 and #10 from the local bus station), which presents the history of glass-making, complete with some fine examples. You can also pay a visit to the famous glassworks (daily 9am–2.30pm; guided tours with reservation, 120Kč; ℡353 449 455), established in 1857 by Ludwig Moser.

Walking in the hills

Of all the spas, Karlovy Vary's constitutional **walks** are the most physically taxing and visually rewarding. You can let the **funicular** (*lanová draha*) take the strain by hopping aboard one of the trains (daily: Feb–May & Sept–Dec 9am–6pm; June–Aug till 7pm; every 15min; 60Kč one way) from behind the *Grand Hotel Pupp* up to the Diana rozhledna and *Diana* restaurant. Alternatively, you can climb up through the beech and oak trees to the wooden crucifix above Stará louka, and then on to the spectacular panorama where the **Peter the Great Memorial** commemorates the visiting Russian tsar and his dozen or so royal hangers-on. In season you can enjoy the (not so perfect) view northwards from the *Jelení skok* restaurant (Tues–Sun 10am–6pm).

The road below *Jelení skok* slopes down to **Zámecký vrch**, where Turgenev stayed at no. 22 in 1874–75 and which the English aristocracy used to ascend in order to absolve their sins at the red-brick Anglican church of **sv Lukáš** (Evangelical and Methodist services are still held here, although not in English). Clearly visible, high on the opposite bank, is the *Imperial* sanatorium, a huge fortress hotel built in 1912 to rival *Pupp* and flying in the face of the popular Art Nouveau architecture of the spa; it was converted into a hospital during World War II, handed over to the Soviets during the Communist period, and has only recently been turned back into a hotel (it even has its own funicular to transport guests to and from the spa below).

An alternative route back down to the Sadová kolonáda is the street of **Sadová** itself, which is lined with some of the most gloriously flamboyant mansions in the whole spa. Topping the lot, though, is the fabulous white Russian Orthodox church of **sv Petr and Pavel** (daily 10am–5pm), built to serve the visiting Russian aristocracy and now equally popular with the spa's current crop of Russian visitors. The church's stunning exterior, crowned by a series of gilded onion domes, is its finest asset.

Eating, drinking and entertainment

Inexpensive meals are rare in Karlovy Vary – and often the calibre of what's on offer is less than you'd expect. That said, there are some pleasant surprises. Restaurants that double as pubs and hotel bars remain the most popular places to have a drink. The all-night casinos, which have been sprouting up near the bus station, should be visited as a last resort.

Karlovy Vary's **cultural life** is pretty varied, from classical concerts at the former *Kurhaus* (Lázně III) and occasionally at *Pupp*, to the rock club *Rotes*

Becherovka

Karlovy Vary is, of course, the home of one of the country's most peculiar and popular drinks, **becherovka**, a liqueur made from a secret recipe of nineteen different herbs, which really does ease digestion and is fondly referred to as Karlovy Vary's "thirteenth spring". It was actually invented by the unlikely sounding Scot, Dr Frobig, in 1805, but only launched commercially two years later by the enterprising Dr Jan Becher. It's available in bars and restaurants all over town (and just about anywhere else in the country). Be warned: it's an acquired taste – a little like cough mixture – and perhaps best drunk with tonic, ice and a slice (ask for a *beton*). The company's factory shop is on T.G. Masaryka 57, near náměstí Republiky, as is the **Jan Becher Museum** (daily 9am–5pm; 100Kč; ☏353 170 177, ⓦwww.becherovka.cz), where you can tour the old cellars and experience the delights of a liqueur-tasting.

Berlin, Jaltská 7, which also serves as a gallery. The town also hosts the celebrated **International Film Festival** in July (ⓦwww.kviff.com), which attracts at least a handful of big names.

Restaurants and cafés

Charleston Bulharská 1. Smart pub with a British feel serving Czech staples that can be washed down with one of several beers on tap.

Dobrá čajovna Varšavská 13. Enjoy a healthy cup of tea in this down-to-earth antidote to the town's prevailing air of coffee-and-cake overindulgence.

Elefant café Stará louka 30. The nearest Karlovy Vary comes to an elegant Habsburg-style café, and as a result very popular – even if the cakes and coffees take second billing to the refined interior and the people-watching on Stará louka.

Embassy Nová louka 21. One of the oldest Baroque houses in the spa, the *Embassy* offers a fresh and superlative take on traditional Czech cuisine.

Grand Hotel Pupp Mírové nám. 2. If you're looking for opulence, you might as well head for the *Grand Hotel Pupp*, whose bar and restaurant boast unrivalled Neoclassical decor.

Pizzeria Capri Stará Louka 42. The best pizza in town, as well as pasta favourites likes spaghetti carbonara, in this warm approximation of a New York pizza shop – but it doesn't come cheap.

U Švejka Stará louka 10. More than a little incongruous on Stará louka, the welcoming *U Švejka* offers a typical Czech pub atmosphere, with the Good Soldier himself sitting by the entrance. A Kozel porter makes an ideal match for the smoked pork neck in plum sauce with potato dumplings.

Loket

The tiny hilltop town of **LOKET** (Elbogan) is an exquisite, virtually undiscovered, miniature gem, just 12km west of the crowds of Karlovy Vary. It takes its name from the sharp bend in the River Ohře – *loket* means elbow – which provides the town with its dramatic setting. The fourteenth-century **hrad** (daily: April–Oct 9am–4.30pm; Nov–March 9am–3.30pm; ⓦwww .hradloket.cz; 80Kč), which slots into the precipitous fortifications, displays porcelain manufactured in the town over the last couple of centuries; you can also explore the castle's former prison, climb the lookout tower, explore the ruined Romanesque rotunda, and enjoy the tacky permanent exhibition on ghosts, plus the occasional concert, medieval market and fencing match. In July, during the *Loketské kulturní léto* **festival** (ⓦwww.loketfestival.info), the castle provides a backdrop to opera performances. The pretty main square is overlooked by the **Hotel Bílý kůň**, where Goethe met his last love, Ulrike von Lewetzow, he in his 70s, she a mere 17. Hardly surprisingly, she refused his marriage proposal – his *Marienbader Elegie* describes the event – and then remained single throughout her long life. The rest of Loket's picturesque streets form a garland around the base of the castle, sheltering half-timbered houses and secluded courtyards like Sklenařská, where the redundant

▲ Loket castle

German sign *Glaser Gasse* remains unmolested since the forced expulsions of 1945 stripped the town of its German-speaking inhabitants.

Practicalities

Loket's **information centre** (April–Dec daily 10am–noon & 1–5pm; Jan–March Tues–Sat 10am–noon & 1–5pm; ☎352 684 123, ⓦ www.loket.cz) is at T.G. Masaryka 12, near the bridge. The best **place to stay** is the *Hotel Císar Ferdinand* (☎352 327 130, ⓦ www.hotel-loket.cz; ④), in the grandiose former post office at the top of the main square, with its own brewpub serving an excellent half-dark sv Florián beer. Cheaper is the amiable **hostel** *Lazy River* (☎352 684 587, ⓦ www.lazyriverhostel.com; ①–②), at Kostelní 72, conveniently located between the square and the castle.

Loket is easily accessible by **bus** from Karlovy Vary, but by far the most inspiring way of getting there is to walk the seventeen-kilometre-long, blue-marked track from Karlovy Vary, which crosses over to the left bank of the River Ohře at the halfway point and passes the giant pillar-like rocks of the **Svatošské skály** (Hans Heiling Felsen), which have inspired writers from Goethe to the Brothers Grimm.

Travel details

Trains

Connections with Prague: Domážlice (2 daily; 2hr 30min); Františkovy Lázně (4 daily; 3hr 40min); Karlovy Vary (3 daily; 4hr 5min–5hr 10min); Mariánské Lázně/Cheb (10 daily; 2hr 55min/3hr 25min); Plzeň (hourly; 1hr 40min).

Cheb to: Františkovy Lázně (19–22 daily; 15min); Karlovy Vary (20–24 daily; 50min–1hr 5min); Mariánské Lázně (17–19 daily; 25–35min);

Nürnberg (1 daily; 2hr); Plzeň (15–17 daily; 1hr 35min– 2hr 10min).
Domážlice to: Klatovy (5–6 daily; 1hr).
Karlovy Vary to: Kadaň (17–19 daily; 55min–1hr 10min).
Klatovy to: Železná Ruda (6–8 daily; 1hr 20min).
Mariánské Lázně to: Karlovy Vary (6–7 daily; 1hr 40min–2hr 20min); Teplá (7–9 daily; 30–35min).
Plzeň to: Domážlice (11–16 daily; 50min–1hr 50min); Furth-im-Wald (2 daily; 1hr 20min); Klatovy (9–16 daily; 45min–1hr); Munich (3 daily; 4hr 20min–7hr); Stříbro (14–17 daily; 25–50min); Železná Ruda (3–4 daily; 2hr 20min–2hr 30min).

Buses

Connections with Prague: Karlovy Vary (hourly; 2hr 10min–2hr 20min); Plzeň (hourly; 1hr 25min–1hr 50min).
Karlovy Vary to: Františkovy Lázně (1–3 daily; 1hr); Loket (Mon–Sat 1–2 hourly, 8 on Sun; 25–30min).
Plzeň to: Horšovský Týn (Mon–Sat 1–2 hourly, 5 on Sun; 1hr); Karlovy Vary (Mon–Sat hourly, 8 on Sun; 1hr 30min–1hr 45min).

North Bohemia

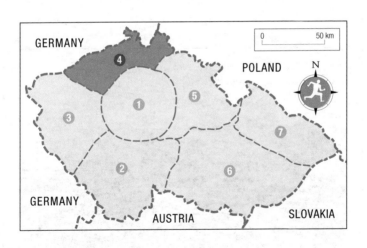

CHAPTER 4 # Highlights

* **Terezín** Habsburg-era fortress, used as a transit camp and "model ghetto" by the Nazis, which now stands as a chilling memorial to the Holocaust. **See p.244**

* **Litoměřice** Ecclesiastical town with a remarkable collection of Baroque churches designed by the Broggio family. **See p.247**

* **České Švýcarsko** Hilly, wooded border region with bizarre sandstone rock formations and boat trips along the Kamenice River. **See p.253**

* **Liberec** North Bohemia's busiest town boasts a splendid neo-Renaissance town hall and an excellent modern art gallery. **See p.258**

▲ České Švýcarsko

North Bohemia

North Bohemia (Severní Čechy) became a byword for the ecological disaster facing the country in the Communist era. Its forests all but disappeared, weakened by acid rain and finished off by parasites, its villages were bulldozed to make way for opencast mines, and its citizens literally choked to death – all due to the brown-coal-burning power stations that have provided the region with employment for the last hundred years. As in other parts of the country though, laborious environmental clean-up efforts have finally turned the tide; green landscapes again prevail in summertime, and the air, even in winter, is far cleaner than a decade ago. Parts of North Bohemia are popular with Czech and German tourists, in particular the eastern half of the region, where the industrial landscape gives way to areas of outstanding natural beauty like **České Švčcarsko** and the **České středohoří**, and towns of architectural finesse, like **Litoměřice**.

Geographically, the region is divided by the River Labe (Elbe) into two roughly equal halves. To the east, where the frontier mountains are slightly less pronounced, two rich German-speaking cities developed: **Liberec** (Reichenberg), built on the cloth industry, and **Jablonec** (Gablonz), famed for its jewellery. In addition, much of Bohemia's world-famous crystal and glass is still based in the smaller settlements located in the very north of the region. To the west of the Labe lie the **Krušné hory** (Erzegebirge or Ore Mountains), which, as their name suggests, were once a valuable source of iron ore and other minerals. Nowadays, however, the mountains are better known for their depleted forests (albeit slowly coming back to life), and for their brown coal deposits that have permanently altered landscapes and cityscapes alike.

Historically, the region has been part of Bohemia since the first Přemyslid princes, but from very early on, large numbers of Germans from neighbouring Saxony drifted over the ill-defined border, some taking up their traditional wood-based crafts, others working in the mines that sprang up along the base of the mountains. By the end of the nineteenth century, **factories** and **mines** had become as much a part of the landscape of North Bohemia as mountains and chateaux. Then, with the collapse of the empire, the new Czechoslovak state inherited three-quarters of the Habsburg Empire's industry, and at a stroke became the world's tenth most industrialized country.

German and Czech miners remained loyal to the Left until the disastrous slump of the 1930s, when the majority of North Bohemia's German-speakers put their trust in the Sudeten German Party or SdP, with disastrous

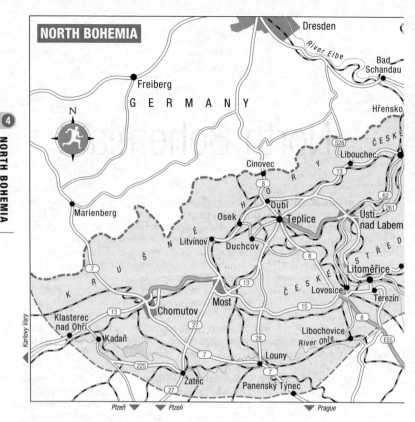

consequences for the country – and for Europe. Allied bombings took their toll during the war, and with the backing of the Big Three (Churchill, Roosevelt and Stalin) at Potsdam, the German-speaking population was forcibly (and bloodily) expelled in 1945. Economic necessity ensured that North Bohemia was quickly rebuilt and resettled, but its land and lives were irrevocably marred by forty years of unbridled industrialization under the Communists.

While the rest of Europe was belatedly tempering sulphur emissions and increasing fuel efficiency, the Czechs were steadily sinking to fortieth place in the world league of industrial powers and rising to first place for male mortality rates, cancer and stillbirths. It's easy to blame all these calamities on the factory fetishism of the Communists, but damage to the forests of the Krušné hory was noted well before 1948, and smog levels irritated the citizens of North Bohemia for the best part of the twentieth century. Meanwhile, the brown-coal industry that caused much of the havoc is being wound down as power generation has shifted to the nuclear plant at Temelín, and new filters on the remaining smoke-stacks have brought forth dramatic improvements. The downside is that these measures are likely to leave the region with one of the highest unemployment rates in the Czech Republic, something that can only exacerbate the smouldering tensions between the Czechs and **Roma** who have shared this polluted home since 1945.

Up the River Ohře

There are five historic towns along the **River Ohře** (Eger), ignored by most travellers eager to reach Karlovy Vary and the spas of West Bohemia. With your own car, they can all be covered in a day; by public transport (preferably bus), it's best to concentrate on just one or two. If you're driving, be sure to take in one of the best **views** in the entire region, from the ridge shortly after Panenský Týnec on route 7: in the foreground, bizarre hillocks rise up like giant molehills, behind, the entire range of the Krušné hory is stretched out in all its distant glory (close up it's not so pretty).

Libochovice

The first place of interest along the Ohře is **LIBOCHOVICE** (Libokowitz), a sleepy village nestling in the shadow of the Rožmberks' mighty ruined fortress of Házmburk, whose Gothic profile is a prominent landmark. Libochovice has a **zámek** (April & Oct Sat & Sun 9am–noon & 1–4pm; May, June & Sept Tues–Sun 9am–noon & 1–5pm; July & Aug Tues–Sun 9am–noon & 1–6pm; tour in English 100Kč) of its own, given a Baroque cladding by the Lobkowicz family when they took it over in the seventeenth century, but with many of its original Gothic features intact. The entrance is presided over by a brooding bust

237

of one of the heroes of the Czech national revival movement, Jan Evangelista Purkyně, father of Czech medicine, who was born in the chateau in 1787. Two lasting Lobkowicz additions provide the highlight of the chateau tour: the rather splendid *sala terrena* featuring trompe l'oeil frescoes by Italian artists, and the grandiose Saturn Hall. You could picnic with the noisy peacocks that stalk the carefully manicured French gardens (open till 7pm), have a snack at the café in the courtyard of the chateau, enjoy good Czech **food** at the *Zámecký šenk* next door, or go for a cheap pizza at *Il Vulcano* nearby.

Louny

LOUNY (Laun) is the first of the medieval fortified towns on route 7 (the road from Prague to Chomutov), its perfect Gothic appearance nearly completely marred by fire in 1517 but for the strikingly beautiful church of **sv Mikuláš** (May–Sept Tues–Sun 10am–5pm; Oct–April Tues–Fri 2–4pm, Sat & Sun 1–4pm), whose spiky, tent-like triple roof, the town's most famous landmark, is thought to have been rebuilt by the German mason Benedikt Ried (he used a similar design to great effect on the cathedral in Kutná Hora; see p.145), who died here in 1534. Inside, be sure to check out the ribbed vaulting, intricately carved limewood altars, barleysugar pillars and remarkable knobbly filigree work; you can also climb the tower.

Around the back of the church in Pivovarská, the local museum occupies the **Dům rytířů sokolů z Mor** (Tues–Fri 10am–5pm, Sat & Sun 1–5pm), with its distinctive Gothic stone oriel window and wedge-shaped roof. Roughly opposite is the **Galerie Benedikta Rejta** (Tues–Sun 10am–5pm), in a huge former brewery, whose interiors seem too large for the modest exhibition of modern Czech art within. The town's nineteenth-century synagogue, on Hilbertova, now houses the district archives. The impressive **Žatecká brána**, Louny's only remaining medieval gateway, marks the beginning of a pleasant river walk along the town's surviving ramparts on the northern edge of the old town.

Louny is less than an hour's drive from Prague airport. The main train station is 1km or so east of the old town, while Louny předměstí, a short walk south of the old town, is only good for trains to Rakovník, and the once daily České Budějovice–Most express. If you need a place **to stay**, the **tourist office** (Mon, Tues & Thurs 6am–5pm, Wed till 6pm, Fri till 4pm; ☎415 621 102, Ⓦwww.mulouny.cz), at Mírové náměstí 35, can help. Or try the *Hotel Union* (☎415 653 330, Ⓦwww.hotel-union.cz; ❷), in the shadow of sv Mikuláš on Beneše z Loun, with its own half-decent **restaurant** serving the local **beer**. There are good pizzas and grilled meats (and great views over the ramparts) to be had at the outdoor terrace at *Vivaldi*, or the usual Czech staples (plus the odd surprise, like eel in mustard sauce) at *U Daliborky*, both east of the main square on Hilbertova.

Žatec

ŽATEC (Saaz), 24km up the Ohře from Louny, is the centre of the Czech hop-growing region. In summer, from here as far south as Rakovník (Rakonitz), the roads are hemmed in by endless tall, green groves of hop vines. Red Saaz **hops** are considered among the finest in the world for brewing beer, and, way back in the twelfth century, were already being sent down the Elbe to the Hamburg hop market.

There's even a small hop garden on the arcaded main square of the attractive old town, which sits on a hilltop, across the river from the two train stations.

The square itself is centred on a vast Baroque plague column and overlooked by the onion-domed **radnice**, whose (47m) **tower** (Mon & Wed 8–11.45am & 12.45–5pm, Tues & Thurs 8–11am & noon–3pm, Fri 8–11am & noon–2.30pm) offers great views. Behind the radnice is the town's synagogue – once the second largest in the republic – and the town's former Jesuit **church**, guarded by a wonderful gallery of beatific sculptures. The town brewery (not open to the public) occupies pride of place in the nearby thirteenth-century castle.

You can find out more about the local hop industry from the town's **Chmelářské muzeum** (May–Oct Mon–Sat 10am–5pm; 50Kč), in a former hop warehouse on náměstí Prokopa Velkého, a couple of blocks south of the old town. Žatec's biggest annual binge is the **hop festival** *Dočesná*, held in the square at the beginning of September. The choice of **accommodation** is better in Louny or Kadaň, but if you need to stay, *U hada* on the main square (℡415 711 000, ⓦwww.uhada-zatec.cz; ❸) is the best choice, with its own decent restaurant and *vinárna*.

Kadaň

Very much in the same mould as Louny and Žatec, **KADAŇ** (Kaaden), 22km west, is an altogether more picturesque halt on the Ohře. From the train station, you enter the old town through the round, whitewashed barbican of the **Žatecká brána**. The town suffered badly during the Thirty Years' War, the population was driven out in 1945, and the whole place lived under a dusty air of neglect for the following fifty years. Now the town's handsome eighteenth-century buildings have all been more or less restored to their former glory, and the place has really come alive once more. The most striking sights on the partially arcaded town square are the prickly white conical octagonal spire of the **radnice** (tours summer Sat & Sun 10am, noon & 3pm), which looks like a minaret of a West African mosque, and the twin red onion domes of the imposing **Děkanský kostel**, which contains some good Baroque furnishings. Roughly opposite the radnice, you'll find **Katová ulička** (Hangman's Lane), Bohemia's narrowest street, which is barely more than a passage, the light straining to make its way past the maze of buttresses. The hangman himself used to live in the small white house below the gate at the end of the lane, which has since been converted into a cute little tea and spice shop. From the end of Katová ulička, you gain access to the best-preserved part of the town walls or **hradby** (April–Oct 6am–8pm; Nov–March 8am–2pm), which lead round to the southern tip of town, where Kadaň's **hrad**, a modest provincial seat, sits overlooking the Ohře. Out of the centre, along the road to Klášterec nad Ohří, a former Franciscan monastery houses the **Městské muzeum** (May, June & Sept Sat & Sun 10am–4pm; July & Aug daily 10am–4pm; 50Kč), with an exhibition devoted to the town's history, though more interesting are the sixteenth-century tombs of the Lobkowicz family (including Václav Lobkowicz featured in his panoply) in the monastery church and the fifteenth-century chapterhouse – one of the oldest in Bohemia and with fine vaulting.

The **tourist office** (Mon & Wed 8.30am–5pm, Tues, Thurs & Fri 8.30am–4pm, Sat & Sun 9am–noon; ⓦwww.mesto-kadan.cz) is in the radnice. **Accommodation** isn't a problem, with the lovely pension *Horoskop* (℡474 342 684, ⓦwww.pension-kadan.cz; ❸), across from the hrad, the best of several good central places to stay. A nice alternative is the small *Hotel Tercier* (℡&ⓕ474 345 234; ❷), Žatecká 566, standing on top of the town walls; its **restaurant** is a bizarre cave-like place, with kitsch prehistoric monsters sticking out of the walls. There are several **campsites**; the *Hradec* (mid-April to Sept; ☎605 497 169, ⓦwww.atchradec.com), 3km southeast of town off route 224, enjoys the nicest position, on the banks of the Ohře, not far from Hradec train station.

Klášterec nad Ohří

KLÁŠTEREC NAD OHŘÍ (Klösterle-an-der-Eger), 5km west of Kadaň, is the pretty quadrilateral seat of one of the many branches of the Thun family. Although, as the name suggests, the town was originally centred on a Benedictine monastery, it was the Thuns who really determined its present appearance, commissioning the two colourful Baroque churches and establishing the porcelain factory and spa facilities that made the town wealthy in the previous two centuries.

The Thuns' **zámek**, built up the hill from the village in 1646, houses a **Muzeum porcelánu** (guided tours only; on the hour April–Oct Tues–Sun 9am–noon & 1–5pm), containing over 6000 pieces of local and imported china from the vast collection belonging to Prague's UPM (Decorative Arts Museum); replicas can be purchased in the museum shop. The wonderful **gardens** (*zámecká zahrada*) sloping down to the river, are filled with over forty varieties of rare trees and dotted with Baroque sculptures by Brokoff. To get inside the family vault or **Thunská hrobka**, you need to ask at the museum, though it offers little of interest besides the odd quadruple-barrelled name – viz. Josef Oswald II Thun-Hohenstein-Salm-Reifferscheid, who has barely enough room on his coffin to fit his aristocratic credentials. The guide disappointedly concedes that all that remains of the first Thun of Klášterec is "a skull and a few bones" – rather impressive, considering that he died some 300 years ago and when all that's left of another, eighteenth-century, Thun is a shoe.

The chateau is a 1.5km trek from the main bus or train station. The **tourist office** (Mon–Fri 8.30–11.30am & noon–5pm; June–Aug also Sat & Sun 10am–4pm), left of the church, offers local information. There are a few places to **stay**, including the *Hotel Slavie* (☎474 375 211, ⓦwww.hotelslavie.wz.cz; ❷), opposite the gardens on Tyršova; ugly from the outside it has a pleasant, friendly **restaurant** serving local food.

The North Bohemian brown-coal basin

The **North Bohemian brown-coal basin** contrives to be even less enticing than it sounds. Stretching the 60km from Kadaň to Ústí nad Labem, it comprises an almost continuous rash of opencast mines, factories and prefabricated towns, earning it the nickname *Černý trojhelník* (black triangle). The majority of the country's brown coal (lignite) is mined here, most of it from just 10m below the surface. As a result, huge tracts of land at the foot of the **Krušné hory** have been transformed by giant diggers that crawl across fields of brown sludge like the last surviving cockroaches in a post-nuclear desert. Around one hundred villages have been bulldozed, rail and road links shifted, and the entire town of Most flattened to make way for the ever-expanding mines.

Not only is the stuff extracted here, but much of it is burnt locally, and brown coal is by far the filthiest and most harmful of all fossil fuels. To the credit of the Czech government (and not a little pushing from the EU), filters have been installed in the main power stations at Tušimice and Prunéřov, less than 5km to the north and east of Kadaň, and the smoky yellow clouds that used to billow through the valley are now much less lethal. On certain winter days, when the nearby mountains cause thermal inversions, the smog can still be intense and authorities resort to distributing filter masks to local schoolchildren; but in the summer the pollution levels drop dramatically, and you'll hardly notice the effect. Nonetheless, the character of the region has been forever altered, and aside from a couple of engaging stops – or indeed to view the spectacle itself – there is little reason to visit.

Most

Situated at the heart of the brown-coal basin, **MOST** (Brüx) is a sort of architectural paean to the *panelák*, the prefabricated high-rise blocks that are perhaps the Communists' most striking visual legacy. The only historic building to survive the town's demolition in the 1960s was the late-Gothic church of **Nanebevzetí Panna Maria** (April & Oct Wed–Sun 9am–4pm; May–Sept Tues–Sun 9am–6pm; signed "přesunutý kostel"), which was transported in one piece on a specially built railway to the edge of the mine, 841m away (the move took 28 days). Designed by Jakob Heilmann of Schweinfurt, a pupil of Benedikt Ried, in the early sixteenth century, it's now something of a lonesome sight, stranded between a motorway and the edge of the mining area, a short walk upriver from the train station. The original altar and numerous statues were preserved and reinstalled after the move, lending an odd juxtaposition to the otherwise clean, modern setup of the interior. Ask to see the video in the crypt that lauds the state's wonderful achievement in shifting the church – a hollow feat given that they relocated it above a polluted underground lake, whose sulphurous liquid has to be drained off to prevent the site from flooding. If your morbid fascination is captured, head for the vast **local museum** (Tues–Fri 9am–5pm, Sat & Sun 1–5pm), visible to the west beneath the hilltop castle of Hněvín.

Duchcov

At first, **DUCHCOV** (Dux), 20km northeast of Most, appears no different from the other brown-coal basin towns, encircled as it is by coal mines. But in this unlikely town there's a grandly conceived Baroque **zámek** (April & Oct Wed–Sun 9am–4pm; May–Sept Tues–Sun 9am–6pm; 100Kč), designed by Jean-Baptiste Mathey, which once hosted emperors and kings, as well as artistic luminaries such as Schiller, Goethe and Beethoven. The chateau's former librarian was none other than **Giacomo Casanova** (1725–98), who took refuge here at the invitation of Count Waldstein. Broke, almost impotent and painfully aware of his age, Casanova whiled away his final, fairly miserable thirteen years writing his steamy memoirs, the twelve-volume *Histoire de ma vie*. He took a vow of celibacy on entering Duchcov, though rumours continued to link him with various women, including the leading lady at the premiere of Mozart's *Don Giovanni* in Prague. The Venetians would like Casanova's remains, but no one is sure where they are; it's likely they have disappeared under the opencast mines.

The tour guides are well aware that today's trickle of visitors is more concerned with Casanova than with the chateau's period furniture, and so save the exhibition dedicated to the world's most famous bounder till last. Duchcov also boasts a vast collection of Czech **Baroque art**, including sculptures by Brokoff and Braun, and a series of obsequious portraits of the Waldstein family, mostly by Václav Vavřinec Reiner, who is also responsible for the fresco in the Great Hall. Much of the chateau park, along with the Baroque hospital designed by Octavio Broggio, was bulldozed in the 1950s by the Communists, who (wrongly) suspected that large coal deposits lay beneath the gardens. The priceless frescoes were shifted to a purpose-built concrete pavilion, where – forlorn, badly lit and brutally restored – they remain today; to see the frescoes, you must endure a thirty-minute guided tour (same hours as the chateau).

Valdštejn on Masarykova, just by the chateau, serves up standard Czech **food**, like dumplings with goulash.

Teplice

Feeling very much forgotten in the northwest corner of this polluted region lies the traumatized town of **TEPLICE-ŠANOV** (Teplitz-Schönau), the fourth spa of the once celebrated quartet of Bohemian resorts that included Mariánské Lázně, Františkovy Lázně and Karlovy Vary (see Chapter 3). In the early nineteenth century it featured the likes of Beethoven, Liszt and Wagner on its *Kurliste*; by the 1880s, however, the mining industry had already inflicted its first blow on Teplice's idyllic way of life: the nearby Döllinger mine breached an underwater lake, flooding the natural springs, which subsequently had to be artificially pumped to the surface. The lingering smell of lignite was a characteristic of the town even then, and is now complemented by several additional chemical vapours. In addition, Teplice now has more than its fair share of social problems: there's a large and vocal skinhead movement here, which has come to blows with the town's Vietnamese and Roma communities on several occasions in recent years. All this doesn't make for a great introduction to the town, but elements of the old spa have survived, and if you're in the area, Teplice merits at least an afternoon's halt.

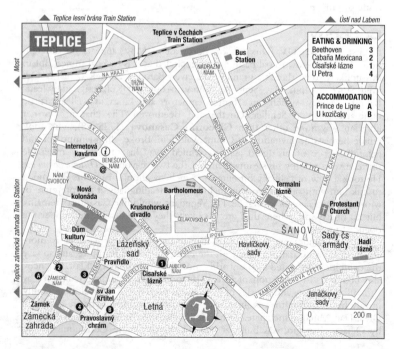

The Town

Arriving at the main train station, **Teplice v Čechách**, with its rich neo-Renaissance frescoes adorning the vaulted ceiling, injects a sense of hope; this is soon dispelled by block after block of silent and peeling late nineteenth-century houses as you head for the centre via 28 října or the main street, Masarykova třída, one block south.

At the end of Masarykova, behind the rather brutal Krušnohorské divadlo (an uncharacteristic, late work by Helmer and Fellner), the spa proper begins. Even the old *Kur Garten* – now the **Lázeňský sad** – has a somewhat diseased air about it, despite the lively sounds of birdlife. Nowadays, the Communist-era white concrete **Dům kultury** is the dominant feature of the park, fronted by the **Nová kolonáda**, a glorified greenhouse made from some of Bohemia's great glass surplus.

Only when you cross the valley to the brightly coloured Neoclassical houses on **Lázeňská** is it possible to make the imaginative leap into Teplice's arcadian past. Beethoven once stayed in a house on Lázeňská, and it was in Teplice that he wrote his famous love letter to a woman he called his "Immortal Beloved", but whose identity still remains a mystery. Beyond Lázeňská lies the town's monumental **zámek**, seat of the Clary-Aldringen family until 1945, when they and most other *Teplitzer* took flight from the approaching Red Army. It was here, in 1813, that Tsar Alexander I, the Emperor Franz I and Kaiser Friedrich Wilhelm of Prussia concluded the "Holy Alliance" against Napoleon. The countless rooms of the chateau are now part of the local **museum** (tours on the hour Tues–Sun 10am–noon & 1–5pm; 40Kč), with memorials to Beethoven, Pushkin and (of course) Goethe, wall-to-wall Biedermeyer, displays of historical clocks, old coins, ceramics and spa porcelain, and much else besides. The obligatory guided tour takes you also through the castle's courtyard, where there are remains of the medieval basilica, with a well-preserved Romanesque crypt.

Outside the main gates of the chateau is the cobbled expanse of **Zámecké náměstí**, centred on Matthias Bernhard Braun's flamboyant charcoaled plague column. To the east, there are two churches: the first is the **Pravoslavný chrám**, a neo-Gothic Orthodox church; the second is the more handsome Baroque church of **sv Jan Křtitel**, whose richly painted interior is worth a peek. Hot water dribbles through a sculpted boar's mouth into the occasional tourist's palms from the original spring, known as the **Pravřídlo** (Urquelle), which is set into the wall opposite the southeast corner of the church on Lázeňská. Further east still, a splendid staircase, the Ptačí schody (Birds' Staircase), takes you past the twin turrets of the *Švejk U Petra* restaurant to the blissful **zámecká zahrada**, which spreads itself around two lakes still "enlivened with swans", just as Baedeker noted approvingly back in 1905.

Practicalities

The main **bus terminal** and **train station** (Teplice v Čechách) are next to each other just off Masarykova; Teplice zámecká zahrada train station, to the west of the chateau garden, is served only by slow trains to Lovosice. The efficient **tourist office** (Mon–Fri 8am–5pm; Ⓦ www.teplice.cz), in the middle of Benešovo náměstí, should be able to help find **accommodation**. You can check **email** at the simple *Internetová kavárna* on Benešovo náměstí, near *Vienna*. By far Teplice's nicest (and most expensive) place to stay is the *Hotel Prince de Ligne* (☏ 417 537 733, Ⓦ www.princedeligne.cz; ➎), a renovated late nineteenth-century hotel overlooking Zámecké náměstí. Cheaper is the pension *U kozičky*

(☎417 816 411, ⊛www.ukozicky.cz; ❹), Rooseveltova 262, between the wooded hill of Letná and a busy road (ask for a room overlooking the former), which has a restaurant with a terrace overlooking the zámek.

One of the best **restaurants** in town is *U Petra*, on the zámecká zahrada staircase, which serves up Chateaubriand for around 200Kč. Other options include the *Beethoven*, a nearby daytime-only place (you can also buy warm *oplatký* here), and the quite cheap *Cabaña Mexicana* (Tues–Sat from 4pm), next door to *Prince de Ligne*. There's also a pleasant **café** on the first floor of the smart nineteenth-century Čísařské lázně.

Terezín

The old road from Prague to Berlin passes through the fortress town of **TEREZÍN** (Theresienstadt), just over 60km northwest of the capital. Built in the 1780s by the Habsburgs to defend the northern border against Prussia, it was capable of accommodating 14,500 soldiers and hundreds of prisoners. In 1941 the population was ejected and the whole town turned into a **Jewish ghetto**, and used as a transit camp for Jews whose final destination was Auschwitz.

Hlavná pevnost

Although the **Hlavná pevnost** (Main Fortress) has never been put to the test in battle, Terezín remains intact as a garrison town. Today, it's an eerie, soulless place, built to a dour eighteenth-century grid plan, its bare streets empty apart from the residual civilian population and visitors making their way between the various museums and memorials. As you enter, the red-brick zigzag fortifications are still an awesome sight, though the huge moat has been put to good use by local gardening enthusiasts.

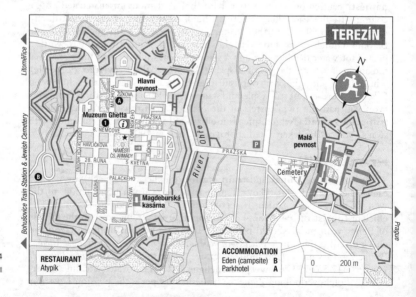

A brief history of the ghetto

In October 1941 Reinhard Heydrich and the Nazi high command decided to turn the whole of Terezín into a **Jewish ghetto**. It was an obvious choice: fully fortified, close to the main Prague–Dresden railway line, and with an SS prison already established in the Malá pevnost (Small Fortress) nearby. The original inhabitants of the town – less than 3500 people – were moved out, and transports began arriving at Terezín from many parts of central Europe. Within a year, nearly 60,000 Jews were interned here in appallingly overcrowded conditions; the monthly death rate rose to 4000. In October 1942, the first transport left for Auschwitz. By the end of the war, 140,000 Jews had passed through Terezín; fewer than 17,500 remained when the ghetto was finally liberated on May 8, 1945. Most of those in the camp when the Red Army arrived had been brought to Terezín on forced marches from other concentration camps. Even after liberation, typhus killed many who had survived this far.

One of the perverse ironies of Terezín is that it was used by the Nazis as a cover for the real purpose of the *Endlösung* or "Final Solution", formalized at the Wannsee conference in January 1942 (at which Heydrich was present). The ghetto was made to appear self-governing, with its own council or **Judenrat**, its own bank printing (worthless) ghetto money, its own shops selling goods confiscated from the internees on arrival, and even a café on the main square. For a while, a special "Terezín family camp" was even set up in Auschwitz, to continue the deception. The deportees were kept in mixed barracks, allowed to wear civilian clothes and – the main purpose of the whole thing – send letters back to their loved ones in Terezín telling them they were OK. After six months' "quarantine", they were sent to the gas chambers.

Despite the fact that Terezín was being used by the Nazis as cynical propaganda, the ghetto population turned their unprecedented freedom to their own advantage. Since almost the entire Jewish population of the Protectorate (and Jews from many other parts of Europe) passed through Terezín, the ghetto had an enormous number of outstanding Jewish artists, musicians, scholars and writers (most of whom subsequently perished in the camps). Thus, in addition to the officially sponsored activities, countless clandestine cultural events were organized in the cellars and attics of the barracks: teachers gave lessons to children, puppet-theatre productions were held, and literary evenings were put on.

Towards the end of 1943, the so-called **Verschönerung** or "beautification" of the ghetto was implemented, in preparation for the arrival of the International Red Cross inspectors. Streets were given names instead of numbers, and the whole place was decked out as if it were a spa town. When the International Red Cross asked to inspect one of the Nazi camps, they were brought here and treated to a week of Jewish cultural events. A circus tent was set up in the main square; a children's pavilion erected in the park; numerous performances of Hans Krása's children's opera, *Brundibár* (Bumble Bee), staged; and a jazz band, called the Ghetto Swingers, performed in the bandstand on the main square. The Red Cross visited Terezín twice, once in June 1944, and again in April 1945; both times the delegates filed positive reports.

Muzeum Ghetta

The first place to head for is the **Muzeum Ghetta** (Ghetto Museum; daily: April–Oct 9am–6pm; Nov–March 9am–5.30pm; 160Kč, 200Kč including Malá pevnost and Magdeburská kasárna), which was opened in 1991, on the fiftieth anniversary of the arrival of the first transports to Terezín. After the war, the Communists had followed the consistent Soviet line by deliberately underplaying the Jewish perspective on Terezín. Instead, the emphasis was on the Malá pevnost, where the majority of victims were not Jewish, and on the war as an anti-fascist struggle, in which good (Communism and the Soviet Union) had triumphed over evil (fascism and Nazi Germany). It wasn't until the Prague Spring of 1968 that the idea of a museum dedicated to the history of the Jewish ghetto first emerged. In the 1970s, however, the intended building was turned into a Museum of the Ministry of the Interior instead. Now that it finally exists, this extremely informative and well-laid-out exhibition at last attempts to do some justice to the extraordinary and tragic events which took place here between 1941 and 1945, including displays on the measures that led inexorably to the *Endlösung* (Final Solution). There's also a fascinating video (with English subtitles) showing clips of the Nazi propaganda film shot in Terezín – *Hitler Gives the Jews a Town* – intercut with harrowing interviews with survivors.

Magdeburská kasárna

The **Magdeburská kasárna** (Magdeburg Barracks; same hours as the Muzeum Ghetta), former seat of the *Freizeitgestaltung* – part of the *Judenrat*, the Jewish self-governing council – in the south of the ghetto, has been turned into a fascinating museum concentrating on the remarkable artistic life of Terezín. First off, however, there's a reconstructed women's dormitory, with three-tier bunks and all the luggage and belongings in place to give some kind of idea of the cramped living conditions endured by the ghetto inhabitants. The first exhibition room has displays on the various Jewish musicians who passed through Terezín, including Pavel Haas, a pupil of Janáček, Hans Krása, a pupil of Zemlinsky, who wrote the score for *Brundibár*, and Karel Ančerl, who survived the Holocaust to become conductor of the Czech Philharmonic. The final room concentrates on the writers who contributed to the ghetto's underground magazines, but the greatest space is given over to the work of Terezín's numerous artists. Many were put to work by the SS, who set up a graphics department headed by cartoonist Bedřich Fritta, producing visual propaganda to proclaim how smoothly the ghetto ran. In addition, there are many clandestine works, ranging from portraits of inmates to harrowing depictions of the cramped dormitories, the effects of starvation, and the transports. These provide some of the most vivid and deeply affecting insights into the reality of ghetto life in the whole of Terezín, and it was for this "propaganda of horror" that several artists, including Fritta, were eventually deported to Auschwitz.

Malá pevnost

On the other side of the River Ohře, east down Pražská, lies the **Malá pevnost** (Small Fortress; April–Oct 8am–6pm; Nov–March 8am–4.30pm), built as a military prison in the 1780s, at the same time as the main fortress. The prison's most famous inmate was the young Bosnian Serb, **Gavrilo Princip**, who succeeded in assassinating Archduke Ferdinand in Sarajevo in 1914, and was interned and died here during World War I. In 1940 it was turned into an **SS prison** by Heydrich, and after the war it became the official memorial and museum of Terezín. The majority of the 32,000 inmates who passed through the prison were active in the resistance (and, more often than not, Communists). Some 2500 inmates perished in the prison, while another 8000 subsequently died in the concentration camps. The vast cemetery laid out by the entrance contains the graves of over 2300 individuals, plus numerous other corpses, and is perhaps rather insensitively dominated by a large Christian cross, plus a smaller Star of David.

There are guides available, or else you can simply use the brief self-guided (English) tour sheet. The infamous Nazi refrain *Arbeit Macht Frei* (Work Brings

Freedom) is daubed across the entrance on the left, which leads to the exemplary washrooms, still as they were when built for the Red Cross tour of inspection. The rest of the camp has been left empty but intact, and graphically evokes the cramped conditions under which the prisoners were kept half-starved and badly clothed, subject to indiscriminate cruelty and execution. One building houses a permanent exhibition on the nearby **Litoměřice concentration camp**, where over 18,000 prisoners were forced to construct underground arms factories that the Nazis hoped to conceal from the Allies. The prison's **main exhibition** is displayed in the SS barracks opposite the luxurious home of the camp Kommandant and his family. A short documentary, intelligible in any language, is regularly shown in the cinema that was set up in 1942 to entertain the SS guards.

Practicalities

Terezín is about an hour's **bus** ride from Prague's Florenc bus terminal, or a short hop from Litoměřice, just 3km to the north; the bus drops you off in front of the tourist office on B. Némcove around the corner from the museum. The nearest **train station** to Terezín (from which the transports used to leave) is at Bohušovice nad Ohří, on the main Prague–Děčín line; occasional buses run to and from Terezín, or else it's a winding three-kilometre walk southwest of the main fortress. It's difficult to imagine a less appealing place **to stay**, but stay you may, at the badly run-down *Parkhotel*, on Máchova (☎416 782 260, ⓦwww .hotelterezin.cz; ❸), or at the **campsite** *Eden* (April–Oct), just west of town. Otherwise, the **tourist office** (Mon–Thurs 8am–5pm, Fri 8am–1.30pm, Sun 9am–3pm) can advise you on the many possibilities in Litoměřice. The only acceptable **restaurant** in the centre is the simple but clean *Atypík*, on Máchova, a block west of the museum.

Litoměřice and around

LITOMĚŘICE (Leitmeritz), 3km north of Terezín, at the confluence of the Ohře and the Labe rivers, is arguably the most appealing town in North Bohemia. It has been an ecclesiastical centre since the Přemyslid Spytihněv II founded a collegiate chapter here in 1057. From the eleventh century onwards, German craftsmen flooded into Litoměřice, thanks to its strategic trading position on the Labe, and it soon became the third or fourth city of Bohemia. Having survived the Hussite Wars by the skin of its teeth, it was devastated in the Thirty Years' War, but its most recent upheaval came in 1945, when virtually the entire population (which was predominantly German-speaking) was forcibly expelled. After 1989 the town began to pick up the pieces after forty years of neglect. Restoration work continues, and the re-establishment here of a Catholic seminary has brought some pride back to the town.

Though the main reason people come is to pay their respects at Terezín, Litoměřice is also of interest. The entire place is a virtual museum to **Octavio Broggio**, who was born here in 1668 and, along with his father Giulio, redesigned the town's many churches following the arrival of the Jesuits and the establishment of a Catholic bishopric in the mid-seventeenth century. The reason for this zealous re-Catholicization was Litoměřice's rather too eager conversion to the heretical beliefs of the Hussites and its disastrous allegiance to the Protestants in the Thirty Years' War.

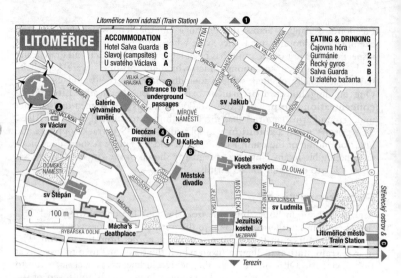

▼ Terezín

The Town

Stepping out of the train station, you're greeted by the last bastion of the old town walls across the road; behind it lies the historical quarter, entered via the wide boulevard of Dlouhá. The first church you come to is the hybrid structure of **Kostel všech svatých** (All Saints) at the top of the street, which started life as a Romanesque church and now boasts the only Gothic spires left on the skyline, a beautiful wedge-shaped affair reminiscent of Prague's right bank, plus three smaller spikier ones behind. Its present Baroque facade was designed by Broggio, but the oppressively low ceiling and dusty furnishings are disappointing, with the notable exception of the fifteenth-century panel painting by the Master of Litoměřice. More impressive is the light-infused interior of the nearby **Jezuitský kostel** (Jesuit Church), another work by Broggio, whose ceiling is adorned with colourful frescoes.

The town's vast cobbled marketplace, **Mírové náměstí**, once one of the most important in Bohemia, now boasts only a couple of buildings from before the Thirty Years' War. The best known is the **Mrázovský dům**, at no. 15 on the south side of the square, whose owner at the time, a devout Hussite, had a huge wooden *kalich* (chalice) – the symbol of all Hussites – plonked on the roof in 1537. Ask at the tourist office (in the same building) for a guided tour (April–Oct Mon–Sat 10am–5pm, Sun 10am–3.30pm). The other building that stands out is the arcaded fourteenth-century **radnice**, at the eastern end of the square, topped by a shapely Renaissance gable. It now serves as the town **museum** (Tues–Sun 10am–5pm; 25Kč), worth a quick spin if only for the coffered sixteenth-century ceiling of the council hall; there's still precious little mention in the exhibition of the 1945 expulsions. On hot summer days you can cool off in the **underground tunnels and cellars** (*historické sklepy*; May–Sept 11am–3pm; the entrance is in the restaurant *Radniční sklípek*, Mirové náměstí 21; 40Kč) that stretch beneath the square and surrounding buildings. In medieval times the three-storey tunnels and cellars were used for storage and as a refuge during sieges; the guided tour lasts twenty minutes.

The art galleries

In the western corner of the square is the town's excellent **Diecézní muzeum** (Tues–Sun: April–Sept 9am–noon & 1–6pm; Oct–March closes 5pm; 20Kč). As befits a rich ecclesiastical region, there are a lot of very fine religious paintings here, beginning with the serene *Madonna with Child in an Enclosed Garden*, an early oil painting from 1494. In the gruesome *Donor, Christ and Death*, Christ's flesh appears almost translucent, while Death appears as a skeleton tightly wrapped in skin. Among the museum's most valuable paintings is Lucas Cranach the Elder's *St Anthony the Hermit*, which depicts the saint being tempted heavenwards by a grisly collection of devilish animals. The most remarkable section of the gallery, however, is the timber-built building at the back of the museum, which contains a vast collection of "naive art": works from the last century by local amateur artists on a variety of themes from the religious to the political, from landscapes to portraits.

A few doors up nearby Michalská, the **Galerie výtvarného umění** (Gallery of Fine Art; Tues–Sun: April–Sept 9am–noon & 1–6pm; Oct–March closes 5pm; 32Kč) occupies a wonderfully rambling sixteenth-century building, whose inner courtyard is draped in ivy and echoes to the trickle of a modern fountain. Temporary exhibitions supplement the small permanent collection of late nineteenth- and early twentieth-century Czech canvases, including Impressionist work by Jan Preisler, Antonín Hudeček and Antonín Slavíček, plus a few pieces of Baroque art, and a bizarre Gothic statue of Mary Magdalene, depicted with her hair covering her entire body except her knees. There's more Gothic art on the ground floor, in particular the surviving panels of the early sixteenth-century winged altar by the Master of Litoměřice, whose paintings are peopled by folk with expressive, almost grotesque faces, their poses and gestures remarkably sophisticated for the period. Baroque dwarfs and other more modern sculptures pepper the gallery's terrace overlooking the ramparts.

Around sv Štěpán

On a promontory 500m southwest of the town centre, the **Dómský pahorek** (Cathedral Hill), where the bishop and his entourage once held residence, was originally entirely separate from the town, with its own fortifications. The small Orthodox chapel of **sv Václav** (St Wenceslas) on the northern slope is perhaps the younger Broggio's finest work, grand despite its cramped proportions and location, though suffering a little from a gaudy salmon-pink and silver-grey facelift. But the real reason to come out here is to wonder at the former cathedral of **sv Štěpán** (St Stephen), which looks out onto the quiet, grassy enclosure of Dómské náměstí. Redesigned by Giulio Broggio (among others) in the seventeenth century, sv Štěpán marked the start of the extensive rebuilding of Litoměřice. The cathedral's ceiling is disappointing, but the dark wood and the gloomy altar paintings from the school of Cranach the Elder add atmosphere. Outside, the freestanding Italianate campanile, designed by the Viennese architect Heinrich Ferstel in the 1880s, gives a peculiarly Tuscan touch.

A path along the north side of sv Štěpán leads down the cobbled lane of Máchova, where the Czech poet **Karel Hynek Mácha** died in 1836; there's a commemoration plaque at no. 3. In true Romantic style, Mácha died of consumption at the age of 26. His most famous poem, *Máj* (May), was hijacked by the Communists as their May Day anthem, but remains a popular love poem. He used to be buried in the local cemetery, but when the Nazis drew up the Sudetenland borders, Litoměřice lay inside the Greater German Reich, so the Czechs dug up the poet and reinterred him in the Vyšehrad cemetery in Prague (see p.117). Once you've reached the bottom of the cathedral hill, the stairway of the Máchovy schody will take you back up into town.

Practicalities

All **buses** terminate at the Litoměřice město **train station**, at the southeast corner of the old town, terminus for trains to Mělník and Ústí nad Labem; trains to Lovosice, Úštěk and Česká Lípa depart from Litoměřice horní nádraží, to the north of the old town. The **tourist office** (May–Sept Mon–Fri 8am–6pm, Sat 8am–5.30pm, Sun 9.30am–4pm; Oct–April Mon & Wed 8am–5pm, Tues & Thurs 8am–4.15pm, Fri 8am–4pm, Sat 8–11am; ☎416 732 440, ⓦwww.litomerice.cz), in the dům U Kalicha on Mírové náměstí, can arrange **private rooms**. You can access the **internet** in the regional library on the opposite side of the square.

If you want to treat yourself, stay at the friendly *Hotel Salva Guarda* (☎416 732 506, ⓦwww.salva-guarda.cz; ❸), in a lovely sgraffitoed building on Mírové náměstí and named after the house's sixteenth-century owner, who was an imperial bodyguard. Another excellent choice is ⚒ *U svatého Václava* (☎416 737 500, ⓦwww.upfront.cz/penzion; ❸), a pretty little pension with comfortable and sunny rooms across from sv Václav. There's also the *Slavoj* **campsite** (May–Sept; ☎416 734 481) with bungalows, near the open-air cinema (*letní kino*) on Střelecký ostrov, the woody island on the river, just south of the Litoměřice město train station.

The best **restaurant** in town is the *Salva Guarda,* which serves Czech and international dishes. *Gurmánie,* a sleek, cavernous place on the west side of the main square, offers cafeteria-style meals, sandwiches and snacks; *U zlatého bažanta*, a couple of doors west from the tourist office, combines a typical Czech restaurant, a shop selling old furniture, and a pleasant **café**. Just east of the square, *Řecký gyros* (closed Sat & Sun) serves Greek-style fast food, while to the north on Tylova across from the leafy Jiráskovy sady, the *Čajovna hóra* is a popular, relaxing spot for tea and coffee.

Ploskovice and Úštěk

An easy day-trip from Litoměřice, the village of **PLOSKOVICE**, 6km to the northeast off route 15, hides one of Octavio Broggio's few secular works, a summer **zámek** (April–Oct Tues–Sat 9am–5pm, Sun 10am–3pm; 70Kč; tour in English 150Kč; ⓦwww.zamek-ploskovice.cz). After his abdication in 1848, this became a favourite summer watering hole for the Habsburg emperor Ferdinand I, who commissioned the exuberant Rococo plasterwork – sometimes frivolous, sometimes tasteless, always fun. The beautiful walled grounds (daily dawn–dusk) are flourishing, their fountains frothing forth. The main **bus stop** is directly by the zámek; to reach it from the **train station**, follow the little stream north for 1km. Simple Czech food is served at the **restaurant** *U zámku,* opposite the bus stop.

Bypassed by the main road – and, it seems, by the entire last three centuries – **ÚŠTĚK** (Auscha) originally grew up around a now-ruined medieval fortress. On one side of the main square there's a line of fourteenth-century burgher houses, which, unusually for Bohemia, still retain their original triangular gables of wood or slate. The **Jezuitský kostel**, built after the devastating fire of 1765, occupies centre stage in the square, and features a trompe l'oeil main altar, a Karel Škréta altarpiece and several fine wooden sculptures. Some 200m from the church, down Kamenná, in among the geese and hens, there are some fascinating wooden shacks known as **ptačí domky** (birds' houses). Perched on top of each other on the highest ledge of the steeply terraced banks, they provided ad hoc accommodation for Jewish families who were forced to live in ghettos until at least 1848, and for the Italian workers who built the town's railway link in the late nineteenth century. The inconspicuous, apricot-coloured synagogue nearby has recently been renovated and is open to the public (☎606 460 912).

Practicalities

It's fifty minutes by train from Litoměřice and about another half-a-kilometres walk from the train station east to the old town. If you're **camping**, head for the *Chmelař* site (May–Sept) by the pleasant sandy shores of Chmelař lake (boat rental available in season), behind the train station, or try *Zátiší* (April–Oct), at 1 máje 4. You'll also find several modest **pensions**, and a couple of good **restaurants**: *Restaurace na růžku*, in a pink building off the main square, and *Restaurace pod podloubím*, behind the church on the square. In the nearby library there's a **tourist office** (9am–5pm: July & Aug daily; rest of the year Mon–Fri) with **internet** access.

Doksy, Máchovo jezero and Bezděz

From Ploskovice trains take about 90min (change in Česká Lípa) to reach **DOKSY** on the southernmost sandy shores of the **Máchovo jezero**. The lake, created in medieval times, has been a popular recreational spot since nineteenth-century Romantics such as Karel Hynek Mácha (after whom the lake is named) used to trek out here. Nowadays it's surrounded by hotels, bungalows and campsites: the lakeside *Klůček* **campsite** (May–Sept) is the nearest to Doksy train station. There's a mercifully small museum dedicated to Mácha in Doksy itself, though you're infinitely better off going on the poet's favourite walk: the eight-kilometre hike southeast along the red-marked Máchova cesta up to the ruined hilltop **hrad Bezděz** (Bösig; April & Oct Sat & Sun 9am–4pm; May–Sept Tues–Sun 9am–5pm; 50Kč), its outline clearly visible for miles around. It was one of the most important castles in Bohemia until its destruction in the Thirty Years' War, but there's not much to see now aside from a Gothic chapel and, of course, the unbeatable view from the top of the hill (604m) – still, at least you get to explore it without taking a guided tour. You can take the train another two stops to Bezděz to cut the walking distance down to just 2km.

Ústí nad Labem

Some 20kim north, on the other side of the beautiful České středohoří (Central Bohemian Hills), which part only to allow the River Labe to slither through, lies the vast metropolis of **ÚSTÍ NAD LABEM** (Aussig). From a small town, Aussig grew rapidly into the second largest port on the Labe (Elbe) after Hamburg, and the busiest in the Habsburg Empire. Solidly German-speaking and heavily industrialized, Aussig suffered terrible bomb damage during World War II. Worse was to follow. On July 30, 1945, Ústí's sugar refinery, being used to store ammunition confiscated from the Germans, was blown up, killing fourteen Czechs and triggering a riot. The attack was blamed on die-hard Nazis, and enraged Czechs stormed through the town, dragging off any German they could find, and lynching hundreds before throwing them into the Labe. The incident is thought to have been instrumental in persuading President Beneš to declare the three million ethnic Germans living in Czechoslovakia enemies of the state and call for their forceful expulsion from the country.

Ústí was resettled after the war and its industries further expanded; today, with a population of just under 100,000, it's the third largest city in Bohemia. Given its aesthetic limitations, and its almost unbearable historical baggage, most people give the place a wide berth. If, however, you find yourself here for whatever reason, you can while away an hour or so quite easily.

Trains usually stop at Ústí for only four or five minutes, which is long enough for most people – one whiff of the air and a glance at the discoloured river tells you that this is yet another chemical town. For those venturing into town, it's just a couple of blocks west from the main train station to Ústí's chief sights, the Dominican church of **sv Vojtěch**, given a Baroque facelift by Octavio Broggio in the 1730s, and the fourteenth-century cathedral of **Nanebevzetí Panny Marie**. Destroyed by the Hussites during their bloody occupation of the town in 1426, the cathedral was rebuilt in late-Gothic style, and has been nicely restored. The building's outrageously leaning steeple is the result of bomb damage in World War II.

The main square, **Mírové náměstí**, has had its entire northern side ripped out, and is now only really remarkable for the surviving Socialist Realist mosaic, depicting the inevitable road from the workers' revolution to world peace, which adorns the headquarters of the local council. West of the main square, overlooking the concrete paving stones of Lidické náměstí, is the final building worthy of mention: the town's theatre or **Městské divadlo**, built in 1909 in the style of the Viennese Secession.

On the opposite side of the Labe from the city centre is the suburb of **Střekov** (Schreckenstein), dominated by its ruined **hrad** (mid-March to Oct daily 9.30am–4.30pm; Nov & Dec Sat & Sun 9.30am–4.30pm; 60Kč; bus #1 from both the train and bus stations), a nightmare fairy-tale pile built into a bleak, black rocky outcrop high above the river. Like the Lorelei on the Rhine, it was much loved by the nineteenth-century Romantics, and provided inspiration for one of Wagner's operas (*Tannhäuser*). Set amid the tantalizing hills of the České středohoří, it's easy to see why – and to forget for a moment that this lovely landscape has been pockmarked with industrial zones. Now the ruins are back in the hands of the Lobkowicz family, you're free to explore, and revel in the incredible views up the hilly Labe valley and over to Ústí's grim smokestacks and awesome *paneláky*. The castle kitchen is now the *Wágnerka* **café** and **restaurant**, with a shady terrace from which you can watch the barges negotiating the lock below.

Practicalities

Ústí's **bus station** is just south of Lidické náměstí, a couple of blocks west of the main square. Travelling by fast train from Prague, Dresden or Berlin, you're most likely to arrive at Ústí's main **train station**, hlavní nádraží, at the southeast corner of the old town by the river (24hr left-luggage); trains from Litoměřice and Mělník pass through Střekov station, on the other side of the river, and terminate at Ústí nad Labem západ, which is another couple of blocks west of the bus station, down Revoluční.

The **tourist office** (Mon–Fri 8am–5pm, Sat 8am–noon; ☎475 220 233, ⓦ www.usti-nl.cz) is at Hradiště 9, between the train station and the main square. If you need to **stay the night**, you might as well enjoy the Communist-era luxury of the *Hotel Bohemia*, the high-rise monstrosity on the main square, Mírové náměstí (☎475 311 111, ⓦ www.ihbohemia.com; ❹). Less pricey is the *Hotel Palace* (☎475 220 953; ❶–❷), Malá Hradební 57, near the train station; rooms overlooking the noisy street are cheaper.

České Švýcarsko

The area of sandstone rocks around Děčín is popularly known as **České Švýcarsko** (Bohemian Switzerland), a nickname coined by artists of the Romantic movement, though the landscape is in fact far from alpine. The River Labe drives a deep wedge into the geographical defences of Bohemia, forging a grand valley through the dense forests, interrupted by outcrops of sandstone rock welded into truly fantastic shapes. While it has always been a popular spot for weekend recreation, it was only in 2000 that a small portion of České Švýcarsko (ⓦwww.ceskesvycarsko.cz) was officially designated a national park, the **Národní Park České Švýcarsko** (ⓦwww.npcs.cz), and while the park certainly contains some of the most precious natural treasures of the region, the entire area surrounding **Děčín** is greatly appealing.

Like the other *skalní města* rock "cities" in the Český ráj (see p.267) and the Broumov region (see p.284), the whole area was formed when volcanic rock thrust its way to the surface, causing fissures and cracks that later widened. The result is probably the most impressive geological amusement park in the country, a dense network of mini-canyons and bluffs all covered in a blanket of woodland – spectacular stuff, and a favourite with rock climbers, but also fairly easy **hiking** country.

Whichever part in the České Švýcarsko you're heading for, it's a good idea to get hold of a proper walking **map**; those available from local tourist offices and bookshops mark all campsites and footpaths in the area, including those on the German side. **Transport** throughout the region is not great – just infrequent rural bus services to most places – though the distances are small enough to make hiking an attractive proposition. In season, there's plenty of inexpensive **private accommodation**, making it possible for non-campers to spend more than just a day in the countryside.

Děčín

Despite being German-speaking for most of the last thousand years, **DĚČÍN** has long been the geographical gateway to Bohemia, its castle rising up to the east as you enter the country from Dresden. Modern Děčín is really two towns – **Děčín** (Tetschen) itself on the east bank and **Podmokly** (Bodenbach) on the west – amalgamated in 1942 but still divided by the River Labe, which has always been the driving force behind the town's economy. As a busy industrial port, its attractions are limited, but its position on the river is quite dramatic, and, lying at the heart of České Švýcarsko, it serves as a convenient base for exploring the region.

Podmokly

The main point of arrival is Děčín's grubby **hlavní nádraží** in **Podmokly**, which looks out onto a mass of grey concrete and an unsightly supermarket. It's not a great start, but then Podmokly was a late developer, only coming into existence in 1850 through the amalgamation of three villages on the left bank. Sixty years of furious building followed, funded by the town's flourishing shipping industry, the results of which are still visible in the four or five blocks west of the station.

With time to kill and an interest in stuffed birds, medieval Madonnas or navigation, you can spend a happy hour in the **Oblastní muzeum** (Tues–Sun 9am–noon & 1–5pm; 30Kč), in a former hunting lodge on třída České Mládeže. A more miraculous sight is the Moorish Art Nouveau **synagogue**, round the

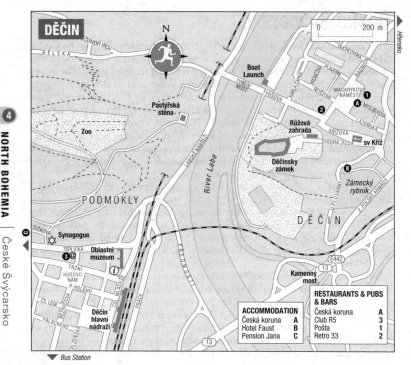

ACCOMMODATION

Česká koruna	A
Hotel Faust	B
Pension Jana	C

RESTAURANTS & PUBS & BARS

Česká koruna	A
Club R5	3
Pošta	1
Retro 33	2

▼ Bus Station

corner on Žižkova, dating from 1907, which was saved from being torched on *Kristallnacht* by a local German, and is one of the few to survive in what was Sudetenland. Nowadays, given a slightly injudicious lick of garish yellow and blue paint, it is used by the local Jewish community for exhibitions (Mon–Fri 8am–3pm) and services.

You could also head for the meringue-coloured mansion atop the precipitous **Pastýřská stěna** (Hirtenfelswände or Shepherd's Wall); follow signs for the zoo up the hill past the synagogue. At the top there's a small **café** and restaurant with an incredible view over Děčín, and, a little further back from the cliff, a small **zoo** (daily: May–Aug 8am–7pm; April & Sept 8am–6pm; Oct–March 8am–4pm; 80Kč), with grizzly bears, llamas, capybaras, lynxes and wolves.

Děčín

To cross the river to **Děčín** from Podmokly, follow the crowds onto the buses from outside the station (buy your ticket from a newsagent), or continue downstream from Podmolky's Oblastní muzeum until you reach the Tyršův most. Děčín itself is much older than Podmokly, as evidenced by the austerely impressive **Děčínský zámek** (Schloss Tetschen-Bodenbach) at its centre, elevated above the town and river on an isolated lump of rock. The chateau's mostly Baroque appearance dates from the time of the Thun-Hohensteins, but it has been much abused since the family sold it to the state in the 1930s. Used as a barracks by the Germans, Czechs and lastly Russians, there's not much left of the original interior; part of it has been given over to the **Oblastní museum** (Tues–Sun 9am–noon & 1–5pm), with the castle's arsenal and a selection of local Baroque art on display.

The chief attraction of the chateau, however, is the **Růžová zahrada** (daily: April & Sept–Oct 10am–6pm; May–Aug 10am–8pm; 12Kč), a truly wonderful Baroque rose garden, laid out on a terrace cut into the north face of the rock high above the town. At one end is a befrescoed *sala terrena*, while at the far end is an ornate Baroque belvedere peppered with statuary. To gain access to the garden (and the chateau), you must walk up the sloping **Dlouhá jízda**, a gloomy three-hundred-metre-long drive cut into the rock. Directly below the garden are the distinctive black dome and twin tower lanterns of the salmon-pink Baroque church of **sv Kříž**, which has a richly painted and furnished interior. Two other sights worth noting are the striking 1906 Art Nouveau **fountain** on Děčín's main square, Masarykovo náměstí, and to the south of the castle, the slowly disintegrating stone bridge or **Kamenný most**, over the River Ploučnice, punctuated by Brokoff's Baroque statuary.

Practicalities

Most **trains** end up at Děčín hlavní nádraží in Podmokly, which has a left-luggage office; all international trains to and from Germany stop here. The **bus** station is a few blocks south. The town's main **tourist office** (Mon–Fri 9am–5pm, Sat 9am–noon; ☏412 531 333, ⓦ www.mmdecin.cz) is around the corner from Podmokly's Oblastní muzeum on an alleyway off Tržní; there's also a small tourist office in the zámek (☏412 518 905, ⓦ www.zamekdecin.cz). Both can provide information on **river cruises** on the Labe to Hřensko and further afield. To go **online**, head for *Club R5*, Thomayerova 25/3, in Podmokly.

For **accommodation**, walk over or catch any bus to Děčín proper, where your best bets are the comfortable *Česká koruna* (☏412 516 104, ⓦ www .hotelceskakoruna.cz; ❸), on Masarykovo náměstí, or *Hotel Faust*, U plovárny 43 (☏412 518 859, ⓦ www.hotelfaust.cz; ❸), just south of the zámek. If you have your own transport, consider the pleasant *Pension Jana* (☏412 544 571, ⓦ www .penzionjana.cz; ❸), a couple of kilometres out of town on route 13 to Teplice. The **restaurant** at the *Česká koruna* features fish from Třeboň, while the nearby smoky *Pošta* is good for a beer, with a view onto the square. Cheap Czech food and beer is served at the affable *Retro 33* one block south of the main square on Tyršova.

Exploring České Švýcarsko

The popular **Jetřichovické stěny**, mostly within national park boundaries to the northeast of Děčín, is topographically more interesting and covers a much greater area than its western counterparts. At its base runs the Kamenice River, accessible in parts only by boat (for boat trips, see p.257). The smaller, less spectacular range to the west, the **Děčínské stěny**, doesn't suffer the same human congestion and can easily be reached on a day's hike from Děčín itself.

Děčínské stěny

If your sole aim is to see the sandstone rocks, it's simplest to catch one of the few buses a day from Děčín to Tisá, or to take the train to Libouchec station and walk the 2.5km north (and up) to Tisá. If, however, you're intent on a day's walking, follow the red-marked path from the Tyršův most in Děčín for 10km to **Děčínský Sněžník** (723m), a giant table mountain thrust up above the decaying tree line, on top of which stands a handsome sandstone look-out tower (*rozhledna*; April–Oct Mon–Fri 10am–5pm, Sat & Sun 9am–5pm; Nov–March when the weather allows), erected in 1864 by Count Thun-Hohenstein. The red-marked path eschews the direct route to Tisá and instead heads north to Ostrov, the last village before the border, where there's the luxury *Hotel Ostrov* (☏475 222 428,

@www.hotelostrov.com; ❹), and a simple **campsite** with bungalows (April to mid-Nov) by a pretty lake, overlooked by the cliffs of the Ostrovské skály. The nearest border crossing (24hr) is at Petrovice, northwest of Tisá.

From the village of **TISÁ** itself, the **Tiské stěny** appear like a gloomy black wall – climb the hill and the whole sandstone "city" opens up before you. Sandy trails crisscross this secret gully, and it's fairly simple to get to the top of one or two of the gigantic boulders without any specialist equipment (the best viewpoint is to the left of the ticket office). You could spend hours here, exploring, picnicking and taking in the panoramic views. Via **Děčínský Sněžník**, it's a full day's walk from Děčín, but there's plenty of private **accommodation** in the village, including the nice pension *Zlatá koruna* (☏475 222 526, @www.zlata-koruna.com; ❷), en route to the ticket office; as well as the *Pod Císařem* **campsite** 2km northeast of Tisá in Ostrov (mid-March to Dec; ☏475 222 013, @www.podcisarem.cz), with an on-site pub-restaurant.

Hřensko

Despite its dramatic mountainous setting, **HŘENSKO** (Herrnskretchen), at 116m above sea level, is in fact the lowest point in Bohemia. It was once a pretty village on the right bank of the Labe, dotted with half-timbered houses and redolent of Saxony on the opposite bank. However, Hřensko currently makes its living out of the German day-trippers flocking to the nearby rocks, and with their former East German neighbours now flush with euros, business is booming. Nightclubs line the road coming into Hřensko, and the village itself is barely visible under the sheer number of shops and garden-gnome stalls, the majority run by the republic's Vietnamese minority. It's unlikely you'll want to **stay** here, though there are several hotels to choose from; try the decent, four-storey *Hotel Labe* (☏412 554 088, @www.hotel.labe.cz; ❷), by the river front, which has pastel-coloured rooms with TV, or the luxury *Hotel Praha* (☏412 554 006, @www.hotel-hrensko.cz; ❺), with comfortable rooms and sauna, in the stylish edifice at the eastern end of the village. Both have **restaurants**.

Jetřichovické stěny

The only way to get to the **Jetřichovické stěny** and the Kamenice gorge is by **bus**, with three or four a day making the roundabout journey to Jetřichovice, via Hřensko, Tři prameny, Mezní Louka and Mezná; if you're driving, note that there is no parking between Hřensko and Mezní Louka, but there are additional daily buses between the two.

By far the most popular destination is the **Pravčická brána** (@www.pbrana .cz), at 30m long and 21m high the largest natural stone bridge in Europe. It's a truly breathtaking sight, though not one you're likely to enjoy alone unless you get there very early or out of season. Hop off the bus at Tři prameny, a clearing 3km up the road from Hřensko, and walk the remaining 2km along the trail marked in red. To get close to the bridge (as opposed to walking across it, which is forbidden), you'll have to pay an admission fee. The German border is less than 1km away, but the red-marked path that appears to head towards it actually rejoins the road 4.5km further east at **MEZNÍ LOUKA**, where you can take your pick from the **hotel** (☏412 511 603, @www.mezni-louka.cz; ❸) of the same name, or the **campsite** opposite, with bungalows (April–Oct; ☏412 554 084).

From Mezní Louka, the red-marked path continues another 14km to Jetřichovice, meandering through the southern part of the complex of mini-canyons, taking in the **Malá Pravčická brána**, a smaller version of the bridge, and a couple of ruinous border castles. **JETŘICHOVICE** is a lovely old Saxon hamlet made up of huge wooden farmsteads typical of the region. Several serve as pensions: ⚞ *Dřevák* (☎412 555 015, Ⓦwww.drevak.eu; ❸), an idyllic woodframe home with an impeccable restaurant in the centre of the village, is one of the best places to stay in the entire region. There is also a **campsite**, *U Ferdinanda*, 1.5km south, across a ford, with bungalows and a swimming pool (May–Sept).

The Kamenice gorge

Another option from Mezní Louka is to walk the 2km southwest to **MEZNÁ**, an unassuming little village that basks in a sunny meadow above the River Kamenice. Several basic pensions offer affordable rooms: *Pension Na vyhlídce* (☎412 554 065, Ⓦwww.penzionnavyhlidce.eu; ❷) has its own **restaurant**, as does *Pension Čedos* (☎412 554 064, Ⓦwww.cedos.tym.cz; ❶–❷), which offers cheap, simple (and clean) rooms without en-suite facilities. The latter enjoys a better location, with a summer terrace providing great views of the surrounding wooded hills.

From the village green, a green-marked path plunges 30m into the cool, dank shade of the river, traversed by the wooden bridge Mezní můstek. Here you have a choice of heading up or down the **Kamenice gorge** to landing stages, where boatmen punt you along a short but dramatic **boat trip** down (or up) the river. The trips are justifiably popular, but boats run every ten- to twenty-minutes, so you shouldn't have to wait long. The downstream trip, along the **Tichá soutěska** (quiet gorge; Easter to Nov daily 9am–6pm), drops you at the edge of Hřensko (see opposite) – you can alternatively pick it up via the yellow-marked path in Hřensko; this is perhaps the more dramatic of the two, and certainly the longer. The upstream boat unloads its passengers just 500m further up the **Divoká soutěska** (Easter to Nov daily 9am–5pm). With the latter trip, you can return to Mezní Louka via the blue-marked path, or continue along first the blue- then the yellow-marked path up a shallower gorge to Jetřichovice, about 5km east.

Česká Kamenice and Benešov nad Ploučnicí

With your own transport, **ČESKÁ KAMENICE** (Böhmisch Kamnitz), 18km east of Děčín on route 13, makes a great alternative base for exploring České Švýcarsko. For a start, it's a lot more pleasant to rest up in than Děčín, with its interesting blend of nineteenth-century Habsburg edifices, the odd wooden folk building and a splendid Baroque pilgrimage chapel. The best **hotel** of a rather limited selection is the clean, nicely furnished *Slávie* (☎412 582 538; ❷), náměstí Míru 208. The **tourist office** (May–Sept Mon–Fri 9am–5pm, Sat 9am–1pm; Oct–April Mon–Fri 9am–4pm, Sat 9–11am; ☎412 582 600, Ⓦwww.ceskakamenice.cz) is on the main square, náměstí Míru, where you'll also find plenty of **restaurants and pubs**.

Five kilometres east of Česká Kamenice, on the other side of Kamenický Šenov, is another, much rarer geological phenomenon: the **Panská skála** (Herrnhausfelsen), a series of polygonal basalt columns that look like a miniature Giant's Causeway minus the sea. The result of a massive subterranean explosion millions of years ago – during which molten basalt was spewed out onto the surface and cooled into what are, essentially, crystals – they make a strange, supernatural sight in this unassuming countryside, but are too small to be really awe-inspiring. Unlike Northern Ireland's tourist attraction, the Panská skála are easily missed, even though they're only 500m south of route 13; look for the village of Prachen and ask the bus driver to tell you when to get out.

Halfway between Děčín and Česká Kamenice, and easily reached from either by train, is **BENEŠOV NAD PLOUČNICÍ**, a pretty little town characterized by its two connected **zámky** (April & Oct Wed–Sun 9am–4pm; May–Sept Tues–Sun 9am–6pm; 120Kč). The lower one is a neo-Gothic hunting lodge with meticulously restored interiors; the upper boasts Renaissance ceilings and an offbeat collection of Japanese and Chinese art. There is ample **accommodation**, though scout around before resorting to the rather dour *Jelen* (℡412 586 223; ❶), on the attractive main square; a safer bet, particularly for a longer stay, is one of the two basic self-service apartments at no. 6 on the square (℡412 586 262; ❷) – look for the "Apartma" sign. The nearest **campsite**, *Slunce* (mid-May to mid-Sept; ℡722 785 684, Ⓦwww.akslunce.wz.cz), is in the village of Žandov, 10km southeast of Benešov, on the road to Česká Lípa (and 2km north of the train station Police-Žandov on the Benešov–Česká Lípa railway line).

Liberec and around

Lying comfortably in the broad east–west sweep of the Nisa Valley, framed by the Jizera Mountains to the north and the isolated peak of Ještěd to the south, **LIBEREC** (Reichenberg) couldn't hope for a grander location. The city itself, made prosperous and enormous by its famous textile industry, can't quite live up to its setting, but it's lively and bustling, with a smattering of interesting buildings and a couple of fairly good museums, all of which could keep you happily amused for the best part of a day.

Arrival, information and accommodation

The **train station** has a left-luggage office (4am–11.30pm) and lockers. From here (and the adjacent bus station), walk, or jump on tram #2 heading down 1 máje, to Soukenné náměstí, which is overlooked on one side by the city's eyesore Tesco superstore, and on the other by one of the functionalist Baťa shops designed by Vladimír Karfík in the 1930s. From here, it's a short steep walk up Pražská to the main square, **Benešovo náměstí**, where – in the town hall – you'll find the efficient **tourist office** (June–Sept Mon–Fri 8.30am–6pm, Sat & Sun 9am–noon; Oct–May Mon–Fri 8.30am–6pm & Sat 9am–noon; ℡485 101 709, Ⓦwww.infolbc.cz), which can arrange very reasonable private **accommodation**. Liberec's hotels tend to be pricey, relying as they do on German tourists and business travellers. The nearest **campsite**, well equipped and with a pool, is the *Stadión Pavlovice*, Letná (May–Sept; ℡485 123 468, Ⓦwww.autocamp-liberec.cz), in the midst of a housing estate (bus #12 from the town hall, or #24 & #26 from behind the Divadlo F.X. Šaldy). The Krajská vědecká knihovna (State Research Library) has **internet** access (Mon, Wed & Thurs 10am–7pm, Fri 10am–8pm, Sat 10am–2pm).

Hotels and pensions

Grandhotel Zlatý lev Gutenbergova 3 ℡485 256 700, Ⓦwww.zlatylev.cz. Vast, turn-of-the-twentieth-century building with luxurious rooms and all amenities, conveniently located behind the chateau. ❺

Ještěd Horní Hanychov ℡485 104 291, Ⓦwww.hotel.jested.cz. Unbeatable location, view and kitsch 1960s decor in the TV tower on top of the mountain of the same name. ❸

Hotel Praha Železná 2 ℡485 102 655, Ⓦwww.hotelpraha.net. Very comfortable hotel on the edge of the main square, which has preserved its original Art Nouveau entrance foyer, and a few other period fittings. ❹

Hotel Radnice Moskevská 11 ℡602 222 365, Ⓦwww.hotelradnice.cz. Well-appointed four-star, on the edge of the main square, with spacious, if dull, rooms. ❺

Pension U muzea Vítězná 24 ℡485 102 693, Ⓦwww.penzionumuzea.cz. Large nineteenth-century villa in the leafy district near the Severočeské museum. ❷

Unihotel Voroněžská 1329/13 ℡485 352 211, wunihotel.vslib.cz. A real cheapie, just north of the main square, in a high-rise university complex. ❷

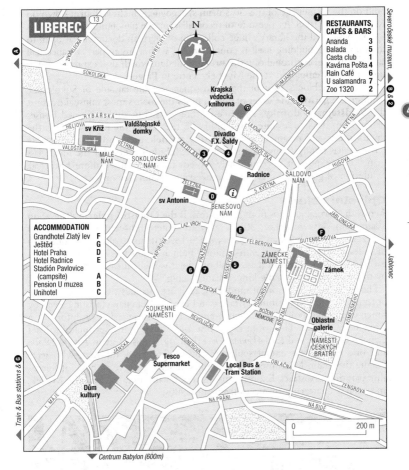

LIBEREC 13

N

Severočeské muzeum

RESTAURANTS, CAFÉS & BARS

Ananda	3
Balada	5
Casta club	1
Kavárna Pošta	4
Rain Café	6
U salamandra	7
Zoo 1320	2

DVOŘECKÁ

RUPRECHTICKÁ

SOKOLSKÁ

RUMJANCEVOVA

VORONĚŽSKÁ

Krajská vědecká knihovna

@

RYBÁŘSKÁ

HELJOVA

sv Kříž

Valdštejnské domky

VALDŠTEJNSKÁ

MALÉ NÁM.

VĚTRNÁ

SOKOLOVSKÉ NÁM.

FRÝDLANTSKÁ

ŽELEZNÁ

Divadlo F.X. Šaldy

SOKOLSKÁ

JULIOVÁ

5. KVĚTNA

HUSOVA

Radnice

ŠALDOVO NÁM.

5. KVĚTNA

JABLONECKÁ

sv Antonín

BENEŠOVO NÁM.

LAZ. VRCH

PAPÍROVÁ

PRAŽSKÁ

FELBEROVA

MOSKEVSKÁ

GUTENBERGOVA

ZÁMECKÉ NÁMĚSTÍ

Zámek

6 7 5

JEZDECKÁ

ZÁMEČNICKÁ

RUMUNSKÁ

BOŽENY NĚMCOVE

BŘEZINA

Oblastní galerie

NÁMĚSTÍ ČESKÝCH BRATŘÍ

KOMENSKÉHO

SOUKENNÉ NÁMĚSTÍ

REVOLUČNÍ

FUGNEROVA

JÁNSKÁ

Tesco Supermarket

Local Bus & Tram Station

OBLAČNÁ

ZENGROVA

1. MÁJE

Dům kultury

NA PRÁNI

NA BIDĚ

0   200 m

ACCOMMODATION

Grandhotel Zlatý lev	F
Ještěd	G
Hotel Praha	D
Hotel Radnice	E
Stadión Pavlovice (campsite)	A
Pension U muzea	B
Unihotel	C

◀ *Train & Bus stations & G*

▲ *Jablonec*

▲ *B & 2*

▼ *Centrum Babylon (600m)*

The City

Dominating the attractive main square of **Benešovo náměstí**, Liberec's magnificent, cathedral-like **radnice** (guided tours April & May Sat 10am–noon; June–Sept Mon–Fri 9am–4pm, Sat 10am–noon) is probably the most telling monument the chauvinistic Reichenberger could have bestowed on the city. Purposely designed to recall Vienna's own Rathaus, its lofty trio of neo-Renaissance copper cupolas completes the effect with an impressive Flemish flourish. Liberec has the distinction of being one of the few places outside Prague where there was any real fighting following the Warsaw Pact invasion of 1968; a small memorial to the right of the town hall steps commemorates those who died.

Behind the radnice is the city's theatre, **Divadlo F.X. Šaldy** (Ⓦwww .saldovo-divadlo.cz), a typically solid, showy affair designed by the Viennese architects Helmer and Fellner in the 1880s. While you're admiring the theatre, you can also check the atmospheric pressure on the nineteenth-century weather machine opposite the main facade. On Rumjancevova, behind the theatre, the **Krajská vědecká knihovna** (State Research Library; Ⓦwww.kvkli.cz) was built on the former site of the city's main synagogue, which was burnt down on *Kristallnacht* in 1938. As a gesture of reconciliation, the new building also houses a synagogue, and the library's huge collection of German documents is open to the public. The building itself is contemporary, with a large open entrance hall and plenty of glass throughout; the structure design, which uses exposed steel, is similar to that employed at the Myslbek centre in Prague.

A couple of blocks west of the main square, on the far side of Sokolovské náměstí, the narrow side street of Větrná hides the town's most unusual treasure, the **Valdštejnské domky**, a terrace of three crisscross timber-framed houses dating from the late seventeenth century. To the east of the main square is the town's rouge-and-cream sixteenth-century **zámek**, previously owned by the Clam-Gallas family. Converted into a vast exhibition centre for the local glass giants, Glassexport, it is temporarily closed. There's another, more historical, exhibition of glassmaking at the Severočeské muzeum (see opposite).

Oblastní galerie

Across the formal gardens from the chateau is the **Oblastní galerie** (Tues–Sun 10am–6pm; Ⓦ www.ogl.cz; 30Kč), a white nineteenth-century building off 8. března that has been an art gallery since 1873. Its unusually large collection includes a series of nineteenth-century French landscapes and some much earlier Dutch and Flemish masters, all of which were bequeathed to the gallery by the local German textile king, Johann Liebig.

The excellent collection of modern Czech art includes two striking female portraits by the Impressionists Jiránek and Hudeček, a characteristic canvas by super-weird Symbolist Josef Váchal, and a lovely swaggering sculpture of a woman by Šaloun. The room of Cubist and Fauvist canvases includes Josef Čapek's much reproduced *Woman Over the City*, Kubišta's grim *Kiss of Death*, and one of the few extant sculptures by Otakar Švec, the man who gave Prague the Stalin Monument. In the postwar section there's a bevy of Surrealist paintings, Abstract Expressionist works by the likes of Mikuláš Medek, and even a smattering of pieces from the 1980s.

▲ Benešovo náměstí, Liberec

Konrad Henlein in Reichenberg

Sited just the wrong side of the historical borders of Germany, the Reichenbergers made up for this geographical oversight with their ardent pan-Germanism. Appropriately enough, it was the home town of **Konrad Henlein**, born in the nearby village of Reichenau (Rychnov) in 1898 and destined to become the leader of the Sudeten German Party (SdP). Henlein played an unheroic role in World War I, and after a spell as a bank clerk in Reichenau he became a gym teacher in the German-speaking town of Asch (Aš) in West Bohemia. The combined effects of the slump and the events in neighbouring Nazi Germany and fascist Austria excited the Sudeten Germans, who proclaimed Henlein their Führer at a huge rally outside Saaz (Žatec) in 1933. Under Henlein, the SdP began to demand autonomy and self-determination for the German-speaking border districts of Bohemia and Moravia, and in the 1935 elections they won roughly two-thirds of the Sudeten German vote (thus becoming the largest single party in the country).

Yet despite his nationalist credentials, and the fact that the Nazis subsidized the SdP, Henlein was disliked in Nazi circles, due to his links with the **Kamaradschaftbund**, a secretive organization inspired by Austrian clerical fascism rather than German National Socialism. The Nazis preferred the leader of the SdP's radical wing, **Karl Hermann Frank**, a one-eyed bookseller from Karlsbad, who wanted Sudetenland to be ceded to Germany. During the course of 1938, impressed by the Nazi takeover in Austria, Henlein foolishly agreed to push for the secession of Sudetenland. When the Nazis took over Sudetenland later that year, Henlein's closest associates, particularly those in the Kamaradschaftbund, were arrested and sent off to the camps. Henlein himself was too prominent a public figure to be interned; instead, he was appointed Gauleiter of Sudetenland, a position of little power, while Frank was eventually elevated to State Secretary, the second most powerful man in the Nazi Protectorate. In 1945 Henlein committed suicide after being captured by the Americans, while Frank was tried and hanged for war crimes in Prague in 1946.

Severočeské muzeum and around

Liberec's grandest museum is the **Severočeské muzeum** (Tues–Sun 9am–5pm; 40Kč), a wonderful period piece from the 1890s built in a theatrical neo-Renaissance style. The museum lies a couple of tram stops (tram #2) up 5. května, which turns into Masarykova, a long, leafy avenue flanked by decadent turn-of-the-twentieth-century mansions, once the property of a wealthy Reichenberger, now converted into pensions, flats, clinics and the like. Inside the museum, the old Communist-era displays on local and natural history are eminently skippable, but the glassware, jewellery and bronzework upstairs make a visit worthwhile. In addition to the locally produced stuff, there's an Art Nouveau lamp and vase by Lötz and another by Gallé, plus a Cubist tea set by Janák, some Wiener Werkstätte silverwork and some wacky shaggy tapestries from the 1970s.

At the top of the road is the city's chief park, and the popular **Botanická zahrada** (Botanical Gardens; daily: April–Oct 8am–6pm; Nov–March until 4pm; 80Kč), famous for their orchids. Here, too, you'll find the oldest **zoo** (zoologická zahrada; daily: April–Oct 8am–6pm; Nov–March until 5pm; 90Kč) in Bohemia, which boasts Europe's largest collection of birds of prey and two white tigers, as well as the usual array of elephants, pumas, chimpanzees and the like.

Ještěd and Centrum Babylon

Liberec's top hotel – in every sense – sits on the summit of **Ještěd** (1012m) or Jeschken, from where you can look over into Poland and Germany on a clear day. Even if you don't stay the night (see p.258), be sure to check out the bar-cum-diner and the restaurant with its crazy mirrors, neither of which would look out of place in a 1960s sci-fi series. To get there from the centre of town, take tram #2 to the end of the line (Dolní Hanychov), then bus #33 to the **cable car** (*lanovka*), which runs to the summit and hotel at least hourly (Mon 8am & 2–7pm, Tues–Sun 8am–7pm, out of season till 6pm; 80Kč return).

Liberec also boasts the largest covered **amusement park** in the country, the Centrum Babylon (℡485 251 311, ⓦwww.centrumbabylon.cz; 290Kč for a day pass), with a set of swimming pools (daily 10am–10pm), a funfair (daily 10am–8pm) and a casino. It's at Nitranská 1, a ten-minute walk southeast of the train station.

Eating and drinking

Liberec is home to perhaps the finest café in the country outside Prague – the *Kavárna Pošta*.

Ananda Frýdlantská 210/12. Laid-back vegetarian restaurant just northwest of the main square, with a good selection of hot and cold dishes as well as a buffet.

Balada Moskevská 13. A cosy place with good pasta and Svijany beer.

Casta club Tržní nám. 11. Late-night drinking spot that has live bands most nights.

🏃 **Kavárna Pošta** naměstí Dr. Beneše 24, on the corner of Mariánská. Across from the theatre, and decorated in white and gold Neoclassical style, with dazzling chandeliers, the *Pošta*

conjures up late nineteenth-century Reichenberg beautifully – and its cakes are suitably sumptuous.

Rain Café Pražská 28. Popular modern restaurant and cafe with vivid decor and straightforward Czech meals.

U salamandra Pražská 13. Halfway down Pražská, this big, modern pub doles out heaps of Czech food and mugs of Gambrinus. Closed Sun.

Zoo 1320 Masarykova 1320. Slightly upscale restaurant with a summer terrace opposite the Severočeské museum. Serves a variety of filling dishes, including fish, pasta, pizza and steaks.

Jablonec nad Nisou

JABLONEC NAD NISOU (Gablonz) starts where the southwestern suburbs of Liberec end. It began life as a small Czech village, but was cut short in its prime by the Hussite Wars, when the whole area was laid waste by the neighbouring Catholic Lusatians. From the sixteenth century onwards, it was better known as Gablonz, the name used by the Saxon glassmakers who began to settle in the area, but it wasn't until the late nineteenth century that the town's **jewellery trade** took off. By the early 1900s Gablonz was exporting its produce to all corners of the globe, and its burghers grew very rich indeed, erecting private mansions fit for millionaires and lavish public buildings. Everything changed in 1945, when almost the entire German-speaking population of 100,000 was expelled, throwing the local glass industry into crisis (the Communists solved the problem by using forced labour in the factories). Meanwhile, uniquely for German refugees from eastern Europe, nearly a fifth of the exiled townsfolk stayed together and resettled in a suburb of Kaufbeuren, in Bavarian Swabia, which they named Neugablonz after their Bohemian home town.

The main reason for venturing into Jablonec is to visit the engaging **Muzeum skla a bižuterie** (Glass and Jewellery Museum; Tues–Sun 9am–5pm, Wed 9am–6pm; ⓦwww.msb-jablonec.cz), downhill from the town hall, in the palatial Zimmer & Schmidt building on U muzea, east off Dolní náměstí. The museum boasts a three-metre-high tower of bangles set against a backdrop of hundreds of earrings, and – on the stairs – the longest necklace in the world, 220m long and made in just four hours by local art students (it shows). Among the best items are the Lötz and Moser glass, the works by Adolf Loos, the Secession and Art Deco hatpins and the incredible collection of early twentieth-century jet jewellery.

A second branch of the museum in the **Galerie Belveder** (Tues–Sun 9am–noon & 12.30–5pm), at Mlýnská 27, a ten-minute walk along Smetanova and Nad Mlýnem from behind the Nová radnice, boasts an eclectic array of objects, including coins, medals, hairslides and cuff links from various historical periods.

The rest of the town centre has a number of dour, though impressive, 1930s structures, most notably the **Nová radnice**, whose slimline clock tower dominates the skyline. Up the hill from the town hall, the gargantuan brick-built church, **Nejsvětější Srdce Páně** (Most Sacred Heart of Our Lord), towers over Horní náměstí; local boy Josef Zasche was the architect responsible. The former wealth of the town is obvious from the leafy suburbs, though many of the buildings have been neglected. One that has been beautifully restored is the town theatre or **Městské divadlo**, designed by the ubiquitous Helmer and Fellner in 1907 and located west down Generála Mrázka; another is the graceful **Starokatolický kostel** (open for services only), a minimalist Art Nouveau church designed by Josef Zasche in 1900, 500m or so east of the centre, just off route 4 to Tanvald.

Practicalities

You can reach Jablonec on **tram** #16 from Liberec, which winds its way scenically and slowly up the Nisa Valley and deposits you close to the main **train station** to the southwest of the town centre. The choice of accommodation is limited, though the **tourist office** (Mon–Fri 8am–5pm, Sat 8am–noon; ☎485 357 335, ⓦ www.mestojablonec.cz), on the main square, should be able to help. The best **hotel** is the fairly brutally modernized late nineteenth-century *Rehavital* on Jugoslavská (☎483 317 591, ⓦ www.rehavital.cz; ❹), which has a sauna, a gym and an excellent restaurant; alternatively, there's the looming, high-rise *Hotel Merkur* (☎483 312 741, ⓦ www.hotelmerkur.cz; ❸), on Anenské náměstí, at the southwestern corner of the centre, which offers simply furnished rooms and its own restaurant and bar.

Cheap Czech **food** is available at the timber-decorated bistro *Adam + Eva* (closed Sun), on Mírové náměstí. For decent pizzas, head for *Pizzeria Franco*, just down from the radnice at Lidická 15; close by at no. 1 is *Balada*, a funky place (with a twin in Liberec) that has a stab at some unusual dishes.

Jizerské hory

Northeast of Liberec, the **Jizerské hory** (Isergebirge) form the western edge of the Krkonoše mountain range, which, in turn, makes up the northern border of Bohemia. Like their eastern neighbours, they have been very badly affected by acid rain, though extensive replanting has softened the impact visually. In fact, on first sight the mountains are undeniably dramatic, rising suddenly from Liberec's northern suburbs to heights of over 1000m. Large numbers of Czech and German tourists flock here in summer and winter – you can follow suit by taking tram #3 from Liberec, or bus #1 from Jablonec to Janov or Bedřichov.

Frýdlant

It was neither an old stronghold nor a new mansion, but a rambling pile consisting of innumerable small buildings closely packed together and of one or two storeys; if K had not known that it was a castle he might have taken it for a little town.

Franz Kafka, *The Castle*

No one is quite sure which castle Kafka had in mind when he wrote his novel, but a strong candidate is surely the hybrid sprawling castle at **FRÝDLANT** (Friedland), a town on the north side of the frontier mountains, forty minutes by train from Liberec. Like his fictional character K, Kafka himself came here on business, though not as a land surveyor but as an accident insurance clerk, a job he did for most of his brief life. In Kafka's time the **hrad** and **zámek** (Tues–Sun: April & Oct 9am–3.30pm; May, June & Sept 9am–4pm; July & Aug 9am–4.30pm; 190Kč for both) were still owned by the Clam-Gallas clan, but its most famous proprietor was Albrecht von Waldstein, Duke of Friedland, whose statue stands within the castle precincts. Such was the fame of Waldstein that the Clam-Gallas family opened the castle to the public as early as 1801. The guided tour (up to 2hr) might be a bit much for some people, but the interior is, for once, richly furnished with period pieces and in good condition, having been a museum now for two hundred years. The complex is on a wooded basalt hill over the river, a short walk southeast of the train station and town centre.

If you want to stay, try the large, friendly *Frýdlant* **campsite** (May–Sept) by a bend in the river beyond the castle, or the campsite (May–Sept) in **HEJNICE**, 10km southeast (30min by train; change at Raspenava), a village dominated by its towering **pilgrimage church**, with an attractive frescoed interior. Hejnice also has **hotels** and pensions; try the *Lázně Libverda* (T482 368 111, Wwww .lazne-libverda.cz; ❷), a small spa complex. You can cross the border into **Poland** just 13km north of Frýdlant at Habartice-Zawidów, on the road to Zgorzelec/Görlitz.

Travel details

Trains

Connections with Prague – Hlavní nádraží: Bohušovice (1 daily; 1hr); Chomutov (4 daily; 2hr 25min–2hr 45min); Děčín (4–5 daily; 1hr 35min–1hr 50min); Kadaň (2 daily; 3hr); Louny (1 daily; 1hr 50min); Most (3 daily; 2hr 30min); Ústí nad Labem (6 daily; 1hr 15min–1hr 25min); Žatec (1 daily; 2hr).
Connections with Prague – Holešovice: Děčín (2–3 daily; 1hr 20min); Ústí nad Labem (3–4 daily; 1hr 5min–1hr 15min).
Connections with Prague – Masarykovo nádraží: Bohušovice (up to 1 daily; 1hr); Chomutov (5 daily; 2hr 20min–2hr 50min); Děčín (3–4 daily; 1hr 40min); Kadaň (1 daily; 2hr 50min); Louny (1 daily; 1hr 50min); Most (3 daily; 2hr 30min); Ústí nad Labem (5–6 daily; 1hr 20min); Žatec (2 daily; 2hr).
Česká Lípa to: Benešov nad Ploučnicí (14–17 daily; 20–30min); Děčín (14 daily; 35–55min); Liberec (14–15 daily; 1hr 10min–1hr 30min); Litoměřice (8–9 daily; 1hr 10min); Mimoň (14–16 daily; 20–30min).
Chomutov to: Kadaň (hourly; 10–15min); Karlovy Vary (17–19 daily; 1hr 20min); Klášterec nad Ohří (16–20 daily; 20min); Most (29–31 daily; 20–25min); Plzeň (3 daily; 2hr 25min); Ústí nad Labem (hourly; 1hr 10min–1hr 25min); Žatec (10–14 daily; 20–30min).

Děčín to: Benešov nad Ploučnicí (every 1–2hr; 15–20min); Česká Kamenice (9–11 daily; 35–50min); Liberec (6 daily; 2hr–2hr 50min); Ústí nad Labem (every 1–2hr; 20–30min).
Liberec to: Frýdlant (11–14 daily; 35–40min); Jablonec nad Nisou (every 1–2hr; 25–30min); Turnov (13–18 daily; 40–55min).
Litoměřice to: Mělník (18–19 daily; 30–40min); Ploskovice (every 2–3hr; 12min); Úštěk (8–9 daily; 30min); Ústí nad Labem (15–22 daily; 25–30min).
Louny to: Libochovice (6–9 daily; 35–45min); Most (12–16 daily; 30–45min); Žatec (6–7 daily; 35min).
Most to: Děčín (3 daily; 1hr 10min); Duchcov (every 30min–1hr; 15–25min); Ústí nad Labem (hourly; 45min–1hr).

Buses

Connections with Prague: Liberec (hourly; 1hr 10min–1hr 40min); Litoměřice (hourly Mon–Fri; 1hr–1hr 50min); Louny (hourly; 1hr 15min); Terezín (15 daily Mon–Fri, 2 daily Sat & Sun; 1hr).
Česká Kamenice to: Jetřichovice (Mon–Fri 4 daily; 25min).
Děčín to: Hřensko (4 daily Mon–Fri; 20min); Mezná (3 daily Mon–Fri; 35min).
Jablonec to: Harrachov (6–10 daily; 1hr 5min–1hr 15min).

East Bohemia

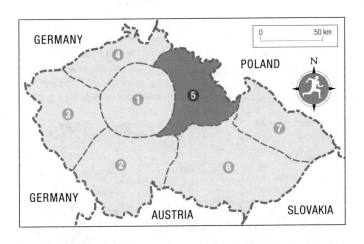

CHAPTER 5

Highlights

✳ **Český ráj** Great rambling countryside, dotted with ruined castles, sandstone protrusions, chateaux and folk architecture. See p.267

✳ **Adršpach rocks** A bizarre rock "city" that rises out of the woods to the east of the Krknoše mountains. See p.282

✳ **Nové Město nad Metují** Picture-postcard square and a chateau whose interior includes work by early twentieth-century architects. See p.286

✳ **Hradec Králové** A picturesque old town standing opposite an innovative new town, built between the wars by Rondo-Cubist architects. See p.288

✳ **Kuks** Long-defunct spa with the finest array of Baroque statues outside Prague. See p.294

✳ **Pardubice** As well as its old town and chateau, Pardubice boasts a Rondo-Cubist crematorium and the world's most challenging steeplechase course. See p.296

✳ **Litomyšl** Attractive town with Renaissance chateau and the extraordinarily weird Portmonbeum, designed by Josef Váchal in the early twentieth century. See p.299

▲ Kuks

East Bohemia

ast Bohemia (Východní Čechy) is probably the most difficult Czech region to categorize. It has none of the polluting industry of its immediate neighbours, though it has suffered indirectly from their excesses; it contains some of the flattest landscape in Bohemia, but also its highest peaks; historically it has been predominantly Czech, though pockets of German settlement have left their mark in the culture and architecture. Lastly, the region has never really enjoyed fixed boundaries, a confusion compounded by the administrative borders currently in operation, which have arbitrarily added on parts of Moravia.

For variety of scenery, however, East Bohemia is hard to beat. Along the northern border with Poland, the peaks of the **Krkonoše** and the **Orlické hory** form an almost continuous mountain range, with excellent opportunities for hiking and skiing. The lower-lying **Český ráj**, to the south, and the area around **Broumov** to the east are wonderfully pastoral, and typically Bohemian, landscapes of rocky sandstone covered in thick forest. Further south still, the terrain on either side of the River Labe – the Polabí, as it is known – is flat, fertile and, for the most part, fairly dull. But the towns of the river basin do much to make up for it – **Hradec Králové**, the regional capital, and its historic rival, **Pardubice**, both boast handsomely preserved historic centres.

Český ráj

Less than 100km from Prague, the sandstone rocks and densely wooded hills of the **Český ráj** (Bohemian Paradise) have been a popular spot for weekending Praguers for over a century. Although the Český ráj is officially limited to a small nature reserve southeast of Turnov, the term is loosely applied to the entire swathe of hills from Mnichovo Hradiště to Jičín. **Turnov** is the most convenient base for exploring the region, though **Jičín** is infinitely more appealing, with its preserved seventeenth-century old town. More interesting than either is the surrounding **countryside**: ruined fortresses, bizarre rock formations and traditional folk architecture, all smothered in a blanket of pine forests.

From Turnov, local **trains** run roughly every two hours to Jičín, and local **buses** from both towns infrequently wind their way through the otherwise inaccessible villages nearby. Generally, though, the distances are so small – Turnov to Jičín, for example, is just 24km – that you'd be better off buying a map and **walking** along the network of marked footpaths.

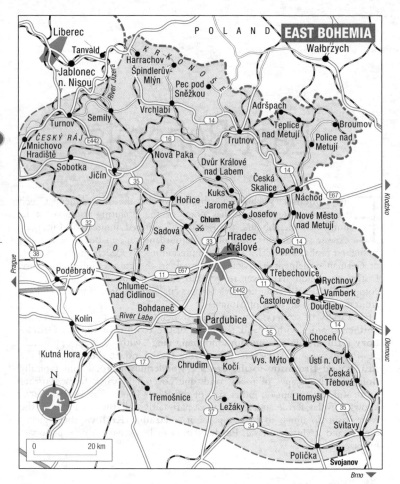

EAST BOHEMIA

POLAND

Liberec
Tanvald
Harrachov
Jablonec n. Nisou
Špindlerův-Mlýn
Pec pod Sněžkou
Wałbrzych

K R K O N O Š E

River Jizera

Turnov
Semily
Vrchlabí
Adršpach
14
Teplice nad Metují
Broumov

ČESKÝ RÁJ
E442
16
Trutnov
Police nad Metují

Mnichovo Hradiště
Sobotka
Jičín
Nová Paka
Dvůr Králové nad Labem
Česká Skalice

35
Hořice
Kuks
Náchod
E67
Klodzko

32
Jaroměř
Chlum
Josefov
Nové Město nad Metují

Sadová
33
Hradec Králové
Opočno
14

P O L A B Í
11 E67
Třebechovice
Rychnov
Vamberk

Poděbrady
Chlumec nad Cidlinou
E442
11
Doudleby
Olomouc

Bohdaneč
River Labe
Pardubice
Častolovice

Kolín
35
Choceň
14

Kutná Hora
17
Chrudim
Kočí
Vys. Mýto
Ústí n. Orl.
Česká Třebová

N

Třemošnice
Ležáky
Litomyšl
35

37
34
Svitavy

0   20 km

Polička
Svojanov

Brno

Prague
38

Turnov and around

TURNOV (Turnau), as the name suggests, can be less than stimulating, though its main square is lively enough, and the town has done a good job promoting itself as the logistical and accommodation centre for the region. The **tourist office** (July & Aug Mon–Fri 8am–6pm, Sat 9am–4pm, Sun 9am–2pm; Sept–June Mon–Fri 8am–5pm, Sat 9am–noon; ☏481 366 255, ⓦwww.turnov.cz or www.bohemian-paradise.info), on the main square, can help find **accommodation**, including private rooms, as can Čechotour, on Nádražní near the train station, a ten-minute walk west of the old town on the other side of the river. The best **hotel**, the late nineteenth-century *Korunní Princ* on the main square (☏481 313 520, ⓦwww.korunniprinc.cz; ❸), has pleasantly furnished en suites with satellite TV and a good, spacious restaurant serving up Czech specialities and fish dishes. The smaller and quieter *Cleopatra* (☏481 322 417, ⓦwww.cleopatra.cz; ❸), just up from the main square on 5 května, also has a pleasant restaurant. There's a simple **pension**, *U svatého Jana* (☏481 323 325, www.svatyjan.euroregin.cz; ❷), behind the *Korunní Princ*, down Hluboká. As for **restaurants**, the *U belgického dvora* (closed Sat eve), down from the *Korunní Princ*, serves Czech food, with an even cheaper branch (closed Sat afternoon & Sun) around the corner at Hluboká 285.

On the outskirts of Turnov lies the chateau of **Hrubý Rohozec** (April & Oct Sat & Sun 9am–4pm; May–Sept Tues–Sun 9am–5pm; ⓦwww.hruby -rohozec.cz; short tour 45Kč, long tour 70Kč), high up on the left bank of the Jizera river. A Gothic castle redesigned in the Renaissance, it's a welcome contrast to the rest of the town, and its interior gives some great views and a series of handsome chambers. Ask for an *anglický text* or book an English-speaking tour (☎481 321 012). If you want a drink or a bite to eat, head for restaurant of the local **brewery**, *Pivovar Rohozec*, 1.5km northwest of the chateau in Malý Rohozec.

Malá Skála

About 10km northeast of Turnov, the wonderful little village of **MALÁ SKÁLA** is accessible by train and bus. Nothing much happens here, but it's a pretty base for hikes into the surrounding hills. A steep red-marked path leads from behind the train station to the **Suché skály** (Dry Rocks) and a number of caves used during the Counter-Reformation as safe houses for persecuted Protestants. A green-marked path then leads to the hamlet of **PROSIČKA**, after which the blue-marked path heads back to Malá Skála; the whole route can easily be covered in a half day. Another red-marked path from Malá Skála follows a ridge on the other side of the river, from where the view across the valley to the ruined castle of **Frýdštejn** (May–Oct Tues–Sun 10am–5pm; ⓦwww.frydstejn.cz; 40Kč) is reward for your pains. You could extend the day by dropping into the castle and continuing up the blue-marked path to the viewing tower atop Kopanina (657m), returning to Malá Skála via the green-marked path. There's a **campsite** (ⓦautocampmalaskala.infohelp.cz; May–Sept) on the right bank of the river, and a delightful **pension** with a very good restaurant, *Teta Marta* (☎483 392 140, ⓦwww.tetamarta.net; ❷), 1km up the road to Frýdštejn. Right near the train station, the larger *Hotel Skála* (☎483 392 299, ⓦwww.hotelskala.cz; ❷) is a reasonable enough place that also serves up steaks and chops from its outdoor grill.

Valdštejn and Hruboskalské skalní město

A lovely two-kilometre walk through the woods along either the red- or green-marked path from the Turnov-město train station (one stop down the Jičín line) brings you to the former Gothic stronghold of **Valdštejn** (9am–4.30pm: April & Oct Sat & Sun; May–Sept daily; 35Kč), ancestral seat of the Waldsteins for many years. Already in ruins by the late sixteenth century, it was occupied by vagrants, and later attempts to restore it never came to fruition. Its position, however, remains impressive – as does the eighteenth-century stone bridge flanked by Baroque statues.

Another 2km southeast, the first (and arguably the best) of Český ráj's skalné města (sandstone cities), **Hruboskalské skalní město**, unfolds amid the trees. It's easy to spend hours clambering up and down the bluffs and dodging the crevices, whose names – Myší díra (Mouse Hole), Dračí věž (Dragon's Tower) and Sahara – give some idea of the variety of rock formations. Viewpoints, like Zamecká vyhlídka or Mariánská vyhlídka, range high above the treeline, with the protruding stone slabs emerging from the pine trees like ossified giants. The nearby castle of **Hrubá skála**, popular with Czech film crews, is a colossal nineteenth-century reconstruction of the Gothic original. It's now a wonderful

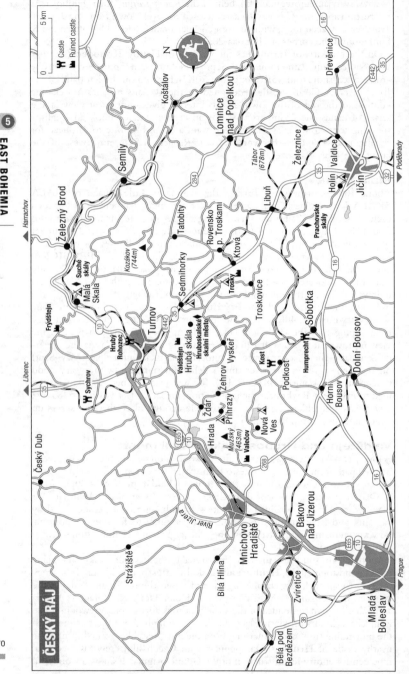

ČESKÝ RÁJ

and reasonably priced **hotel**, *Zámek Hrubá Skála* (☎481 659 111, ⓦwww
.hrubaskala.cz; ❹), with a baronial **restaurant** open to non-residents. From
here, a green-marked path descends through the Myší díra and the Dračí skály,
zigzagging down to the large lakeside **campsite**, *Sedmihorky* (all year; ⓦwww
.campsedmihorky.cz), near the Karlovice-Sedmihorky station on the Turnov–
Jičín line. Also down here is a well-sited spa hotel, *Lázně Sedmihorky* (☎481 550
111, ⓦwww.sedmihorky.cz; ❸).

Trosky

The spectacular ruined castle of **Trosky** (April & Oct Sat & Sun 8.30am–4pm;
May & Sept Tues–Sun 8.30am–4pm; June–Aug Tues–Sun 8.30am–6pm;
ⓦwww.trosky.cz; 40Kč), which literally means "rubble", 5km southeast of
Hrubá skála, is the Český ráj's number-one landmark. Its twin Gothic towers,
Bába (Grandmother) and Panna (Virgin), were built on volcanic basalt rocks
that burst through the sandstone strata millions of years ago. You can climb the
ridge between Bába and Panna (the higher of the two) for a far-reaching view
of the Jizera basin. The flash **hotel** and restaurant complex, *Trosky* (☎&ⓕ481
382 290; ❷), by the castle car park, offers cheap and decent doubles, and there
are two very basic **campsites** – *Svitačka* (May–Sept), a short way to the south,
and *Vidlák* (June–Aug), 2km northwest along the red-marked path, by the lake
of the same name, with a cheap but passable *hospoda* across the road. Three or
four **buses** a day run to Trosky from Turnov; trains are slower but more frequent
and deliver you at Ktová station on the Jičín line, from where it's a three-
kilometre walk uphill along the green-marked path.

Jičín and around

At the southeastern tip of the Český ráj, where the fertile plain of the River
Labe touches the foothills of the Krkonoše, **JIČÍN** (Gitschin), an hour by train
from Turnov, is easily the most rewarding stop in the region. Its location, close
to some of the Český ráj's most dramatic scenery, makes it a convenient base for
some easy hiking, while its Renaissance zámek and arcaded square make it an
attractive place to stay. Jičín is also very accessible, with good bus connections
throughout the region.

The Town

Jičín is closely associated with the infamous **Albrecht von Waldstein**, who,
during his brief and meteoric rise to eminence, owned almost every chateau in
the region. Waldstein confiscated Jičín early in the Thirty Years' War, and chose
this rather unlikely town as the capital of his new personal empire, the Duchy
of Friedland. He established a hospital to ensure his workers were not incapaci-
tated for long, insisted everyone attend the Jesuit college he founded, and
established a mint; but for his murder, he would no doubt have fulfilled his plans
for a bishopric and a university.

In the 1620s he rebuilt the main square – now named **Valdštejnovo náměstí**
in his honour – in stone, in a late-Renaissance style, full of light touches.
Waldstein even lent the local burghers money to adapt their houses to suit his
plans. One side is still dominated by Waldstein's **zámek** (Tues–Fri 9am–5pm,
Sat & Sun 9am–noon & 12.30–5pm; 60Kč), which now contains a dull local
museum and, in the converted riding school, an art gallery, as well as the great
conference hall in which the leaders of the three great European powers, Russia,
Austria and Prussia, formed the Holy Alliance against Napoleon in 1813. A
covered passage connects the chateau's eastern wing with the **Jesuit church**

Waldstein

Albrecht von Waldstein (known to the Czechs as Albrecht z Valdštejna, and to the English as Wallenstein – the name given to him by the German playwright Schiller in his tragic trilogy) was the most notorious warlord of the Thirty Years' War. If the imperial astrologer Johannes Kepler is to be believed, this is because he was born at 4pm on September 14, 1583. According to Kepler's horoscope, Waldstein was destined to be greedy, deceitful, unloved and unloving. Sure enough, at an early age he tried to kill a servant, for which he was expelled from his Lutheran school. Recuperating in Italy, he converted to Catholicism (an astute career move) and married a wealthy widow who conveniently died shortly after. Waldstein used his new fortune to cultivate a friendship with Prince Ferdinand, heir to the Habsburg Empire, who in turn thought that a tame Bohemian noble could come in handy.

Within five years of the **Battle of Bílá hora** in 1620, Waldstein owned a quarter of Bohemia, either by compulsory purchase or in return for money or troops loaned to Ferdinand. It was a good time to go into property: Ferdinand's imperial armies, who were busy restoring Catholicism throughout Europe, provided a ready-made market for agricultural produce. And as a rising general, Waldstein could get away with a certain amount of insider trading, marching armies with as many as 125,000 men over enemy territory or land owned by rivals, laying waste to fields and then selling his troops supplies from his own pristine Bohemian estates.

As Waldstein ranged further afield in Germany, conquering **Jutland**, **Pomerania**, **Alsace** and most of **Brandenburg** on Ferdinand's behalf, his demands for reward grew ever more outrageous. Already duke of Friedland and governor of Prague, Waldstein was appointed duke of Mecklenburg in 1628. This upset not only the existing duke, who had backed Ferdinand's opponents, but even the emperor's loyalist supporters. If Ferdinand thought fit to hand one of the greatest German titles to this Czech upstart, was any family's inheritance secure? Soon, though, Waldstein's services became too expensive for Ferdinand, so the duke was relieved of his command.

In 1630 Saxons occupied Prague, and the emperor was forced to reinstate Waldstein. Ferdinand couldn't afford to do without the supplies from Waldstein's estates, but knew he was mortgaging large chunks of the empire to pay for his services. More alarmingly, there were persistent rumours that Waldstein was about to declare himself king of Bohemia and defect to the French enemy. In 1634 Waldstein openly rebelled against Ferdinand, who immediately hatched a plot to **murder** Waldstein, sending a motley posse including English, Irish and Scottish mercenaries to the border town of Cheb, where they cut the general down in his nightshirt as he tried to rise from his sickbed. Some see Waldstein as the first man to unify Germany since Charlemagne, others see him as a wily Czech hero. In reality, he was probably just an ambitious, violent man, as his stars had predicted.

next door, allowing the nobility to avoid their unsavoury subjects while en route to Mass. But this steeple-less Baroque church is eclipsed by the mighty sixteenth-century **Valdická brána** (April, May & Sept Tues–Sun 2–5pm; June–Aug daily 9am–5pm; 20Kč) close by, whose restored tower gallery offers a panoramic view over the town.

One of Waldstein's more endearing additions to the town is the **lipová alej** (now known as Revoluční), a 2km-long avenue of 1200 lime trees planted in two dead-straight lines by Waldstein's soldiers. At the far end is the once princely garden of **Libosad**, now an overgrown spinney but still worth a wander. The melancholy of its Renaissance loggia, last repaired at the end of the First Republic, is matched by the nearby Jewish cemetery, which boasts some finely carved tombstones.

Practicalities

The **tourist office** (late May to mid-Sept Mon–Fri 8am–6pm, Sat 9am–4pm, Sun 10am–5pm; rest of the year Mon–Fri 9am–5pm, Sat 9am–noon; ☎493 534 390, ⓦwww.jicin.org), in the zámek, has **internet access** and can find **accommodation**, including private rooms. *U České koruny* (May to mid-Sept; ☎493 531 241; ➋), on the main square, is the best of the central pensions; there is also the friendly *Albrecht* (☎493 532 544; ➋), with just a pair of rooms in a family home 1km down the lime-tree avenue that leads to Valdice at Revoluční 712. Perhaps the best hotel in town is the comfortable *Hotel Jičín* (☎493 544 250, ⓦwww.hoteljicin.cz; ➍), two blocks east of the main square at Havlíčkova 21, which has spotless, well-appointed en suites with satellite TV and an excellent restaurant serving hearty Czech cuisine. Some 16km down route 16 to Mladá Boleslav, the *Rumcajs* **campsite** (May–Sept; ☎736 250 185) has wooden chalets.

There are plenty of unusual **restaurants** in the old town: *U piráta*, outside the Valdická brana at Husova 127, backs up its off-beat buccaneer theme with trout, tuna and even shark in addition to standard Czech dishes. Creative and filling pizzas, as well as "food for those who say meat is meat", are served on the pleasing patio at *Pizzerie U Henryho*, behind *U České koruny* on the main square, while agreeable Chinese food is on the menu at the aptly named *China Restaurant*, on Jiráskova, northeast of the main square.

Prachovské skály

Despite the very real attractions of the town, most people come to Jičín to see the **Prachovské scaly** (50Kč), a series of sandstone and basalt towers hidden in woods 8km to the northwest. To get there, it's a gentle walk along the yellow-marked path, via the *Rumcajs* campsite; local buses also make the fifteen-minute ride. The rocks may lack the subtlety of the Hruboskalské skalní, but make up for it in sheer size and area; their name derives from the dust (*prach*) that covers the forest floor, forming a carpet of sand. In high season, swarms of climbers cling to the silent, grey rocks like a plague of locusts, but it's possible to find a tranquil spot at other times; try the green- or yellow-marked path. Note that the viewpoints on the south side of the skalní město (such as Vyhlídka míru or Vyhlídka Českého ráje) are better than those opposite. Dorm **beds** are available in the primitive *ubytovna* right by the rocks, but these are usually booked solid in summer; try instead a private room, or the *Parkhotel Skalní město* (☎493 525 011, ⓦwww.skalnimesto.cz; ➌), a fine place back down the road to Jičín.

Sobotka and around

Compared with Turnov or Jičín, **SOBOTKA** is off the beaten track: 13km from either place, with limited accommodation, and only accessible by train from Jičín (50min; change at Libuň). Unless you're camping (and hiking) or staying in one of the handful of pensions, it's no good as a base for exploring, though it does harbour some good examples of the local brightly painted half-timbered architecture and – just northwest of the town, on a strange conical hill – the striking seventeenth-century **Humprecht hunting lodge** (April & Oct Sat & Sun 9–11.30am & 1–3.30pm; May, June & Sept Tues–Sun 9–11.30am & 1–4.30pm; July & Aug Tues–Sun 9am–5pm), named after its eccentric aristo-cratic instigator, Jan Humprecht Černín. It's a bizarre building, worth a peek if only for the trompe l'oeil dining room, a windowless sixteen-metre-high oval cylinder with the acoustics of a cathedral. On the other side of the hill from Sobotka is a rudimentary **campsite** (mid-June to Sept) and a swimming pool.

The best **hotel** is the *Ort* (☎493 571 137, ⓦwww.ceskyraj.cz/hotelort; ❸),
2km to the north in Nepřívěc, which offers decent (if smallish) two- to four-
bed rooms, as well as bike rental and a sauna.

Podkost

Up to five buses daily (weekdays only) cover the 3km northwest from Sobotka
to **PODKOST**, a small settlement by a pond at the edge of the Žehrov forest.
The village is dominated in every way by **Hrad Kost** (April & Oct Wed–Sun
9am–4pm; May, June & Sept Tues–Sun 9–5pm; July & Aug daily 9am–6pm;
100Kč; ⓦwww.kinskycastles.com), which sits on top of a gigantic sandstone
pedestal and sports a characteristic rectangular keep. Thanks to a fire in 1635, after
which it was used as a granary, Kost was spared the attentions of later architectural
trends and retains its fourteenth-century flavour, making it the best-preserved
castle in the Český ráj. There's a choice of tours: *Kinskych v Čechách* takes you
around the state rooms, while *Mučírna* follows torture through the ages. You can
stay in a self-catering apartment in a castle gate (☎493 517 144; ❺), or in the
village at the *Helikar* (☎493 571 127; ❷), which also has dorm beds (❶).

Valečov and around

You're more likely to find suitable accommodation at **NOVÁ VES**, another
4km northwest along the scenic red-marked path through the woods of the
Žehrovský les. This tiny village has three campsites and plenty of pensions along
the shores of the nearby **Komárovský rybník**. North of the lake a matrix of
paths crisscrosses the complex rock systems within the forest, emerging 3km
later at a campsite (May–Sept) in Příhrazy. Paths spread west from here and back
into the woods until they reach Mužský (463m), from where it's another 2km
uphill to the prehistoric burial ground of Hrada and the rocky viewpoint at
Drábské světničky. The truly amazing sight of **Valečov** (April & Oct Sat & Sun
9am–5pm; May & June Tues–Sun 9am–6pm; July & Aug daily 9am–6pm; Sept
Tues–Sun 9am–5pm; Nov–March Sat & Sun 10am–4.30pm; 35Kč), a ruined
fort cut into the rock, lies another 2km to the south at the southwestern edge
of the woodland. On a day-hike, you could easily do a round trip from Nová
Ves or Příhrazy by heading east from Valečov, or continuing another 3km west
on the red-marked path to the station at Mnichovo Hradiště (see below), on the
main line to Prague.

Mnichovo Hradiště

Another base for the area around Valečov is the small industrial town of
MNICHOVO HRADIŠTĚ (Münchengrätz), in the southwest corner of the
Český ráj. The main square has a handsome neo-Renaissance radnice smothered
in sgraffito, as well as one of the region's better **hotels**, *U hroznu* (☎326 771
617; ❸), with its own *vinárna*. Buses stop right on the main square; the **train
station** is some five blocks southeast.

   The town's attractive Renaissance **zámek** (April & Oct Sat & Sun 8.45am–
3pm; May–Sept Tues–Sun 8.45am–4pm; 90Kč), 1km north of the main square,
was owned by the Waldstein family up to 1945. The main fifty-minute guided
tour (*1 okruh*; 90Kč) takes you through the chateau's beautiful period interiors;
a fifteen-minute tour takes you round the early nineteenth-century theatre
(*2 okruh*; 40Kč); and a thirty-minute tour takes in the ornate Baroque chapel of
sv Anna (*3 okruh*; 40Kč), in the chateau grounds, last resting place of Albrecht
von Waldstein, who was murdered in Cheb (Eger) in 1634 (see p.221). Initially
buried in Valdice, outside Jičín, the general's body wasn't brought to Mnichovo

Hradiště until the eighteenth century, by which time the family couldn't afford the lavish mausoleum Albrecht himself had hoped for – instead, all you see is a modest plaque that was erected in 1934. The chapel still merits a visit, if only for its impressive stucco ceilings and the adjacent lapidarium.

The Krkonoše

The **Krkonoše** (Giant Mountains), the highest mountains in Bohemia, formed part of the historical northeastern border of its ancient kingdom. They were uninhabited until the sixteenth and seventeenth centuries, when glass-making and ore-mining brought the first German and Italian settlers to the Riesengebirge, as they were then known. The mountains' beauty ensured an early tourist trade, and, for resorts like **Špindlerův Mlýn** and **Pec pod Sněžkou**, tourism remains the sole industry. Despite being one of the few protected national parks in the country, the Krkonoše suffered considerably from **acid rain** in the decades up to the 1990s – much of which was caused by heavy industries over the borders in East Germany and Poland. Once the trees were badly affected, insects did the rest, transforming them into grey husks. Extensive felling aimed to stop the spread of the destructive insects, but it was a bit like a smoker removing their lungs to prevent cancer. For many, the fate of Bohemia's ancient forests was the most damning indictment of the Communists' forty years of mismanagement.

In the last two decades, however, the condition of the mountains has improved remarkably, with plenty of new tree planting and rebirth on the heels of much stricter emissions controls in both Poland and the Czech Republic. Czechs will reassure you that things here were never as bad as in the Krušné hory (see p.240) anyway, and it's true: while in summer you can't avoid the relics of barren hillsides and ashen tree trunks, if you stay in the largely unspoiled valley, or come in winter when the snow obscures much of the damage, it's possible to remain oblivious.

Vrchlabí

VRCHLABÍ (Hohenelbe) is the hub of the Krkonoše for transport and supplies, but not as well situated for skiing or hiking as the other main towns. Vrchlabí's long main street stretches for 3km along the banks of the Labe, taking you past the pleasing gardens and zoo of the sixteenth-century chateau and a number of traditional wooden, arcaded folk buildings around the centre. A trio of folk houses at the far end of the street (náměstí Míru) – one in stone, flanked by two timber-framed neighbours – have been converted into the small **Krkonošské muzeum** (June–Oct Mon–Sat 9am–noon & 1–4.30pm; Nov–May Mon–Fri 9am–noon & 1–4pm; 40Kč), containing, among other things, folk art and glassware. Displays on regional life through the ages (Tues–Sun 8am–5.30pm) and the local environment (Tues–Sun 8am–3.30pm) feature at the museum's other branch, located in the former Augustan monastery on Husova, a five-minute walk to the west. Attached to the museum on náměstí Míru, a **Krkonošský národní park office** (KRNAP; June–Oct Mon–Sat 9am–noon & 1–4.30pm; Nov–May Mon–Fri 9am–noon & 1–4pm) has maps and weather information.

Practicalities

Reservations are recommended for the direct **buses** from Prague, some of which continue on to Špindlerův Mlýn (see p.277); if you're travelling by **train**,

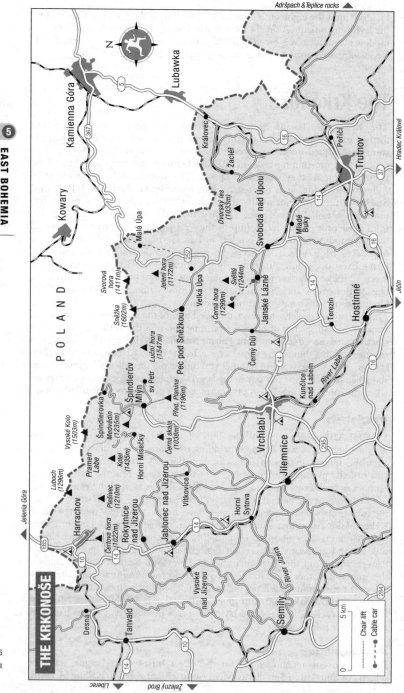

THE KRKONOŠE

N

P O L A N D

Kamienna Góra

Kowary

Lubawka

Królovec

Žacléř

Dvorský les
(1033m)

Svoboda nad Úpou

Mladé Buky

Trutnov

Poříčí

Malá Úpa

Svorová
hora
(1411m)

Jelení hora
(1172m)

Sněžka
(1602m)

Velká Úpa

Světlá
(1244m)

Černá hora
(1299m)

Janské Lázně

Hostinné

Vysoké Kolo
(1503m)

Luční hora
(1547m)

Pec pod Sněžkou

Terezín

Špindlerův
Mlýn

sv Petr

Před. Planina
(1196m)

Černý Důl

Kunčice
nad Labem

Luboch
(1296m)

Pramen
Labe

Špindlerovka

Medvědín
(1235m)

Kotel
(1435m)

Horní Mísečky

Černá skála
(1038m)

Vrchlabí

River Labe

Harrachov

Plešivec
(1210m)

Čertova hora
(1022m)

Rokytnice
nad Jizerou

Jablonec nad Jizerou

Vitkovice

Horní
Sytova

Jilemnice

Desná

Tanvald

Vysoké
nad Jizerou

River Jizera

Semily

Jelenia Góra ▲

Liberec ▲

Železný Brod ▲

Hradec Králové ▼

Jičín ▼

5 km

0   5 km

· · · · · Chair lift

—·—·— Cable car

you'll need to change at Kunčice nad Labem, 4km south. Vrchlabí's **tourist office** (Mon–Fri 9am–12.30pm & 1.30–5pm; ☏499 422 136, ⓦwww.vrchlabi .cz) is in the radnice on the main square, náměstí T.G. Masaryka. For room booking and tour services right across the Krkonoše, check out also the ING Tours travel agency (Mon–Fri 8am–6pm, Sat 8am–noon; ☏499 453 623, ⓦwww.ingtours.cz) in the IT Centrum near the square. This complex also contains the best **supermarket** in town, though there's one next to the bus station as well.

Hotels boil down to the *Labuť* (☏499 421 964, ⓦwww.hotellabut.cz; ❷) on the main street, Krkonošská, and the equally good *U svatého Vavřince* (☏499 421 044; ❸), in a large yellow building on náměstí Míru. There are also many small, central **pensions**, with self-service apartments (☏499 421 260; ❷) above the *Klasika* pizzeria and steakhouse just beyond *Labuť*. Of the three local **campsites**, the *Vejsplachy* (mid-June to Sept), just south of route 14, has the best position, alongside a lake. *Klasika* is a local favourite for **food**, while the *Krušovická restaurace* on the main square has an outdoor grill – and an **internet café** upstairs.

Špindlerův Mlýn and around

No doubt **ŠPINDLERŮV MLÝN** (Spindlermühle), 15km north up the Labe Valley, was once an idyllic, isolated mountain hamlet. Successive generations, however, have found it difficult to resist exploiting a town where seven valleys meet, and countless private pensions and hotels lie scattered across the hillsides. Still, the place retains a cosy feel, and makes a fine base for a few days of outdoor activity. The River Labe, here still a stream, flows through its tiny centre.

It's important to book **accommodation** in advance during the high seasons. The booking office of the Info Pavilon (☏499 523 364, ⓦwww .spindleruvmlyninfo.cz), in the centre, can help, as well as provide ski rental. This is a private agency with ties to particular local hotels; if you prefer impartial advice, make for the **tourist office** (daily 9–11.30am & 12.30–5pm; ⓦwww .mestospindleruvmlyn.cz), hidden beyond the post office on the other side of the stream. Recommendable hotels include the lovely wood-panelled mountain lodge *Start Hotel* (☏499 433 305, ⓦwww.hotelstart.cz; ❹), Horská 17, which stands on a slope just west of the central area. Equally well appointed is the ⚝ *Hotel Praha* (☏499 523 516, ⓦwww.hotelprahaspindl.cz; ❸), Okružní 118, north of centre, with a slight Art Nouveau theme and a nice restaurant with a terrace overlooking the town. Lower-end rooms can be found in the pretty *Pension U Čeňků* (☏499 523 700, ⓦwww.ucenku.cz; ❷), near the tourist office. There are two fairly pricey **campsites** a couple of kilometres north of the central area, both open all year.

You can grab a bite **to eat** in the terrace pizzeria in the Pavilon, by the edge of the stream. The aforementioned hotels have good restaurants, and the *Pension U Čeňků* a cute patio from which to sip a beer or eat filling Czech food. *Abacante*, on the street to the far left when you cross the river into town, serves Mexican food, while the *Špindlerovská hospoda* right in town is a decent pub with good food. If you're driving, know that **parking** is severely restricted in town, and unless your hotel has reserved space you'll have to pay an exorbitant fee to leave your vehicle at the car park just to the south.

Outdoor activities

Other than hanging around alongside the pretty riverbanks or poking into shops, there's little else to do other than ride the year-round Medvědín **chairlift**

Krkonoše practicalities

Accommodation

The Krkonoše has long been the country's top outdoor resort area, which means **accommodation** should be booked in advance at the height of the winter ski season, and in July and August. Luckily, the entire mountain range is teeming with cheap **private rooms**, which can be booked through numerous accommodation agencies in the resorts. Špindlerův Mlýn and Jánské Lázně are undoubtedly the prettiest towns in which to stay; theoretically, you can also sleep at one of the **bouda** (chalets) dotted across the mountains, originally hideouts for fleeing Protestants in the seventeenth century, but even these often require advance planning. Armed with a map, you could head for *Josefova bouda* (℡499 523 422, Ⓦwww.josefovabouda .cz; ❷), near the end of the bus line from Špindlerův Mlýn to Špindlerova bouda, or to *Bradlerovy boudy* (℡499 422 056, Ⓦwww.bradlerovy-boudy.cz; ❷), along the green-marked trail east of the source of the Labe (*pramen Labe*; see below). The former is conveniently situated near the Slezské sedlo (pass), the meeting point of several very attractive walking trails; the latter boasts a pleasantly quiet location and can serve as a base for exploring the western part of the main ridge. Positioned in a beautiful location, although not so pretty itself, is *Labská bouda* (℡499 421 755, Ⓦwww.labskabouda.cz; ❷), at the edge of the Labe Valley. An hour's walk west of Sněžka, along a blue-marked path, stands the area's largest, wooden *Luční bouda* (℡499 736 144, Ⓦwww.lucnibouda.cz; ❷), where during World War II Luftwaffe pilots were trained. **Camping** is one way to ensure a place for the night, although facilities are somewhat restricted. Within the strict boundaries of the national park are just two sites, though plenty more lie along the fringes.

Getting around

Buses are the quickest way to get around, with plenty of fast connections to Prague and throughout east Bohemia. **Trains** can get you as far as Harrachov, Vrchlabí and Trutnov, though these connections can be awkward. There are also numerous **chair-lifts** that operate even in summer. However, **hiking** is undoubtedly the best way of

(*lánová dráha*; daily every 30min 8am–6pm; 150Kč return) up the mountain of the same name (1235m); follow the signs from the left bank of the river. You could also try the year-round **bobsleigh track** (*bobová dráha*; snowless days only 10am–6pm; Ⓦwww.bobovka.cz; 80Kč) nearby. Several outfitters in the centre offer **ski** and **mountain bike** rental and activity tours; try Skolmax (℡605 339 359, Ⓦwww.skolmax.cz).

The **River Labe**, which flows into the North Sea (as the Elbe) near Hamburg, has its source in the Krkonoše. It takes about three hours to **hike** to the source (*pramen Labe*): a long, boulder-strewn walk along the valley, followed by a short, sharp climb out of the forest. Characteristically for the Krkonoše, the upper plateau is disappointingly flat and boggy, and the source itself (500m from the Polish border) no great sight. If you're carrying your pack with you, continue for three hours along the blue-marked track to Harrachov (see opposite). Otherwise, it's around two hours back to Špindlerův Mlýn, via Horní Mísečky and Medvědín. Another worthwhile trek is along the red-marked path to *Luční bouda* (see above), a huge chalet at the edge of Krkonoše's largest (and potentially dangerous) marsh. It takes two hours from Svatý Petr and includes an extremely steep climb up the Kozí hřbety. From the *bouda* you can descend to Špindlerův Mlýn along the beautiful, V-shaped Bílé Labe valley (blue markers; 2hr).

getting around, since each valley is basically a long, winding dead end for motor vehicles, with pretty hefty parking fees (and sometimes queues) aimed at dissuading drivers from bringing their vehicles into the park. There are now three 24-hour **border crossings into Poland**: Harrachov–Jakuszyce, Královec–Lubawka and Pomezní Boudy–Przełęcz Okraj. More convenient for walkers are four additional tourist border crossings on the ridge itself (daily: April–Sept 8am–8pm; Oct–March 9am–4pm), only accessible on foot.

Hiking

For those intent on serious **hiking**, a detailed **map** of the mountains, showing the network of colour-coded marked paths, is essential. Warm clothing is also important, no matter what the season – the summits are battered by wind almost every day, and have an average annual temperature of around freezing. Persistent mist – around for about 300 days in the year – makes sticking to the marked paths a must. In winter, most of the high-level paths are closed, and recently, even in summer, several have been closed to give the mountains a rest. To find out the latest details, head for the tourist information offices in any of the resorts. Keep in mind, too, that you will hardly be alone on the trails, as the mountains are immensely popular among Czechs, Poles and Germans.

Skiing

The Krkonoše is also the most popular region in the Czech Republic for **skiing**, since it receives by far the longest and most reliable snowfall in the country. Pec pod Sněžkou is the largest resort, followed by Špindlerův Mlýn and Harrachov. Queues for lifts everywhere can be long and slow, but are more than compensated for by the cheapness of the ski passes and accommodation – although these have risen to levels formidable to the average Czech. Lift tickets cost upwards of 600Kč per day, and ski rental is easily had for around 250Kč per day. In summer, numerous outlets in each resort offer mountain bike rental – ask at the tourist office for the cycling map.

Harrachov

Five buses and three trains a day (change at nearby Tanvald or Turnov) make the journey from Prague to the westernmost resort in the Krkonoše, **HARRACHOV** (Harrachsdorf), whose cottages are scattered about the Mumlava Valley. Harrachov is a ski resort, so unless you're aiming for the slopes, your time is best spent hiking the surrounding mountains. The official national park tourist office, KRNAP (daily 8am–noon & 1–4.30pm), close to the bus station, can help with maps and walking suggestions. As for sights, there's been a working **glassworks** here since 1712, which you can tour (book a day or two in advance); the adjacent **Muzeum skla** (Glass Museum; Mon–Fri 9am–5pm, Sat & Sun 9am–1pm; ⓦwww.sklarnaharrachov.cz) has a small sample of glassware throughout the ages, as well as a shop (Mon–Fri 8am–2pm). There's also a **Lyžařské muzeum** (Ski Museum; Tues–Sun 9–11.30am & noon–4pm), further up the road, which traces the history of skiing and celebrates Harrachov's occasional hosting of one round of the world ski-jump champion-ships (most recently in January 2008). The **Hornické muzeum** (Mining Museum; daily 10am–6pm; ⓦwww.ados-harrachov.cz), near the main car park, features a collection of minerals as well as the leftovers of a mineral mine that functioned here until the early 1990s. You can take an hour-long guided tour down into the extensive system of tunnels, whose total length exceeds 20km.

Accommodation here tends to be cheaper than in the neighbouring resorts, but it can be hard to get a room in high season. On the main road at the western edge of town the **tourist office**, MIC (Mon–Fri 9am–5pm, Sat & Sun 10am–4pm; out of season Mon–Fri 9am–3pm; ⓦwww.harrachov.cz), can help. There are dozens of pensions all over the valley; near the MIC office in Harrachov you'll find the pleasing *Pension Ploc* (☎481 528 194, ⓦwww .pensionploc.euroregin.cz; ❷), owned by a former Czech ski-jumping champion, and the partly wooden *Hotel Šedý vlk* (☎481 528 159; ❸), with a gym, pool and sauna. These facilities are also available at the large *Sporthotel Rýžoviště* (☎481 528 102, ⓦwww.harrachov.cz/sporthotel; ❷), in the hamlet of Rýžoviště, southeast of the centre. There's also a **campsite** (all year; ☎481 529 536, ⓦwww.camp.harrachov.cz) up the road towards the Polish border.

The hotels have good **restaurants**, and there's the *Restaurant Novosad*, with its own brewery, at the glassworks. Halfway up the **chairlift** to Čertova hora, *Myslivna* offers Czech meals and excellent views.

Pec pod Sněžkou and Janské Lázně

The sole attribute of **PEC POD SNĚŽKOU** (Petzer) is its proximity to the mountains. In winter this becomes the Czech Republic's chief ski centre, strung along an endless winding road. In summer it's the main hiking base for climbing **Sněžka** (Schneekoppe or Snow Peak), at 1602m the highest mountain in Bohemia and the most impressive in the entire range. Its bleak, grey summit rises above the tree line, relieving walkers of the painful sight of gently expiring pines, and making for a fine panorama – which you'll likely share with literally hundreds of others. If you don't fancy the six-kilometre ascent, take the **chairlift** (daily: Oct–April hourly 8am–6pm; May–Sept 8am–7pm; 330Kč return) from the village, which will take you in two stages to the top. The border, signified by white-and-red stone markers, divides the rounded summit; the seventeenth-century wooden chapel of sv Vavřinec (St Lawrence), a dull restaurant and a couple of snack stands are at the top.

Many Czechs use the chairlift as a launching pad for further **hiking**. To the east of the summit, a path follows the narrow mountain ridge (which also marks the border) for 2.5km to another peak, Svorová hora (Czarna Kopa to the Poles). To the west, there's a steep drop, again along the ridge, to *Slezská bouda*, a decent restaurant on the Polish side. To reach Špindlerův Mlýn from here (3hr 30min), follow the blue markers (via *Luční bouda*) forking off to the left – the red-and-blue ones veer into Polish territory.

Practicalities

There are regular **buses from Prague** to Pec pod Sněžkou, plus the occasional two or three to Janské Lázně (see opposite) and many to Trutnov. The Krkonoše National Park **information centre** (daily 7.30am–noon & 12.30–6pm; out of season Mon–Fri 7.30am–noon & 12.30–4pm), on the main road up from the bus station, has good maps and can provide hiking and skiing information. There is a second national park visitors' centre (same hours) with mundane exhibits on local flora and fauna, 2km up Obří důl, a valley to the north of town that provides an alternate hiking route to Sněžka. Ski rental is available from dozens of shops around town.

Pec has no campsite and its **hotels** are generally overpriced and booked up, but the concentration of private rooms strewn across the hills is even denser here than in other Krkonoše resorts. The **Turista** information and travel agency (daily: winter 9am–6pm, shorter hours out of ski season; ☎499 736 280,

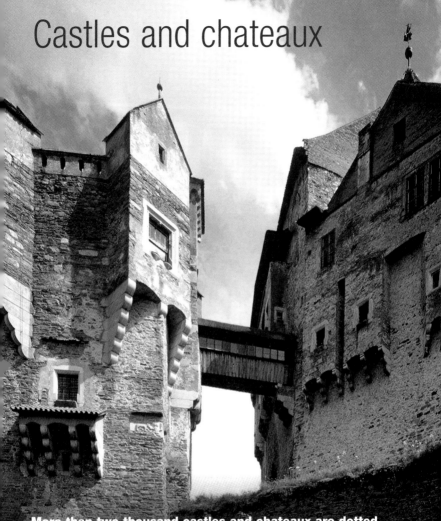

Castles and chateaux

More than two thousand castles and chateaux are dotted about the Czech countryside, and while the luxurious chateaux of the Loire or the rugged castles of Scotland may be better known, the best Czech fortresses and palaces easily rival the finest in Europe. They range from rambling ruins, crumbling away on hilltops, that reflect the strategic role the country played in central Europe in the Middle Ages, to gargantuan, sumptuous affairs financed by the enormous wealth accrued by the Habsburgs and their blue-blooded supporters in more recent history. A visit is one of the chief pleasures of any trip to the country.

Bouzov ▲

Hrubý Rohozec ▼

Whose castle is it?

Just like the Czech people themselves, stately homes in the Czech Republic have been through some turbulent times over the last century. The merry-go-round began in 1918 with the collapse of the Austro-Hungarian Empire, after which castles such as **Konopiště**, the lavishly furnished former home of the Archduke Franz Ferdinand, and all other Habsburg-owned properties were confiscated by the new republic. Twenty years later, the Nazis marched into Czechoslovakia and requisitioned numerous piles: they had a particular penchant for neo-Gothic fantasy castles like **Bouzov**. In 1945, many aristocratic families, like the Colloredo-Mansfeld family at **Opočno**, had their property expropriated either for being Nazi collaborators, or simply as ethnic Germans. In 1948, the Communists took over and appropriated all the country's remaining castles and chateaux, turning some into army barracks, prisons or colleges, and the rest into tourist attractions. Since 1989, many properties have been slowly returned to their pre-1948 owners (or their heirs), though most have stayed open to the public. Nevertheless, a tangle of lawsuits rumble on: Karel de Fours Walderode was recently cleared of Nazi collaboration and his heirs are currently hoping to reclaim the clifftop chateau of **Hrubý Rohozec**; the Kinský family have had less success and were recently declared to have been ethnic Germans. Most famously, the **Liechtenstein** royal family are still seeking to reclaim more than four thousand square kilometres of Czech territory, plus their attendant properties, including the vast neo-Gothic chateau of **Lednice**, taken from them in 1945.

Prague Castle

With so many dramatic castles and chateaux in the Czech countryside, it's easy to forget that probably the most impressive of all is **Prague Castle** (Pražský hrad), known to the Czechs simply as the Hrad. Not only does it dominate the capital's skyline, it also contains some of the city's best art and architecture from across the centuries, including the country's finest **cathedral**, a building that took nearly six hundred years to complete. More than any other castle in the country, the Hrad embodies the vicissitudes of Czech history. Parts of the complex, such as the **Basilica of sv Jiří**, date as far back as the twelfth century, while characteristic flourishes, like the fir-tree flag poles and the copper-canopied **Bull Staircase**, date only from the 1920s. The modern fanfare and the toy soldier costumes of the popular **Changing of the Guard** were devised only after the fall of Communism.

▲ Lednice

▼ Prague Castle

The Hrad has, of course, also been a seat of power for over a millennium, starting with the Přemyslid princes in the ninth century and continuing, since 1918, as the presidential palace. The early Bohemian kings were elected under the vast ribbed-vaulting of the **Vladislavský sál**, and the modern republic's presidents continue to be sworn in there. The Habsburg Emperor Rudolf II made the castle his main seat of power, and invited artists and alchemists from across Europe to his court – his legacy can be seen in the tiny houses of the **Zlata ulička** built into the walls to house the imperial guard, and in the remnants of his once great art collection. What's truly remarkable about Prague Castle, though, is that it remains a living, breathing institution and not a museum piece.

Kroměříž ▲

Jaroměřice nad Rokytnou ▼

Český Krumlov ▼

Top 10 castles and chateaux

▶▶ **Bouzov** (see p.363). Pompously impressive neo-Gothic castle that once belonged to the Teutonic Knights and was later used by the Nazi SS.

▶▶ **Český Krumlov** (see p.182). The Krumlovský zámek dominates this beautiful town, and boasts a perfectly preserved Rococo theatre.

▶▶ **Jaroměřice nad Rokytnou** (see p.335). Colossal Baroque chateau with formal gardens and its very own, vast, domed and frescoed church.

▶▶ **Jindřichův Hradec** (see p.172). This lakeside chateau has a triple-tiered Renaissance loggia and some very fine Italian stuccowork.

▶▶ **Kroměříž** (see p.349). Seat of the Bishop of Olomouc, this town chateau boasts some stunning Baroque interiors, and an impressive art collection.

▶▶ **Lednice** (see p.328). Without doubt the best of the region's neo-Gothic extrava-ganzas, with vast gardens, furnished with a mock-ruined castle and a minaret.

▶▶ **Nové Město nad Metují** (see p.286). What makes this seventeenth-century chateau stand out from the rest is the interior redecoration, undertaken by Slovak folk architect Dušan Jurkovič and Czech Cubist Pavel Janák from 1906 onwards.

▶▶ **Pernštejn** (see p.323). The most impressive medieval castle in Moravia, this late Gothic pile rises majestically above the treetops of the forests north-west of Brno.

▶▶ **Střekov** (see p.252). Inspiration for Wagner's opera *Tannhäuser*, this is the ultimate clifftop ruin, with awesome views over the River Labe (Elbe) and the city of Ústí nad Labem.

▶▶ **Vranov** (see p.333). Cliff-top zámek which contains a domed hall and a chapel by the outstanding Baroque architect Johann Bernhard Fischer von Erlach.

ⓦwww.turistapec.cz) in the centre of town handles the whole range of accommodation, including cheap rooms and chalets (*boudy*) that can make a nice escape from the crowds. There is also an information stand down the road from the bus station with an electronic board posting hotel and **pension** vacancies; you can call from the free telephone. One well-priced, comfortable option is *Penzion Veronika* (ⓣ499 736 135, ⓦwww.veronikapec.wz.cz; ❸), with its own restaurant, a short drive or steep ten-minute walk uphill to the west of the centre, beyond the eyesore that is the *Hotel Horizont*. *Pension Nikola* (ⓣ499 736 151, ⓦwww.nikolapec.cz; ❸), near the park information centre, is a little pricier. If you can pay more, the plush and central *Hotel Hořec* (ⓣ499 736 422, ⓕ499 736 424; ❺) is a good deal.

Many hotels and pensions have their own **restaurants**, and the *Hospoda na Peci* across from the Turista office provides a smoky mountain-lodge atmosphere to go with your cheap beer and goulash. Up the road toward the *Pension Nikola*, *Enzian Gril* is a tasty little pub and grill with outside tables around the back.

Janské Lázně

JANSKÉ LÁZNĚ (Johannisbad), hidden away in a sheltered, fertile valley on the southern edge of the national park, has a different atmosphere from the other resorts, and as such is probably the nicest and cheapest place to base yourself in the entire Krkonoše. Visitors tend to come here to take the cure rather than climb the surrounding peaks, although even the lazy can reach the top of Černá hora on the hourly cable car (8am–6pm). On a hot summer's day all the classic images of spa life converge on the stretch of lawn in front of the modest Kolonáda: a brass band plays oompah tunes in slightly lackadaisical fashion, while the elderly and disabled spill from the tearoom on to the benches outside. The best **place to stay** is the friendly, cosy *Villa Ludmila* (ⓣ499 875 260, ⓦwww.villa-ludmila.cz; ❷), followed by the more rustic *Lesní dům* (ⓣ499 875 385, ⓦwww.lesnidum.cz; ❷), which has a sauna and hot tub and its own **restaurant**.

Trutnov

The modern factories and housing complexes that ring Bohemia's easternmost textile town, **TRUTNOV** (Trautenau), signal the end of the national park, though the town is easily within striking distance of the Krkonoše and an equally good base for exploring the Adršpach and Teplice rocks (see p.282).

The busy arcaded main square, **Krakonošovo náměstí**, downstream and uphill from the railway station, has been beautifully restored. Alongside its plague column stands a fountain depicting Krakonoš (Rübezahl to the Germans), the sylvan spirit who guards the Giant Mountains and gave them their Czech name. Both are best appreciated from one of the cafés under the arcades of the main square. Perhaps Trutnov's biggest claim to fame is that in the early 1970s **Václav Havel** worked in the local brewery, which produces a very good beer called, predictably enough, Krakonoš. His experiences provided material for *Audience*, one of three plays centred around the character Vaněk (a lightly disguised version of himself). The brewery lies roughly halfway between the train station and the main square.

Practicalities

The **tourist office** (Mon–Fri 9am–6pm, Sat 9am–noon; ⓣ499 818 245, ⓦwww.trutnov.cz) in the radnice can point you towards **private rooms**, or you could try one of Trutnov's **hotels**: the *Grand* (ⓣ499 819 270, ⓦwww.grandtu.cz; ❸) has seen better days but is conveniently located on the main square; the nicer *Adam* (℡ 499 811 955, Ⓦ www.hotel-adam.cz; ④) has spacious, simple rooms in an arcaded house near the square on Havlíčkova. Both have their own **restaurants**; the *No. 1*, on Horská between the bus station and the square, is also recommended for good, cheap pub grub. The *Dolce Vita* **campsite** (all year; Ⓦ www.dolce.cz) is by a small lake, 4km southwest of Trutnov – take the blue-marked path from the centre of town. Trutnov's annual **open-air music festival** (mid-Aug; Ⓦ festivaltrutnov.cz) is the country's largest rock festival, featuring Czech bands and the odd headliner from the West.

East to Broumov

Between Trutnov and Broumov, some 30km east, lie two seemingly innocuous hilly strips smothered in trees, which only on much closer inspection reveal themselves to be riddled with sandstone protrusions and weird rock formations on the same lines as those in the Český ráj (see p.267). Distances here are small and the gradients gentle, making it ideal for a bit of none-too-strenuous – but no less spectacular – **hiking**. If you want to explore the rocks, get hold of the detailed *Teplicko-Adršpašské skály/Broumovské stěny* **map** before you start; it shows all the colour-coded footpaths and campsites. Local **buses** do serve the more out-of-the-way places like Broumov, but it's worth taking advantage of the slow but scenic **train** service from Trutnov to Teplice nad Metují, via Adršpach.

The Adršpach and Teplice rocks

The **Adršpach and Teplice rocks** (Teplicko-Adršpašské skály), 15km east of Trutnov, rise up out of the pine forest like petrified phalluses. Some even take trees with them as they launch themselves into the air. German tourists have flocked here since the nineteenth century, though nowadays they are outnumbered by Czech rock climbers and ramblers. The rocks are concentrated in two separate *skalní města* (rock "cities"): the Adršpach rocks, just south of the village of the same name, and the Teplice rocks, 2km south through the woods. The latter can also be approached from the villages of Janovice or Teplice **nad Metují**.

Adršpach

ADRŠPACH (Adersbach) train station (one stop on from Horní Adršpach) lies at the northern extremity of the rock system, though you can't really miss it, since some of the rocks have crept right up to the station itself. There are two entrances close to each other (open roughly till dusk; 60Kč), and a nearby kiosk with the **tourist office** (Mon–Fri 7–11.30am & noon–3pm; Ⓦ www.skalyadrspach.cz). Once through the perimeter fence, the outside world recedes and you're surrounded by new sensations – sand underfoot, the scent of pine, boulders and shady trees. Most of the sandstone rocks are dangerous to climb without the correct equipment and experience, so you'll probably have to content yourself with strolling and gawping at the formations best described by their nicknames: Babiččina lenoška (Grandmother's Armchair), Španělská stěna (Spanish Wall) and the ironic Trpaslík (Dwarf).

The green-marked path winds its way along and over a stream, through narrow clefts between the rocks, eventually bringing you to a couple of waterfalls (*vodopády*). From here, steps hewn out of the rock lead up to the Adršpašské jezírko, a lake trapped above ground level between the rocks, where jovial boatmen pole you along in rafts a short distance to the other side. From here,

▲ Adršpach rocks

the yellow-marked path continues through the woods for 2km to the entrance to the Teplice rocks (see below). If you fancy a swim or a spot of nude bathing, head for the Pískovna lake to the east of the Adršpach entrance, with its dramatic backdrop of craggy rocks and pine trees. The *Hotel Lesní zátiší* (☎491 586 202; ❸), by the entrance to the rocks, offers decent **rooms** and **food**. More comfortable is the *Pension Adršpach* (☎491 586 102, ⓦwww.adrspach-skaly .cz; ❸), on the road to Teplice nad Metují, which also has a restaurant.

Teplice

The easiest approach for the **Teplické skalní město** is from Teplice nad Metují-skály station, just across the river from the entrance (usually open until 6pm, June–Aug till 8pm; ⓦwww.teplickeskaly.cz; 50Kč) to the rocks. A blue-marked path heads west for 2km, after which you reach the Anenské údolí, the main valley of the *skalní město* – another theatrical burst of geological abnormalities that form a narrow valley of rocks. Right by the woods' edge you can also explore the rock fortress of **Střmen**, which once served as a Hussite hideout (accessible by a system of ladders and steps). The *Hotel Orlík* (☎491 581 025, ⓦorlik.hotel-cz.com; ❷) is next to the entrance to the rocks, though you'd be better off heading for the well-run and friendly *Penzion U Skalního potoka* (☎491 581 317, ⓦwww.penzion.adrspach.cz; ❸), which has six pleasant rooms behind the ticket office (best to reserve at least several days in advance).

Alternatively, **TEPLICE NAD METUJÍ** (Wekelsdorf) itself, 2km east, is a functional base, with a supermarket, a cinema, several pensions and a couple of hotels. There's also the *Bučnice* **campsite** (May–Sept; ⓦwww.autokemp.wz.cz), 1km up the road from Teplice nad Metují-skály station. If you're a keen rock climber, then the long-running **Festival of Mountaineering Films** (Medzinárodní horolezecký filmový festival; ⓦwww.teplicenadmetuji.cz), held here on the last weekend of August, is well worth checking out. Though basically an excuse for a lot of boozing and boasting, it attracts people from all over Europe who come to share their experiences, many demonstrating their skills on the local formations.

Broumov

BROUMOV (Braunau), a predominantly German-speaking town before the war, 30km due east of Trutnov, is probably the best place to base yourself if you're thinking of exploring the Broumov walls. The town is particularly impressive from a distance, with its colossal Baroque **Benediktinský klášter**, perched on a sandstone pedestal above the River Stěnava. The monastery was used by the Communists to incarcerate much of the country's Benedictine priesthood after 1948, most of whom passed their remaining days here. During the 1960s numerous nuns were also imprisoned here – up to 300 at one point – and forced to labour in local factories and fields, until they too eventually died. This sad recent past seems to echo throughout the monastery, which stands mostly unused and lonely. Hourly guided **tours** (April–Oct Tues–Sat 9–11am & 1–4pm, Sun 10–11am & 2–4pm; 65Kč) lead through the stunning Baroque chapel, designed by Kilian Ignaz Dientzenhofer, Bohemia's foremost ecclesiastical architect, who lived here from 1727 to 1738; it features paintings by his contemporary Vratislav Vavřinec Reiner. Upstairs, the musty library contains what is said to be the only copy of the Shroud of Turin in central Europe.

Before leaving town, take time to look at the Silesian fourteenth-century **wooden church** (the oldest in the country) on the Křinice road out of the centre. With a car and a passion for **Baroque churches**, you could also happily spend a morning exploring the local Stěnava valley, with its numerous churches designed in the eighteenth century by Dientzenhofer.

Practicalities

The **train** and **bus stations** lie close to each other five- to ten-minutes' walk southeast of the old town. Set in its own grounds to the southwest of the centre off Šalounova and with an excellent restaurant, the *Hotel Veba* (☎491 580 211, ⓦwww.hotel.veba.cz; ❸) is the best **place to stay**. More central is the Communist-era *Hotel Praha* (☎491 523 786, ⓦwww.hotel-praha.cz; ❸) on the main square. In the radnice, a couple of doors to the left, the **tourist office** (May & Sept Mon–Fri 8am–4pm, June–Aug Mon–Sat 8am–noon, Oct–April Mon–Thurs 8am–4pm, Fri 8am–3pm; ⓦwww.broumov.net) can help with private rooms. Try to sample the local beer, Opat, if the **restaurants** at *Veba* and *Praha* still offer it – the larger national brands are doing a good job of taking over pub menus. If you follow the red-marked trail heading southwest to the chapel of Panna Maria Sněžná (2hr) you'll find a nineteenth-century mountain hut with an atmospheric restaurant (closed Mon & Tues) serving simple, hearty food.

The Broumov walls

The **Broumov walls** (Broumovské stěny) make up a thin sandstone ridge that almost cuts Broumov off from the rest of the country. From the west, there's no indication of the approaching precipice, from which a wonderful vista sweeps out over to Broumov and beyond into Poland, but from the east, the ridge is clearly spread out before you. The best place to appreciate the view is from Dientzenhofer's chapel of **Panna Maria Sněžná**, in among the boulders at the edge of the big drop. The best rock formations are 9km south of here, close to the highest point of the wall, **Božanovský Špičák** (733m), only a few hundred metres from the Polish border. You can approach the Dientzenhofer chapel from either Police nad Metují, 5km to the southwest, or Broumov, 6km to the east. To get to the rocks around Božanovský Špičák, take the bus from Police to Machov, or the train from Broumov to Božanov, and walk the final 3.5km.

Náchod and around

Cowering at the base of its large, lordly seat, built to guard the gateway to Bohemia from Silesia, **NÁCHOD** is one of the few Czech border towns that has been predominantly Czech for most of its life. Even the Nazis stopped short of annexing it when they marched into the Sudetenland in 1938, since at the time there were only four German-speaking families in the whole town. Nowadays, most people just stop off in order to break the journey and spend their last remaining crowns en route to Poland. Although the Polish border is a couple of kilometres east of the town centre, Náchod actually makes a useful base for exploring the surrounding area, including the two exceptional **chateaux** at Nové Město nad Metují and Opočno.

The town is a lot better looking than your average border town: the main square, **náměstí T.G. Masaryka**, in particular, looks striking. Its two most winsome buildings are the fourteenth-century church of **sv Vavřinec** (St Lawrence) at the centre, its entrance flanked by two fat square towers sporting comically large wooden onion domes, and the Art Nouveau *Hotel U beránka*, with sinewy lines and detailed mosaic lettering and interior light fittings. At one corner of the square, the town **museum** (Tues–Sun 9am–noon & 1–5pm; 30Kč) has a quite good display on local history that includes folk dress and dioramas describing the 1866 Austro-Prussian wars waged in the area.

Peeking out of the foliage, high above the town, and a very stiff climb from the main square, is Náchod's sprawling, unassailable, sgraffitoed **zámek** (March & Nov Sat & Sun 10am–4pm *malý okruh* only; April & Oct Sat & Sun 10am–4pm; May–Aug Tues–Sun 9am–5pm; Sept Tues–Sun 9am–4pm). The original Gothic structure survives only in the pretty round tower in the centre; everything else is the result of building projects spanning the Renaissance and Baroque periods. There's a choice of two guided tours: the first-floor Piccolomini tour (*1 okruh*; 75Kč) includes exhibits accrued over the centuries by descendants of the Italian Ottavio Piccolomini-Pieri, Waldstein's bodyguard, who was given the castle by Ferdinand II after informing the emperor of Waldstein's secret plans (see p.272), while the second-floor tour (*2 okruh*; 70Kč) focuses on the the castle art collection courtesy of the exiled Duke of Kurland, and takes you round the Russian paintings (see below). The *malý okruh* (short tour; 15Kč) allows unguided access to the tower, the dungeons and the viewing terrace.

The former riding school, or **jízdárna** (Tues–Sun 9am–noon & 1–5pm), beyond the bear-inhabited moat by the car park, houses a surprisingly healthy collection of **Russian paintings**. The highlights include two finely studied female portraits by Ilya Repin, the most famous of the "Wanderers" who broke away from the official Russian academy of art, better known for his epic works filled with fiery bearded figures like the *Trial of Christ*. The leader of the Wanderers, Ivan Kramskoy, is responsible for the superbly aloof portrait of an aristocratic lady in a carriage, with a St Petersburg palace as a backdrop. Also on display are works by Serov and Makovsky, but best of all by far are the wildly colourful depictions of peasant women by turn-of-the-twentieth-century artist Filip Malyavin, who was a lay brother on Mount Athos in Greece before he took up painting full-time.

Náchod practicalities

The town's **train** and **bus stations** are both five-minutes' walk east of the centre, at the end of Kamenice. The **tourist office** (Mon–Fri 8am–5.30pm, Sat 8.30–11.30am; ☎491 420 420, ⊛www.icnachod.cz), in a travel agency near the

The Cowards in Náchod

The exiled writer **Josef Škvorecký** was born and bred in Náchod – a "narrow cleavage between the mountains", as he characteristically dubbed it. During his wartime adolescence he was joined by film-director-to-be **Miloš Forman**, then only a young boy, who came to stay with his uncle when his parents were sent to a concentration camp from which they never returned. Later, in the cultural thaw of the 1960s, before they were both forced to emigrate, the two men planned (unsuccessfully) to make a film based on *The Cowards*, Škvorecký's most famous novel. Set in "a small Bohemian town" (ie Náchod) in the last few days of the war, the book caused a sensation when it was published (briefly) in 1958 because of its bawdy treatment of Czech resistance to the Nazis. Škvorecký also set the action of a later novel, *The Miracle Game*, in the nearby village of Hronov. In both novels, and in *The Engineer of Human Souls*, the name of the main character is Danny Smiřický, after Náchod's local aristo family.

square at Kamenice 144, should be able to help with **accommodation**. *U beránka* (☎491 433 118, ⓦ www.hotel-beranek.cz; ❸) is a comfortable option and probably the town's greatest institution: a hotel, café, theatre and restaurant (serving the local Primátor beer as well as traditional Czech food) in one. The nearby *U města Prahy* (☎491 421 817, ⓦ web.quick.cz/hotpraha; ❷) is a simple, reasonably priced hotel, also with a restaurant and *vinárna*. Náchod's pretty riverside **campsite** (mid-May to mid-Sept) is by the woods 1.5km east of the centre, signposted down Běloveská.

Nové Město nad Metují

NOVÉ MĚSTO NAD METUJÍ, 9km south of Náchod, has a stunning old town square, with one of the country's most interesting chateaux crouched in one corner. While the town's modern quarter sprawls unattractively over the lower ground, the staré město sits quietly – and prettily – on a high spur hemmed in by the River Metuje, a tributary of the River Labe. Restored sixteenth-century houses line each side of the rectangular arcaded main square, **Husovo náměstí**; the set of cream-coloured gables along the north side are the most photographed.

What makes Nové Město's old town extra special is its remarkable seventeenth-century **zámek** (April & Oct Sat & Sun 9am–4pm; May, June & Sept Tues–Sun 9am–4pm; July & Aug daily 9am–5pm; 50Kč/80Kč), which looks out across the Labe basin (known as the Polabí) from the northeast corner of the square. After piecemeal alterations, it fell into disrepair in the nineteenth century, until the industrialist Josef Bartoň bought the place in 1908 and commissioned the quirky Slovak architect **Dušan Jurkovič** to entirely redesign it – which he did, most notably with the timber-framed structures, redolent of his native land, in the terraced gardens (May–Sept), and the bizarre wall-to-wall leather vaulting of the Žebrový sál (Ribbed Hall). The other rooms are lavishly furnished in every period from the original Renaissance to Cubism, including highly unusual works by Czech Cubists like **Pavel Janák**. Bartoň eventually died here in 1951, at the ripe old age of 98. In an uncharacteristically magnanimous gesture, the Communists had allowed him and his wife (and their cook) to live out their last days in three rooms at the top of the chateau. The place is now back in the hands of the Bartoň family, who live here and run it with great efficiency. Check out the set of dwarves by the Baroque sculptor Braun, standing along the terrace and bridge across the moat, and for a great view over the square and gardens, climb the castle's tower (this can be done without a guide).

An extra treat is on hand in the outlying village of **Slavoňov**, where a precious little wooden church, dating from 1533, boasts an exquisite wood-panelled interior, virtually all its surfaces painted in simple, rich designs. The flat ceiling panels are each distinct, while the almost cartoon-like paintings on the choir depict local scenes and nobility. Ask the tourist office in Nové Město to call ahead to the friar's office so that someone will be on hand to let you in. To get to Slavoňov, follow the yellow-marked path 4km through the woods from Nové Město's main square, or catch the occasional bus which leaves from there too.

Practicalities

Nové Město nad Metují is a beautiful eight-kilometre **walk** from Náchod down the winding River Metuje (yellow-marked path, followed by red). If you arrive by **train**, you'll end up 2km northwest of the chateau, in Nové Město's new town; infrequent local buses link the old town square with the station, or you can follow the blue markers. Coming by **bus** from Náchod or Hradec Králové, you can alight at Husovo náměstí itself. The **tourist office** (May–Sept Mon–Fri 8am–5pm, Sat & Sun 9am–noon & 1–5pm; Oct–April Tues–Fri 8am–5pm, Sat & Sun 1–4pm; Ⓦwww.muzeum-nmnm.cz/infocentrum.htm), diagonally opposite the zámek, can set you up in a private room or nearby **pension**. There's another branch in the modern art gallery Zázvorka, just off the square. *Hotel U Broučka* (☎491 472 571; ❷), on Husovo náměstí offers simple en-suite rooms and a pleasant **restaurant**.

Opočno

Ten kilometres south of Nové Město nad Metují is the town of **OPOČNO**, whose **zámek** (April & Oct Sat & Sun 9–11.30am & 12.30–4pm; May, June & Sept Tues–Sun 9–11.30am & 12.30–5pm; July & Aug closes 6pm) is spectacularly poised on a knife's edge above the Polabí plain. The main attraction is the triple-decker loggia, built in the sixteenth century by Italian architects around the chateau's three-sided courtyard. Clinging to the chateau's foundations is the lovely wooded **zámecký park** (daily: April–Sept 7am–8pm; Oct–March 8am–3pm; free) with a summer palace or *letohrádek* used for art exhibitions. All this, and the view, can be appreciated without having to take either of the guided tours, though it would be a shame to miss these if you've made it this far. The short tour (60Kč) takes you round beautifully restored rooms containing sundry precious possessions of the Colloredo family, who owned the place until 1945; the last remaining family member is in the process of reacquiring it. On the long tour (90Kč) you also get to visit Opočno's famous armoury: a priceless collection of rifles, swords, a Roman helmet and even a well-worn chastity belt.

Buses are the most direct means of getting to Opočno; several connect with Hradec Králové daily. The **train** station (Opočno pod Orlickými horami) is a good 2km below the town to the west. Of **places to stay**, *Hotel Jordánek* (☎494 667 555, Ⓦwww.jordanek.cz; ❶–❷), quietly located at Nádražní 447, on the road to the train station, offers decent en suites with TV; it also has a pleasant (and popular in the evenings) **restaurant** serving traditional food.

The Babiččino údolí

Some 10km west of Náchod by train, the town of **ČESKÁ SKALICE** marks the beginning of the Úpa Valley, better known as the **Babiččino údolí** after the novel that has made it famous, *Babička* (Grandmother) by **Božena Němcová**

(1820–62). A precise and realistic portrait of Czech peasant life in the mid-nineteenth century, dominated by the kindly wisdom of the story's grandmother figure, the tale is still required reading for Czechs of all ages. Němcová's tragic life is almost as well known as the tale itself: forced to marry at 17 to a man more than twice her age, Němcová wrote, "The years of my childhood were the most beautiful of my life. When I married I wept over my lost liberty, over the dreams and ideals forever ruined". Moving in Czech republican and literary circles in the 1840s, she caused outrage with her numerous passionate and very public affairs. Her independent spirit, her championing of women's education and her involvement in the 1848 revolution have endeared her to many Czech women. Nowadays, she is still a household name, and one of the few Czech women to have entered the country's literary canon.

There are several museums dedicated to Němcová in the area, two in Česká Skalice itself. The first is in her old schoolhouse, the timber-framed **Barunčina škola** (May & June Tues–Sun 8am–5pm; July & Aug daily 9am–5pm; Sept Tues–Sun 9am–4pm), northwest off the main square up B. Němcové; the second is in the former pub, *U bílého českého lva*, in which she got married, now part of the town's **Textilní muzeum** (Textile Museum; same hours plus Oct–April Mon–Fri 8am–3pm; ⓦ www.bozenanemcova.cz), further up B. Němcové and across the river. Her **birthplace** in Červený Kostelec, 8km north of Česká Skalice, is also now a museum (times as for the škola). Perhaps the most rewarding for non-Czech-speakers is **Ratibořice**, 2.5km north of Česká Skalice (April & Oct Sat & Sun 10am–3pm; May & Sept Tues–Sun 9am–4pm; June–Aug Tues–Sun 9am–5pm; tours only), the pretty little pink chateau with green shutters where Němcová's father was equerry, and her mother laundress.

You can also explore the gentle **valley** that was her childhood haunt and the main inspiration for the book – a very beautiful place in its own right.

Hradec Králové

Capital of East Bohemia and the largest city on the fertile plain known as the Polabí, **HRADEC KRÁLOVÉ** (Königgrätz) has a typically handsome historical quarter, paid for by the rich trade that used to pass through en route to Silesia. But there's another side to the town, too. To the west of the medieval centre is one of the great urban projects of the interwar Republic, built by the leading modern Czech architects of the day. The two towns don't really blend in with one another – in fact, they barely communicate – and these days the staré město is more like a museum piece. Even if you don't particularly take to the new town, it's a fascinating testimony to the early optimism of the First Republic, and gives the whole of Hradec Králové a unique, expansive and prosperous atmosphere.

Hradec Králové spreads itself out on both banks of the Labe: on the left bank, the **staré město** (old town) sits on an oval rock between the Labe and the Orlice rivers; the **nové město** (new town) begins as soon as you leave the old town, straddling the river and then composing itself in fairly logical fashion between the river and the station to the west.

Arrival, information and accommodation

The **train** and **bus** stations are in the nové město. To reach the staré město, take bus #5, #6, #11, #15 or #17, all of which plough down Gočárova, or trolleybus

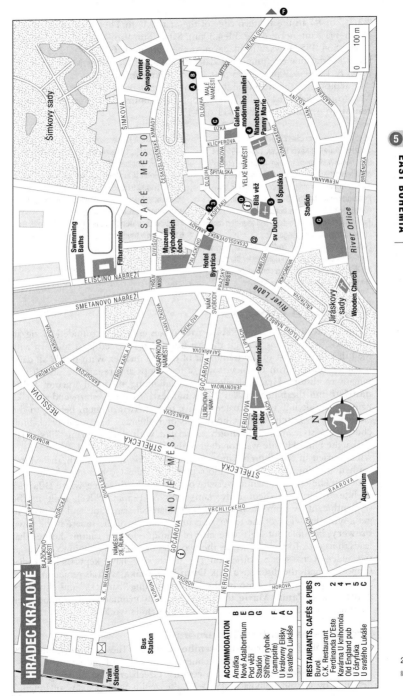

HRADEC KRÁLOVÉ

Train Station

Bus Station

Šimkovy sady

Swimming Baths

Filharmonie

STARÉ MĚSTO

Former Synagogue

Galerie moderního umění

Nanebevzeti Panny Marie

Muzeum východních čech

Hotel Bystrica

Bilá věž

sv Duch

U Špulaků

Stadión

River Orlice

Jiráskovy sady

Wooden Church

Ambrožův sbor

Gymnázium

NOVÉ MĚSTO

Aquarium

River Labe

ACCOMMODATION

Amátka	B
Nové Adalbertinum	E
Pod věží	D
Stadión	G
Stříbrný rybník (campsite)	F
U královny Elišky	A
U svatého Lukáše	C

RESTAURANTS, CAFÉS & PUBS

Buvol	3
C.K. Restaurant	
Ferdinanda D'Este	2
Kavárna U knihomola	4
Old England pub	1
U čányfuka	5
U svatého Lukáše	C

#2, #3 or #7 to the western edge of the Staré Město. There's a **tourist office** (Mon–Fri 8am–noon & 12.30–4.30pm, Sat & Sun 9am–noon & 12.30–3pm; ☏ 495 534 485, ✪ www.ic-hk.cz) near the stations at Gočarova 1225, with a more central branch (June–Sept daily 10am–4pm; Oct–May Mon–Fri 8am–noon & 12.30–4.30pm; ☏ 495 580 492) at Velké náměstí 165.

In addition to the **hotels** and pensions, the *Stříbrný rybník* **campsite** (mid-May to mid-Sept), by a lake, is very popular in summer. It has cabins and **bike rental**. To get there, take bus #11 or #17.

Accommodation

Penzion Amátka Kavčí Plácek 120 ☏ 495 514 935, ✪ www.sweb.cz/amatka. A simple, cheap pension at the corner of the Malé náměstí, the quieter of the two main squares in the old town. ❷
Penzion Nové Adalbertinum Velké nám. 32 ☏ 495 063 111, ✪ www.noveadalbertinum.cz. Tastefully refurbished doubles and four-bed rooms in the former Jesuit college. ❸
Pod věží Velké náměstí ☏ 495 514 932, ✪ www .pod-vezi.cz. Little pension right under the tower (as its name states), offering comfortable, airy rooms overlooking the square. ❸

Hotel Stadión Komenského 1214 ☏ 495 514 664. A basic hotel just outside the staré město by the ice hockey stadium. ❷
🏃 **Hotel U královny Elišky** Malé nám. 117 ☏ 495 518 052, ✪ www.hotel -ukralovnyelisky.info. An excellent four-star hotel with sauna, next door to *Amátka*. ❻
Penzion U svatého Lukáše Úzká 208 ☏ 495 518 616, ✪ www.usvateholukase.com. Another nice place with rooms around a quiet courtyard, just off the main square. ❸

The staré město

In the eighteenth century, the **staré město** was entirely surrounded by zigzag red-brick fortifications, though they've now been replaced by a modern ring road that keeps most of the traffic out of the old quarter. With nearly all daily business conducted in the new town, a few shops and restaurants are all that remain to disturb Hradec Králové's two adjoining medieval squares, **Velké náměstí** and the much smaller **Malé náměstí**. At the western end of Velké náměstí, the skyline is punctuated by five towers. Two of them belong to the church of **sv Duch** (Holy Ghost), one of Bohemia's few great brick-built churches, a style more commonly associated with neighbouring Silesia. Jan Žižka, the blind Hussite warrior, died of the plague here in 1424, and was for a while buried in this church. Given its grand Gothic scale, though, the white-washed interior, filled for the most part with neo-Gothic furnishings, is a letdown. The church's twin towers are outreached by the once-white **Bílá věž** (White Tower; April–Sept daily 9am–noon & 1–5pm; 25Kč), built in the sixteenth century from the profits of Bohemian–Silesian trade, and *the* place to get a bird's-eye view of the town. Also in this corner of the square is the town **brewery**, invisible but for the terrace of Baroque former canons' houses that leads to its gate. To the east, where the two sides of the square begin to converge, the older Renaissance houses on the north side have kept their arcades. Opposite stands the distinctive pink **Dům U Špuláka**, with its projecting oriel and copper dome, and, close by, the Jesuits' Baroque "barracks" and church of **Nanebevzetí Panny Marie**, the latter beautifully maintained, its trompe l'oeil altarpiece providing a suitable repository for Brandl's work.

The Galerie moderního umění

Hradec Králové's **Galerie moderního umění** (Tues–Sun 9am–noon & 1–6pm; 30Kč), opposite the Jesuit church, houses one of the country's finest permanent collections of twentieth-century Czech art. The building itself – designed by Osvald Polívka in 1910–12, the genius behind many of Prague's finest Art Nouveau structures – is also a treat: five storeys high, with a large, oval glass-roofed atrium at the centre.

The ground floor is given over to temporary exhibitions, while on the first floor the collection of works by fin-de-siècle artists is entirely in keeping with its surroundings. Among the highlights are a couple of lesser-known **Mucha** drawings, an early **Kupka**, and a whole series by **Jan Preisler**, including a study for the mural which now adorns the former *Hotel Bystrica*. The unexpected pleasure is **Josef Váchal**'s work, in particular the mysterious *Satanic Invocation* (*Vzývaci d'abla*), which spills over onto its carved wooden frame. Several wood sculptures by **Bílek** and three bronze reliefs by **Sucharda** make for a fairly comprehensive overview of Czech Secessionist art. The floor ends with the beginnings of the Czech obsession with Cubism, most famously **Emil Filla**'s own version of *Les Demoiselles d'Avignon* and *Salome's Dance*.

The second floor is dominated by Czech Cubist and Fauvist painters, interspersed with a few from the Realist and Surrealist schools prominent in the 1920s. **Josef Šíma**'s semi-surreal work is probably the most original (he was a member of the avant-garde group *Devětsil*), though only two canvases and a pen-and-ink sketch are on display. Postwar art up to 1968 is the subject of the third floor, interesting if only for the fact that many of the artists, like **Mikuláš Medek**, have only relatively recently been exhibited in public galleries. The views from the top floor should be incentive enough to get you up there, along with more post-1968 material, like the psychedelic *Přátelé*; patently political works, however, like *Red Wall* (*Červená zeď*) are the exception. Surrealism was always frowned upon, hence artists like **Jiří Kolář**, two of whose classic collages are shown here, are much better known in the West.

The nové město

Most of what you now see outside the old town is the result of an architectural master plan outlined between 1909 and 1911, though much of the work wasn't carried out until the 1920s. Building began on a grand scale with the **Muzeum východních čech** (Tues–Sun 9am–5pm; ⓦ www.muzeumhk.cz; 50Kč) on the leafy waterfront, designed by the father of the Czech modern movement, **Jan Kotěra**. With the rest of central Europe still under the hold of the Viennese Secession, Kotěra's museum, crowned with one of his characteristic domes, represents a shot across the bows of contemporary taste, finished in what was at the time an unconventional mixture of red brick and concrete rendering. The entrance is guarded by two colossal sphynx-like janitors, but otherwise the ornamentation is low-key – as is the exhibition inside, a straightforward though attractive display of nineteenth- and twentieth-century arts and crafts, books and posters, plus a model of the town from 1865, showing the fortifications intact. Kotěra is also responsible for the distinctive **Pražský most** (Prague Bridge), with its squat kiosks at either end and wrought-iron arch decorated with fairy lights.

Further down the Labe embankment is the Hradec Králové Filharmonie building, a stern structure that hosts a good orchestral concert series. Just beyond is an excellent **swimming pool**, designed in the 1920s, equipped with an artificial wave machine, sauna, massage parlour and, of course, a pub.

Gočár's new town

Kotěra died shortly after World War I, and it was left to one of his pupils, **Josef Gočár**, to complete the construction of the new town. Gočár had been among the foremost exponents of Czech Cubist architecture before the war, but, along with Pavel Janák, he changed tack in the 1920s and attempted to establish a specifically Czechoslovak style of architecture that incorporated prewar Cubism. It was dubbed "Rondo-Cubism" because of its recurrent semicircular motifs, and though few projects got off the ground, elements of the style are reflected in the appealing homogeneity of the new town. On a sunny day, the pastel shades of the buildings provide a cool and refreshing backdrop; bad weather brings out the brutalism that underlies much of Gočár's work.

This brutalism is most evident in his largest commission, the **Státní gymnázium** on the right bank, a sprawling series of buildings with an L-shaped, four-storey, red-brick structure, fronted by an atypically slender bronze nude by Jan Štursa. Up the side of the school, on V lipkách, is a later, still more uncompromising work, the Protestant **Ambrožův sbor**, built in functionalist style on a striking angular site. But by far Gočár's most successful set-piece is **Masarykovo náměstí**, two blocks north, which basks in the sun at the heart of the new town, shaped like a big slice of lemon sponge, with a pivotal statue of Masaryk back in its rightful place after a forty-year absence. If you're travelling by train, be sure to admire the **train station**'s splendidly modernist design, again by Gočár, in particular the slimline 1930s clock tower.

Hradec Králové's mini **aquarium** (Obří akvárium; Tues–Sun 9am–6pm; July & Aug also Mon 11am–4pm; ⓦwww.obriakvarium.cz; 90Kč) is at Baarova 10, a ten-minute walk south of the new town in an otherwise faceless neighbourhood. Its centrepiece is a walk-through glass tunnel in a tank of Amazonian fish, while a small construction of a rainforest helps you forget briefly that you're still in central Europe.

Eating, drinking and nightlife

In addition to the **restaurants** in the pensions, of which the tasteful *U svatého Lukáše* is the best, there are plenty of places in the old town dishing up the usual plain but filling food. For a Habsburg Empire atmosphere try *C.K. Restaurant Ferdinanda D'Este*, on V Kopečku, with tables on a little patio. Another pleasant option is the *U čáryfuka* (closed Sun), an elegant restaurant with a vast menu in the shadow of the church of sv Duch. *Kavárna U knihomola* (At the Bookworm), opposite the modern art gallery, makes a soothingly hip spot for coffee or a light lunch. **Nightlife** is rather slow, but the *Buvol* on V Kopečku is a lively Czech-Irish pub open until 2am and the *Old England* pub, also on V Kopečku, is open nonstop.

Around Hradec Králové

The flat expanse around Hradec Králové, known as the **Polabí**, is a fertile region whose hedgeless cornfields stretch as far as the eye can see. It's dreary to look at, baking hot in summer and covered in a misty drizzle most of the winter, but there are several places worth a day-trip or overnight stop within easy reach of Hradec Králové by bus or train.

Třebechovice and Častolovice

TŘEBECHOVICE POD OREBEM, 11km east of Hradec Králové along route 11, is a nondescript town, famous only for its wood-carved Nativity scene or *Betlém*, housed in a purpose-built **museum** (Tues–Sun: May–Sept 9am–noon & 1–5pm; Oct–April closes 4pm; ⓦwww.betlem.cz; 50Kč). It all began in 1871, when local joiner Josef Probošt and his wood-carving friend, Josef Kapucián, set out to create the largest Nativity scene in the world. Only the death of Kapucián forty years later brought the project to an end, by which time the two men had carved 400 moving figures, many of them modelled on their friends and neighbours. If you think that's kitsch, take a look at the museum's other room, which displays *Betlém* scenes in glass, pottery and paper.

Eighteen kilometres on is the Renaissance chateau of **Častolovice** (April & Oct Sat & Sun 9am–6pm; May–Sept Tues–Sun 9am–6pm; ⓦwww.zamek -castolovice.cz), recently returned to the Šternberk family, who acquired it back in 1694. It's a hybrid pile, right by route 11, with a huge English-style park stretching away to the north. The inner courtyard is particularly beautiful, as is the glorious Rytířský sál (Knights' Hall), with a Renaissance painted panel ceiling and portraits of various regional noblemen.

Jaroměř and Josefov

JAROMĚŘ, 36km northeast of Hradec Králové and accessible by train, is a pleasant enough town with a curving cobbled square. The main attraction is one of Gočár's early works, the **Wenke department store**, on route 33, the busy main road from Hradec Králové to the Polish border. In this exceedingly unpromising street (now called Husova) in 1911, Gočár undertook one of the first self-conscious experiments in Cubist architecture. It's an imaginative, eclectic work, quite unlike the much plainer Cubism of Prague's Vyšehrad villas or the nearby spa of Bohdaneč, the plate-glass facade topped by a Neoclassical upper floor and the monochrome, geometric interior still intact. Instead of selling goods, it now serves as the **Městské muzeum a galerie** (April–Nov Tues–Fri 9am–5pm, Sat & Sun 1–5pm), its tiny art gallery displaying works by all three of Jaroměř's home-grown artists: the sculptors Otakar Španiel and Josef Wagner, and the *Devětsil* painter Josef Šíma, whose wilfully optimistic painting of Jaroměř is just one of a number of his works on show. If you want to **stay**, try one of the hotels on the square: *Hotel 28* (☎491 815 311; ❷), with decent, clean rooms and a pizzeria; or the basic *U dvou jelenů* (☎491 815 230; ❶).

One kilometre south of Jaroměř, where the Labe and the Metuje rivers converge, is the fortress town of **JOSEFOV** (Josefstadt). In the 1780s the Habsburgs created three fortified towns along the northern border with their new enemy, Prussia: Hradec Králové (which has since lost its walls), Terezín and Josefov – the last two purpose-built from scratch and preserved as they were. Terezín was put to terrible use by the Nazis during World War II (see p.244), but Josefov remains the great white elephant of the empire, never having witnessed a single battle. Their mutual designs are unerringly similar: two fortresses (one large, one small), identikit eighteenth-century streets, and a grid plan whose monotony is broken only by the imposing **Empire Church** on the main square. Again like Terezín, Josefov is still a garrison town, though there aren't many soldiers left; the empty buildings have mostly been taken over by Roma families. Though not a great day out, it's worth taking a stroll along the thick zigzag trail of red-brick fortifications, now topped by beautiful tree-lined paths, with views across the wheat fields of the Polabí. If you're really keen, you can even visit the town's **underground tunnel system**, where costumed soldiers lead you through claustrophobic candle-lit passageways; follow the signs to the Podzemí (April & Oct Sat & Sun 9am–noon & 1–4pm; May–Sept Tues–Sun 9am–noon & 1–5pm).

Kuks and around

Magnificently poised above a rustic village of timber-framed cottages, the great complex of Baroque spa buildings at **KUKS**, 5km north of Jaroměř, on the banks of the Labe, was the creation of the enlightened Bohemian dilettante Count Franz Anton Graf von Sporck (Špork in Czech). Work began, largely according to Sporck's own designs, in the 1690s, after the discovery of a nearby mineral spring with healing properties – by 1730 he had created his own private **spa resort**, with a garden maze, a hospital, a concert hall (complete with its own orchestra) and a racecourse (surrounded by statues of dwarves). For a while, Kuks' social life was on a par with the likes of Karlsbad; then, in 1738, the impresario died, and on December 22, 1740, disaster struck when the river broke its banks, destroying all the buildings on the left bank and, worse still, the springs themselves.

All that remains of the original spa is an overgrown monumental stairway leading nowhere, and, on the right bank, the hospital building fronted by **Matthias Bernhard Braun**'s famous terrace, now the chief reason for visiting Kuks. Sporck became the Tyrolean sculptor's chief patron in Bohemia, commissioning from him a series of **allegorical statues** intended to elevate the minds of his spa guests: to the west, the twelve *Vices* culminate in the grim *Angel of Grievous Death*; to the east, the twelve *Virtues* end with the *Angel of Blessed Death*. Over the years the elements have not been kind to Braun's work, whose originals, including a few surviving dwarves, have retreated inside the hospital building and now provide the highlight of the 45-minute guided tour (April & Oct Sat & Sun 9am–noon & 1–3pm; May–Aug Tues–Sun until 5pm; Sept Tues–Sun until 4pm). Also on the tour is the beautifully restored eighteenth-century pharmacy and Baroque chapel; Sporck's subterranean mausoleum is no longer on show.

There's a good **restaurant**, *Zámecká vinárna*, next to the zámek, ladling out huge portions of meat and gravy. Buses will either drop you at the main road, a short walk north of the village, or in the village itself; the **train station** lies to the south, behind the hospital building and formal gardens (follow the blue-marked path).

Betlém

One stop along the tracks, or a steep 5km walk along the blue-marked path, upriver from Kuks, is **Betlém** (Bethlehem), Braun's outdoor Nativity sculpture park, again sponsored by Sporck. It's an unlikely, ingenious location, deep in the midst of a silver birch wood, and used to include several working springs, including one that shot water high up into the foliage. However, centuries of neglect, pilfering and weathering have taken their toll (many of the sculptures have been covered with cheap wooden roof shelters in a much-belated attempt to prevent any further damage) and what you see now are the few survivors of what would once have been a remarkable open-air *atelier* – exclusively the ones that Braun hacked out of various boulders he found strewn about the wood. In contrast to Kuks, the theme here is more explicitly religious, with the best-preserved sculptural groups depicting The Journey of the Magi and the Nativity. The dishevelled man crawling out of his cave, and looking very much like a 3-D representation of William Blake's *Fall of Man*, is in fact an obscure Egyptian hermit called Garinus.

Dvůr Králové nad Labem

DVŮR KRÁLOVÉ NAD LABEM, 8km northwest of Kuks, is familiar to postwar generations of Czech kids as the site of the country's largest **zoo** (daily

9am–6pm or dusk; 150Kč; ⓦ www.zoodk.cz). As underfunded eastern European zoos go, Dvůr Králové has tried harder than most to make the animals' lives bearable, but a safari park it is not. There's a *dětský koutek* (kids' corner), where children can stroke the more domesticated animals, and a "safari" consisting of a free bus ride through a series of open enclosures containing a serious surfeit of antelopes. The safari bus sets off from the far side of the zoo – a long way to walk for smaller kids, so it's best to take the horse and cart or mini-train there. The zoo lies 1km west of town, on Štefánikova, and is well signposted.

Dvůr Králové **bus station** is on 17 listopadu; to get to the main square, walk north two blocks, then left down Švehlova. The **train station** lies 2km southwest of the centre; a bus meets all trains and drops passengers in the centre, or you can walk down 5 května, which becomes 28 října before crossing the river, after which it's due north up Riegrova and Revoluční to the main square. The **tourist office** (Mon–Fri 8am–5pm, Sat 9am–1pm; ☎ 499 321 742, Ⓔ info@mudk.cz) can be found on the arcaded main square; nearby, on Revoluční, is the small, peaceful *Pension na náměstí* (☎ 499 329 129, ⓦ penzion .nanamesti.cz; ❷), run by a private travel agency.

Hořice

Just about every Czech sculptor over the last hundred years was trained at the School of Masonry and Sculpture founded in 1884 at **HOŘICE V PODKRKONOŠÍ**, 23km northwest of Hradec Králové. As a result, the town now boasts one of the country's richest collections of sculpture and plays host to an annual **International Symposium of Contemporary Sculpture** in July and August (ⓦ www.symposiumhorice.cz). There are sculptures all over town and exhibitions of contemporary works in the town **museum** (Tues–Fri 9am–noon & 1–5pm) on the main square, but the largest collection is in the **Galerie plastik** (Tues–Sun 9am–noon & 1–5pm), halfway up the sv Gothard hill to the east of town (5min walk down Janderova). Half the gallery is given over to temporary exhibitions, but the permanent collection is still impressive. All the leading lights of Czech sculpture are represented here, even Šaloun, famous for his Jan Hus Monument in Prague, and Bílek, neither of whom actually studied here, as well as one of the few extant works by Otakar Švec, the man responsible for Prague's since-dynamited Stalin Monument. In the meadows and orchards to the north of the gallery is the **symposium area**, with previous years' exhibits out on show. To the east is the local **cemetery** (*hřbitov*), which has a wonderful triumphal arch over the entrance and a scattering of well-sculpted headstones. To the west, the **Smetanovy sady** are dotted with mostly nineteenth-century sculptures of leading figures of the Czech national revival.

Despite the town's enormous artistic treasures, it sees few visitors. The helpful **tourist office** (Mon–Fri 7.30am–5pm, Sat & Sun 8am–noon; ⓦ www.horice .org) is in the pretty radnice on the main square; you can **stay** at the nearby *Hotel Královský Dvůr* (☎ 493 624 527, ⓦ www.kralovskydvur.com; ❷). Of the three **campsites** in the area, the nearest is the *U věže* (March–Nov), 1km north of town on the road to Dvůr Králové. The **train station** (Hořice v Podkrkonoší) lies 1km south of town down Husova (there's an occasional connecting bus).

Chlumec nad Cidlinou

CHLUMEC NAD CIDLINOU, 29km west of Hradec Králové, in the middle of the featureless, dusty Polabí, was the scene of one of the largest peasant uprisings in the country in 1775, after which 3000 of those who had taken part were burned to death in a nearby farm. Just over fifty years before that bloody incident, Count Kinský built himself one of Bohemia's most exquisite provincial chateaux, **Karlova Koruna** (April & Oct Sat & Sun 9am–noon & 1–4pm; May & June Tues–Sun 8am–noon & 1–5pm; July & Aug Tues–Sun 8am–5pm; Sept Tues–Sun 9am–noon & 1–5pm; 50Kč). Begun in 1721 by Giovanni Santini, it stands on a rare patch of raised ground to the northwest of the town, south of the train station. Santini's ground plan is a simple but intriguing triple-winged affair, dominated by a central circular hall, with a two-storey pink-and-grey marble dome and a grand staircase leading to the upper balcony. The building's exterior and grounds are both in need of some tidying up, however. In the grounds, the modest Baroque pleasure house displays copies of Braun's statuary.

Pardubice and around

There's always been a certain amount of rivalry between the two big cities of the Polabí, Hradec Králové and **PARDUBICE**, just under 20km to the south. On balance, Pardubice's historical core is probably more immediately appealing than Hradec Králové's, and it has a lovely chateau, but its new town lacks the cohesion of its neighbour, which makes the whole place feel a lot smaller. Throughout the horse-racing world, Pardubice is best known for its **steeple-chase course** (second only to Liverpool's Aintree for difficulty), where the *Velká Pardubická* (first run in 1874) takes place in early October – usually accompanied by protests by Czech animal rights activists.

Arrival, information and accommodation

You could visit Pardubice on a day-trip from Hradec Králové (it's only 30min away by train); the **train** and **bus stations** lie at the end of Palackého in the

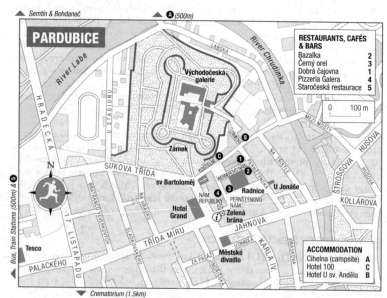

new town, a busy thoroughfare and the beginning of Pardubice's long parade of shops. It's a good ten-minute walk from here (or a short ride on trolley bus #2) northeast to the old town, much of it along Míru, a busy commercial street. Pardubice's modern and helpful **tourist office** (daily 9am–6pm; ⓦwww .ipardubice.cz), nameští Republiky 1, provides **internet access**.

There are a few reasonable **hotels** in the old town. *Hotel 100* (☎466 511 179, ⓦwww.hotel100.cz; ❸) has a fine location and clean rooms on Kostelní; *U sv Anděla* (☎466 535 656, ⓦwww.hotelzlandel.pardubicko.com; ❸), down the street on Zámecká, is a tad larger and dearer, but similarly well kept. The *Cihelna* **campsite** (June to mid-Oct; ☎466 415 833) is just north of the river up K. cihelně. Note that accommodation is impossible to find over the weekend of the **Velká Pardubická** (ⓦwww.vpcp.cz) in early October, unless you book well in advance.

The Town

The section of **Míru** from the bus and train stations to the old town contains an arresting threesome of late Secession buildings on the left-hand side, with *U lva* at the centre, distinguished by the two tiny lion heads on its gable. Míru comes to an end at **náměstí Republiky**, which marks the transition from the new town to the old. At one end, the striking Art Nouveau **Městské divadlo** (town theatre) is a deliberately Czech structure, designed by Antonín Balšánek (who collaborated with Polívka on Prague's Obecní dům), its magnificent facade flanked by multicoloured mosaics: Libuše founding Prague on one side and a blind Žižka leading the Hussites into battle on the other. The other truly arresting building on the square is the church of **sv Bartoloměj**, originally Gothic but more memorable for the Renaissance additions to its exterior – courtesy of local bigwigs, the Pernštejns – which makes up for its lack of a tower with a syringe-like central spike. Josef Gočár worked in Pardubice, as well as in Hradec Králové: the squat, grey Komerční banka and the *Hotel Grand* opposite are both his.

The soaring Gothic gateway, **Zelená brána** (May–Sept Tues–Sun 9am–noon & 1–5pm; Oct Sat & Sun only; 15Kč), with its twisted uppermost tower and wonderful baubled spikes, makes for a memorable entrance to the old town, and a good place from which to survey it. The main square, **Pernštýnovo náměstí**, is an intimate affair, an effect made all the more pronounced by the tall three-storey buildings on each side, handsome gabled sixteenth- and eighteenth-century houses for the most part, with the exception of the flamboyant neo-Renaissance **radnice**. The sculptural decoration throughout the old town is remarkable, at its most striking on **U Jonáše**, whose plaster-work includes an exuberant depiction of Jonah at the moment of digestion by the whale. Inside there's a branch of the Východočeská galerie (Tues–Fri noon–6pm, Sat & Sun 10am–6pm) with a permanent exhibition of Czech nineteenth- and twentieth-century art, including works by the locally born artist Jaroslav Grus. A handful of picturesque backstreets spread north from here, with the buttressed beauty of Bartolomějská or the crumbling facades of Pernštýnská both leading to the romantic embankment, Wernerovo nábřeší, whose drooping willow trees provide a perfect spot of shade in summer.

At this point, you should head up Zámecká, and cross the vast dry moat to the **zámek** (Tues–Sun 10am–6pm; 60Kč), which, protected by an impressive series of walls, gates and barbicans, occupies more space than the entire staré město. The chateau's sgraffitoed appearance, and its beautiful loggia in the main courtyard, among which a happy congregation of peacocks and turkeys struts

Janák's crematorium and Gočár's spa

Pardubice boasts two fine buildings from a unique period in Czech architectural history. The first is the town's crematorium on Pod břízkami (trolley bus #1 from náměstí Republiky), designed by **Pavel Janák** in the 1920s, and, with its feast of semicircular motifs and garish colours, one of the finest extant Rondo-Cubist buildings in the country. The other architectural gem is **Josef Gočár**'s sanatorium at the nearby spa of Bohdaneč, accessible on trolley bus #3 (via Semtín). Built in 1909, it was, in all probability, the first Cubist structure ever built.

its stuff, date from the sixteenth century when it became the chief seat of the powerful Pernštejn family. The latter were also responsible for the chateau's precious Renaissance wall paintings, which have been partially preserved in the **Rytířské sály** on the first floor. There are trompe l'oeil doorframes and decorative motifs, plus two very large pictures: the first is of Moses being given the ten commandments, while the second (and best preserved) features Delilah cutting the hair of the sleeping Samson, while a phalanx of Philistines arrives hotfoot. You can see the frescoes – and the tiny arms collection and the local museum, which are also in the chateau – without a guided tour; just make sure you buy the useful English information leaflets when you purchase your ticket.

On the other side of the outer courtyard, the **Východočeská galerie** (Tues–Fri noon–6pm, Sat & Sun 10am–6pm) contains a small collection of modern Czech art on the first floor. The gallery owns works by all the major Czech artists of the last century, from Čapek to Medek, but only a few pieces stick out: Kamil Lhoták's realist canvases from the 1940s and 1950s, the giant *Human Egg* by Eva Kmentová, and a great little pair of papier-mâché wellingtons called *Homage to Jules Verne* by Jiří Kolář.

Eating, drinking and entertainment

There's a very pleasant *Dobrá čajovna* on Pernštýnská, and a great little *vinárna* named *Bazalka* across the way, which serves good salads at its wicker tables. You'll also find several **restaurants** on the old town square, most of which have outdoor seating: *Černý orel* serves upscale steak dishes, while *Pizzeria Galera* (whose entrance is actually on Bartolomějská) has decent fish and Italian entrées. If you want to taste the town's famous 19° porter, the strong, dark **beer** brewed here since 1890, head for the *Staročeská restaurace* at the Pernštejn brewery on Palackého, halfway from the station into town.

Chrudim, Kočí and Ležáky

Twelve kilometres south of Pardubice, the pretty little town of **CHRUDIM** springs into life in early July for its annual **Puppet Festival**. At other times of the year, it's still worth the short train ride to visit the marvellous **Muzeum loutkářských kultur** (Puppet Museum; April, May & Sept Tues–Sun 9am–noon & 1–5pm; June–Aug Tues–Sun 9am–noon & 1–6pm; Oct–March Thurs & Fri 9am–noon & 1–5pm, Sat & Sun 1–5pm; 20Kč), in the splendid sixteenth-century Mydlářovský dům on Břetislavova, just off the main square. The Czech Lands have a long tradition of puppetry, going back to the country's peasant roots, and the museum holds marionettes and puppets donated from all over the world. If you're looking for cheap **accommodation**, head for the *Sporthotel* (☏469 621 028; ❶), on Tyršovo náměstí, 200m from the main square, which has spacious rooms without en-suite facilities.

The village of **KOČÍ**, 4km east of Chrudim on route 17, boasts the unusual Gothic church of **sv Bartoloměj**, founded in 1397 by Queen Žofiá, wife of Václav IV. At first glance it appears to be made of timber, but its brick body is simply enveloped by a wooden cover. This effect is intensified by the Baroque, wooden, arcaded bridge (18m long) that connects the church with the road. To see the interior, which has Gothic cross vaulting, you need to find the custodian (ask at house no. 40).

Southeast of Chrudim off route 37, in a quiet, shady glen, is a memorial to the village of **LEŽÁKY**, which suffered an even worse fate than Lidice (see p.155). On June 24, 1942, the SS rounded up the village's entire adult population and shot all 56 of them; two children were deemed fit for Germanization and the rest were sent off to the camps. The motive for Ležáky's destruction was the same as for Lidice's: Hitler wanted revenge for the assassination of Reinhard Heydrich, Reichsprotektor of Bohemia and Moravia. Exactly two weeks after Lidice was wiped out, Ležáky suffered the same fate for concealing a resistance transmitter. Today the foundation stones of the houses, which were all burned down, are all that remain, and these have been carefully rearranged and topped with memorial stones. The main difference between Ležáky and Lidice, though, is that no new town was built here: the road simply passes through, with signs to mark the boundaries. A **museum** (May–Sept Tues–Sun 9am–5pm; 10Kč) displays photographs of the destruction, as well as of each of the victims. There are no buses to Ležáky, only a few daily services from Chrudim to Miřetice, 2km west.

Litomyšl and around

For a small town in the northern reaches of the Bohemian-Moravian Uplands, **LITOMYŠL** (Leitomischl) has big ideas. In 1992 a School for Restoration and Conservation was founded here and immediately set to work restoring the Portmoneum, a house decorated with fantastical murals and furniture by Josef Váchal, which opened the following year. Soon after, the town pulled off an even more amazing coup by getting seven presidents of central Europe – including Václav Havel, Lech Walesa and Richard von Weizsäcker – to meet here for a summit.

The town's picturesque main square, **Smetanovo náměstí**, is strung out like a juicy fat Czech sausage and lined with almost uninterrupted arcades, a pastel parade of Baroque and Neoclassical facades. The sixteenth-century **U rytířů**, at no. 110 (May–Sept Tues–Sun 10am–noon & 1–5pm; Oct–April 9am–noon & 1–4pm; 20Kč), is the finest of the lot, decorated with medieval knights and merchants holding bags of money, clinging mischievously to their carved columns; the building hosts art exhibitions, worth checking out if only to admire the coffered Renaissance ceiling inside. The town's most famous son is the composer **Bedřich Smetana**, who was born here in 1824, hence Jan Štursa's effete statue of the composer at the northwest corner of the main square. Every year at the end of June the town puts on a ten-day **international opera festival**, *Smetanova Litomyšl*, in his honour.

Northeast of the main square, a knot of ramshackle backstreets, punctuated by churches, leads up to the town's most celebrated monument, the Pernštejns' **zámek** (April & Oct Sat & Sun 9am–noon & 1–4pm; May–Sept Tues–Sun 9am–noon & 1–5pm; 90Kč), a smart, sgraffitoed affair that bursts into frivolous gables and finials on its roof and which boasts one of Bohemia's finest triple-decker loggias inside. The main guided tour (*1 okruh*) leads you through state and banquet rooms richly decorated in porcelain and period furniture. The highlight, though, is the remarkable late eighteenth-century theatre where the young Smetana made his debut as a pianist, accompanied by much of the original scenery painted by Josef Platzer. The alternative tour (*2 okruh*) features the less spectacular guest rooms, the pretty chateau chapel and a remarkable collection of historical keyboard instruments. The chateau's former riding school, across the courtyard, houses the **Muzeum antického sochařství a architektury** (May–Oct Tues–Sun 9am–noon & 1–5pm; 30Kč), a bizarre collection of plaster and bronze casts of Greek and Roman classical statues from museums around the world. Also worth catching is the contemporary art displayed nearby in the chateau's cellars, the **Zámecké sklepní** (April & Oct Sat & Sun 9am–4pm; May–Sept 9am–5pm; 20Kč), including an impressive collection of lifesize statues by Olbram Zoubek and modern ceramcis by Jiří Dudycha.

Smetana himself was born in the chateau's former brewery, one of eighteen children to an upwardly mobile brewer. The building now houses the **Rodný byt Smetany** (April & Oct Sat & Sun 9am–noon & 1–4pm; May–Sept Tues–Sun 9am–noon & 1–5pm; Ⓦwww.rml.cz; 20Kč), a modest memorial museum to the composer. Smetana was a veritable *Wunderkind*, playing in a string quartet at the age of 5 and composing his first symphony at 8, but a year before that, the family moved to Jindřichův Hradec. Catalyzed by the events of 1848, Smetana became a leading figure in the Czech national revival (despite German being his mother tongue), helping to found Prague's Národní divadlo. In 1874 he had to resign as the theatre's chief conductor after becoming deaf through a syphilitic infection. He went on to promote the nationalist cause through works like *Má vlast* ("My Country"), a symphonic poem inspired by Czech legends, but sadly ended his days in a mental asylum.

A short walk southeast of the chateau, at Terézy Novákové 75, is without doubt Litomyšl's most extraordinary and unique artistic treasure, the **Portmoneum** (May–Oct Tues–Sun 9am–noon & 1–5pm; 60Kč). From the outside, it looks like any other provincial town house, but inside, the walls, ceilings and furniture of two rooms are decorated with the strange and wonderful work of the self-taught artist **Josef Váchal** (1884–1969), from the early 1920s. Váchal's ghoulish art is difficult to categorize: the ceiling in one room is a whirlwind of devils, spirits and sinful creatures; elsewhere are cherubs, Kupkaesque celestial orbs of light, quotations from Hindu religious texts and a Crucifixion, while Váchal himself appears at one point as a rat-catcher. The man who wanted his house decorated with such disturbing murals was **Josef Portman** (after whom the house is named), a civil servant, amateur printer and collector of Váchal's art, who died here in 1968.

Practicalities

Litomyšl lies on a little-used branch line from Choceň, so buses are the easiest way to get here. The **bus station** is on Mařákova, five-minutes' walk southeast of the centre, a pleasant stroll along (and across) the River Loučná; the **train station** is five-minutes' walk west of the old town, again along (and across) the river. The efficient **tourist office** (April–Sept Mon–Fri 9am–7pm, Sat & Sun 9am–3pm; Oct–March Mon–Fri 8.30am–6pm, Sat 9am–2pm; ☏461 612 161, Ⓦwww.litomysl.cz/ic) on the west side of the main square can help with **accommodation**. Also on the main square, the upmarket *Zlatá hvězda* (☏461 615 338, Ⓦwww.zlatahvezda.com; ❸), where Havel stayed, is the town's finest

Schindler's Svitavy

When Spielberg's Holocaust film, *Schindler's List*, reached the Czech Republic in 1994, it was premiered in **Svitavy** (Zwittau), a small Moravian town (currently in East Bohemia) 20km southeast of Litomyšl. The simple reason for this was that the "hero" of the film, Nazi industrialist **Oskar Schindler**, was born here in 1908, son of an insurance salesman, at Iglauerstrasse (now Poličská) 24. In Svitavy, he was known as a hard-drinking womanizer who was expelled from school for falsifying his school report and some years later arrested in the *Hotel Ungar*, on the town's main square, for supplying the German Abwehr with information.

Schindler became a member of the Nazi Party early on and, during the war, he used his Party contacts to establish a kitchenware factory in Kraków, using Jewish slave labour. It was here that Schindler began to shelter Jews, hiring them even though they were too sick or weak to work, in order to save them from certain death in the nearby camps. In 1943 he took 900 Jewish workers with him and set up an armaments factory in Brněnec, a town 15km south of Svitavy. In fact, Schindler made sure that not a single weapon actually produced at the factory and by the end of the war he had saved 1200 Jews from deportation. He died in 1974 in Hildesheim in Germany, though his remains were transferred to Israel as a mark of gratitude.

The majority of Svitavy's population (most of whom were German-speaking) were expelled after the war, and only a few of the older inhabitants can remember Schindler from his Svitavy days. The film therefore came as something of a revelation to many of Svitavy's residents, who had previously been told only the Communists' postwar version of events: that Schindler was simply the Nazi chief of the local concentration camp. Despite the release of the film, the town council still had to overcome fierce local opposition in order to erect a memorial plaque – in Czech and German – in the park opposite Schindler's birthplace. The plaque was eventually unveiled by the republic's Chief Rabbi shortly after the film's premiere.

hotel. The little *Pension Pod klášterem* (℡ 461 615 901, Ⓦ www.podklasterem .cz; ❷), crouched on B. Němcové in the shadow of the Piarist church, is comfortable enough; you could also stay in the smart self-catering apartment in the former brewery where Smetana was born (℡ 461 612 575, Ⓦ apartment .smetana-litomysl.com; ❷). *Primátor* **campsite** (May–Sept; ℡ 461 612 238, Ⓦ www.camplitomysl.cz), with bungalows, lies 2km southeast of the town centre, off route 35/E442 to Moravská Třebová. *Zlatá hvězda* has an excellent **restaurant** and surprisingly good prices, or you can lunch at the fine *Zámecká restaurace* in the chateau grounds. The best place for a cup of tea is the quiet, Indian-style *Čajovna v muzeu* in the regional museum building.

Polička

The Bohemian-Moravian Uplands are clearly a musically fertile region: Mahler spent his childhood in Jihlava (see p.340), while the town of **POLIČKA**, 18km south of Litomyšl, produced **Bohuslav Martinů**, who was born in 1890 at the top of the 75-metre-tall fairytale neo-Gothic tower of the church of sv Jakub, just west of the main square. The composer's father – a cobbler by trade – was also the local watchman, and the single room in which the family of five lived until 1902 has to be one of the most memorable memorials to any composer. To climb the tower, you must buy a ticket from the local **museum** (May–Aug Tues–Sun 9am–5pm; Sept–April Tues–Sun 9am–noon & 12.30–4pm; 40Kč), on Tylova, north off the main square, where you can see an exhibition and watch a video on Martinů's life. Despite spending much of his life in exile, Martinů always carried a postcard of the view from the tower, and twenty years after his death in a Swiss hospital in 1959 he was finally buried in the town cemetery, within sight of the tower.

Apart from the composer, there's little other reason for coming to Polička, which had its aesthetic charms altered in a devastating fire in 1845. You can explore the town's beautifully preserved and pretty impressive **fortifications** (April & Oct Mon–Fri 9am–4pm; May & Sept Mon–Fri 9am–4pm, Sat 1–4pm; June Mon–Fri 9am–5pm, Sat & Sun 1–4pm; July & Aug Mon–Fri 9am–5pm, Sat 9am–4pm) with a guide from the **tourist office** (Mon–Fri 8.30am–6pm, Sat 9am–2pm; ⓦwww.policka-mesto.cz) on the main square. The **train station** is north of the town, off route 359 to Litomyšl, but only connects with Svitavy and Česká Třebová, not Litomyšl. The best place to **stay** is the pretty blue *Penzion U purkmistra* (☎461 722 310, ⓦwww.upurkmistra.cz; ❷), on Riegrova near the church of sv Jakub, and there's a **campsite** (May–Sept), 1.5km south of the town off route 360 to Nové Město na Moravě.

Travel details

Trains

Connections with Prague: Hradec Králové (12–16 daily; 1hr 25min–1hr 45min); Pardubice (30 daily; 1hr 10min–1hr 30min); Trutnov (1–2 daily; 3hr–3hr 20min); Turnov (8–12 daily; 2–3hr).

Hradec Králové to: Častolovice/(5 daily; 40min); Chlumec nad Cidlinou (every 1–2hr; 20–40min); Dvůr Králové (7 daily; 40min); Hořice (11–17 daily; 30–50min); Jaroměř (hourly; 20–30min); Jičín (11–15 daily; 1hr 15min–1hr 25min); Kuks (1 daily; 30min); Pardubice (1–2 hr; 25–30min); Třebechovice pod Orebem (15–20 daily; 15min).

Náchod to: Nové Město nad Metují/Opočno (9–18 daily; 15–25min/25–35min); Teplice nad Metují (11–18 daily; 30–40min).

Pardubice to: Chrudim (hourly; 20–30min); Liberec (7 daily; 3hr–3hr 30min).

Trutnov to: Adršpach/Teplice nad Metují (7–9 daily; 1hr/1hr 15min); Česká Skalice/Jaroměř (13–17 daily; 1hr/1hr 15min); Chlumec nad Cidlinou (9 daily; 2hr–2hr 30min); Kunčice nad Labem (11–15 daily; 30min).

Turnov to: Hradec Králové (13–14 daily; 2hr–2hr 30min); Jičín (9–10 daily; 50min–1hr)

Buses

Connections with Prague: Harrachov (up to 5 daily; 3hr); Hradec Králové (hourly; 1hr 30min–2hr); Jičín (7–15 daily; 1hr 10min–2hr); Litomyšl (4–7 daily; 3hr–3hr 30min); Náchod (5–18 daily; 2hr 30min–3hr); Pec pod Sněžkou (2–7 daily; 3hr–3hr 30min); Špindlerův Mlýn (up to 6 daily; 2hr 30min–3hr); Trutnov (5–12 daily; 2hr 45min); Vrchlabí (7–11 daily; 2–3hr).

Hradec Králové to: Jaroměř (over 30 daily Mon–Fri, 6 daily Sat & Sun; 25min–1hr); Kuks (13 daily Mon–Fri; 30–45min); Litomyšl (hourly; 1hr 10min–1hr 30min); Náchod (25 daily Mon–Fri, 5 daily Sat & Sun; 1hr); Nové Město nad Metují (3–10 daily; 45min–1hr 10min); Pec pod Sněžkou (1–2 daily; 1hr 35min–2hr); Trutnov (up to 7 daily; 1hr–1hr 30min); Vrchlabí (3–8 daily; 1hr 30min).

Jičín to: Turnov (2–15 daily; 30min–1hr).

Náchod to: Broumov (7–20 daily; 45min–1hr); Nové Město nad Metují (1–2 hr Mon–Fri; 15–30min).

Trutnov to: Janské Lázně (hourly; 30min); Pec pod Sněžkou (hourly; 35–50min); Vrchlabí (up to 10 daily; 35–50min).

Vrchlabí to: Špindlerův Mlýn (16–22 daily; 20min).

South Moravia

A t first sight, the landscape of **South Moravia** (Jižní Morava) appears little different from that of much of Bohemia, a mixture of rolling hills and dense forests. Only as you move south towards Vienna does the land become noticeably more plump and fertile, with the orchards and vineyards continuing into Austria itself. **Brno** is the obvious starting point: an engaging city, whose attractions are often underrated due to its heavy industrial base and peripheral housing estates. Brno is also within easy distance of a host of sights, most notably Moravia's karst region, the Moravský kras, which boasts the country's most spectacular **limestone caves**, and the atmospheric medieval castle of **Pernštejn**.

South of Brno a string of pretty villages, towns and chateaux punctuate the **River Dyje** (Thaya) as it meanders along the Austrian border. Historically, the land on either side of the Dyje was for centuries German-speaking, its buildings designed by Austrian architects and its sights set firmly on Vienna, just 60km to the south. However, as in the rest of the country, the ethnic German population was forcibly removed from South Moravia after 1945. The region's viticulture kept going on private plots even after nationalization in 1948, but in every other way the last half century has driven a great wedge between two previously identical regions on either side of the river. **Mikulov**, on the main road from Vienna, is a great introduction to the region; close by, at the chateaux of **Lednice** and **Valtice**, the Liechtensteins had their base for many centuries. Further west, another border town, **Znojmo**, harbours the country's most precious medieval frescoes, and is a great jumping-off point for the **Podyjí** national park, formed by the damming of the Dyje and dotted with castles and chateaux. Further west still, on the Bohemian border, **Telč** and **Slavonice** are two of the most beautiful Renaissance towns anywhere in Europe. Yet while Telč is a popular stop-off on whirlwind tours of the country, Slavonice – every bit as perfect – sees far fewer visitors. Both towns sit at the southern end of the **Bohemian-Moravian Uplands** or Vysočina, a poor and sparsely populated area that separates Bohemia and Moravia, and which is viewed by most travellers only through a window en route to Brno. **Jihlava** is the area's most convenient starting point, but it won't hold you long. More compelling is the pilgrimage church at **Žďár nad Sázavou**, another of Santini's Baroque-Gothic confections.

East of Brno, the landscape around the River Morava is visually uninspiring, but the wine and rich folk heritage are good reasons for stopping. To the south, the area known as **Slovácko** hosts the country's two largest **folk festivals**, in Vlčnov and Strážnice. Further north, the provincial treasure house and graceful

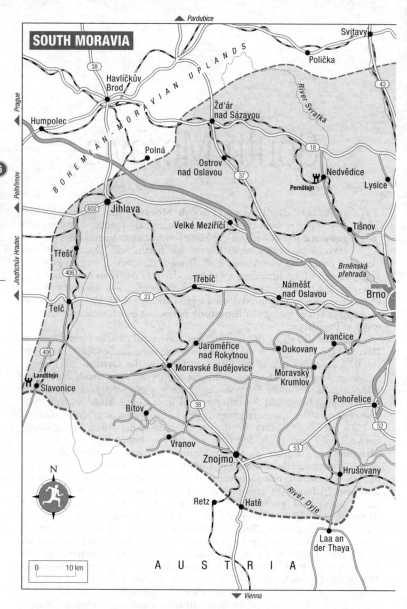

SOUTH MORAVIA

gardens of **Kroměříž** provide a fascinating contrast with modernist **Zlín**, where the multinational Baťa shoe empire has its roots.

Transport is fairly good throughout Moravia, though the train system is not as comprehensive as that of Bohemia, petering out in the Vysočina and degenerating into a series of complex branch lines along the more industrialized River Morava. In such instances, buses are invariably quicker and more direct.

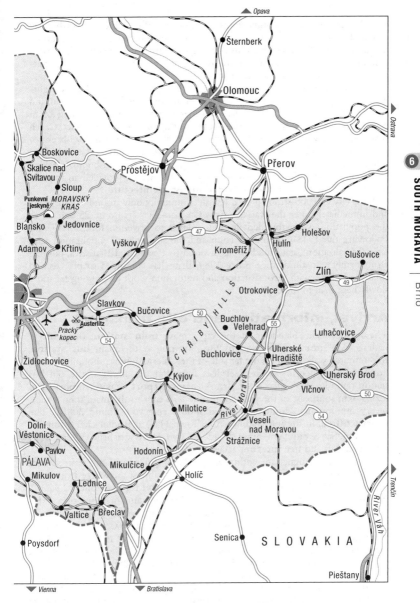

Brno

BRNO (Brünn) "welcomes the visitor with new constructions", as one Communist-era tourist brochure euphemistically put it. In fact, the high-rise *paneláky* that surround the Moravian capital play a major part in discouraging travellers from stopping here. But as the second-largest city in the Czech Republic, with a population of 400,000, a couple of really good museums and art galleries, a handful of other sights and a fair bit of nightlife, it's worth a day or two. For the most part, though, the city receives few foreign visitors outside the annual trade fairs, which has its advantages: tourists are welcomed here with genuine interest, and the pace of life is endearingly (some might say infuriatingly) provincial compared with that of Prague.

Brno was a late developer, being no bigger than Olomouc until the late eighteenth century. However, the town's first cloth factory was founded in 1766, and within fifteen years was followed by another twenty. With the building of an engineering plant early in the next century, the city began to attract Czech workers, along with Austrian, German, English and, in particular, Jewish entrepreneurs, making it the second largest city in the Czech Lands by the end of the nineteenth century. Between the wars, Brno enjoyed a cultural boom, heralded by the 1928 Exhibition of Contemporary Culture, which provided an impetus for much of the city's pioneering **functionalist architecture**.

Of the city's 10,000-strong prewar Jewish community, only around 670 survived, and immediately after the war, the city's German-speakers (some 25 percent of the population) were rounded up and ordered to leave, on foot, for Vienna. Following the 1948 Communist coup and the subsequent centralization (and later federalization), state funds were diverted to Prague and Bratislava, pushing Brno firmly into third place. Since 1989, Brno has continued to play second fiddle to Prague, with reconstruction and restoration work progressing far more slowly here than in the capital.

Arrival, information and city transport

The fin-de-siècle splendour of the city's main **train station**, Brno hlavní nádraží, is a great introduction to the city; not so the main **bus station**, five-minutes' walk south on the far side of the Galerie Vaňkova shopping centre. Some buses (especially express services from Prague) arrive at the old bus station opposite the *Grand Hotel*. Brno's Tuřany **airport** (ⓦ www.airport-brno .cz) is 6km southeast of the city centre: bus #76 runs to the main train station (every 30min–1hr; 22min) and a taxi should cost you around 300Kč. The **tourist office,** in the stará radnice (Old Town Hall) at Radnická 8 (Mon–Fri 8am–6pm, Sat & Sun 9am–5pm; ☎542 211 090, ⓦ www.ticbrno.cz), has well-informed staff and free **internet** access.

Most of Brno's sights are within easy walking distance of the train station, although **trams** (ⓦ www.dpmb.cz) will take you almost anywhere in the city within minutes. You need to buy either a 10Kč **ticket** for two zones (2 *pásma*), which will last you ten minutes without changing trams or buses, or a 15Kč ticket, again for two zones, which is valid for sixty minutes and allows changes between trams or buses. Tickets must be bought from news kiosks or yellow ticket machines and punched on board; you might want to buy a 24-hour *celodenní jízdenka*, 60Kč for one zone (which should suffice for sightseeing purposes), or 190Kč for all zones. A couple of trams run all night, but many have been replaced by night buses which run along the old tram routes – all gather together in front of the station on the hour, every hour. The same tickets are valid for the city's **buses** and **trolleybuses**, which congregate at Moravské náměstí and Mendlovo náměstí, though you're unlikely to need to use them unless you're staying right out in suburbia.

Accommodation

Finding **accommodation** in Brno is relatively easy, though prices are fairly high, thanks to the various trade fairs (when rates can double or even triple).

The tourist office can arrange cheap **private rooms**, though many on their books are out of the centre. The most central **hostel** is the *Travellers' Hostel* at Jánská 22 (☎542 213 573), but it's only open in July and August. The rest of the year, you'll have to head for the *Student Pension Palacký* (☎541 641 111), a high-rise block on the far northern edge of the city at the end of Kolejní; take tram #12 or #13 to their terminus and then trolleybus #53 to the end of the line. There are several **campsites** along the shores of the Brněnská přehrada (Brno Dam), 10km northwest of the city centre; the nearest is *Radka* (June–Aug), on the east bank beyond the hostel-style *Hotel Přehrada* (☎546 210 167) and the Sokolské swimming pool; to reach the dam, take tram #1, #3 or #11.

Amphone Třída kpt. Jaroše 29 ☎545 428 310, ⓦwww.amphone.cz. On a tree-lined boulevard just 10min walk from the city centre, this is a good budget choice – although the smallish en-suite rooms are beginning to show wear and tear. ❸

Pegas Jakubská 4 ☎542 210 104. Small, basic rooms right in the old town above the micro-brewery/pub of the same name (although it's not especially noisy). Prices are creeping up due to the central location. ❺

Pod Špilberkem Pekařská 10 ☎543 235 003, ⓦwww.hotelpodspilberkem.cz. Slightly old-fashioned but perfectly habitable en suites just west of the centre, and within walking distance of pretty much everything you need. ❹

Pyramida Zahradnická 19 ☎543 427 310. Perfectly comfortable and pleasant Communist-era high-rise a couple of tram stops southwest of the old town, near Výstaviště. ❸

Royal Ricc Starobrněnská 10 ☎542 219 262, ⓦwww.romantichotels.cz. Brno's luxury hotel of choice, with a lovely position in the backstreets of the old town, and the odd original Renaissance feature and tasteful repro furnishings. ❼

Slavia Solniční 15–17 ☎542 321 249, ⓦwww .slavia.hotel.cz. Communist-era hotel that's pretty comfortable, very central and competitively priced. ❻

Slovan Lidická 23 ☎533 422 111, ⓦwww .hotelslovan.cz. Bland but comfortable en suites in a six-storey block, diagonally opposite the Janáčkovo divadlo. ❹

The City

One of the nicest things about Brno is its compact and almost entirely traffic-free historical centre. The main action goes on within this small, egg-shaped old town, which is encircled by a swathe of parks and the inner ring road. Around **Zelný trh** and **náměstí Svobody** you'll find most of the city's shops and markets. In the southwestern corner raised above the old town are the quieter streets around **Petrov**, the lesser of Brno's two hills, topped by the cathedral. Further west, the squat fortress of **Špilberk** looks down on the old town to the east and Staré Brno to the south, site of the original early medieval settlement. Worth a visit, but even further from the centre, are Brno's **Technické muzeum** and the city's two modernist architectural landmarks: the exhibition grounds of **Výstaviště** and – on the opposite side of town – Mies van der Rohe's **Vila Tugendhat**.

Masarykova and Zelný trh

Masarykova, with its cobbles, steaming manholes and defunct tram lines, has a definite buzz in the afternoon after work, with a steady stream of people ploughing up and down to and from náměstí Svobody (see p.311). The street's tall mansions, laden with a fantastic mantle of decorations, perfectly express the confidence of the city's late-nineteenth-century industrialists.

Immediately to the left as you head up Masarykova from the train station is Kapucínské náměstí, where you'll find the macabre **Kapucínská hrobka** (Tues–Sat 9am–noon & 2–4.30pm, Sun 11–11.45am & 2–4.30pm), a gruesome collection of dead monks and notables mummified in the crypt of the Capuchin church. Until the eighteenth century, Brno's moneyed classes forked out large sums to be buried here in the monks' simple common grave, hoping to find a

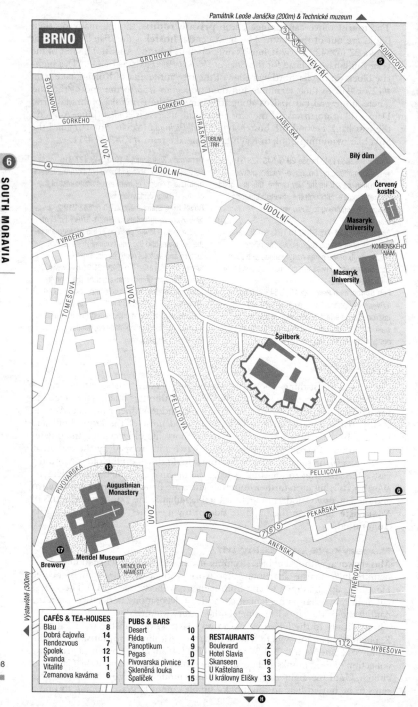

BRNO

GROHOVA

STOJANOVA

GORKÉHO

GORKÉHO

UVOZ

JIRÁSKOVA

OBILNÍ TRH

KOUNICOVA

VEVEŘÍ

JASELSKÁ

Bílý dům

Červený kostel

Masaryk University

ÚDOLNÍ

ÚDOLNÍ

KOMENSKÉHO NÁM.

Masaryk University

TVRDÉHO

TOMEŠOVA

UVOZ

Špilberk

PELLICOVA

PELLICOVA

PIVOVARSKÁ

Augustinian Monastery

UVOZ

PEKAŘSKÁ

ANENSKÁ

LEITNEROVA

Mendel Museum

MENDLOVO NÁMĚSTÍ

Brewery

Výstaviště (300m)

HYBEŠOVA

CAFÉS & TEA-HOUSES	
Blau	8
Dobrá čajovňa	14
Rendezvous	7
Spolek	12
Švanda	11
Vitalité	1
Zemanova kavárna	6

PUBS & BARS	
Desert	10
Fléda	4
Panoptikum	9
Pegas	D
Pivovarska pivnice	17
Skleněná louka	5
Špalíček	15

RESTAURANTS	
Boulevard	2
Hotel Slavia	C
Skanseen	16
U Kaštelana	3
U královny Elišky	13

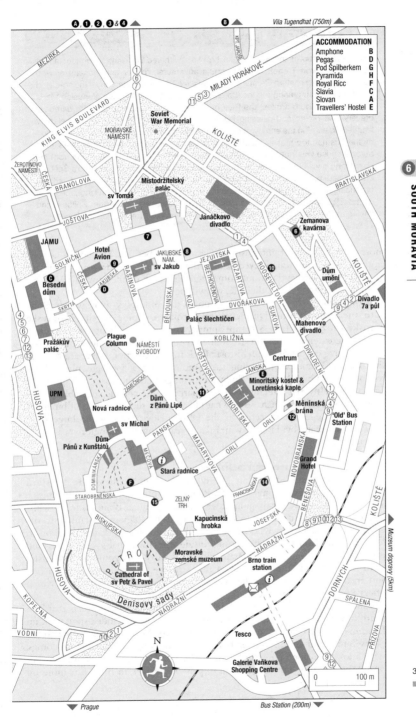

A 1 2 3 & 4　　　　**B**　　　Vila Tugendhat (750m)

ACCOMMODATION
Amphone	B
Pegas	D
Pod Špilberkem	G
Pyramida	H
Royal Ricc	F
Slavia	C
Slovan	A
Travellers' Hostel	E

MEZÍRKA

KPT. JAROŠE

MILADY HORÁKOVÉ

KING ELVIS BOULEVARD

17 5 3

MORAVSKÉ NÁMĚSTÍ

Soviet War Memorial

KOLIŠTĚ

ŽEROTÍNOVO NÁMĚSTÍ

ČESKÁ

BRANOLOVA

BRATISLAVSKÁ

Místodržitelský palác

sv Tomáš

JOŠTOVA

Janáčkovo divadlo

Zemanova kavárna **6**

JAMU

SOLNIČNÍ

ČESKÁ

7

Hotel Avion **9**

JAKUBSKÉ NÁM. **8**

JAKUBSKÁ

RAŠÍNOVA

sv Jakub

JEZUITSKÁ

MOZARTOVA

ROOSEVELTOVA

1 4

BEETHOVENOVA

10

Dům umění

KOLIŠTĚ

C

Besední dům

SKRYTÁ

D

BĚHOUNSKÁ

KOZÍ

DVOŘÁKOVA

SUKOVA

Divadlo 7a půl **2**

9 4

4 5 6 7 12 13

Pražákův palác

Plague Column

NÁMĚSTÍ SVOBODY

Palác šlechtičen

KOBLIŽNÁ

Mahenovo divadlo

POŠTOVSKÁ

JÁNSKÁ

Centrum

HUSOVA

UPM

ZÁMEČNICKÁ

Dům z Pánů Lipé

11

MINORITSKÁ

Minoritský kostel & Loretánská kaple **E**

ORLÍ

Měnínská brána

1 2

9

'Old' Bus Station

Nová radnice

sv Michal

PÁNSKÁ

MASARYKOVA

ORLÍ

12

NOVOBRANSKÁ

BENEŠOVA

Dům Pánů z Kunštátů

DOMINIKÁNSKÁ

MEČOVÁ

Stará radnice **i**

F

FRANCISKÁNSKÁ

14

Grand Hotel

KOLIŠTĚ

STAROBRNĚNSKÁ

15

ZELNÝ TRH

JOSEFSKÁ

Muzeum dopravy (5km)

BISKUPSKÁ

Kapucínská hrobka

NÁDRAŽNÍ

8 9 10 12 13

DORNYCH

SPÁLENÁ

Moravské zemské muzeum

Brno train station

HUSOVA

P E T R O V

Cathedral of sv Petr & Pavel

Denisovy sady

NÁDRAŽNÍ

i

PŘÍZOVA

KOPEČNÁ

VODNÍ

10 2 1

Tesco

N

Galerie Vaňkova Shopping Centre

9 12

0　　　100 m

▼ Prague　　　　　　　Bus Station (200m) ▼

Baron Trenck (1711–49)

Most charismatic of the Kapucínská hrobka's withered denizens is without doubt **Baron Franz von Trenck**, an aristocratic adventurer, dueller and womanizer who inherited lands in eastern Croatia and raised a fea3rsome private army – the so-called **Pandours** – from among the local peasants and brigands. Fighting alongside Maria Theresa's Habsburg armies, the Pandours garnered a reputation for both daredevil bravery and raping-and-pillaging lawlesness, catapulting Trenck into the celebrity league and earning the enmity of his military colleagues. Regarded as a loose cannon by the Austrian top brass, Trenck was framed on trumped-up treason charges – the baron's cause was not helped when he attempted to throw the trial judge from his box during a visit to the theatre. Condemned to life imprisonment in Brno's Špilberk prison (see p.315), Trenck set about writing his Munchhausen-esque memoirs, producing a racy bestseller which was translated into most European languages. The memoirs closed with a fanciful account of their author escaping from Špilberk and fleeing to Belgium with his mistress. In real life, however, Trenck died in his cell.

short cut to heaven – righteousness by association, perhaps. The bodies lie fully clothed, some with hollow-eyed skulls, others frozen in the last painful grimace of death. Just to drive the point home, signs in Czech chime in with "What we are, they once were; what they are, we will be".

To the west of the crypt steps lead up to the Biskupský dvůr, which, along with the neighbouring Dietrichsteinský palác, is home to the **Moravské zemské muzeum** (Tues–Sat 9am–5pm; Ⓦ www.mzm.cz). Brno is at the centre of quite an extensive area of early human settlement, and the museum contains an impressive collection of prehistoric finds from the region (there are more in the Anthropos annexe, including the famous *Venus of Věstonice*, plus a large section on the Great Moravian Empire. Opening out to the north of Kapucínské náměstí is **Zelný trh** (literally "cabbage market"), the chaotic vegetable market on a sloping cobbled square, somewhat ill-served by the mishmash of buildings that line its edges. At its centre is the petrified diarrhoea of the huge (dry) *Parnassus* fountain by Fischer von Erlach, featuring mythological beasts and Hercules himself .

The stará and nová radnice

Tucked down a side street, but clearly visible from Zelný trh, is the **stará radnice**, whose best feature is Anton Pilgram's Gothic doorway on Radnická. The tallest of the five thistly pinnacles above the statue of Blind Justice is deliberately twisted as if it's about to fall on your head – Pilgram's testament to the corrupt town aldermen who shortchanged him for his work (he went on to help furnish Vienna's Stephansdom). Inside, the town hall's courtyards and passageways are home to the **Brněnský drak** (Brno dragon), the **Brněnské kolo** (Brno wheel), the town's main tourist office, an exhibition space, a café and an observation tower (*vyhlídková věž*; April–Sept daily 9am–5pm), which offers a panorama across the city's red-tiled rooftops.

Round the back of the stará radnice, the handful of cobbled streets that lead south towards Petrov hill are the nearest Brno gets to a secluded spot: walk up Dominikanská to take a quick look inside the **Dům pánů z Kunštátu** (Tues–Sun 10am–6pm), one of Brno's few surviving Renaissance buildings, with a lovely arcaded courtyard and, inside, a café, temporary exhibitions put on by the city museum, and a small display on Janáček in Brno (for more on Janáček, see p.314).

The Brno mascots

Countless local legends surround the **Brněnský drak** (Brno "dragon", in fact a stuffed alligator), which hangs from the ceiling of the town hall entrance. The standard version is that the marauding beast was tricked into eating a carcass stuffed full of lime, upon which it rushed down to the River Svratka and quenched its thirst, causing the lime to expand and its stomach to burst. The most likely origin of the creature is that it was a gift from the Turkish sultan to Archduke Matthias, who in turn bequeathed it to Brno in an attempt to ingratiate himself with the local aristocrats. The other town mascot displayed here is the **Brněnské kolo** (Brno wheel), made in 1636 by a cartwright from Lednice, who bet a friend that he could fell a tree, make a wheel and roll it to Brno (some 50km away), all before sunset. He won the bet and the wheel has been given pride of place in the stará radnice ever since, though the story goes that following his great feat people began to suspect that the cartwright was in league with the devil: his business fell off and he died in poverty.

Petrov

Continue up Biskupská to **Petrov**, the smaller of the city's two central hills. At the top stands the **Cathedral of sv Petr and Pavel**, whose needle-sharp neo-Gothic spires from 1901 dominate the skyline. The cathedral holds a special place in Brno's history for having been instrumental in saving the town from the Swedes during the Thirty Years' War. After months besieging the town during the course of 1645, the Swedish general Tortennson decided to make one last attempt at taking the town, declaring he would give up at noon if the town hadn't surrendered. In a fit of inspiration, the bell-ringer, seeing that the town was on the brink of defeat, decided to ring the noon bells an hour early. The Swedes gave up their attack, the city was saved, and as a reward the Habsburg Emperor switched the Moravian capital from Olomouc to Brno (well, so the story goes). The clock strikes twelve at 11am to this day. Inside the lofty nave, there's a valuable fourteenth-century *Madonna and Child*, but the most intriguing art treasures are the aluminium *Stations of the Cross*, by Jiří Marek. Constructed in the early 1960s, these get progressively more outrageous and abstract as the story unfolds, until the final relief is no more than flailing limbs and anguished metal.

The cathedral is not the only reason to climb Petrov: from the nearby **Denisovy sady**, tucked into the city ramparts, there's a far-reaching view over the great plain south to Vienna, and an interesting angle on the cathedral itself. In among the trees and courting couples, a slender obelisk, resting on several squashed lions, commemorates the end of the Napoleonic Wars (the Battle of Austerlitz took place just outside Brno – see p.324), lining up perfectly with the avenue of Husova which leads to the red-brick Protestant church, known as the **Červený kostel** (Red Church), and, beyond it, the bright white former Party headquarters, known as the **Bílý dům** (White House).

Náměstí Svobody

Back down on Masarykova, follow the flow north and you'll end up at **náměstí Svobody**, the city's main square since the early thirteenth century. The medieval church that once stood at its centre was torn down in 1870, leaving only a Baroque plague column. Still, in summer, you can sit out, drink coffee and admire the square's finer buildings, which together span almost four centuries. The earliest is the **Dům z panů Lipé** (House of the Lords of Lipá), with an ornate Renaissance facade decorated with sgraffito, added as late as 1938. Though the building's arcaded courtyard has been brutally converted into a muzak-filled shopping mall, it's worth venturing inside and taking the lift to the rooftop **viewing platform** (*vyhlídková terasa*), which gives great views over the old town, the cathedral and Špilberk. A few doors along, at no. 15, the **Kleinův palác** was designed around 1848 in neo-Renaissance style by Theophil Hansen, the Danish architect responsible for some of the finest buildings on Vienna's Ringstrasse; the Klein family owned a nearby ironworks, hence the elegant wrought-iron oriel windows held up

▲ Petrov, Brno

with miniature Atlantes. Opposite, and lacking in such subtlety, is **Dům u čtyř mamlasů** (House of the Four Idiots), belonging to another of Brno's richest nineteenth-century Jewish industrialists, whose four muscle-bound employees struggle to hold up both his building and their loincloths. And in the 1930s, the functionalist **Moravská banka** (now the Komerční banka), designed by Arnošt Wiesner and Bohuslav Fuchs, was erected in the northwest corner of the square.

Heading north from náměstí Svobody, a stream of people flows past the book and record shops, pubs and cafés on **Česká**, wolfing down takeaways and ice cream on the way and, at the top, waiting for the trams and buses that congregate on Joštova, which marks the end of the old town. On the northeast corner of the square is the **Palác šlechtičen** (Noblewomen's Palace), which was founded in the 1670s as a school for twelve orphaned girls; four from poor families, four from burgher families and four from noble families. The building hosts temporary ethnographic exhibitions (Tues–Sat 9am–5pm).

North and east of náměstí Svobody

Clearly visible to the north of náměstí Svobody, up Rašínova, is the late Gothic church of **sv Jakub** (St James), with its distinctive onion dome and needle spire. Erected and paid for by the local burghers, it took two centuries to complete, and is perhaps best known for the sixteenth-century copulating couple on the south side of the tower. The pulpit in particular is worth a look: the stone base dates from 1526 and features three exquisite relief scenes – the Nativity, Jesus in the Temple and the Mount of Olives – and a lovely lion beneath the pedestal; above is a much later multi-tiered wooden tester packed with saints.

The finest architectural work of the Grimm brothers (there really were two of them) was the **Minoritský kostel** on the corner of Minoritská and Jánská, whose vivacious frontage makes the most of its cramped site. The right-hand portal leads to the main gilded nave, whose interior represents much the best slice of Baroque in town, high to the point of giddiness, an effect that's intensified by the illusionistic frescoes. Linked to the church next door by double doors in the north aisle is an equally stunning chapel, with a steep altar staircase that must be ascended on bended knee, and full-size colour terracotta statues of Jesus and the two robbers looking down from the gallery above. The greater part of the church is taken up with a **Loretánská kaple** (Loreto Chapel), its outer walls smothered in grisaille depictions of the miracle; the atmospheric red-brick interior holds the standard Black Madonna and Child set against a rich marble backdrop.

At the bottom of Jánská, the seven-storey department store **Centrum**, built in 1928 by the shoe magnate Tomáš Baťa, still cuts a bold figure. Beyond lies one of Brno's finest late nineteenth-century buildings, the **Mahenovo divadlo**, a forthright structure designed by Helmer and Fellner, exuding the municipal confidence of its original German patrons with its Corinthian columns and pediment. Its insides are smothered in gold sculpturing and glittering chandeliers, and it had the distinction of being the first theatre in the Austro-Hungarian Empire to be fitted with electric light bulbs. In total contrast to the flamboyant Mahenovo is Bohuslav Fuchs' squat functionalist **Dům umění** (Tues–Sun 10am–6pm; ⓦwww.dumb.cz), which hosts some of the city's most innovative exhibitions and theatre performances. A little further up Rooseveltova from the Mahenovo is the grey and scruffy-looking **Janáčkovo divadlo**, built in the 1960s as the country's largest opera house.

Although he was born in Hukvaldy (see p.378), in northern Moravia, **Leoš Janáček** (1854–1928) moved to Brno at the age of 11 and spent most of his life here, first as a chorister and then teacher and choirmaster at the local Augustinian monastery. Battling against the prejudices of the German-speaking town administration, he managed to drag Czech music out of the pub and into the concert hall, eventually founding the Brno Conservatoire and Organ School in 1882. All but one of his operas were premiered in Brno, and as a composer he remained virtually unknown outside Moravia until well into his 60s, when he began the last and most prolific creative period of his life. For much of the twentieth century, Janáček was overshadowed by his compatriots, Smetana (whom the Communists were particularly keen on) and Dvořák (whom the West has always revered), but in the last couple of decades his music has become increasingly popular, with works such as *Jenůfa* enjoying international acclaim.

Across the park from the opera house named after him, at the junction of Kounicova and Smetanova, is the **Památník Leoše Janáčka** (Mon–Fri 9am–noon & 1–4pm), in the cottage where the composer lived, at the back of the Organ School. Along with some period furniture and personal possessions you can see Čapek's original designs for the première of *The Makropulos Case*, and a BBC cartoon version of *The Cunning Little Vixen*. Unlike his predecessors, Smetana and Dvořák, Janáček chose not to be buried in Prague's illustrious Vyšehrad cemetery, opting instead for Brno's municipal one. If you're on the Janáček trail, bus #62 from outside Tesco, behind the train station, terminates at the main entrance off Jihlavská; or else tram #5, #7 or #8 will take you to within walking distance – the cemetery is easy enough to spot, thanks to the bright white pinnacles of Arnošt Wiesner's strikingly modern crematorium, designed in 1930.

Moravská galerie

Brno's **Moravská galerie** (Wed–Sun 10am–6pm, Thurs until 7pm; ⓦwww .moravska-galerie.cz; 80Kč) has one of the best art collections in the country, spread out over three premises. Probably the most universally appealing is the applied art collection in the Uměleckoprůmyslové muzeum or **UPM**, on Husova, which forms the western limit of the old town. The richly decorated ground floor plays host to wacky installations and temporary exhibitions of anything from avant-garde photomontages to the work of the local art school. The gallery's imaginatively designed permanent applied arts collection starts on the first floor, and continues on the top floor, with captions in Czech and English throughout.

The museum begins with a room devoted to medieval craftsmanship, the centrepiece of which is a wonderful silver-gilt crozier from the 1330s belonging to the abbots of Rajhrad. The highlight of the Renaissance room is an incredible seventeenth-century Swiss ceramic stove with matching seta, all smothered in pictorial depictions of the months of the year. After a room of Baroque and Rococo glassware, snuff boxes, fans and pocket watches, and the simple, almost modernist lines of the Biedermeier or Empire period, you reach a whole selection of Thonet furniture. Thonet, whose factories were mostly located in Moravia, fitted out the fin-de-siècle cafés of the Habsburg Empire with their bentwood chairs and tables. The Art Nouveau or Secession section is particularly rewarding, with a vast, curvaceous Gaillard sideboard, iridescent Lötz glassware from Klášterský Mlýn and a Klimt clay *jardinière*.

Further up Husova is the Moravská galerie's **Pražákův palác**, another sturdy nineteenth-century edifice, designed by Theophil Hansen and now housing an excellent permanent collection of twentieth-century Czech art. The pictures are rehung every year or so, but you're bound to see at least some of the gallery's best works, which include sculptures by Bílek, Štursa and Gutfreund; early Cubist works by Kubišta and Procházka, plus later pieces by Josef Čapek and Šíma; black-and-white photographs by Sudek and others; political works by Nepraš; and abstracts by Mikuláš Medek.

The third Moravská galerie building is the **Místodržitelský palác**, the former residence of the governor of Moravia, originally built as an Augustinian monastery at the eastern end of Joštova. Under the Communists it served as a museum of the working class, but it now hosts temporary exhibitions, plus a small permanent collection that includes a smattering of Gothic works, a few minor Baroque works by fresco specialists Kremser Schmidt, Maultbertsch and Daniel Gran, and some sentimental Biedermeier paintings. The final room contains the palace's only truly memorable works: a portrait of a woman by Hans Makart, painted with his characteristically dark, chocolate-brown palette, and Max Švabinský's striking *Red Sunshade*.

Špilberk

Skulking on a thickly wooded hill to the west of Husova and barely visible through the trees, the ugly, squat fortress of **Špilberk** (ⓦ www.spilberk.cz) acquired a reputation as one of the most god-awful prisons in the Habsburg Empire. As you walk up through the castle grounds, a monument featuring a wolf suckling Romulus and Remus commemorates the many Italians who died here, having been incarcerated fighting for their country's freedom in the northern regions – then under Austrian rule – of what is now Italy. The testimony of one Italian inmate, the poet Count Silvio Pellico, so shocked the empire's middle classes that the prison was closed down in 1855. In 1880 it was opened as a tourist attraction by the local military commander, Costa-Rosetti, who installed a model torture chamber and wrote the guide himself, recounting and embellishing myths and legends associated with the place. Sixty years later, it was put back into use by the Nazis who confined, tortured and killed countless prisoners here during the war.

Underneath the fortress's eastern gate lurks the entrance to the atmospheric **kasematy** (dungeons; Tues–Sun: May–Sept 9am–6pm; Oct–April 9am–5pm; 60Kč). Most chilling is the reconstruction of the so-called "dark cells" in the north wing, installed by the great reforming Emperor Josef II, who first turned the barracks into a prison. In these, prisoners were chained by the neck and hands in complete darkness and given only bread and water – a practice eventually stopped by Josef II's successor, Leopold II. Silvio Pellico and his contemporaries were actually incarcerated in the upper storey of the fortress, in – as it were – the best cells. Make sure you pick up a leaflet with a plan, since the place is a veritable labyrinth. For the best view over Brno, head for the **rozhledna** (May–Sept Tues–Sun 9am–6pm; April & Oct Sat & Sun 9am–5pm; 30Kč), the fortress's observation tower.

Beyond the eastern gate and across the moat lies Špilberk's central courtyard and the **Muzeum města Brna** (Museum of the City of Brno; May–Sept Tues–Sun 9am–6pm; April & Oct Tues–Sun 9am–5pm; Nov–March Wed–Sun 10am–5pm; 140Kč), which is best taken at a canter. Temporary exhibitions take place on the ground floor, along with a permanent display on the history of the prison. On the second floor, Baroque statues and sixteenth-century votive paintings from the church of sv Jakub, paid for by rich local burghers and painted by Dutch masters, hang alongside a decent collection of eighteenth- and nineteenth-century portraits of rich local townsfolk. Works from the first half of the last century include a good spread by Antonín Procházka, from his Cubist *Girl with Garland* to the loose brushwork of *Bathing Horses* from the 1940s. Also worthy of note are Jaroslav Král's Cubist paintings, such as his portrait of Cubist architect Emil Králík; František Foltýn's pastel-shaded abstract works; and the minimalist egg cups and glasses designed by Bohuslav Fuchs.

The top floor includes a section on Brno's **interwar architecture**, with photos, architectural drawings and a few pieces of original furniture by the likes of Adolf Loos, Alvar Aalto and Mies van der Rohe. The work of functionalist architect Bohuslav Fuchs (see opposite) occupies centre stage, although there's also a section on the Nový dům colony (see opposite) and the original plans for the (unrealized) Centrum skyscraper.

You exit via a Baroque chapel decorated by the family of Baron von Trenck (see p.310) to serve as a memorial to one of Špilberk's most famous prisoners – macabre frescoes of skeletons bearing posies of flowers symbolize life's transience. The chapel also contains a display of photomontages by anti-Nazi artist John Heartfield, who lived in Brno between 1933 and 1938.

Gregor Mendel and the Augustinian monastery

The area south of the Špilberk hill, where the first settlements sprang up in the early Middle Ages, is known as **Staré Brno**. Few traces of these survive and nowadays there's nothing particularly interesting about this part of town, with the exception of the fourteenth-century **Augustinian monastery** on Mendlovo náměstí. Despite its unpromising locale – the square is little more than a glorified bus terminal – the monastery's **Bazilika** is one of Brno's finest Gothic buildings, its interior walls and pillars smothered in delicate geometric patterning dating from 1905. Take a look at the church's *Black Madonna* icon set beneath a silver crown at the high altar, which dates from the thirteenth century and which, it was believed, protected the city from foreign troops. The best time to visit is just before a service (Tues, Thurs, Fri & Sun 5.45–7.15pm); tours can also be arranged from the Mendel museum (see below).

The monastery is best known for one of its monks, **Gregor Mendel** (1822–84), whose experiments in the abbey gardens with cultivating and hybridizing peas and bees eventually led to the discovery of the principles of heredity and, subsequently, genetics. Despite the publication of several seminal papers outlining his discoveries, his work was ignored by the scientific establishment of the day, and in 1868 he gave up his research to become the monastery's abbot. Only after his death was he acknowledged as one of the greats of modern biology. Apart from his glasses and the tools of his trade, there's not much of Mendel the man in the **Mendel museum** (April–Oct daily 10am–6pm; Nov–March Wed–Sun 10am–6pm; 80Kč) in the west wing of the monastery. Instead, interactive computers explain the basics, while art installations provoke visitors into thinking about the ethical minefield of genetics. Before you leave, don't miss the monks' eighteenth-century **refectory**, opposite the ticket office, with its florid Art Nouveau stuccowork and vast relief depicting the abbot ascending into heaven.

Výstaviště and around

Southwest of the city centre, where the River Svratka opens up to the plain (tram #1 from the station), is the **Výstaviště** (Ⓦ www.bvv.cz) or exhibition grounds. The main buildings were laid out in 1928 for the city's Exhibition of Contemporary Culture, and most of the leading Czech architects of the day were involved in the scheme, which prompted a flurry of functionalist building projects across the city's burgeoning suburbs.

Fuchs and Functionalism

Although Brno produced two great modern architects in Adolf Loos and Jan Kotěra, they spent most of their time in Vienna and Prague respectively, and it was left to another Moravian, **Bohuslav Fuchs**, who began working here in 1923, to shape the face of modern Brno. Fuchs and his functionalist cohorts turned their hand to everything from the town's crematorium to the Protestant church on Botanická, its interior decoration as "low-church" and prosaic as you can get. Fuchs' hand is everywhere in the city, in the low-slung post office extension to the main train station, in the Alfa *pasáž* off Jánská, in the slimline *Hotel Avion*, on Česká, and in Výstaviště itself. His most famous works are the open-plan boarding school and Vesna girls' school (on Lipová, just north of Výstaviště), two simple four-storey functionalist buildings, way ahead of their time. Perhaps the best way to appreciate Fuchs' work, though, is to head out to the outdoor swimming pool he built in the city's eastern suburbs, just off Zábrdovická (tram #2 or #3; stop Vojenská nemocnice), where you can laze by the pool and take in the culture at the same time.

As you approach the concave entrance to the trade fair grounds, you're greeted by *Atomový věk* (Atomic Age), a classic Social Realist sculpture on a towering plinth. Inside the grounds, the first building you come to is **Pavilón A**, a vast exhibition hall built in 1928, with distinctive concrete parabolic arches; two constructivist red-brick buildings, to the south, also date from the original 1928 exhibition. At the end of the main avenue, you'll find the two postwar additions which have kept closest to the spirit of the original concept: **Pavilón G**, with its glass encased tower, a 1990s reconstruction of an original 1928 building, and the circular crystal-and-concrete **Pavilón Z**, the largest building on the site. The only building which predates the exhibition is the eighteenth-century **zámek**, which features a marble hall on the ground floor designed in 1924 by Brno-born arch-minimalist Adolf Loos.

The part of the 1928 exhibition that really caused a sensation was the **Nový dům** settlement, worth a look if you're keen on Bauhaus-style architecture. Inspired by the Weissenhofsiedlung built a year earlier in Stuttgart, Bohuslav Fuchs and various others designed a series of boxy, white, concrete villas by the woods of the Wilsonův les, north of Výstaviště, up Žabovřeská (tram #1 from Výstaviště), in the streets of Drnovická and Petřvaldská. The brief for each architect was to create modest two-storey houses for middle-income families, using standard fittings and ordinary materials to keep the unit cost down. Many are now grey, peeling and overrun by vegetation, and it takes a leap of imagination to appreciate the shock of the new that these buildings must have aroused at the time.

Vila Tugendhat

On the opposite side of town, in the northeastern suburb of Černá Pole, modernist guru Mies van der Rohe built the **Vila Tugendhat** (hourly guided tours Wed–Sun 10am–6pm; ☎545 212 118, ⊛www.tugendhat-villa.cz; 120Kč) in the same functionalist style as the Nový dům settlement, but to a very different brief: the Tugendhats, an exceptionally rich Jewish family who ran a number of the city's textile factories, wanted a state-of-the-art house kitted out in the most expensive gear money could buy. It was completed in 1930, but the family had barely eight years to enjoy the luxury of the place before fleeing to South America (with most of the period furniture) in the wake of the Nazi invasion. For the next fifty years it was put to many uses – both the Nazis and Communists were particularly partial to it for exclusive social functions. From the street, you enter through the top floor, but the main living space is actually downstairs, open-plan for the most part and originally decked out in minimalist monochrome furnishings offset by colourful Persian carpets. The Communists' "modernization" after the war was depressingly thorough, and the huge unbroken front window, which looked out over the garden and the whole cityscape beyond it, has been replaced by a series of much smaller panes, being all the Communists' glassworks could muster. The house is at Černopolní 45, off Merhautova, itself a continuation of M. Horákové (tram #3, #5 or #11; stop Dětská nemocnice). It's very popular, so book ahead.

Technické muzeum

Brno's **Technické muzeum** (Tues–Sun 9am–5pm; Ⓦ www.technicalmuseum .cz; 60Kč) is in the far northern suburb of Královo Pole, by the terminus of tram #13. Head first for the museum's **Panoptikon** (April–Oct daily 9am–5pm; Nov–March Mon–Fri 9am–5pm), a large wooden stereoscope built in 1890 and designed to allow several viewers to see its three-dimensional slides simultaneously. The exhibition itself kicks off with a host of beautiful **vintage and veteran cars** from a lovely 1910 Austro-Daimler to a postwar Praga limo – look out, too, for the Z4, made by Brno's own Zbrojovka car factory. On the ground floor there's some pretty technical stuff on steam engines and turbines, with a section on Viktor Kaplan, who invented his turbine while working in Brno. With labelling mostly in Czech, it's probably best to head for the more visually engaging exhibits on the second floor, including dioramas and mechanical music boxes, model planes, old radios, TVs and telephones. On the top floor is the **Experimentárium**, the museum's excellent hands-on section.

Eating and drinking

There's no shortage of good **places to eat and drink** in Brno, but equally, there's nothing like the choice of cuisines available in Prague. Brno also has nowhere near the same volume of expats, so prices are uniformly low, and the clientele predominantly Czech. Most night-time drinking takes place in the **pubs** – which are also the cheapest places to eat simple, traditional **Czech food** – although there's a fair selection of late-opening bars and clubs for the party-hard crowd. Locally brewed **Starobrno** beer is very much the tipple of choice, although you'll find all major Czech brews fairly well represented in Brno's bars and pubs.

Cafés and tea-houses

Blau Jakubské náměstí. Designer café, decked out in (you guessed it) blue, and something of a media hangout, due to it being located in the same building as Czech TV's Brno studios. Mon–Fri 8am–10pm, Sat 11am–10pm, Sun 2–10pm.

Dobrá čajovňa Franciskánská 6. With oriental carpets and cushions strewn around the first-floor rooms of a galleried building, this has the look and feel of an Ottoman-era caravanserai. Big choice of teas and hookah-pipe tobaccos. Daily 11am–11pm.

Rendezvous Moravské náměstí. Small café decked out in citrus-fruit colours opposite the Místodržitelský palác, serving toasted sandwiches and sweet and savoury *palačinky*. Mon–Thurs

8am–10pm, Fri 8am–11pm, Sat & Sun 10am–10pm.

Spolek Orlí 22. Pleasant bookshop café with an imaginative veggie-friendly menu featuring soups, risotto, pasta and *palačinky*. Mon–Sat 10am–10pm, Sun noon–10pm.

Švanda Poštovská 8d (Alfa pasáž). Smoky modernist café in the functionalist Alfa pasáž. Mon–Sat 10.30am–midnight, Sun 4pm–midnight.

Vitalité Lidická 26. Self-service healthy-eating canteen with soups, stews, salads and fish. Smart but slightly sterile, it's a bit like eating in a Scandinavian furniture showroom. Mon–Fri 9.30am–6pm, Sat 11am–3pm.

Zemanova kavárna Jezuitská 6 Ⓦ www .zemanka.cz. In the park just off Jezuitská, this luscious white cube of a building is an exact replica of Fuchs' functionalist café of 1923, which was torn down by the Communists in order to build the Janáčkovo divadlo. Great for cakes and coffee and a solid menu of light meals. Mon–Fri 10am–10pm, Sat & Sun 11am–10pm.

Restaurants

Boulevard Lidická 12 ⓦ www.boulevardrestaurant.cz. Upscale, stylish eatery particularly good for fish and seafood, as well as the midlle-European meat standards. With three-course set lunches at 250Kč, and main dishes hovering around the 300Kč mark, it's twice as expensive as the regular pubs and restaurants in town, but probably worth the splurge. Daily noon–midnight.

Skanseen Peharská 76. Tasty and filling pork and dumplings in a theatrical peasant-hut interior, crammed with rustic knick-knacks. Daily 11am–midnight.

Hotel Slavia Solniční 15–17. Experience classy central European meat dishes in a semi-formal, slightly old-fashioned atmosphere that hasn't changed much since Communist times in this excellent hotel restaurant. Daily noon–11pm.

U Kaštelana Kotlařska 51a ☏ 541 213 497, ⓦ www.ukastelana.cz. In an old brewery 10min walk north of the old town (head up Lidická and turn left after passing Lužánký park), this is the gourmet restaurant of choice, mixing classic French cuisine with Japanese sushi and a handful of Czech-Moravian classics – all immaculately prepared and presented. With mains starting at 300Kč (and moving steeply upwards if you opt for the shark or the steak), this is worth saving for a treat. Mon–Sat noon–midnight.

U královny Elišky Mendlovo nám. 1B ⓦ www.ukralovnyelisky.cz. Atmospheric cellar *vinárna* tucked into the hillside behind the Augustinian monastery, offering the whole Moravian caboodle, including live folk music. Turns into an upmarket disco-pub on weekend nights. Tues–Sat 7pm–3am.

Pubs

Panoptikum Jakubská 9. Bright, modern pub-restaurant with a handsome selection of draught beers and a good – if rather standard – range of Czech food. Sun–Thurs 11am–2am, Fri & Sat 11am–4am.

Pegas Jakubská 4. If there are any foreigners in town, it's guaranteed they'll be drinking here – and fair enough, for this is a large and very pleasant pub that brews its own light and dark beers on the premises. Also serves up a decent goulash with dumplings. Mon–Fri 9am–midnight, Sun 10am–10pm.

Pivovarská pivnice Mendlovo náměstí. The true Starobrno experience: a pub right by the brewery itself, perfectly served 12-degree Starobrno and the rarer 14-degree Baron Trenck. The indoor bar area is a bit rough and ready, although the outdoor terrace – with wooden benches and a stage for live music – is much more of a family venue. Daily 10am–midnight.

Špalíček Zelný trh 12. A Starobrno pub with a solid menu of Czech pork and poultry favourites. Tables outside in summer overlooking the vegetable market. Daily 11am–11pm.

Bars and clubs

Desert Rooseveltová ⓦ www.dodesertu.com. Multi-chambered cellar decorated in brash pop-art style and frequented by mildly bohemian, non-mainstream-music types. Regular gigs and DJ nights in the back room. Daily 7pm–2am or later.

Fléda Štefánikova 24 ⓦ www.fleda.cz. Basement-bound jazz pub with frequent live performances, a 20min walk north of the centre but well worth the trek.

Skleněná louka Kounicova 23 ⓦ www.sklenenalouka.cz. Barrel-vaulted cellar bar with occasional live music, catering for a slightly alter-native, rocky crowd. The Atrium bar on the ground floor of the same building goes for ear-splitting house and techno, and there's an arty daytime *čajovna* under the eaves on the top floor. Mon–Fri 6pm–1am, Sat & Sun 6pm–2am.

Entertainment

Lovers of classical music, opera and drama are well catered for, with two big opera houses/theatres, a philharmonic orchestra, and numerous smaller venues. To find out what's on, get hold of the monthly **listings** pamphlet *Kam v Brně* (ⓦ www.kultura-brno.cz) from the tourist office. The Mahenovo divadlo, which boasts the most ornate interior, mostly puts on plays in Czech; while the Janáčkovo divadlo stages **opera and ballet**. Tickets for both can be bought in advance from the box office at Dvořákova 11 (Mon–Fri 8am–5.30pm, Sat 9am–noon; ⓦ www.ndbrno.cz), or from the venue itself half an hour before the performance starts. The Besední dům, home to the Státní filharmonie Brno (ⓦ www.sfb.cz), hosts regular **classical concerts**. For chamber music, check out the concert hall of the local music academy, JAMU, on Komenského náměstí. There's an excellent **art-house cinema**, Kino Art, at Cihlářská 19 (Ⓦ www.kinoartbrno.cz), a short way up Lidická from Moravské náměstí. The city hosts its own week-long European film festival, **Dny evropského filmu** (Ⓦ www.eurofilmfest.cz) in February; a festival of spiritual music at Petrov around Easter, **Velikonoiní festival duchovní hudby**; a summer music festival and occasional open-air opera in the Špilberk courtyard; and in late September/early October, a three-week-long **international classical music festival**, known as Moravský podzim (Ⓦ www.mhfb.cz).

Listings

Books Barvič & Novotný, Česká 13. Brno's best-stocked bookshop, with lots of maps, English-language guides, CDs and posters. Daily until 7pm.

Currency exchange Komerční banka, náměstí Svobody 21. 24hr exchange at the main train station.

Hospital Bratislavská 2; emergency medical attention ☏ 555.

Left luggage The main train station has 24hr left luggage and lockers.

Newspapers The newsagents in the train station and the kiosk opposite the main train station has the best selection of foreign newspapers.

Pharmacy All-night service at Koblížna 7 ☏ 542 210 222.

Police The main police station is at Kounicova 46.

Post office The most convenient post office is next door to the train station. It runs a 24hr telephone exchange.

Taxis Ranks outside the station and on Solniční, or dial ☏ 542 321 321 for City Taxi.

Around Brno

The area around Brno is rich in potential day-trips, the most popular of which is to the limestone caves of the **Moravský kras**, closely followed by the castle of **Pernštejn** and the battlefield at **Slavkov** (Austerlitz). Potentially more interesting than any of those, however, is the Renaissance chateau at **Moravský Krumlov**, which houses a museum dedicated to the work of the Art Nouveau painter Alfons Mucha.

Moravský kras

Moravia's number-one tourist attraction, the limestone **karst region** of the **Moravský kras** (Ⓦ www.smk.cz), lies just over 25km northeast of Brno. The most popular (and rewarding) of the caves to visit is the **Punkevní jeskyně**, which has a fantastic array of stalactites and stalagmites and includes an underground river, a giant chasm and the possibility of a cable-car ride. Quite apart from the caves, the whole karst region boasts some dramatic and varied scenery, smothered in a thick coating of coniferous forest and riddled with marked paths, providing great **walking** country. If you're not in a hurry, the three **churches** in Křtiny, Jedovnice and Senetářov and the town of Boskovice deserve a visit, providing a more relaxed alternative to the crush of tourists along the Punkva river.

The caves

The **Punkevní jeskyně** lies at the deepest part of the gorge – get there early, or get the tourist office to book in advance for you, as tickets can sell out for the whole day in high season. In the summer, tours run every fifteen minutes and take around an hour (April–June & Sept Mon 10am–3.50pm, Tues–Sun

8.20am–3.50pm; July & Aug Mon 10am–3.50pm, Tues–Sun 8.20am–5pm; Oct Tues–Fri 8.40am–2pm, Sat & Sun 8.20am–3.40pm; Nov–March Tues–Sun 8.40am–2pm; ☎516 418 602, ⓦwww.cavemk.cz; 150Kč). After a series of five chambers, you come to the bottom of the **Propast Macocha** (Macocha Abyss), a gigantic 138-metre mossy chasm created when the roof of one of the caves collapsed. The first man to descend into the abyss and return alive was Father "Lazarus" Erker in 1728, almost two hundred years before the caves themselves were properly explored. From the abyss, you're taken by boat 500m along the slimy underground Punkva river, which gives the cave its name. Just beyond the entrance to the caves, there's a very steep **cable car** (*lanová dráha*), which can whisk you swiftly to the top of the abyss, so you can look down on where you've just been. If you're going to take the Eko-Train (*vlaček*) and the cable car, be sure to buy a *Kombi-Karte* when you first set out.

The other caves open to the public are only slightly less spectacular, and the queues are far shorter. The **Kateřinská jeskyně** (30min tour: Feb & March Tues–Sun 10am, noon & 2pm; April & Oct Tues–Sun 8.20am–4pm; May–Sept daily 8.20am–4pm; 60Kč), 1.5km before the Punkevní jeskyně at the point where the Punkva river re-emerges, is the largest single cave in the karst region, one huge "cathedral" of rock formations, 100m long and 20m high.

Practicalities

To get to the caves by public transport, catch a morning **train** from Brno to BLANSKO station (not Blansko město), and walk 200m south to the bus station. From here, **buses** depart for **SKALNÍ MLÝN**, location of the main ticket office and information centre for the **Punkevní jeskyně** caves. Before setting out, check with the Brno tourist office (see p.306) that trains and buses connect. All visitors to the caves must either walk the 1.5km from Skalní Mlýn or catch the regular **Eko-Train** service; there are also bikes for hire. Alternatively, it's a very nice five-kilometre walk through the woods all the way from Blansko station along the green-marked path. Make sure you take some warm clothing, as the temperature in the caves is a constant 8.7°C.

The **hotel** *Skálni Mlýn* (☎516 418 113, ⓦwww.smk.cz; ❸), in Skálni Mlýn itself, is busy with tourists, but the perfect place to stay if you're keen to visit several of the caves. The nicest **campsite** in the region is *Relaxa* (May–Sept; ☎602 795 703, ⓦwww.camprelaxa.cz) in Sloup, north of the caves; you'll have to walk the 5km to the caves if you've no transport.

Křtiny, Jedovnice and Senetářov

Although buses run to Křtiny, the most rewarding way to reach the village is to take the train from Brno to Adamov zastávka (not Adamov itself) and walk east up the **Josefovské údolí** (the blue-marked path follows the road), a steep, craggy valley with remnants of the original primeval forest cover and open-air stalagmites. After 3km, at the top of the valley, there's a special nature trail round a mini-karst region of around five caves, none of which is actually accessible. Another 3km further east along the blue path, and out of the woods, leaps the enormous dome and tower of the pilgrimage church of **KŘTINY**, designed by the Baroque genius Giovanni Santini. One door is usually open to let you inside, where the nave has been handed over to a series of interlinking frescoed domes that fuse into one, giving the church a Byzantine feel. The interior decor is gaudy High Baroque, with technicolour cherubs and saints strewn about the place, but the overall effect is satisfyingly impressive and unified.

Taking the yellow-marked path, skirt the edge of the woods to the northeast, which rise gently past the understated summit of Proklest (574m). Six kilometres on from Křtiny, you emerge from the trees at the small lake by the village of **JEDOVNICE**, no beauty itself, thanks to a fire in 1822, which also torched the late eighteenth-century village church. From the outside the latter looks hurriedly restored; the interior, however, redesigned in the 1960s, contains symbolic art, stained glass and, as the centrepiece, a striking **altar** painting by Mikuláš Medek, *persona non grata* in Czechoslovakia in the 1950s for his penchant for abstract art, surrealism and social comment. His choice of colours is didactic: a blue cross for hope, and red for the chaos of the world. Unless it's a Sunday, you'll have to get the key from the *kaplan* who lives opposite the church and who can also furnish you with an *anglický text*.

There's no escaping the modernity of Ludvík Kolek's concrete church at **SENETÁŘOV**, completed in 1971, 4km down the road to Výskov; it's built in the shape of a ship, its "mast" visible as you approach from the plateau – though as a concept, its symbolism is reminiscent of the work of Santini. It's an uncompromising building, with huge plate-glass panels at the west end, through which you can clearly see the main altarpiece, an abstract version of the Last Supper against a vivid blue background. But it's Medek's *Stations of the Cross*, on the north wall and difficult to see without getting inside, that are the most striking. Starting with a deep red crown of thorns, the pictures progress in bold, simple colours and symbols, fusing into one long fourteen-piece canvas and signalling an original working of an otherwise hackneyed theme.

Buses from Brno and Blansko run regularly to Jedovnice, passing through Křtiny and occasionally continuing to Senetářov. Křtiny is a good base, with several new pensions such as the *Santini* (☎516 439 432 or 723 426 776; ❸) and the *Olšovec* **campsite** (April–Oct; Ⓦ www.olsovec.cz) on the southeastern corner of the lake in Jedovnice.

Boskovice

BOSKOVICE, 17km north of Blansko, guards the Svitava valley. On the whole, it's a sleepy little place, with a modest chateau and a ruined hilltop castle, though it does have one of the best-preserved Jewish quarters in Moravia. Jews began to settle in Boskovice from the fifteenth century onwards, and from 1727 they were incarcerated in a ghetto, with five gates, one of which remains to this day. By the mid-nineteenth century, Jews made up a third of the town's population of around six thousand. To find out more about the town's Jewish history, head for the town's seventeenth-century **synagogue** (April & Oct Sat & Sun 1–5pm; May–Sept Tues–Fri 9am–5pm, Sat & Sun 1–5pm; 30Kč), south of the main square on Antonína Trapla, whose walls and vaults feature beautifully preserved frescoes of flora and fauna. The exhibition inside has photos of the community in its prime and of the transport in March 1942, which sent the town's 458 Jews to Terezín.

Just off the main square on Hradní, a modest town museum hosts changing exhibitions of local interest. Five-minutes' walk further on stands the town's **zámek** (Tues–Sun: June–Aug 9am–6pm; May & Sept 9am–5pm; 80Kč), a former monastery adapted as an aristocratic home in the 1820s, and currently containing a clutch of well-restored Neoclassical interiors. It was handed back to its former owners, the Mensdorff-Pouillys, in the 1990s, along with the ruined **hrad** (April & Oct Sat & Sun 10am–4pm; May & Sept Tues–Sun 10am–5pm; June–Aug daily 9am–6pm; 30Kč), which is a five-minute walk further south through the woods.

For something much more mind-blowing, however, you should head out to the **Westernové městečko Boskovice** (from 10am: May & June Sat & Sun;

July & Aug Tues–Sun; @www.wildwest.cz), a wild west theme park about 2km northeast of the town along the blue-marked path. Saloons, rodeos and open-air extravaganzas are just some of the attractions, and you can even stay the night on set or in a wagon around a campfire.

Practicalities

Boskovice is a perfectly feasible base for exploring the whole of the Moravský kras, if you have your own transport. To get there by **train** from Brno or Blansko, you need to change at Skalice nad Svitavou. Best place **to stay** is the *Penzion pod Zámkem*, just off the main square at Hradní 4 (T516 456 056, @www.penzionpodzamkem.cz; ❸), offering neat en-suite doubles and a handful of triples and quads. If it's full, then the *Hotel Slavia* by the train station (T501 454 126, @www.bosnet.cz/hotel-slavia; ❸) is a reasonable alternative. Although the name might suggest a Jewish theme, the barrel-vaulted *Makkabi* **restaurant** at Velanova 8 offers straightforward Czech pork-and-potato dishes, plus locally brewed Černa Hora beer. The *Literární* **čajovňa**, just up from the synagogue on U císařské, doles out speciality teas by the potful – you can sit on a normal chair or on a bed strewn with teddy bears – as well as selling books, Hindu effigies, darbuka drums and other essentials. If all the hippy stuff is a bit much, head round the corner to the funky *Kafírna Dogvil* on Zborovská, which serves up strong doses of coffee.

Spread over a long weekend in mid-July, the Boskovice **Festival** (@www .unijazz.cz) is a hip and well-attended cultural event involving jazz gigs, literary readings, art shows and drama. Reserve accommodation well in advance or visit from Brno on the train.

Pernštejn

The Gothic stronghold of **Pernštejn**, a picture-perfect medieval castle, is one of the most popular, and easiest day-trips from Brno; the picturesque **train** journey up the Svratka Valley to the nearest station, **NEDVĚDICE**, takes just over an hour. From the platform, the castle is visible to the west; to get there follow the yellow-marked track. Beyond its series of outer defences, the **hrad** (July & Aug Tues–Sun 9am–noon & 1–5pm; May, June & Sept closes 4pm; April & Oct Sat & Sun 9am–noon & 1–3pm; 80Kč) is a truly dramatic sight, with kestrels circling the dizzying sheer walls. Originally built in the thirteenth century, it has been left a jumble of unpredictable angles and extras from various reconstructions, including a death-defying covered wooden bridge that spans the castle's main keeps. There are four guided tours: *trasa A* is the standard hour-long tour; *trasa B*, twenty minutes longer, takes in the nineteenth-century period interiors; *trasa C*, also twenty minutes longer, concentrates on the dungeons and the attics; *trasa D* is a thirty-minute canter through the chapel, sacristy and clock tower.

Moravský Krumlov

Squeezed into a tight bend of the Rokytná river, southwest of Brno, is **MORAVSKÝ KRUMLOV**, whose **zámek**, to the west of town, boasts a delicate arcaded loggia from 1557, and an **art gallery** (Tues–Sun: April–June, Sept & Oct 9am–noon & 1–4pm; July & Aug closes 5pm; 60Kč) dedicated to one of the better-known Czech artists, **Alfons Mucha** (1860–1939), who was born in the mining town of Ivančice, a few kilometres to the north. The Mucha Museum in Prague (see p.111) may have a finer selection of works from Mucha's most popular period, when he was living in Paris, but you do get to see here one major piece missing from that collection, the *Slovanská epopej* (Slav Epic), a cycle of twenty monumental canvases commissioned by an American millionaire. In Czech terms they're well-worn themes – Komenský fleeing the "fatherland", the Battle of Vítkov and so on – but they were obviously heartfelt for Mucha, who saw the project as his life's work. In the end he paid for his nationalism with his life: dragged in for questioning by the Gestapo after the 1939 Nazi invasion, he died shortly after being released. In this slightly forlorn chateau, Mucha's gloomy, melodramatic paintings take on a fascination all of their own.

Trains from Brno are fairly frequent and direct (those from Znojmo or Mikulov require a change at Hrušovany nad Jevišovkou), but the station is a good 2km east of the town; **buses** from Brno and Znojmo will drop you in the centre, but timings are only really any good from Znojmo.

Slavkov and the Battle of Austerlitz

Twenty kilometres by train across the flat plain east of Brno, **SLAVKOV** (Austerlitz) would be just another humble ribbon village were it not for the great mass of Martinelli's late Baroque **zámek** (May–Sept 9am–5pm; April, Oct & Nov 9am–4pm; Ⓦwww.zamek-slavkov.cz; 55Kč). Like so many chateaux close to the Austrian border, its contents were quickly and judiciously removed by their owners before the arrival of the Red Army in 1945; in their place are changing exhibitions, usually on a military theme. The highlight of the 45-minute guided tour is the central concave hall, **Sál předků**, which has the most incredible acoustics. Every whisper of sound in the giant dome echoes for a full ten seconds, while outside not one word can be heard. Martinelli also designed the village's imposing Neoclassical church, with its massive Corinthian portico; inside are some great high-relief sculptures along the walls and above the high altar.

On December 2, 1805, in the fields between Slavkov and Brno, the Austrians and Russians received a decisive drubbing at the hands of the numerically inferior Napoleonic troops in the **Battle of Austerlitz** (also known as the "Battle of the Three Emperors"). The Austrians and Russians committed themselves early, charging into the morning fog to attack the French on both flanks. From his vantage point on the Žuráň hill to the north, Napoleon, confident of victory, held back until the enemy had established its position, and then attacked at their weakest point, the central commanding heights of the Pratzen hill (Pracký kopec), splitting their forces and throwing them into disarray. It was all over by lunchtime, with over 24,000 troops dead. After the battle, all three emperors signed a peace treaty, marking an end to Napoleon's eastern campaign until the fateful march on Moscow in 1812. There's a graphic description of the battle in Tolstoy's epic novel *War and Peace*.

Just over one hundred years later, on the strategic Pratzen hill, 8km southwest of Slavkov, the **Mohyla míru** (Monument of Peace) was erected on the instigation of a local pacifist priest, and paid for by the governments of France, Austria and Russia, who within three years of pledging the money were once again at war with one another. There's a superb view of the surrounding killing fields, now just a series of ploughed fields peppered with crosses and dotted with the odd little Calvary. The tent-like stone monument, designed by the Art Nouveau architect Josef Fanta, contains a small chapel, and nearby there's a **museum** (April Tues–Sun 9am–5pm; May, June & Sept daily 9am–5pm; July & Aug daily 9am–6pm; Oct–March Tues–Sun 9am–3.30pm; Ⓦwww.muzeumbrnenska.cz; 75Kč), including the obligatory toy soldier mock-up of the battle. Military enthusiasts without their own transport have a choice of uphill walks: 2km to the southeast from Ponětovice train station, 3km to the northeast from Sokolnice train station, or 1.5km to the south from the bus stop in Prace. On the anniversary of the battle, the Friends of the French Revolution treat onlookers to a chilly re-enactment.

There's a **tourist office** next door to the zámek (April, May & Sept–Nov Tues–Sun 9am–4pm; June–Aug Mon–Sat 9am–noon & 12.30–5pm, Sun 11am–5pm; Dec–March Mon–Fri 9am–4pm). For **food**, head for the *Hotel Sokolský dům*, which also offers **rooms** (☎544 221 103, Ⓦwww.hotel sokolskydum.cz; ❸). Another good option is the *Stará pošta* (☎517 375 985, Ⓦwww.staraposta.cz; ❻), 4km northwest of Slavkov, on the north side of the motorway, where Napoleon stayed before the battle; it serves decent food, has very nicely furnished rooms, and offers horse-drawn tours of the battlefield in the summer.

Bučovice

Ten kilometres further east, and accessible by train from Brno, the **zámek** (May–Sept: Tues–Sun 9am–noon & 1–4pm; April & Oct Sat & Sun only; 60Kč) at **BUČOVICE**, circled by kestrels, gets a fraction of the visitors of Slavkov, partly perhaps because of its unpromising exterior: a dull grey fortress with four ugly squat towers. None of it prepares you for the subtle, slender Italianate arcading of the courtyard's three-sided loggia, with each set of supporting columns topped by a different carved motif. At the centre of the courtyard a chunky stone fountain was added a few generations later, out of keeping with the rest of the masonry. The towers, the gardens and countless rooms once matched the charm and elegance of the courtyard, but the Liechtensteins, who obtained the chateau through marriage in 1597, soon turned it into little more than a storage house for the family records, scattering its original furnishings among their many other Moravian residences.

The only things they couldn't remove were the original sixteenth-century **ceiling decorations**, a fantastical mantle of sculpture and paint, coating just five or so rooms, none more than 6m across. The first few are just a warm-up for the thick stucco of the **císařský sál**, with the bejewelled relief figures of Mars, Diana, a half-naked Europa and, most magnificent of all, the Emperor Charles V trampling a turbaned Turk into the paintwork. But the decoration of the **zaječí sál** (The Hall of Hares) is the real star turn, an anthropomorphic work thought to be one of the few from that period still in existence. It's a comical scene, with the hares exacting their revenge on man and his closest ally, the dog. The aftermath of the hares' revolution sees them sitting in judgement (wigs and all) over their defeated enemies, as well as indulging in more highbrow activities – hare as Rembrandt, hare as scholar and so on.

Mikulov and around

Clinging on to the southern tip of the **Pavlovské vrchy**, the last hills before the Austrian plain, **MIKULOV** (Nikolsburg) is one of South Moravia's minor gems. Slap bang in the middle of the wine-producing region, it's been a border post for centuries – hence the narrow streets and siege mentality of much of the architecture. The town still functions as a busy crossing between the two countries; if you're driving from Vienna, it's a great introduction to the country and, given its strategic locale, surprisingly tourist-free except after the grape **harvest** in late September, when the first bouquet is being tried and tested in vast quantities at the local *sklepy* (wine caves) on the edge of town.

Raised above the jumble of red rooftops is the **zámek** (Tues–Sun: April & Oct 9am–4pm; May–Sept 9am–5pm; Ⓦwww.rmm.cz; art gallery 20Kč, museum and art gallery 70Kč), an imposing complex built right into the rocky hill on the west side of town. Used by the Gestapo to hoard confiscated art objects, it was blown to smithereens by them in the last days of the war in a final nihilistic gesture. Rebuilt in the 1950s, it now houses the local museum and a large portrait collection, mostly Habsburg royalty, Dietrichsteins and cardinals, though the future George III makes a surprising appearance.

From 1575 onwards, the castle and town were in the hands of the fervently Catholic Dietrichsteins, who established various religious edifices and institutions here. They're also responsible for the hint of Renaissance in the town and the main square itself, which is called simply **Náměstí**, appealingly misshapen and centred on a vast, ornate Trinity column. **U rytířů**, on the corner of the square, has a sixteenth-century sgraffito facade, depicting, among other things, Noah's flood, with the ark in a sea of drowning sinners. Behind the column, the Dietrichsteins built the church of sv Anna, with a Loreto chapel – this popular pilgrimage church burned down in the town fire of 1784. The imposing Neoclassical facade that you now see, with its stumpy square towers, dates from the mid-nineteenth century, when the Dietrichsteins decided to turn the church into the family mausoleum or **Dietrichštejnská hrobka** (guided tours every 30min; April–Oct Tues–Sun 10am–6pm; 40Kč). The main reason to wander inside is for the views from amid the angels on the church's roof. The family was also responsible for the series of chapels visible to the east of the town on the bleak, exposed limestone hill of **Svatý kopeček**, well worth the climb for the view across the vineyards towards Vienna.

Mikulov boasted one of the most important Jewish communities in central Europe until the advent of the Nazis: in the mid-nineteenth century it was the second largest in the Czech Lands, with twelve synagogues, and was the seat of the chief rabbi (Landesrabbiner) of Moravia from the sixteenth century until 1851. The old **Jewish ghetto** lies to the west of the castle, where the town's sixteenth-century **synagogue** (mid-May to Sept Tues–Sun 10am–5pm), on Husova, has been renovated. Uniquely for a Czech synagogue, the Baroque interior is in the Lvov style, with a four-columned pink marble pillar over the *bimah*; the main body of the building is used for temporary exhibitions while the women's gallery houses an exhibition on Jewish religious practices. Round the corner in Brněnská, a rugged path leads to the overgrown medieval **Jewish cemetery** (Židovský hřbitov; closed Sat), with over four thousand graves and some finely carved marble tombstones dating back to 1605; to get into it, you'll need to pick up the key from the synagogue or the tourist office.

Practicalities

The town is rarely busy, except during the September wine festival, the majority of visitors pausing for a couple of hours at the most before moving on. The town centre is ten-minutes' walk northeast of the **train station**: take the footbridge over the main road and continue up the hill. There's a **tourist office** on the main square (May–Sept daily 8am–6pm; Oct–April Mon–Fri 8.30am–noon & 1–5pm, Sat & Sun 9am–4pm; ☎519 510 855, Ⓦwww.mikulov.cz), which can help with accommodation. The *Tanzberg*, in the former house of Rabbi Löw at Husova 8 (☎519 510 692, Ⓦwww.hotel-tanzberg.cz; ❸), offers bright and airy en-suite **rooms** with house-plants, TV and wi-fi; the nearby *Templ*, Husova 50 (☎519 323 095, ⓦwww.templ.cz; ❹) combines olde-worlde features and winding staircases with comfortable en suites – the top-floor attic rooms are the cosiest. *Pension Moravia* (☎777 634 560, ⓦwww.moravia.penzion.com; ❷), behind the main square at Poštovní 1, has tiny but perfectly adequate en suites equipped with minuscule TVs – breakfast is delivered to your room on a tray. **Bike rental** is available from the *Templ* hotel. The *Tanzberg* and *Templ* **restaurants** serve local and international dishes in elegant surroundings; *Restaurace pod radnicí* on the main square concentrates on Czech pub food, and the *Petit Café*, occupying a leafy courtyard opposite the *pod radnicí*, specializes in *palačinky*.

Pálava

Mikulov is the starting point for hiking and exploring the **Pavlovské vrchy**, a big, bulging ridge of rugged and treeless limestone hills, and the surrounding region, known as the **Pálava**. Since the damming of the Dyje and the creation of the artificial Nový mlýn lake, the rare plant life on the Pavlovské vrchy has suffered badly. On the plus side, the lake has attracted much greater numbers of waterfowl, as well as eagles, falcons and black and red kites, and the whole area is now a protected region. It's also good, gentle **hiking country**, with wide-angle views on both sides and a couple of picturesque ruined castles along the ten-kilometre red-marked path to **DOLNÍ VĚSTONICE**.

Archeological research has been going on here since 1924, when an early Stone Age settlement was discovered. Brno's Moravské zemské muzeum (see p.314) displays the best findings, which include wolves' teeth jewellery and clay figurines such as the voluptuous *Venus of Věstonice*, a tiny female fertility figure. However, there is a small **Archaeologická expozice** (Tues–Sun 8am–noon & 1–5pm; 20Kč) in Dolní Věstonice, which, despite the lack of information in English, exhibits some interesting finds: skulls, a woolly mammoth's tooth, and several animal and fertility statues, including, inevitably, a copy of the aforementioned Venus. From Dolní Věstonice you can either walk another 4km to the station on the main Brno–Břeclav line at Popice or catch one of the hourly buses back to Mikulov. *Vinařský dům* (☎519 515 395, ⓦwww.silinek.nakupujeme.cz; ❷) is a lovely seventeenth-century **pension** in Pavlov, 3km east of Dolní Věstonice. Alternatively, there are several **campsites** along the shores of the Nový mlýn lake – *Merkur* (mid-April to Oct; ⓦwww.pasohlavky.cz), near Pasohlávky, 10km north of Mikulov, has its own lagoons, bungalows, windsurfing and bike rental.

Lednicko-Valtický areál

To the southeast of Mikulov, nose to nose with the Austrian border, is the UNESCO-protected **Lednicko-Valtický areál**, a landscape dominated by the twin residences of the Liechtensteins, one of the most powerful landowning families in the country until 1945 (see box, p.328). The chateaux lie 7km apart at either end of a dead-straight lime-tree avenue, in a vast, magnificent stately park, dotted with follies – including a sixty-metre minaret – and fish ponds and surrounded by acres of lovely woodland. Being in a low-lying area prone to flooding, mosquitoes can be something of a problem in summer – especially worth bearing in mind if you're camping. It's also worth noting that accommodation in the area tends to be fully booked in the middle of August when there's a **Baroque Music Festival** in Valtice.

The Liechtensteins

The **Liechtensteins** (of Grand Duchy fame) were for many centuries one of the most powerful families in the Czech Lands, particularly in Moravia. At their peak in the seventeenth century they owned no fewer than 99 estates – one more and they would have had to maintain a standing army in the service of the Emperor. The one who made the most of all this wealth was Prince-Bishop Karl Eusebius von Liechtenstein-Kastelcorn, who came into the family fortune in 1627, and whose motto – "Money exists only that one may leave beautiful monuments to eternal and undying remembrance" – can be seen in practice all over Moravia.

Like nearly all the ethnic Germans who lived in Czechoslovakia, the Liechtensteins were forced to leave in 1945 and retreat to their minuscule alpine country. For the next 45 years it looked like the long history of the Liechtensteins in the Czech Lands had come to an end. Then, in 1990, the new government passed a law of *restituce* (restitution), which meant that all property confiscated by the Communists from 1948 onwards was to be handed back to its original owners. Despite having had their property taken from them in the earlier appropriations of 1918 and 1945, the Liechtensteins continue to request compensation from the Czech government for the seizure of their former residences, which comprise something like 1600 square kilometres of land – ten times the area of present-day Liechtenstein.

Lednice

The most popular of the two chateaux is undoubtedly the family's summer residence at **LEDNICE** (Eisgrub). Part of the Liechtenstein estate since 1243, the **zámek** (April, Sept & Oct Sat & Sun 9am–noon & 1–4pm; May–Aug closes 5pm; ⓦwww.lednice.cz; 100Kč) was subjected to a lavish rebuild job in the 1840s, which turned it into a neo-Gothic extravaganza. Part of the chateau is occupied by an exhibition devoted to agriculture, but there's plenty to look at on the main guided tour, with vivid, over-the-top Romantic interiors crowding each of its wood-panelled rooms. If fake medievalism doesn't turn you on, however, head instead for the chateau's vast wrought-iron and glass palm house or **palmový skleník** (April & Oct Tues–Sun 9am–noon & 1–3.30pm; May–Sept Tues–Sun 9am–noon & 1–5.30pm; Nov, Dec, Feb & March Sat & Sun 9am–noon & 1–3.30pm; 50Kč).

Best of all in Lednice is the expansive, watery **Zámecký park**, home to numerous herons, grebes and storks, as well as regular falconry displays in summer. Piqued by local objections to their plan for a colossal church, the Liechtensteins decided in 1797 to further alienate the village by building the largest **minaret** (April & Oct Sat & Sun 10am–4pm; May–Aug Tues–Sun 10am–6pm; Sept Tues–Sun 10am–5pm; 20Kč) outside the Islamic world, which dominates the view of the park from the chateau; it's equally impressive close up, smothered in Arabic script, golden baubles and crescent moons, and you can climb to the top (60m) for great views. Further east is the Janův hrad or **Janohrad** (April & Oct Sat & Sun 9am–4.45pm; May–Sept Tues–Sun 9am–4.45pm; 30Kč), a ruined "Gothick" castle, round which there are guided tours every 45 minutes.

You can explore the park on foot, or catch one of the **boats** (ⓦwww.1plavebni .cz) that head off from the first bridge you come to for the minaret (every 20–30min; 25min; 80Kč) and the hrad (hourly; 45min; 120Kč).

Practicalities

From the drab town of **Břeclav**, east of Valtice, you can take the lovely red 1955 Tatra diesel train to Lednice (April–Sept Sat & Sun; mid-May to mid-June

Tues–Sun) or even go by **boat** up the Dyje (July & Aug Sat & Sun; Ⓦwww
.lodnidoprava.com). Lednice's **tourist office** is on the main square at zámecké
náměstí 68 (Mon & Wed 8am–5pm, Tues & Thurs 8am–2pm; ☎519 340 986,
Ⓦwww.lednice.cz). The best **accommodation** is *My Hotel* (☎519 340 130,
Ⓦwww.myhotel.cz; ❻), a large, modern hotel on the road to Podivín, with bike
rental and good disabled access; alternatively, there's the *Pension Jordán* (☎519
340 285, Ⓦwww.pensionjordan.cz; ❸), which has clean, brightly painted
en-suite rooms. The *Zámecká restaurace*, just inside the chateau gates, serves
inexpensive Czech **food** and beer.

Valtice

VALTICE (Feldsberg), 7km southwest of Lednice, was ceded to the Czechs by
the Austrians during a minor border adjustment dictated by the 1920 Treaty of
St Germain. From the end of the English-style gardens of the town's enormous
Baroque **zámek** (Tues–Sun: May–Aug 9am–6pm; Sept 9am–5pm; Oct 9am–
4pm; Ⓦwww.valtice.cz; 80Kč) you used to be able to see the watchtowers of
the Iron Curtain in among the chateau's vineyards (which incidentally produce
a good Moravian red). Once the family's foremost residence – over and above
Liechtenstein itself – Valtice looks great from the outside, but was cleaned out
just before the end of World War II, leaving its beautifully restored interior
relentlessly bare. However, the east wing has been converted into a budget hotel
and restaurant that does a brisk trade with holidaying Austrians.

In addition to those in Lednice's chateau grounds, Josef Kornhäusel and Josef
Hardtmuth constructed several more grand **follies** for the Liechtensteins in the
early nineteenth century amid the woods of the **Boří les** and the ponds that
lie between Lednice and Valtice. To reach the Boří les, take the scenic red-
marked path from Valtice train station, 2km through the woods, part of the way
along a tree-lined avenue, to the triumphal arch called **Rendezvous**, which
contains a concert hall and ballroom on the top floor. Another 1.5km deeper
into the woods brings you to the Neo-Gothic chapel of **sv Hubert**, a popular
picnic spot, and then for a similar distance north to the **Chrám tří grácií**, a
curving colonnade sheltering a copy of the *Three Graces*; on the opposite bank
of the nearby pond stands another Kornhäusel folly, the **Rybniční zámeček**.

A short way east of the Tří Grácií, by the railway line, stands the **Nový dvůr**,
an ornate structure with a central rotunda-cum-cowshed, which featured glass
partitions, built by the Liechtensteins for rearing sheep, rare-breed cattle and more
latterly horses. Beyond, on the other side of the railway, is the **Apollonův chrám**,
a Neoclassical pavilion overlooking one of the two fifteenth-century fish ponds,
now a popular summer swimming spot. A couple of kilometres west of the Tří
Grácií, on the other side of the village of **HLOHOVEC** (Bischofswarth), is the
Hraniční zámeček, which used to stand on the historic border between Austria
and Moravia (hence its name – *hranice* meaning "border"), and now houses a very
smart hotel and restaurant (see p.330).

Practicalities

Several buses a day on weekdays, two at weekends, run **between Lednice
and Valtice**. Valtice is also just ten minutes by **train** from Mikulov and fifteen
from Břeclav, 8km to the east. The **tourist office** on the main square (daily
9am–5pm; ☎519 352 978, Ⓦwww.radnice-valtice.cz) is a mine of local information. *Hubertus* (☎530 503 465, Ⓦwww.hotelhubertus.cz; ❸), in the
chateau, offers plain but good-value **accommodation**; the *Apollon* (☎519
352 625, Ⓦwww.hotel-apollon.cz; ❸), set in its own gardens up the *lipovej alej*

at P. Bezruče 720, is another good option. You can sample local **wines** and nibble snacks at *Vinoteka*, opposite the church; the next-door-but-one *Albero* offers filling Czech staples in a garden courtyard. A better **restaurant**, with views across one of the lakes, can be found in the *Hraniční zámeček* (☎519 354 353, Ⓦwww.hranicnizamecek.cz; ❹), in **Hlohovec**, which also offers excellent rooms, some with facilities for the disabled.

Znojmo

Perched spectacularly above the deep valley of the River Dyje, **ZNOJMO** (Znaim) boasts one of the biggest, best-restored and most atmospheric old towns in western Moravia. With irregular squares linked by zigzagging alleys, it's the perfect place to indulge in aimless urban strolls. There's also plenty to see, with the **castle museum** and Romanesque rotunda topping the list. Znojmo receives a lot of Austrian and German day-trippers, but most have left by early evening.

Arrival, information and accommodation

Trains run fairly frequently from Mikulov to Znojmo, taking around an hour; there are hourly **buses** from Brno and good bus connections with Jihlava too. The old town is a brisk hike from the station: head up 17 listopadu to Marianské náměstí, then west along Pontassievská and Zámečnická.

The **tourist office**, with branches at Obroková 10 and on the approach road to the hrad (☎515 222 552; July & Aug Tues 9am–5pm, Wed–Sat 9am–4pm, Sun 9am–6pm; Sept–June Tues–Sat 9am–4.30pm, Sun 9am–5pm; Ⓦwww.znojmocity.cz), can help with **accommodation**. There are two good

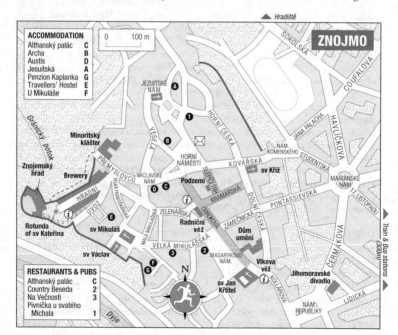

campsites to the north of Znojmo: the family-run *Country* (May–Oct; Ⓦwww.camping-country.com), in Hluboké Mašůvky, 7km up route 361, and the lakeside *Výr* (June–Sept) near Výrovice, 10km away, off route 399 to Plaveč. There's no shortage of well-priced **hotels** and **pensions**, plus a welcoming **hostel**, the *Travellers'*, just below the cathedral at Staré Město 22 (☎515 221 489, Ⓦwww.travellers.cz), which offers bunks in four- to six-person dorms (300–350Kč per person) and a couple of doubles (❷) with shared facilities.

Unless otherwise stated, **breakfast** is included in the rates in the reviews below.

Hotels and pensions

Althanský palác Horní nam. 3 ☎515 221 192, Ⓦwww.althanskypalac.cz. Historical building where Emperor Charles IV once stopped off, offering three storeys of en-suite rooms which improve the higher up you go: the ground-floor doubles are on the poky side, while top-floor rooms come with hardwood floors, attic ceilings and (in most cases) full-sized tubs. ❹–❺

Archa Vlková 4 ☎515 225 062, Ⓦwww .pensionarcha.cz. Fifteenth-century building overlooking a cobbled alley, housing a handful of two-person studios with kitchenettes. Breakfast on request for a few extra koruny. ❷

Austis Václavské nám. 5 ☎515 241 949, Ⓦwww.austisznojmo.cz. Owned by a Prague-based construction company but still friendly and intimate, this pension features functional, subtly decorated en suites. As so often in these old buildings, the attic rooms offer most mosphere. ❷

Jesuitská Jesuitská 5 ☎515 221 440 or 603 830 130, Ⓦwww.jesuitska.cz. Prim ten-bed pension opposite the Jesuit church with en-suite rooms decked out in soft, chintzy colours. Free wi-fi throughout. ❷

Penzion Kaplanka U Branky 6 ☎515 226 947 or 775 552 212, Ⓦwww.kaplanka.cz. Friendly pension occupying a fifteenth-century former hostel for the local clergy, offering simple, functional rooms with basin and TV. There's a WC/shower shared between every two or three rooms. The grassy garden features fish pond, barbecue facilities, and a wonderful view of the Dyje valley. No breakfast, but there is a communal kitchen. ❷

U Mikuláše Mikulášské nám. 8 ☎515 220 856. Eccentrically decorated pension above the U Rolanda café, with rooms (some en suite, some with shared facilities) arranged around a tightly spiralling staircase. Breakfast can be ordered in the downstairs café for a handful of extra koruny. ❷

The Town

Znojmo's main square, **Masarykovo náměstí**, centres on a Marian column with striking pink sandstone plinth and four accompanying saints. A couple of attractive surviving buildings on the east side of the square also deserve attention: the **Měšťanský dům**, which has a very fine sixteenth-century stone portal and matching pilasters, and the **Dům umění** (Tues–Sun 9–11.30am & noon–5pm; 30Kč), a beautiful Renaissance building, two doors down. The latter has an arcaded courtyard out back, diamond vaulting on the first floor, and a small collection of Gothic and Baroque art.

At the top of the square, the late-Gothic pinnacled and baubled **radniční věž** (May–Sept Mon–Fri 9am–6pm, Sat & Sun 9am–5pm; Oct–April Mon–Fri 9am–6pm, Sat 9am–noon; 10Kč) is all that's left of the old town hall, burnt down by the Nazis in the closing stages of the war. From this soaring romantic affair, its uppermost gallery twisting at an angle to the main body, the view through its wooden hatches is spectacular. One block east on Slepičí trh (Chicken Market) is the entrance to the town's underground tunnels or **podzemí** (April Mon–Sat 10am–4pm; May–June & Sept daily 9am–4pm; July & Aug daily 9am–5pm; Oct Sat 10am–4pm; 30Kč) that run under the old town; originally built for defensive purposes, they were later used for storing wine.

A wander from here along the narrow lane of Velká Mikulášska leads to the oldest part of Znojmo – a tight web of alleyways woven round the cathedral of **sv Mikuláš**, a plain Gothic hall church sporting an unusual gable embellished with blind arcading. Inside, it has retained its elegant Gothic net vaulting and slender round pillars, but the most amazing thing is its Baroque pulpit: a giant globe, with its top sliced off, crowned by a sounding board of free-flying clouds, sunbursts, cherubs and saints. Take a look, too, at the glass coffin underneath the organ loft, containing the macabre clothed skeleton of a Christian martyr. Set at a right angle to the cathedral is the much smaller **chapel of sv Václav**, tucked into the town walls, from which you get a commanding view up and down the Dyje valley as it blends into the Austrian plain. The chapel itself is a curious building, built literally on top of its Gothic predecessor in the sixteenth century, when the town's fortifications against the Turks were erected (and smothered the old building). The church now belongs to the local Orthodox community, and the priest will happily show you round the chapel and the bare Gothic original.

"Better a living brewery than a dead castle", goes one of the more obscure Czech proverbs, and as far as **Znojemský hrad** (May–Sept Tues–Sun 9am–5pm; Ⓦwww.znojmuz.cz; 45Kč) goes it's hard to disagree. The parts that didn't become a brewery have since been turned into a local **museum** distinguished, for the most part, by its trompe l'oeil Baroque fresco in the oval entrance hall, glorifying the Deblín family, who rebuilt the chateau in 1720 only to run out of male heirs in 1784. To reach the museum, take the special path (daily: May–Sept 9am–9pm; Oct–April 9.30am–8pm) that runs along the perimeter of the brewery. The castle's most precious relic is the **Rotunda** (times as above), home to the best-preserved twelfth-century frescoes in the country, including contemporary portraits of the Přemyslid princes. Note that access might be restricted in bad weather in order to protect the paintings.

The local museum in the former **Minoritský klášter** (Mon–Fri 9–11.30am & noon–5pm; plus May–Aug Sat & Sun same hours; 30Kč), opposite the brewery, is worth skipping in favour of a scramble in the thickly wooded deep gorge of the Podyjí national park, which begins as soon as you leave the town walls at the end of Přemyslovců. It's a gentle wander round the foot of the castle to the chapel of sv Václav, but for a longer **walk** and an unbeatable vista of Znojmo and the Dyje, take the blue-marked path down to the stream and then the green-marked path past the Stations of the Cross, up to the village and nunnery of Hradiště; bus #1 runs back into town.

Eating and drinking

There are plenty of **restaurants** to choose from, although many of the more tourist-oriented places shut their doors once the day-trippers have departed. Wherever you eat, try *kyselá okurka*: **pickled gherkins** flavoured with paprika. Znojmo stages its own **wine festival**, *Znojemské vinobraní*, in the middle of September.

Althanský palác Horní nam. 3. Fine dining in a semi-formal hotel restaurant, with fancy steaks, skewer-grilled meats and pan-fried fish dishes predominating. Sizeable wine list, and courtyard seating in summer. Mon–Sat 10am–11pm, Sun till 10pm.

Country Beseda Masarykovo nám. 22. An interesting mix of Czech and American food, with dishes like Kuřecí prsa Bronko Billy. Mon–Fri 10am–11pm, Sat & Sun 11am–11pm.

Na Věčnosti Velká Mikulášská 11 Ⓦwww .navecnosti.cz. A real find: a pleasant, mostly veggie restaurant-gallery, which offers *bryndzové halušky* (cheesy noodles), a range of *smažený sýr*, pasta and even fish dishes. The brick-vaulted cellar bar has habit-forming Dudák beer and features regular live music. Restaurant Mon–Fri 11am–10pm, Sat & Sun 11am–midnight; bar daily 6pm–1am.

Pivnička U svatého Michala Divišovo nam. 12. The ice cream and cake shop at street level leads to a wood-panelled first-floor beer bar with a small outdoor terrace. Dalešice beer on tap, and a fine range of snacks from toasted sandwiches to plates of prosciutto. Mon–Sat 10am–10pm, Sun 4–10pm.

Podyjí

The meandering River Dyje and the artificial Vranov lake to the west of Znojmo are part of the heavily forested and very pretty **Podyjí** national park, which provides a summer playground for large numbers of holidaying Czechs. There are plenty of opportunities for swimming and lazing around, plus a couple of interesting chateaux and lots of hiking possibilities. Without your own transport, getting about can be time-consuming, so you might want to plan to spend at least two or three days in the area.

Vranov

The village of **VRANOV NAD DYJÍ** (Frain), 20km west of Znojmo, is a scruffy place, but it sits below an incredible cliff-top **zámek** (April & Oct Sat & Sun 9am–noon & 1–4pm; May, June & Sept Tues–Sun 9am–noon & 1–5pm; July & Aug 9am–noon & 1–6pm; 130Kč; ⓦ www.zamekvranov.cz), magnificently poised on a knife's edge above the Dyje. Originally a medieval stronghold, it was converted into a beautiful Baroque chateau by the Viennese genius Johann Bernhard Fischer von Erlach after a fire in 1665. Nothing else on the guided tour of the sprawling complex (not even the medieval sauna) can quite compare to Fischer's trump card at the far end – the cavernous dome of the **Sál předků** (Ancestors' Hall), whose truly awesome overall effect is as much due to Rottmayr's wild frescoes as to Fischer's great oval skylights: its frenzied, over-the-top paintings depict the (fictitious) achievements of the Althan family who commissioned the work. One other piece of Fischer von Erlach genius worth inspecting is the palace's tiny **chapel** (June & Sept Sat & Sun 9am–5pm; July & Aug Tues–Sun 9am–6pm; 30Kč), a visit to which is not included in the chateau tour. Again, it's the frescoes, executed by a pupil of Rottmayr, that make the place so special: the main fresco features the Archangel Michael smiting Satan's followers who tumble over the cornice itself, while in the side chapels skeletons frolic and angels pray.

From the village, it's a fifteen-minute walk to the dam (*přehrada*) and the sandy **beach** known as **Vranovská pláž**, accessible via the footbridge across the lake. From May to September there's a fair bit of life here: a couple of **campsites** (May–Sept), chalets, boat rental, a few shops and an occasional **boat service** up the lake to Bítov and beyond. Sun-worshippers lie shoulder to shoulder on the beach in the high season, but it's easy to lose the crowd by picking a rocky spot further upstream.

One of the most interesting **walks** in the area is to take the red-marked path from Vranov village along the Dyje, then up into the woods and hills until you reach the road which runs from Čížov to the Austrian border (6km). From here, it's just 2km by either the blue-marked path by the road, or the green-marked path through the woods via the Hardeggská vyhlídka, a lookout post from which you can view the picturesque Austrian border village of Hardegg with its own castle (April to mid-Nov 9am–5pm; July & Aug till 6pm; €6.50), accessible via a small footbridge. The round trip will take all day, so carry a picnic, or some euros in order to grab a bite to eat in Hardegg.

Practicalities

Buses run regularly from Znojmo to Vranov at the weekend, less often during the week. You could also take the more frequent **train** to Sumná station and walk the 4km along the green-marked path to Vranov. Here you can **stay** above the friendly, family-run *Country Saloon* courtyard pub (☎733 501 754, ⓦ www .country.saloon.web.wo.cz; ❷) or in the en-suite rooms of the grandiose

Zámecký hotel (☎515 296 101, Ⓦwww.zameckyhotel.cz; ❸), some of which have views of the chateau.

Bítov

The village of **BÍTOV**, 8km west up the lake, and high above the shore, is nowhere near as dramatically situated as Vranov. It does, however, have at least one good **place to stay**: the popular café/pension *U Tesařů* on the main square (☎515 294 616, Ⓦutesaru.hyperlinx.cz; ❷), which offers modern, comfortable rooms and decent Czech food. The nearby *Bítov-Horka* **campsite** (May–Sept; Ⓦwww.camp-bitov.cz) is ideally situated down by the lakeside. The only way to get from Vranov to Bítov – apart from hitching or walking – is to take the **boat** from the Vranovská pláž (see p.333). There are just one or two buses from Znojmo to Bítov; connections with Jihlava (see p.338) are much the same.

The ruined castle that can be seen from the lake is the fourteenth-century fort of **Cornštejn** (July & Aug daily 9am–5pm), which unfortunately can be explored only with a guide. Bítov's own **hrad** (April & Oct Sat & Sun 9am–noon & 1–4pm; May, June–Sept Tues–Sun 9am–noon & 1–5pm; July & Aug closes 6pm) has weathered slightly better and lies 2.5km to the west of the village, along the red-marked path. Like Vranov, it boasts a classic defensive location on a spit of grey rock high above the river, which the flooding of the valley has diminished only slightly, and for this reason alone it's worth clambering up to enjoy the view. In the courtyard there's a lovely, cool thirteenth-century **wine cellar** where you can taste and buy the local wine, and an *občerstvení* where you can get a snack and a glass of beer, but inside, lacking Fischer's ingenious touch, the castle's not a patch on Vranov. The hour-long **guided tour** (*trasa 1*; 85Kč) through the contrived neo-Gothic decor and soulless, unlived-in rooms is enlivened only by a pack of stuffed dogs. The castle's second floor is occupied by the **armoury** (*trasa 2*; 85Kč), with a wide-ranging collection of seventeenth-century weapons.

Třebíč and around

TŘEBÍČ, 70km due west of Brno, is best known for its Romanesque basilica and its restored Jewish ghetto – both protected by UNESCO since 2003. In most other respects, it's a fairly nondescript town, though it does serve as a useful jumping-off point for the Baroque chateau of **Jaroměřice nad Rokytnou**.

Třebíč's main square, **Karlovo náměstí**, is not as pretty as those in Telč (see p.336) or Slavonice (p.337), though its grandiose scale gives some hint of the town's medieval importance. Immediately south of the square, the **Městská věž** (May–Sept daily 10am–5pm; 10Kč), offers a good overview of the town from its terrace. Třebíč's former glory is almost entirely down to the **Benedictine monastery**, which was founded in 1101 on a hill just north of the centre on the north bank of the River Jihlava. The monastery was closed down as early as the fifteenth century, and transformed into a chateau, which houses the local **museum** (April–June, Sept & Oct Tues–Sun 8am–noon & 1–5pm; July & Aug daily 8am–5pm; Nov–March Tues–Sun 8am–noon & 1–4pm; Ⓦwww.zamek -trebic.cz; 30Kč), whose displays include a large selection of nativity scenes. However, it's the former monastery church, the big grey **Basilica of sv Prokop** (Tues–Thurs 9am–noon & 1–5pm, Fri 9am–noon & 1–4.30pm, Sat–Mon 1–5pm), that's the real draw. Although heavily restored in the Baroque period, and again between the wars, the church retains much of its original mid-thirteenth-century architecture, a transitional style between Romanesque and Gothic, particularly in the vast north portal, the chancel, the galleried apse and the crypt.

Back down in the town, squeezed up against a hill, the northern bank of the river was for centuries the town's **Jewish ghetto**, known as Zámostí. Třebíč's Jewish population peaked at the end of the eighteenth century, at over 1700 (nearly 60 percent of the total population of the town), but by the 1930s had dwindled to just 300, most of whom subsequently perished in the Holocaust. Architecturally, the ghetto remains remarkably intact – it's currently home to many of the town's local Romanies, though with renovation (and gentrification) continuing apace, probably not for long. Consisting of little more than two parallel cobbled streets, the ghetto was originally approached from Žerotinovo náměstí, just north of the bridge, via a narrow alley which was sealed off by a chain on the Sabbath. At the western end of the ghetto, on Tiché náměstí, is the former **Přední synagoga** (Front Synagogue), which had to be reduced in height in the Baroque period after complaints by the Countess of Valdštejn; it was handed over to the Czechoslovak Hussite Church in the 1950s. At the eastern end of the two streets you can visit the **Zadní synagoga** (Rear Synagogue; daily 10am–noon & 1–5pm), whose walls are painted in Hebrew script and decorated with vegetal and floral motives. In the women's gallery there's an exhibition on Jewish Třebíč, and, in the main body of the synagogue, a memorial to the 290 Jews who died in the Holocaust. To reach the **Jewish cemetery** (Židovský hřbitov; daily: March–April & Oct 8am–6pm; May–Sept 8am–8pm; Nov–Feb 9am–4pm; free), which contains some three thousand graves dating from the seventeenth century to the 1930s, follow the signs up the hill and down Hrádek.

Třebíč practicalities

Třebíč is on the main line from Brno to Jihlava, and the **train station** is fifteen-minutes' walk south of the main square; the **bus station** lies a block or so west of the main square on Komenského náměstí, while the **tourist office** has branches in the town hall, at the western end of the main square (Mon–Fri 9am–noon & 1–6pm, Sat & Sun till 5pm; ☎568 847 070, ⓦwww.kviztrebic.cz), and in the courtyard of the basilica (Tues–Fri 9am–noon & 1–5pm, Sat–Mon 1–5pm).

The *Travellers'* **hostel**, Žerotínovo náměstí 19 (☎568 422 594, ⓦwww.travellers.cz), provides bunk-bed dorms (260–350Kč per person) and en-suite doubles (❷) in the atmospheric, timber-beamed rooms of a galleried former coaching inn. More comfortable is the *Penzion U synagogy* (☎568 610 023 or 775 707 506; ❷), offering characterful en suites next door to the Žádní synagoga – although reception is often unstaffed in the mornings and evenings. Ugly on the outside, *Hotel Slavia*, Karlovo náměstí 5 (☎568 848 560, ⓦwww.hotel-trebic.cz; ❹) offers standard three-star comforts with free wi-fi.

For **food** and **beer**, ⌁ *U Dubu*, squeezed into the arched entrance to the *Travellers' Hostel* building, mixes traditional Czech pork-chop dishes with Mediterranean-inspired salads, pastas and fish – look out for the cheap daily specials. *Betlém*, uphill from the main square at Haaskova 10, serves hearty portions of meat, goulash and good draught beer in a quirky pub environment, while *U Barborky*, just uphill from the basilica on na Barbare, is a raucous rock-oriented pub with a pizzeria upstairs.

Jaroměřice nad Rokytnou

The small town of **JAROMĚŘICE NAD ROKYTNOU**, 14km south of Třebíč, is overwhelmed by its gargantuan russet-and-cream Baroque **zámek**

(April & Oct Sat & Sun 9am–noon & 1–4pm; May, June & Sept Tues–Sun 9am–noon & 1–5pm; July & Aug closes 6pm), built over the course of 37 years by the wealthy and extravagant Johann Adam von Questenberg. For the most part it's the work of Dominico d'Angeli, but the two Austrian architects Jakob Prandtauer and Johann Lukas von Hildebrandt also appear to have been involved at various stages. The highlights of the chateau are the elegant Rococo halls, the Hlavní sál and the Táneční sál, where Questenberg used to put on lavish classical concerts. To see these you must join *trasa A* (45min; 85Kč); *trasa B* (25min; 50Kč) only takes you round the later interiors and the porcelain collection. Alternatively, you could skip both tours and spend the morning exploring the great domed and frescoed chapel (now the local parish church) or pottering around the formal gardens. Even better, come during July and August, when the chateau stages a **festival** of classical music. Jaroměřice is on the **train** line from Znojmo to Jihlava, but from Třebíč you have to change trains, which means you'd be better off travelling by bus. Note that the train station is 2km west of town, in the village of Popovice. If you're stuck overnight, check out the kitsch decor in the lumbering Communist-era monolith that is the *Hotel Opera* (☎568 440 230, ⓦwww.hotelopera.cz; ❷).

Telč

It's no exaggeration to say that the last momentous event in **TELČ** (Teltsch) was the great fire of 1530, which wiped out all the town's wooden Gothic houses and forced it to start afresh. This fortuitous disaster made Telč what it is: a perfect sixteenth-century provincial town. Squeezed between two fish ponds, the Štěpnický to the east and the Ulický to the west, the **staré město** is little more than two medieval gate towers, one huge wedge-shaped square and a chateau. Renaissance arcades extend the length of the main square, **náměstí Zachariáše z Hradce**, lined with pastel-coloured houses (including the town's fire station) that display a breathtaking variety of gables and pediments, none less than two hundred and fifty years old. At the eastern end of the square, you can climb the **věž sv Ducha** (June–Sept Mon–Sat 10am–noon & 1–5pm) for an overview.

At the narrow western end of the square, the **zámek** (Tues–Sun: April & Oct 9am–noon & 1–4pm; May–Sept until 5pm; 140Kč; ⓦwww.zamek-telc.cz) in no way disturbs the sixteenth-century atmosphere of the town; it too was badly damaged in the fire and had to be rebuilt in similar fashion. Like the chateau at the nearby Bohemian town of Jindřichův Hradec (see p.172), it was the inspiration of Zachariáš of Hradec, whose passion for all things Italian is again strongly in evidence. Of the two guided tours, choose the hour-long *trasa A*, which concentrates on the Renaissance-era rooms and their exceptional array of period ceilings. The shorter *trasa B* features living spaces from later periods; also quite fun, the whole place feeling refreshingly intimate and low-key after the pomposity of the region's Baroque chateaux.

Even if you don't take a guided tour, look inside the chateau's exquisite All Saints' **chapel**, opposite the ticket office. The chapel was built in 1580 as the last resting place of Zachariáš of Hradec and his wife Kateřina of Valdštejn, who lie, arms outstretched in prayer, surrounded by a beautiful, multicoloured wrought-iron grille. The decor is surprisingly upbeat, and the stuccowork is outstanding, with gilded trumpets erupting from a farrago of plump fruits. In the central relief on the ceiling of the nave, a host of skeletons is being restored to life on the Day of Judgement.

You can also stroll through the cloistered formal garden at leisure, and visit the **Galerie Jana Zrzavého** (April, Sept & Oct Tues–Sun 9am–noon & 1–4pm; May–Aug closes 5pm; Nov–March Tues–Fri 9am–noon & 1–4pm, Sat 9am–1pm) in the east wing, dedicated to the Surrealist painter Jan Zrzavý (1890–1977). Born in nearby Havlíčkův Brod, Zrzavý's early works were Post-Impressionist, but he quickly adopted his own dreamlike, slightly surreal style. His paintings are definitely an acquired taste, though by no means monotonous; particularly striking are his pallid, grey, virtually uninhabited Breton landscapes painted between the wars.

The local branch of the **muzeum Vysočiny** (times as for the zámek) is housed in the chateau, too, with a model of the town, a miniature Bethlehem scene and displays on local history. More intriguing, though, is the exquisite ceramic World War I memorial, at the end of the covered passageway that leads to the town's church. Although the adjacent World War II memorial doesn't explicitly say so, it's clear that the majority of the town's victims in the last war were from the local Jewish community.

Telč is at its busiest at the turn of July and August when it hosts the two-week-long **Prázdniný v Telči festival** (Ⓦ www.prazdninyvtelci.cz) of folk, country and fusion music.

Practicalities

The **train station** is a ten-minute walk east of the old town along Masarykova, but with direct trains only connecting with Jihlava, you're more likely to find yourself arriving at the nearby **bus station**. The helpful **tourist office** (May–June & Sept Mon–Fri 8am–5pm, Sat & Sun 10am–5pm; July & Aug closes 6pm; Oct Mon–Fri 8am–5pm, Sat & Sun 10am–4pm; Nov–April Mon & Wed 8am–5pm, Tues & Thurs 8am–4pm, Fri 8am–3pm; Ⓦ www.telc-etc.cz), at no. 10 on the main square, can book **pensions** and **private rooms**. *Hotel Celerin* (Ⓣ 567 243 477, Ⓦ www.hotelcelerin.cz; ➍) enjoys a great location, at no. 43, at the wide end of the main square – the best rooms face the square or are in the wood-beamed attic. Square-side views are also on offer at the *Černý orel* (Ⓣ 567 243 222, Ⓦ www.cernyorel.cz; ➍), at no. 7, though there is less in the way of character inside. The *Pantof* **hostel**, at no. 42 on the square (May–Oct only; Ⓣ 776 887 466, Ⓦ www.pantof.com), offers cosy dorms for 350Kč per person and one double room (➊), although there is frequently no one at reception – call in advance rather than just turning up. The nearest **campsite** is the *Velkopařezitý* lakeside site (all year), 7km northwest of Telč. *U Marušky*, just off the square on Palackeho, serves solid Czech **food** and draught beers, in an atmospheric room stuffed with domestic bric-a-brac. The next-door *Šenk pod věží* hedges its bets with both local food and workaday pizzas – the outdoor terrace overlooking the former moat is the main selling point. The coolest night-time hangout is *Antoniana* on Palackeho, a café-bar that also serves as a photography gallery.

Slavonice

SLAVONICE (Zlabings), 25km south of Telč and a stone's throw from the Austrian border, is in many ways even more remarkable. It's a monument to a prosperity that lasted for just one hundred years, shattered by the Thirty Years' War, which halved the population, then dealt its deathblow in the 1730s when the post road from Prague to Vienna was rerouted via Jihlava. In 1945 the forced removal of the local German-speaking inhabitants emptied Slavonice, and matters deteriorated even further when the Iron Curtain wrapped itself around the village, severing road and rail links with the West.

Even now, the **staré město** – not much larger than the one at Telč – still has a strange and haunting beauty. The impression is further enhanced by the bizarre biblical and apocalyptic sixteenth-century "strip cartoons" played out on the houses in monochrome sgraffito. The best place to start is at the tourist office (see below), on **náměstí Míru**, the larger of the town's two squares; note the stunning diamond vaulting in the entrance hall. From here, a steep staircase descends to the thirteenth-century **Podzemní chodby** (underground tunnels; July & Aug daily 9am–noon & 1–6pm; 50Kč) running under a line of houses and the square itself. Known locally as *U itala* – the friendly owner is Italian – the former **Lutheran prayer room** (Protestantská modlitebna; May–Sept daily 10am–noon & 1–5pm) is at no. 517 on Horní náměstí. Here, on the first floor, you can see the exceptional wall paintings of the Apocalypse, which miraculously survived the Counter-Reformation: look, in particular, for the mischievous depiction of the Devil as a crocodile wearing the papal crown, not to mention the horse-riding Whore of Babylon. To round off your trip, climb the **Městská věž** (May & Sept Sat & Sun 10am–noon & 1–5pm; June–Aug daily 9am–noon & 1–6pm; 20Kč), attached to the town's central church.

Practicalities

Trains from Telč take fifty minutes, from Jihlava an incredible two hours (with a change at Kostelec u Jihlavy); the train station lies five-minutes' walk south of the town centre, and a short walk from the **Austrian border** (daily 6am–10pm) and town of Fratres. Slavonice is also connected by the occasional **bus** to Jindřichův Hradec and points west. Most people come to Slavonice on a day-trip, but the **tourist office** on náměstí Míru (April & Oct Mon–Fri 10am–4pm; May daily 10am–noon & 1–5pm; June–Sept daily 9am–noon & 1–5pm; Nov–March Mon–Fri 10am–noon & 1–4pm; ⓦwww.i.slavonice-mesto.cz) can help if you wish to **stay**. Choices on náměstí Míru include the *Hotel Alfa* (ⓣ384 493 261, ⓦhotelalfa.wbs.cz; ❶–❷), which is basically a pub with simple rooms upstairs; the intimate twelve-room *U růže* (ⓣ384 493 004, ⓦwww.dumuruze.cz; ❹), with a small swimming pool and sauna on site; and *Hotel Arkáda* (ⓣ384 408 408, ⓦwww.hotelarkada.cz; ❸), in the arcaded house opposite *Alfa*, which has pleasant one- to four-bed en-suite rooms. At *Appetito*, also on the main square, you can eat traditional Czech **food** in a courtyard out back.

Jihlava

When silver deposits were discovered in the nearby hills in the 1240s, **JIHLAVA** (Iglau) was transformed overnight from a tiny Moravian village into one of the biggest mining towns in central Europe. Scores of German miners settled here, and by the end of the century Jihlava boasted two hospitals, two monasteries and, most importantly, the royal mint. The veins of silver ran out in the fourteenth century, but the town continued to flourish thanks to the cloth trade, reaching its zenith around the latter half of the sixteenth century when over 700 master spinners worked in the town. The expulsion of ethnic Germans from this *Sprachinsel* (language-island) after 1945 changed the face of the town forever.

Though the town is not as appealing a place to stay as Třebíč or Telč, it has enough sights to warrant a day-trip. It retains a surprisingly attractive staré

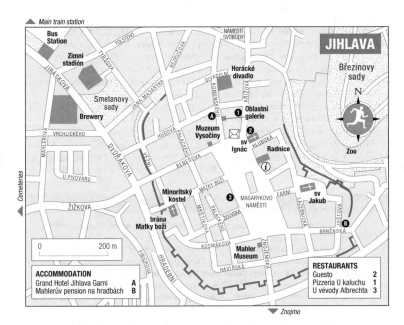

město, despite the decision of a Communist town council to plonk a mud-brown, multi-storey car park/supermarket right in the middle of the cobbled main square, **Masarykovo náměstí**. If you can ignore the eyesore, the square is actually a wonderfully expansive space. Sloping steeply to the south and lined with restrained Baroque and Rococo houses, it sports two fountains, and a Marian column, beside which is a plaque to Evžen Plocek, the 41-year-old who set himself alight on April 4, 1969, in protest against the Soviet invasion. At the top of the square, at no. 58, the **muzeum Vysočiny** (Tues–Sun 9am–noon & 12.30–5pm; ⓦmuzeum.ji.cz; 30Kč) is one of the few Renaissance houses to survive the 1523 fire, and its covered inner courtyard, with arcaded gallery, patchy murals and diamond vaulting, is perfectly preserved. The museum's collections of stuffed animals and mushrooms are less remarkable, though it does boast a well-preserved eighteenth-century pharmacy from nearby Polná.

You can see different kinds of interior design in the **oblastní galerie Vysočiny** (Tues–Sun 9am–12.30pm & 1–5pm; 30Kč), around the corner at Komenského 10, north of the main square, which houses a small but excellent collection of nineteenth- and twentieth-century Czech art. You can also head down into the extensive catacombs, known as **katakomby** (daily: April 10am–4pm; May & Sept 9am–4pm; June–Aug 9am–5pm; tours on the hour; 40Kč) or *historické podzemí*. The entrance is beside the imposing early Baroque facade of the Jesuit church of **sv Ignác**, built at the top of the square in the 1680s. Unfortunately, the church is usually closed, so to see the ceiling fresco and the stupendous trompe l'oeil main altar, you'll need to time your visit with one of the services.

Apart from the Jesuit church, all the town's other churches comply with medieval requirements and are set back from the square. The most obvious of these is the church of **sv Jakub** (St James), east of the square down Farní, whose two plain stone towers and steeply pitched, chevroned roof rise majestically above the surrounding burgher houses. The church is best admired from afar, though it's also possible to climb its northern **tower** (May & Sept Sat & Sun 10am–1pm & 2–6pm; June–Aug Tues–Sun same hours; 10Kč) for a panoramic view over the town. You can peek at the spectacular gilded Baroque altarpieces, but if you want a closer look you'll have to ask for the key or wait for a church service. The town walls run round the back of the church, and in the leafy gorge below are the woods of the Březinovy sady.

For a town built on silver, Jihlava lacks the vestiges of prosperity that grace, for example, Kutná Hora. A few finely carved portals and the remnants of fifteenth-century frescoes survive here and there, but just one gateway, **brána Matky boží** (July & Aug Mon–Fri 9am–6pm, Sat & Sun 10am–1pm & 2–6pm; April–June & Sept Mon–Fri 8am–5pm, Sat & Sun 10am–1pm & 2–5pm; March & Oct Mon–Fri 8am–5pm; 10Kč), guarding the road from the west, is all that's left

Mahler in Iglau

"I am thrice homeless, as a native of Bohemia in Austria, as an Austrian among Germans and as a Jew throughout the world. Everywhere an intruder, never welcomed." **Gustav Mahler**'s predicament was typical of the Jews of *Mitteleuropa*, and it only exacerbated his already highly strung personality. Prone to Wagnerian excesses and bouts of extreme pessimism, he would frequently work himself into a state of nervous collapse when composing or conducting. It was this Teutonic temperament as much as his German-speaking background that separated him from his more laid-back Czech musical contemporaries.

Mahler was born in 1860 in the nearby village of **Kaliště** (Kalischt) on the Bohemian side of the border, the second son of Bernhard Mahler, an ambitious Jewish businessman. The same year, the Mahlers, who were the only non-Czechs in the entire village, moved to **Iglau** (Jihlava), where there had been a strong Jewish community since the mid-fourteenth century. The family moved to **Wienerstrasse** (now Znojemská) 4, and Mahler's father opened a pub, by all accounts a drunken dive that proved a big success. Bernhard was able eventually to open his own distillery, but at home there was little to rejoice about. Judging by his frequent court appearances, Bernhard was a bad-tempered, violent man, while his wife, Marie, a frail woman whose minor heart condition was only worsened by her fourteen pregnancies (only six children survived to adulthood).

Mahler went to school at the German Gymnasium on Hluboká (some fifty years after Smetana), but showed more musical, than academic, promise. At the age of just 10, he made his first public appearance as a pianist at the town's municipal theatre, then in a converted church on **Komenského**. A local farmer persuaded Bernhard to send his boy to **Prague** to study music, but Mahler returned homesick after less than a year. After completing his studies in **Jihlava**, where he later claimed "I didn't learn anything", he was accepted as a student at the Vienna conservatoire. Mahler then enjoyed a fairly stormy career as a conductor that included stints at, among other places, Olomouc and Prague, before finally settling in **Vienna**, the place with which he is most closely associated. His links with Jihlava were permanently severed in 1889, when both his parents died, the family property was sold, and his remaining siblings moved away.

Mahler's parents' grave still stands in the Jewish cemetery, 1km west on U cvičiště, off Žižkova, close to the municipal cemetery. Dedicated fans who wish to track down **Mahler's birthplace** should be aware that there are several villages called Kaliště in Bohemia: the correct one is listed in map indexes as **Kaliště** (Pelhřimov), roughly 7km northwest of Humpolec, and confusingly not Kaliště (Jihlava). The building in which the composer was born is now the *Penzion Mahler* (☎565 546 528, ⓦwww.en .mahler-penzion.cz; ➋), with a pub downstairs and a small concert hall hosting occasional events.

of the town's five gates. Nearby is the beautifully restored **Minoritský kostel**, a remarkable little church that dates back to around 1250. The building's antiquity – it's the oldest stone building in the town – is evident in the thick Romanesque pillars and fragments of medieval frescoes in the nave. However, the Baroque fittings are no less interesting, particularly the technicolour Crucifixion scene opposite the pulpit, which is played out in front of a ruched silver drape. Make sure you venture into the choir to admire the mural depicting the medieval town, located above the sedilia.

Just off the south end of the square at Znojemska 4, **Gustav Mahler**'s childhood home now serves as a **museum** (daily 10am–noon & 1–5pm; 20Kč) dedicated to the composer's life and times. Renovated in 2008, it's short on authentic Mahler memorabilia but strong on presentation, with period photographs of Jihlava and a scattering of nineteenth-century domestic trinkets conveying an evocative sense of the composer's early years.

Practicalities

The **main train station** – simply called Jihlava – is a good 2km northeast of the town centre, so hop on trolleybus #A or #B; slow trains to or from Tábor, Jindřichův Hradec or České Budějovice also stop at **Jihlava-město**, 1km north of the old town – there are no trolleybuses, but it's an easy walk to the staré město along třída Legionářů. From the **bus station**, northwest of the old town, it's a five-minute walk to the main square. Jihlava's **tourist office** (Mon–Fri 8am–5pm, Sat 8am–noon; July & Aug also Sun 8.30am–5pm; ☎567 167 158, Ⓦwww.jihlava.cz), in the radnice on the main square, can organize **private rooms** (❷). The most atmospheric place to stay is *Mahlerův pension na hradbách*, just off the square at Brněnská 31 (☎567 303 300, Ⓦwww .mahleruvpenzion.cz; ❸), with smart en suites with TV and fridge, and a handful of three- and four-person apartments (2400Kč), in a building once used by Mahler's liquor-trading father as a storehouse and shop. A useful fallback is the *Grandhotel Jihlava Garni*, Husová 1 (☎567 121 011, Ⓦwww .grandjihlava.cz; ❷–❹) a splendid Art Nouveau building offering smart, functional, mostly en-suite, rooms. Local buses run to the lakeside *Pávov* **campsite** (May–Sept), 4km north of Jihlava, not far from the motorway. Jihlava's most aesthetically pleasing **restaurant** is *U vévody Albrechta* (closed Sun), in a banquet room decorated with Renaissance frescoes, on the first floor at no. 41 on the west side of the main square. Pub-restaurant *Guesto*, just off the square at Křížová 2, doles out a trusty range of Czech dishes and good draught beer, while *Pizzerie U Kalichu*, just down the street at Křížová 11 (Ⓦwww.pizzerieukalichu.cz), serves thin-crust pies and salads.

Žďár nad Sázavou

The highest point in the Bohemian-Moravian Uplands, or Vysočina, is around 40km northeast of Jihlava, though the whole range is actually more like a high rolling plateau. This has always been a poor region, but it's worth heading out into the hinterland to see the **Cistercian monastery** near **ŽĎÁR NAD SÁZAVOU** (Ⓦwww.zdarns.cz). Established in the thirteenth century, the town has grown hugely since World War II to become one of the largest in these parts, producing, among other things, ice skates. The monastery complex itself lies a three-kilometre walk (or short bus #2 ride) north through the grey new town – instructive if nothing else. As you approach the woods and fishponds, you'll see a small bridge decorated with the familiar figures of eighteenth-century saints; on the other side lies the monastery, now back in the hands of the Kinský family.

A **ticket office** near the entrance gate provides information on the whole complex, which is the work of **Giovanni Santini** (who also had a hand in the monasteries of Plasy and Kladruby, near Plzeň), perhaps the most gifted architect of the Czech Counter-Reformation. His two great talents were marrying Gothic and Baroque forms in a new way, and producing buildings with a humour and irony often lacking in eighteenth-century architecture. The monastery church isn't a particularly good example, but the wooded hill to the south of the complex conceals one that is: the UNESCO-protected **Zelená hora** (Green Hill) pilgrimage church (May–Sept Tues–Sun 9am–5pm; April & Oct Sat & Sun 9am–5pm; 60Kč). It's a unique and intriguing structure, with zigzag cemetery walls forming a decagon of cloisters around the central star-shaped church, a giant mushroom sprouting a half-formed, almost Byzantine dome, dedicated to sv Jan Nepomucký (St John of Nepomuk). The interior is filled with details of his martyrdom, along with symbolic and numerical references to the saint and the Cistercians. On the pulpit, a gilded relief depicts his being thrown off the Charles Bridge in Prague by the king's men, while everywhere in macabre repetition are the saint's severed tongue and the stars that appeared above his head. Back in the main part of the monastery there's a **Muzeum knihy** (Book Museum; April & Oct Sat & Sun 8am–noon & 12.30–4pm; May, June & Sept Tues–Sun same hours; July & Aug Tues–Sun 9am–noon & 12.30–5pm), housed in the Santini-designed stables, with swirling zigzag patterning on the ceiling. The exhibition on Santini himself and other personalities of the local Baroque (daily 9am–5pm) is in the former convent, along with a display of old pianos.

Practicalities

Žďár is just an hour's fast train ride from Brno; the town centre is 1km north of the train station, and it's another 2km to the monastery (both sections are covered by bus #2). The **tourist office**, náměstí Republiky 24 (mid-June to mid-Sept Mon–Fri 8am–noon & 1–6pm, Sat 8am–noon & 1–7pm, Sun 8am–noon & 1–2pm; mid-Sept to mid-June Mon–Fri 8am–noon & 1–5pm, Sat 8am–noon; ☎566 628 539, ⓦwww.zdarns.cz), can help with accommodation, although there's usually no problem finding a room: **hotels** include *U labutě*, náměstí Republiky 70 (☎566 622 949, ⓦwww.hotelulabute.cz; ❷), offering simply furnished but smart en suites in an old roadside inn, and the less attractive *Hotelový dům Morava* (☎566 625 826, ⓔmorava@cerum.cz; ❶), a brick-and-concrete ziggurat below the square offering spartan doubles, triples and quads. *Teferna*, a decent *hostinec* by the monastery, serves Starobrno. A little further up the road you come to the *Pilská nádrž* lakeside **campsite** (May–Sept).

The Slovácko region

What the Labe basin is to the Bohemians, the **Slovácko region**, around the plains of the River Morava 50km east of Brno, is to the Moravians. They settled in this fertile land around the late eighth century, taking their name from the river and eventually lending it to the short-lived Great Moravian Empire, the first coherent political unit in the region to be ruled by Slavs and the subject of intense archeological research (and controversy) over the last forty years. Ethnically, it's a grey area where Moravians and Slovaks happily coexist – the local dialect and customs are virtually indistinguishable from West Slovakia. Tomáš Garrigue Masaryk, Czechoslovakia's founder and first president, hailed from here, and his mixed parentage – his mother was German-speaking, his father a Slovak peasant – was typical of the region in the nineteenth century. For the visitor, though, it's a dour, undistinguished landscape – flat, low farming country, with just the occasional factory or ribbon village to break the monotony – and most people pass through en route to more established sights. In summer this can be a great mistake, for almost every village in the area has its own **folk festival**, and in early autumn the local **wine caves** are bursting with life and ready to demonstrate the region's legendary and lavish hospitality.

Uherské Hradiště and around

The industrial town of **UHERSKÉ HRADIŠTĚ** (Ungarisch-Hradisch) sees few visitors at the best of times, and the only reason travellers stray into its shapeless centre is in their search for the **Pamatník Velké Moravy** (April–Oct daily 9am–noon & 12.30–5pm; 30Kč), suspected site of the capital of the Great Moravian Empire, the short-lived ninth-century state which once covered Moravia, Slovakia, Bohemia and parts of western Hungary. The site is north of the centre, across the Morava, on Jezuitská in a part of town known confusingly as Staré Město (10min by foot; follow the white signs to *památník*). The remains, housed in a concrete bunker, include the foundations of a ninth-century church, discovered in 1949, and a lot of bones and broken crockery – a specialist's paradise, but less gripping for the rest of us.

Arriving at Uherské Hradiště by **bus**, simply walk west along Velehradská třída to the centre; arriving by train is more complicated – **trains** travelling north or south tend to arrive at Staré Město u Uherského Hradiště on the north bank of the river, while trains from the east arrive in the southern suburb of Kunovice. The more central Uherské Hradiště station, southwest of the main square, is only served by the occasional shuttle service between the two. The best place to **stay** is the *Hotel Slunce* (☏572 432 640, ⓦwww.synothotels.com; ⓖ), on the main square, opposite the church; it's an efficient, modern place, with a few surviving features from its Renaissance days. For something cheaper in the town's vicinity, ask at the **tourist office** (daily 8am–6pm; ☏572 525 525, ⓦwww.mic.uh.cz), also on the main square, to the right of the church.

Velehrad

The **Cistercian monastery** at **VELEHRAD**, just 9km across the fields from Uherské Hradiště, is one of the most important pilgrimage sites in the Czech Republic. It's an impressive sight, too, with the twin ochre towers of its **bazilika** (daily 7am–7pm) set against the backdrop of the Chřiby hills, a low beech-covered ridge that separates Brno from the Morava basin. Served by regular **buses** from Uherské Hradiště, it's an easy half-day trip.

The monastery's importance as an object of pilgrimage derives from the belief (now proved to be false) that it was the seat of **St Methodius** who arrived in Moravia in 863 to begin the conversion of the central European Slavs to Christianity. The 1100th anniversary of St Methodius's death on July 5, 1985, attracted over 150,000 pilgrims from across Czechoslovakia, the largest single unofficial gathering in the country since the first anniversary of the Soviet invasion in August 1969 (July 5 is now a national holiday). Five years later, Velehrad entertained Pope John Paul II, and half a million people turned up. The church owes its gigantic scale to the foundations of the original Romanesque church on which it's built. This burned down in 1681 after being sacked several times by marauding Protestants, but you can visit its remains in the crypt's **lapidárium** (July & Aug daily 9am–6pm; June daily 9am–noon & 1–6pm; April, May, Sept & Oct Tues–Sun 9am–noon & 1–5pm; 40Kč). Inside the church itself, the artistry may be lacking in finesse, but the faded glory of the frescoed nave, suffused with a pink-grey light and empty but for the bent old women who come here for their daily prayers, is bewilderingly powerful.

At the edge of the village, en route to Uherské Hradiště, is the **Archeoskanzen** (May–Sept daily 9am–5pm; Oct–April Tues–Sun 9am–4pm; Ⓦ www.archeoskanzen.cz; 50Kč), a reconstructed Great Moravian settlement. Surrounded by a tall palisade, the *skanzen* contains various wooden structures, including a sheep run and church.

Buchlovice and Buchlov

Four kilometres west of Velehrad, still just out of reach of the Chřiby hills, the village of **BUCHLOVICE** (Buchlowitz) is easily accessible by bus from Uherské Hradiště. Here you'll find the Berchtolds' pretty little eighteenth-century **zámek** (April & Oct Tues–Sun 9am–noon & 1–3pm; May, June & Sept Tues–Sun 9am–noon & 1–4pm; July & Aug daily 9am–noon & 1–5pm; Ⓦ www.zamek-buchlovice.cz; 80Kč, park only 20Kč), a warm and hospitable country house with a lovely arboretum bursting with rhododendrons, fuschias and peacocks. The renovated house, composed of two symmetrically opposed semicircles around a central octagon, still contains most of its original Rococo furniture, left behind by the family when they fled to Austria in 1945. Another prize exhibit abandoned in haste was a leaf from the tree beneath which Mary Queen of Scots was executed.

A stiff three-and-a-half-kilometre climb up into the forest of the Chřiby hills will take you to the Gothic hrad of **Buchlov** (April & Oct Sat & Sun 9am–3pm; May, June & Sept Tues–Sun 8am–4pm; July & Aug daily 9am–5pm; 85Kč), which couldn't be more dissimilar. In bad weather, as the mist whips round the bastions, it's hard to imagine a more forbidding place, but in summer the view over the treetops is terrific and the whole place has a cool, breezy feel to it. Founded as a royal seat by the Přemyslids in the thirteenth century, it has suffered none of the painful neo-Gothicizing of other medieval castles – in fact the Berchtolds turned it into a museum as early as the late nineteenth century. Heavy, rusty keys open up a series of sparsely furnished rooms lit only by thin slit windows, and dungeons in which the Habsburgs used to confine the odd rebellious Hungarian. If you're on for a bit of hiking, the stillness and extraordinary beauty of the surrounding beech forests are difficult to match, but be sure to stock up with provisions, as there are few shops in the area. There's a **restaurant** in the castle, and a *Smraďavka* **campsite** (April–Oct), 2km southeast of Buchlovice.

Strážnice and around

On the last weekend of June, thousands converge on the otherwise unexceptional town of **STRÁŽNICE** (Strassnitz), 20km or so southwest of Uherské Hradiště, for the annual **International Folk Festival** (Ⓦ www.nulk.cz) – the largest in the country. During the festival, held in three purpose-built stadiums in the grounds of the local chateau, hotels are booked solid; reseve well in advance or bring a sleeping bag.

At any other time of the year, there's only enough to keep you occupied for an hour or two. Though no work of art itself, the **zámek**, ten-minutes' walk north of the centre, off the road to Bzeneč, contains an exceptionally good **folk museum** (May–Oct Tues–Sun 8am–5pm; 40Kč). En route to the chateau, you'll pass the town's excellent **skanzen** (May, June, Sept & Oct Tues–Fri 9am–4pm; Sat & Sun 9am–5pm; July & Aug daily 9am–5pm; 55Kč), with numerous restored thatched, timber-built cottages and peasant gear from the outlying villages.

The **train station** is five-minutes' walk south of the town centre. Except during the festival, it should be easy enough to **stay** at the *Strážnice* (☎518 332 444, ⓦwww.hotelstraznice.cz; ➌), which offers comfiortable en-suites and a good restaurant; or the more basic *Turistická ubytovna TJ Strážnice* (☎518 334 501; ➊), east of town, behind the *skanzen*. *Strážnice*, behind the zámek (May–Oct; ⓦwww.camp-straznice.cz), is a well-equipped **campsite** with a pool, restaurant, and four-person bungalows (800Kč). A good **place to eat** Czech food and meet the locals is the popular (and smoky) restaurant *Na rynku*, on náměstí Svobody, which turns into a **pub** in the evening.

Wine caves and festivals around Strážnice

Strážnice makes a good base for visiting a number of private *sklepy* or **wine caves**. Perhaps the easiest to visit for those without their own transport are the Plže caves at **PETROV**, a thin settlement strung out along the main road from Hodonín, one stop down the railway line from Strážnice. Hidden from sight, on the other side of the railway track, are around eighty whitewashed stone caves more than two hundred years old, some beautifully decorated with intricate floral designs, others with just a simple deep-blue stripe. Around late September there are usually one or two locals overseeing their new harvest who'll be happy to show you around and no doubt invite you to sample (and of course buy) some of their wine. During the rest of the summer, merry-making goes on on weekend evenings. Those with their own transport and a taste for the stuff could check out **Polesovice**, 12km north, or **Mutěnice**, 15km west, or better still the thatched *sklepy* at **Prušánky**.

Countless **festivals** in the area include the Dolmácké slavnosti, held every three years in Hluk (the next one is in 2011), and pilgrimages to places like Blatnice, held in September. The most famous after Strážnice is the annual *Jízda králů* (Ride of the Kings) held over the weekend of Whitsuntide (the last Sun in May) in **VLČNOV**, which lies south of route 50 between Uherské Hradiště and the pistol-producing town of Uherský Brod. Young villagers in traditional costumes ride through the town on horseback, and folk concerts and dances are staged all weekend.

Luhačovice

Some 27km east of Uherské Hradiště is the genteel spa town of **LUHAČO-VICE**, decidedly lush after the rather demure Morava valley but without the pomp and majesty of the west Bohemian spas. Although its springs are mentioned as far back as the twelfth century, nothing much was done about developing the place until it was bought up in 1902 and building began on the first of Slovak Dušan Jurkovič's quirky, 'folksy, half-timbered villas, which have become the spa's hallmark.

The largest of these, the **Dům Dušana Jurkoviče** (now a hotel), dominates the central spa gardens spreading northeast from the train station. The beams are purely decorative, occasionally breaking out into a swirling flourish, and the roof is a playful pagoda-type affair, creating a uniquely Slovak folk version of Art Nouveau. The blot on Luhačovice's copybook is the **Kolonáda**, a graceless curving concrete colonnade that's nevertheless a good place to sit and the world go by. The rest of the spa forms a snake-like promenade boxed in by shrubs and trees, with folksy bridges spanning the gently trickling river. Soon enough you hit another cluster of Jurkovič buildings, one of which is the open-air natural spring **swimming pool**. The villas continue into the leafy suburbs, but unless you fancy a hike into the surrounding woods or are staying at the lakeside **campsite** (May–Oct) 1km up the main road, there's no reason to continue walking. If you're interested in the folk traditions of the area, and the history of the spa, hop across to the west bank of the stream to the museum in the **vila Lipová** (April–Oct Tues–Sun 9am–noon & 1–5pm; Nov & March Thurs 9am–noon & 1–4pm; 30Kč).

Although Luhacovice lies at the end of a branch line from Uherský Brod, getting here from Moravia's major cities by rail involves several changes. A handful of direct **buses** run from Brno to Luhačovice, and there are several more connections via Zlín or Uherské Hradiště. The **bus** and **train stations** are at the southwestern end of the spa, ten-minutes' walk from the centre, where, at Masarykova 950, there's an efficient **tourist office** (Mon–Fri: March–May & Oct 8am–5pm; June–Sept 8am–6pm; Nov–Feb 8am–4pm; Ⓦwww .luhacovice.cz). Reasonable **accommodation** can be found all over the spa, but call ahead at least a day in advance. The pension-style *Hotel Lužná* (☎577 131 112, Ⓦwww.hotelluzna.cz; ❸) lies just south of the spa proper on Solné. Between the centre and the spa, on pedestrianized Dr. Veselého, is the simple but tidy *Hotel Vltava* (☎577 131 376; ❷). If you're heading into Slovakia, the scenic train journey from Uherský Brod through the White Carpathians to Trenčianska Teplá is as good a way as any to get there.

Zlín

Hidden in a gentle green valley east of the Morava, **ZLÍN** is one of the most fascinating Moravian towns. Despite appearances, it's not just another factory town, it is *the* factory town – a museum of functionalist architecture and the inspiration of one man, **Tomáš Baťa** (pronounced "Batya"). When Baťa founded his company in 1894 with his brother and sister, Zlín's population was less than 3000. Now, with suburbs trailing along the River Dřevnice, it's approaching 90,000. The town's heyday was during the First Republic, when Baťa planned and started to build the ultimate production-line city, a place where workers would be provided with good housing, schooling, leisure facilities and a fair wage. "Work collectively, live individually" was one of Baťa's favourite aphorisms, and all along the approach roads to the town centre you can see the red-brick shoe-box houses that Baťa constructed for his workers as "temporary accommo-dation" – houses that have lasted better than anything built after 1948. The combined effects of Allied bombing, nationalization and economic stagnation have left only a hint of the model garden city Baťa had in mind. Zlín can't hope to appeal to everyone's aesthetic tastes, but it does present an entirely different side of the country from the usual provincial medieval staré město.

Baťa was a long-standing patron of modern art, which he felt would reflect the thrust and modernity of his own business. In 1911 he had his own **villa** built on the north side of the river by the leading Czech architect of the time, Jan Kotěra; it's a very understated affair, virtually devoid of ornamentation, and

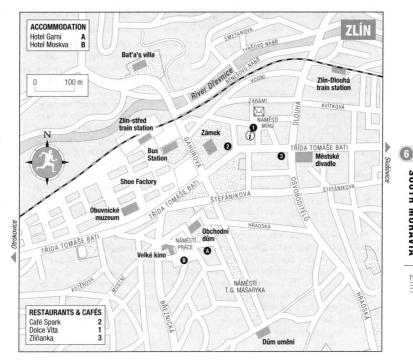

now institutionalized. In the late 1920s Le Corbusier was called in to design the town, but after an abortive sketch of the place, this chance of a lifetime fell to local-born architect **František Gahura**, who had studied under Kotěra.

Zlín literally revolves around the **shoe factory** itself. Its sixteen-storey office building, called *mrakodrap* (skyscraper), was designed by one-time apprentice to Le Corbusier Vladimír Karfík, and nowadays serves as the city's administration office. The style – concrete frame, red-brick infill and plate-glass windows – was intended to be "the leitmotif of Zlín's architecture", as Gahura put it, and is indeed typical of all the town's original 1930s buildings, later copied and barbarized by undistinguished postwar architects. Baťa's own office was a huge, air-conditioned, glass-encased lift, capable of visiting every floor. Near the *mrakodrap* is Zlín's main "sight", **Obuvnické muzeum** (Shoe Museum; April–Oct Tues–Sun 10am–noon & 1–5pm; Nov, Dec, Feb & March Tues–Fri only), a wonderful 1930s-style display with shoes from all over the world – from medieval *boty* to the sad attempts of the Communist Svit factory in Zlín – plus a good section on Baťa himself. The rest of the complex is filled with wholesale houses and stores (production having been transferred to the east).

Directly opposite the main entrance, across třída Tomáše Bati, is Karfík's plate-glass department store, **Obchodní dům**, which naturally includes a shoe shop. Beyond here, on náměstí Práce (Work Square), lies Gahura's 1931 **Velké kino**, which holds 2000 movie-goers – now unfortunately redone with new white vinyl siding, it's undistinguished – and the eleven-storey Společenský dům, built by Karfík and Lorenz in 1932–33 and now occupied by the **Hotel Moskva**.

Baťa

Son of a local cobbler, **Tomáš Baťa** worked his way up from nothing to become the First Republic's most famous millionaire. He grew rich supplying the Austro-Hungarian army with its boots during World War I, and between the wars quickly became the largest **manufacturer of shoes** in the world, producing over 50 million pairs annually. Baťa became Zlín's mayor in 1923, but died in a plane crash in 1932 at the peak of his power, and although his work was continued by his son (also called Tomáš), the firm and most of the family were forced to leave the country in 1938. Tomáš junior elected to go to Canada, taking his own management team (one hundred families) and shoemaking machinery with him. There, he quickly set about building another model factory town, known as Bataville, just outside Ottawa, and the company continued to expand into the vast multinational it is today; much of its production now takes place in low-cost Asia.

Nationalization in 1945 robbed Baťa of the company's spiritual home, and in 1949 zealous Party hacks added insult to injury by renaming the town **Gottwaldov** after the country's notorious first Communist president, Klement Gottwald, also known as the "Stalinist butcher". It was no doubt seen as a just revenge on Baťa, who rid his shop floor of Communists by decree in the 1920s. Soon after November 1989, Tomáš junior paid his first visit to Zlín for over forty years, and the whole town turned out to greet him, draping banners out of their windows proclaiming *"ať žije Zlín"* (Long live Zlín). In 1990 the town once more became officially known as Zlín, but due to alleged Nazi collaboration by members of his family, Baťa was unable to reclaim the factory through restitution. Nevertheless, Baťa now has a significant stake in the shoe market, with numerous outlets across the country, including the flagship modernist store on Wenceslas Square in Prague.

Gahura's master plan was never fully realized, and much of the town is accidental and ill-conceived. Only the sloping green of **náměstí T.G. Masaryka**, flanked by more boxy buildings, gives some idea of the trajectory of Gahura's ideas. The first block on the left is Gahura's Masarykovy Školy, where Baťa pursued his revolutionary teaching methods still admired today. At the top of this leafy space is the **Dům umění** (Mon–Fri 9am–5pm, Sat & Sun 9am–noon & 1–5pm), designed by Gahura in 1932 as a memorial to Baťa, where his statue, some memorabilia, and the wreckage of the biplane in which he crashed, used to stand. It now serves as the concert hall for the town's orchestra and for exhibitions of contemporary art – appropriate enough, given Baťa's tireless patronage of the **avant-garde**, which he not only utilized in his photographic advertising but also produced in the film studios that were built here between the wars, where many of the country's renowned animation films are still made.

The only other place of interest is the modest country **zámek** (Tues–Sun 9am–noon & 1–5pm) in the park opposite the factory, which houses the town's **Muzeum jihovýchodní Moravy** (South Moravian Museum) boasting a small, but excellent, collection of **twentieth-century Czech art**, ranging from the Cubists Kubišta, Filla, Čapek and Procházka, to wacky Pop Art sculptures from the 1960s and more contemporary works.

Curiously, Zlín is also the birthplace of two unlikely bedfellows: the playwright **Tom Stoppard** and Donald Trump's ex-wife, **Ivana** (née Zelníčková).

Practicalities

Zlín is an easy day-trip from Brno, Kroměříž or Olomouc, although approaching by train can involve a roundabout journey: it's located on a branch line which departs the main Břeclav–Přerov route at the junction town of Otrokovice. Zlín's **train** and **bus stations** are just a few minutes' walk from the centre and everything there is to see. The **tourist office** (June–Sept Mon–Thurs 6am–6pm, Fri 6am–5pm, Sat 9am–noon; Oct–May closed Sat; Ⓦwww.mestozlin.cz) can be found in the radnice on náměstí Míru.

Accommodation is overpriced, catering mostly for business clientele. At one time, *the* hotel to stay at was Gahura's high-rise *Hotel Moskva* (Ⓣ577 561 111, Ⓦwww.moskva-zlin.cz; ❹), on náměstí Práce, though it's become something of an all-purpose building housing offices, pseudo-glitzy shops and the centre of the town's fairly dubious nightlife. Next door, you can enjoy the gleaming white decor – and less fuss – of the *Hotel Garni* (Ⓣ577 212 074, Ⓦwww .hotelgarnizlin.cz; ❸). Both places offer free **wi-fi**. For **eating**, *Dolce Vita*, náměstí Míru 12, serves up steaks, pastas and sandwiches in a bright, pop-art interior with tables on the square in summer. You can relax over a coffee and cake at the *Café Spark*, in a glass pavilion in the park opposite the zámek; the nearby *Zlíňanka*, třída Tomáše Bati 18, is an old-fashioned, frumpily decorated little place with great ice cream.

Kroměříž and around

KROMĚŘÍŽ (Kremsier), 30km or so up the Morava from Uherské Hradiště and seat of the bishops of Olomouc from the Middle Ages to the nineteenth century, is one of Moravia's most graceful towns. Its once-powerful German-speaking population has long since gone, and nowadays the town feels pleasantly provincial, famous only for its Moravian male-voice choir and folk music tradition. Though quiet, Kroměříž is definitely worth a day-trip, if only for the chateau's rich collections and the town's very beautiful and extensive gardens.

Savagely set upon by the Swedish army in the Thirty Years' War, Kroměříž was rebuilt by order of **Prince-Bishop Karl Eusebius von Liechtenstein-Kastelcorn**, a pathological builder (see p.328) and a member of the richest dynasty in Moravia at the time. Vast sums were spent not only on hiring Italian architects, but also on enriching the chateau's art collection and establishing a musical life to rival Vienna. Liechtenstein founded a college for choristers, maintained a thirty-piece court orchestra and employed a series of prestigious *Kapellmeister*, though nowadays, aside from the chateau's extensive archives, there's little evidence of the courtly life.

The staré město

Set back from the banks of the River Morava, the centre of the staré město is the former marketplace of **Velké náměstí**. A broad, gracious square, its sea of cobblestones is interrupted only by the lime trees that surround a gilded plague column and fountain (there's an even better column and fountain ensemble on Riegrovo náměstí). Arcades have survived here and there round the square, the radnice has a fine white Renaissance tower, and the houses themselves, though they have suffered over the years, are now prettily painted up. Jánská, just off the square, hides the town's finest ensemble: a flourish of terraced canons' houses with bright Empire frontages.

Arcibiskupský zámek

The houses at the northern corner of Velké náměstí part to reveal the UNESCO-protected **Arcibiskupský zámek** (Archbishop's Palace; April & Oct Sat & Sun

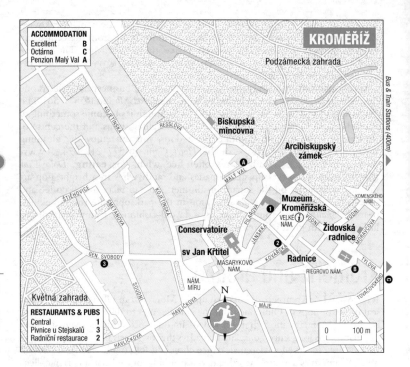

Within the image:

KROMĚŘÍŽ

ACCOMMODATION
Excellent **B**
Octárna **C**
Penzion Malý Val **A**

Podzámecká zahrada

Bus & Train Stations (400m)

RESSLOVA

KOJETÍNSKÁ

STIEHOVICE

SMETANOVA

KOJETÍNSKÁ

GEN. SVOBODY

SOUDNÍ

Květná zahrada

Biskupská mincovna

Arcibiskupský zámek

MALÝ VAL

A

PILAŘOVA

Muzeum Kroměřížská

1

VELKÉ *(i)* NÁM.

KOMENSKÉHO NÁM.

VODNÍ

Conservatoire

sv Jan Křtitel

JÁNSKÁ

KOVÁŘSKÁ

2

MASARYKOVO NÁM.

NÁM. MÍRU

Radnice

Židovská radnice

MORÁCOVA

RIEGROVO NÁM.

TYLOVA

TOVAČOVSKÉHO

B

C

3

HAVLÍČKOVA

N

1. MÁJE

RESTAURANTS & PUBS
Central **1**
Pivnice u Stejskalů **3**
Radniční restaurace **2**

HAVLÍČKOVA

0   100 m

9am–4pm; May, June & Sept Tues–Sun 9am–5pm; July & Aug until 6pm; tour in English 180Kč; ⓦ www.azz.cz), a vast Baroque fortress whose severity is relieved only by the fifteenth-century lanterned tower, sole survivor of the Swedes' rampage in the Thirty Years' War. Inside, the chateau is a gentler Rococo than its uncompromising exterior might suggest. The dark wood and marble decor of the small **Manský sál**, where the bishops held court, is overwhelmed by Maulbertsch's celebratory frescoes, which bear down on guests from the unusually low ceiling. The archbishop's bedroom rather alarmingly contains a double bed – the official story being that it was for his parents when they came to visit.

The showpiece of the palace is the fiddly white-and-gold excess of the **Sněmovní sál**, as high and mighty as anything in Prague, and featured in Miloš Forman's film *Amadeus*. In the first three months of 1849, Reichstag delegates from all parts of the Habsburg Empire met to thrash out a new liberal constitution in the face of the revolutionary events of the previous year. In the end, though, the Kremsier Constitution that came out of these brainstorming sessions and acknowledged "equality of national rights" was unceremoniously ditched by the new imperial government, who drew up their own version. Police were sent to Kremsier to close down the Reichstag, with orders to arrest the most radical delegates. The Habsburgs' final bout of absolutism had begun. After – or instead of – the main guided tour (*trasa 1 – historické sály*) you can visit the **Zámecká obrazárna** (Chateau Gallery), which contains what's left of the Liechtensteins' vast art collection, still the best selection of sixteenth- and seventeenth-century European paintings in Moravia. There's plenty of bucolic frolicking supplied by the Flemish masters, including an earthy Breughel, a trompe l'oeil Hoogstraten, and a more sober portrait of Charles I of England and his wife Henrietta by

6

SOUTH MORAVIA | Kroměříž and around

Van Dyck. Others worth noting are Veronese's awestruck bearded *Apostles*, Cranach's gruesome *Beheading of St John the Baptist*, and the gallery's prize possession, *Apollo Punishing Marsyas*, a late Titian. At the end of your visit, climb the **tower** to admire the panorama of neighbouring streets and gardens.

The rest of the staré město

The **Muzeum Kroměřížska** (Tues–Sun 9am–noon & 1–5pm; 40Kč), on the main square, contains a large collection of work by Max Švabinský, a late-nineteenth-century artist and graphicist who was born at Panská 11 in 1872. There's no denying his skill nor his prolific output, but he's a mite too gushy and Romantic for some, and the drawings of nudes and tigers, not to mention his collection of exotic butterflies and stuffed birds, displayed here are unlikely to make many converts. Of the town's churches, the Gothic **sv Mořic** is the oldest, but its innards were ripped out by fire in 1836 and rebuilt without much feeling. A better bet is the Baroque church of **sv Jan Křtitel** at the top of Jánská, whose sensuous lines and frescoed oval dome combine to form one of the showpieces of Moravian Baroque. Lastly, it's worth wandering round to Moravcova in the easternmost corner of the old town, which was formerly the Jewish **ghetto**. Jewish communities in places like Kroměříž, Uherské Hradiště and Prostějov were among the largest in the Czech Lands before World War II, and since they provided many essential services the local bigwigs left them alone. The **Židovská radnice** (Jewish Town Hall) here – one of the few outside Prague – is remarkable not for its architectural beauty but for its mere existence, the result of a magnanimous gesture by the prince-bishop for services rendered in the Thirty Years' War; today it serves as a cultural centre and gives little hint of its previous life.

The gardens

Like Olomouc (see p.355), Kroměříž is a place as rich in gardens as in buildings. The watery **Podzámecká zahrada** (daily: summer 7am–7pm; winter 7am–4pm) established by one of the green-fingered Chotek family who held the archbishopric in the 1830s, stretches right down to the Morava, covering an area twice the size of the old town. Having long since lost its formality, it's now a pleasantly unruly park, reeking of wild garlic in spring and hiding an aviary and menagerie, harbouring raccoons, baboons and parrots, plus a deer park and a few stalking peacocks. Ten-minutes' walk west of the chateau is the early Baroque **Květná zahrada** (daily: summer 7am–7pm; winter 7am–4pm; 20Kč), more formal but also more beautiful and generally in a better state of repair. The garden was laid out by the Liechtensteins in the 1670s, and one of its many charms is a huge domed rotunda with a **Foucault pendulum** – one of just four in the world.

Practicalities

The **train station** and the **bus station** are on the opposite bank of the River Morava from the chateau gardens; head down Vejvanovského to reach the old town. The **tourist office** (Mon–Fri 9am–5pm, Sat & Sun 9am–3pm; ⓦwww .mesto-kromeriz.cz), on Velké náměstí, can arrange private rooms, but charges 20Kč for each call. There's plenty of characterful **accommodation**: the *Octárna*, in a former vinegar distillery at Tovačovského 318 (ⓣ573 505 655, ⓦwww .octarna.eu; ❹), offers soothing en suites with TV, desk space and free wi-fi; the family-run *Excellent* (ⓣ573 333 023, ⓦwww.excellent.tunker.com; ❸) is a cosy B&B with a sauna and internet access; and the *Penzion Malý Val*, Malý Val 1541 (ⓣ573 332 496, ⓦwww.malyval.cz; ❸), has en suite rooms in a bright, modern building. *Radniční restaurace*, Kovářská 20, a wine **restaurant** in the cellars of the town hall, serves delicious food and a good range of wines from Valtice, while the

Central on the main square contains a workmanlike restaurant on the ground floor and weekend dances in the café upstairs (closed Sun). *Pivnice u Stejskalů*, on the way to the Květná zahrada at Generala Svobody 13, offers simple, inexpensive Czech food and good draught beer. You can buy the local **wine** and have a tour of the cellars at the *Arcibiskupské zámecké sklepy*, behind the archway beside the chateau.

Holešov

HOLEŠOV (Holleschau), 15km northeast of Kroměříž on route 432 (and just 15min by train), makes an interesting day-trip. The town had one of the largest Jewish communities in Moravia, peaking at around 1700 in the mid-nineteenth century. It also has the dubious distinction of being a victim of the last Jewish pogrom on Czech soil in December 1918, during which two Jews were killed. The old ghetto lies to the northwest of the town square, náměstí dr. E. Beneše, centred on the unique, Polish-style **Šachova synagoga** (9am–noon & 1–5pm: April–June, Sept & Oct Wed–Sun; July & Aug Tues–Sun; Nov–March Fri–Sun), on Příční. Built in 1560, the synagogue retains its remarkably ornate eighteenth-century interior. On the second floor there's an exhibition on, and a few relics from, the town's Jewish history. Further north, in a kink of the River Rusava, lies the **Jewish cemetery** (Židovský hřbitov), with graves dating back to 1647. The **train** and **bus stations** lie ten-minutes' walk west of the square, where there's a friendly **tourist office** (Mon–Fri 8.30am–8pm, Sat & Sun 8.30am–4pm; Ⓦwww.holesov.mic.cz).

Travel details

Trains

Connections with Prague: Brno (every 1–2hr; 2hr 40min–3hr 40min); Žďár nad Sázavou (7 daily; 2hr 10min–2hr 20min).

Brno to: Blansko (hourly; 20–30min); Bratislava (8 daily; 1hr 30min–2hr); Bučovice (hourly; 35–50min); České Budějovice (4 daily; 4hr 25min); Jihlava (every 1–2hr; 1hr 55min–3hr 20min); Kroměříž (1–2 daily; 1hr 20min); Moravský Krumlov (hourly; 45–50min); Náměšť nad Oslavou (hourly; 45min–1hr; 45min); Olomouc (up to 7 daily; 1hr 25min); Pardubice (every 2hr; 1hr 35min–1hr 50min); Slavkov (hourly; 25–35min); Třebíč (every 1–2hr; 1hr 10min–1hr 45min); Vienna (5 daily; 1hr 45min); Žďár nad Sázavou (hourly; 1hr 5min–1hr 35min); Znojmo (1 daily; 1hr 55min).

Telč to: Slavonice (2–8 daily; 50min–1hr).

Znojmo to: Jaroměřice nad Rokytnou (every 2hr; 50min–1hr 40min); Jihlava (2 daily; 2hr–2hr 20min); Mikulov (every 1–2hr; 1hr–1hr 45min); Retz (4–8 daily; 22min); Šatov (up to 8 daily; 12min); Valtice (every 1–2hr; 1hr 20min).

Buses

Connections with Prague: Brno (every 30min–1hr; 2hr 20min–3hr 30min); Znojmo (2 daily; 3hr 10min–3hr 25min).

Brno to: Buchlovice (up to hourly; 55min–1hr 25min); Jaroměřice nad Rokytnou (2–7 daily; 1hr 30min–1hr 55min); Jedovnice (24 daily Mon–Fri; 45min); Kroměříž (hourly Mon–Fri, 2–4 daily Sat & Sun; 1hr 10min–1hr 40min); Křtiny (hourly Mon–Fri; 35min); Luhačovice (1–6 daily; 2hr 15min–2hr 55min); Mikulov (19–20 daily Mon–Fri; 45min–1hr 40min); Moravský Krumlov (2–13 daily; 50min–1hr 10min); Telč (2–6 daily; 1hr 55min); Uherské Hradiště (hourly Mon–Fri, up to 7 daily Sat & Sun; 1hr 50min); Zlín (hourly Mon–Fri, 4 daily Sat & Sun; 1hr 50min–2hr 25min); Znojmo (up to 8 daily; 1hr–1hr 15min).

Jihlava to: Telč (hourly Mon–Fri; 40min–1hr).

Uherské Hradiště to: Buchlovice (up to hourly; 10–30min); Kroměříž (1 daily; 1hr 20min); Luhačovice (3 daily Mon–Fri; 40min–1hr 25min); Strážnice (8 daily Mon–Fri; 45min–1hr 10min); Trenčín (7–10 daily; 1hr 10min–1hr 40min); Velehrad (3–11 daily; 10–25min); Zlín (every 30min Mon–Fri, 2 daily Sat & Sun; 35min–1hr 10min).

7

North Moravia

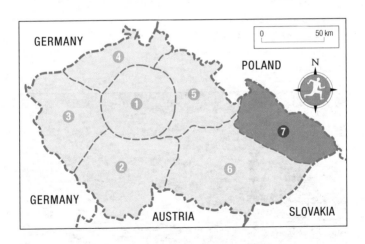

CHAPTER 7

Highlights

✳ **Olomouc** With its cobbled squares, fountains and Baroque churches, Moravia's most handsome city is the perfect base from which to tour the region. See p.355

✳ **Ostrava nightlife** An exploding number of bars and clubs has transformed Moravia's erstwhile home of heavy industry into the Czech Republic's undisputed Friday-night capital. See p.370

✳ **Wooden churches in the Beskydy** The densely wooded countryside of the Beskydy boasts the largest concentration of wooden churches in the Czech Republic. See p.375

✳ **Štramberk** Hilly Beskydy village with a remarkable array of wooden architecture in situ. See p.375

✳ **Rožnov pod Radhoštěm** The country's largest and most impressive open-air museum or *skanzen*. See p.379

▲ Štramberk

North Moravia

espite its historical status as the heartland of the Czech Republic's coal and steel industry, **North Moravia** (Severní Morava) is not the never-ending conglomeration of factories that its critics would have you believe. In fact, the north boasts some of Moravia's wildest and most varied countryside, including the **Jeseníky**, the region's highest peaks, which brush up against the Polish border to the north. To the east, near the border with Slovakia, the villages of the **Beskydy** are a treasure-trove of Moravian folk culture. Wooden houses and churches are dotted along the valleys, and a range of traditional timber buildings has been gathered together and restored in the republic's largest open-air museum in **Rožnov pod Radhoštěm**. In addition to its folk culture and hiking potential, the Beskydy is endowed with some intriguing museums: a large car collection at the technical museum in **Kopřivnice**, a hat museum in **Nový Jičín**, and two memorials to famous local boys – Sigmund Freud, who was born in **Příbor**, and Leoš Janáček, who lived and composed in **Hukvaldy**.

The region's two largest cities typify North Moravia's contradictions: **Ostrava**, the country's largest mining and steel town, is a place rich in industrial heritage whose considerable charms – like its no-holds-barred nightlife – are not immediately apparent; **Olomouc**, on the other hand, the old medieval capital on the banks of the River Morava, is easily Moravia's most attractive and relaxing city, unambiguously postcard-pretty.

Olomouc

OLOMOUC (pronounced "Olla-moats" and known to the city's sizeable prewar German-speaking community as Olmütz) is easily the most immediately satisfying of Moravia's three big cities, thanks to its well-preserved staré město, sloping cobbled squares, Baroque fountains, and healthy quota of university students. Occupying the crucial Morava crossing point on the road to Kraków, Olomouc was actually the capital of Moravia from 1187 to 1641 and the seat of a bishopric (later archbishopric) for even longer. All this attracted the destructive attention of Swedish troops in the Thirty Years' War, and their occupation in the 1640s left the town for dead. During this period, Brno took over as capital, in reward for its heroic stand against the Swedes; only the wealth of the church and its strategic trading position kept Olomouc alive. Meanwhile, the military threat from Prussia confined the town to within its eighteenth-century red-brick fortifications, and only after these were finally torn down in 1888 did the city begin to evolve into the industrial centre it is today.

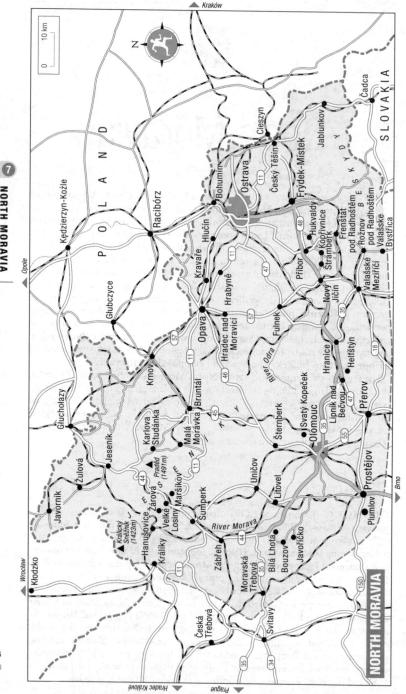

▲ *Kraków*

SLOVAKIA

◄ *Opole*

Čadca

Jablunkov

Cieszyn

Bohumín

Ostrava

Český Těšín

Frýdek-Místek

11

Hukvaldy

48

Kopřivnice

Frenštát
pod Radhoštěm

B E

S K Y D Y

Rožnov
pod Radhoštěm

Kravaře

Hlučín

Štramberk

Příbor

Valašské
Meziříčí

Valašské
Bystřice

Hrabyně

11

47

Nový
Jičín

35

Opava

Hradec nad
Moravicí

Fulnek

57

Glubczyce

57

Krnov

11

River Odra

46

Hranice

Helfštýn

18

Racibórz

Kędzierzyn-Koźle

P   O   L   A   N   D

Bruntál

45

Svatý Kopeček

Lipník nad
Bečvou

Přerov

47

Sternberk

Karlova
Studánka

Malá
Morávka

Olomouc

35

Głuchołazy

Jeseník

Praděd
(1491m)

11

Uničov

Prostějov

55

Žulová

44

Litovel

◄ *Brno*

Javorník

Žárová

Velké
Losiny

Šumperk

River Morava

Plumlov

Klodzko

Králický
Sněžník
(1423m)

Hanušovice

Králíky

Zábřeh

Bílá Lhota

Bouzov

Javoříčko

44

150

◄ *Wrocław*

11

Moravská
Třebová

35

◄ *Hradec Králové*

◄ *Prague*

Česká
Třebová

Svitavy

35

34

N

0   10 km

N

NORTH MORAVIA

If you're coming in late April, late August or late October, you may well coincide with one of the huge flower shows, or **Flora Olomouc** (ⓦ www .flora-ol.cz), which bring hordes of Czech visitors to the city – hotels fill up quickly at these times and it's advisable to book well in advance.

Arrival, information and accommodation

The **train station** is 2km east of the old town, and the **bus terminal** is 1km beyond this. On arrival, walk or take any **tram** from the train station heading west up Masarykova and get off after three or four stops; from the bus station take tram #4, which proceeds down Masarykova, or tram #5, which runs along třída Svobody south of the old town. The city is divided into two zones; to go to the centre of town you need only an inner zone ticket (*vnitřní jízdenka*), which you should buy from a machine or news kiosk; there is also a one-day ticket (*jednodenní lístek*), available from the main bus station. The **tourist office**, in the arcades on the north side of the radnice (daily 9am–7pm; ☏585 513 385, ⓦ www.olomoucko.cz or www.olomouc-tourism.cz), provides information as well as booking **private rooms**.

Accommodation

With a clutch of comfy **pensions**, Olomouc offers plenty of choice for the independent traveller – although the best places are quite small and advance booking is recommended. The city also has a welcoming, superbly central **hostel**, 🏃 *Poets' Corner*, Sokolská 1 (☏777 570 730, ⓦ www.hostelolomouc .com), run by people who know their stuff when it comes to travel in Moravia. It's spread over two floors of an apartment building, with two eight-bunk dorms (from 350Kč) plus doubles (❷) and triples with homely old furniture. There's a spacious kitchen, cosy living room, and wi-fi throughout. If you want to **camp**, head to the site in Šternberk (see p.364).

🏃 **Antika** Wurmova 1 ☏731 560 264 or 608 470 160, ⓦ www.antika.cz. A popular place that should be reserved well in advance, with three apartments (sleeping 2–3) decorated with folksy furnishings, fancy textiles and antiques. One apartment comes with kitchenette, the other two boast toaster, kettle and a fridge regularly refilled with breakfast eats. Wi-fi throughout. No credit cards. ❹

Arigone Univerzitní 20 ☏585 232 351, ⓦ arigone .web.tiscali.cz. Lovely hotel with original wood ceilings and parquet floors. Small, so book in advance. ❹

Gemo Pavelčákova 22 ☏585 222 115, ⓦ www .hotel-gemo.cz. Something of a modern eyesore from the outside, this is an efficiently run, centrally located business hotel, offering all mod cons. ❼

Na hradbách Hrnčířská 3 ☏585 233 243, ⓦ www.pensionnahradbach.wz.cz. Small, inexpensive, pension with two doubles and two triples,

hidden away in one of the city's prettiest, quietest backstreets. ❸

Na hradě Michalská 4 ☏585 203 231, ⓦ www .penzionnahrade.cz. An all-mod-cons pension in an ancient town house, offering stylish en suites with TV, a/c and cable internet access. There's a secluded back garden with sun-loungers. ❹

U anděla Hrnčířská 10 ☏585 228 775, ⓦ www .uandela.cz. Rooms above a restaurant in a cute cobbled alley. A couple of en suites with TV and fridge, and a couple of studios with kitchenettes. ❷

U dómu Dómská 4 ☏585 220 502, ⓕ585 220 501. Small, centrally located 20-bed B&B, near the cathedral. ❹

🏃 **U Jakuba** 8 května 9 ☏585 209 995, ⓦ www.pensionujakuba.com. Stylish pension in a beautifully renovated fifteenth-century house, offering bright en suites and a couple of two-person apartments. Your host, Jakub, is in fact a friendly small dog. Wi-fi throughout. ❷

The City

Despite being a quarter the size of Brno, Olomouc has the same buzz, with its main arteries clogged with shoppers in the afternoon rush. The **staré město** is a strange contorted shape, squeezed in the middle by an arm of the Morava.

OLOMOUC

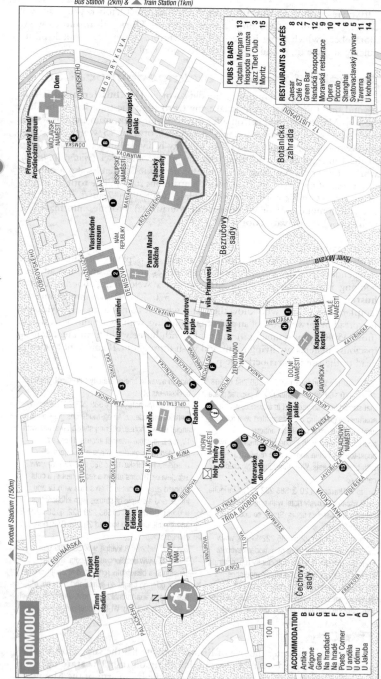

Bus Station (2km) & ▲ Train Station (1km)

◄ Football Stadium (150m)

Flora Exhibition Grounds (300m) ►

River Morava

PUBS & BARS

Captain Morgan's	13
Hospoda u muzea	1
Jazz Tibet Club	3
Moritz	15

RESTAURANTS & CAFÉS

Caesar	8
Café 87	2
Green Bar	7
Hanácká hospoda	12
Moravská restaurace	9
Opera	10
Piccolo	4
Shanghai	6
Svatováclavský pivovar	5
Taverna	11
U kohouta	14

ACCOMMODATION

Antika	B
Arigone	E
Gemo	G
Na hradbách	H
Na hradě	F
Poets' Corner	C
U anděla	I
U dómu	A
U Jakuba	D

0   100 m

N

Předmětské hrad/
Arcidiecézní muzeum
Dóm

Arcibiskupský
palác

Palacký
University

Biskupské
náměstí

Vlastivědné
muzeum

Panna Maria
Sněžná

Muzeum umění

Šarkandrova
kaple

sv Michal

via Primavesi

Kapucínský
kostel

sv Mořic

Radnice

Horní
náměstí
Holy Trinity
Column

Moravské
divadlo

Haunschildův
palác

Dolní
náměstí

Former
Edison
Cinema

Puppet
Theatre

Zimní
stadión

Čechovy
sady

Bezručovy
sady

Botanická
zahrada

Malé
náměstí

Palachovo
náměstí

Horní and Dolní náměstí

In the western half of the staré město, all roads lead to the city's two central cobbled main squares, which are hinged to each other at right angles. The lower of the two, Dolní náměstí, is more or less triangular, but the upper one, **Horní náměstí**, is thoroughly irregular. At its centre is the **radnice**, a cream-coloured amalgamation of buildings and styles with the occasional late-Gothic or Renaissance gesture – a freestanding flight of steps, the handsome lanterned tower soaring up to its conclusion of baubles and pinnacles, and, tucked round the back, a lonely oriel window above a self-portrait of the mason holding out his hand for more money from the miserly town council. But it's the north side that draws the crowds, with the **astronomical clock** originally built by Master Hanuš, like its more famous successor in Prague, but destroyed in World War II. The rather soulless workerist remake chimes all right, but the hourly mechanical show of proletarians is disappointing.

Far more action-packed is the monumental, polygonal **Holy Trinity Column** (Sousoší nejsvětější Trojice), erected in the first half of the eighteenth century to the west of the radnice, its ornamental urns sprouting dramatic gilded flames. The largest plague column in the Czech Republic, it's big enough to be a chapel and in some ways acts like one: inside you'll find a nun telling the stories of the saints featured on the outside (daily 9am–noon). Set into the west facade of the square is the **Moravské divadlo**, a Neoclassical theatre where the young Gustav Mahler arrived as the newly appointed *Kapellmeister* in 1883. The local press took an instant dislike to him: according to his own words, "from the moment I crossed the threshold . . . I felt like a man who is awaiting the judgement of God". No doubt there was a strong element of kneejerk anti-Semitism in his hostile reception, but this was not helped by Mahler's autocratic style, which caused a number of the local prima donnas to live up to their name. He lasted just three months.

Olomouc makes a big fuss of its **fountains** (*kašna*), which grace each one of its six ancient market squares. Horní náměstí boasts three of them: Hercules, looking unusually athletic for his years; a vigorous depiction of Julius Caesar to the east of the radnice; and one dedicated to the ancient Greek poet Arion, featuring several turtles and Arion embracing a dolphin. Jupiter and Neptune can be found in **Dolní náměstí**, which has a dustier feel to it, sloping down to the characteristically low-key Capuchin church. Of all the square's subdued Baroque facades, it's the **Haunschildův palác**, on the corner with Lafayettova, which stands out, its single Renaissance oriel decorated with scenes from Ovid.

Sv Mořic and the side streets

North of Horní náměstí, off Opletalova, is the church of **sv Mořic**, an oddly mutant building – from the west at least – defended like a Norman fort and overcome inside by a thick coat of pink paint that makes the original Gothic interior difficult to stomach. It does, however, boast the Engler organ, the largest in the Czech Republic; an ugly, dark, wooden affair with over 10,000 dirty grey pipes and a fair few cherubs, it sounds better than it looks (there's an organ festival held here in early Sept). You can also climb the church **tower** (May–Sept Mon–Fri 9.15–11.45am & 12.30–4pm, Sat 9.15–11.45am & 12.45–4pm, Sun 1–4pm) for an overview of the staré město.

Two of the city's best-looking backstreets, Školní and Michalská, lead southeast from Horní náměstí up to the long slope of Žerotínovo náměstí, which features an appealing ensemble of lime trees, streetlamps and Baroque statuary at its upper end. Overlooking them all is the Italianate church of **sv Michal**, whose rather plain facade hides a cool, spacious interior clad in the masterly excess of High

Baroque. Three octagonal saucer domes rise up in Byzantine fashion atop Roman pilasters with gilded Corinthian capitals so large their acanthus leaves bear fruit. There's a very high cherub count on the side altars and a wonderful silver relief of sheep on the gilded pulpit. Close to sv Michal, on the corner of Univerzitní, is the late-nineteenth-century **vila Primavesi**, designed in the Viennese Secession style by, among others, the local sculptor Anton Hanak and the Viennese architect Josef Hofmann for the Primavesi family who went on to finance the Wiener Werkstätte in the 1920s. It now houses the **Galerie Primavesi** (Tues–Fri 8.30am–12.30pm & 1–5pm, Sat 8.30am–12.30pm; donation requested), which puts on temporary exhibitions of modern art and photography.

It's also worth checking out the mini-dome of the neo-Baroque **Sarkandrova kaple**, which replaced the old prison on Mahlerova at the beginning of the twentieth century. The chapel takes its name from a Catholic priest of Silesian origin, **Jan Sarkander** (1576–1620), who was incarcerated in the aforementioned prison and died after being tortured by local Protestants. In 1995 Pope John Paul II visited Olomouc and officially canonized Sarkander, whose relics now rest in the gilded casket opposite the pulpit in the local cathedral (see opposite). His canonization angered the local non-Catholic community, who claimed that Sarkander was a willing instrument of the Counter-Reformation, taking over the parish of Holešov after the local Protestants had been kicked out by the Jesuits.

Muzeum umění to the Dóm

Firmly wedged between the two sections of the staré město is the obligatory Jesuit church of **Panna Maria Sněžná**, deemed to be particularly necessary in a city where Protestantism spread like wildfire among the German community during the sixteenth century. Jutting out into the road, the church marks the former gateway from the old town to the archbishop's territory to the east, where the great mass of the former Jesuit College, now the **Palacký University**, dominates the neighbouring square, náměstí Republiky.

Above the Divadlo hudby, on the opposite side of the square, is the **Muzeum umění** (Tues–Sun 10am–6pm; Ⓦ www.olmuart.cz; 50Kč), which hosts major exhibitions of contemporary art. There's something of a permanent collection in the attic, which features Art Nouveau stained glass from the vila Primavesi, modernist furniture by Anton Hanak, and a model of his strange *Child over an Ordinary Day* (a cherub standing over a four-headed plinth around which four snakes have wrapped themselves), originally positioned under the pergola in the vila Primavesi's garden. There's a good deal of turn-of-the-twentieth-century Czech art, including stylized Beskydy village-scapes courtesy of the great promoter of local folk culture Bohumír Jaroněk. You can also gain access to the gallery's *vyhlídkova věž* (lookout tower) for a rooftop view over Olomouc. Next door is the town's **Vlastivědné muzeum** (April–Sept Tues–Sun 9am–6pm; Oct–March Wed–Sun 10am–5pm; Ⓦ www.vmo.cz; 30Kč), housed in the former Poor Clares' convent and cloisters, with a pretty dull permanent display on the region's natural history.

The trams and cars hurtling across the cobbles make this one of Olomouc's least accommodating squares, so, after admiring the Bernini-esque Triton fountain, you'd do well to slip down Mariánská to leafy **Biskupské náměstí**, one of the most peaceful spots in town. Among its fine Baroque buildings, erected after the destructive occupation of the Swedes, is the **Arcibiskupský palác** (Archbishop's Palace; closed to the public), financed by the multimillion-aire Bishop Liechtenstein in the 1660s; it was here, at a safe distance from Vienna, that the 18-year-old Franz Josef I was proclaimed emperor in 1848. On the other side of the tramlines, the Cathedral of sv Václav, or **Dóm**, started life as a twelfth-century Romanesque basilica, but, as with Brno and Prague, the current structure is mostly the result of nineteenth-century neo-Gothic restoration, which included the addition of the 100-metre-high eastern spire. However, the nave is bright and airy, its walls and pillars prettily painted in imitation of the great Romanesque churches of the West; the modern, high-relief Stations of the Cross are quite striking, and the **krypta** (Tues & Thurs–Sat 9am–5pm, Wed 9am–4pm, Sun 11am–5pm) has a wonderful display of gory reliquaries and priestly sartorial wealth.

A former episcopal palace next door now holds the **Arcidiecézní muzeum** (Tues–Sun 10am–6pm; 50Kč), with a stunning collection of Gothic paintings and sculpture, much of it atmospherically located in the Romanesque halls and passageways of the basement – the surviving remnant of the palace's twelfth-century original. Visitors can also inspect the *rajski dvůr* or "paradise yard", a cloistered garden, while Renaissance frescoed corridors lead down to the restored chapel of sv Jan Křtitel (St John the Baptist), in which are exhibited fine statuary and fragments of the original palace.

Beyond the staré město

The Habsburg defences to the west of the staré město were torn down in the late nineteenth century to make way for what is now a long, busy thoroughfare known as **třída Svobody**. Starting in the north with the former **Edison cinema**, a late-Secession building from 1913 decorated with caryatids worshipping light bulbs, it continues with the familiar trail of Habsburg bureaucratic architecture. Halfway down on the west side of the street, a leftover water tower is the only survivor on Palachovo náměstí, a square that contained a synagogue until the Nazis burnt it down in 1939, and where a double statue of Stalin and Lenin subsequently stood. The former (and only the former) was defaced badly towards the end of the 1980s, apparently by an outraged Gorbachev-supporting Soviet soldier; neither survived the iconoclasm of November 1989, and the square is now named after the 1969 martyr Jan Palach (see p.108).

If you're tired of Olomouc's uneven cobbles, the best places to head for are the **parks**, which practically encircle the town. A couple of blocks of fin-de-siècle houses stand between Svobody and a long, well-maintained patchwork strip of crisscross paths, flowerbeds and manicured lawns. The Flora Výstaviště exhibition grounds, which host the thrice-yearly flower festival (see p.357), also contain the palm- and cactus-filled *skleníki* or glasshouses belonging to the city's **botanical gardens** (botanická zahrada; daily: March–April 9.30am–5pm; May–Sept 9.30am–6pm), which are worth visiting at any time of the year.

Some 8km northeast of the centre, the twin clock towers of the gleaming yellow-and-white Baroque pilgrimage church dominate the hill of **Svatý kopeček** (Heiligberg). Perched 200m above the plain and flanked by its vast convent wings, the site and scale are truly spectacular. Viewed close up the building itself doesn't always live up to expectations, but the views are spectacular and the adjoining zoo is well worth visiting (daily 8am–7pm or dusk); bus #11 from Olomouc train station will take you there.

Eating, drinking and nightlife

There are several set-piece **restaurants** on and around Olomouc's two main squares, while **pubs** are sprinkled liberally throughout the centre. Be sure to try out the city's famously pungent local cheese, *Olomoucký sýr*, known also as *tvarůžky*. For a big city, Olomouc goes to bed pretty early. As far as **entertainment** goes, the Moravské divadlo (Ⓦwww.moravskedivadlo.cz), on Horní námestí, puts on a good selection of opera as well as regular concerts by the city's philharmonic orchestra. *Jazz Tibet Club* at Sokolská 48 (Ⓦ www.jazzclub .olomouc.com) features live music (jazz, blues or funk) two or three times a week, with concerts kicking off at around 8pm. In late May, Olomouc has its **Spring Music Festival** (Olomoucké hudební jaro), when concerts are spread evenly around the city's churches, monasteries and other venues. For a full rundown of what's on during your stay, buy the **listings** magazine *Info* at the tourist office.

Restaurants and cafés

Caesar Horní námestí. Popular pizzeria in the radnice, with prime-position seating on the main square. The dreary interior is not as atmospheric as it could be. Daily 9am–1am.

Café 87 1 máje 29. Bright, funky café next door to the Muzeum umení, serving egg-and-bacon breakfasts, toasted sandwiches, croissants, cakes and shakes. Daily 8am–9pm.

Green Bar Ztracena 1. Canteen-style self-service displaying a tempting range of soups, salads and vegetarian mains. Tasty, inexpensive and central, this is the busiest place in the city at around noon. Mon–Fri 10am–5pm, Sat 9am–2pm.

Hanácká hospoda Dolní nám. 38. A large, crowded restaurant in the Haunschilduv palác, with a wide choice of Czech dishes and moderate prices. Mon–Sat 10am–midnight, Sun 10am–8pm.

Moravská restaurace Horní nám. 23. Slap bang next to the theatre on the main square, with traditional Moravian menu and wait-staff in folksy costume; this is where the coach parties invariably end up. Good list of Moravian wines. Daily 11.30am–11pm.

Opera Horní námestí. Main-square café with plentiful cakes and ice cream, a roomy interior with a children's play area, and an outdoor terrace looking out towards the plague column and fountain. Mon–Sat 9am–11pm, Sun 9am–9pm.

Piccolo 8 kvetna. Buzzing little place on the ground floor of the Prior department store, deservedly popular with local caffeine addicts. Your best bet for an early coffee and croissant. Mon–Fri 8am–5pm, Sat 8am–noon.

Shanghai Horní nám. 8. Spacious Chinese restaurant, on an upper floor opposite the radnice, with large windows offering an unbeatable view over

the square. Great-value lunchtime specials. Daily 11am–11pm.

Svatovaclavský pivovar Riegerova. Restaurant-brewery serving up delicious own-brand beer and a solid menu of goulash-and-dumplings main courses. Mon–Sat 11am–midnight, Sun 11am–10pm.

Taverna Pavelčaková. Good pizza and pasta in a homely checked-tablecloth dining room. Cute garden patio at the back. Sun–Thurs 10.30am–11pm, Fri & Sat till midnight.

U kohouta Lafayettová 3. Arguably the best restaurant in Olomouc, with the most eccentric opening hours, frequently closing at weekends and taking an entire month off in summer. Their reputation is based on great steaks and fine fish, although the own-recipe goulash is also good. Mon–Fri 10am–9pm, Sat open if the owner feels like it.

Pubs and bars

Captain Morgan's Mlynská 2. Hip, dark café/bar in the old fortifications, with a succession of vaulted rooms, an outside patio, and DJ-driven dance-pop at weekends. Daily 10am–2am.

Hospoda u muzea 1 máje. Boasting a nautical porthole in the doorway and known as *ponorka* ("submarine"), this claustrophic tunnel of a bar is popular with a generation-spanning crew of arty nonconformists. Service is frighteningly efficient: take a seat and mugs of Pilsner will arrive on your table at regular intervals until you start screaming for mercy. Occasional gigs on the tiny stage. Daily noon–midnight.

Moritz Javoricka. Micro-breweryery pub serving its own rich and cloudy beers, together with a menu of nibbles and grilled meats. Big outdoor terrace in the park across the road. Daily 11am–11pm.

Around Olomouc

Olomouc sits happily in the wide plain of the **Haná region**, famous for its folk costumes and for its songs celebrating the fertility of the land. Naturally enough in a strongly agricultural area, the **harvest festivals** (*Hanácké dožínky* or *dožínkový slavnost*) are the highlight of the year, advertised on posters everywhere in the second half of September. All the places covered below are situated in the Morava plain, and easily reached by bus or train on day-trips from Olomouc, with the exception of Helfštýn and the area round Bouzov, which are really only accessible to those with their own transport.

Helfštýn

If you're heading east from Olomouc into the Beskydy by rail or road, it's difficult to miss the spectacular ruined castle of **Helfštýn** (March & Nov Sat & Sun 9am–4pm; April, Sept & Oct Tues–Sun 9am–5pm; May–Aug Tues–Sun 9am–6pm; 30Kč), which looks down from the wooded hills to the south of River Bečva, above the road-junction town of Lipnik nad Bečvou. Founded sometime in the fourteenth century, it's one of the largest medieval castles in the Czech Republic, and was used by the Hussites as a base from which to attack Olomouc, before being deliberately laid to waste by the Habsburgs following the Thirty Years' War. Sections of the complex have since been restored, but the place is still, for the most part, a ruin and you can wander at will. Concerts, mock battles and various other events are staged here over the summer (check Ⓦwww.helfstyn.cz) and there's a permanent display of modern **blacksmith** artistry in one of the castle wings (*expozice kovářství*; May–Sept Tues–Sun 9am–5pm), plus an annual international blacksmiths' convention, *Hefaiston*, in late August. To get to the castle, you can walk the 5km along the red-marked path from the train station at Lipník nad Bečvou, which is served from Olomouc by regular train (some direct, some involving a change at either Přerov or Hranice na Moravě).

Prostějov and Plumlov

Twenty kilometres and thirty minutes by train from Olomouc, the big textile town of **PROSTĚJOV** (Prossnitz) has a grand and spacious old centre based around a large, well-laid-out main square, Masarykovo náměstí. The town's main architectural highlight is Jan Kotěra's 1908 **Národní dům** (Ⓦwww .narodni-dum.info), northeast of the square near the last remaining bastion of the old town walls and now housing a theatre and restaurant. As in his museum at Hradec Králové (see p.291), Kotěra was moving rapidly away from the "swirl and blob" of the Secession, but here and there the old elements persist in the sweep of the brass door handles and the pattern on the poster frames. Apart from its furniture, the restaurant has been left unmolested, and the bold Klimt-like ceramic relief of *The Three Graces* above the mantelpiece is still as striking as ever. Though considerably less aesthetic, *U krále Ječmínka*, a brewpub one block southeast of the Narodní dům, actually serves the best **food** and **beer** in town.

Five kilometres west of Prostějov stands the imposing slab of the chateau at **PLUMLOV** (Plumenau), one of the Liechtensteins' many fancies. Designed by Prince-Bishop Karl Eusebius von Liechtenstein-Kastelcorn himself, only one wing of the four planned got off the drawing board. Not all of the **zámek** (July & Aug Tues–Sun 10am–noon & 2–6pm; May, June & Sept Sat & Sun 10am–noon & 2–5pm; April & Oct Sat & Sun 1–5pm; 50Kč) is accessible, but you can wander round the courtyards, and visit several atmospheric chambers used as galleries. Below the chateau, beside a reservoir, the Žralok **campsite** (May–Sept) provides good opportunities for swimming.

Bouzov and around

Accessible by bus from Olomouc (with a change at Litovel), the village of **BOUZOV** is nothing but its **hrad** (April & Oct Sat & Sun 9am–3pm; May–Sept

▲ Bouzov

Tues–Sun 9am–4pm; ⓦ www.hrad-bouzov.cz), a Romantic neo-Gothic fortress right on the high point of the *vrchovina*, and perfectly suited as a base for its former proprietors, the Teutonic Knights. Predictably enough, it also took the fancy of the Nazi SS, who used it as a base during World War II. The pompous pseudo-medievalism of the interior is not to everyone's taste, and the place is huge, so there's a choice of guided tours: *trasa 1* (*klasická*; 100Kč) gives you an hour-long whirl around the place; *trasa 2* (*velká*; 150Kč) lasts an extra fifty minutes and is for real enthusiasts, as is *trasa 3* (*mix speciál*; 150Kč). Tours are in Czech only, so non-speakers should ask for an *anglický text*. The most characterful **accommodation** in the area is *Valáškův grunt* (☏ 585 346 312, ⓦ www.valaskuvgrunt .cz; ❸), 2km west in the nearby village of Kozov, a former manor house with plain, homely en suites, an arcaded garden courtyard and a small outdoor pool.

The Jeseníky

Extending east from the Bohemian Krkonoše are the **Jeseníky** (Gesenke), the highest peaks in what is now Moravia. Sparsely populated, the region is worlds apart from the dense network of industrial centres in the north and east of the province, or even the vine-clad hills of the south. The highest reaches, or **Hrubý Jeseník** between Šumperk and Jeseník, have been damaged by acid rain, but the mountains as a whole are peaceful and green. The foothills on either side of the big peaks harbour some low-key **spa resorts** like Lázně Jeseník, Karlova Studánka, and the historical remains of Czech Silesia in **Krnov** and **Opava**.

Šternberk

Some 20km north of Olomouc, you hit the ridge of the Jeseníky foothills at **ŠTERNBERK** (Sternberg), where the annual *Ecce Homo* motor race is held in mid-September over the lethal switchbacks on the road to Opava. The town itself, a long two-kilometre haul north of the train and bus stations, is dominated by its giant Baroque church and **hrad** (April & Oct Sat & Sun 9am–3pm; May–Sept Tues–Sun 9am–4pm), the latter rebuilt in Romantic style in the late nineteenth century. You'll need to take a guided tour: *trasa 1* (90Kč; 50min) leads you through the state rooms and the castle chapel, complete with Gothic statue of the Šternberk Madonna; *trasa 2* (70Kč; 50min) concentrates on art and furniture salvaged from the stately homes of northern Moravia; *trasa 3* (130Kč; 1hr 30min) includes both.

The *U zlatého muflona* **campsite** (mid-May to mid-Sept; ☎585 011 300, Ⓦwww.campsternberk.cz), in Dolní Žleb, 3km north of Šternberk, features partly shaded tent and caravan space as well as four-person chalets (90–120Kč), some with en-suite facilities.

Šumperk

Gateway to the upper Jeseníky, **ŠUMPERK** (Schönberg) has the feel of a mountain town, although it's really a jumping-off point to nearby destinations rather than a resort in its own right. The main drag is **Hlavní třída**, beyond the park to the north of the train station, and, at the far western end of Hlavní, the tiny old town is easy to miss, its neo-Renaissance radnice standing on the pretty little square of **náměstí Míru**. For the panorama of the town and surrounding hills you can climb its **tower** (Mon–Fri & Sun: June & Sept 9am–3pm; July & Aug 9am–noon & 1–5pm), though far better **views**, including the whole range of the Jeseníky, are from the hilltop **Rozhledna na Háji** (March, April & Oct Sat & Sun 10am–4pm; May, June & Sept Sat & Sun 10am–5pm; July & Aug Tues–Sun 10am–5pm; Nov–Feb Sat & Sun 10am–3pm), a 30-metre-tall viewing tower just west of the town (the blue markers followed by the green). The **tourist office** in the local museum by the park (Mon 8am–noon & 12.30–5pm, Tues–Fri 8am–5pm; ☎583 214 000, Ⓦwww.infosumperk.cz) can advise on **accommodation**.

Velké Losiny

Some 9km northeast of Šumperk, the tiny spa of **VELKÉ LOSINY** (Gross-Ullersdorf) is one of the last oases of civilization before you hit the deserted heights of the Jeseníky. The town's Renaissance **zámek** (April & Oct Sat & Sun 9am–noon & 1–4pm; May–Aug Tues–Sun 8am–noon & 1–5pm; Sept Tues–Sun 9am–noon & 1–4pm; Ⓦwww.losiny-zamek.cz; 40Kč) is set in particularly lush grounds beside a tributary of the River Desná. It's a three-winged, triple-decker structure, part Renaissance and part Baroque, opening out into a beautifully restored sixteenth-century arcaded loggia, and for once the guided tour is really worthwhile. The chateau was the northernmost property of the extremely wealthy Žerotín family, but was inhabited for less than a hundred years; its grandest chamber is the Knights' Hall, which has retained its original parquet floor and leather wall hangings. Strong supporters of the Unity of Brethren, the Žerotíns were stripped of their wealth after the Battle of Bílá hora and the chateau was left empty – except as a venue for the region's notorious witch trials (56 sentenced to death) during the Counter-Reformation.

Velké Losiny is also home to the country's one remaining **paper mill** or *papírna* (April–June & Sept Tues–Fri 9am–5pm, Sat & Sun 9am–noon & 12.30–5pm; July–Aug also Mon 10am–2pm; Oct–March Tues–Fri 9am–3pm, Sat & Sun 9am–noon & 12.30–4pm; 30Kč), which still produces handmade paper. Built in the 1590s by the Žerotín family, and still bearing the family's coat of arms on its watermark, the mill is situated between the chateau and the spa and houses a small museum on the history of paper. The **train** and **bus stations** are in the spa itself, from which the chateau is a pleasant one-kilometre walk south. Those especially interested in **wooden churches** might consider visiting the nearby villages of **ŽÁROVÁ**, 3km northwest of Velké Losiny, and **MARŠÍKOV**, 2km to the east. Both churches were built at the beginning of the seventeenth century, in the Renaissance style, using wood from the demolished church in Velké Losiny. Ask around for the keys.

Velké Losiny is a more attractive place to stay than Šumperk and there's plenty of **accommodation**: the central *Hotel Praděd*, Lažeňska 4 (☎583 248 215, ⓦwww.hotel-praded.cz; ❹) offers smart en suites with TV; while *Penzion Přerovka*, northeast of the train station at Revoluční 12 (☎583 248 334, ⓦwww .prerovka.cz; ❷), is an unfussy family-run B&B with garden.

Hrubý Jeseník

The River Desná peters out before the real climb into the central mountain range of **Hrubý Jeseník**. A bus from Šumperk runs roughly every two hours via the northernmost train station, Kouty nad Desnou, to the saddle of Červeno-horské sedlo (1013m) and beyond. The ascent by route 44 from Kouty is via a dramatic series of hairpin bends, but the top of the pass is a disappointment. The tourist board may talk of "mountain meadows and pastures", but the reality is low-lying scrub and moorland: any spruce or pine trees that dare to rise above this are new growth, only recently conquering the effects of acid rain. There's a restaurant by the roadside for beer and food, and an impromptu and very basic **campsite**, 500m away to the northwest, along with plenty of private rooms. For a better view, take the 45-minute walk northwest to **Červená hora** (1333m); it's another ninety minutes to **Šerák** (1351m), which looks down onto the Ramzovské sedlo, the much lower pass to the west that the railway from Šumperk to Jeseník wisely opts for. A chairlift from Šerák will take you down to the campsite and train station at Ramzová, in the valley bottom. Alternatively, you could walk two hours east from Červenohorské sedlo to **Praděd** (The Great Grandfather), at 1491m the highest and most barren peak in the range.

Below and to the east of Praděd is the picturesque Silesian spa resort of **KARLOVA STUDÁNKA**, strung out along the valley of the bubbling River Bílá Opava. The spa has a useful **information centre** (daily 9am–5pm; out of season closes 4pm; ☎554 772 004, ⓦwww.jeseniky-praded.cz), and is dotted with cold fizzy springs (with an extraordinarily high iron content) and attractive dark-brown weatherboarded spa buildings, many with cream shutters and balconies for enjoying the fresh mountain air. Most of the **accommodation** in the spa is for patients, but you could try the *Hotel Džbán* (☎554 772 014, ⓔhoteldzban@seznam.cz; ❸), in the centre of town, which has pleasant rooms (some overlooking the spa park) and a restaurant downstairs. There's also the *Dolina* **campsite** (mid-May to Sept), 7km northeast of the spa near Vrbno pod Pradědem (Würbenthal). Another option is to stay in **MALÁ MORÁVKA**, 8km to the south down route 445, which has the advantage of being at the end of an idyllic little branch line from Bruntál (trains don't always run daily on this line so check it's running; more reliable are the frequent bus connections with Bruntál). M Servis acts as a **tourist office** (in season daily 8am–6pm; ⓦwww .malamoravka.cz) and can help with accommodation in the area; you can rent bikes and skis there, too. There are numerous inexpensive pensions and rooms along the valley between here and Karlova Studánka, so **accommodation** shouldn't be a problem.

Jeseník and around

On the other side of the pass, the road plunges down with equal ferocity to **JESENÍK** (Freiwaldau), a fairly nondescript town busy in summer with Polish day-trippers. Over the stream, north of the main square in the Smetanovy sady, there's a wonderful Art Nouveau monument to local farmer Vincent Priessnitz, founder of the nearby spa (see below), presiding godlike over the skinny and ill on his right and the "cured" (or at least plump) on his left. Otherwise, Jeseník is mainly useful as a base for exploring the surrounding area; there are several reasonably priced hotels and pensions, and a **campsite** (all year; ©camp -bobrovnik@iol.cz) with a swimming pool less than 2km west along the valley en route to another spa resort, Lipová Lázně.

Two kilometres above the town, with fantastic views south to the Jeseníky and north into Poland, is **LÁZNĚ JESENÍK** (Gräfenberg). Here Priessnitz established one of the most famous Silesian spas in the nineteenth century, where the likes of Russian writer Gogol and King Carol I of Romania took the cure. Nowadays, the only grandish spa building is the grey rendered **Priessnitz Sanatorium**, built in 1910. Scattered about the surrounding countryside, and interspersed with numerous monuments erected by grateful patients, are the **natural springs**, which provide hot and sulphuric refreshment on the obligatory constitutionals (you can buy a map from the Priessnitz Sanatorium). If you'd prefer to get clean away from people, and particularly sickly spa patients, make your way to the viewpoint from the summit of Zlatý chlum, 2km east of Jeseník.

From Lipová Lázně, a tiny, picturesque branch line heads northeast, eventually terminating at Javorník (see below), in the northernmost Silesian salient. The first stop, though, is Lipová Lázně jeskyně, just over the ridge from the entrance to the **Jeskyně na pomezí** (July & Aug daily 9am–5pm; May–June, Sept & Oct Tues–Sun 9am–4pm; 80Kč), a mini-karst cave system with colourful stalactites and stalagmites in the shape of fruit, vegetables and fungi. Another two stops along the line is **ŽULOVÁ** (Friedeberg), whose local fortress, precipitously situated on a moated island of rock, was converted into a church in the nineteenth century. Beyond Žulová, the countryside flattens out as it slips into Poland, and the train continues to **JAVORNÍK** (Jauernig), where the local chateau, **Janský vrch** (April & Oct Sat & Sun 9am–noon & 1–3pm; May–Aug Tues–Sun 8am–noon & 1–4pm; Sept Tues–Sun 9am–noon & 1–3pm; 70Kč), perches high above the village. There's a choice of guided tours: the 45-minute *trasa 1* takes you around the period interior, which features a collection of historical pipes and ornate smoking devices, as well as a small theatre, where the composer **Carl Ditters von Dittersdorf** used to stage operas (when he wasn't being the local forest warden); the thirty-minute *trasa 2* whisks you round the servants' quarters, the chapel and the lookout tower.

Krnov

As if to underline the arbitrary nature of the region's current borders, the railway line from Jeseník passes in and out of Polish territory en route to **KRNOV** (Jägerndorf), famous for its Rieger-Kloss organ factory – the largest in Europe – established here in 1873. The town was flattened in World War II and the current population of 26,000 is only two-thirds of the town's prewar level – but it's still worth a brief stopover if you're heading for Opava or into Poland just 3km away.

From the town's otherwise nondescript main square, **Hlavní náměstí**, two buildings stand out: the salmon-pink-and-white **radnice** from 1902, topped by an excitable clock tower, modelled on the one in the Viennese suburb of Währing and decorated with patterned tiling; and the late-nineteenth-century **spořitelna**, a savings bank in two shades of green. Beyond the Atlantes who guard the entrance to the latter, you can see the beautifully restored foyer and staircase, its stained glass, ironwork and plastering smothered in Art Nouveau floral motifs. On the ground floor is the *Dynasty* café and restaurant, restored and slightly modernized, but with enough of its original fittings – brass chandeliers, wooden panelling and so forth – to give some idea of its glory days. To the west, on Zámecké náměstí, one side of the street features an unusual arcade held up by round, squat pillars, while beyond, to the north, lies the so-called **Švedská zed'** (Swedish Wall), a short, surviving stretch of the town's fortifications with decorative Renaissance battlements, later used in the unsuccessful defence of the town against the Swedes during the Thirty Years' War.

Krnov's main **train station** is 1km west of the centre along Mikulášská, though most trains heading to or from Opava and Ostrava also stop at Krnov-Cvilín, about 500m northeast of the centre down Hlubčická. The **tourist office**, at Hlavní náměstí 25 (mid-May to mid-Sept Mon–Fri 8am–6pm, Sat & Sun 9am–2pm; mid-Sept to mid-May Mon–Fri 9am–5pm, Sat 9am–1pm; ☎554 614 612, ⓦwww.krnov.mic.cz), can help you find private rooms. Otherwise, the best **accommodation** option is the *Hotel Pepa*, Zámecké náměstí (☎554 611 005, ⓦwww.pepa.hotel-cz.com; ❹), offering plain en suites in a historical town house. For a taste of un-renovated Communist-era kitsch, try *Hotel Praha* (☎554 610 741, ⓦwww.praha.hotel-cz.com; ❷), west of the historical core at Revoluční 10.

Opava and around

Right by the Polish border, 24km southeast of Krnov, **OPAVA** (Troppau) is one of the oldest towns in the country, an important trading centre on the Amber Road from the Adriatic to the Baltic Sea, but perhaps better known as **Troppau**, capital of Austrian (and later Czech) Silesia (see box opposite). Badly damaged in the last few weeks of World War II, it nevertheless retains enough grandiose nineteenth-century buildings to give some idea of how it looked in its heyday. Much has been rebuilt since 1945, and while Opava may not merit a detour, it's a good place to break a journey or do a bit of chateau-seeing.

The most spectacular reminder of the town's former days, the huge church of **Nanebevzetí Panny Marie**, lies in the west of the old town, built in Silesian Gothic style in the late fourteenth century, and sheltering a lovely crown-shaped high altar. East of this giant red-brick church is the town's main square, **Horní náměstí**, above which rises the tall tower of the old *Schmetterhaus*, or **Hláska**, symbol of the town's forgotten prosperity, where foreign merchants were permitted to sell their wares. Opposite this stands another object of civic pride, the neo-Baroque **Slezské divadlo**. Opava's best-looking street is Masarykova třída, lined with noble Baroque palaces that once belonged to the likes of General Blücher and one of Beethoven's chief patrons, Count Razumovský. The **Silesian Diet** used to meet in the Jesuit college at the northern end of the street, while the Minorite monastery, further south, was the venue for the 1820 Troppau Conference, when the "Holy Alliance" of Austria, Russia and Prussia met to thrash out a common policy towards the revolutionary stirrings of post-Napoleonic Europe.

Set in the town's pretty semicircle of parks to the east is the grandiose **Slezské zemské muzeum** (Tues–Sat 9am–noon & 1–4pm, Sun 9am–noon & 2–4pm; ⓦwww.szmo.cz; 30Kč), built in neo-Renaissance style in 1893. It has been

From 1335 onwards, **Silesia** (Slezsko in Czech) was an integral part of the Historic Lands of the Bohemian Crown. In the 1740s the majority of it was carelessly lost to the Prussians by the young Habsburg Empress Maria Theresa. The three remaining Duchies – Troppau (Opava), Jägerndorf (Krnov) and Teschen (Těšín) – became known as **Austrian Silesia**, with Troppau as their capital, separated from each other by the Moravian salient around Ostrava. The population, though predominantly German, contained large numbers of Czechs and Poles – a mishmash typical of the region and one which caused often violent clashes and interminable territorial disputes. In 1920, after a few bloody skirmishes, the new state of Czechoslovakia lost part of Těšín to Poland and gained part of Hlučín from Germany, and in 1928 **Czech Silesia** was amalgamated with Moravia. This last act, in particular, annoyed the violently irredentist prewar German population. However, like the majority of the country's German-speaking minority, they were expelled in 1945, making the whole issue of a separate Silesia fairly redundant.

painstakingly restored since the war and houses a large but uninspiring exhibition that manages to avoid all the most controversial aspects of Silesian history. Opava does have one superb piece of twentieth-century architecture, the **church of sv Hedvik**, about 500m up Krnovská, one block to the south. The western facade is striking, made from big slabs of rusticated stone with concrete infill, plastered with giant Latin lettering and rising vertically in steps to form a strictly geometric tower. Begun in 1933 by local architect Leopold Bauer, it was used as a storehouse by the Nazis and Communists, and was only finished and opened for religious services in 1992.

Opava has two **train stations**; the main one – and the most central – is Opava východ, at the southeastern corner of the old town. The town suffers from a dearth of accommodation, which makes the regional **tourist office** (Mon–Fri 8am–6pm, Sat 8–11am; ☎553 756 143, ⓦwww.infocentrum.opava.cz), on the main square behind the radnice, especially useful. Cosiest of the **hotels** is the *Iberia*, just off the main square at Pekařská 11 (☎553 776 700, ⓦwww.hoteliberia .cz; ④), offering smart en suites in a tastefully restored old town house. The ungainly sixty-room *Koruna*, náměstí Republiky 17 (☎777 747 047, ⓦwww .hotelkoruna.cz; ④), presents an acceptable alternative. As for **food**, *U bílého koníčka*, on Dolní náměstí, is a vaulted beer hall, serving mugs of Gambrinus and all the usual Czech dishes, while *Stará Tiskárna*, facing a stretch of park at Beethovenova 3, offers a tasty repertoire of steaks and a restful outdoor terrace.

Hradec nad Moravicí

The castle high above the town of **HRADEC NAD MORAVICÍ**, 8km south on route 57, appears at first sight to be a neo-Gothic pile straight out of a Hammer Horror film. In fact, the red-brick castle's magnificent gateway opens up to reveal another, earlier, Neoclassical zámek covered in smooth white plaster. The **Červený zámek**, or *Rotes Schloss* as the red-brick castle was known, is now occupied by the hotel of the same name, while the **Bílý zámek** or *Weisses Schloss* contains a collection of porcelain and paintings (April, Oct & Dec Sat & Sun 10am–noon & 1–4pm; May–Sept Tues–Sun 9am–noon & 1–5pm; 120Kč). The latter used to belong to the Lichnovský family, who invited performances from the likes of Beethoven, Liszt and Paganini – in early June there's a Beethoven music festival, *Beethovenův hradec*, held here. On a clear day it's well worth exploring the lovely grounds that stretch out along the ridge beyond the white castle.

Hrabyně

No one driving between Ostrava and Opava on route 11 can fail to notice the ugly great slab of concrete which crowns the strategic heights around the village of **Hrabyně**. In the final few weeks of World War II, the Red Army was forced to engage in a costly pitched battle for the area, and in the 1980s, the sycophantic Communist regime decided to erect this bombastic **tribute** to the fallen, at a cost of millions of crowns. Thus was proved the indissoluble friendship between Czechoslovakia and the Soviet Union – "Together with the Soviet Union for ever and ever and never any other way", as the slogans used to say. The army vehicles that used to be scattered across the hilltop now line the alley behind the structure, and the monument gives out superb views north into Poland. Inside, there's a typically lavish but dull permanent display on the military operation, and rather more enlightening temporary **exhibitions**, also on a military theme (April–June, Sept & Oct Thurs & Fri 9am–3.30pm, Sat & Sun 11am–5pm; July & Aug Tues–Fri 9am–5pm, Sat & Sun 11am–5pm).

Although Hradec is an easy day-trip from Opava or Ostrava, it's worth considering an overnight stay in the *Červený zámek* **hotel** (☎553 783 021, ⓦwww.cervenyzamek.hotel-cz.com; ❸), with a restaurant open to non-guests. There's also the *Hradec* **campsite** (May–Sept) a short way to the south of the town and castles, along route 57.

Ostrava

Having spent decades as the kind of place you'd be best advised to avoid, **OSTRAVA** (Ostrau) is emerging onto the must-do list for Moravia-bound travellers. Long dismissed as a grim coal-and-steel town blighted by environmental pollution, the Czech Republic's third-largest city experienced an almost total economic collapse in the 1990s. Heavy industry's decline did however bring an immediate improvement in the air quality, and Ostrava – drip-fed back to life with European Union funds – set about reinventing itself as a forward-looking post-industrial metropolis. Former eyesores like the Karolina coking plant were levelled (it's being turned into a shopping mall), while red-brick factories found themselves preserved as heritage sites. Crucial to Ostrava's new image is its growing reputation for hedonism-fuelled **nightlife**, thanks in large part to the popularity of Stodolní – a pedestrianized street which constitutes a single uninterrupted strip of bars and clubs.

Arrival and information

Ostrava's main **train station**, Ostrava hlavní nádraží, is around 2km north of the city centre (tram #1, #2 or #8). Trains from Krnov and Opava terminate at Ostrava-Svinov (most fast trains also call here), 5km west of the centre (tram #4, #8 or #9). One or two trains an hour from the main train station (including trains to and from Český Těšín) will take you to the most central of the city terminals, Ostrava střed, next door to the main **bus station** and just ten-minutes' walk west of the centre (tram #1, #2 or #6). The helpful **tourist office** (ⓦwww.ostravinfo.cz) has branches at the main train station (Mon–Fri 7am–6pm, Sat 7am–noon & 12.30–3pm, Sun 10am–noon & 12.30–6pm; ☎596 136 218), in the town centre at Nádražní 7 (Mon–Fri 7am–6pm, Sat 8am–2pm; ☎596 123 913) and at Ostrava Svinov train station (Mon–Fri

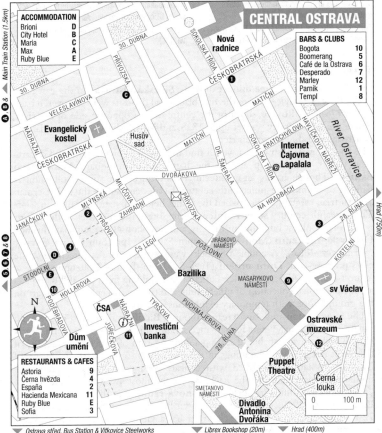

ACCOMMODATION

Brioni	D
City Hotel	B
Maria	C
Max	A
Ruby Blue	E

CENTRAL OSTRAVA

BARS & CLUBS

Bogota	10
Boomerang	5
Café de la Ostrava	6
Desperado	7
Marley	12
Parnik	1
Templ	8

RESTAURANTS & CAFES

Astoria	9
Černa hvězda	4
España	2
Hacienda Mexicana	11
Ruby Blue	E
Sofia	3

7am–8pm, Sat 7am–noon & 12.30–3pm, Sun 12.30–4pm & 4.30–8.30pm;
☏597 310 174).

The Librex bookshop, Smetanovo náměstí (daily 9am–7pm) sells a good
range of maps and has free **internet** access. You can also check your emails at
the hippyish *Internet čajovna Lapalala*, Sokolska 20 (Mon–Fri 10am–9pm, Sat
& Sun 4–9pm).

Accommodation

Ostrava's **hotels** fill up quickly, especially at weekends, so it's worth ringing in
advance or starting your search early in the day.

Brioni Stodolní 8 ☏599 500 000, ⓦwww
.hotelbrioni.cz. Conveniently central bolt-hole offering
roomy en suites decked out in warm but not always
co-ordinated colours. Wi-fi throughout. ❼

City Hotel Macharova 16 ☏596 134 090, ⓦwww
.hotelcity-ostrava.cz. Inexpensive, but comfortable,
modernized hotel within walking distance of the
main train station. ❸

Maria Přívozská 23 ☏596 110 676, ⓦwww
.hotel-maria.cz. You'll find simply decorated en
suites at this decent, mid-range hotel in a convenient downtown location. ❹

Max Nádraží 186 ☏595 136 790, ⓦwww
.hotelmax-ostrava.com. Inexpensive hotel right by
the station. The en suites with small TVs are on the
careworn side, but basically clean and secure. Solid

Czech meat and dumplings in the downstairs restaurant. ❸
Ruby Blue Stodolní 11 ☎ 597 609 111, Ⓦ www .rubyblue.cz. Designer hotel in the heart of the nightlife district, mixing minimalist furnishings with warm blood-orange textiles. All rooms come with swanky modern bathrooms, flat-screen TVs and wi-fi. ❺

The City

Ostrava divides into three distinct districts: **Slezská Ostrava**, on the east bank of the River Ostravice, where the first black-coal deposits were discovered back in the 1760s; **Vítkovice**, south of the centre on the opposite side of the river, where the first foundry was set up in 1828; and **Moravská Ostrava**, the largely pedestrianized downtown district.

It's in Moravská Ostrava that you'll find most of the town's shops and department stores, bunched up around the handsome main square, **Masarykovo náměstí**. Though hardly an architectural masterpiece, the square still vaunts a handful of swanky late-nineteenth-century facades erected by the rich German and Austrian capitalists who owned the mines here until nationalization in 1945. The sixteenth-century **stará radnice**, in the southeastern corner of the square, is one of the oldest buildings in the city and now houses the less than thrilling **Ostravské muzeum** (Mon–Fri 9am–5pm, Sat 9am–1pm, Sun 1–5pm; Ⓦ www .ostrmuz.cz; 40Kč). A couple of blocks west of the square at Jurečkova 9, the city's purpose-built **Dům umění** (Tues–Sat 10am–1pm & 1.30–6pm; Ⓦ www .gvuostrava.cz; 50Kč), a red-brick Functionalist building from the 1920s, displays an unexceptional collection of nineteenth- and twentieth-century Czech art on the ground floor, with temporary exhibitions upstairs.

The huge salmon-pink-and-cream-coloured **Bazilika**, northwest of the main square, built in a heavy neo-Renaissance style in the 1880s, is the second largest church in Moravia, capable of seating a congregation of four thousand. One of the finest Art Nouveau buildings in the city stands to the north at the top of Milíčova, its facade decorated with delicate floral stuccowork – ignore the modern extension around the back. By far the most awesome monument to Ostrava's former municipal pride is the **nová radnice**, at the end of 30 dubna. Erected in the 1920s, it is the largest town hall in the country, and its slender, 72-metre-high, copper-clad clock tower has a viewing platform (daily: May–Oct 9am–7pm; Nov–April 9am–5pm).

A couple of blocks south of Ostrava's main square, the grassy **Černá louka** park is strewn with exhibition pavilions hosting trade fairs and antique markets (check Ⓦ www.cerna-louka.cz to see what's on). At the far end of the park a footbridge leads to the opposite bank of the Ostravice, where you can pick up an ascending path to the local **hrad**. Built in the thirteenth century to guard the border between Moravia and Silesia, the castle has been much changed over the centuries – mining subsidence caused it to sink 17m in the 1980s, and it was only in 2004 that the city felt fit to re-open it. The castle boasts an attractive courtyard and rewarding **museum** (May–Sept Tues–Sun 10am–6pm; Oct–April Fri–Sun 11am–4pm; 60Kč), featuring arms and armour from the Thirty Years' War and a gruesome display of torture instruments.

Industrial Ostrava

Ostrava's once mighty coal and steel industries went into steep decline in the 1990s, although there is plenty of visual evidence of the city's former role, with skeletal pitheads looming over downtown areas and suburbs alike. Steel is still forged at the huge Arcelor Mittal works in Kunčice, 5km to the southeast, its slender smoke-billowing chimneys clearly visible from the city centre. Closer to hand, the now dormant **Vitkovice steelworks** immediately south of central

Ostrava have been declared an industrial heritage zone, with antiquated derricks and silver snaking pipes preserved as monuments to the region's manufacturing past. Trams #1 and #2 from Nádražní run past the site should you wish to take a closer look.

Those with a passionate interest in the local mining industry should hop on bus #34, #52 or #56 at the top of Sokolská třída, east of the main train station, which provide a regular service north across the River Odra to the suburb of Petřkovice (get off at the U Jana stop). Here, at the now defunct Anselm mine (once owned by the Rothschilds), there's a **Hornický skanzen**, or open-air mining museum (daily 9am–6pm; guided tours on the hour; Ⓦ www .muzeumokd.cz; 150Kč), where you can descend into the pit, inspect the seams and take a look at the exhibition in the manager's villa.

Eating, drinking, nightlife and entertainment

Although Ostrava doesn't offer the greatest range of **eating** opportunities, there's a handful of reasonable restaurants spread throughout the city centre. For **snack food** head for the open-air grill stalls along Stodolní, where you can feast handsomely on sausage, *pleskavice* (Balkan beef patties) and skewered shish kebabs. **Drinking** is concentrated on the bar-lined Stodolní and a few adjoining streets, although a brace of worthwhile **nightlife** venues stand some distance away from the main party strip. If it's the Stodolní experience you're aiming for then Friday is undoubtedly the best time to come, although you'll find something going on here almost every night.

Ostrava also boasts a good **philharmonic orchestra** (Ⓦ www.jfo.cz), which plays in various venues across the city, while the Divadlo Antonína Dvořáka (Ⓦ www.ndm.cz) puts on a range of opera, ballet and theatre. The tourist information office at Nádražní 7 (see p.370) is a good place to ask about programmes and tickets. Predictably enough, Janáček, who died in Ostrava, is the subject of the city's May music festival, **Janáčkův máj** (Ⓦ www.janackuvmaj.cz), which features top-notch contemporary-classical performances as well as pieces by the local boy himself. For pop-rock fans, **Colours of Ostrava** (first or second week of July; Ⓦ www.colours.cz) is a major musical event involving an international line-up of rock, pop, jazz and dance acts. Unusually for festivals of this nature, the open-air stages are spread throughout the town, turning the centre into one vast party zone.

Restaurants and cafés

Astoria Masarykovo náměstí. Roomy square-side restaurant doling out pizzas, steaks and Balkan grills. The interior is chintzy in the extreme, but there are good views.

Černá hvězda Stodolní 2. This split-level café-bar is one of the few drinking venues along Stodolní that works just as well as a daytime coffee-and-cakes venue as a place for knocking back potent cocktails at night. Tasty ciabatta sandwiches too. Mon–Thurs 7.30am–11pm, Fri 7.30am–midnight, Sat 1pm–midnight, Sun 1–11pm.

España Tyršova 31. Spanish-themed restaurant with chicken and seafood dishes predominating, in rooms adorned with maritime bric-a-brac. Closed Sun.

Hacienda Mexicana Nádražni 305. Roomy Mexican restaurant decked out to look like the set of a spaghetti western. All the usual Mexican-themed dishes are here, although you should really save room for the steaks.

Ruby Blue Stodolní 11. Impossibly cool designer restaurant on three floors, aimed at the more affluent of Stodolní's bar-hoppers. The international menu features affordable pastas and salads, alongside more expensive steaks and fish.

Sofia 28 řína. Inexpensive, friendly and unassuming place in an upstairs room, specializing in Balkan dishes – *Sofia*'s grilled meatballs and fresh vegetable salads are probably better than those you'll get in the Bulgarian capital itself. Mon–Fri 11am–9pm.

Bars and clubs

Bogota Poděbradova 18. Grungy bar with punk and ska on the sound system, several tables of bar football, and a secluded roof terrace. A tiny stage hosts occasional bands. Mon–Fri 11am–2am, Sat 5pm–3am, Sun 6pm–midnight.

Boomerang Stodolní 22. Barn-sized disco-pub that attracts a hedonistic, up-for-anything crowd on Friday nights. A connecting door leads to the *Havana* pub, which is marginally more sedate. Mon–Thurs 5pm–1am, Fri & Sat 5pm–4am.

Café de la Ostrava Stodolní 28. Quirky café-bar with eccentric art on the walls and plenty of nooks and crannies to slump into. Pilsner Urquell, Radegast and Gambrinus on tap; funk, hip-hop and soul on the sound system. Mon–Thurs noon–2am, Fri noon–4am, Sat 5pm–4am, Sun 5pm–2am.

Desperado Stodolní 31. Dark, atmospheric bar with a slightly silly Wild West/Mexican Revolution theme. There's a disco in what looks like a stable out back, and a big courtyard for mingling. Mon–Thurs 5pm–3am, Fri & Sat 6pm–4am.

Marley Černá Louka ⓦ marley.ov-kluby.net. Roomy club with attention-grabbing graffiti-style murals, and a DJ policy that runs from reggae through hip-hop to the wilder regions of electronic dance music. Wed & Thurs 3pm–1am, Fri & Sat 4pm–6am.

Parnik Sokolská třída 26 ⓦ www.klub-parnik.cz. Offering something of a slightly more grown-up vibe to the Stodolní drinking scene, this well-equipped gig venue has a regular programme of jazz, blues and "adult" rock. Look out for posters: opening times depend on what's on.

Templ Stodolní 20. A somewhat characterless disco-pub most nights of the week, *Templ* comes into its own when alternative bands or DJs climb onto the stage. Look out for posters or simply stick your head round the door to see what's on. Tues–Thurs 11am–1am, Fri 11am–4am, Sat 6pm–4am.

The Beskydy

Despite their proximity, the hilly **Beskydy** region and the Ostrava coal basin are poles apart. In the foothills there's a whole cluster of interesting sights not far from (and including) **Nový Jičín**. Further south and east, into hiking country proper, the old Wallachian traditions have been preserved both in situ, in the more inaccessible villages, and at the open-air folk museum or *skanzen* at **Rožnov pod Radhoštěm**.

Nový Jičín

NOVÝ JIČÍN (Neu-Titschein) is a typical one-square town on the main road from Olomouc to Ostrava. That said, that one square, Masarykovo náměstí, is particularly fine, with wide, whitewashed arcades tunnelling their way under a host of restrained, late-Baroque facades in pastel colours. The **radnice** is an unusual white, boxy affair rebuilt in the 1930s, its wonderfully jagged gable a reminder of its seventeenth-century origins. However, the one building that stands out (literally) from the rest is the **stará pošta**, where Tsar Alexander I and General Suvorov have both stayed the night; its pretty two-storey loggia dates from the town's boom time in the sixteenth century when it bought its independence from the Žerotín family.

Nowadays, the town's chief attraction is its **Kloboučnické muzeum** (Hat Museum; April–Oct Tues–Fri 8am–noon & 1–4pm, Sat & Sun 9am–3pm; Nov–March closed Sat), laid out in the Žerotíns' old chateau, accessed through the covered passageway of Lidická beneath the radnice. Thankfully, the present exploits of the old state hat enterprise, Tonak (based in the town), are only lightly touched on, leaving most of the museum to a wonderful variety of hats produced in Nový Jičín since 1799 by the original firms of Hückel, Peschel and Böhm. The bit that gets the Czechs going is the array of hats worn by famous national personages – a bit esoteric for non-Czechs, though some might be stirred by the sight of Masaryk's topper.

The **tourist office** (Mon–Fri 8am–5pm, Sat & Sun 9am–noon; ⓦ www .novyjicin.cz), on Úzká near the chateau, can help find **accommodation** in the area – although with both Olomouc and Štramberk a quick bus ride away, you're unlikely to need to stay.

Although numerous timber-framed houses were torn down during the course of the nineteenth century, the wooden churches of the Beskydy region fared a little better. Below is a selection of the region's best examples.

Bílá 25km east of Rožnov pod Radhoštěm. A mountain hamlet near the Slovak border boasts an untypical, slender Scandinavian church, brought from Sweden by Cardinal Fürstenberg and built here in 1875.

Bystřice nad Olší 12km southeast of Český Těšín. Polish/Czech town in the Olše valley, with a wooden neo-Gothic Catholic church, built in 1896 to replace the sixteenth-century stone one.

Guty 11km south of Český Těšín. Probably the most striking of all the Beskydy's wooden churches, with its bulky Lemk-style western tower erected in 1781 above the narthex (entrance porch).

Hodslavice 8km south of Nový Jičín. Birthplace of Czech nationalist and historian František Palacký, one of the chief political figures of the nineteenth-century Czech national revival. Hodslavice also boasts the sixteenth-century wooden church of sv Ondřej.

Kunčice pod Ondřejníkem 4km east of Frenštát pod Radhoštěm. This mountain village was a favourite summer resort of the wealthy steel and coal magnates of Ostrava, one of whom, in 1931, brought an entire Greek-Catholic church over from what is now Ukraine for his wedding.

Radhošť 6km south of Frenštát pod Radhoštěm. You have to climb a mountain to see the wooden chapel of sv Cyril & Metoděj, built in neo-Byzantine style in 1905, from which there's an unbeatable view across the Beskydy.

Rybí 4km northwest of Štramberk. Fifteenth-century Gothic church with shingled roof, tower and onion dome steeple, plus a dinky little sundial in its main gable.

Štramberk and around

Eight kilometres east of Nový Jičín, the smokestack settlement of **ŠTRAMBERK** (Strallenburg; ⓦ www.stramberk.cz) is one of the best places to take your first dip into Wallachian culture. Clumped under the conic Bílá hora (not to be confused with *the* Bílá hora in Prague) like an ancient funeral pyre, Štramberk feels very old indeed, yet many of its wooden cottages were built as recently as the first half of the nineteenth century. Its virtue is in displaying Wallachian architecture in situ, the cottages simply constructed out of whole tree trunks, unpainted and free of tourists rather than cooped and mummified in a sanitized *skanzen*.

Arrival and information and accommodation

Thirty-minutes' walk east of the village, Štramberk's **train station** is served by the Studenka–Veřovice branch line and enjoys good connections with both Ostrava and Olomouc. In addition, Kopřivnice-Nový Jičín **buses** pick up and drop off at the Bílá Hora stop, ten-minutes' walk downhill from Štramberk's square. The helpful **tourist office** (Tues–Sun 9am–noon & 12.30–4pm), just off the main square in the same building as the Zdeněk Burian Museum, can fill you in on public transport times.

Hotels and pensions

Gong ⓣ 556 852 900, ⓦ www.hotel-gong.cz. Modern building 10min walk downhill from the centre, offering en suites with TV and wi-fi, plus the

added comforts of an on-site sauna and small indoor pool. ❹

Roubenka ⓣ 556 852 566, ⓦ www.roubenkahotel .cz. Stylish en suites in a trio of modern timber-clad

Wallachian culture

As far as anybody can make out, the **Wallachs** or **Vlachs** were semi-nomadic sheep and goat farmers who settled the mountainous areas of eastern Moravia and western Slovakia in the fifteenth century. Although their name clearly derives from the Romanian Vlachs, it is believed that they arrived from eastern Poland and Ukraine, and the name Vlach is simply a generic term for sheep farmer. Whatever their true origins, they were certainly considered a race apart by the surrounding Slav peasants. Successive Habsburg military campaigns against the Vlachs in the seventeenth century destroyed their separate identity, and nowadays Wallachian culture lives on only in the folk customs and distinctive wooden architecture of the region.

buildings, in the lower part of the village – to get there head down Dolní from the post office. ④ **Šipka** Náměstí 37 ☏ 556 852 181, ⓦ www .hotelsipka.cz. Cosy, intimate hotel on the main square offering "standard" en suites with TV, minibar and wi-fi. "Lux" rooms have higher ceilings and more desk space. ③–④

Stará škola Náměstí 18 ☏ 556 852 697, ⓦ www .penzionstaraskola.cz. Pleasant but functional rooms in a characterful creaky-floored building. With en-suite doubles, triples and quads, it's a good place for groups or families. ②

The village

Though little more than a hillside village, Štramberk does have a nominal main square. At one end are several stone buildings in folk Baroque style, behind which rises up the galleried wooden *klopačka* (belfry) of the original church. At the other end is an old Jesuit church painted in sherbet orange, next door to the small **Muzeum Štramberk** (April–Oct Tues–Sun 9am–noon & 1–5pm; Nov–March until 4pm & closed Sat; 20Kč), which has a coma-inducing display of fossils on the ground floor, and a far livelier folk-craft collection upstairs. Ascending via alleys round the side of the church takes you past some of Štramberk's most picturesque houses and ultimately brings you to the one remaining tower of a castle that was laid waste by the Tatars. Popularly known as the **Trúba**, or "tube", it is now a lookout post offering fantastic views of the surrounding hills (April & Oct daily 9am–5pm; May–Sept daily 9am–7pm; Nov–March Fri–Sun 10am–4pm; 20Kč).

Just below the main square, the **Zdeněk Burian Museum** (May–Sept Tues–Sun 9am–noon & 12.30–5pm; Oct–April until 4pm; 20Kč) is dedicated to the work of the prolific painter who was born in nearby Kopřivnice and spent his childhood in Štramberk. Burian (1905–81) was a book illustrator and palaeontologist, but is perhaps best known (to Czechs, at any rate) for his painstaking representations of the world of prehistoric humans. His inspiration came from the nearby **Šipka cave**, beneath the limestone hill of Kotouč (532m), where remains of Neanderthal man were discovered in the late nineteenth century. The caves are a short walk through the woods of the Národní sad, signposted off the road to Kopřivnice. You can also reach Kopřivnice by taking the path climbing Bílá Hora, which is topped with an ugly (but high) **lookout tower** (*rozhledna*; May–Oct Tues–Sun 8am–6pm; 30Kč), offering an unbeatable view across the mountains.

Eating and drinking

The **restaurant** of the *Hotel Šipka* offers a solid menu of steak, pork and chicken dishes, as well as excellent-value daily specials which tend to run out by early evening. Also on the village square, *Městský pivovar* serves up Czech meat-and-dumpling favourites, washed down with their delicious own-brewed beer. Pretty much every shop in the village sells the local speciality, *Štramberské uší* (Štramberk Ears), honeyed gingerbread (often filled with cream), which commemorates a particularly gruesome legend: during the Tatar invasion, the local people were saved by a judiciously timed flood which kept the marauders at bay – when the waters subsided, so the story goes, sacks full of the ears of Tatar victims were found.

Around Štramberk: Kopřivnice

On the other side of Bílá hora from Štramberk (and an easy 30min walk), the bland factory town of **KOPŘIVNICE** (Nesselsdorf) has a brace of fine museums. Most compelling is the **Technické muzeum** (May–Sept Tues–Sun 9am–5pm; Oct–April until 4pm; Ⓦ www.tatramuseum.cz; 75Kč), a blue-and-white pavilion in the centre of town that celebrates the output of the local Tatra car factory – even if spark plugs don't usually fire your imagination, there are some wonderful old cars here. Unlike the popular and ubiquitous Škoda, Tatra cars have always aimed to be exclusive: the first model, which came out in 1897, was called the President, and from 1948 onwards that's exactly who rode in them. The silent and powerful black Tatra limos, looking like something out of a gangster movie, became the ultimate symbol of Party privilege. Ordinary mortals could buy any colour they liked except black – the colour reserved for Party functionaries. Tatra found life hard in the post-Communist world: with the Party no longer in a position to pay for its usual bulk order, production of luxury cars stopped in 1999, although a reduced number of their Tonka-tough trucks are still in production.

Standing in a park beside Kopřivnice's train station, the turreted Neoclassical **Šustalova vila** (Tues–Sun: May–Sept 9am–5pm; Oct–April till 4pm; 30Kč) is a beautifully restored example of the houses that local industrialists built for themselves in the late nineteenth century. Orginally owned by the Šustala carriage-maker family, the villa now serves as a museum of the Kopřivnice **porcelain** industry with a small but incandescent display of jugs and plates. There's also a section devoted to childrens' book illustrator Zdeněk Burian. The **café** in the basement is a good place to unwind before moving on.

Příbor

Just 5km and one train station north of Kopřivnice, **PŘÍBOR** (Freiberg) bears no little resemblance to Nový Jičín (see p.374), with a similarly pleasant, arcaded

Freud in Freiberg

Born in 1856 to a hard-up Jewish wool merchant and his third wife, **Sigmund Freud** had no hesitation in ascribing significance to events that took place during the family's brief sojourn here. "Of one thing I am certain," he wrote later, "deep within me, although overlaid, there continues to live the happy child from Freiberg, the first-born child of a young mother who received from this air, from this soil, the first indelible impressions". Things were not always so idyllic, and Freud later used a number of events from his early childhood to prove psychoanalytical theories. The family maidservant, "my instructress in sexual matters" in Freud's own words, was a local Czech woman who used to drag him off to the nearby Catholic church and in Freud's eyes was responsible for his "Rome neurosis". She was eventually sacked for alleged theft (and for encouraging baby Sigmund to thieve, too) and sent to prison. Things weren't too hot on the Oedipal front, either, Freud suspecting his half-brother of being the father of his younger sister, Anna.

main square. However, as the native town of **Sigmund Freud**, Příbor has a much greater claim to fame. Although the family's financial problems forced them to leave for Vienna when Sigmund was only 4, it's difficult to resist the chance to visit the place where Freud went through his oral and anal phases. Freud's **birthplace**, in an alley just below the square (Tues–Sun: April–Sept 9am–5pm; Oct–March 9am–4pm; 40Kč), is now a small museum which makes up for the lack of authentic exhibits with an inventive words-and-pictures display and a witty English-language film about Freud's childhood. The local **Muzeum v Příboře** (Tues & Thurs 8am–noon & 1–4pm, Sun 9am–noon; 30Kč), in the former monastery on Lidická, also boasts a Freud memorial room – an uninspiring affair filled with photos of learned, bearded men (including Jung) at conferences on psychoanalysis.

Hukvaldy

Moravians hold **Leoš Janáček** much dearer to their hearts than Freud, and his birth village of **HUKVALDY**, 6km east of Příbor, has become a modest shrine to the composer. The village itself is appealing, nestling in a wooded hill on top of which sits a ruined **hrad** (April & Oct Sat & Sun 9am–4pm; May–Aug Tues–Sun 9am–6pm; Sept Tues–Sun 9am–5pm; 40Kč), complete with deer park – there's a statue of the Cunning Little Vixen in the woods. The composer's **museum**, housed in his sandy-yellow cottage, is pleasantly low-key (April & Oct Sat & Sun 10am–noon & 1–4.30pm; May & Sept Tues–Sun 10am–noon & 1–5pm; June–Aug Tues–Sun till 6pm), containing just a little modest furniture and his lectern (he always composed standing up). However, it's the gentle pastoral setting, an element underlying all Janáček's music, that provides the most instructive impression of the place. If you come here in July, you'll coincide with the **Janáčkovy Hukvaldy** (Ⓦwww.janackovy-hukvaldy.cz), an international music festival which includes concerts in the castle and open-air opera performances. Should you wish to **stay**, try the *Hukvaldský dvůr* (Ⓣ558 699 241, Ⓦwww.volny.cz/hukvaldsky.dvur; ❷), in the village, or ask at the tourist office (April–Oct Mon & Wed 7–11am & noon–5pm, Tues 7–11am & noon–3pm, Fri 7–11am; Ⓣ558 699 221) opposite. For food and superb **beer**, head 1km north of the village to *U zastávky* (Ⓦwww.pivovar-hukvaldy.cz), a micro-brewery in Dolní Sklenov. Eight **buses** a day link Hukvaldy with Ostrava, and a few more run irregularly to Kopřivnice and Příbor.

Janáček in Hukvaldy

Leoš Janáček (1854–1928) was the fifth of nine children – too many for his impecunious father who taught at the local school. Thus, at the age of 11, the boy was sent to Brno to be a chorister, and from then on he made his home in the city, battling against the prejudices of the powerful German elite who ruled over the Moravian classical music scene. When at last he achieved recognition outside Moravia, through the success of the opera *Jenůfa*, he was already in his 60s. Having bought a cottage in Hukvaldy, he spent his last, most fruitful years based here and in Brno, composing such works as *The Glagolitic Mass*, *The Cunning Little Vixen* and *From the House of the Dead*. The music of this period was fired by his obsessive love for a woman called Kamila Strösslová, wife of a Jewish antique dealer in Písek, who had sent him food parcels throughout World War I. Although he never left his wife, Janáček wrote over 700 letters to Kamila, the most passionate ones written almost daily in the last sixteen months of his life. In August 1928 he caught a chill searching for her son in the nearby woods, and died in a hospital in Ostrava.

Into the hills of the Beskydy

Between the sparsely wooded pastureland around Nový Jičín and the Rožnovská Bečva valley to the south are the **hills of the Beskydy**. Starting off in North Moravia and entering Poland, they actually extend right over into Ukraine, shadowing the much higher Carpathian range to the south. Spruce has gradually given way to pine, which, though damaged by acid rain, is not too badly affected by pollutants, and in the westernmost reaches patches of beech forest still exist.

Frenštát

A former cold war army base, **FRENŠTÁT POD RADHOŠTĚM** has been considerably spruced up in the post-Communist period, and the main square, which is peppered with Baroque statuary, is very pretty indeed. Though not exactly in the thick of the Beskydy, it's easily the chief starting point for people heading off into the hills. The **train and bus stations** are 1km east of the main square, where you'll find the **tourist office** (Mon–Fri 8.30am–noon & 12.30–5pm, Sat 8.30–11.30am; July & Aug also Sun 8.30–11.30am; ℡556 836 916, Ⓦwww.frenstat.info) in the radnice, and a couple of decent **hotels**: the *Přerov* (℡556 835 991, Ⓦwww.jetcom.cz/prerov; ❷) is cheap and friendly, with a restaurant on the ground floor and a cellar **pub** a few doors down, named after Oliver Hardy; a touch nicer is the adjacent *Radhošt'* (℡556 839 839, Ⓦwww.hotelradhost.cz; ❷). The *Frenštát* **campsite** (May to mid-Oct; ℡556 836 624) lies on the north bank of the river, 1km northwest of the town centre.

Radhošt' and Pustevny

Both Frenštát and Rožnov (see below) dub themselves *pod* – "under" – **Radhošt'**, which, thanks to its legends, is the Beskydy's most famous (though not tallest) peak. The view from the summit (1129m) is still pretty good, and there's a fanciful wooden chapel, done out in neo-Byzantine style. Two kilometres east, there's a statue of Radegast, the mountain's legendary pagan god (who lends his name to the famous local beer). Another kilometre east lies **Pustevny** – a series of late nineteenth-century timber-slat buildings designed by Dušan Jurkovič, including the fantastical hotel, the *Tanečnica* (℡556 835 341, Ⓦwww.tanecnica.cz; ❸), named after the nearby mountain, and the equally comfortable *Maměnka* (℡556 836 207, Ⓦwww.libusin-mamenka.cz; ❸). You can reach Pustevny by **chairlift** (*lanovka*; Mon–Fri 8am–4pm, Sat & Sun 7am–6pm on the hr, in winter every other hr) from Trojanovice-Ráztoka, 6km southeast of Frenštát. You can also get there by **bus** from Rožnov pod Radhoštěm (3–4 daily). Campers can follow the yellow- and/or green-marked path down to the *Kněhyně* **campsite** (all year) with bungalows in Prostřední Bečva.

Rožnov pod Radhoštěm

Halfway up the Rožnovská Bečva valley, on the south side of Radhošt', lies the former spa town of **ROŽNOV POD RADHOŠTĚM**, home to the Czech Republic's biggest and most popular **skanzen** of folk architecture. The open-air museum – officially entitled **Valašské muzeum v přírodě** – is divided into three parts, each with different opening hours (50–60Kč each, combined admission 120Kč, family pass 240Kč; Ⓦwww.vmp.cz). Note that guided tours are compulsory in the Mlýnská dolina; they're usually in Czech, so ask for the *anglický text*. The main entrance to the museum lies across the river from the train station.

The moving force behind the first section, the Wooden Town or **Dřevené městečko** (Jan–March & Oct Tues–Sun 9am–4pm; April & Sept daily 9am–5pm; May–Aug daily 8am–6pm; Christmas season daily 9am–4pm), was local artist Bohumír Jaroněk, who was inspired by the outdoor folk museum in Stockholm (from which the word *skanzen* derives). In 1925 Rožnov's eighteenth-century wooden radnice was moved from the main square to its present site, followed by a number of other superb timber buildings from the town and neighbouring villages like Větřkovice u Příbora, which supplied the beautiful seventeenth-century wooden church (where services are still held). There are Wallachian beehives decorated with grimacing faces, a smithy and even a couple of *hospoda* selling food and warm *slivovice*. The second section, the Wallachian Village or **Valašská dědina** (April exteriors only Sat & Sun 10am–5pm; May–Aug daily 9am–6pm; Sept daily 10am–5pm), was built in the 1970s on a hillside across the road from the Dřevěné městečko. It takes a more erudite approach, attempting to re-create a typical highland sheep-farming settlement – the traditional Wallachian community – complete with a variety of farm animals and organic crops, plus a schoolhouse, dairy and blacksmith. Enthusiastic guides take you round the third section, **Mlýnská dolina** (Mill Valley; daily: May–Aug 9am–6pm; Sept 9am–5pm), which is centred around an old flour mill and includes a water-powered blacksmith's and sawmill, peopled by period-dressed artisans.

Rožnov's **tourist office**, in the radnice on the main square (May–Sept daily 8am–noon & 1–6pm; Oct–April Mon–Fri 8.30am–noon & 1–4pm; Ⓦwww .roznov.cz), can help with **accommodation**. One of the best hotels in town is the flashy *Eroplán* across the river from the *skanzen* at Horní Paseky 451 (Ⓣ571 648 014, Ⓦwww.eroplan.cz; ❸), with sauna, weights room and its own restaurant. *Hotel AGH*, just off the main square at Čechova 142 (Ⓣ571 625 666, Ⓦwww.hotel-agh .cz; ❹), offers tasteful rooms and a good restaurant. **Campsites** are thick on the ground east of the *skanzen*, with one on either side of the road to Prostřední Bečva – the *Rožnov* (all year) and the *Sport* (mid-June to mid-Sept) – and a third, *Pod lipami* (July & Aug), 3km up the road in Dolní Bečva. The *Rožnovský rynek* **restaurant**, inside the Společenský dům (a nineteenth-century spa building in the park just west of the *skanzen*), serves up local cuisine in a folksy interior intended to re-create the atmosphere of a nineteenth-century Wallachian inn.

Český Těšín

If you fancy a jaunt into **Poland**, the easiest place to visit is probably **ČESKÝ TĚŠÍN** (Cieszyn), 55km northeast of Rožnov (although it's easiest to get here on one of the regular commuter trains from Ostrava). Following World War I the town was claimed by both Poland and Czechoslovakia, and ended up being split down the middle with the River Olše (Olza) serving as the frontier. The Poles got the best deal, ending up with the well-preserved old town on the right bank, while the Czechs were left with a frumpy nineteenth-century suburb. With an attractive brace of squares and a grid of cobbled streets, the Polish part of town is worth a wander, and there's no passport control on the bridge joining one side to the other.

Central, opposite Český Těšín train station at Nádražní 16 (Ⓣ558 713 113, Ⓦwww.hotel-central.cz; ❷), offers unexciting but adequate en-suite **rooms** with TV and wi-fi, and boasts a Mexican restaurant that gets lively at weekends. Over on the other side of town, Cieszyn **bus** station provides onward connections to Kraków and beyond.

Travel details

Trains

Connections with Prague: Olomouc (1–2 hourly; 3hr 10min–3hr 30min); Ostrava (every 2–3hr; 3hr 50min–5hr 30min).

Jeseník to: Javorník (3 daily; 1hr 5min–1hr 15min); Žulová (4 daily; 30–40min).

Lipová Lázně to: Javorník (3 daily; 1hr–1hr 15min); Žulová (3 daily; 30–40min).

Olomouc to: Jeseník (3 daily; 2hr 15min–3hr 45min); Krnov (every 1–2hr; 1hr 45min–2hr 15min); Lipová Lázně (3 daily; 2hr 5min–3hr 30min); Opava (up to 9 daily; 2hr 20min–3hr 20min); Ostrava (every 1–2hr; 1hr 15min–2hr); Prostějov (every 1–2hr; 15–25min); Šumperk (10 daily; 1hr 10min–1hr 35min).

Opava to: Hradec nad Moravicí (every 1–2hr; 12min); Jeseník (4 daily; 2hr–2hr 10min); Krnov (hourly; 30–45min); Ostrava (hourly; 30–50min).

Ostrava to: Český Těšín (1–2 hourly; 40–55min).

Šumperk to: Jeseník (9 daily; 1hr 45min–2hr 15min); Lipová Lázně (8–9 daily; 1hr 25min–1hr 45min).

Buses

Connections with Prague: Nový Jičín (2 daily; 5hr); Olomouc (up to 8 daily; 3hr 50min–5hr); Ostrava (6–7 daily; 5hr 20min–7hr 30min).

Nový Jičín to: Frenštát pod Radhoštěm (hourly; 40min); Kopřivnice (hourly; 30–45min); Příbor (hourly; 25min); Štramberk (1–2 hourly; 15–35 min).

Olomouc to: Nový Jičín (up to 9 daily; 50min–1hr 15min); Opava (4 daily Mon–Fri; 1hr 50min–2hr); Ostrava (up to 15 daily; 1hr 30min–2hr 10min); Příbor (up to 5 daily Mon–Fri; 1hr 20min–1hr 30min); Rožnov pod Radhoštěm (1–2 daily; 1hr 25min–1hr 55min).

Rožnov pod Radhoštěm to: Frenštát pod Radhoštěm (1–2 hourly; 15–30min); Valašská Bystřice (1–2 hourly; 20–25min).

Contexts

Contexts

History

Czechoslovakia had been in existence for a mere 74 years when it officially split into the Czech Republic and Slovakia on January 1, 1993. Before that period, the Czechs had been firmly under the sway of their German, Polish or Habsburg neighbours for more than a millennium. Although never quite in full control of its historical destiny, Bohemia, nevertheless, has consistently played a pivotal role in European history, prompting the famous pronouncement (attributed to Bismarck) that "he who holds Bohemia holds mid-Europe".

Beginnings

According to Roman records, the area now covered by the Czech Republic was inhabited as early as 500 BC by **Celtic tribes**: the Boii, who settled in Bohemia (which bears their name), and the Cotini, who inhabited Moravia (and parts of Slovakia). Very little is known about either tribe except that around 100 BC they were driven from these territories by two **Germanic tribes**: the Marcomanni, who occupied Bohemia, and the Quadi, who took over from the Cotini. These later semi-nomadic tribes proved awkward opponents for the Roman Empire, which wisely chose the River Danube as its natural eastern border.

The disintegration of the Roman Empire in the fifth century AD corresponded with a series of raids into central Europe by eastern tribes: firstly the **Huns**, who displaced the Marcomanni and Quadi, and later the **Avars**, who replaced the Huns around the sixth century, settling a vast area including the Hungarian plains and parts of what are now Slovakia and the Czech Republic. About the same time, the **Slav tribes** entered Europe from east of the Carpathian mountains, and appear to have been subjugated by the Avars, at the beginning at least. Their first successful rebellion seems not to have taken place until the seventh century, under the Frankish leadership of **Samo** (624–658 AD), though the kingdom he created died with him.

The Great Moravian Empire

The next written record of the Slavs in this region isn't until the eighth century, when East Frankish (Germanic) chroniclers reported that a people known as the **Moravians** had established themselves around the River Morava, a tributary of the Danube, which now forms part of the border between the Czech Republic and Slovakia. It was an alliance of Moravians and Franks (under Charlemagne) that finally expelled the Avars from central Europe in 796 AD, clearing the way for the establishment of the **Great Moravian Empire** (**Velká Morava**), which at its peak also included Slovakia, Bohemia and parts of Hungary and Poland. This was the first and last time (until the establishment of Czechoslovakia, for which it served as a useful precedent) that Czechs and Slovaks were united under one ruler (though both sides argue over whether the empire was more Czech or Slovak in character).

The first attested ruler of the empire, **Mojmír** (836–846 AD), found himself at the political and religious crossroads of Europe, under pressure from two sides: from the west, where the Franks and Bavarians (both Germanic tribes) were jostling for position with the Roman papacy; and from the east, where the Patriarch of Byzantium was keen to extend his influence across eastern Europe. The Germans pulled off the first coup, by helping to oust Mojmír and replace him with his nephew, **Rastislav** (846–870 AD). However, Rastislav proved to be nobody's puppet and, dissatisfied with the German missionaries, he called on the Byzantine Emperor to send some missionaries who knew the Slav language. SS **Cyril and Methodius** were sent and given the job of making a written language and introducing Christianity, using the Slav liturgy and Eastern rites. Rastislav, in turn, was captured and blinded by his nephew, **Svätopluk** (871–894 AD), again in cahoots with the Germans. Eventually, however, Svätopluk also managed to defeat the Germans, at the Battle of Devín in 873, and during his reign – nearly a quarter of a century – the empire reached its greatest extension.

Svätopluk died shortly before the **Magyar invasion** of 896, an event that heralded the end of the Great Moravian Empire and a significant break in Czech history. The Slavs to the west of the River Morava (the Czechs) swore allegiance to the Frankish Emperor, Arnulf; while those to the east (the Slovaks) found themselves under the yoke of the Magyars.

The Přemyslid dynasty

There is evidence that Bohemian dukes were forced in 806 to pay a yearly tribute of 500 pieces of silver and 120 oxen to the Carolingian Empire (a precedent the Nazis were keen to exploit as proof of German hegemony over Bohemia). These early Bohemian dukes "lived like animals, brutal and without knowledge", according to one chronicler. All that was to change when the earliest recorded Přemyslid duke, **Bořivoj** (852/53–888/89 AD) appeared on the scene. The first Christian ruler of Prague, Bořivoj was baptized in the ninth century, along with his wife Ludmila, by the Byzantine missionaries Cyril and Methodius (see above). Other than being the first to build a castle on Hradčany, nothing very certain is known about Bořivoj, nor about any of the other early Přemyslid rulers, although there are numerous legends, most famously that of **Prince Václav** (St Wenceslas), who was martyred by his pagan brother Boleslav the Cruel in 929 AD.

Cut off from Byzantium by the Hungarian kingdom, Bohemia lived under the shadow of the **Holy Roman Empire** from the start. In 950, Emperor Otto I led an expedition against Bohemia, making the kingdom officially subject to the empire and its king one of the seven electors of the Emperor. In 973 AD, under Boleslav the Pious (967–999 AD), a bishopric was founded in Prague, subordinate to the archbishopric of Mainz. Thus, by the end of the first millennium, German influence was already beginning to make itself felt in Bohemian history.

The **thirteenth century** was the high point of Přemyslid rule over Bohemia. With the Emperor Frederick II preoccupied with Mediterranean affairs and dynastic problems, and the Hungarians and Poles busy trying to repulse the Mongol invasions from 1220 onwards, the Přemyslids were able to assert their independence. In 1212, Otakar I (1198–1230) managed to extract a "**Golden Bull**" (formal edict) from the Emperor, securing the royal title for himself and his descendants (who thereafter became kings of Bohemia).

The discovery of silver and gold mines in the Czech Lands heralded a big shift in the population from the countryside to the towns. Large-scale **German colonization** was generally encouraged by the Přemyslids in Bohemia and Moravia. German miners and craftsmen founded whole towns – including Kutná Hora and Jihlava – in the interior of the country, where German civil rights were guaranteed them. At the same time, the territories of the Bohemian crown were increased to include not only Bohemia and Moravia, but also Silesia and Lusatia to the north (now divided between Germany and Poland).

The beginning of the fourteenth century saw a series of dynastic disputes – messy even by medieval standards – that started with the death of Václav II from consumption and excess in 1305. The following year, the murder of his heirless teenage son, Václav III, marked the **end of the Přemyslid dynasty** (he had four sisters, but female succession was not recognized in Bohemia). The nobles' first choice of successor, the Habsburg Albert I, was murdered by his own nephew, and when Albert's son, Rudolf I, died of dysentery not long afterwards, Bohemia was once more left without heirs.

The Luxembourg dynasty

The crisis was finally solved when the Czech nobles offered the throne to **John of Luxembourg** (1310–46), who was married to Václav III's youngest sister. German by birth and educated in France, King John spent most of his reign participating in foreign wars, with Bohemia footing the bill, until his death on the field at Crécy in 1346. His son, **Charles IV** (1346–78), was wounded in the same battle but, thankfully for the Czechs, lived to tell the tale.

It was Charles who ushered in the Czech nation's **golden age**. Although born and bred in France, Charles was a Bohemian at heart (his mother was Czech and his real name was Václav); he was also extremely intelligent, speaking five languages fluently and even writing an autobiography. In 1346, he became not only king of Bohemia, but also, by election, Holy Roman Emperor. Two years later he founded a university in Prague and began to promote the city as the cultural capital of central Europe, erecting rich Gothic monuments – many of which still survive – and numerous ecclesiastical institutions. As Emperor, Charles issued many Golden Bull edicts that strengthened Bohemia's position, promoted Czech as the official language alongside Latin and German, and presided over a period of relative peace in central Europe, while western Europe was tearing itself apart in the Hundred Years' War.

Charles' son, **Václav IV** (1378–1419), who assumed the throne in 1378, was no match. Stories that he roasted a cook alive on his own spit, shot a monk whilst hunting, and tried his own hand at beheading people with an axe, are almost certainly myths. Nevertheless, he was a legendary drinker, prone to violent outbursts, and so unpopular with the powers that be that he was imprisoned twice – once by his own nobles, and once by his brother, Sigismund. His reign was also characterized by religious divisions within the Czech Lands and Europe as a whole, beginning with the **Great Schism** (1378–1417), when rival popes held court in Rome and Avignon. This was a severe blow to Rome's centralizing power, which might otherwise have successfully rebuffed the assault on the Church that got under way in the Czech Lands towards the end of the fourteenth century.

The Czech Reformation

The attack was led by the peasant-born preacher **Jan Hus**. A follower of the English reformer John Wycliffe, Hus preached at Prague's Betlémská kaple (see p.97), in the language of the masses (ie Czech), against the wealth, corruption and hierarchical tendencies within the Church at the time. Although a devout, mild-mannered man, he became embroiled in a dispute between the conservative clergy, led by the archbishop and backed by the pope in Rome, and the Wycliffian Czechs at the university. When the archbishop gave the order to burn the book of Wycliffe, Václav backed Hus and his followers, for political and personal reasons (Hus was, among other things, the confessor to his wife, Queen Sophie).

There's little doubt that Václav used Hus and the Wycliffites to further his own political cause. He had been deposed as Holy Roman Emperor in 1400 and, as a result, bore a grudge against the current Emperor, Ruprecht of the Palatinate, and his chief backer, Pope Gregory XII in Rome. His chosen battleground was Prague's university, which was divided into four "nations" with equal voting rights: the Saxons, Poles and Bavarians, who supported Václav's enemies, and the Bohemians, who were mostly Wycliffites. In 1409 Václav issued the **Kutná Hora Decree**, which rigged the voting within the university giving the Bohemian "nation" three votes, and the rest a total of one. The other "nations", who made up the majority of the students and teachers, left Prague in protest.

Three years later the alliance between the king and the Wycliffites broke down. Widening his attacks on the Church, Hus began to preach against the sale of religious indulgences to fund the inter-papal wars, thus incurring the enmity of Václav, who received a percentage of the sales. In 1412, Hus and his followers were expelled from the university and excommunicated, and spent the next two years as itinerant preachers spreading their reformist gospel throughout Bohemia. Hus was then summoned to the **Council of Constance** to answer charges of heresy. Despite a guarantee of safe conduct from the Emperor Sigismund, Hus was condemned to death and, having refused to renounce his beliefs, was burned at the stake on July 6, 1415.

Hus' martyrdom sparked off a **widespread rebellion** in Bohemia, initially uniting virtually all Bohemians – clergy and laity, peasant and noble (including many of Hus' former opponents) – against the decision of the council and, by inference, against the established Church and its conservative clergy. The Hussites immediately set about reforming Church practices, most famously by administering communion *sub utraque specie* ("in both kinds", ie bread and wine) to the laity, as opposed to the established practice of reserving the wine for the clergy.

The Hussite Wars: 1419–34

In 1419, Václav inadvertently provoked large-scale rioting by endorsing the readmission of anti-Hussite priests to their parishes. In the ensuing violence, several Catholic councillors were thrown to their death from the windows of Prague's Novoměstská radnice, in Prague's **first defenestration** (see p.112). Václav himself was so enraged (not to say terrified) by the mob that he suffered a heart attack and died, "roaring like a lion", according to a contemporary chronicler. The pope, meanwhile, declared an international crusade against the Czech heretics, under the leadership of Václav's brother and heir, the Emperor Sigismund.

Already, though, cracks were appearing in the Hussite camp. The more radical reformers, who became known as the **Táborites**, after their south Bohemian base, Tábor, broadened their attacks on the Church hierarchy to include all figures of authority and privilege. Their message found a ready audience among the oppressed classes in Prague and the Bohemian countryside, who went round eagerly destroying Church property and massacring Catholics. Such actions were deeply disturbing to the Czech nobility and their supporters, who backed the more moderate Hussites – known as the **Utraquists** (from the Latin *sub utraque specie*) – whose criticisms were confined to religious matters.

For the moment, however, the common Catholic enemy prevented a serious split among the Hussites, and, under the inspirational military leadership of the Táborite **Jan Žižka**, the Hussites' (mostly peasant) army enjoyed some miraculous early victories over the numerically superior "crusaders", most notably at the Battle of Vítkov in Prague in 1420. The Bohemian Diet quickly drew up the **Four Articles of Prague**, which were essentially a compromise between the two Hussite camps, outlining the basic tenets on which all Hussites could agree, including communion "in both kinds". The Táborites, meanwhile, continued to burn, loot and pillage ecclesiastical institutions from Prague to the far reaches of what is now Slovakia.

At the **Council of Basel** in 1433, Rome reached a compromise with the Utraquists over the Four Articles in return for ceasing hostilities. The peasant-based Táborites rightly saw the deal as a victory for the Bohemian nobility and the status quo, and vowed to continue the fight. However, the Utraquists, now in cahoots with the Catholic forces, easily defeated the remaining Táborites at the **Battle of Lipany**, outside Kolín, in 1434. The Táborites were forced to withdraw to the fortress town of Tábor. Poor old Sigismund, who had spent the best part of his life fighting the Hussites, died just three years later.

Compromise

Despite the agreement of the Council of Basel, the pope refused to acknowledge the Utraquist church in Bohemia. The Utraquists nevertheless consolidated their position by electing the gifted **Jiří of Poděbrady** as first regent and then king of Bohemia (1458–71). The first and last Hussite king, George (Jiří to the Czechs), is remembered primarily for his commitment to promoting religious tolerance and his far-sighted efforts to establish some sort of "Peace Confederation" in Europe.

On George's death, the Bohemian Estates handed the crown to the **Polish Jagiellonian dynasty**, who ruled in absentia and effectively relinquished the reins of power to the Czech nobility. In 1526, the last of the Jagiellonians, King Louis, was defeated by the Turks at the Battle of Mohács and died fleeing the battlefield, leaving no heir to the throne. The Roman Catholic Habsburg Ferdinand I (1526–64) was elected king of Bohemia – and what was left of Hungary – in order to fill the power vacuum, marking the **beginning of Habsburg rule** over the Czech Lands. Ferdinand adroitly secured automatic hereditary succession over the Bohemian throne for his dynasty, in return for accepting the agreement laid down at the Council of Basel back in 1433. With the Turks at the gates of Vienna, he had little choice but to compromise at this stage, but in 1545, the international situation eased somewhat with the establishment of an armistice with the Turks.

In 1546, the Utraquist Bohemian nobility provocatively joined the powerful Protestant Schmalkaldic League in their (ultimately unsuccessful) war against the Holy Roman Emperor Charles V. When armed conflict broke out in

Bohemia, however, victory fell to Ferdinand, who took the opportunity to extend the influence of Catholicism in the Czech Lands, executing several leading Protestant nobles, persecuting the reformist Unity of Czech Brethren who had figured prominently in the rebellion, and inviting Jesuit missionaries to establish churches and seminaries in the Czech Lands.

Like Václav IV, **Emperor Rudolf II** (1576–1611), Ferdinand's eventual successor, was moody and wayward, and by the end of his reign Bohemia was once more rushing headlong into a major international confrontation. But Rudolf also shared characteristics with Václav's father, Charles, in his love of the arts, and in his passion for Prague, which he re-established as the royal seat, in preference to Vienna, which was once more under threat from the Turks. Czechs tend to regard Rudolfine Prague as a second golden age, but as far as the Catholic Church was concerned, Rudolf's religious tolerance and indecision were a disaster. In the early 1600s, his melancholy began to veer close to insanity, a condition he had inherited from his Spanish grandmother, Joanna the Mad. And in 1611, the heirless Rudolf was forced to abdicate by his brother **Matthias**, to save the Habsburg house from ruin. Ardently Catholic, but equally heirless, Matthias proposed his cousin **Ferdinand II** as his successor in 1617. This was the last straw for Bohemia's mostly Protestant nobility, and the following year conflict erupted again.

Counter-Reformation to Enlightenment

On May 23, 1618, two Catholic nobles were thrown out of the windows of Prague Castle – the country's **second defenestration** (see p.74) – an event that's now taken as the official beginning of the complex religious and dynastic conflicts collectively known as the **Thirty Years' War** (1618–48). Following the defenestration, the Bohemian Diet expelled the Jesuits and elected the youthful Protestant "winter king", Frederick of the Palatinate, to the throne. In the first decisive set-to of the war, the Protestants were defeated at the **Battle of Bílá hora** (Battle of the White Mountain), which took place on November 8, 1620, on the outskirts of Prague. In the aftermath, 27 Protestant nobles were executed on Prague's Staroměstské náměstí, and the heads of ten of them displayed on the Charles Bridge.

It wasn't until the Protestant Saxons occupied Prague in 1632 that the heads were finally taken down and given a proper burial. The Catholics eventually drove the Saxons out, but for the last ten years of the war, Bohemia and Moravia became the main battleground between the new champions of the Protestant cause – the Swedes – and the imperial Catholic forces. In 1648, the final battle of the war was fought in Prague, when the Swedes seized Malá Strana, but failed to take Staré Město, thanks to the stubborn resistance of Prague's Jewish and newly Catholicized student populations on the Charles Bridge.

The Thirty Years' War ended with the **Peace of Westphalia**, which, for the Czechs, was as disastrous as the war itself. An estimated five-sixths of the Bohemian nobility went into exile, their properties handed over to loyal Catholic families from Austria, Spain, France and Italy. The country was devastated, towns and cities laid waste, and the total population reduced by almost two-thirds. On top of all that, the Czech Lands and Slovakia were now decisively under Catholic influence, and the full force of the **Counter-Reformation** was brought to bear on its people. All forms of Protestantism were outlawed, the education system handed over to the Jesuits and, in 1651 alone, over two hundred "witches" burned at the stake in Bohemia.

The next two centuries of Habsburg rule are known to the Czechs as the **Dark Ages**. The focus of the empire shifted back to Vienna, the Habsburgs' absolutist grip catapulted the remaining nobility into intensive Germanization, while fresh waves of German immigrants reduced Czech to a despised dialect spoken by peasants, artisans and servants. The situation was so bad that Prague and most other urban centres became practically all-German cities. By the end of the eighteenth century, the Czech language was on the verge of dying, with government, scholarship and literature exclusively in German. For the newly ensconced Germanized aristocracy, of course, the good times rolled, and the country was endowed with numerous Baroque palaces and monuments.

After a century of iron-fisted Habsburg rule, the accession of Charles VI's daughter, **Maria Theresa** (1740–80) marked the beginning of the **Enlightenment** in the empire. The Empress acknowledged the need for reform and, despite her own attachment to the Jesuits, followed the lead of Spain, Portugal and France in expelling the order in 1773. But it was her son, **Joseph II** (1780–90), who brought about the most radical changes to the social structure of the Habsburg lands. His 1781 **Edict of Tolerance** (Toleranzpatent) allowed a large degree of freedom of worship for the first time in over 150 years, and went a long way towards lifting the restrictions on Jews. The next year, he ordered the dissolution of the monasteries and embarked upon the abolition of serfdom. Despite his reforms, though, Joseph was not universally popular. Catholics – by now some ninety percent of the population – viewed him with disdain. His centralization and bureaucratization placed power in the hands of the Austrian civil service, and thus helped to entrench the **Germanization** of the Czech Lands. He also offended the Czechs by breaking with tradition and not holding an official coronation ceremony in Prague.

The Czech national revival

The Habsburgs' enlightened rule inadvertently provided the basis for the economic prosperity and social changes of the **Industrial Revolution**, which in turn fuelled the Czech national revival of the nineteenth century. The textile, glass, coal and iron industries began to grow, drawing ever more Czechs in from the countryside and swamping the hitherto mostly Germanized towns and cities. An embryonic Czech bourgeoisie emerged and, thanks to Maria Theresa's educational reforms, new educational and economic opportunities were given to the Czech lower classes.

For the first half of the century, the **Czech national revival** or *národní obrození* was confined to the new Czech intelligentsia, led by philologists like Josef Dobrovský and Josef Jungmann at Prague's Charles University or Karolinum. Language disputes (in schools, universities and public offices) remained at the forefront of Czech nationalism throughout the nineteenth century, only later developing into demands for political autonomy. The leading figure of the time was the Moravian Protestant and historian **František Palacký**, who wrote the first history of the Czech nation, rehabilitating Hus and the Czech reformists in the process. He was in many ways typical of the early Czech nationalists – pan-Slavist and virulently anti-German, but not yet entirely anti-Habsburg.

1848 and the Dual Monarchy

The fall of the French monarchy in February 1848 prompted a crisis in the Habsburg Empire. The new bourgeoisie, of Czech-, German- and Hungarian-speakers, began to make political demands: freedom of the press, of assembly, of religious creeds and, in the nature of the empire, more rights for its constituent nationalities. In the **Czech Lands**, liberal opinion became polarized between the Czech- and German-speakers. Palacký and his followers were against the dissolution of the empire and argued instead for a kind of multinational federation. Since the empire contained a majority of Slavs, the ethnic Germans were utterly opposed to Palacký's scheme, campaigning instead for unification with Germany to secure their interests. So when Palacký was invited to the Pan-German National Assembly in Frankfurt in May, he refused. Instead, he convened a **Pan-Slav Congress** the following month, which met in Prague. Meanwhile, the radicals and students (on both sides) took to the streets, erecting barricades and giving the forces of reaction an excuse to declare martial law. In June, the Habsburg military commander bombarded Prague; the next morning the city capitulated – the counter-revolution in the Czech Lands had begun.

1848 left the absolutist Habsburg Empire shaken but fundamentally unchanged. The one great positive achievement in 1848 was the **emancipation of the peasants** and of the empire's **Jewish population**. Otherwise, events only served to highlight the sharp differences between German and Czech aspirations in the Czech Lands. The Habsburg recovery was, however, short-lived. In 1859 and again in 1866, the new Emperor, Francis Joseph I, suffered humiliating defeats at the hands of the Italians and Prussians respectively. In order to buy some more time, the compromise or *Ausgleich* of 1867 was drawn up, establishing the so-called **Dual Monarchy** of Austria-Hungary – two independent states united under one ruler.

The *Ausgleich* came as a bitter disappointment for the Czechs, who remained second-class citizens while the Magyars became the Austrians' equals. The Czechs' failure to bend the Emperor's ear was no doubt partly due to the absence of a Czech aristocracy that could bring its social weight to bear at the Viennese court. Nevertheless, the *Ausgleich* did mark an end to the absolutism of the immediate post-1848 period, and, compared to the Hungarians, the Austrians were positively enlightened in the wide range of civil liberties they granted, culminating in universal male suffrage in 1907.

Under Dualism, the Czech **national revival** flourished – and splintered. The liberals and conservatives known as the **Old Czechs**, backed by the new Czech industrialists, advocated working within the existing legislature to achieve their aims. By 1890, though, the more radical **Young Czechs** had gained the upper hand and instigated a policy of non-cooperation with Vienna. The most famous political figure to emerge from the ranks of the Young Czechs was the Prague university professor **Tomáš Garrigue Masaryk**, who founded his own Realist Party in 1900. Masaryk hailed from the Moravian borderlands where Slovaks and Czechs lived harmoniously and advocated the (then rather quirky) concept of closer cooperation between the Czechs and Slovaks.

World War I

At the outbreak of **World War I**, the Czechs and Slovaks showed little enthusiasm for fighting alongside their old enemies, the Austrians and Hungarians, against their Slav brothers, the Russians and Serbs. As the war progressed, large numbers defected to form the **Czechoslovak Legion**, which fought on the Eastern Front against the Austrians. Masaryk travelled to the USA to curry favour for a new Czechoslovak state, while his two deputies, the Czech Edvard Beneš and the Slovak Milan Štefánik, did the same in Britain and France.

Meanwhile, the Legion, now numbering around 100,000 men, became embroiled in the Russian revolutions of 1917 and, when the Bolsheviks made peace with Germany, found itself cut off from the homeland. The uneasy cooperation between the Reds and the Legion broke down when Trotsky demanded that they hand over their weapons before heading off on their legendary **anabasis**, or march back home, via Vladivostok. The soldiers refused and became further involved in the Civil War, for a while controlling large parts of Siberia and, most importantly, the Trans-Siberian Railway, before arriving back to a tumultuous reception in their new joint republic.

In the summer of 1918, the Allies finally recognized Masaryk's provisional government. On October 28, 1918, as the Habsburg Empire began to collapse, the first **Czechoslovak Republic** was declared in Prague. Meanwhile, the German-speaking border regions of Bohemia and Moravia (later to become known as the Sudetenland) declared themselves autonomous provinces of the new republic of Deutsch-Österreich (German-Austria), which it was hoped would eventually unite with Germany itself. The new Czechoslovak government was having none of it, but it took the intervention of Czechoslovak troops before control of the border regions was wrested from the secessionists.

In Slovakia, any qualms the Slovaks may have had about accepting rule from Prague were superseded by fear of Hungarian military action. Košice (Kassa), Bratislava (Poszony) and various other Hungarian-speaking regions were only wrested from Hungarian control in January 1919. Soon afterwards, Béla Kun's Hungarian Red Army reoccupied much of the country, and was only booted out by the Czechoslovak Legion in the summer of 1919. In June 1920 the **Treaty of Trianon** confirmed the controversial new Slovak–Hungarian border along the Danube, leaving some 750,000 Hungarians on Czechoslovak soil, and a correspondingly large number of Slovaks within Hungarian territory.

Last to opt in favour of the new republic was **Ruthenia** (officially known as Sub-Carpatho-Ruthenia), a rural backwater of the old Hungarian Kingdom that became part of Czechoslovakia in the Treaty of St Germain in September 1919. Its incorporation was largely due to the campaigning efforts of Ruthenians who had emigrated to the US. For the new republic, the province was a strategic bonus but a huge drain on resources.

The First Republic

The new nation of Czechoslovakia began **postwar life** in an enviable economic position – tenth in the world industrial league table – having inherited seventy to eighty percent of Austria-Hungary's industry intact. Less enviable was the diverse make-up of its population – a melange of minorities that would in the end prove its downfall. Along with the six million Czechs and two million Slovaks who initially backed the republic, there were over three million Germans and 600,000 Hungarians, not to mention sundry other Ruthenians (Rusyns), Jews and Poles.

That Czechoslovakia's democracy survived as long as it did is down to the powerful political presence and skill of **Masaryk**, the country's first, and longest-serving, president (1918–35), who shared executive power with the cabinet. His vision of social democracy, stamped on the nation's new constitution, was extremely liberal (if a little bureaucratic and centralized), aimed at ameliorating any ethnic and class tensions by means of universal suffrage, land reform and, more specifically, the Language Law, which ensured bilinguality to any area where the minority exceeded twenty percent.

The elections of 1920 reflected the mood of the time, ushering in the left-liberal alliance of the **Pětka** ("The Five"), a coalition of five parties led by the Agrarian Antonín Švehla, whose slogan "We have agreed that we will agree" became the keystone of the republic's consensus politics between the wars. Gradually, all the other parties (except the Fascists and Communists) – including even the far-right Slovak People's Party (HSMS) and most of the Sudeten German parties – began to participate in (or at least not disrupt) parliamentary proceedings. On the eve of the Wall Street Crash, the republic was enjoying an economic boom, a cultural renaissance and a temporary *modus vivendi* among its minorities.

The 1930s

The 1929 Wall Street Crash plunged the country into crisis. Economic hardship was quickly followed by **political instability**. In Slovakia, the HSMS fed off the anti-Czech resentment fuelled by Prague's manic centralization, and the appointment of Czechs to positions of power throughout the region. Taking an increasingly nationalist/separatist position, the HSMS was by far the largest party in Slovakia, consistently polling around thirty percent. In Ruthenia, the elections of 1935 gave only 37 percent of the vote to parties supporting the republic, the rest going to the Communists, pro-Magyars and other autonomist groups.

But the most intractable of the minority problems was that of the Sudeten Germans, who lived in the heavily industrialized border regions of Bohemia and Moravia. Nationalist sentiment had always run high in the Sudetenland, many of whose German-speakers resented being included in the new republic, but it was only after the Crash that the extremist parties began to make significant electoral gains. Encouraged by the rise of Nazism in Germany, and aided by rocketing Sudeten German unemployment, the far-right **Sudeten German Party** (SdP), led by gym teacher Konrad Henlein, was able to win over sixty percent of the German-speaking vote in the 1935 elections.

Although constantly denying any wish to secede from the republic, the activities of Henlein and the SdP were increasingly funded and directed from Nazi Germany. To make matters worse, the Czechs suffered a severe blow to their morale with the death of Masaryk late in 1937, leaving the country like "a lighthouse high on a cliff with the waves crashing on it on all sides", as his less capable Socialist successor, Edvard Beneš, put it. With the Nazi annexation of Austria (the *Anschluss*) on March 11, 1938, Hitler was free to focus his attention on the Sudetenland, calling Henlein to Berlin on March 28 and instructing him to call for autonomy.

The Munich Crisis and World War II

On April 24, 1938, the SdP launched its final propaganda offensive in the **Karlsbad Decrees**, demanding (without defining) "complete autonomy". As this would clearly have meant surrendering the entire Czechoslovak border defences, not to mention causing economic havoc, Beneš refused to bow to the SdP's demands. Armed conflict was only narrowly avoided and, by the beginning of September, Beneš was forced to acquiesce to some sort of autonomy. On Hitler's orders, Henlein refused Beneš's offer and called openly for the secession of the Sudetenland to the German Reich.

On September 15, as Henlein fled to Germany, the British prime minister, Neville Chamberlain, flew to Berchtesgaden on his own ill-conceived initiative to "appease" the Führer. A week later, Chamberlain flew again to Germany, this time to Bad Godesburg, vowing to the British public that the country would not go to war (in his famous words) "because of a quarrel in a far-away country between people of whom we know nothing". Nevertheless, the French issued draft papers, the British Navy was mobilized, and the whole of Europe fully expected war.

Then, in the early hours of September 30, in one of the most treacherous and self-interested acts of modern European diplomacy, prime ministers Chamberlain (for Britain) and Daladier (for France) signed the **Munich Diktat** with Mussolini and Hitler, agreeing – without consulting the Czechoslovak government – to all of Hitler's demands. The British and French public were genuinely relieved, and Chamberlain flew back to cheering home crowds, waving his famous piece of paper that guaranteed "peace in our time".

Betrayed by his only Western allies and fearing bloodshed, Beneš capitulated, against the wishes of most Czechs. Had Beneš not given in, however, it's doubtful anything would have come of Czech armed resistance, surrounded as they were by vastly superior hostile powers. Beneš resigned on October 5 and left the country. In Slovakia many Slovaks viewed the Munich Diktat as a blessing in disguise, and on October 6 they declared their own autonomous government in Žilina. On October 15, **German troops occupied Sudetenland**, to the dismay of the forty percent of Sudeten Germans who hadn't voted for Henlein (not to mention the half a million Czechs and Jews).

However, the "rump" **Second Republic** (officially known as Czecho-Slovakia), was not long in existence before it too collapsed. On March 15, 1939, Hitler informed Hácha of the imminent Nazi occupation of what was left of the Czech Lands, and persuaded him to demobilize the army, again against the wishes of many Czechs. The invading German army encountered no resistance (nor any response from the Second Republic's supposed guarantors, Britain and France) and swiftly set up the Nazi **Protectorate of Bohemia and Moravia**. At the same time, with the approval of the Germans, **Slovak independence** was declared.

In the Czech Lands, during the first few months of the occupation, left-wing activists were arrested and Jews placed under the infamous **Nuremburg Laws**, but Nazi rule in the Protectorate at that time was not as harsh as it was to become – the economy even enjoyed a mini-boom. Then in late October and November 1939, Czech students began a series of demonstrations against the Nazis, who responded by closing down all institutions of higher education. Calm was restored until 1941, when Himmler's deputy in the SS, **Reinhard Heydrich**, was put in charge of the Protectorate. Arrests and deportations followed, reaching fever pitch after Heydrich was assassinated by the Czech resistance in June 1942 (see p.113). The reprisals were swift and brutal, culminating in the destruction of the villages of Lidice and Ležáky. Meanwhile, the "final solution" was meted out on the country's remaining Jews, who were transported first to the ghetto in Terezín, and then on to the extermination camps. The rest of the Czech population was frightened into submission, and there were very few acts of active resistance in the Czech Lands until the Prague Uprising of May 1945.

By the end of 1944, Czechoslovak and Russian troops had begun to liberate the country, starting with Ruthenia, which Stalin decided to take as war booty despite having guaranteed to maintain Czechoslovakia's pre-Munich borders. On April 4, 1945, under Beneš's leadership, the provisional **Národní fronta** government – a coalition of Social Democrats, Socialists and Communists – was established. On May 5, the people of Prague finally rose up against the Nazis, many hoping to prompt an American offensive from Plzeň, recently captured by General Patton's Third Army. In the end, the Americans made the politically disastrous (but militarily wise) decision not to cross the previously agreed upon demarcation line. The Praguers held out against the Nazis until May 9, when the Russians finally entered the city.

The Third Republic

Violent reprisals against suspected collaborators and the German-speaking population in general began as soon as the country was liberated. All Germans were given the same food rations as the Jews had been given during the war. Starvation, summary executions and worse resulted in the deaths of thousands of ethnic Germans. With considerable popular backing and the tacit approval of the Red Army, Beneš began to organize the **forced expulsion of the German-speaking population**, referred to euphemistically by Czechs and Slovaks as the *odsun* (transfer). Only those Germans who could prove their antifascist credentials were permitted to stay – the Czechs and Slovaks were not called on to prove the same – and by the summer of 1947, nearly 2.5 million Germans had been kicked out or had fled in fear. On this occasion, Sudeten German objections were brushed aside by the Allies, who had given Beneš the go-ahead for the *odsun* at the postwar Potsdam Conference. Attempts by Beneš to expel Slovakia's Hungarian-speaking minority in similar fashion, however, proved unsuccessful.

On October 28, 1945, sixty percent of the country's industry was nationalized. Confiscated Sudeten German property was handed out by the largely Communist-controlled police force, and in a spirit of optimism and/or opportunism, people began to join the Communist Party (KSČ) in droves, membership more than doubling in less than a year. In the **May 1946 elections**, the Party reaped the rewards of their enthusiastic support for the *odsun*, of Stalin's vocal opposition to Munich, and of the recent Soviet liberation, emerging as the strongest single party in the Czech Lands, with up to forty percent of the vote (the largest ever for a European communist party in a multiparty election). President Beneš appointed the KSČ leader, **Klement Gottwald**, prime minister of another Národní fronta coalition, with several, strategically important, cabinet portfolios going to Party members, including the ministries of the Interior, Finance, Labour and Social Affairs, Agriculture and Information.

Gottwald assured everyone of the KSČ's commitment to parliamentary democracy and, initially at least, even agreed to participate in the Americans' Marshall Plan (the only Eastern Bloc country to do so). Stalin immediately summoned Gottwald to Moscow, and on his return the KSČ denounced the plan. By the end of 1947, the Communists were losing support as the harvest failed, the economy faltered and malpractices within the Communist-controlled Ministry of the Interior were uncovered. In response, the KSČ warned the nation of imminent "counter-revolutionary plots", and argued for greater nationalization and land reform.

Then in February 1948 – officially known as **Victorious February** – the latest in a series of scandals hit the Ministry of the Interior, prompting the twelve non-Communist cabinet ministers to resign en masse in the hope that this would force a physically weak President Beneš to dismiss Gottwald. No attempt was made to rally popular support against the Communists. Beneš received over 5000 resolutions supporting the Communists and just 150 opposing them. Stalin sent word to Gottwald to take advantage of the crisis and ask for military assistance – Soviet troops began massing on the Hungarian border. It was the one time in his life when Gottwald disobeyed Stalin; instead, by exploiting divisions within the Social Democrats, Gottwald was able to maintain his majority in parliament. The KSČ took to the streets (and the airwaves), arming "workers' militia" units to defend the country against counter-revolution, calling a general strike and finally, on February 25, organizing the country's biggest-ever demonstration in Prague. The same day, Gottwald went to an indecisive (and increasingly ill) Beneš with his new cabinet, all Party members or "fellow travellers". Beneš accepted Gottwald's nominees, and the most popular Communist coup in eastern Europe was complete, without bloodshed and without the direct intervention of the Soviets. In the aftermath of the coup, thousands of Czechs and Slovaks fled abroad.

The People's Republic

Following Victorious February, the Party began to consolidate its position, a relatively easy task given its immense popular support and control of the army, police force, workers' militia and trade unions. A **new constitution** confirming the "leading role" of the Communist Party and the "dictatorship of the proletariat" was passed by parliament on May 9, 1948. President Beneš refused to sign, resigned in favour of Gottwald, and died (of natural causes) shortly afterwards. Those political parties that were not banned or forcibly merged with the KSČ were prescribed fixed-percentage representation and subsumed within the so-called "multiparty" Národní fronta.

With the Cold War in full swing, the **Stalinization** of Czechoslovak society was quick to follow. In the Party's first Five Year Plan, ninety percent of industry was nationalized, heavy industry (and, in particular, the defence industry) was given a massive boost, and compulsory collectivization forced through. Party membership reached an all-time high of 2.5 million, with "class-conscious" Party cadres rewarded with positions of power. "Class enemies" (and their children), on the other hand, suffered discrimination, and it wasn't long before the Czechoslovak mining "gulags" began to fill up with the regime's political opponents – "kulaks", priests and "bourgeois oppositionists" – who numbered over 100,000 at their peak.

Having incarcerated most of its external opponents, the KSČ, with a little prompting from Stalin, embarked upon a ruthless period of internal bloodletting. As the economy nose-dived, the press was filled with calls for intensified "class struggle", rumours of impending "counter-revolution" and reports of economic sabotage by fifth columnists. An atmosphere of fear and confusion was created to justify **large-scale arrests of Party members** with an "international" background – those with a wartime connection with the West, Spanish Civil War veterans, Jews and Slovak nationalists.

In the early 1950s, the Party organized a series of Stalinist **show trials** in Prague, the most spectacular of which was that of Rudolf Slánský who, second only to Gottwald in the KSČ before his arrest, was sentenced to death as a "Trotskyist-Titoist-Zionist". Gottwald himself died in mysterious circumstances in March 1953, nine days after attending **Stalin's funeral** in Moscow. The nation heaved a sigh of relief, but the regime seemed as unrepentant as ever, and the arrests and show-trials continued. Then, on May 30, the new Communist leadership announced drastic currency devaluation, effectively reducing wages by ten percent while raising prices. The result was a wave of isolated **workers' demonstrations** and rioting in Prague, Plzeň and the Ostrava mining region. Czechoslovak army units called in to suppress the demonstrations proved unreliable, and it was left to the heavily armed workers' militia and police to disperse the crowds and make the predictable arrests and summary executions.

In 1954, in the last of the show trials, Gustáv Husák, the post-1968 president, was given life imprisonment, along with other leading Slovak comrades. So complete were the Party purges of the early 1950s, so sycophantic (and scared) was the surviving leadership, that Khrushchev's 1956 thaw was virtually ignored by the KSČ. An attempted rebellion in the Writers' Union Congress was rebuffed and an enquiry into the show trials made several minor security officials scapegoats for the "malpractices". The genuine mass base of the KSČ remained loyal to the Party for the most part; Prague basked under the largest statue of Stalin in the world; and in 1957, the unreconstructed neo-Stalinist **Antonín Novotný** – alleged to have been a spy for the Gestapo during the war – became first secretary and president.

Reformism and invasion

The first rumblings of protest against Czechoslovakia's hardline leadership appeared in the official press in 1963. At first, the criticisms were confined to the country's worsening economic stagnation, but soon they developed into more generalized protests against the KSČ leadership. Novotný responded by ordering the belated release and rehabilitation of victims of the 1950s purges, permitting a slight cultural thaw and easing travel restrictions to the West. In effect, he was simply buying time. The half-hearted economic reforms announced in the 1965 **New Economic Model** failed to halt the recession, and the minor political reforms instigated by the KSČ only increased the pressure for greater reforms within the Party.

In 1967 Novotný attempted a pre-emptive strike against his opponents. Several leading writers were imprisoned, Slovak Party leaders were branded as "bourgeois nationalists", and the economists were called on to produce results or else forgo their reform programme. Instead of eliminating the opposition, however, Novotný unwittingly united them. Despite Novotný's plea to the Soviets, Brezhnev refused to back a leader whom he regarded as "Khrushchev's man in Prague". On January 5, 1968, Novotný was replaced as First Secretary by the young Slovak leader **Alexander Dubček**, and on March 22 was dislodged from the presidency by the Czech war hero Ludvík Svoboda.

1968: The Prague Spring

By inclination, Dubček was a moderate, cautious reformer, the perfect compromise candidate – but he was continually swept along by the sheer force of the reform movement. The virtual **abolition of censorship** was probably the single most significant step Dubček took. It transformed what had hitherto been an internal Party debate into a popular mass movement. Civil society, for years muffled by the paranoia and strictures of Stalinism, suddenly sprang into life in the dynamic optimism of the first few months of 1968, the so-called "**Prague Spring**". In April, the KSČ published their Action Programme, proposing what became popularly known as "socialism with a human face" – federalization, freedom of assembly and expression, and democratization of parliament.

Throughout the spring and summer, the reform movement gathered momentum. The Social Democrat Party (forcibly merged with the KSČ after 1948) re-formed, anti-Soviet polemics appeared in the press and, most famously of all, the writer and lifelong Party member Ludvík Vaculík published his personal manifesto entitled "**Two Thousand Words**", calling for radical de-Stalinization within the Party. Dubček and the moderates denounced the manifesto and reaffirmed the country's support for the Warsaw Pact military alliance. Meanwhile, the Soviets and their hardline allies – Gomuľka in Poland and Ulbricht in the GDR – took a very grave view of the Czechoslovak developments on their doorstep, and began to call for the suppression of "counter-revolutionary elements" and the reimposition of censorship.

As the summer wore on, it became clear that the Soviets were planning military intervention. Warsaw Pact manoeuvres were held in Czechoslovakia in late June, a Warsaw Pact conference (without Czechoslovak participation) was convened in mid-July and, at the beginning of August, the Soviets and the KSČ leadership met for **emergency bilateral talks** at Čierná nad Tisou on the Czechoslovak–Soviet border. Brezhnev's hardline deputy, Alexei Kosygin, made his less-than-subtle threat that "your border is our border", but did agree to withdraw Soviet troops (stationed in the country since the June manoeuvres) and gave the go-ahead to the KSČ's special Party Congress scheduled for September 9.

In the early hours of August 21, fearing defeat for the hardliners at the forth-coming KSČ Congress and claiming to have been invited to provide "fraternal assistance", the Soviets gave the order for the **invasion of Czechoslovakia** to be carried out by Warsaw Pact forces (only Romania refused to take part). Dubček and the KSČ reformists immediately condemned the invasion before being arrested and flown to Moscow for "negotiations". President Svoboda refused to condone the formation of a new government under the hardliner Alois Indra, and the people took to the streets in protest, employing every form of nonviolent resistance in the book. Apart from individual acts of martyrdom, like the self-immolation of **Jan Palach** on Prague's Wenceslas Square, casualties were light compared to the Hungarian uprising of 1956 – the cost in terms of the following twenty years was much greater.

Normalization

In April 1969 StB agents provoked anti-Soviet riots during the celebrations of the country's double ice hockey victory over the USSR. On this pretext, another Slovak, **Gustáv Husák**, replaced the broken Dubček as First Secretary and instigated his infamous policy of "**normalization**". Over 150,000 fled the country before the borders closed, around 500,000 were expelled from the Party, and an estimated one million people lost their jobs or were demoted. Inexorably, the KSČ reasserted its absolute control over the state and society.

The only part of the reform package to survive the invasion was **federalization**, which gave the Slovaks greater freedom from Prague (on paper at least), though even this was severely watered down in 1971. Dubček, like countless others, was forced to give up his job, working for the next twenty years as a minor official in the Slovak forestry commission.

An unwritten social contract was struck between rulers and ruled during the 1970s, whereby the country was guaranteed a tolerable standard of living (second only to that of the GDR in Eastern Europe) in return for its passive collaboration. Husák's security apparatus quashed all forms of dissent during the early 1970s, and it wasn't until the middle of the decade that an organized opposition was strong enough to show its face. In 1976, the punk rock band "The Plastic People of the Universe" was arrested and charged with the familiar "crimes against the state". The dissidents who rallied to their defence – from former KSČ members to right-wing intellectuals – agreed to form **Charter 77** (*Charta 77*), with the purpose of monitoring human rights abuses in the country (which had recently signed the Helsinki Agreement on human rights). One of the organization's prime movers and initial spokespersons was the absurdist Czech playwright **Václav Havel**. Over the next decade, Havel, along with many others, endured relentless persecution (including long prison sentences) in pursuit of its ideals. The initial gathering of 243 signatories increased to over 1000 by 1980, causing panic in the moral vacuum of the Party apparatus, but consistently failed to stir a fearful and cynical populace into action.

In the late 1970s and early **1980s**, the inefficiencies of the economy prevented the government from fulfilling its side of the social contract. As living standards began to fall, cynicism, alcoholism, absenteeism and outright dissent became widespread, especially among the younger (post-1968) generation. The arrest and imprisonment in the mid-1980s of the **Jazz Section** of the Musicians' Union, who disseminated "subversive" pop music (like pirate copies of "Live Aid"), highlighted the ludicrously harsh nature of the regime. Pop concerts, annual religious pilgrimages and, of course, the anniversary of the Soviet invasion all caused regular confrontations between the security forces and certain sections of the population. Yet still a mass movement like Poland's Solidarity failed to emerge.

With the advent of **Mikhail Gorbachev**, the KSČ was put in an awkward position, as it tried desperately to separate perestroika from comparisons with the reforms of the Prague Spring. Husák and his cronies had prided themselves on being second only to Honecker's GDR as the most stable and orthodox of the Soviet satellites – now the font of orthodoxy, the Soviet Union, was turning against them. In 1987, **Miloš Jakeš** – the hardliner who oversaw Husák's normalization purges – took over smoothly from Husák as general (first) secretary and introduced *přestavba* (restructuring), Czechoslovakia's lukewarm version of perestroika.

The Velvet Revolution

Everything appeared to be going swimmingly for the KSČ as it entered **1989**. Under the surface, however, things were increasingly strained, with divisions developing in the KSČ leadership as the country's economic performance worsened. The protest movement, meanwhile, was gathering momentum: even the Catholic Church had begun to voice dissatisfaction, compiling a staggering 500,000 signatures calling for greater freedom of worship. But the

21st anniversary of the Soviet invasion produced a demonstration of only 10,000, which was swiftly and violently dispersed.

During the summer, however, more serious cracks began to appear in Czechoslovakia's staunch hardline ally, the GDR. The trickle of East Germans fleeing to the West turned into a mass exodus, forcing Honecker to resign and, by the end of October, prompting nightly mass demonstrations on the streets of Leipzig and Dresden. The opening of the Berlin Wall on November 9 left Czechoslovakia, Romania and Albania alone on the Eastern European stage, still clinging to the old truths.

All eyes were now turned upon Czechoslovakia. Reformists within the KSČ plotted an internal coup to overthrow Jakeš, in anticipation of a Soviet denunciation of the 1968 invasion. Their half-baked plan to foment unrest backfired, however. On Friday **November 17**, a 50,000-strong peaceful demonstration organized by the official Communist youth organization was viciously attacked by the riot police. Over 100 arrests, 500 injuries and one death were reported – the fatality was in fact an StB (secret police) *agent provocateur*. Ultimately, events overtook whatever plans the KSČ reformists may have had. The demonstration became known as the *masakr* (massacre), and Prague's students began an occupation strike, joined soon by the city's actors, who together called for an end to the Communist Party's "leading role" and a general strike to be held for two hours on November 27.

Civic Forum

On Sunday November 19, on Václav Havel's initiative, the established opposition groups such as Charter 77 met and agreed to form Občanské fórum or **Civic Forum**. Their demands were simple: the resignation of the present hardline leadership, including Husák and Jakeš; an inquiry into the police actions of November 17; an amnesty for all political prisoners; and support for the general strike.

On the Monday evening, the first of the really big **nationwide demonstrations** took place – the biggest since the 1968 invasion – with more than 200,000 people pouring into Prague's Wenceslas Square. This time the police held back, and rumours of troop deployments proved false. Every night for a week people poured into the main squares in towns and cities across the country, repeating the calls for democracy, freedom and the end to the Party's monopoly of power. As the week dragged on, the Communist media tentatively began to report events, and the KSČ leadership started to splinter under the strain, with the prime minister, **Ladislav Adamec**, alone in sticking his neck out and holding talks with the opposition.

The end of one-party rule

On Friday evening, Dubček, the ousted 1968 leader, appeared alongside Havel before a crowd of over 300,000 in Prague, and in a matter of hours the entire Jakeš leadership had resigned. The weekend brought the largest demonstrations the country had ever seen – over 750,000 people in Prague alone. At the invitation of Civic Forum, Adamec addressed the crowd, only to get booed off the platform. On Monday November 27, eighty percent of the country's workforce joined the two-hour **general strike**, including many of the Party's previously stalwart allies, the miners and engineers. The following day, the Party agreed to the end of one-party rule and the formation of a new "coalition government".

A temporary halt to the nightly demonstrations was called and the country waited expectantly for the "broad coalition" cabinet promised by Prime Minister Adamec. On December 3, another Communist-dominated line-up was announced by the Party and immediately denounced by Civic Forum, who called for a fresh wave of demonstrations and another general strike for December 11. Adamec promptly resigned and was replaced by **Marián Čalfa**. On December 10, one day before the second threatened general strike, Čalfa announced his provisional "**Government of National Understanding**", with Communists in the minority for the first time since 1948 and multiparty elections planned for June 1990. Having sworn in the new government, President Husák, architect of the post-1968 "normalization", finally threw in the towel.

By the time the new Čalfa government was announced, the students and actors had been on strike for over three weeks. The pace of change had surprised everyone involved, but there was still the issue of the election of a new president. Posters shot up all round the capital urging "**HAVEL NA HRAD**" (Havel to the Castle – the seat of the presidency). The students were determined to see his election through, continuing their occupation strike until Havel was officially elected president by a unanimous vote of the Federal Assembly on December 29.

The 1990 elections

Czechoslovakia started the new decade full of optimism. On the surface, the country had a lot more going for it than its immediate neighbours (with the possible exception of the GDR). The Communist Party had been swept from power without bloodshed, and, unlike the rest of Eastern Europe, Czechoslovakia had a strong, interwar democratic tradition with which to identify – Masaryk's First Republic. Despite **Communist economic mismanagement**, the country still had a relatively high standard of living, a skilled workforce and a manageable foreign debt.

In reality, however, the situation was different. Not only was the country economically in a worse state than most people had imagined, it was environmentally devastated, and its people were suffering from what Havel described as "post-prison psychosis" – an inability to think or act for themselves. The country had to go through the painful transition "from being a big fish in a small pond to being a sickly adolescent trout in a hatchery". As a result, it came increasingly to rely on its newfound saviour, the humble playwright-president Václav Havel.

In most people's eyes "Saint Václav" could do no wrong, though he himself was not out to woo his electorate. His call for the rapid withdrawal of Soviet troops was popular enough, but his apology for the postwar expulsion of Sudeten Germans was deeply resented, as was his generous amnesty that eased the country's overcrowded prisons. The amnesty was blamed by many for the huge **rise in crime**.

In addition, there was still plenty of talk about the possibility of "counter-revolution", given the thousands of unemployed StB at large. Inevitably, accusations of previous StB involvement rocked each political party in turn in the run-up to the first free elections. The controversial **lustrace** (literally "lustration" or "cleansing") law, which barred all those on StB files from public office for the following five years, ended the career of many a politician and public figure, on the basis of often highly unreliable StB reports.

Despite all the inevitable hiccups and the increasingly vocal Slovak nationalists, Civic Forum remained high in the opinion polls. The **June 1990
elections** produced a record-breaking 99 percent turnout. With around sixty
percent of the vote, Civic Forum were clear victors (the Communists got just
thirteen percent), and Havel immediately set about forming a broad "Coalition
of National Sacrifice", including everyone from Christian Democrats to
former Communists.

The main concern of the new government was how to transform an outdated
command-system economy into a **market economy** able to compete with its
EU neighbours. The argument over the speed and model of economic reform
caused Civic Forum to split into two separate parties: the centre-left Občanské
hnutí or Civic Movement (OH), led by the foreign minister and former
dissident Jiří Dienstbier, who favoured a more gradualist approach; and
Občanská demokratická strana or the right-wing **Civic Democratic Party**
(ODS), headed by the finance minister **Václav Klaus**, who pronounced that
the country should "walk the tightrope to Thatcherism".

One of the first acts of the new government was to pass a controversial **restitution law**, handing back small businesses and property to those from whom
it had been expropriated after the 1948 Communist coup – excluding Jewish
families driven out in 1938 by the Nazis, and, of course, the millions of Sudeten
Germans who were forced to flee the country after the war. A law was eventually passed to cover the Jewish expropriations, but the Sudeten German issue
remains unresolved.

The Slovak crisis

One of the most intractable issues facing post-Communist Czechoslovakia – to
the surprise of many Czechs – turned out to be the **Slovak problem**. Having
been the victim of Prague-inspired centralization from just about every Czech
leader from Masaryk to Gottwald, the Slovaks were in no mood to suffer
second-class citizenship any longer. In the aftermath of 1989, feelings were
running high, and, more than once, the spectre of a "Slovak UDI" was threatened by Slovak politicians hoping to boost their popularity by appealing to
voters' nationalism. Despite the tireless campaigning and negotiating by both
sides, a compromise agreement failed to emerge.

The differences between the Czechs and Slovaks came to a head in the
summer of 1990, when it came to deciding on a new name for the country. In
what became known as the **great hyphen debate**, the Slovaks insisted that a
hyphen be inserted in "Czechoslovakia". The demand was greeted with ridicule
by most Czechs; Havel was one of the few who had some sympathy.

The **June 1992 elections** soon became an unofficial referendum on the future
of the federation. Events moved rapidly towards the break-up of the republic
after the resounding victory of the Movement for a Democratic Slovakia
(HZDS), under the wily, populist politician and former boxer **Vladimír Mečiar**,
popularly known as "Vladko", who, in retrospect, was quite clearly seeking
Slovak independence, though he never explicitly said so during the campaign. In
the Czech Lands, the right-wing ODS emerged as the largest single party, under
the leadership of Václav Klaus, who – ever the economist – was not going to shed
tears over losing the economically backward Slovak half of the country.

Talks between the two sides got nowhere, despite the fact that polls in both
republics consistently showed majority support for the federation. The HZDS

then blocked the re-election of Havel, who had committed himself entirely to the pro-federation cause. Havel promptly resigned, leaving the country without a president, and Klaus and Mečiar were forced to discuss the terms of what has become known as the "Velvet Divorce". On January 1, 1993, after 74 years of troubled existence, Czechoslovakia was officially divided into two.

The Czech Republic

Generally speaking, post-Communist life has been much kinder to the Czechs than to the Slovaks. While the Slovaks had the misfortune of being led by the increasingly wayward and isolated Mečiar, the Czech Republic enjoyed a long period of **political stability**, jumped to the front of the queue for the EU and NATO, and was widely held up as a shining example to the rest of the former Eastern Bloc. Klaus and his party, the ODS, proved themselves the most durable of all the new political forces to emerge in the former Eastern Bloc. Nevertheless, in the **1996 elections**, although the ODS again emerged as the largest single party, it failed to gain an outright majority. They repeated the failure again in the first elections for the Czech Senate, the upper house of the Czech parliament. The electorate was distinctly unenthusiastic about the idea of another chamber full of overpaid politicians, and a derisory thirty percent turned out to vote in the second round. In the end, however, it was – predictably enough – a series of corruption scandals that eventually prompted **Klaus's resignation** as prime minister in 1997.

One of the biggest problems to emerge in the 1990s was the issue of **Czech racism towards the Roma minority**. The topic became world news in 1997, when a misleading documentary broadcast on Czech TV showed life for the handful of Czech Roma who had emigrated to Canada as a proverbial bed of roses. At last, the documentary seemed to suggest, they had found a life free from the racism and unemployment that is the reality for most of the Czech Republic's estimated quarter of a million gypsies. The programme prompted a minor exodus of up to one thousand Czech Roma to Canada. Another documentary, this time extolling life for Czech Roma in Britain, had a similar effect, with several hundred Roma seeking political asylum on arrival at Dover.

Stalemate and apathy

The **1998 elections** proved that the Czechs had grown tired of Klaus's dry, rather arrogant, leadership. However, what really did it for Klaus was that for the first time since he took power, the economy had begun to falter. The **ČSSD** or Social Democrats, under **Miloš Zeman**, emerged as the largest single party, promising to pay more attention to social issues. Unable to form a majority government, Zeman followed the Austrian example, and decided to make an "**opposition agreement**" with the ODS. This Faustian pact was dubbed the "Toleranzpatent" by the press, after the 1781 Edict of Tolerance issued by Joseph II (see p.391). The Czech public were unimpressed, and in 2000, thousands turned out in Wenceslas Square for the *Díky a odejděte* (Thank you, now leave) protest, asking for the resignation of both Zeman and Klaus.

Havel stepped down in 2003 after ten years as Czech president, to be replaced by his old sparring partner, Václav Klaus. No Czech president is ever likely to enjoy the same moral stature, though even Havel's standing is no longer what it used to be, particularly at home. His marriage to the actress Dagmar Veškrnová, seventeen years his junior, in 1997, less than a year after his first wife, Olga, died of cancer, was frowned upon by many. And his very public fall-out with his sister-in-law, Olga Havlová, over the family inheritance of the multimillion crown Lucerna complex in Prague, didn't do him any favours either.

Czechs have steadily become increasingly disillusioned with their politicians, with just 58 percent turning out for the **2002 elections**, and 18 percent of them voting for the Communists. Nevertheless, in 2003, 55 percent of the population turned out to vote in the **EU referendum**, with a convincing 77 percent voting in favour of joining. Despite growing cynicism towards politics of any kind, Czechs genuinely celebrated their entry into the EU in 2004; for many, it was the culmination of everything they had fought for in 1968 and 1989, a final exorcism of the enforced isolation of the Communist period.

EU accession has been fairly positive for the Czechs. The economy has recovered from the recession, so there has been no great flight of labour from the country as there has been in Poland. The most persistent problem is corruption and the Czech political system itself, which continues to produce weak minority governments. One of the sticking blocks is that the Communists continue to receive around 15 percent of the vote, but are shunned by all the other parties. The June 2006 elections were a case in point, with left and right gaining exactly 100 seats each. It took until January 2007 before Mirek Topolánek of the ODS succeeded in winning a vote of confidence for his coalition government.

Books

A great deal of Czech fiction and poetry has been translated into English and is easily available, and the key moments in Czech twentieth-century history are also well covered. Those tagged with the 🏃 symbol are particularly recommended.

History, politics and society

Peter Demetz *Prague in Black and Gold: The History of a City*. Demetz's scholary account of more than a thousand years of central European history and culture is determinedly un-partisan and refreshingly antinationalist. Prague in Danger is a moving account of the war years, during which he lived in Nazi-occupied Prague as a "first-degree half-Jew".

R.J.W. Evans *Rudolf II and His World*. First published in 1973, and still the best account there is of the alchemy-mad Emperor, but not as salacious as one might hope given the subject matter.

Jan Kaplan & Krystyna Nosarze-wska *Prague: The Turbulent Century*. This is the first real attempt to cover the twentieth-century history of Prague warts and all. The text isn't as good as it should be, but the range of photographs and images is incredible.

Karel Kaplan *The Short March*. An excellent account of the electoral rise and rise of the Communists in Czechoslovakia after the war, which culminated in the bloodless coup of February 1948. *Report on the Murder of the General Secretary* is a detailed study of the most famous of the anti-Semitic Stalinist show trials, that of Rudolf Slánský, number two in the Party until his arrest.

🏃 **Callum MacDonald** *The Killing of SS Obergruppenführer Reinhard Heydrich*. Gripping tale of the build-up to the most successful and controversial act of wartime

resistance, which took place in May 1942, and prompted horrific reprisals by the Nazis on the Czechs.

Callum MacDonald & Jan Kaplan *Prague in the Shadow of the Swastika*. Excellent account of the city under Nazi occupation, with incisive, readable text illustrated by copious black-and-white photos.

Jirí Musil (ed) *The End of Czechoslovakia*. Academics from both the Czech and Slovak Republics attempt to explain why Czechoslovakia split into two countries just at the point when it seemed so successful.

Derek Sayer *The Coast of Bohemia*. A very readable cultural history, concentrating on Bohemia and Prague, which aims to dispel the ignorance shown by the Shakespearean quote of the title. Particularly illuminating on the subject of twentieth-century artists.

Kieran Williams *The Prague Spring and its Aftermath: Czechoslovak Politics, 1968–70*. This book draws on declassified archives to analyse the attempted reforms under Dubček and to take a new look at the 1968 Prague Spring.

🏃 **Elizabeth Wiskemann** *Czechs and Germans*. Researched and written in the build-up towards Munich, this is the most fascinating and fair treatment of the Sudeten problem. Meticulous in her detail, vast in her scope, Wiskemann manages to suffuse the weighty text with enough anecdotes to keep you gripped. Unique.

Essays, memoirs and biography

Karel Čapek *Talks with T.G. Masaryk.* Čapek was a personal (and political) friend of Masaryk, and his diaries, journals, reminiscences and letters give great insights into the man who personified the First Republic.

Timothy Garton Ash *We The People: The Revolutions of 89.* A personal, anecdotal, eyewitness account of the Velvet Revolution (and the events in Poland, Berlin and Budapest) – by far the most compelling of all the post-1989 books. Published as *The Magic Lantern* in the US.

Patrick Leigh Fermor *A Time of Gifts.* The first volume of Leigh Fermor's trilogy based on his epic walk along the Rhine and Danube rivers in 1933–34. In the last quarter of the book he reaches Czechoslovakia, indulging in a quick jaunt to Prague before crossing the border into Hungary. Written forty years later in dense, luscious and highly crafted prose, it's an evocative and poignant insight into the culture of *Mitteleuropa* between the wars.

Václav Havel The first essay in *Living in Truth* is "Power of the Powerless", Havel's lucid, damning indictment of the inactivity of the Czechoslovak masses in the face of "normalization". *Letters to Olga* is a collection of Havel's letters written under great duress (and heavy censorship) from prison in the early 1980s to his wife – by turns philosophizing, nagging, effusing and whingeing. *Disturbing the Peace* is probably Havel's most accessible work, a series of autobiographical questions and answers in which he talks interestingly about his childhood, the events of 1968 when he was in Liberec, and the path to Charter 77 and beyond. *Summer Meditations* are post-1989 essays by the playwright-president, while *The Art of the Impossible* is a collection of speeches given after becoming the country's president in 1990. *To the Castle and Back* is a strange mixture of reminiscences, interviews and the philosophy of commonsense from a man who initially subtitled the book *My Strange Life as a Fairy Tale Hero.*

Miroslav Holub *The Dimension of the Present Moment*; *Shedding Life: Disease, Politics and Other Human Conditions.* Two books of short philosophical musings/essays on life and the universe by this unusual, clever scientist-poet.

Leoš Janáček *Intimate Letters.* Some of the countless letters written by the elderly composer Leoš Janáček to Kamila Strösslová, a young married woman with whom he fell passionately in love in later life.

John Keane *Vaclav Havel: A Political Tragedy in Six Acts.* The first book to tell both sides of the Havel story: Havel the dissident playwright and civil rights activist who played a key role in the 1989 Velvet Revolution, and Havel the ageing and increasingly ill president, who, in many people's opinion, simply stayed on the stage too long.

Heda Margolius Kovaly *Prague Farewell* (*Under a Cruel Star* in the US). Autobiography starting in the concentration camps of World War II and ending with the author's flight from Czechoslovakia in 1968. Married to one of the Party officials executed in the 1952 Slánský trial, she tells her story simply and without bitterness. The best account there is on the fear and paranoia whipped up during the Stalinist terror.

Milan Kundera *Testaments Betrayed.* Fascinating essays on a range of subjects, from the formation of historical reputation to the problems of translations.

Benjamin Kuras *Czechs and Balances, Is There Life After Marx?* Witty, light, typically Czech takes on national identity and Central European politics; *As Golems Go* is a more mystical look at Rabbi Löw's philosophy and the Kabbalah.

Ivan Margolius *Reflections of Prague: Journeys through the 20th Century.* Fascinating memoir of life in Prague before, during and after the war. Margolius is the son of one of the eleven Party members who were executed in the 1952 Slánsky show trial.

Ota Pavel *How I Came to Know Fish.* Pavel's childhood innocence shines through particularly when his Jewish father and two brothers are sent to a concentration camp and he and his mother have to scrape by.

Angelo Maria Ripellino *Magic Prague.* A wide-ranging look at the bizarre array of historical and literary characters who have lived in Prague, from the mad antics of the court of Rudolf II to the escapades of Jaroslav Hašek. Scholarly, rambling and richly written.

Anna Robertson *No Going Back to Moldova.* Simple and unaffected account of a childhood spent in a convent boarding school in Moravian Silesia and an early adulthood spent in Prague. Robertson was later deported as a Sudeten German and settled in England.

Josef Škvorecký *Talkin' Moscow Blues.* Without doubt the most user-friendly of Škvorecký's works, containing a collection of essays on his wartime childhood, Czech jazz, literature and contemporary politics, all told in his inimitable, irreverent and infuriating way. Published as *Head for the Blues* in the US.

Ludvík Vaculík *A Cup of Coffee With My Interrogator.* A Party member until 1968, and signatory of Charter 77, Vaculík revived the *feuilleton* – a short political critique once much loved in central Europe. This collection dates from 1968 onwards.

Zbyněk Zeman *The Masaryks – The Making of Czechoslovakia.* Written in the 1970s while Zeman was in exile, this is a very readable, none too sentimental biography of the country's founder Tomáš Garrigue Masaryk, and his son Jan Masaryk, the postwar Foreign Minister who died in mysterious circumstances shortly after the 1948 Communist coup.

Czech fiction

Josef Čapek *Stories about Doggie and Pussycat.* Josef Čapek (Karel's older brother) was a Cubist artist of some renown, and also a children's writer. These simple stories about a dog and a cat are wonderfully illustrated and seriously postmodern.

Karel Čapek *Towards a Radical Centre.* Čapek, the literary and journalistic spokesperson for Masaryk's First Republic, is better known in the West for his plays, some of which, such as *R.U.R.*, feature in this anthology. Probably the best of his novel writing is contained in the trilogy *Three Novels*, set in Czechoslovakia in the 1930s. His *Letters from England* had the distinction of being banned by the Nazis and the Communists for its naive admiration of England in the 1920s.

Daniela Fischerová *Fingers Pointing Somewhere Else.* Subtly nuanced, varied collection of short stories from dissident playwright Fisherová.

Ladislav Fuks *The Cremator.* About a man who works in a crematorium in occupied Prague and is about to throw in his lot with the Nazis when he discovers that his wife is half-Jewish; *Mr Theodore Mundstock* is set in 1942 Prague, as the city's Jews wait to be transported to Terezín.

Jaroslav Hašek *The Good Soldier Švejk*. This classic, by Bohemia's most bohemian writer, is a rambling, picaresque tale of Czechoslovakia's famous fictional fifth columnist, Švejk, who wreaks havoc in the Austro-Hungarian army during World War I.

Václav Havel *Selected Plays 1963–87*; *Selected Plays 1984–87*. Havel's plays are not renowned for being easy. *The Memorandum* is one of his earliest works, a classic absurdist drama that, in many ways, sets the tone for much of his later work, of which the *Three Vaněk Plays*, featuring Ferdinand Vaněk, Havel's alter ego, are perhaps the most successful. The 1980s collection includes *Largo Desolato*, *Temptation* and *Redevelopment*; freedom of thought, Faustian opportunism and town-planning as metaphors of life under the Communists.

Daniela Hodrova et al *Povídky: Short Stories by Czech Women*. This collection brings together women of different generations and from different backgrounds to provide a many-sided perspective.

Bohumil Hrabal From this thoroughly mischievous writer, the slim but superb *Closely Observed Trains* is a postwar classic, set in the last days of the war and relentlessly unheroic; it was made into an equally brilliant film by Jiří Menzl. *I Served the King of England* follows the antihero Dítě, who works at the Hotel Paříž, through the decade after 1938. *Too Loud a Solitude*, about a waste-paper disposer under the Communists, was also made into a film by Menzl.

Alois Jirásek *Old Czech Legends*. A major figure in the nineteenth-century Czech *národní obrození*,

Jirásek popularized Bohemia's legendary past. This collection includes all the classic texts, including the story of the founding of the city by the prophetess Libuše.

Franz Kafka A German-Jewish Praguer, Kafka has drawn the darker side of central Europe – its claustrophobia, paranoia and unfathomable bureaucracy – better than anyone else, both in a rural setting, as in *The Castle*, and in an urban one, in one of the great novels of the twentieth century, *The Trial*.

Ivan Klíma A survivor of Terezín, Klíma is a writer in the Kundera mould as far as sexual politics goes, but his stories are a lot lighter. *Judge on Trial*, written in the 1970s, is one of his best, concerning the moral dilemmas of a Communist judge. *Waiting for the Dark, Waiting for the Light* is a pessimistic novel set before, during and after the Velvet Revolution of 1989. *The Spirit of Prague* is a very readable collection of biographical and more general articles and essays on subjects ranging from Klíma's childhood experiences in Terezín to the current situation in Prague. His latest novels, *Ultimate Intimacy*, *No Saints or Angels* and *Love and Garbage*, are set in the cynical post-revolutionary Czech Republic, while *Between Security and Insecurity* is a more serious consideration of moral values in today's world.

Pavel Kohout *I am Snowing: The Confessions of a Woman of Prague* is set in the uneasy period just after the fall of Communism during the *lustrace* controversy (see p.402). *The Widow Killer* is a thriller about a naive Czech detective partnered with a Gestapo agent in the last months of World War II.

Milan Kundera Kundera is the country's most popular writer – at least with non-Czechs. His early books are very obviously "political",

C

CONTEXTS | Books

409

particularly *The Book of Laughter and Forgetting*, which led the Communists to revoke Kundera's citizenship. *The Joke*, written while he was still living in his home country, and in many ways his best work, is set in the very unfunny era of the Stalinist purges. Its clear, humorous style is far removed from the carefully poised posturing of his most famous work, *The Unbearable Lightness of Being*, set in and after 1968, and successfully turned into a film some twenty years later. *Testaments Betrayed*, on the other hand, is a fascinating series of essays about a range of subjects from the formation of historical reputation to the problems of translations. Kundera now writes in French.

Arnošt Lustig *Diamonds of the Night; Night and Hope; Darkness Casts No Shadow; A Prayer for Kateřina Horovitová; Lovely Green Eyes.* A Prague Jew exiled since 1968, Lustig spent World War II in Terezín, Buchenwald and Auschwitz, and his novels and short stories are consistently set in the Terezín camp.

Gustav Meyrink Another of Prague's weird and wonderful characters, Meyrink started out as a bank manager, but soon became involved in cabalism, alchemy and drug experimentation. His *Golem*, based on Rabbi Löw's monster, is one of the classic versions of the tale, set in the Jewish quarter. *The Angel of the West Window* is a historical novel about John Dee, an English alchemist invited to Prague in the late sixteenth century by Rudolf II.

Božena Němcová *The Grandmother.* One of the best-loved Czech novels of the nineteenth century, *Babička* (as it's known in Czech) is the story of a young girl's childhood with her granny in the Bohemian countryside.

Jan Neruda *Prague Tales.* Not to be confused with the Chilean Pablo Neruda (who took his name from the Czech writer). These are short,

bittersweet snapshots of life in Malá Strana at the end of the last century.

Ivan Olbracht *The Sorrowful Eyes of Hannah Karajich.* This moving novel set in the vanished world of a Jewish village in Carpatho-Ruthenia shows the effects of Zionism and the terror of Hitler; his more famous work is *Nicola the Outlaw*, a sort of Ruthenian Robin Hood.

Iva Pekárková *Truck Stop Rainbows.* A heroine who attempts to fight, often by using sexual politics, against the grim realities of the Communist system in Czechoslovakia in the 1980s.

Karel Poláček *What Ownership's All About.* A darkly comic novel set in a Prague tenement block, dealing with the issue of fascism and appeasement, by a Jewish-Czech Praguer who died in the camps in 1944.

Rainer Maria Rilke *Two Stories of Prague.* Both tales deal with the artificiality of Prague's now defunct German-speaking community, whose claustrophobic parochialism drove the author into self-imposed exile in 1899 (for more on Rilke see Poetry, below).

Peter Sís *The Three Golden Keys.* Short, hauntingly illustrated children's book set in Prague, by Czech-born American Sís.

Josef Škvorecký *The Cowards; The Miracle Game; The Swell Season; The Bass Saxophone; Miss Silver's Past; Dvořák in Love; The Engineer of Human Souls; The Republic of Whores.* A prolific writer and relentless anti-Communist, Škvorecký is typically Bohemian in his bawdy sense of humour and irreverence for all high moralizing. The *Cowards* (which briefly saw the light of day in 1958) is the tale of a group of irresponsible young men in the last days of the war, an antidote to the lofty prose from official authors at the time, but hampered by its dated Americanized translation. *The Miracle Game* enjoys a better translation and is set against the backdrop of the Prague Spring. Less well known (and understandably so) are Škvorecký's detective stories featuring a podgy, depressive Czech cop, Lieutenant Boruvka, which he first wrote in the 1960s when his more serious work was banned. His latest Boruvka book, and the first of his books written in English, is *Two Murders in My Double Life*, a mystery set in the Czech Republic and Canada, where he now lives.

🏃 **Zdena Tomin** Although Czech-born, Tomin writes in English (the language of her exile since 1980); she has a style and

fluency all her own. *Stalin's Shoe* is the compelling and complex story of a girl coming to terms with her Stalinist childhood, while *The Coast of Bohemia* is based on Tomin's experiences of the late 1970s dissident movement, when she was an active member of Charter 77.

Ludvík Vaculík *The Guinea Pigs.* Vaculík was expelled from the Party in the 1968 Prague Spring; this novel, set in Prague, catalogues the slow dehumanization of Czech society after the Soviet invasion.

Jiří Weil *Life With a Star; Mendelssohn is on the Roof.* Two novels written just after the war and based on Weil's experiences as a Czech Jew in hiding in Nazi-occupied Prague.

Poetry

Jaroslav Čejka, Michal Černík and Karel Sýs *The New Czech Poetry.* Slim, interesting volume by three Czech poets all in their late 40s at the time and all very different. Čejka is of the Holub school, and comes across simply and strongly; Černík is similarly direct; Sýs the least convincing.

Sylva Fischerová *The Tremor of Racehorses: Selected Poems.* Poet and novelist Fischerová in many ways continues in the Holub tradition. Her poems are by turns powerful, obtuse and personal, and were written in exile in Switzerland and Germany after fleeing in 1968.

Josef Hanzlík *Selected Poems.* Refreshingly accessible collection of poems written over the last 35 years by a poet of Havel's generation.

Miroslav Holub Holub is a scientist and scholar, and his poetry reflects this unique fusion of master poet and chief immunologist. Regularly banned in his own country, he is the Czech poet *par excellence* – classically

trained, erudite, liberal and Westward-leaning. The full range of his work, including some previously unpublished poems, can be found in *Intensive Care: Selected and New Poems* and *Poems Before and After: Collected English Translations*.

Rainer Maria Rilke *Selected Poetry.* Rilke's Prague upbringing was unexceptional – except that his mother brought him up as a girl until the age of 6. He later became the greatest German-speaking lyric poet of the interwar period, writing haunting, emotional, sensual verse that attempts to grapple with the ineffable.

Marcela Rydlová-Herlich (ed) *Treasury of Czech Love Poems.* A good way to get a taste of Czech poetry, with more than 33 – mostly twentieth-century – poets represented.

Jaroslav Seifert *The Poetry of Jaroslav Seifert.* Czechoslovakia's only author to win the Nobel prize for literature, Seifert was a founder-member of the

Communist Party and the avant-garde arts movement *Devětsil*, later falling from grace and signing the Charter in his old age. His longevity means that his work covers some of the most turbulent times in Czech history, but his irrepressible lasciviousness has been known to irritate.

Literature by foreign writers

David Brierley *On Leaving a Prague Window*. Very readable thriller set in post-Communist Prague, which shows that past connection with dissidents can still lead to violence.

Bruce Chatwin *Utz*. Chatwin is one of the "exotic" school of travel writers, hence this slim, intriguing and mostly true-to-life account of an avid crockery collector from Prague's Jewish quarter.

Lionel Davidson *The Night of Wenceslas*. This Cold War thriller, set in pre-1968 Czechoslovakia, launched Davidson's career as a spy-writer.

Martha Gellhorn *A Stricken Field*. The semi-autobiographical story of an American journalist who arrives in Prague just as the Nazis march into Sudetenland is a fascinating, if senti-mental, insight into the panic and confusion in "rump" Czechoslovakia after the Munich Diktat. First published in 1940.

Kathy Kacer *Clara's War*. The story of a young girl and her family who are sent from Prague to Terezín in 1943. The horror is played down as the book is aimed at children aged around 10, but nevertheless it's based on truth.

Jill Paton Walsh *A Desert in Bohemia*. A gripping story set against the aftermath of World War II and the subsequent political upheaval in Czechoslovakia.

Philip Roth *Prague Orgy*. Novella about a world-famous Jewish novelist (ie Roth) who goes to Communist Prague to recover some unpublished Jewish stories. A coda to the author's Zuckerman trilogy.

Art, photography and film

Czech Modernism 1900–1945 Wide-ranging and superbly illustrated, this American publication records the journey of the Czech modern movement through Cubism and Surrealism to Modernism and the avant-garde. The accompanying essays by leading art and film critics cover fine art, architecture, film, photography and theatre.

Devětsil – Czech Avant-Garde Art, Architecture and Design of the 1920s and 30s Published to accompany the 1990 Devětsil exhibition at Oxford, this is the definitive account of interwar Czechoslovakia's most famous left-wing art movement, which attracted artists from every discipline.

Invasion Prague 68 Josef Koudelka. A vivid photographic record of the turbulent days after the invasion of Czechoslovakia by the Warsaw Pact countries.

Prague – A Guide to Twentieth-century Architecture Ivan Margolius. Dinky little pocket guide to all the major modern landmarks of Prague (including a black-and-white photo of each building), from the Art Nouveau Obecní dům, through functionalism and Cubism, to the Fred & Ginger building.

Language

Language

Czech

he official language of the Czech Republic is **Czech** (český), a highly complex Slav tongue. Though – unless you're here for some time – you're not likely to make any great inroads into it, any attempt to speak Czech will be heartily appreciated. English is widely spoken in hotels and restaurants, though less so in shops and museums, and among the older generation at least, German is still the most widely spoken second language. Russian, once the compulsory second language, has been virtually wiped off the school curriculum.

Pronunciation

English-speakers often find Czech impossibly difficult to pronounce. In fact, it's not half as daunting as it might first appear. Apart from a few special letters, each letter and syllable is pronounced as it's written, with virtually no letter unvoiced. The trick is always to **stress the first syllable** of a word, no matter what its length; otherwise you'll render it unintelligible. Note that there is no definite or indefinite article, and word endings change according to their function in the sentence.

Short and long vowels

Czech has both **short** and **long vowels** (the latter being denoted by a variety of accents). The trick is to lengthen the vowel without affecting the principal stress of the word, which is invariably on the first syllable.

a like the u in c**u**p
á as in f**a**ther
e as in p**e**t
é as in f**ai**r
ě like the y in y**e**s
i or y as in p**i**t

í or ý as in s**ea**t
o as in n**o**t
ó as in d**oo**r
u like the oo in b**oo**k
ů or ú like the oo in f**oo**l

Vowel combinations and diphthongs

There are very few diphthongs in Czech. Combinations of vowels not mentioned below should be pronounced as two separate syllables.

au like the ou in f**ou**l
ou like the oe in f**oe**

There are very few **teach yourself Czech** guides available and each has drawbacks. *Colloquial Czech*, by James Naughton, is good, but a bit fast and furious for most people; *Teach Yourself Czech* is a bit dry for some. Numerous **Czech phrasebooks** are available, not least the *Czech Rough Guide Phrasebook*, laid out dictionary-style for instant access. A good online dictionary is ⓦ www.slovnik.cz and you can practise your Czech online at ⓦ www.locallingo.com.

The alphabet

In the Czech alphabet, letters that feature a háček (as in the á of the word itself) are considered separate letters and appear in Czech indexes immediately after their more familiar cousins. More confusingly, the consonant combination of ch is also considered as a separate letter and appears in Czech indexes after the letter h. In the index of this book, we use the English system, so words beginning with c, č and ch all appear under c.

Consonants and accents

There are no silent **consonants**, but r and l can form a syllable if standing between two other consonants or at the end of a word, as in Brno (Br–no) or Vltava (Vl–ta–va). The consonants listed below are those that differ substantially from the English. Accents look daunting, but the only one that causes a lot of problems is ř, probably the most difficult letter to say in the entire language.

c like the **ts** in boats
č like the **ch** in chicken
ch like the **ch** in the Scottish loch
ď like the **d** in duped
g always as in **goat**, never as in general
h always as in **have**, but more energetic
j like the **y** in yoke
kd pronounced as **gd**
ľ like the **lli** in colliery

mě pronounced as **mnye**
ň like the **n** in nuance
p softer than the English p
r as in **rip**, but often rolled
ř like the sound of **r** and **ž** combined
š like the **sh** in shop
ť like the **t** in tutor
ž like the **s** in pleasure; at the end of a word, like the **sh** in shop

Basic words and phrases

Basics

Yes	ano	Today	dnes
No	ne	Yesterday	včera
Excuse me/please/ don't mention it	prosím	Tomorrow	zítra
		The day after tomorrow	pozítra
You're welcome	není zač		
Sorry	pardon	Now	hnet
Thank you	děkuju	Later	později
OK	dobrá	Leave me alone	dej mi pokoj
Bon appétit	dobrou chuť	Go away	jdi pryč
Bon voyage	šťastnou cestu	Help!	pomoc!
Hello/goodbye (informal)	ahoj	This one	tento
		A little	trochu
Goodbye (formal)	na shledanou	Large–small	velký–malý
Good day	dobrý den	More–less	více–méně
Good morning	dobré ráno	Good–bad	dobrý–zpatný
Good evening	dobrý večer	Hot–cold	horký–studený
Good night (when leaving)	dobrou noc	With–without	s–bez
		How are you?	jak se máte?

Getting around

Over here	tady	By foot	pěšky
Over there	tam	By taxi	taxíkem
Left	nalevo	Ticket	jízdenka
Right	napravo	Railway station	nádraží
Straight on	rovně	Bus station	autobusové nádraží
Where is …?	kde je …?	Bus stop	autobusová zastávka
How do I get to Brno?	jak se dostanu do Brna?	When's the next train to Prague?	kdy jede další vlak do Prahy?
How do I get to the university?	jak se dostanu k univerzitě?	Is it going to Brno?	jede to do Brna?
By bus	autobusem	Do I have to change?	musím přestupovat?
By train	vlakem	Do I have to have a reservation?	musím mit místenku?
By car	autem		

Questions and answers

Do you speak English?	mluvíte anglicky?	Why?	proč?
		How much is it?	kolík to stojí?
I don't speak German	nemluvím německy	Are there any rooms available?	máte volné pokoje?
I don't understand	nerozumím	I want a double room	chtěl bych dvou lůžkovy pokoj
I understand	rozumím		
Speak slowly	mluvte pomalu	For one night	na jednu noc
How do you say that in Czech?	jak se tohle vekne česky	With shower	se sprchou
		Are these seats free?	je tu volno?
Could you write it down for me?	mužete mí to napsat?	May we (sit down)?	můžeme?
		The bill please	zaplatím prosím
What	co	Do you have …?	máte …?
Where	kde	We don't have	nemáme
When	kdy	We do have	máme

Some signs

Entrance	vchod	Danger!	pozor!
Exit	východ	Hospital	nemocnice
Toilets	záchod	No smoking	kouření zakázáno
Men	muži	No bathing	koupání zakázáno
Women	ženy	No entry	vstup zakázáno
Gentlemen	pánové	Arrivals	příjezd
Ladies	dámy	Departure	odjezd
Open	otevřeno	Police	policie
Closed	zavřeno		

Days of the week

Monday	pondělí	Thursday	čtvrtek
Tuesday	úterý	Friday	pátek
Wednesday	středa	Saturday	sobota

Sunday	neděle	Month	měsíc
Day	den	Year	rok
Week	týden		

Numbers

0	nula	21	dvacetjedna
1	jeden	30	třícet
2	dva	40	čtyřícet
3	tří	50	padesát
4	čtyří	60	šedesát
5	pět	70	sedmdesát
6	šest	80	osumdesát
7	sedm	90	devadesát
8	osum	100	sto
9	devět	101	sto jedna
10	deset	155	sto padesát pět
11	jedenáct	200	dvěstě
12	dvanáct	300	tři sta
13	třínáct	400	čtyři sta
14	čtrnáct	500	pět set
15	patnáct	600	šest set
16	šestnáct	700	sedm set
17	sedmnáct	800	osum set
18	osmnáct	900	devět set
19	devatenáct	1000	tisíc
20	dvacet		

Months of the year

Many Slav languages have their own highly individual systems in which the words for the names of the months are descriptive nouns sometimes beautifully apt for the month in question.

January	leden	ice	August	srpen	sickle
February	únor	renewal	September	zaří	blazing
March	březen	birch	October	říjen	rutting
April	duben	oak	November	listopad	leaves falling
May	květen	blossom	December	prosinec	slaughter of
June	červen	red			the pig
July	červenec	redder			

Some foreign countries

Australia	Austálie	Great Britain	Velká Britanie
Austria	Rakousko	Hungary	Maďarsko
Canada	Kanada	Netherlands	Nizozemí
Ireland	Irsko	New Zealands	Novy Zéland
Germany	Německo	US	Spojené státy americké

Food and drink glossary

Basics

chléb	bread	pečivo	pastry
chlebíček	(open) sandwich	pepř	pepper
cukr	sugar	polévka	soup
hořice	mustard	předkrmy	starters
houska	round roll	přílohy	side dishes
jídla na	main dishes	rohlík	finger roll
knedlíky	dumplings	ryby	fish
křen	horseradish	rýže	rice
lžíce	spoon	šálek	cup
máslo	butter	sklenice	glass
maso	meat	snídaně	breakfast
med	honey	sůl	salt
mléko	milk	talíř	plate
moučník	dessert	tartarská omáčka	tartare sauce
nápoje	drinks	teštoviny	noodles, pasta
nůž	knife	večeře	supper/dinner
oběd	lunch	vejce	eggs
objednávku	to order	vidlička	fork
obloha	garnish	volské oko	fried egg
ocet	vinegar	zeleniny	vegetables
ovoce	fruit		

Soups

boršč	beetroot soup	kuřecí	thin chicken soup
bramborová	potato soup	rajská	tomato soup
čočková	lentil soup	zeleninová	vegetable soup
fazolová	bean soup	zelná	sauerkraut and meat soup
hovězí vývar	beef broth		
hrachová	pea soup		

Fish

kapr	carp	sardinka	sardine
losos	salmon	štika	pike
makrela	mackerel	treska	cod
platýs	flounder	úhoř	eel
pstruh	trout	zavináč	herring/rollmop
rybí filé	fillet of fish		

Meat dishes

bažant	pheasant	kýta	leg
biftek	beef steak	ledvinky	kidneys
čevapčiči	spicy meatballs	řízek	steak
dršťky	tripe	roštěná	sirloin
drůbež	poultry	salám	salami
guláš	goulash	sekaná	meat loaf
hovězí	beef	skopové	maso mutton
husa	goose	slanina	bacon
játra	liver	šunka	ham
jazyk	tongue	svíčková	fillet of beef
kachna	duck	telecí	veal
karbanátky	minced meat rissoles	vepřové	pork
klobásy	sausages	vepřové řízek	breaded pork cutlet
kotleta	cutlet		or schnitzel
kuře	chicken	žebírko	ribs

Vegetables

brambory	potatoes	kyselá okurka	pickled gherkin
brokolice	broccoli	kyselé zelí	sauerkraut
celer	celery	lečo	ratatouille
česnek	garlic	lilek	aubergine
chřest	asparagus	okurka	cucumber
cibule	onion	pórek	leek
čočka	lentils	rajče	tomato
fazole	beans	ředkev	radish
houby	mushrooms	řepná bulva	beetroot
hranolky	chips, French fries	špenát	spinach
hrášek	peas	žampiony	mushroom
karotka	carrot	zelí	cabbage
květák	cauliflower		

Fruit, cheese and nuts

banán	banana	maliny	raspberries
borůvky	blueberries	mandle	almonds
broskev	peach	měkký sýr	soft cheese
bryndza	goat's cheese in brine	meruňka	apricot
citrón	lemon	niva	semi-soft, crumbly,
grep	grapefruit		blue cheese
hermelín	Czech brie	oříšky	peanuts
hrozny	grapes	oštěpek	heavily smoked curd
hruška	pear		cheese
jablko	apple	ostružiny	blackberries
jahody	strawberries	parenica	rolled strips of lightly
kompot	stewed fruit		smoked curd cheese

pivní sýr	cheese flavoured with beer	tvaroh	fresh curd cheese
pomeranč	orange	urda	soft, fresh, whey cheese
rozinky	raisins	uzený sýr	smoked cheese
švestky	plums	vlašské ořechy	walnuts
třešně	cherries		

Common terms

čerstvý	fresh	(za)pečený	baked/roast
domácí	home-made	plněný	stuffed
duzený	stew/casserole	sladký	sweet
grilovaný	roast on the spit	slaný	salted
kyselý	sour	smažený	fried in breadcrumbs
m.m. (maštěny máslem)	with melted butter	studený	cold
		syrový	raw
na kmíně	with caraway seeds	sýrový	cheesy
na roztu	grilled	teplý	hot
na smetaně	in cream sauce	uzený	smoked
na zdraví!	cheers!	vařený	boiled
nadívaný	stuffed	znojemský	with gherkins
nakládaný	pickled		

Drinks

bílé víno	white wine	led	ice
burčák	young wine	minerálka	mineral water
čaj	tea	mléko	milk
červené víno	red wine	pivo	beer
destiláty	spirits	suché víno	dry wine
káva	coffee	svařák	mulled wine
koňak	brandy	vinný střik	white wine with soda
láhev	bottle	víno	wine

An A–Z of street names

After 1989, most of the streets named after erstwhile stars of the Communist Party disappeared. This was not the first (nor the last) time that the sign writers had put their brushes to use: after World War I, the old Habsburg names were replaced by Czech ones; then under the Nazis, the streets were named after Hitler and his cronies, only for the Czech names to be reinstated in 1945; under the Communists, the names were changed once (or twice) more. The following names are currently the most popular in the Czech Republic; remember that street names always appear in the genitive or adjectival form: Palacký street as Palackého, for example, or Hus street as Husova.

5 května (May 5). The day of the Prague Uprising against the Nazis in 1945.

17 listopadu (November 17). Commemorates the anti-Nazi demonstration of Nov 17, 1939, after which the Nazis closed down all Czech institutions of higher education. The November 17, 1989 demonstration was held to commemorate the 1939 one, but, after the attack by the police, signalled the beginning of the Velvet Revolution.

28 října (Oct 28). Anniversary of the foundation of Czechoslovakia in 1918.

29 August The day the unsuccessful Slovak National Uprising against the Nazis began in 1944.

Beneš, Edvard (1884–1948). Hero to some, traitor to others, Beneš was president from 1935 until 1938, when he resigned, having refused to lead the country into bloodshed over the Munich Crisis, and again from 1945 until 1948, when he acquiesced to the Communist coup.

Bezruč, Petr (1867–1958). Pen name of the Czech poet Vladimír Vayek, who wrote about the hardships of the Ostrava mining region.

Čapek, Karel (1890–1938). Czech writer, journalist and unofficial spokesperson for the First Republic. His most famous works are The Insect Play and R.U.R., which introduced the word robot into the English language.

Čech, Svatopluk (1846–1908). Extreme Czech nationalist and poet whose best-known work is Songs of a Slave.

Chelčicky, Petr (born c.1390). Extreme pacifist Hussite preacher who disapproved of the violence of Žižka and his Taborite army.

Dobrovský, Josef (1753–1829). Jesuit-taught pioneer in Czech philology. Wrote the seminal text The History of Czech Language and Literature.

Duklianské hrdiny (The Dukla Heroes). The name given to the soldiers who died capturing the Dukla Pass in October 1944, the first decisive battle in the liberation of the country from the Nazis.

Dvořák, Antonín (1841–1904). Perhaps the most famous of all Czech composers, whose best-known work, the New World Symphony, was inspired by his extensive sojourn in the US.

Havlíček-Borovský, Karel (1821–56). Satirical poet, journalist and nationalist, exiled to the Tyrol by the Austrian authorities after 1848.

Horáková, Milada (1901–50). Socialist parliamentary deputy who was killed in the Stalinist purges.

Hus, Jan (1370–1415). Rector of Prague University and reformist preacher who was burnt at the stake as a heretic by the Council of Constance (see p.194).

Janácek, Leos (1854–1928). Moravian-born composer, based in Brno for most of his life, whose operas in particular have become quite widely performed in the West.

Jirásek, Alois (1851–1930). Writer for children and adults who popularized Czech legends and became a key figure in the national revival.

Jiří z Poděbrad (1458–71). The only Hussite and last Czech king of Bohemia, better known to the English as George of Poděbrady.

Jungmann, Josef (1773–1847). Prolific Czech translator and author of the seminal History of Czech Literature and the first Czech dictionary.

Karl IV (1346–78). Luxembourgeois king of Bohemia and Holy Roman Emperor responsible for Prague's golden age in the fourteenth century. Better known to the English as Charles IV.

Komenský, Jan Amos (1592–1670). Leader of the Protestant Unity of Czech Brethren. Forced to flee the country and settle in England during the Counter-Reformation. Better known to the English as Comenius.

Lidice Bohemian village outside Prague which fell victim to the Nazis in June 1942 in retaliation for the murder of Reinhard Heydrich: the male inhabitants were shot, the women and children were sent to the camps and the entire place was burnt to the ground.

Mácha, Karel Hynek (1810–36). Romantic nationalist poet and great admirer of Byron and Keats, who, like them, died young. His most famous poem is *Máj*, published just months before his death.

Masaryk, Tomáš Garrigue (1850–1937). Professor of philosophy at Prague University, President of the Republic (1918–35). His name is synonymous with the First Republic and was removed from all street signs after the 1948 coup. Now back with a vengeance.

Němcová, Božena (1820–62). Highly popular writer who got involved with the nationalist movement and shocked with her unorthodox behaviour. Her most famous book is *Grandmother*.

Neruda, Jan (1834–91). Poet and journalist for the Národní listy. Wrote famous short stories describing Prague's Malá Strana.

Opletal, Jan (1915–39). Czech student killed by Nazis in 1939 during anti-Nazi demonstration.

Palach, Jan (1947–69). Philosophy student who committed suicide by self-immolation in protest against the 1968 Soviet invasion.

Palacký, František (1798–1876). Nationalist historian, Czech MP in Vienna and leading figure in the events of 1848.

Pavlov, I.P. (1849–1936). Russian Nobel prize-winning scientist, famous for his experiments on dogs (hence, "Pavlov's dogs"), from which he developed the theory of conditioned reflexes.

Purkyně, Jan Evangelista (1787–1869). Czech doctor, natural scientist and pioneer in experimental physiology who became professor of physiology at Prague and then Wrocław universities.

Ressel, Josef (1793–1857). Fascinatingly enough, the Czech inventor of the screw-propeller.

Rieger, Ladislav (1818–1903). Nineteenth-century Czech politician and one of the leading figures in the events of 1848 and its aftermath.

Smetana, Bedřich (1824–84). Popular Czech composer and fervent nationalist whose *Má vlast* (My Homeland) traditionally opens the Prague Spring Music Festival.

Sokol (Falcon). Physical education movement founded in 1862 and very much modelled on its German counterpart. The organization was a driving force during the Czech national revival, but was banned by the Nazis and later the Communists.

Štefánik, Milan Rastislav (died 1919). Slovak explorer and fighter pilot who fought and campaigned for Czechoslovakia during World War I.

Štúr, Ľudovít (1815–56). Slovak nationalist who led the 1848 revolt against the Hungarians and argued for a Slovak language distinct from Czech.

Svoboda, Ludvík (1895–1979). Victorious Czech general from World War II who acquiesced to the 1948 Communist coup and was Communist president during the Prague Spring in 1968 and until 1975.

Tyl, Josef Kajetán (1808–56). Czech playwright and composer of the Czech national anthem, "Where is my Home?"

Wilson, Woodrow (1856–1924). US president who oversaw the peace settlement after World War I, and was therefore seen by many as one of the founders of Czechoslovakia.

Wolker, Jiří (1900–24). Czech Communist who died of TB aged 24 and whose one volume of poetry was lauded by the Communists as the first truly proletarian writing.

Žižka, Jan (died 1424). Brilliant, blind military leader of the Táborites, the radical faction of the Hussites.

A glossary of words and terms

brána gate.

čajovna tea-house.

český Bohemian.

chata chalet-type bungalow, country cottage or mountain hut.

chrám large church.

cukrárna pastry shop.

divadlo theatre.

dóm cathedral.

dům/dom house.

dům kultury communal arts and social centre; literally "house of culture".

hora mountain.

hospoda pub.

hostinec pub.

hrad castle.

hranice border.

hřbitov cemetery.

jeskyně cave.

jezero lake.

kámen rock.

kaple chapel.

kašna fountain.

katedrála cathedral.

kavárna coffee house.

klášter monastery.

kostel church.

koupaliště swimming pool.

Labe River Elbe.

lanovka funicular or cable car.

lázně spa.

les forest.

malý small.

město town; staré město – old town, nové město – new town, dolní město – lower town, horní město – upper town.

moravský Moravian.

most bridge.

nábřeží embankment.

nádraží train station.

náměstí square.

Nisa River Neisse.

Odra River Oder.

okruh route (of a guided tour).

ostrov island.

památník memorial or monument.

paneláky prefabricated high-rise housing.

pasáž indoor shopping mall.

pivnice pub.

pokladna ticket office.

pramen natural spring.

prohlídka viewpoint.

radnice town hall.

řeka river.

restaurace restaurant.

sad park.

sál room or hall (in a chateau or castle).

schody steps.

sedlo saddle (of a mountain).

skála crag/rock.

skanzen an open-air folk museum, with reconstructed folk art and architecture.

staré město old town.

svatý/svatá saint – often abbreviated to sv.

teplice spa.

trasa route (of a guided tour).

třída avenue.

ulice street.

velký large.

věž tower.

vinárna wine bar or cellar.

Vltava River Moldau.

vrchovina uplands.

vrchy hills.

vyhlídková věž viewing tower.

výstava exhibition.

zahrada gardens.

zámek chateau.

An architectural glossary

Ambulatory Passage round the back of the altar, in continuation of the aisles.

Art Nouveau Sinuous and stylized form of architecture and decorative arts. Imported from Vienna and Budapest in 1900–10 and therefore known in Czechoslovakia as the Secession rather than Jugendstil, the German term.

Baroque Expansive, exuberant architectural style of the seventeenth and mid-eighteenth centuries, characterized by ornate decoration, complex spatial arrangement and grand vistas.

Beautiful Style Also known as the Soft Style of painting. Developed in Bohemia in the fourteenth century, it became very popular in Germany.

Bimah The central, raised, section of a synagogue from which the Torah is read aloud.

Chancel Part of the church where the altar is placed, usually at the east end.

Empire A highly decorative Neoclassical style of architecture and decorative arts practised in the first part of the nineteenth century.

Fresco Mural painting applied to wet plaster, so that the colours immediately soak into the wall.

Functionalism Plain, boxy, modernist architectural style, prevalent in the late 1920s and 1930s in Czechoslovakia, often using plate-glass curtain walls and open-plan interiors.

Gothic Architectural style prevalent from the twelfth to the sixteenth century, characterized by pointed arches and ribbed vaulting.

Loggia Covered area on the side of a building, often arcaded.

Nave Main body of a church, usually the western end.

Neoclassical Late eighteenth- and early nineteenth-century style of architecture and design returning to classical Greek and Roman models as a reaction against Baroque and Rococo excesses.

Oriel A bay window, usually projecting from an upper floor.

Predella Small panel below the main scenes of an altarpiece.

Rococo Highly florid, fiddly though (occasionally) graceful style of architecture and interior design, forming the last phase of Baroque.

Romanesque Solid architectural style of the late tenth to thirteenth centuries, characterized by round-headed arches and geometrical precision.

Secession Style of early twentieth-century art and architecture based in Germany and Austria and a reaction against the academic establishment (see also "Art Nouveau").

Sgraffito Monochrome plaster decoration effected by means of scraping back the first white layer to reveal the black underneath.

Shingle Wooden roof tiles.

Stucco Plaster used for decorative effects.

Tympanum Area above doorway or within a pediment.

Historical and political terms

Czech Lands A phrase used to denote Bohemia and Moravia.

First Republic The new Czechoslovak Republic founded by Masaryk after World War II, made up of Bohemia, Moravia, Silesia, Slovakia and Ruthenia, dismantled by the Nazis in 1938–39.

Great Moravian Empire The first Slav state covering much of what is now Czechoslovakia, which ended shortly after the Magyar invasion of 896 AD.

Greek-Catholic Church Formed from various breakaways from the Eastern (Orthodox) Church in the sixteenth century, the Greek-Catholic Church retains many Orthodox practices and rituals but is affiliated to the Roman Catholic Church. Also known as the Uniate Church.

Habsburgs The most powerful royal family in central Europe, whose power base was Vienna. They held the Bohemian and Hungarian thrones from 1526 to 1918, and by marriage and diplomacy acquired territories all over Europe.

Historic Provinces Land traditionally belonging to the Bohemian crown, including Bohemia, Egerland, Moravia, Silesia and Lusatia.

Holy Roman Empire Name given to the loose confederation of German states (including for a while the Czech Lands) which lasted from 800 until 1806.

Hussites Name given to Czech religious reformers who ostensibly followed the teachings of Jan Hus (1370–1415).

Jagiellonians Polish-Lithuanian dynasty who ruled the Czech Lands from 1471 to 1526.

Magyars The people who ruled over the Hungarian Kingdom and now predominate in modern-day Hungary.

Mitteleuropa Literally German for "central Europe", but it also conveys the idea of a multilingual central European culture, lost after the break-up of the Habsburg Empire.

Národní fronta Literally the National Front,

the dummy coalition of parties dominated by the Communists which ruled the country until December 1989.

Národní obrození Czech "national revival" movement of the nineteenth century, which sought to rediscover the lost identity of the Czech people, particularly their history and language.

Přemyslid The dynasty of Czech princes and kings who ruled over the Historic Lands of Bohemia from the ninth century to 1306.

Ruthenia Officially Sub-Carpatho-Ruthenia, the easternmost province of the First Republic, annexed by the Soviet Union at the end of World War II.

Sudetenland Name given to mostly German-speaking border regions of the Czech Lands, awarded to Nazi Germany in the Munich Diktat of September 1938.

Velvet Revolution The popular protests of November/December 1989 which brought an end to 41 years of Communist rule. Also known as the Gentle Revolution.

Abbreviations

ČD (České dráhy) Czech Railways.

CKM (Cestovní kanceláu mládeze) Youth Travel Organization.

ČSAD (Česká státní automobilová doprava) Czech state bus company.

KSČ (Komunistická strana československá) The Czechoslovak Communist Party (now defunct).

KSČM Communist Party of Bohemia and Moravia (still functioning).

ODS (Občanská demokratická strana) Civic Democratic Party – right-wing faction of Civic Forum.

SdP Sudeten German Party (Sudetendeutsche Partei), the main proto-Nazi Party in Czechoslovakia in the late 1930s.

StB (Státní bezpečnost) The Communist secret police (now disbanded).

Travel store

UK & Ireland
Britain
Devon & Cornwall
Dublin **D**
Edinburgh **D**
England
Ireland
The Lake District
London
London **D**
London Mini Guide
Scotland
Scottish Highlands
 & Islands
Wales

Europe
Algarve **D**
Amsterdam
Amsterdam **D**
Andalucía
Athens **D**
Austria
Baltic States
Barcelona
Barcelona **D**
Belgium &
 Luxembourg
Berlin
Brittany & Normandy
Bruges **D**
Brussels
Budapest
Bulgaria
Copenhagen
Corsica
Crete
Croatia
Cyprus
Czech & Slovak
 Republics
Denmark
Dodecanese & East
 Aegean Islands
Dordogne & The Lot
Europe on a Budget
Florence & Siena
Florence **D**
France
Germany
Gran Canaria **D**
Greece
Greek Islands
Hungary

Ibiza & Formentera **D**
Iceland
Ionian Islands
Italy
The Italian Lakes
Languedoc &
 Roussillon
Lanzarote &
 Fuerteventura **D**
Lisbon **D**
The Loire Valley
Madeira **D**
Madrid **D**
Mallorca **D**
Mallorca & Menorca
Malta & Gozo **D**
Moscow
The Netherlands
Norway
Paris
Paris **D**
Paris Mini Guide
Poland
Portugal
Prague
Prague **D**
Provence
 & the Côte D'Azur
Pyrenees
Romania
Rome
Rome **D**
Sardinia
Scandinavia
Sicily
Slovenia
Spain
St Petersburg
Sweden
Switzerland
Tenerife &
 La Gomera **D**
Turkey
Tuscany & Umbria
Venice & The Veneto
Venice **D**
Vienna

Asia
Bali & Lombok
Bangkok
Beijing
Cambodia
China

Goa
Hong Kong & Macau
Hong Kong
 & Macau **D**
India
Indonesia
Japan
Kerala
Korea
Laos
Malaysia, Singapore
 & Brunei
Nepal
The Philippines
Rajasthan, Dehli
 & Agra
Shanghai
Singapore
Singapore **D**
South India
Southeast Asia on a
 Budget
Sri Lanka
Taiwan
Thailand
Thailand's Beaches
 & Islands
Tokyo
Vietnam

Australasia
Australia
East Coast Australia
Fiji
Melbourne
New Zealand
Sydney
Tasmania

North America
Alaska
Baja California
Boston
California
Canada
Chicago
Colorado
Florida
The Grand Canyon
Hawaii
Honolulu **D**
Las Vegas **D**
Los Angeles &
 Southern California
Maui **D**

Miami & South Florida
Montréal
New England
New York City
New York City **D**
New York City Mini
Orlando & Walt
 Disney World® **D**
Oregon &
 Washington
San Francisco
San Francisco **D**
Seattle
Southwest USA
Toronto
USA
Vancouver
Washington DC
Yellowstone & The
 Grand Tetons
Yosemite

**Caribbean
& Latin America**
Antigua & Barbuda **D**
Argentina
Bahamas
Barbados **D**
Belize
Bolivia
Brazil
Buenos Aires
Cancùn & Cozumel **D**
Caribbean
Central America on a
 Budget
Chile
Costa Rica
Cuba
Dominican Republic
Ecuador
Guatemala
Jamaica
Mexico
Peru
Puerto Rico
St Lucia **D**
South America on a
 Budget
Trinidad & Tobago
Yucatán

D: Rough Guide
DIRECTIONS for
short breaks

Available from all good bookstores

For more information go to www.roughguides.com

ROUGH GUIDES

Visit us online

www.roughguides.com

Information on over 25,000 destinations around the world

ROUGH GUIDES   **BROADEN YOUR HORIZONS**

NOTES

NOTES

NOTES

Small print and

Index

A Rough Guide to Rough Guides

Published in 1982, the first Rough Guide – to Greece – was a student scheme that became a publishing phenomenon. Mark Ellingham, a recent graduate in English from Bristol University, had been travelling in Greece the previous summer and couldn't find the right guidebook. With a small group of friends he wrote his own guide, combining a highly contemporary, journalistic style with a thoroughly practical approach to travellers' needs.

The immediate success of the book spawned a series that rapidly covered dozens of destinations. And, in addition to impecunious backpackers, Rough Guides soon acquired a much broader and older readership that relished the guides' wit and inquisitiveness as much as their enthusiastic, critical approach and value-for-money ethos.

These days, Rough Guides include recommendations from shoestring to luxury and cover more than 200 destinations around the globe, including almost every country in the Americas and Europe, more than half of Africa and most of Asia and Australasia. Our ever-growing team of authors and photographers is spread all over the world, particularly in Europe, the USA and Australia.

In the early 1990s, Rough Guides branched out of travel, with the publication of Rough Guides to World Music, Classical Music and the Internet. All three have become benchmark titles in their fields, spearheading the publication of a wide range of books under the Rough Guide name.

Including the travel series, Rough Guides now number more than 350 titles, covering: phrasebooks, waterproof maps, music guides from Opera to Heavy Metal, reference works as diverse as Conspiracy Theories and Shakespeare, and popular culture books from iPods to Poker. Rough Guides also produce a series of more than 120 World Music CDs in partnership with World Music Network.

Visit www.roughguides.com to see our latest publications.

Rough Guide travel images are available for commercial licensing at www.roughguidespictures.com

Rough Guide credits

Text editor: Samantha Cook
Layout: Umesh Aggarwal
Cartography: Karobi Gogoi
Picture editor: Mark Thomas
Production: Rebecca Short
Proofreader: Susannah Wight
Cover design: Chloë Roberts
Editorial: London Ruth Blackmore, Andy Turner, Keith Drew, Edward Aves, Alice Park, Lucy White, Jo Kirby, James Smart, Natasha Foges, Róisín Cameron, Emma Traynor, James Rice, Emma Gibbs, Kathryn Lane, Christina Valhouli, Monica Woods, Mani Ramaswamy, Alison Roberts, Harry Wilson, Lucy Cowie, Helen Ochyra, Joe Staines, Peter Buckley, Matthew Milton, Tracy Hopkins, Ruth Tidball; **New York** Andrew Rosenberg, Steven Horak, AnneLise Sorensen, Ella Steim, Anna Owens, Sean Mahoney, Paula Neudorf; **Delhi** Madhavi Singh, Karen D'Souza, Lubna Shaheen
Design & Pictures: London Scott Stickland, Dan May, Diana Jarvis, Nicole Newman, Sarah Cummins, Emily Taylor; **Delhi** Ajay Verma, Jessica Subramanian, Ankur Guha, Pradeep Thapliyal, Sachin Tanwar, Anita Singh, Nikhil Agarwal
Production: Vicky Baldwin

Cartography: **London** Maxine Repath, Ed Wright, Katie Lloyd-Jones; **Delhi** Rajesh Chhibber, Ashutosh Bharti, Rajesh Mishra, Animesh Pathak, Jasbir Sandhu, Alakananda Roy, Swati Handoo, Deshpal Dabas
Online: London George Atwell, Faye Hellon, Jeanette Angell, Fergus Day, Justine Bright, Clare Bryson, Áine Fearon, Adrian Low, Ezgi Celebi, Amber Bloomfield; **Delhi** Amit Verma, Rahul Kumar, Narender Kumar, Ravi Yadav, Debojit Borah, Rakesh Kumar, Ganesh Sharma, Shisir Basumatari
Marketing & Publicity: London Liz Statham, Niki Hanmer, Louise Maher, Jess Carter, Vanessa Godden, Vivienne Watton, Anna Paynton, Rachel Sprackett, Libby Jellie, Laura Vipond; **New York** Geoff Colquitt, Nancy Lambert, Katy Ball; **Delhi** Ragini Govind
Manager India: Punita Singh
Reference Director: Andrew Lockett
Operations Manager: Helen Phillips
PA to Publishing Director: Nicola Henderson
Publishing Director: Martin Dunford
Commercial Manager: Gino Magnotta
Managing Director: John Duhigg

Publishing information

This first edition published May 2009 by
Rough Guides Ltd,
80 Strand, London WC2R 0RL
345 Hudson St, 4th Floor,
New York, NY 10014, USA
14 Local Shopping Centre, Panchsheel Park,
New Delhi 110017, India
Distributed by the Penguin Group
Penguin Books Ltd,
80 Strand, London WC2R 0RL
Penguin Group (USA)
375 Hudson Street, NY 10014, USA
Penguin Group (Australia)
250 Camberwell Road, Camberwell,
Victoria 3124, Australia
Penguin Group (Canada)
195 Harry Walker Parkway N, Newmarket, ON,
L3Y 7B3 Canada
Penguin Group (NZ)
67 Apollo Drive, Mairangi Bay, Auckland 1310,
New Zealand

Cover concept by Peter Dyer.

Typeset in Bembo and Helvetica to an original design by Henry Iles.

Printed and bound in China

© Rob Humphreys

No part of this book may be reproduced in any form without permission from the publisher except for the quotation of brief passages in reviews.

448pp includes index

A catalogue record for this book is available from the British Library.

ISBN: 978-1-84836-036-5

The publishers and authors have done their best to ensure the accuracy and currency of all the information in **The Rough Guide to The Czech Republic**, however, they can accept no responsibility for any loss, injury, or inconvenience sustained by any traveller as a result of information or advice contained in the guide.

1   3   5   7   9   8   6   4   2

Help us update

We've gone to a lot of effort to ensure that the first edition of **The Rough Guide to The Czech Republic** is accurate and up to date. However, things change – places get "discovered", opening hours are notoriously fickle, restaurants and rooms raise prices or lower standards. If you feel we've got it wrong or left something out, we'd like to know, and if you can remember the address, the price, the hours, the phone number, so much the better.

Please send your comments with the subject line "**Rough Guide Czech Republic Update**" to ®mail@roughguides.com. We'll credit all contributions and send a copy of the next edition (or any other Rough Guide if you prefer) for the very best emails.

Have your questions answered and tell others about your trip at ®community.roughguides.com

Acknowledgements

Rob Humphreys thanks Sam for even bothering to attempt to engage with the lower-case issue and other things. Thanks too to Kate for enduring a bumpy ride along the Labe, to Pavla for gifts from Brno and Jon for going Moravian with enthusiasm.

Steven Horak would like to thank Sam for being such a pleasure to work with, her patience and her support throughout the project. Thanks as well to all the helpful staff at tourist offices throughout Bohemia – your assistance truly was invaluable – and to Rob, whose suggestions were always spot on. Lastly, for enduring with good humour my prolonged fascination with all things Czech, thanks to my family and friends – particularly my mom, without whom it would not have been possible.

Jonathan Bousfield would like to thank Sam Cook, Ashley Davies, Matthew Sweney and all the household at Poet's Corner.

Readers' letters

Thanks to all the readers who have taken the time to write in with comments and suggestions (and apologies if we've inadvertently omitted or misspelt anyone's name):

Peter Bartos, Alan Brady, Simon Cowper, Gel Goldsby, Colin Groom, Alex Hetwer, Frank Higbie, Catherine Jones, Dorothy Kurpanik, Tony Madigan, Arthur & Pamela Mawson, Boyd McClymont, Hilary McDowell, Fab Marsani, Marek Mráz, Maureen Poole, Vince Raison, Sharon Roberts, Chris Shallow, D. F. Wilson, Mrs Rosemary P. Worsley.

SMALL PRINT

Photo credits

All photos © Rough Guides except the following:

Title page
Telč © Alberto Paredes/Alamy

Full page
Malá Strana district of Prague © Clay McLachlan/ Getty Images

Introduction
Detail of stained glass in the Obecní Dům © Hemis/Axiom Photo Agency
Train © Rob Humphreys
Červená Lhota © Profimedia International/Alamy
View over Prague © Stuart Dee/Getty Images
Hiking in Sumava National Park © Profimedia International/Alamy
Wooden church © Isifa Image service/Alamy
Folk festival © JTB Photo Communications/Alamy

Things not to miss
01 Žd'ár nad Sázavou © Isifa Image Service/ Alamy
02 Rožnov pod Radhoštěm © Kirstine Lundbak/ Alamy
03 Veletržni palác © Rob Humphreys
04 Český ráj © Steven Horak
05 Třeboňsko © Profimedia International/Alamy
06 Plzeň brewery © Chris Fredrriksson/Alamy
07 Telč © Karen Su/Alamy
09 Karlovy Vary © Steven Horak
10 Terezín © Steven Horak
11 Burčák © Jiri Rezac/Alamy
12 Litomyšl © Profimedia International/Alamy
13 Mariánské Lázně © Chris Howes/Wild Places Photography/Alamy
14 Pernštejn © Isifa Image Service/Alamy
15 České Švýcarsko © Profimedia International/ Alamy
16 Roast pork and dumplings © Isifa Image Service/Alamy
18 Český Krumlov © Steven Horak
20 Moravský kras © Vova Pomortzeff/Alamy
21 Nové Město nad Metují © Profimedia International/Alamy
22 Hiking in the Sumava © Profimedia International/Alamy
23 Budvar beer © Jiri Rezac/Alamy

24 Strážnice Folk Festival © JTP Photo Communications/Alamy
25 Slavonice © Imagebroker/Alamy

Czech beer colour section
Barman pouring beer © Yadid Levy/Alamy
Copper brewing pans © Chris Howes/Alamy
Barman in Prague © Alberto Paredes/Alamy
Bar sign © Eddie Gerald/Alamy
Beer advertisment © Kirstine Lundbak/Alamy
Prague pub © Chris Fredriksson/Alamy
Beer label © Imagebroker/Alamy
Beer hall © Yadid Levy/Alamy

Castles and chateaux colour section
Pernštejn Castle © Isifa Images Service/Alamy
Bouzov © Profimedia International/Alamy
Hrubý Rohozec © Profimedia International/Alamy
Lednice © Isifa Images Service/Alamy
Prague Castle © Stephen Simpson/Getty Images
Kroměřiž © Isifa Images Service/Alamy
Jaroměřice nad Rokytnou © Isifa Images Service/ Alamy
Český Krumlov © Jon Arnold Images/Alamy

Black and whites
p.158 Sumava National Park © Isifa Images Service/Alamy
p.166 Tábor © Isifa Images Service/Alamy
p.183 Český Krumlov © Chris Howes/Alamy
p.202 Kladruby monastery © Interfotobildagentur/ Alamy
p.227 Karlovy Vary © Stephen Saks Photography/ Alamy
p.231 Loket Castle © Chris Howes/Alamy
p.260 Benešovo náměstí, Liberec © Profimedia International/Alamy
p.266 Kuks © Profimedia International/Alamy
p.283 Adršpach rocks © Profimedia International/ Alamy
p.302 Telč © Radek Detinsky/Alamy
p.312 Petrov, Brno © Rob Humphreys
p.354 Štramberk © Profimedia International/ Alamy
p.364 Bouzov © Profimedia International/Alamy

SMALL PRINT

Index

Map entries are in colour.

INDEX

445